Thank you for purchasing the third supplement to the twentieth edition of Clerk & Lindsell on Torts

 ## Don't miss important updates

So that you have all the latest information, **Clerk & Lindsell on Torts** is supplemented regularly. Sign up today for a Standing Order to ensure you receive the updating supplements as soon as they publish. Setting up a Standing Order with Sweet & Maxwell is hassle-free, simply tick, complete and return this FREEPOST card and we'll do the rest.

You may cancel your Standing Order at any time by writing to us at Thomson Reuters, PO Box 1000, Andover, SP10 9AH stating the Standing Order you wish to cancel.

Alternatively, if you have purchased your copy of **Clerk & Li** ~~...~~ pplier, please ask your supplier to ensure that you are registered t ~~...~~

All goods are subject to our 30 day Satisfaction Guarantee

D0531238

Yes, please send me new supplements and /or new editions of **Clerk & Lindsell on Torts** to be invoiced on publication, until I cancel the standing order in writing.

☐ [All new editions]

☐ [All new supplements to the 20th edition]

☐ [All new supplements and editions]

Title .... Name ....

Organisation ....

Job title ....

Address ....

....

Postcode ....

Telephone ....

Email ....

S&M account number (if known) ....

PO number ....

All orders are accepted subject to the terms of this order form and our Terms of Trading. (see www.sweetandmaxwell.co.uk). By submitting this order form I confirm that I accept these terms and I am authorised to sign on behalf of the customer.

Signed .... Job Title ....

Print Name .... Date ....

UK VAT Number: GB 900 5487 43. Irish VAT Number: IE 9513874E. For customers in an EU member state (except UK & Ireland) please supply your VAT Number. VAT No [   ]

(BC007) V9 (12.2011) JL / KG

SWEET & MAXWELL

THOMSON REUTERS

THOMSON REUTERS

FREEPOST

PO BOX 1000

ANDOVER

SP10 9AH

UNITED KINGDOM

THE COMMON LAW LIBRARY

TORTS

THE COMMON LAW LIBRARY

CLERK & LINDSELL

ON

TORTS

THIRD SUPPLEMENT TO THE
TWENTIETH EDITION

Up-to-date to
August 2013

SWEET & MAXWELL

 THOMSON REUTERS

First Edition	(1889)	J. F. Clerk and W.H.B. Lindsell
Second Edition	(1896)	" " " "
Third Edition	(1904)	Wyatt Paine
Fourth Edition	(1906)	" " " "
Fifth Edition	(1909)	" " " "
Sixth Edition	(1912)	" " " "
Seventh Edition	(1921)	" " " "
Eighth Edition	(1929)	W. A. Macfarlane and G.W. Wrangham
Ninth Edition	(1937)	Under the General Editorship of Harold Porter
Tenth Edition	(1947)	" " " "
Eleventh Edition	(1954)	Under the General Editorship of John Burke and Peter Allsop
Twelfth Edition	(1961)	General Editor: A. L. Armitage
Thirteenth Edition	(1969)	" " " "
Fourteenth Edition	(1975)	General Editor: Sir Arthur L. Armitage and R. W. M. Dias
Fifteenth Edition	(1982)	General Editor: R. W. M. Dias
Sixteenth Edition	(1989)	" " " "
Seventeenth Edition	(1995)	General Editor: Margaret R. Brazier
Second Impression	(1996)	" " " "
Third Impression	(1998)	" " " "
Eighteenth Edition	(2000)	General Editor: Anthony M. Dugdale
Second Impression	(2003)	" " " "
Nineteenth Edition	(2006)	General Editors: Anthony M. Dugdale and Michael A. Jones
Twentieth Edition	(2010)	General Editor: Michael A. Jones
		Consultant Editor: Anthony M. Dugdale

Published in 2013 by

Sweet & Maxwell,
100 Avenue Road, London NW3 3PF
Part of Thomson Reuters (Professional) UK Limited
(Registered in England & Wales, Company No 1679046.
Registered Office and address for service:
Aldgate House, 33 Aldgate High Street, London EC3N 1DL)
For further information on our products and services, visit:
http://www.sweetandmaxwell.co.uk

Typeset by LBJ Typesetting Ltd of Kingsclere
Printed and bound by CPI Group (UK) Ltd, Croydon, CR0 4YY

No natural forests were destroyed to make this product;

only farmed timber was used and re-planted.

British Library Cataloguing in Publication Data

A CIP catalogue record for this book
is available from the British Library

ISBN 978–0–41403–108–1

HOW TO USE THIS SUPPLEMENT

This is the Third Cumulative Supplement to the Twentieth Edition of *Clerk and Lindsell on Torts*, and has been compiled according to the structure of the main volume.

At the beginning of each chapter of this Supplement is a mini table of contents from the main volume. Where a heading in this table of contents has been marked with a square pointer, this indicates that there is relevent information in the Supplement to which the reader should refer. Material that is new to the Cumulative Supplement is indicated by the symbol ■. Material that has been included from the previous Supplement is indicated by the symbol □.

Within each Chapter, updating information is referenced to the relevant paragraph in the main volume.

TABLE OF CASES

1044807 Alberta Ltd v Brae Centre Ltd [2008] ABCA 397; (2008) 302 D.L.R. (4th) 252
    CA (Alberta) 24–15, 24–36, 24–55
32Red Plc v WHG (International) Ltd [2013] EWHC 815 (Ch) 25–83
32Red Plc v WHG (International) Ltd; sub nom. WHG (International) Ltd v 32 Red Plc
    [2012] EWCA Civ 19; [2012] E.T.M.R. 14; [2012] R.P.C. 19 . . . . 25–76, 25–81
A (A Minor) v A Health & Social Services Trust [2011] NICA 28; [2012] N.I. 77 10–104
A Lloyd's Syndicate v X. *See* Lloyd's Syndicate v X
A Local Authority v E [2012] EWHC 1639 (COP); [2012] 2 F.C.R. 523; [2012] H.R.L.R.
    29; (2012) 15 C.C.L. Rep. 511; [2012] Med. L.R. 472; (2012) 127 B.M.L.R. 133 10–53
A v Bottrill [2002] UKPC 44; [2003] 1 A.C. 449; [2002] 3 W.L.R. 1406; (2003) 70
    B.M.L.R. 198; (2002) 146 S.J.L.B. 207 28–146
A v Chief Constable of Hampshire [2012] EWHC 1517 (QB) 14–35
A v Essex CC [2003] EWCA Civ 1848; [2004] 1 W.L.R. 1881; [2004] 1 F.L.R. 749; [2004]
    1 F.C.R. 660; [2004] B.L.G.R. 587; (2004) 7 C.C.L. Rep. 98; [2004] Fam. Law 238;
    (2004) 148 S.J.L.B. 27 8–43
A v Essex CC; B v Suffolk CC; S v Hertfordshire CC; J v Worcestershire CC [2010] UKSC
    33; [2011] 1 A.C. 280; [2010] 3 W.L.R. 509; [2010] 4 All E.R. 199; [2010] P.T.S.R.
    1332; [2010] H.R.L.R. 32; [2010] U.K.H.R.R. 937; 30 B.H.R.C. 1; [2010] E.L.R.
    531; (2010) 13 C.C.L. Rep. 314; (2010) 154(28) S.J.L.B. 30 . . . . 14–89, 14–96
A&E Television Networks LLC v Discovery Communications Europe Ltd [2013] EWHC
    109 (Ch); [2013] E.T.M.R. 3 . . . . 25–81, 25–82, 26–17
A&L Plumbing Ltd v Ridge Tool Co [2010] 350 Sask. R. 148 11–30
AAA v Associated Newspapers Ltd [2013] EWCA Civ 554 . . . . 27–39, 27–40, 27–41
AB v Home Office. *See* B v Home Office
AB v Ministry of Defence. *See* B v Ministry of Defence
Abbey v Gilligan [2012] EWHC 3217 (QB); [2013] E.M.L.R. 12 . . . . 27–08, 27–12, 27–27,
                                                        27–39, 27–41, 27–44
Abramova v Oxford Institute of Legal Practice [2011] EWHC 613 (QB); [2011] E.L.R.
    385 . . . . 8–200, 14–61
ACC Bank Plc v Johnston & Co [2010] IEHC 236; [2010] 4 I.R. 605; [2011] P.N.L.R. 19 . . . 10–126
Acte IARD Societe v Ettax Societe [2010] E.C.C. 24 11–46
Adams v Law Society of England and Wales [2012] EWHC 980 (QB) 6–28, 14–113, 14–115
Adams v Thomson Holidays Ltd [2009] EWHC 2559 (QB) 12–07
Addis v Campbell [2011] EWCA Civ 906 . . . . 8–153, 21–26
Adelson v Anderson [2011] EWHC 2497 (QB) 22–201
Adorian v Commissioner of Police of the Metropolis [2009] EWCA Civ 18; [2009] 1
    W.L.R. 1859; [2009] 4 All E.R. 227; [2009] C.P. Rep. 21; [2009] Po. L.R. 38; (2009)
    106(6) L.S.G. 18 15–134
AEG v Bilka Lavprisvarehus A/S (C–402/03). *See* Skov AEG v Bilka Lavprisvarehus
    A/S (C–402/03)
Aerotel Ltd v Telco Holdings Ltd; Macrossan's Patent Application (No.0314464.9) [2006]
    EWCA Civ 1371; [2007] 1 All E.R. 225; [2007] Bus. L.R. 634; [2006] Info. T.L.R.
    215; [2007] R.P.C. 7; (2007) 30(4) I.P.D. 30025; (2006) 156 N.L.J. 1687 25–94
African Strategic Investment (Holdings) Ltd (formerly Randgold Resources (Holdings)
    Ltd) v Main [2011] EWHC 2223 (Ch) 4–28
Agribrands Purina Canada Inc v Kasamekas [2011] ONCA 460; (2011) 334 D.L.R. (4th)
    714 24–100
AI Enterprises Ltd v Bram Enterprises Ltd [2012] NBCA 33; (2012) 350 D.L.R. (4th) 601
    . . . . 24–70, 24–73
AIB Group (UK) Plc v Mark Redler & Co Solicitors [2013] EWCA Civ 45; [2013] P.N.L.R.
    19; [2013] 8 E.G. 106 (C.S.); (2013) 157(7) S.J.L.B. 3 . . . . 10–23, 10–33, 10–119, 10–147

Ajinomoto Sweeteners Europe SAS v Asda Stores Ltd [2010] EWCA Civ 609; [2011] Q.B.
    497; [2011] 2 W.L.R. 91; [2010] 4 All E.R. 1029; [2010] E.M.L.R. 23; [2010] F.S.R.
    30; (2010) 107(24) L.S.G. 17; (2010) 160 N.L.J. 842 23–03
Akhtar v Brewster [2012] EWHC 3521 (Ch) 19–75
Aktas v Adepta; Dixie v British Polythene Industries Plc [2010] EWCA Civ 1170; [2011]
    Q.B. 894; [2011] 2 W.L.R. 945; [2011] 2 All E.R. 536; [2011] C.P. Rep. 9; [2011]
    P.I.Q.R. P. 32–56
Al Hassan-Daniel v Revenue and Customs Commissioners [2010] EWCA Civ 1443;
    [2011] Q.B. 866; [2011] 2 W.L.R. 488; [2011] 2 All E.R. 31; [2011] H.R.L.R. 9;
    [2011] U.K.H.R.R. 1; (2011) 108(1) L.S.G. 14; (2011) 161 N.L.J. 64. . . . . 3–03, 3–04
Al Khudairi v Abbey Brokers Ltd [2010] EWHC 1486 (Ch); [2010] P.N.L.R. 32 18–11
Al-Amoudi v Kifle [2011] EWHC 2037 (QB) 22–224, 22–226
Al-Ghabra v HM Treasury; Ahmed v HM Treasury [2010] UKSC 1; [2010] 2 A.C. 697;
    [2010] 2 W.L.R. 325; [2010] 2 All E.R. 799; [2010] E.M.L.R. 15; [2010] H.R.L.R.
    14; [2010] U.K.H.R.R. 181; (2010) 107(6) L.S.G. 18; (2010) 154(4) S.J.L.B. 29;
    [2010] N.P.C. 8 . . . . 14–87, 27–47
Al-Jedda v United Kingdom (27021/08) (2011) 53 E.H.R.R. 23; 30 B.H.R.C. 637 ECtHR . . . 14–73
Al-Skeini v United Kingdom (55721/07) (2011) 53 E.H.R.R. 18; 30 B.H.R.C. 561; [2011]
    Inquest L.R. 73 14–73
Alanov v Chief Constable of Sussex [2012] EWCA Civ 234 . . . . 14–69A, 15–69
Albert Packaging Ltd v Nampak Cartons & Healthcare Ltd [2011] EWPCC 15; [2011]
    F.S.R. 32 25–59
Alexander v Freshwater Properties Ltd [2012] EWCA Civ 1048 12–57
Alexander v Mercouris [1979] 1 W.L.R. 1270; [1979] 3 All E.R. 305; (1979) 252 E.G. 911;
    (1979) 123 S.J. 604 CA (Civ Div) 8–130
Alfa Laval Tumba AB v Separator Spares International Ltd [2012] EWCA Civ 1569;
    [2013] 1 W.L.R. 1110; [2013] 2 All E.R. 463; [2013] 2 All E.R. (Comm) 177; [2013]
    C.P. Rep. 9; [2013] I.L.Pr. 10; [2013] I.C.R. 455; [2013] F.S.R. 22. 7–02
Ali Ghaith v Indesit Company UK Ltd [2012] EWCA Civ 642 2–12
Ali v Bradford MDC [2010] EWCA Civ 1282; [2012] 1 W.L.R. 161; [2011] 3 All E.R. 348;
    [2011] P.T.S.R. 1534; [2011] R.T.R. 20; [2011] P.I.Q.R. P6; [2010] N.P.C. 113 9–11,
                                                                                                    14–49, 20–193
Ali v Lord Grey School Governors; sub nom. A v Headteacher and Governors of Lord Grey
    School [2006] UKHL 14; [2006] 2 A.C. 363; [2006] 2 W.L.R. 690; [2006] 2 All E.R.
    457; [2006] H.R.L.R. 20; [2006] U.K.H.R.R. 591; 20 B.H.R.C. 295; [2006] E.L.R.
    223. 14–96
Allen v Gulf Oil Refining Ltd [1981] A.C. 1001; [1981] 2 W.L.R. 188; [1981] 1 All E.R.
    353; [1981] J.P.L. 353; (1981) 125 S.J. 101 HL. 20–87
Allen v Hounga; Hounga v Allen [2012] EWCA Civ 609; [2012] I.R.L.R. 685; [2012] Eq.
    L.R. 679 3–40
Alleslev-Krofchak v Valcom Ltd [2010] ONCA 557; (2010) 322 D.L.R. (4th) 193. . . . 24–26, 24–73
AlleslevKrofchak v Valcom [2010] ONCA 557; (2010) 322 D.L.R. (4th) 193 CA (Ont). 24–70
Alleyne v Commissioner of Police of the Metropolis [2012] EWHC 3955 (QB). 15–49, 19–61
Allison v London Underground Ltd [2008] EWCA Civ 71; [2008] I.C.R. 719; [2008]
    I.R.L.R. 440; [2008] P.I.Q.R. P10; (2008) 105(8) L.S.G. 24; (2008) 152(8) S.J.L.B.
    34. . . . . 13–36, 13–54
Allstate Life Insurance Co v Australia and New Zealand Banking Group Ltd (1995) 130
    A.L.R. 469. 24–15
AM v News Group Newspapers Ltd [2012] EWHC 308 (QB). 27–46
Ambrosiadou v Coward [2011] EWCA Civ 409; [2011] E.M.L.R. 21; [2011] 2 F.L.R. 617;
    [2011] Fam. Law 690 27–47
Amin v Imran Khan & Partners [2011] EWHC 2958 (QB) 14–114
AMM v HXW [2010] EWHC 2457 (QB); (2010) 160 N.L.J. 1425 27–47
AMP v Persons Unknown [2011] EWHC 3454 (TCC); [2011] Info. T.L.R. 25; (2012)
    156(2) S.J.L.B. 31. . . . . 15–19, 27–44
An Informer v Chief Constable [2012] EWCA Civ 197; [2013] Q.B. 579; [2013] 2 W.L.R.
    694; [2012] 3 All E.R. 601 . . . . 8–55, 14–30
Anam v Secretary of State for the Home Department. See R. (on the application of Anam)
    v Secretary of State for the Home Department

Andrews v Barnett Waddingham (A Firm) [2006] EWCA Civ 93; [2006] P.N.L.R. 24;
   [2006] Pens. L.R. 101. 2–175
Anheuser-Busch Inc v Budejovicky Budvar Narodni Podnik (C–96/09 P) [2011] E.T.M.R.
   31. 25–79
Anns v Merton LBC; sub nom. Anns v Walcroft Property Co Ltd [1978] A.C. 728; [1977]
   2 W.L.R. 1024; [1977] 2 All E.R. 492; 75 L.G.R. 555; (1977) 243 E.G. 523; (1988) 4
   Const. L.J. 100; [1977] J.P.L. 514; (1987) 84 L.S.G. 319; (1987) 137 N.L.J. 794;
   (1977) 121 S.J. 377 HL. 8–113
Anslow v Norton Aluminium Ltd [2012] EWHC 2610. 20–29
Apis-Hristovich EOOD v Lakorda AD (C–545/07) [2009] Bus. L.R. 1554; [2009] E.C.R.
   I–1627; [2009] 3 C.M.L.R. 3; [2009] E.C.D.R. 13. 25–08
Apison v Dilnot [2011] EWHC 869 (QB). 23–03
APW v WPA [2012] EWHC 3151 (QB) 15–19, 27–46
Armstrong DLW GmbH v Winnington Networks Ltd [2012] EWHC 10 (Ch); [2013] Ch.
   156; [2012] 3 W.L.R. 835; [2012] 3 All E.R. 425; [2012] Bus. L.R. 1199; (2012)
   109(5) L.S.G. 20; (2012) 162 N.L.J. 181; [2012] Env. L.R. D4. 17–35
Armstrong v Keepmoat Homes Ltd Unreported February 3, 2012 QBD 12–25
Arrowhead Capital Finance Ltd (In Liquidation) v KPMG LLP [2012] EWHC 1801
   (Comm); [2012] P.N.L.R. 30 10–197
ASG v GSA [2009] EWCA Civ 1574 27–47
Ashley v Chief Constable of Sussex [2008] UKHL 25; [2008] 1 A.C. 962; [2008] 2 W.L.R.
   975; [2008] 3 All E.R. 573; [2008] Po. L.R. 203; (2008) 158 N.L.J. 632; (2008)
   152(17) S.J.L.B. 29. 15–52
Ashton v Turner [1981] Q.B. 137; [1980] 3 W.L.R. 736; [1980] 3 All E.R. 870; [1981]
   R.T.R. 54; (1980) 124 S.J. 792 QBD 3–18
Asmussen v Filtrona United Kingdom Ltd [2011] EWHC 1734 (QB) 2–50, 13–21A
Associated Newspapers Group Ltd v Wade [1979] 1 W.L.R. 697; [1979] I.C.R. 664; [1979]
   I.R.L.R. 201; (1979) 123 S.J. 250 CA (Civ Div) 24–177
Astellas Pharma v Stop Huntingdon Animal Cruelty [2011] EWCA Civ 752; (2011)
   155(26) S.J.L.B. 27. 5–79
Attorney General of Trinidad and Tobago v Ramanoop [2005] UKPC 15; [2006] 1 A.C.
   328; [2005] 2 W.L.R. 1324. 1–12
Austin v Commissioner of Police of the Metropolis [2009] UKHL 5; [2009] 1 A.C. 564;
   [2009] 2 W.L.R. 372; [2009] 3 All E.R. 455; [2009] H.R.L.R. 16; [2009] U.K.H.R.R.
   581; 26 B.H.R.C. 642; [2009] Po. L.R. 66; (2009) 153(4) S.J.L.B. 29 14–80
Austin v Southwark LBC [2010] UKSC 28; [2011] 1 A.C. 355; [2010] 3 W.L.R. 144;
   [2010] 4 All E.R. 16; [2010] P.T.S.R. 1311; [2010] H.L.R. 38; [2011] 1 P. & C.R. 8;
   [2010] 3 E.G.L.R. 45; [2010] 35 E.G. 94; [2010] 26 E.G. 90 (C.S.); (2010) 107(27)
   L.S.G. 16; (2010) 154(25) S.J.L.B. 42; [2010] N.P.C. 71. 20–63
Austin v United Kingdom (39692/09); Black v United Kingdom (40713/09); Lowenthal v
   United Kingdom (41008/09) (2012) 55 E.H.R.R. 14; 32 B.H.R.C. 618; [2012] Crim.
   L.R. 544 ECtHR 14–80, 15–64
Avrora Fine Arts Investment Ltd v Christie, Manson & Woods Ltd [2012] EWHC 2198
   (Ch); [2012] P.N.L.R. 35. 10–20
AXA General Insurance Ltd, Petitioners; sub nom. AXA General Insurance Ltd v Lord
   Advocate; AXA General Insurance Ltd v HM Advocate [2011] UKSC 46; [2012] 1
   A.C. 868; [2011] 3 W.L.R. 871; 2012 S.C. (U.K.S.C.) 122; 2011 S.L.T. 1061; [2012]
   H.R.L.R. 3; [2011] U.K.H.R.R. 1221; (2011) 122 B.M.L.R. 149; (2011) 108(41)
   L.S.G. 22. . . . . 1–27, 8–85, 13–03
Axel Springer AG v Germany (39954/08) [2012] E.M.L.R. 15; (2012) 55 E.H.R.R. 6; 32
   B.H.R.C. 493 ECtHR 27–38, 27–41
Aziz v Lim [2012] EWHC 915 (QB). 17–107, 17–125
B v Home Office; sub nom. AB v Home Office [2012] EWHC 226 (QB); [2012] 4 All E.R.
   276. 9–48
B v Ministry of Defence; sub nom. Ministry of Defence v AB; AB v Ministry of Defence
   [2012] UKSC 9; [2013] 1 A.C. 78; [2012] 2 W.L.R. 643; [2012] 3 All E.R. 673;
   [2012] P.I.Q.R. P13; [2012] Med. L.R. 306; (2012) 125 B.M.L.R. 69; (2012) 109(22)
   L.S.G. 19; (2012) 156(11) S.J.L.B. 3 . . . . 2–29—2–34, 2–64, 5–09, 32–42, 32–45,
                                           32–51, 32–56, 32–59

Bacardi-Martini Beverages Ltd v Thomas Hardy Packaging Ltd; sub nom. Messer UK Ltd
  v Thomas Hardy Packaging Ltd; Messer UK Ltd v Bacardi-Martini Beverages Ltd
  [2002] EWCA Civ 549; [2002] 2 All E.R. (Comm) 335; [2002] 2 Lloyd's Rep. 379 11–23
Bacon v Nacional Suiza CIA Seguros y Reseguros SA [2010] EWHC 2017 (QB); [2010]
  I.L.Pr. 46 7–14
Bailey v Graham; sub nom. Bailey v Graham (aka Levi Roots) [2012] EWCA Civ 1469 27–10
Bailey v Ministry of Defence [2008] EWCA Civ 883; [2009] 1 W.L.R. 1052; [2008] LS
  Law Medical 481; (2008) 103 B.M.L.R. 134 .... 2–29—2–34
Baker v Quantum Clothing Group Ltd; Grabowski v Pretty Polly Ltd; Parkes v Meridian
  Ltd; Baxter v Meridian Ltd [2011] UKSC 17; [2011] 1 W.L.R. 1003; [2011] 4 All
  E.R. 223; [2011] I.C.R. 523; [2011] P.I.Q.R. P14; (2011) 108(17) L.S.G. 13; (2011)
  155(15) S.J.L.B. 38 .... 8–142, 8–165, 9–17, 13–21, 13–21A, 13–30, 13–32, 13–33
Baker v TE Hopkins & Son Ltd; Ward v TE Hopkins & Son Ltd [1959] 1 W.L.R. 966;
  [1959] 3 All E.R. 225; (1959) 103 S.J. 812 CA 3–78
Balfour Beatty Engineering Services Ltd v Unite the Union [2012] EWHC 267 (QB);
  [2012] I.C.R. 822; [2012] I.R.L.R. 452 ..... 5–85, 24–112, 24–145, 24–146, 24–147, 24–163
Bangle v Lafreniere [2012] BCSC 256 17–98
Banque Bruxelles Lambert SA v Eagle Star Insurance Co Ltd [1994] 2 E.G.L.R. 108 10–181
Barclay-Watt v Alpha Panereti Public Ltd Unreported November 23, 2012 7–03
Barker v Corus UK Ltd; Murray (Deceased) v British Shipbuilders (Hydrodynamics) Ltd;
  Patterson (Deceased) v Smiths Dock Ltd; sub nom. Barker v Saint Gobain Pipelines Plc
  [2006] UKHL 20; [2006] 2 A.C. 572; [2006] 2 W.L.R. 1027; [2006] 3 All E.R. 785;
  [2006] I.C.R. 809; [2006] P.I.Q.R. P26; (2006) 89 B.M.L.R. 1; (2006) 103(20) L.S.G.
  27; (2006) 156 N.L.J. 796; (2006) 150 S.J.L.B. 606; [2006] N.P.C. 50 ...... 2–58—2–68, 2–62,
                                                                             28–09
Barr v Biffa Waste Services Ltd [2012] EWCA Civ 312; [2012] 3 All E.R. 380; 141 Con.
  L.R. 1; [2012] 13 E.G. 90 (C.S.); (2012) 109(14) L.S.G. 21; (2012) 156(12) S.J.L.B.
  31 .... 20–10, 20–14, 20–87, 20–107
Barratt Homes Ltd v Dwr Cymru Cyfyngedig (Welsh Water); sub nom. Dwr Cymru
  Cyfyngedig (Welsh Water) v Barratt Homes Ltd [2009] UKSC 13; [2010] 1 All E.R.
  965; [2010] 1 All E.R. 976; [2010] P.T.S.R. 651; 128 Con. L.R. 1; [2010] Env. L.R.
  14; [2010] 1 P. & C.R. 25; [2010] 1 E.G.L.R. 139; [2010] J.P.L. 721; [2009] 50 E.G.
  67 (C.S.); [2009] N.P.C. 140 .... 8–192, 9–09, 20–134
Barrett v Enfield LBC [2001] 2 A.C. 550; [1999] 3 W.L.R. 79; [1999] 3 All E.R. 193;
  [1999] 2 F.L.R. 426; [1999] 2 F.C.R. 434; (1999) 1 L.G.L.R. 829; [1999] B.L.G.R.
  473; (1999) 11 Admin. L.R. 839; [1999] Ed. C.R. 833; (1999) 2 C.C.L. Rep. 203;
  [1999] P.I.Q.R. P272; (1999) 49 B.M.L.R. 1; [1999] Fam. Law 622; (1999) 96(28)
  L.S.G. 27; (1999) 143 S.J.L.B. 183 HL 14–13
Baturina v Times Newspapers Ltd [2011] EWCA Civ 308; [2011] 1 W.L.R. 1526; [2011]
  E.M.L.R. 19; [2011] H.R.L.R. 22; 5 A.L.R. Int'l 877 22–65
Baxendale-Walker v Middleton [2011] EWHC 998 (QB) 5–94, 10–41, 14–116, 24–90, 24–95
Baxter v Mannion [2011] EWCA Civ 120; [2011] 1 W.L.R. 1594; [2011] 2 All E.R. 574;
  [2011] 2 E.G.L.R. 29; [2011] 20 E.G. 114; (2011) 161 N.L.J. 326; (2011) 155(8)
  S.J.L.B. 31 19–13
Bayerische Motoren Werke AG v Round & Metal Ltd [2012] EWHC 2099 (Pat); [2012]
  E.C.C. 28; [2013] F.S.R. 18; (2012) 109(34) L.S.G. 25; [2013] Bus. L.R. D30 25–69,
                                                                             25–82
Bazley v Wesley Monash IVF Pty Ltd [2010] QSC 118; [2011] 2 Qd R. 207; Re Edwards
  [2011] NSWSC 478; (2011) 4 A.S.T.L.R. 392 17–42
BBC v HarperCollins Publishers Ltd [2010] EWHC 2424 (Ch); [2011] E.M.L.R. 6; (2010)
  107(40) L.S.G. 23; (2010) 160 N.L.J. 1426 .... 27–10, 27–32
BBGP Managing General Partner Ltd v Babcock & Brown Global Partners [2010] EWHC
  2176 (Ch); [2011] Ch. 296; [2011] 2 W.L.R. 496; [2011] 2 All E.R. 297; [2011] Bus.
  L.R. 466; [2010] 2 C.L.C. 248 27–14
Beckett v New South Wales [2013] HCA 17 16–29
Beechwood Birmingham Ltd v Hoyer Group UK Ltd [2010] EWCA Civ 647; [2011] Q.B.
  357; [2010] 3 W.L.R. 1677; [2011] 1 All E.R. (Comm) 460; [2010] Bus. L.R. 1562;
  [2010] R.T.R. 33 .... 28–121, 28–127, 28–128
Belka v Prosperini [2011] EWCA Civ 623 3–72

Benetton Group SpA v G-Star International BV (C–371/06) [2007] E.C.R. I–7709; [2008]
  E.T.M.R. 5. 25–76
Berent v Family Mosaic Housing [2012] EWCA Civ 961; [2012] B.L.R. 488; [2012]
  C.I.L.L. 3213. 20–25
Beresford v Sovereign House Estates Ltd [2012] I.C.R. D9. 4–13
Berezovsky v Abramovich [2011] EWCA Civ 153; [2011] 1 W.L.R. 2290; [2011] 1 C.L.C.
  359; (2011) 108(10) L.S.G. 23 . . . . 24–57, 24–59, 24–61, 24–67, 32–20
Berry v Ashtead Plant Hire Co Ltd [2011] EWCA Civ 1304; [2012] P.I.Q.R. P6 13–13
Best Buy Co Inc v Worldwide Sales Corp Espana SL [2011] EWCA Civ 618; [2011] Bus.
  L.R. 1166; [2011] F.S.R. 30 25–86
Best v Smyth [2010] EWHC 1541 (QB). 3–84
Bezpecnostni Softwarova Asociace – Svaz Softwarove Ochrany v Ministerstvo Kultury
  (C–393/09) [2011] E.C.D.R. 3; [2011] F.S.R. 18 25–07
Bhatt v Fontain Motors Ltd [2010] EWCA Civ 863; [2010] P.I.Q.R. P17 . . . . 13–52, 13–64
Biffa Waste Services Ltd v Maschinenfabrik Ernst Hese GmbH [2008] EWCA Civ 1257;
  [2009] Q.B. 725; [2009] 3 W.L.R. 324; [2009] Bus. L.R. 696; [2009] B.L.R. 1; 122
  Con. L.R. 1; [2009] P.N.L.R. 12; (2008) 152(45) S.J.L.B. 25 . . . . 6–26, 20–73, 20–163
Birch v Ministry of Defence [2013] EWCA Civ 676 14–38
Blair v Chief Constable of Sussex [2012] EWCA Civ 633; (2012) 156(20) S.J.L.B. 31;
  [2012] I.C.R. D33 13–36
Blair-Ford v CRS Adventures Ltd [2012] EWHC 2360 (QB). 8–145, 8–163
Blue Sky One Ltd v Mahan Air; PK Airfinance US Inc v Blue Sky Two Ltd; sub nom. Blue
  Sky One Ltd v Blue Airways LLC [2009] EWHC 3314 (Comm) 17–31, 17–88
Blue Sky One Ltd v Mahan Air; PK Airfinance US Inc v Blue Sky Two Ltd [2010] EWHC
  631 (Comm) 17–81, 17–92, 17–114, 17–115
Bocardo SA v Star Energy UK Onshore Ltd; sub nom. Star Energy UK Onshore Ltd v
  Bocardo SA; Star Energy Weald Basin Ltd v Bocardo SA [2010] UKSC 35; [2011] 1
  A.C. 380; [2010] 3 W.L.R. 654; [2010] 3 All E.R. 975; [2011] B.L.R. 13; [2010] 3
  E.G.L.R. 145; [2010] R.V.R. 339; [2010] 31 E.G. 63 (C.S.); [2010] N.P.C. 88. 19–63
Bodey v Hall [2011] EWHC 2162 (QB); [2012] P.I.Q.R. P1 21–15
Bolam v Friern Hospital Management Committee [1957] 1 W.L.R. 582; [1957] 2 All E.R.
  118; [1955–95] P.N.L.R. 7; (1957) 101 S.J. 357 QBD. 8–200, 14–61
Bolitho (Deceased) v City and Hackney HA [1998] A.C. 232; [1997] 3 W.L.R. 1151;
  [1997] 4 All E.R. 771; [1998] P.I.Q.R. P10; [1998] Lloyd's Rep. Med. 26; (1998) 39
  B.M.L.R. 1; [1998] P.N.L.R. 1; (1997) 94(47) L.S.G. 30; (1997) 141 S.J.L.B. 238 HL
  . . . . 2–116, 10–98
Bonnard v Perryman [1891] 2 Ch. 269; [1891–94] All E.R. Rep. 965 CA. 22–256, 27–47
Bonnington Castings Ltd v Wardlaw; sub nom. Wardlaw v Bonnington Castings Ltd [1956]
  A.C. 613; [1956] 2 W.L.R. 707; [1956] 1 All E.R. 615; 1956 S.C. (H.L.) 26; 1956
  S.L.T. 135; 54 L.G.R. 153; (1956) 100 S.J. 207 HL. . . . . 2–12, 2–29—2–34, 2–34, 2–42
Bowen v National Trust for Places of Historic Interest or Natural Beauty [2011] EWHC
  1992 (QB). 12–29
Boycott v Perrins Guy Williams [2011] EWHC 2969 (Ch); [2012] P.N.L.R. 25 . . . . . . 32–13, 32–75
Boyle v Kodak [1969] 1 W.L.R. 661; [1969] 2 All E.R. 439; 6 K.I.R. 427; (1969) 113 S.J.
  382 HL 13–63
Boyle v MGN Ltd [2012] EWHC 2700 (QB) 22–03
Boyle v Thompsons Solicitors [2012] EWHC 36 (QB); [2012] P.N.L.R. 17 10–139
Brady v Norman [2011] EWCA Civ 107; [2011] C.P. Rep. 23; [2011] E.M.L.R. 16 22–197
Brierly v Kendall, Furnival, Douglass and Taylor, 117 E.R. 1540; (1852) 17 Q.B. 937 KB . . 17–115
Brink's Global Services Inc v Igrox Ltd [2010] EWCA Civ 1207; [2011] I.R.L.R. 343 . . . . . 6–30B
British Airways Plc v Unite the Union [2010] I.R.L.R. 423 [2010] EWCA Civ 669; [2010]
  I.C.R. 1316; [2010] I.R.L.R. 809; (2010) 107(22) L.S.G. 19. . . . . 24–116, 24–147,
                                                                             24–151, 24–163
British Chiropractic Association v Singh [2010] EWCA Civ 350; [2011] 1 W.L.R. 133;
  [2011] E.M.L.R. 1; (2010) 107(15) L.S.G. 17; (2010) 160 N.L.J. 547; (2010) 154(14)
  S.J.L.B. 2. 22–166
British Horseracing Board Ltd v William Hill Organisation Ltd (C–203/02) [2009] Bus.
  L.R. 932; [2004] E.C.R. I–10415; [2005] 1 C.M.L.R. 15; [2005] C.E.C. 68; [2005]
  E.C.D.R. 1; [2005] Info. T.L.R. 157; [2005] R.P.C. 13 25–08

British Industrial Plastics Ltd v Ferguson [1940] 1 All E.R. 479 24–19
British Sky Broadcasting Group Plc v Digital Satellite Warranty Cover Ltd (In Liquidation)
    [2011] EWHC 2662 (Ch); [2012] F.S.R. 14 25–83
British Sky Broadcasting Group Plc v Digital Satellite Warranty Cover Ltd (In Liquidation)
    [2011] EWHC 2662 (Ch); [2012] F.S.R. 14 27–08
British Sky Broadcasting Group Plc v Microsoft Corp [2013] EWHC 1826 (Ch) 26–11, 26–18
British Sugar Plc v James Robertson & Sons Ltd [1997] E.T.M.R. 118; [1996] R.P.C. 281;
    (1996) 19(3) I.P.D. 19023 Ch D 25–74
British Telecommunications Plc v One in a Million Ltd; Marks & Spencer Plc v One in a
    Million Ltd; Virgin Enterprises Ltd v One in a Million Ltd; J Sainsbury Plc v One in
    a Million Ltd; Ladbroke Group Plc v One in a Million Ltd [1999] 1 W.L.R. 903;
    [1998] 4 All E.R. 476; [1999] E.T.M.R. 61; [1997–98] Info. T.L.R. 423; [1998]
    I.T.C.L.R. 146; [2001] E.B.L.R. 2; [1999] F.S.R. 1; [1998] Masons C.L.R. 165;
    (1998) 95(37) L.S.G. 37; (1998) 148 N.L.J. 1179 CA (Civ Div) 26–04
Broker House Insurance Services Ltd v OJS Law [2010] EWHC 3816 (Ch); [2011]
    P.N.L.R. 23 10–147
Broster v Galliard Docklands Ltd [2011] EWHC 1722 (TCC); [2011] B.L.R. 569; 137 Con.
    L.R. 26; [2011] P.N.L.R. 34; [2011] C.I.L.L. 3065. . . . . 8–128, 8–129, 10–184
Brown v East Lothian Council [2013] CSOH 62; 2013 S.L.T. 721; 2013 G.W.D. 16–330 13–51
Brown v InnovatorOne Plc [2012] EWHC 1321 (Comm) 9–13, 9–25
Brown v Richmond upon Thames LBC [2012] EWCA Civ 1384. 13–28
Browne v Associated Newspapers Ltd [2007] EWCA Civ 295; [2008] Q.B. 103; [2007] 3
    W.L.R. 289; [2007] C.P. Rep. 29; [2007] E.M.L.R. 20; (2007) 157 N.L.J. 671 27–39
Broxton v McClelland (No.1) [1995] E.M.L.R. 485 CA (Civ Div) 16–64A
Bruhn Newtech Ltd v Datanetex Ltd [2012] EWPCC 17 25–57
Brumder v Motornet Service and Repairs Ltd [2013] EWCA Civ 195; [2013] 1 W.L.R.
    2783; [2013] 3 All E.R. 412; [2013] B.C.C. 381; [2013] 2 B.C.L.C. 58; [2013] I.C.R.
    1069; [2013] P.I.Q.R. P13. . . . . 3–44, 3–52, 3–113,
                                                          9–65, 13–63
BSB Group Plc v Digital Satellite Warranty Cover Ltd. *See* British Sky Broadcasting
    Group Plc v Digital Satellite Warranty Cover Ltd (In Liquidation)
Budejovicky Budvar Narodni Podnik v Anheuser-Busch Inc (C–482/09) [2012] Bus. L.R.
    298; [2012] E.T.M.R. 2; [2012] R.P.C. 11 25–76
Budejovicky Budvar Narodni Podnik v Anheuser-Busch Inc [2009] EWCA Civ 1022;
    [2010] R.P.C. 7; (2010) 33(1) I.P.D. 33003 25–74
Budejovicky Budvar Narodni Podnik v Anheuser-Busch Inc [2012] EWCA Civ
    880; [2012] 3 All E.R. 1405; [2012] E.T.M.R. 48; [2013] R.P.C. 12; (2012) 109(29)
    L.S.G. 29 25–76
Bunnings Group Ltd v CHEP Australia Ltd [2011] NSWCA 342 CA (NSW) 17–07,
    17–11,   17–72,   17–109
Burin Peninsula Community Development Corp v Grandy [2010] NLCA 69; (2011) 327
    D.L.R. (4th) 752 24–67
Burstein v Times Newspapers Ltd [2001] 1 W.L.R. 579; [2001] E.M.L.R. 14; (2001) 98(8)
    L.S.G. 44; (2001) 145 S.J.L.B. 30 CA (Civ Div) 22–240
Butler-Creagh v Hersham; Cherrilow Ltd v Butler-Creagh [2011] EWHC 2525 (QB) . . . .
    18–44,   18–46
Bux v Slough Metals [1973] 1 W.L.R. 1358; [1974] 1 All E.R. 262; [1974] 1 Lloyd's Rep.
    155; 15 K.I.R. 126; (1973) 117 S.J. 615 CA (Civ Div) 9–17
Buxton v Abertawe Bro Morgannwg University Local Health Board [2010] EWHC 1187
    (QB); (2010) 115 B.M.L.R. 62 10–67
CA (Civ Div) 16–64A
Cadder (Peter) v HM Advocate [2010] UKSC 43; [2010] 1 W.L.R. 2601; 2011 S.C.
    (U.K.S.C.) 13; 2010 S.L.T. 1125; 2010 S.C.L. 1265; 2010 S.C.C.R. 951; [2011]
    H.R.L.R. 1; [2010] U.K.H.R.R. 1171; 30 B.H.R.C. 257; (2010) 107(43) L.S.G. 21;
    (2010) 154(41) S.J.L.B. 30 . . . . 9–14, 9–24, 9–44
Caerphilly CBC v Button [2010] EWCA Civ 1311; [2011] I.C.R. D3 . . . . 13–51, 13–54
Cairns v Modi; KC v MGN Ltd; sub nom. C v MGN Ltd [2012] EWCA Civ 1382; [2013]
    1 W.L.R. 1015; [2013] E.M.L.R. 8 . . . . 22–08, 22–224
Cairns-Jones v Christie Tyler South West Wales Division Ltd [2010] EWCA Civ 1642 32–61

Calix v Attorney General of Trinidad and Tobago [2013] UKPC 15; *Times*, July 16, 2013 . . . 15–42, 16–05

Camatic Pty Ltd v Bluecube Ltd [2012] E.C.D.R. 12 25–64

Cambridge v Makin [2011] EWHC 12 (QB). 22–210

Cambridge v Makin [2012] EWCA Civ 85; [2012] E.M.L.R. 19 . . . . 22–129, 22–210

Campbell v Mirror Group Newspapers Ltd; sub nom. Campbell v MGN Ltd [2004] UKHL
    22; [2004] 2 A.C. 457; [2004] 2 W.L.R. 1232; [2004] 2 All E.R. 995; [2004] E.M.L.R.
    15; [2004] H.R.L.R. 24; [2004] U.K.H.R.R. 648; 16 B.H.R.C. 500; (2004) 101(21)
    L.S.G. 36; (2004) 154 N.L.J. 733; (2004) 148 S.J.L.B. 572. . . . . 27–12, 27–39

Caparo Industries Plc v Dickman [1990] 2 A.C. 605; [1990] 2 W.L.R. 358; [1990] 1 All
    E.R. 568; [1990] B.C.C. 164; [1990] B.C.L.C. 273; [1990] E.C.C. 313; [1955–95]
    P.N.L.R. 523; (1990) 87(12) L.S.G. 42; (1990) 140 N.L.J. 248; (1990) 134 S.J. 494
    HL. 5–46A, 8–106, 13–04, 14–08, 14–38

Caribbean Steel Co Ltd v Price Waterhouse (A Firm) [2013] UKPC 18; [2013]
    P.N.L.R. 27 10–03

Carlgarth, The; Otarama, The; Carlgarth, The; Otarama, The [1927] P. 93 CA 12–17

Carter v Ministry of Justice [2010] EWCA Civ 694 8–167

Cassa di Risparmio della Repubblica di San Marino SpA v Barclays Bank Ltd [2011]
    EWHC 484 (Comm); [2011] 1 C.L.C. 701. 18–14

Castle v Commissioner of Police of the Metropolis; sub nom. R. (on the application of
    Castle) v Commissioner of Police of the Metropolis [2011] EWHC 2317 (Admin);
    [2012] 1 All E.R. 953; (2011) 108(36) L.S.G. 18; (2011) 161 N.L.J. 1252 15–64

Catanzano v Studio London Ltd (Appeal No. UKEAT/0487/11/DM) March 7, 2012 EAT 4–04

Caterpillar Logistics Services (UK) Ltd v Huesca de Crean [2012] EWCA Civ 156; [2012]
    3 All E.R. 129; [2012] C.P. Rep. 22; [2012] I.C.R. 981; [2012] F.S.R. 33. 27–14

Catt v Association of Chief Police Officers; sub nom. Catt v Commissioner of Police of the
    Metropolis [2012] EWHC 1471 (Admin); [2012] H.R.L.R. 23; [2012] P.N.L.R. 27;
    [2012] A.C.D. 91. 14–86

Cavalier v Pope [1906] A.C. 428 HL. 12–83

CDE v MGN Ltd [2010] EWHC 3308 (QB); [2011] 1 F.L.R. 1524; [2011] Fam. Law 360. . . . 27–44

CEF Holdings Ltd v Mundey [2012] EWHC 1524 (QB); [2012] I.R.L.R. 912; [2012]
    F.S.R. 35 27–15

Celaya Emparanza y Galdos Internacional SA (Cegasa) v Proyectos Integrales de
    Balizamiento SL (C–488/10) [2012] E.C.D.R. 17 25–68

Centrafarm BV v Sterling Drug Inc (15/74); Centrafarm BV v Winthrop BV (16/74) [1974]
    E.C.R. 1183; [1974] E.C.R. 1147; [1974] 2 C.M.L.R. 480; [1975] F.S.R. 161 25–102

Centre Hospitalier Universitaire de Besancon v Dutrueux (C–495/10) [2012] 2 C.M.L.R.
    1; [2012] C.E.C. 1054; (2012) 127 B.M.L.R. 1 11–46

Centrotherm Systemtechnik v OHIM (T–434/09) (OJ 2011 C311/43) 25–79

Ceva Logistics Ltd v Lynch (t/a SW Lynch Electrical Contractors); sub nom. Lynch v Ceva
    Logistics Ltd [2011] EWCA Civ 188; [2011] I.C.R. 746. . . . . 13–35, 13–51

Challinor v Juliet Bellis & Co [2013] EWHC 347 (Ch) 10–15

Challinor v Staffordshire CC [2011] EWCA Civ 90 19–31

Chambers v Havering LBC [2011] EWCA Civ 1576; [2012] 1 P. & C.R. 17; [2012] 1 P. &
    C.R. DG15 19–15

Chandler v Cape Plc [2012] EWCA Civ 525; [2012] 1 W.L.R. 3111; [2012] 3 All E.R. 640;
    [2012] I.C.R. 1293; [2012] P.I.Q.R. P17. . . . . 4–04, 5–78A, 13–04

Chartered Institute of Patent Attorneys v Registrar of Trade Marks (C–307/10) [2013] Bus.
    L.R. 740; [2013] C.E.C. 361; [2012] E.T.M.R. 42; [2013] R.P.C. 11. 25–76

Checkprice (UK) Ltd (In Administration) v Revenue and Customs Commissioners. *See*
    R. (on the application of Checkprice (UK) Ltd (In Administration)) v Revenue and
    Customs Commissioners

Chen v Gu [2011] NSWSC 1622. . . . . 10–118, 17–104

Cheng v Tse Wai Chun Paul. *See* Tse Wai Chun Paul v Cheng

Cheung v Zhu (t/a Yang Sing Fish and Chip) [2011] EWHC 2913 (QB) 13–56

Chief Constable of Hampshire v Taylor [2013] EWCA Civ 496; [2013] P.I.Q.R. P20. 2–12,
13–36

Chief Constable of Merseyside v Owens [2012] EWHC 1515 (Admin); (2012)
    176 J.P. 68. 17–47

Chinery v Viall, 157 E.R. 1192; (1860) 5 Hurl. & N. 288 Ct Ex. 17–114
Chocosuisse Union des Fabricants Suisses de Chocolat v Cadbury Ltd [1999] E.T.M.R.
   1020; [1999] R.P.C. 826; (1999) 22(8) I.P.D. 22079 26–16
Chubb Fire Ltd v Vicar of Spalding [2010] EWCA Civ 981; [2010] 2 C.L.C. 277; (2010)
   154(33) S.J.L.B. 29; [2010] N.P.C. 9 2–105
Citation Plc v Ellis Whittam Ltd [2013] EWCA Civ 155 23–17
City of London Corp v Samede [2012] EWCA Civ 160; [2012] 2 All E.R. 1039; [2012]
   P.T.S.R. 1624; [2012] H.R.L.R. 14; [2012] B.L.G.R. 372; (2012) 109(10) L.S.G. 19 . . . 14–93A
City of London Corp v Samede [2012] EWHC 34 (QB); (2012) 109(5) L.S.G. 21 19–70
Clark v Bourne Leisure Ltd [2011] EWCA Civ 753 12–28
Clifford v Chief Constable of the Hertfordshire Constabulary [2011] EWHC 815
   (QB) 14–116, 16–05, 16–54
Clift v Slough BC [2010] EWCA Civ 1484; [2011] 1 W.L.R. 1774; [2011] 3 All E.R. 118;
   [2011] P.T.S.R. 990; [2011] E.M.L.R. 13; [2011] U.K.H.R.R. 248; (2011) 155(1)
   S.J.L.B. 30. . . . . 22–14, 22–119
CMCS Common Market Commercial Services AVV v Taylor; sub nom. Taylor v Stoutt
   [2011] EWHC 324 (Ch); [2011] 3 Costs L.O. 259; [2011] P.N.L.R. 17. 10–121
Co-operative Group (CWS) Ltd v Pritchard; sub nom. Pritchard v Co-operative Group
   (CWS) Ltd [2011] EWCA Civ 329; [2012] Q.B. 320; [2011] 3 W.L.R. 1272; [2012]
   1 All E.R. 205 3–54
Cockbill v Riley [2013] EWHC 656 (QB) 8–193, 12–29
Coco v AN Clark (Engineers) Ltd [1968] F.S.R. 415; [1969] R.P.C. 41 Ch D 27–39
Coles v Hetherton [2012] EWHC 1599 (Comm); [2013] 1 All E.R. (Comm) 453; [2012]
   R.T.R. 33; [2013] Lloyd's Rep. I.R. 9; (2012) 162 N.L.J. 873. 28–124
Collins Stewart Ltd v Financial Times Ltd (No.2) [2005] EWHC 262 (QB); [2006]
   E.M.L.R. 5 28–138
Colloseum Holding AG v Levi Strauss & Co (C–12/12) [2013] Bus. L.R. 768; [2013]
   E.T.M.R. 34. 25–79
Colour Quest Ltd v Total Downstream UK Plc; Total UK Ltd v Chevron Ltd; sub nom.
   Shell UK Ltd v Total UK Ltd [2009] EWHC 540 (Comm); [2009] 2 Lloyd's Rep. 1;
   [2009] 1 C.L.C. 186; (2009) 153(12) S.J.L.B. 29. 6–26
Commissioner of Police of the Metropolis v Times Newspapers Ltd [2011] EWHC 2705
   (QB) 27–12
Commonwealth Life Assurance Society Ltd v Smith (1938) 59 C.L.R. 527; [1938]
   HCA 2 16–29
Connor v Surrey CC [2010] EWCA Civ 286; [2011] Q.B. 429; [2010] 3 W.L.R. 1302;
   [2010] 3 All E.R. 905; [2010] P.T.S.R. 1643; [2010] I.R.L.R. 521; [2010] E.L.R. 363;
   (2010) 13 C.C.L. Rep. 491 . . . . 9–41, 13–25,
                                                                              14–08, 14–51
Contostavlos v Mendahum [2012] EWHC 850 (QB) 27–39
Cook v Telegraph Media Group Ltd [2011] EWHC 1134 (QB) 22–166
Cook v Telegraph Media Group Ltd [2011] EWHC 763 (QB) 22–03, 22–166, 22–167A
Cooper v Crabtree (1882) 20 Ch. D. 589 CA 20–66
Cooper v Turrell [2011] EWHC 3269 (QB) 27–48
Cooperative Group Ltd v John Allen Associates Ltd [2010] EWHC 2300 (TCC); (2012) 28
   Const. L.J. 27 10–189
Copley v Lawn; Maden v Haller [2009] EWCA Civ 580; [2010] 1 All E.R. (Comm) 890;
   [2010] Bus. L.R. 83; [2009] R.T.R. 24; [2009] Lloyd's Rep. I.R. 496; [2009] P.I.Q.R.
   P21 28–09
Corbett v Cumbria Kart Racing Club [2013] EWHC 1362 (QB) 8–145, 12–29
Corr v IBC Vehicles Ltd [2008] UKHL 13; [2008] 1 A.C. 884; [2008] 2 W.L.R. 499; [2008]
   2 All E.R. 943; [2008] I.C.R. 372; [2008] P.I.Q.R. P11; (2008) 105(10) L.S.G. 28;
   (2008) 152(9) S.J.L.B. 30. 2–105
Costa v Imperial London Hotels Ltd [2012] EWCA Civ 672 13–59
Coty Prestige Lancaster Group GmbH v Simex Trading AG (C–127/09) [2010] E.T.M.R.
   41; [2010] F.S.R. 38 25–82
Couch v Attorney General [2010] NZSC 27 28–146
Coulson v News Group Newspapers Ltd [2012] EWCA Civ 1547; [2013] 1 Costs L.O. 117;
   [2013] I.R.L.R. 116. 4–34

Coventry (t/a RDC Promotions) v Lawrence; sub nom. Lawrence v Fen Tigers Ltd;
 Lawrence v Coventry (t/a RDC Promotions) [2012] EWCA Civ 26; [2012] 1 W.L.R.
 2127; [2012] 3 All E.R. 168; [2012] P.T.S.R. 1505; 141 Con. L.R. 79; [2012] Env.
 L.R. 28; [2012] 1 E.G.L.R. 165; [2012] 10 E.G. 88 (C.S.); (2012) 109(11) L.S.G. 21;
 (2012) 156(9) S.J.L.B. 31 . . . . 20–14, 20–85
Cowan v Hopetoun House Preservation Trust [2013] CSOH 9; 2013 Rep. L.R. 62; 2013
 G.W.D. 4–125 12–29
Cowshed Products Ltd v Island Origins Ltd [2010] EWHC 3357 (Ch); [2011] E.T.M.R. 42;
 (2011) 108(3) L.S.G. 17 . . . . 26–20, 25–83
Cox v Ergo Versicherung AG (formerly Victoria) [2012] EWCA Civ 1001 7–13
Crawford Adjusters v Sagicor General Insurance (Cayman) Ltd [2013] UKPC 17; [2013]
 4 All E.R. 8 . . . . 16–01, 16–04, 16–06, 16–08, 16–09,
 16–10, 16–62, 16–64, 16–64A
Crosstown Music Co 1 LLC v Rive Droite Music Ltd [2010] EWCA Civ 1222; [2012] Ch.
 68; [2011] 2 W.L.R. 779; [2011] Bus. L.R. 383; [2011] E.C.D.R. 5; [2011] E.M.L.R.
 7; [2011] F.S.R. 5 25–17
Cruddas v Calvert [2013] EWCA Civ 748 . . . . 22–30, 23–03
Cruddas v Calvert [2013] EWHC 1096 (QB) 23–10
Cruddas v Times Newspapers Ltd. *See* Cruddas v Calvert
CTB v News Group Newspapers Ltd [2011] EWHC 1326 (QB) 27–47
Cullen v Chief Constable of the Royal Ulster Constabulary [2003] UKHL 39; [2003] 1
 W.L.R. 1763; [2004] 2 All E.R. 237; [2003] N.I. 375; [2003] Po. L.R. 337; (2003)
 100(15) L.S.G. 38; (2003) 147 S.J.L.B. 873. . . . . 9–14, 9–24, 9–44
Cumberbatch v Crown Prosecution Service; Ali v Department of Public Prosecutions
 [2009] EWHC 3353 (Admin); (2010) 174 J.P. 149; [2010] M.H.L.R. 9 15–77
Customs and Excise Commissioners v Barclays Bank Plc [2006] UKHL 28; [2007] 1 A.C.
 181; [2006] 3 W.L.R. 1; [2006] 4 All E.R. 256; [2006] 2 All E.R. (Comm) 831;
 [2006] 2 Lloyd's Rep. 327; [2006] 1 C.L.C. 1096; (2006) 103(27) L.S.G. 33; (2006)
 156 N.L.J. 1060; (2006) 150 S.J.L.B. 859 . . . . 8–99, 14–17, 14–56
Customs and Excise Commissioners v Total Network SL; sub nom. Revenue and Customs
 Commissioners v Total Network SL; Total Network SL v Revenue and Customs
 Commissioners [2008] UKHL 19; [2008] 1 A.C. 1174; [2008] 2 W.L.R. 711; [2008]
 2 All E.R. 413; [2008] S.T.C. 644; [2008] Lloyd's Rep. F.C. 275; [2008] B.P.I.R.
 699; [2008] B.T.C. 5216; [2008] B.V.C. 340; [2008] S.T.I. 938; (2008) 152(12)
 S.J.L.B. 29. . . . . 24–73, 24–93, 24–94, 24–100
D v East Berkshire Community NHS Trust. *See* JD v East Berkshire Community Health
 NHS Trust
D&F Estates Ltd v Church Commissioners for England [1989] A.C. 177; [1988] 3 W.L.R.
 368; [1988] 2 All E.R. 992; 41 B.L.R. 1; 15 Con. L.R. 35; [1988] 2 E.G.L.R. 213;
 (1988) 4 Const. L.J. 100; [1988] E.G. 113 (C.S.); (1988) 85(33) L.S.G. 46; (1988)
 138 N.L.J. Rep. 210; (1988) 132 S.J. 1092 HL 8–128
Dahlia Fashion Co Ltd v Broadcast Session Ltd [2012] EWPCC 23 25–59
Dalkia France (Societe) v Moteurs Leroy Somer (Societe) [2010] E.C.C. 32 Cour de
 Cassation (France) 11–46
Dalling v RJ Heale & Co Ltd [2011] EWCA Civ 365. . . . . 2–120, 2–121
Darbishire v Warran [1963] 1 W.L.R. 1067; [1963] 3 All E.R. 310; [1963] 2 Lloyd's Rep.
 187; (1963) 107 S.J. 631 CA. 28–124
Darker v Chief Constable of the West Midlands Police [2001] 1 A.C. 435 10–41
Davis v Catto [2011] CSIH 85; 2012 Rep. L.R. 40; 2012 G.W.D. 3–54. 4–03
Davis v Gell (1924) 35 C.L.R. 275; [1924] HCA 56. 16–29
Davison v Habeeb [2011] EWHC 3031 (QB); [2012] 3 C.M.L.R. 6 . . . . 22–08, 22–67
Dawkins v Carnival Plc (t/a P&O Cruises) [2011] EWCA Civ 1237; [2012] 1 Lloyd's Rep.
 1. . . . . 8–176, 12–07, 12–29
Dawson v Page [2013] CSIH 24; 2013 G.W.D. 13–289 12–09
DC Thomson & Co Ltd v Deakin [1952] Ch. 646; [1952] 2 All E.R. 361; [1952] 2 T.L.R.
 105 CA 24–40
DD v Durham CC [2013] EWCA Civ 96 15–116
De Maudsley v Palumbo [1996] E.M.L.R. 460; [1996] F.S.R. 447 Ch D. 27–10
Dean v Kotsopoulos [2012] ONCA 143 17–44

Dee v Telegraph Media Group Ltd [2010] EWHC 924 (QB); [2010] E.M.L.R. 20; (2010)
160 N.L.J. 653. 22–39
Delaney v Pickett [2011] EWCA Civ 1532; [2012] 1 W.L.R. 2149; [2012] R.T.R. 16;
[2013] Lloyd's Rep. I.R. 24; [2012] P.I.Q.R. P10. . . . . 3–18, 3–33, 3–36
Dennard v PricewaterhouseCoopers LLP [2010] EWHC 812 (Ch) 10–18, 10–204,
10–207
Derbyshire CC v Times Newspapers Ltd [1993] A.C. 534; [1993] 2 W.L.R. 449; [1993]
1 All E.R. 1011; 91 L.G.R. 179; (1993) 143 N.L.J. 283; (1993) 137 S.J.L.B. 52
HL. 5–88, 22–35
Desmond v Chief Constable of Nottinghamshire [2011] EWCA Civ 3; [2011] P.T.S.R.
1369; [2011] 1 F.L.R. 1361; [2011] Fam. Law 358 . . . . 8–43, 8–53, 8–110, 16–01
Desmond v Foreman [2012] EWHC 1900 (QB). 14–31
DFT v TFD [2010] EWHC 2335 (QB) 27–47
DH NHS Foundation Trust v PS [2010] EWHC 1217 (Fam); [2010] 2 F.L.R. 1236; (2010)
13 C.C.L. Rep. 606; [2010] Med. L.R. 320; (2010) 116 B.M.L.R. 142; [2010] Fam.
Law 927 10–61
Dhamija v Sunningdale Joineries Ltd [2010] EWHC 2396 (TCC); [2011] P.N.L.R. 9;
[2010] C.I.L.L. 2937. . . . . 10–21, 10–191
DHL Express France SAS v Chronopost SA (C–235/09) [2012] C.E.C. 22; [2011] E.T.M.R.
33; [2011] F.S.R. 38 25–83
Diageo North America Inc v Intercontinental Brands (ICB) Ltd [2010] EWCA Civ 920;
[2011] 1 All E.R. 242; [2012] Bus. L.R. 401; [2010] E.T.M.R. 57; [2011] R.P.C. 2;
(2010) 154(31) S.J.L.B. 29 26–16
Dickins v O2 Plc [2008] EWCA Civ 1144; [2009] I.R.L.R. 58; (2008) 105(41) L.S.G. 19 13–28
Die BergSpechte Outdoor Reisen und Alpinschule Edi Koblmuller GmbH v Guni
(C–278/08) [2010] E.C.R. I–2517; [2010] E.T.M.R. 33. 25–81
Digicel (St Lucia) Ltd v Cable & Wireless Plc [2010] EWHC 774 (Ch) 9–12
Directmedia Publishing GmbH v Albert-Ludwigs-Universitat Freiburg (C–304/07) [2009]
Bus. L.R. 908; [2008] E.C.R. I–7565; [2009] 1 C.M.L.R. 7; [2009] C.E.C. 166;
[2009] E.C.D.R. 3; [2009] E.M.L.R. 6; [2008] Info. T.L.R. 373; [2009] R.P.C. 10. 25–08
Diver v Loktronic Industries Ltd [2012] NZCA 131; [2012] 2 N.Z.L.R. 131 CA (NZ) 24–15
Divya v Toyo Tire and Rubber Co Ltd (t/a Toyo Tires of Japan) [2011] EWHC 1993 (QB) . . . 11–41
Dobson v Thames Water Utilities Ltd [2011] EWHC 3253 (TCC); 140 Con. L.R. 135. 14–101,
20–29, 20–63, 20–77, 20–90, 20–119, 20–134
Dolphina, The [2011] SGHC 273; [2012] 1 Lloyd's Rep. 304 . . . . 24–93, 24–94, 24–97, 24–98,
24–105
Donoghue v Stevenson; sub nom. McAlister v Stevenson [1932] A.C. 562; 1932 S.C.
(H.L.) 31; 1932 S.L.T. 317; [1932] W.N. 139 HL 11–09, 11–19
Doosan Power Systems Ltd v Babcock International Group Plc [2013] EWHC 1364 (Ch);
[2013] E.T.M.R. 40. . . . . 25–15, 26–18
Dormeuil Freres SA v Feraglow [1990] R.P.C. 449 Ch D. 25–83
Dow Jones & Co Inc v Jameel. See Jameel v Dow Jones & Co Inc
Dowson & Mason v Potter [1986] 1 W.L.R. 1419; [1986] 2 All E.R. 418; (1986) 83 L.S.G.
3429; (1986) 130 S.J. 841 CA (Civ Div) 27–33
Dowson v Chief Constable of Northumbria [2010] EWHC 2612 (QB) 15–21
DPP v Fearon [2010] EWHC 340 (Admin); [2010] 2 Cr. App. R. 22; (2010) 174 J.P. 145;
[2010] Crim. L.R. 646; [2010] A.C.D. 39. 20–03
Drake v Foster Wheeler Ltd [2010] EWHC 2004 (QB); [2011] 1 All E.R. 63; [2011]
P.T.S.R. 1178; [2010] P.I.Q.R. P19; (2010) 116 B.M.L.R. 186; [2010] W.T.L.R. 1715;
(2010) 154(32) S.J.L.B. 29 28–27
Drysdale v Hedges [2012] 3 E.G.L.R. 105; (2012) 162 N.L.J. 1056 QBD. . 8–40, 12–09,
12–83,   12–85
DSG Retail Ltd v Comet Group Plc [2002] EWHC 116 (QB); [2002] U.K.C.L.R. 557;
[2002] F.S.R. 58 25–82
Dubai Aluminium Co Ltd v Salaam; Dubai Aluminium Co Ltd v Amhurst Brown Martin &
Nicholson [2002] UKHL 48; [2003] 2 A.C. 366; [2002] 3 W.L.R. 1913; [2003] 1 All
E.R. 97; [2003] 2 All E.R. (Comm) 451; [2003] 1 Lloyd's Rep. 65; [2003] 1 B.C.L.C.
32; [2003] 1 C.L.C. 1020; [2003] I.R.L.R. 608; [2003] W.T.L.R. 163; (2003) 100(7)
L.S.G. 36; (2002) 146 S.J.L.B. 280 . . . . 5–90, 6–30B

Dublin City Council v Technical Engineering and Electrical Union [2010] IEHC 289;
  [2010] 4 I.R. 667. 24–177
Duke of Brunswick v Harmer, 117 E.R. 75; (1849) 14 Q.B. 185 QB 22–04
Durham v BAI (Run Off) Ltd; sub nom. Fleming v Independent Insurance Co Ltd; Edwards
  v Excess Insurance Co Ltd; Thomas Bates & Son Ltd v BAI (Run Off) Ltd; Akzo
  Nobel UK Ltd v Excess Insurance Co Ltd; Municipal Mutual Insurance Ltd v Zurich
  Insurance Co [2012] UKSC 14; [2012] 1 W.L.R. 867; [2012] 3 All E.R. 1161; [2012]
  2 All E.R. (Comm) 1187; [2012] I.C.R. 574; [2012] Lloyd's Rep. I.R. 371; [2012]
  P.I.Q.R. P14; (2012) 125 B.M.L.R. 137; (2012) 162 N.L.J. 502; (2012) 156(13)
  S.J.L.B. 31. . . . . 2–58—2–68, 2–62,
                                                                                      2–66, 4–39, 28–19
Dwr Cymru Cyfyngedig (Welsh Water) v Barratt Homes Ltd; sub nom. Barratt Homes Ltd
  v Dwr Cymru Cyfyngedig (Welsh Water) [2013] EWCA Civ 233; 147 Con. L.R. 1;
  [2013] Env. L.R. 30. . . . . 9–09, 9–12, 20–30, 20–77, 20–134
Dyson Ltd v Vax Ltd [2011] EWCA Civ 1206; [2013] Bus. L.R. 328; [2012]
  F.S.R. 4 . . . . 25–63, 25–64, 25–68
E v English Province of Our Lady of Charity; sub nom. JGE v English Province of Our
  Lady of Charity; JGE v Portsmouth Roman Catholic Diocesan Trust [2012] EWCA
  Civ 938; [2013] Q.B. 722; [2013] 2 W.L.R. 958; [2012] 4 All E.R. 1152; [2013]
  P.T.S.R. 565; [2012] I.R.L.R. 846; [2012] P.I.Q.R. P19 [2012] EWCA Civ 938;
  [2013] Q.B. 722; [2013] 2 W.L.R. 958; [2012] 4 All E.R. 1152; [2013] P.T.S.R. 565;
  [2012] I.R.L.R. 846; [2012] P.I.Q.R. P19 6–31
E v English Province of Our Lady of Charity; sub nom. JGE v English Province of Our
  Lady of Charity; JGE v Portsmouth Roman Catholic Diocesan Trust [2012] EWCA
  Civ 938; [2013] Q.B. 722; [2013] 2 W.L.R. 958; [2012] 4 All E.R. 1152; [2013]
  P.T.S.R. 565; [2012] I.R.L.R. 846; [2012] P.I.Q.R. P19 6–01
Eaton Mansions (Westminster) Ltd v Stinger Compania de Inversion SA [2012] EWHC
  3354 (Ch); [2012] 49 E.G. 66 (C.S.). 19–63, 19–69, 28–138
Eaton Mansions (Westminster) Ltd v Stinger Compania de Inversion SA [2011] EWCA
  Civ 607; [2011] H.L.R. 42; [2011] L. & T.R. 24 19–01
Ecclestone v Medway NHS Foundation Trust [2013] EWHC 790 (QB) 10–67
eDate Advertising GmbH v X (C–509/09); Martinez v MGN Ltd (C–161/10); sub nom.
  E-Date Advertising GmbH v X (C–509/09) [2012] Q.B. 654; [2012] 3 W.L.R. 227;
  [2012] C.E.C. 837; [2012] I.L.Pr. 8; [2012] E.M.L.R. 12 7–04
Edenwest Ltd v CMS Cameron McKenna [2012] EWHC 1258 (Ch); [2013] B.C.C. 152;
  [2013] 1 B.C.L.C. 525; (2012) 109(22) L.S.G. 20 10–116
EDF Energy Powerlink Ltd v National Union of Rail, Maritime and Transport Workers
  [2009] EWHC 2852 (QB); [2010] I.R.L.R. 114. 24–152
Ediger v Johnston [2013] SCC 18; (2013) 356 D.L.R. (4th) 575 10–96
EDO Technology Ltd (EDO) v Campaign to Smash EDO (Preliminary Issues) [2005]
  EWHC 2490 (QB). 15–21
Edwards v National Coal Board [1949] 1 K.B. 704; [1949] 1 All E.R. 743; 65 T.L.R. 430;
  (1949) 93 S.J. 337 CA. 13–30
Edwin Hill & Partners v First National Finance Corp [1989] 1 W.L.R. 225; [1988] 3 All
  E.R. 801; [1989] B.C.L.C. 89; [1988] 48 E.G. 83; [1988] E.G. 116 (C.S.); (1988)
  85(32) L.S.G. 44; (1988) 138 N.L.J. Rep. 268; (1988) 122 S.J. 1389 CA (Civ Div). 24–55
Egan v Central Manchester and Manchester Children's University Hospitals NHS Trust
  [2008] EWCA Civ 1424; [2009] I.C.R. 585. 13–58
El Naschie v Macmillan Publishers Ltd (t/a Nature Publishing Group) [2012] EWHC 1809
  (QB) 22–72, 22–140
EL v Children's Society [2012] EWHC 365 (QB) 6–31
Eli Lilly & Co v Human Genome Sciences Inc; sub nom. Human Genome Sciences Inc v
  Eli Lilly & Co [2011] UKSC 51; [2012] 1 All E.R. 1154; [2012] R.P.C. 6; (2011)
  108(44) L.S.G. 18; [2012] Bus. L.R. D37 25–94
Ellis v Bristol City Council [2007] EWCA Civ 685; [2007] I.C.R. 1614; [2007] P.I.Q.R.
  P26 13–56
Enfield LBC v Outdoor Plus Ltd [2012] EWCA Civ 608; [2012] C.P. Rep. 35; [2012] 2
  E.G.L.R. 105; [2012] 29 E.G. 86 19–63
Entick v Carrington, 95 E.R. 807; (1765) 2 Wils. K.B. 275 KB 14–38

Environmental Manufacturing LLP v Office for Harmonisation in the Internal Market
(Trade Marks and Designs) (OHIM) (T–570/10) [2012] E.T.M.R. 54. . . . . 25–79, 25–81
Esdale v Dover DC [2010] EWCA Civ 409 12–09
ETK v News Group Newspapers Ltd. *See* K v News Group Newspapers Ltd
Euromoney Institutional Investor Plc v Aviation News Ltd [2013] EWHC 1505
(QB) 22–35, 23–10, 23–18
Eva Maria Painer v Standard VerlagsGmbH et al (C–145/10). *See* Painer v Standard
Verlags GmbH (C–145/10)
Evans (t/a Firecraft) v Focal Point Fires Plc [2009] EWHC 2784 (Ch); [2010] E.T.M.R. 29;
[2010] R.P.C. 15; (2010) 33(1) I.P.D. 33004 25–79
Evegate Publishing Ltd v Newsquest Media (Southern) Ltd [2013] EWHC 1975 (Ch). 26–11
Everett v Comojo (UK) Ltd (t/a Metropolitan) [2011] EWCA Civ 13; [2012] 1 W.L.R. 150;
[2011] 4 All E.R. 315; [2011] P.I.Q.R. P8; (2011) 108(5) L.S.G. 19; (2011) 161 N.L.J.
172; (2011) 155(3) S.J.L.B. 39. . . . . 8–51, 12–04
F Hoffmann La Roche & Co AG v Secretary of State for Trade and Industry [1975] A.C.
295; [1974] 3 W.L.R. 104; [1974] 2 All E.R. 1128; [1975] 3 All E.R. 945; (1973) 117
S.J. 713; (1974) 118 S.J. 500 HL 29–28
Fage UK Ltd v Chobani UK Ltd [2012] EWHC 3755 (Ch) 26–17
Fage UK Ltd v Chobani UK Ltd [2013] EWHC 298 (Ch) 26–17
Fage UK Ltd v Chobani UK Ltd [2013] EWHC 630 (Ch); [2013] E.T.M.R. 28; [2013]
F.S.R. 32; (2013) 157(14) S.J.L.B. 31 26–16
Fairchild v Glenhaven Funeral Services Ltd (t/a GH Dovener & Son); Pendleton v Stone &
Webster Engineering Ltd; Dyson v Leeds City Council (No.2); Matthews v Associated
Portland Cement Manufacturers (1978) Ltd; Fox v Spousal (Midlands) Ltd; Babcock
International Ltd v National Grid Co Plc; Matthews v British Uralite Plc [2002]
UKHL 22; [2003] 1 A.C. 32; [2002] 3 W.L.R. 89; [2002] 3 All E.R. 305; [2002]
I.C.R. 798; [2002] I.R.L.R. 533; [2002] P.I.Q.R. P28; [2002] Lloyd's Rep. Med. 361;
(2002) 67 B.M.L.R. 90; (2002) 152 N.L.J. 998 . . . . 2–42, 2–50, 2–58—2–68,
2–62A, 2–64, 2–66, 13–21A
Federal Bank of the Middle East v Hadkinson (Stay of Action); Hadkinson v Saab (No.1)
[2000] 1 W.L.R. 1695; [2000] 2 All E.R. 395; [2000] C.P.L.R. 295; [2000] B.P.I.R.
597; (2000) 97(12) L.S.G. 42; (2000) 150 N.L.J. 393; (2000) 144 S.J.L.B. 128 CA
(Civ Div). 29–42
Federation Cynologique Internationale v Federacion Canina Internacional de Perros de
Pura Raza (C–561/11) [2013] Bus. L.R. 693; [2013] E.T.M.R. 23 25–83
Ferdinand v MGN Ltd [2011] EWHC 2454 (QB). 27–37, 27–39, 27–41, 27–44, 29–22
Fernquest v City & County of Swansea [2011] EWCA Civ 1712. . . . . 8–51, 8–190
Fiddes v Channel 4 Television Corp [2010] EWCA Civ 730; [2010] 1 W.L.R. 2245; [2011]
E.M.L.R. 3; (2010) 160 N.L.J. 974; (2010) 154(26) S.J.L.B. 29 22–03
Financial Services Authority v Sinaloa Gold Plc; sub nom. Financial Services Authority v
Barclays Bank Plc [2013] UKSC 11; [2013] 2 A.C. 28; [2013] 2 W.L.R. 678; [2013]
2 All E.R. 339; [2013] 1 All E.R. (Comm) 1089; [2013] Bus. L.R. 302; [2013] 1
B.C.L.C. 353; [2013] Lloyd's Rep. F.C. 305; (2013) 163 N.L.J. 267; (2013) 157(9)
S.J.L.B. 31. 29–28
Fine & Country Ltd v Okotoks Ltd (formerly Spicerhaart Ltd); sub nom. Okotoks Ltd
(formerly Spicerhaart Ltd) v Fine & Country Ltd [2013] EWCA Civ 672 . . . . . 25–76, 26–06,
26–14, 26–17
Fiona Trust & Holding Corp v Skarga [2013] EWCA Civ 275. 7–11
Fish & Fish Ltd v Sea Shepherd UK; Steve Irwin, The [2013] EWCA Civ 544; [2013] 3 All
E.R. 867 . . . . 4–04, 17–128
Fitzpatrick v Commissioner of Police of the Metropolis [2012] EWHC 12 (Admin); [2012]
Lloyd's Rep. F.C. 361; (2012) 156(3) S.J.L.B. 39 19–61
Flack v Hudson [2001] Q.B. 698; [2001] 2 W.L.R. 982; [2001] P.I.Q.R. P22; (2000) 97(45)
L.S.G. 40; (2000) 144 S.J.L.B. 281 CA (Civ Div) 21–15
Flood v Times Newspapers Ltd; sub nom. Times Newspapers Ltd v Flood [2010] EWCA
Civ 804; [2011] 1 W.L.R. 153; [2010] E.M.L.R. 26; [2010] H.R.L.R. 30 22–136
Flos SpA v Semeraro Casa e Famiglia SpA (C–168/09) [2011] E.C.D.R. 8; [2011]
R.P.C. 10. 25–54
Foley v Lord Ashcroft [2012] EWCA Civ 423; [2012] E.M.L.R. 25 22–74

Folien Fischer AG v Ritrama SpA (C–133/11) [2013] Q.B. 523; [2013] 2 W.L.R. 373; [2013] C.E.C. 727; [2013] I.L.Pr. 1 7–02

Football Association Premier League Ltd v QC Leisure (C–403/08); Murphy v Media Protection Services Ltd (C–429/08) [2012] All E.R. (EC) 629; [2012] Bus. L.R. 1321; [2012] 1 C.M.L.R. 29; [2012] C.E.C. 242; [2012] E.C.D.R. 8; [2012] F.S.R. 1; (2011) 108(40) L.S.G. 22; (2011) 161 N.L.J. 1415 .... 25–23, 25–28

Football Dataco Ltd v Brittens Pools Ltd; Football Dataco Ltd v Yahoo! UK Ltd; Football Dataco Ltd v Stan James (Abingdon) Ltd [2010] EWCA Civ 1380; [2011] E.C.D.R. 9; [2011] R.P.C. 9 25–08

Football Dataco Ltd v Sportradar GmbH (C–173/11) [2013] 1 C.M.L.R. 29; [2013] F.S.R. 4 .... 7–03, 25–08

Football Dataco Ltd v Sportradar GmbH [2011] EWCA Civ 330; [2011] 1 W.L.R. 3044; [2011] Bus. L.R. 1387; [2011] F.S.R. 20 4–04

Football Dataco Ltd v Sportradar GmbH; Football Dataco Ltd v Stan James (Abingdon) Ltd [2013] EWCA Civ 27; [2013] Bus. L.R. 837; [2013] 2 C.M.L.R. 36; [2013] E.C.C. 12; [2013] F.S.R. 30 .... 4–04, 25–08

Football Dataco Ltd v Yahoo! UK Ltd (C–604/10) [2013] All E.R. (EC) 257; [2012] Bus. L.R. 1753; [2012] 2 C.M.L.R. 24; [2012] E.C.D.R. 10; [2013] F.S.R. 1 25–08

Force India Formula One Team Ltd v 1 Malaysia Racing Team Sdn Bhd; sub nom. Force India Formula One Team Ltd v Aerolab SRL (an Italian company) [2013] EWCA Civ 780.................................... 7–02A, 27–04, 27–08, 27–15, 27–33, 27–34

Francis v Southwark LBC; sub nom. Southwark LBC v Francis [2011] EWCA Civ 1418; [2012] P.T.S.R. 1248; [2012] H.L.R. 16; [2011] N.P.C. 124; [2012] 1 P. & C.R. DG11.. 9–25

Frank Houlgate Investment Co Ltd v Biggart Baillie LLP [2009] CSOH 165; 2010 S.L.T. 527; 2010 S.C.L.R. 527; [2010] P.N.L.R. 13; 2010 Rep. L.R. 32; 2010 G.W.D. 4–71 .. 10–116

Frank Houlgate Investment Co Ltd v Biggart Baillie LLP [2013] CSOH 80; [2013] P.N.L.R. 25; 2013 G.W.D. 20–407.. 18–05

Freeman v Higher Park Farm [2008] EWCA Civ 1185; [2009] P.I.Q.R. P6; (2008) 152(43) S.J.L.B. 32... 21–05, 21–15

Frisdranken Industrie Winters BV v Red Bull GmbH (C–119/10) [2012] C.E.C. 957; [2012] E.T.M.R. 16; [2012] Bus. L.R. D121[2012] C.E.C. 957; [2012] E.T.M.R. 16; [2012] Bus. L.R. D121 25–81

Froom v Butcher [1976] Q.B. 286; [1975] 3 W.L.R. 379; [1975] 3 All E.R. 520; [1975] 2 Lloyd's Rep. 478; [1975] R.T.R. 518; (1975) 119 S.J. 613 CA (Civ Div) 3–84

Fruit of the Loom Inc v Office for Harmonisation in the Internal Market (Trade Marks and Designs) (OHIM) (T–514/10) [2012] E.T.M.R. 44; (2012) 109(28) L.S.G. 20 25–79

FS (Afghanistan) v Secretary of State for the Home Department [2011] EWHC 1858 (QB) 15–75

Fundacion Gala-Salvador Dali v Societe des Auteurs dans les Arts Graphiques et Plastiques (ADAGP) (C–518/08) [2010] E.C.D.R. 13; [2011] F.S.R. 4 25–10

Furmedge v Chester-Le-Street DC; sub nom. Furmedge (Deceased), Re; Collings (Deceased), Re [2011] EWHC 1226 (QB) 4–29, 12–10, 12–29

Furnell v Flaherty [2013] EWHC 377 (QB); [2013] P.T.S.R. D20 .... 8–56, 9–09, 14–54

Future Investments SA v Federation Internationale de Football Association [2010] EWHC 1019 (Ch); [2010] I.L.Pr. 34....................................... 24–70

Future Publishing Ltd v Edge Interactive Media Inc [2011] EWHC 1489 (Ch); [2011] E.T.M.R. 50... 25–15

Fytche v Wincanton Logistics Plc [2004] UKHL 31; [2004] 4 All E.R. 221; [2004] I.C.R. 975; [2004] I.R.L.R. 817; [2005] P.I.Q.R. P5; (2004) 101(31) L.S.G. 25; (2004) 148 S.J.L.B. 825.. 13–36

Galashiels Gas Co Ltd v Millar; sub nom. Millar v Galashiels Gas Co Ltd [1949] A.C. 275; [1949] 1 All E.R. 319; 1949 S.C. (H.L.) 31; 1949 S.L.T. 223; 65 T.L.R. 76; 47 L.G.R. 213; [1949] L.J.R. 540; (1949) 93 S.J. 71 HL 13–48

Galileo International Technology LLC v European Union (formerly European Community) [2011] EWHC 35 (Ch); [2011] E.T.M.R. 22 25–79

Gas and Electricity Markets Authority v Infinis Plc. See R. (on the application of Infinis Plc) v Gas and Electricity Markets Authority

Gatt v Barclays Bank Plc [2013] EWHC 2 (QB) 8–110

Gavin v One Housing Group (formerly Community Housing Association Ltd); sub nom.
Gavin v Community Housing Association Ltd [2013] EWCA Civ 580; [2013] 2 P. &
C.R. 17; [2013] 24 E.G. 100 (C.S.); [2013] 2 P. & C.R. DG12 20–136
Geary v JD Wetherspoon Plc [2011] EWHC 1506 (QB); [2011] N.P.C. 60 . . . . .   3–92, 3–100, 8–53,
12–04, 12–17, 12–41, 12–69
Geddis v Bann Reservoir Proprietors (1878) 3 App. Cas. 430 HL 14–08
General Dental Council's Application, Re; sub nom. General Dental Council v Savery
[2011] EWHC 3011 (Admin); [2012] Med. L.R. 204; [2012] A.C.D. 11. 27–29
General Tire & Rubber Co Ltd v Firestone Tyre & Rubber Co Ltd (No.2) [1975] 1 W.L.R.
819; [1975] 2 All E.R. 173; [1975] F.S.R. 273; [1976] R.P.C. 197; (1975) 119 S.J. 389
HL 27–33
Generics (UK) Ltd v Synaptech Inc (C–427/09) [2012] 1 C.M.L.R. 4; [2012] R.P.C. 4 25–91
Generics (UK) Ltd v Yeda Research and Development Co Ltd [2012] EWCA Civ 726;
[2013] Bus. L.R. 777; [2012] C.P. Rep. 39; [2013] F.S.R. 13 27–14
Getty Images (US) Inc v Office for Harmonisation in the Internal Market (Trade Marks and
Designs) (OHIM) (T–338/11) [2013] E.T.M.R. 19 25–76
Ghaith v Indesit Co UK Ltd [2012] EWCA Civ 642; [2012] I.C.R. D34 . . . . 13–36, 13–58
Giggs v News Group Newspapers Ltd; sub nom. CTB v News Group Newspapers Ltd
[2012] EWHC 431 (QB); [2013] E.M.L.R. 5 27–47
Gillan v United Kingdom (4158/05) (2010) 50 E.H.R.R. 45; 28 B.H.R.C. 420; [2010]
Crim. L.R. 415; (2010) 160 N.L.J. 104 ECtHR 15–89
Gillie v Scottish Borders Council [2013] CSOH 76; 2013 Rep. L.R. 86; 2013 G.W.D.
18–374. 13–53
Gillingham BC v Medway (Chatham Docks) Co Ltd [1993] Q.B. 343; [1992] 3 W.L.R.
449; [1992] 3 All E.R. 923; [1993] Env. L.R. 98; 91 L.G.R. 160; (1992) 63 P. & C.R.
205; [1992] 1 P.L.R. 113; [1992] J.P.L. 458; [1991] E.G. 101 (C.S.); [1991] N.P.C. 97
QBD 20–14
Gimex International Groupe Import Export v Chill Bag Co Ltd [2012] EWPCC 31; [2012]
E.C.D.R. 25. 25–63
Ginty v Belmont Building Supplies Ltd [1959] 1 All E.R. 414 QBD 13–63
Goad v Butcher [2011] EWCA Civ 158 8–179
Gold Shipping Navigation Co SA v Lulu Maritime Ltd; Al Salam 95, The; Jebel Ali, The;
sub nom. Owners of the Pearl of Jebel Ali v Owners of the Pride of Al Salam 95
[2009] EWHC 1365 (Admlty); [2010] 2 All E.R. (Comm) 64; [2009] 2 Lloyd's
Rep. 484 32–78
Goldberg v Miltiadous [2010] EWHC 450 (QB). 18–29
Goldsmith v BCD; Khan v BCD [2011] EWHC 674 (QB); (2011) 108(14) L.S.G. 20 27–47
Goldsmith v Patchcott [2012] EWCA Civ 183; [2012] P.I.Q.R. P11; (2012) 156(9) S.J.L.B.
31. . . . . 21–01, 21–05, 21–08, 21–15
Goldsmith v Sperrings Ltd; Goldsmith v Various Distributors [1977] 1 W.L.R. 478; [1977]
2 All E.R. 566; (1977) 121 S.J. 304
Goodes v East Sussex CC [2000] 1 W.L.R. 1356; [2000] 3 All E.R. 603; [2000] R.T.R. 366;
(2001) 3 L.G.L.R. 6; [2000] B.L.G.R. 465; [2000] P.I.Q.R. P148; [2001] J.P.L. 70;
[2000] E.G. 75 (C.S.); (2000) 97(26) L.S.G. 38; (2000) 150 N.L.J. 949; [2000] N.P.C.
65 HL 8–187
Goodwin v News Group Newspapers Ltd; sub nom. Goodwin v NGN Ltd [2011] EWHC
1437 (QB); [2011] E.M.L.R. 27; [2011] H.R.L.R. 31; (2011) 161 N.L.J. 850. . .   27–39, 27–41,
27–44, 27–47
Goody v Odhams Press [1967] 1 Q.B. 333; [1966] 3 W.L.R. 460; [1966] 3 All E.R. 369;
(1966) 110 S.J. 793 CA. 22–242
Google France Sarl v Louis Vuitton Malletier SA (C–236/08); Google France Sarl v Centre
National de Recherche en Relations Humaines (CNRRH) Sarl (C–238/08); Google
France Sarl v Viaticum SA (C–237/08) [2011] All E.R. (EC) 411; [2011] Bus. L.R. 1;
[2010] E.C.R. I–2417; [2010] E.T.M.R. 30; [2010] R.P.C. 19; 3 A.L.R. Int'l 867. 25–81
Gore v Stannard (t/a Wyvern Tyres). See Stannard (t/a Wyvern Tyres) v Gore
Gorringe v Calderdale MBC; sub nom. Calderdale MBC v Gorringe [2004] UKHL 15;
[2004] 1 W.L.R. 1057; [2004] 2 All E.R. 326; [2004] R.T.R. 27; [2004] P.I.Q.R. P32;
(2004) 101(18) L.S.G. 35; (2004) 148 S.J.L.B. 419. . . . .   8–99, 8–187, 9–09, 9–40, 14–49,
14–51, 14–56, 14–57, 20–193

Gorris v Scott (1873–74) L.R. 9 Ex. 125 Ct Ex. 9–15
Grant v YYH Holdings Pty Ltd [2012] NSWCA 360 17–127
Gray v News Group Newspapers Ltd. *See* Phillips v News Group Newspapers Ltd
Gray v Thames Trains Ltd [2009] UKHL 33; [2009] 1 A.C. 1339; [2009] 3 W.L.R. 167;
    [2009] 4 All E.R. 81; [2009] P.I.Q.R. P22; [2009] LS Law Medical 409; (2009) 108
    B.M.L.R. 205; [2009] M.H.L.R. 73; [2009] Po. L.R. 229; (2009) 159 N.L.J. 925;
    (2009) 153(24) S.J.L.B. 33 . . . . 3–18, 3–33, 3–36
Gray v UVW [2010] EWHC 2367 (QB) 27–47
Great Canadian Railtour Co v Teamsters Local 31 [2012] BCCA 238; (2012) 350 D.L.R.
    (4th) 364 24–59
Green v Eadie [2012] Ch. 363; [2012] 2 W.L.R. 510; [2012] P.N.L.R. 9 Ch D 32–13
Greenmanor Ltd v Laurence Pilford [2012] EWCA Civ 756 19–15
Grieves v FT Everard & Sons Ltd; Quinn v George Clark & Nem Ltd; Mears v RG Carter
    Ltd; Jackson v Brock Plc; Rothwell v Chemical & Insulating Co Ltd; Downey v
    Charles Evans Shopfitters Ltd; Storey v Clellands Shipbuilders Ltd; Topping v
    Benchtown Ltd (formerly Jones Bros (Preston) Ltd); Johnston v NEI International
    Combustion Ltd; Hindson v Pipe House Wharf (Swansea) Ltd [2007] UKHL 39;
    [2008] 1 A.C. 281; [2007] 3 W.L.R. 876; [2007] 4 All E.R. 1047; [2007] I.C.R. 1745;
    [2008] P.I.Q.R. P6; [2008] LS Law Medical 1; (2008) 99 B.M.L.R. 139; (2007)
    104(42) L.S.G. 34; (2007) 157 N.L.J. 1542; (2007) 151 S.J.L.B. 1366 . . . . 2–58—2–68
Grimes v Hawkins [2011] EWHC 2004 (QB) 12–30
Grimme Landmaschinenfabrik GmbH & Co KG v Scott (t/a Scotts Potato Machinery)
    [2009] EWHC 2691 (Pat); [2010] E.C.D.R. 4; [2010] F.S.R. 11 25–62
Ground Gilbey Ltd v Jardine Lloyd Thompson UK Ltd [2011] EWHC 124 (Comm);
    [2012] Lloyd's Rep. I.R. 12; [2011] P.N.L.R. 15 . . . . 10–218, 10–228
Group Lotus Plc v 1Malaysia Racing Team Sdn Bhd [2011] EWHC 1366 (Ch); [2011]
    E.T.M.R. 62. 26–06
Grupo Promer Mon Graphic SA v Office for Harmonisation in the Internal Market
    (Trade Marks and Designs) (OHIM) (T–9/07) [2010] E.C.R. II–981; [2010] E.C.D.R.
    7; [2011] Bus. L.R. D13 . . . . 25–63, 25–68
Guardian News and Media Ltd, Re; sub nom. HM Treasury v Youssef
H v Crown Prosecution Service [2010] EWHC 1374 (Admin); [2012] Q.B. 257; [2012]
    2 W.L.R. 296; [2010] 4 All E.R. 264 15–94
Hall v Cable and Wireless Plc; Martin v Cable and Wireless Plc; Parry v Cable and Wireless
    Plc [2009] EWHC 1793 (Comm); [2011] B.C.C. 543; [2010] 1 B.C.L.C. 95; [2010]
    Bus. L.R. D40 9–25
Hammsersley-Gonsalves v Redcar and Cleveland BC [2012] EWCA Civ 1135; [2012]
    E.L.R. 431 8–199
Hanningfield v Chief Constable of Essex [2013] EWHC 243 (QB) 15–67, 15–86
Haringey LBC v Hines [2010] EWCA Civ 1111; [2011] H.L.R. 6 18–02
Harlan Laboratories UK Ltd v Stop Huntingdon Animal Cruelty (SHAC) [2012] EWHC
    3408 (QB) 15–21
Harms (Inc) Ltd v Martans Club Ltd [1927] 1 Ch. 526 CA 25–07
Harris Springs Ltd v Howes [2007] EWHC 3271 (TCC); [2008] B.L.R. 229 32–75
Harrison v Shepherd Homes Ltd [2012] EWCA Civ 904; 143 Con. L.R. 69; [2012] 3
    E.G.L.R. 83; [2012] 41 E.G. 116; [2012] 28 E.G. 80 (C.S.) 8–130
Harvey v Plymouth City Council [2010] EWCA Civ 860; [2010] P.I.Q.R. P18; (2010)
    154(31) S.J.L.B. 30; [2010] N.P.C. 89 12–17
Hasbro Inc v 123 Nahrmittel GmbH [2011] EWHC 199 (Ch); [2011] E.T.M.R. 25; [2011]
    F.S.R. 21 . . . . 26–11, 25–82
Hassan v Gill [2012] EWCA Civ 1291; [2013] P.I.Q.R. P1 . . . . 8–176, 12–29
Hatcher v ASW Ltd [2010] EWCA Civ 1325 . . . . 12–04, 12–64
Haugesund Kommune v Depfa ACS Bank [2011] EWCA Civ 33; [2011] 3 All E.R. 655;
    [2012] 1 All E.R. (Comm) 65; [2012] Bus. L.R. 230; [2011] 1 C.L.C. 166; 134 Con.
    L.R. 51; [2011] P.N.L.R. 14; (2011) 108(6) L.S.G. 19 . . . . . . 2–175, 10–114, 10–133, 10–140,
                                                                             10–147, 10–179, 10–228
Hayes v Chief Constable of Merseyside [2011] EWCA Civ 911; [2012] 1 W.L.R. 517;
    [2011] 2 Cr. App. R. 30; [2012] Crim. L.R. 35. 15–67

Hayes v Willoughby [2013] UKSC 17; [2013] 1 W.L.R. 935; [2013] 2 All E.R. 405; [2013]
    2 Cr. App. R. 11; [2013] E.M.L.R. 19; (2013) 163(7554) N.L.J. 25 15–21
Hedley Byrne & Co Ltd v Heller & Partners Ltd [1964] A.C. 465; [1963] 3 W.L.R. 101;
    [1963] 2 All E.R. 575; [1963] 1 Lloyd's Rep. 485; (1963) 107 S.J. 454 HL 8–113, 8–126
Henderson (t/a Henderson Group Development) v Wotherspoon [2013] CSOH 113; [2013]
    P.N.L.R. 28; 2013 G.W.D. 25–475 10–152
Hennessey v Aer Lingus Ltd [2012] IEHC 124. 12–07
Henry v News Group Newspapers Ltd [2011] EWHC 1058 (QB) 22–230
Herrmann v Withers LLP [2012] EWHC 1492 (Ch); [2012] 4 Costs L.R. 712; [2012]
    P.N.L.R. 28 .... 10–132, 10–133
Hicks v Faulkner (1878) 8 Q.B.D. 167 QBD 16–37
Hide v Steeplechase Co (Cheltenham) Ltd [2013] EWCA Civ 545; [2013] P.I.Q.R. P22;
    (2013) 163(7562) N.L.J. 16 13–46
Hill v Chief Constable of West Yorkshire [1989] A.C. 53; [1988] 2 W.L.R. 1049; [1988] 2
    All E.R. 238; (1988) 152 L.G. Rev. 709; (1988) 85(20) L.S.G. 34; (1988) 138 N.L.J.
    Rep. 126; (1988) 132 S.J. 700 HL 14–28, 14–30, 14–31
Hill v Fellowes Solicitors LLP; sub nom. Thorpe v Fellowes Solicitors LLP [2011] EWHC
    61 (QB); (2011) 118 B.M.L.R. 122; [2011] P.N.L.R. 13 10–126
Hill v John Barnsley & Sons Ltd [2013] EWHC 520 (QB) 2–50, 13–21A
Hillingdon LBC v Neary [2011] EWHC 1377 (Fam); [2011] 4 All E.R. 584; [2012] 1
    F.L.R. 72; [2011] 3 F.C.R. 448; [2011] Med. L.R. 446; (2011) 122 B.M.L.R. 1; [2011]
    M.H.L.R. 404; [2011] Fam. Law 944; (2011) 108(25) L.S.G. 18 10–61
Hillside (New Media) Ltd v Baasland [2010] EWHC 3336 (Comm); [2010] 2 C.L.C. 986;
    [2010] Info. T.L.R. 409. 7–15
Hirose Electrical UK Ltd v Peak Ingredients Ltd [2011] EWCA Civ 987; [2011] Env. L.R.
    34; [2011] N.P.C. 94 20–10
HKRUK II (CHC) Ltd v Heaney; sub nom. HXRUK II (CHC) Ltd v Heaney [2010]
    EWHC 2245 (Ch); [2010] 3 E.G.L.R. 15; [2010] 44 E.G. 126 .... 20–152, 28–134,
                                                                              29–05
Hodgkinson v Renfrewshire Council [2011] CSOH 142; 2011 G.W.D. 29–639 13–48
Hoffmann-La Roche & Co AG v Secretary for Trade and Industry. See F Hoffmann La
    Roche & Co AG v Secretary of State for Trade and Industry
Hollister Inc v Medik Ostomy Supplies Ltd [2012] EWCA Civ 1419; [2013] Bus. L.R. 428;
    [2013] E.T.M.R. 10; [2013] F.S.R. 24; (2013) 129 B.M.L.R. 173................... 25–83
Holtby v Brigham & Cowan (Hull) Ltd [2000] 3 All E.R. 421; [2000] I.C.R. 1086; [2000]
    P.I.Q.R. Q293; [2000] Lloyd's Rep. Med. 254; (2000) 97(19) L.S.G. 44; (2000) 150
    N.L.J. 544; (2000) 144 S.J.L.B. 212 CA (Civ Div) .... 2–29—2–34
Homawoo v GMF Assurances SA (C–412/10) [2012] I.L.Pr. 2 7–14
Home Office v Mohammed; sub nom. Mohammed v Home Office [2011] EWCA Civ 351;
    [2011] 1 W.L.R. 2862; (2011) 108(15) L.S.G. 21................. 14–17, 14–48, 14–51A
Honda Motor Co Ltd v David Silver Spares Ltd [2010] EWHC 1973 (Ch); [2010] F.S.R.
    40. 25–82
Hook v Eatons Solicitors Unreported July 17, 2012 County Ct (Leeds).................... 13–54
Horrocks v Lowe [1975] A.C. 135; [1974] 2 W.L.R. 282; [1974] 1 All E.R. 662; 72 L.G.R.
    251; (1974) 118 S.J. 149 HL.. 22–84, 23–10
Horton v Sadler [2006] UKHL 27; [2007] 1 A.C. 307; [2006] 2 W.L.R. 1346; [2006] 3 All
    E.R. 1177; [2006] R.T.R. 27; [2006] P.I.Q.R. P30; (2006) 91 B.M.L.R. 60; (2006)
    103(26) L.S.G. 27; (2006) 156 N.L.J. 1024; (2006) 150 S.J.L.B. 808.............. 32–56
Hotel Cipriani Srl v Cipriani (Grosvenor Street) Ltd [2010] EWCA Civ 110; [2010] Bus.
    L.R. 1465; [2010] R.P.C. 16 25–82
Hotel Cipriani Srl v Fred 250 Ltd (formerly Cipriani (Grosvenor Street) Ltd) [2013]
    EWHC 70 (Ch); [2013] E.C.C. 11; [2013] E.T.M.R. 18 25–82
Houlgate Investment Co Ltd v Biggart Baillie LLP. See Frank Houlgate Investment Co Ltd
    v Biggart Baillie LLP
Howarth v Cummins Ltd Unreported June 1, 2012 County Ct (Bristol).................. 13–51
Hufton v Somerset CC [2011] EWCA Civ 789; [2011] E.L.R. 482 12–29
Hughes (A Minor) v Newry & Mourne District Council [2012] NIQB 54.................. 12–29
Hughes v Williams (Deceased); sub nom. Williams v Williams (Deceased) [2013] EWCA
    Civ 455; [2013] P.I.Q.R. P17 3–75

Human Genome Sciences Inc v Eli Lilly & Co. *See* Eli Lilly & Co v Human Genome
   Sciences Inc
Hunt v Evening Standard Ltd [2011] EWHC 272 (QB) 22–240
Hunt v Severs; sub nom. Severs v Hunt [1994] 2 A.C. 350; [1994] 2 W.L.R. 602; [1994] 2
   All E.R. 385; [1994] 2 Lloyd's Rep. 129; [1994] P.I.Q.R. Q60; (1994) 144 N.L.J. 603;
   (1994) 138 S.J.L.B. 104 HL 28–27
Hunt v Times Newspapers (No.1) [2012] EWHC 110 (QB).......................... 22–136
Hunt v Times Newspapers Ltd (No.2) [2013] EWHC 1868 (QB) 22–04, 22–72, 22–136
Hussain v King Edward VII Hospital [2012] EWHC 3441 (QB) 10–93
Hutcheson (formerly WER) v Popdog Ltd (formerly REW) [2011] EWCA Civ 1580;
   [2012] 1 W.L.R. 782; [2012] 2 All E.R. 711; [2012] C.P. Rep. 13; [2012] E.M.L.R.
   13.. 27–47
Hutcheson v News Group Newspapers Ltd; sub nom. KGM v News Group Newspapers Ltd
   [2011] EWCA Civ 808; [2012] E.M.L.R. 2; [2011] U.K.H.R.R. 1329 ... 27–39, 27–44, 27–47
Hutton v General Motors of Canada Ltd [2010] ABQB 606; [2011] W.W.R. 284 ..... 11–31, 11–34
Hyndman v Brown and Bradley [2012] NICA 3 13–40
IAM Group Plc v Chowdrey [2012] EWCA Civ 505; [2012] 2 P. & C.R. 13............... 19–75
Ibrahim v Swansea University [2012] EWHC 290 (QB) 22–32
Ifejika v Ifejika [2010] EWPCC 31; [2012] F.S.R. 6........................... 25–59, 25–65
Ifejika v Ifejika; Ifejika v Lens Care Ltd [2010] EWCA Civ 563; [2010] F.S.R. 29.......... 25–70
IG Index Plc v Colley [2013] EWHC 478 (QB) 18–05
Imerman v Tchenguiz. *See* Tchenguiz v Imerman
Imperial Group Plc v Philip Morris Ltd [1984] R.P.C. 293 Ch D 26–17
Infabrics Ltd v Jaytex Ltd (No.2) [1987] F.S.R. 529 CA (Civ Div) 25–35
Infopaq International A/S v Danske Dagblades Forening (C–5/08) [2012] Bus. L.R. 102;
   [2009] E.C.R. I–6569; [2009] E.C.D.R. 16; [2010] F.S.R. 20 .... 25–07, 25–23
Innovia Films Ltd v Frito-Lay North America Inc [2012] EWHC 790 (Pat); [2012]
   R.P.C. 24 .... 7–02A
Integral Memory Plc v Haines Watt [2012] EWHC 342 (Ch); [2012] S.T.I. 1385 32–75
Interflora Inc v Marks & Spencer Plc (C–323/09) [2013] All E.R. (EC) 519; [2012] Bus.
   L.R. 1440; [2012] C.E.C. 755; [2012] E.T.M.R. 1; [2012] F.S.R. 25–81
Interflora Inc v Marks & Spencer Plc [2013] EWCA Civ 319; [2013] F.S.R. 26 ...... 25–81, 26–17
Interflora Inc v Marks & Spencer Plc; sub nom. Marks & Spencer Plc v Interflora Inc
   [2012] EWCA Civ 1501; [2013] 2 All E.R. 663; [2013] E.T.M.R. 11; [2013] F.S.R.
   21; [2013] Bus. L.R. D46 .... 25–81, 26–17
International Energy Group Ltd v Zurich Insurance Plc UK [2013] EWCA Civ 39; [2013]
   3 All E.R. 395; [2013] 2 All E.R. (Comm) 336; [2013] Lloyd's Rep. I.R. 379; [2013]
   P.I.Q.R. P10... 2–58—2–68, 4–39
International Leisure Ltd v First National Trustee Co UK Ltd [2012] EWHC 1971 (Ch);
   [2013] Ch. 346; [2013] 2 W.L.R. 466; [2012] B.C.C. 738; [2012] P.N.L.R. 34......... 10–16
International Stem Cell Corp v Comptroller General of Patents [2013] EWHC 807 (Ch);
   [2013] 3 C.M.L.R. 14 25–94
Internetportal und Marketing GmbH v Schlicht (C–569/08) [2011] Bus. L.R. 726; [2010]
   E.T.M.R. 48[2011] Bus. L.R. 726; [2010] E.T.M.R. 48 25–76
Inventors Friend Ltd v Leathes Prior (A Firm) [2011] EWHC 711 (QB); [2011] P.N.L.R.
   20.. 10–134
Iqbal v Dean Manson Solicitors [2011] EWCA Civ 123; [2011] C.P. Rep. 26; [2011]
   I.R.L.R. 428; (2011) 108(9) L.S.G. 17; (2011) 161 N.L.J. 288 .... 5–89, 6–55, 15–20
Iqbal v Mansoor; sub nom. Iqbal v Dean Manson Solicitors [2013] EWCA Civ 149; [2013]
   C.P. Rep. 27.. 22–88, 22–92
Iqbal v Prison Officers Association; sub nom. Prison Officers Association v Iqbal [2009]
   EWCA Civ 1312; [2010] Q.B. 732; [2010] 2 W.L.R. 1054; [2010] 2 All E.R. 663;
   [2010] 2 Prison L.R. 123; (2010) 107(1) L.S.G. 14 14–110
Irvine v Talksport Ltd [2002] EWHC 367 (Ch); [2002] 1 W.L.R. 2355; [2002] 2 All E.R.
   414; [2002] E.M.L.R. 32; [2002] F.S.R. 60; (2002) 25(6) I.P.D. 25039; (2002) 99(18)
   L.S.G. 38; (2002) 152 N.L.J. 553; (2002) 146 S.J.L.B. 85..................... 26–18
Islington LBC v Jones [2012] EWHC 1537 (QB)............................... 14–93A
ITV Broadcasting Ltd v TVCatchup Ltd (C–607/11) [2013] Bus. L.R. 1020; [2013] 3
   C.M.L.R. 1; [2013] E.C.D.R. 9... 25–07

Jackson v Harrison [1978] HCA 17; (1978) 138 CLR 438 3–05
Jackson v Murray [2012] CSIH 100; 2013 S.L.T. 153; 2013 S.C.L.R. 429; 2013 Rep. L.R.
    30; 2013 G.W.D. 3–104 3–69
Jain v Trent SHA; sub nom. Trent SHA v Jain [2009] UKHL 4; [2009] 1 A.C. 853; [2009]
    2 W.L.R. 248; [2009] 1 All E.R. 957; [2009] P.T.S.R. 382; [2009] H.R.L.R. 14;
    (2009) 12 C.C.L. Rep. 194; [2009] LS Law Medical 112; (2009) 106 B.M.L.R. 88;
    (2009) 106(5) L.S.G. 14; (2009) 153(4) S.J.L.B. 27 16–06
Jama v Ministry of Justice [2012] EWHC 533 (QB). 14–48
Jameel v Dow Jones & Co Inc; sub nom. Dow Jones & Co Inc v Jameel [2005] EWCA Civ
    75; [2005] Q.B. 946; [2005] 2 W.L.R. 1614; [2005] E.M.L.R. 16; (2005) 149 S.J.L.B.
    181. 22–23
Jameel v Wall Street Journal Europe SPRL (No.3) [2006] UKHL 44; [2007] 1 A.C. 359;
    [2006] 3 W.L.R. 642; [2006] 4 All E.R. 1279; [2007] Bus. L.R. 291; [2007] E.M.L.R.
    2; [2006] H.R.L.R. 41; 21 B.H.R.C. 471; (2006) 103(41) L.S.G. 36; (2006) 156
    N.L.J. 1612; (2006) 150 S.J.L.B. 1392. 22–136
James v United Kingdom (25119/09); Lee v United Kingdom (57877/09); Wells v United
    Kingdom (57715/09) (2013) 56 E.H.R.R. 12; 33 B.H.R.C. 617; (2012) 109(37)
    L.S.G. 20 ECtHR 14–98
JD v East Berkshire Community Health NHS Trust; RK v Oldham NHS Trust; K v
    Dewsbury Healthcare NHS Trust; sub nom. D v East Berkshire Community NHS
    Trust; MAK v Dewsbury Healthcare NHS Trust [2005] UKHL 23; [2005] 2 A.C.
    373; [2005] 2 W.L.R. 993; [2005] 2 All E.R. 443; [2005] 2 F.L.R. 284; [2005] 2
    F.C.R. 81; (2005) 8 C.C.L. Rep. 185; [2005] Lloyd's Rep. Med. 263; (2005) 83
    B.M.L.R. 66; [2005] Fam. Law 615; (2005) 155 N.L.J. 654 8–43
Jean Christian Perfumes Ltd v Thakrar (t/a Brand Distributor and/or Brand Distributors
    Ltd) [2011] EWHC 1383 (Ch); [2011] E.C.C. 27; [2011] F.S.R. 34; [2012] Bus. L.R.
    D50 25–80
Jenson v Faux [2011] EWCA Civ 423; [2011] 1 W.L.R. 3038; [2011] T.C.L.R. 4; [2011]
    H.L.R. 30; [2011] 2 P. & C.R. 11; [2011] C.I.L.L. 3025; [2011] N.P.C. 42 8–130
JGE v Portsmouth Roman Catholic Diocesan Trust. *See* E v English Province of Our Lady
    of   Charity
JIH v News Group Newspapers Ltd [2011] EWCA Civ 42; [2011] 1 W.L.R. 1645; [2011]
    2 All E.R. 324; [2011] C.P. Rep. 17; [2011] E.M.L.R. 15; [2011] 2 F.C.R. 95; (2011)
    108(7) L.S.G. 18; (2011) 161 N.L.J. 211 . . . . 27–47, 29–28A
John Grimes Partnership Ltd v Gubbins [2013] EWCA Civ 37; [2013] B.L.R. 126; 146
    Con. L.R. 26; [2013] P.N.L.R. 17. 10–192
John Smith & Co (Edinburgh) Ltd v Hill [2010] EWHC 1016; [2010] 2 B.C.L.C. 556 . . . 20–65, 20–66
John v Times Newspapers Ltd [2012] EWHC 2751 (QB) 22–27
Johnson (t/a Johnson Butchers) v BJW Property Developments Ltd [2002] EWHC 1131
    (TCC); [2002] 3 All E.R. 574; 86 Con. L.R. 74; [2002] N.P.C. 17 20–155
Johnson v BFI Canada Inc [2010] MBCA 101; (2011) 326 D.L.R. (4th) 497 . . . . 24–02, 24–09,
                                                                               24–55, 24–70
Johnson v Unisys Ltd [2001] UKHL 13; [2003] 1 A.C. 518; [2001] 2 W.L.R. 1076; [2001]
    2 All E.R. 801; [2001] I.C.R. 480; [2001] I.R.L.R. 279; [2001] Emp. L.R. 469 13–26
Johnstone v AMEC Construction Ltd [2010] CSIH 57; 2011 S.C.L.R. 178; 2010 Rep. L.R.
    96; 2010 G.W.D. 26–511 13–48
Jones v Environcom Ltd; sub nom. Woodbrook v Environcom Ltd [2011] EWCA Civ
    1152; [2012] Lloyd's Rep. I.R. 277; [2012] P.N.L.R. 5 . . . . 10–225, 10–227
Jones v Kaney [2011] UKSC 13; [2011] 2 A.C. 398; [2011] 2 W.L.R. 823; [2011] 2 All E.R.
    671; [2011] B.L.R. 283; 135 Con. L.R. 1; [2011] 2 F.L.R. 312; [2012] 2 F.C.R. 372;
    (2011) 119 B.M.L.R. 167; [2011] P.N.L.R. 21; [2011] C.I.L.L. 3037; [2011] Fam.
    Law 1202; [2011] 14 E.G. 95 (C.S.); (2011) 108(15) L.S.G. 19; (2011) 161 N.L.J.
    508; (2011) 155(13) S.J.L.B. 30 . . . . 8–20, 10–41, 14–15, 14–35, 16–72, 16–73
Jones v Ruth [2011] EWCA Civ 804; [2012] 1 W.L.R. 1495; [2012] 1 All E.R. 490; [2011]
    C.I.L.L. 3085. . . . . 15–19, 28–136, 28–152
Jones v Secretary of State for Energy and Climate Change [2012] EWHC 2936 (QB) 2–42
Jose v MacSalvors Plant Hire Ltd [2009] EWCA Civ 1329; [2010] T.C.L.R. 2; [2010]
    C.I.L.L. 2809. 4–30
Joseph v Spiller [2012] EWHC 2958 (QB) 22–241

Joseph v Spiller; sub nom. Spiller v Joseph [2010] UKSC 53; [2011] 1 A.C. 852; [2010] 3
  W.L.R. 1791; [2011] 1 All E.R. 947; [2011] I.C.R. 1; [2011] E.M.L.R. 11; (2010)
  107(48) L.S.G. 13; (2010) 160 N.L.J. 1716 22–165
Joyce v Bowman Law Ltd [2010] EWHC 251 (Ch); [2010] P.N.L.R. 22; [2010] 1 E.G.L.R.
  129 10–142
Joyce v O'Brien [2013] EWCA Civ 546; [2013] Lloyd's Rep. I.R. 523; [2013] P.I.Q.R.
  P23 . . . . 3–18, 3–30, 3–33, 3–34, 3–36
JSC BTA Bank v Ablyazov [2009] EWHC 3267 (Comm); [2010] 1 All E.R. (Comm) 1040;
  [2009] 2 C.L.C. 967 29–42
JSC BTA Bank v Ablyazov [2011] EWHC 1136 (Comm); [2011] 1 W.L.R. 2996 . . . . 16–64A
JSC BTA Bank v Ablyazov [2013] EWCA Civ 928 29–42
JSC BTA Bank v Solodchenko; sub nom. JSC BTA Bank v Kythreotis [2010] EWCA Civ
  1436; [2011] 1 W.L.R. 888; [2011] 4 All E.R. 1240; [2011] 2 All E.R. (Comm) 1063;
  [2010] 2 C.L.C. 925; [2011] 1 P. & C.R. DG21 29–42
Jubilee Motor Policies Syndicate 1231at Lloyd's v Volvo Truck & Bus (Southern) Ltd
  [2010] EWHC 3641 (QB) 4–22
Junior Books Ltd v Veitchi Co Ltd [1983] 1 A.C. 520; [1982] 3 W.L.R. 477; [1982] 3 All
  E.R. 201; 1982 S.C. (H.L.) 244; 1982 S.L.T. 492; [1982] Com. L.R. 221; 21 B.L.R.
  66; (1982) 79 L.S.G. 1413; (1982) 126 S.J. 538 HL 8–113
JW Spear & Sons Ltd v Zynga Inc; sub nom. SCRABBLE Trade Mark [2012] EWHC 3345
  (Ch); [2013] F.S.R. 28 25–76
K v News Group Newspapers Ltd [2011] EWCA Civ 439; [2011] 1 W.L.R. 1827; [2011]
  E.M.L.R. 22; (2011) 108(18) L.S.G. 18 . . . . 27–37, 27–39, 27–44, 27–47, 29–28A
K/S Lincoln v CB Richard Ellis Hotels Ltd [2010] EWHC 1156 (TCC); [2010] P.N.L.R.
  31; (2011) 27 Const. L.J. 50 10–166
Kambadzi v Secretary of State for the Home Department. See R. (on the application of
  Kambadzi) v Secretary of State for the Home Department
KBC Bank Ireland Plc v BCM Hanby Wallace [2012] IEHC 120; [2013] P.N.L.R. 7 10–148,
                                                                             10–153
Kearns v General Council of the Bar [2003] EWCA Civ 331; [2003] 1 W.L.R. 1357; [2003]
  2 All E.R. 534; [2003] E.M.L.R. 27; (2003) 153 N.L.J. 482; (2003) 147 S.J.L.B. 476
  . . . . 22–129, 22–210
Keefe v Isle of Man Steam Packet Co Ltd [2010] EWCA Civ 683 8–170
Kelleher v O'Connor [2010] IEHC 313; [2011] P.N.L.R. 3 10–141
Kenneth Winn-Pope v ES Access Platforms. See Winn-Pope v ES Access Platforms Ltd
KGM v News Group Newspapers Ltd. Se Hutcheson v News Group Newspapers Ltd
Khader v Aziz; Khader v Davenport Lyons [2010] EWCA Civ 716; [2010] 1 W.L.R. 2673;
  [2011] E.M.L.R. 2 . . . . 22–209, 23–13
King v Grundon [2012] EWHC 2719 (QB) 22–242
Kingspan Group Plc v Rockwool Ltd; Rockwool Ltd v Kingspan Group Plc [2011] EWHC
  250 (Ch) 23–21, 25–81, 25–82
Kirin-Amgen Inc v Transkaryotic Therapies Inc (No.2); sub nom. Kirin-Amgen Inc's
  European Patent (No.148605) (No.2); Kirin-Amgen Inc v Hoechst Marion Roussel
  Ltd (No.2) [2004] UKHL 46; [2005] 1 All E.R. 667; [2005] R.P.C. 9; (2005) 28(7)
  I.P.D. 28049; (2004) 148 S.J.L.B. 1249 25–93
Kirkton Investments Ltd v VMH LLP [2011] CSOH 200; [2012] P.N.L.R. 11; 2012 G.W.D.
  1–13 . . . . 10–144, 10–147
Kitechnology BV v Unicor GmbH Plastmaschinen [1994] I.L.Pr. 568; [1995] F.S.R. 765
  CA (Civ Div) 7–02A
KJO v XIM [2011] EWHC 1768 (QB) 22–84
Kmiecic v Isaacs [2011] EWCA Civ 451; [2011] I.C.R. 1269; [2011] P.I.Q.R. P13 12–04
Kolmar Group AG v Traxpo Enterprises Pvt Ltd [2010] EWHC 113 (Comm); [2011] 1 All
  E.R. (Comm) 46; [2010] 2 Lloyd's Rep. 653; [2010] 1 C.L.C. 256 24–67
Koninklijke Philips Electronics NV v Lucheng Meijing Industrial Co Ltd (C–446/09),
  [2012] E.T.M.R. 13 25–84
Kosar v Bank of Scotland Plc (t/a Halifax) [2011] EWHC 1050 (Admin); [2011] B.C.C.
  500; [2011] C.T.L.C. 140; (2011) 108(19) L.S.G. 21 15–20
Kwang Yang Motor Co Ltd v Office for Harmonisation in the Internal Market (Trade
  Marks and Designs) (OHIM) (T–10/08) [2012] E.C.D.R. 2 25–63

L (Vulnerable Adults with Capacity: Court's Jurisdiction), Re; sub nom. A Local Authority
    v DL; DL v A Local Authority [2012] EWCA Civ 253; [2013] Fam. 1; [2012] 3
    W.L.R. 1439; [2012] 3 All E.R. 1064; [2013] 2 F.L.R. 511; [2012] 3 F.C.R. 200;
    [2012] B.L.G.R. 757; (2012) 15 C.C.L. Rep. 267; (2012) 127 B.M.L.R. 24; [2012]
    M.H.L.R. 271; [2012] W.T.L.R. 1713; [2012] Fam. Law 1454; (2012) 162 N.L.J.
    503; (2012) 156(13) S.J.L.B. 31 .... 10–49, 10–61
L'Oreal SA v Bellure NV [2010] EWCA Civ 535; [2010] Bus. L.R. 1579; [2010] E.T.M.R.
    47; [2010] R.P.C. 23; (2010) 107(22) L.S.G. 17; (2010) 154(21) S.J.L.B. 30 .... 25–81, 26–04
L'Oreal SA v eBay International AG (C–324/09) [2012] All E.R. (EC) 501; [2012] Bus.
    L.R. 1369; [2011] E.T.M.R. 52; [2012] E.M.L.R. 6; [2011] R.P.C. 27 25–81
Laboratoires Goemar SA's Trade Mark (No.1); sub nom. Laboratories Goemar SA's Trade
    Mark; LABORATOIRE DE LA MER Trade Mark (No.1) [2002] E.T.M.R. 34; [2002]
    F.S.R. 51 Ch D 25–76
Lagden v O'Connor; Burdis v Livsey; Sen v Steelform Engineering Co Ltd; Dennard v
    Plant; Clark v Ardington Electrical Services; sub nom. Clark v Tull (t/a Ardington
    Electrical Services) [2003] UKHL 64; [2004] 1 A.C. 1067; [2003] 3 W.L.R. 1571;
    [2004] 1 All E.R. 277; [2004] R.T.R. 24; [2004] Lloyd's Rep. I.R. 315; (2003) 153
    N.L.J. 1869; (2003) 147 S.J.L.B. 1430.. 28–10
Lait v Evening Standard Ltd [2011] EWCA Civ 859; [2011] 1 W.L.R. 2973; [2012]
    E.M.L.R. 4 .... 22–167A
Lambert v Barratt Homes Ltd [2010] EWCA Civ 681; [2010] B.L.R. 527; (2010) 131 Con.
    L.R. 29; [2011] H.L.R. 1; [2010] 2 E.G.L.R. 59; [2010] 33 E.G. 72 .... 8–158, 20–95
Lambert v Cardiff CC [2007] EWHC 869; [2007] 3 F.C.R. 148; (2007) 97 B.M.L.R. 101 8–43
Lancashire Fires Ltd v SA Lyons & Co Ltd [1997] I.R.L.R. 113; [1996] F.S.R. 629; (1996)
    19(8) I.P.D. 19068 CA (Civ Div) 27–08
Land Securities Plc v Fladgate Fielder (A Firm) [2009] EWHC 577 (Ch); [2009] 13 E.G.
    143 (C.S.) 16–64
Landor & Hawa International Ltd v Azure Designs Ltd [2006] EWCA Civ 1285; [2006]
    E.C.D.R. 31; [2007] F.S.R. 9; (2007) 30(1) I.P.D. 30003........................ 25–62
Lane v Cullens Solicitors [2011] EWCA Civ 547; [2012] Q.B. 693; [2012] 2 W.L.R. 821;
    [2011] P.N.L.R. 25; [2011] W.T.L.R. 1807; [2011] N.P.C. 46 32–13
Lane v Holloway [1968] 1 Q.B. 379; [1967] 3 W.L.R. 1003; [1967] 3 All E.R. 129; (1967)
    111 S.J. 655 CA (Civ Div) 3–54
Larner v British Steel [1993] 4 All E.R. 102; [1993] I.C.R. 551; [1993] I.R.L.R. 278 CA
    (Civ Div)... 13–33
Lawrence v Fen Tigers Ltd [2011] EWHC 360 (QB); [2011] Env. L.R. D13............... 20–85
Led Technologies Pty Ltd v Roadvision Pty Ltd [2012] FCA 3; (2012) 287 A.L.R. 1 24–19
Lego Juris A/S v Office for Harmonisation in the Internal Market (Trade Marks and
    Designs) (OHIM) (C–48/09 P) [2010] E.T.M.R. 63........................... 25–76
Lehmann Timber, The. See Metall Market OOO v Vitorio Shipping Co Ltd
Leno Merken BV v Hagelkruis Beheer BV (C–149/11) [2013] Bus. L.R. 928; [2013]
    E.T.M.R. 16... 25–79
Les Laboratoires Servier v Apotex Inc [2012] EWCA Civ 593; [2013] Bus. L.R. 80; [2013]
    R.P.C. 21 .... 3–26, 3–31A
Less v Hussain [2012] EWHC 3513 (QB); (2013) 130 B.M.L.R. 51 .... 10–45, 10–85
Levicom International Holdings BV v Linklaters [2010] EWCA Civ 494; [2010] P.N.L.R.
    29; (2010) 107(21) L.S.G. 14....................................... 2–13, 10–146
Lewis v Client Connection Ltd [2011] EWHC 1627 (Ch); [2012] E.T.M.R. 6; (2011)
    108(29) L.S.G. 18... 25–83
Lexi Holdings Plc v DTZ Debenham Tie Leugn Ltd [2010] EWHC 2290 (Ch)............. 3–04
Lightfoot v Go-Ahead Group Plc [2011] EWHC 89 (QB); [2011] R.T.R. 27............... 3–72
Lindner Recyclingtech GmbH v Franssons Verkstader AB [2010] E.C.D.R. 1 25–64
Lindsay v O'Loughnane [2010] EWHC 529 (QB); [2012] B.C.C. 153 18–08,
    18–53
Linklaters Business Services (formerly Hackwood Services Co) v Sir Robert McAlpine
    Ltd [2010] EWHC 1145 (TCC); [2010] B.L.R. 537; 130 Con. L.R. 111; [2010] N.P.C.
    61.. 8–128
Linklaters Business Services v Sir Robert McAlpine Ltd [2010] EWHC 2931 (TCC); 133
    Con. L.R. 21 .... 11–19, 11–24

Lister v Hesley Hall Ltd [2001] UKHL 22; [2002] 1 A.C. 215; [2001] 2 W.L.R. 1311;
    [2001] 2 All E.R. 769; [2001] I.C.R. 665; [2001] I.R.L.R. 472; [2001] Emp. L.R. 819;
    [2001] 2 F.L.R. 307; [2001] 2 F.C.R. 97; (2001) 3 L.G.L.R. 49; [2001] E.L.R. 422;
    [2001] Fam. Law 595; (2001) 98(24) L.S.G. 45; (2001) 151 N.L.J. 728; (2001) 145
    S.J.L.B. 126; [2001] N.P.C. 89 . . . . 6–30A, 6–30B, 6–31
Lloyd v Grace Smith & Co Ltd [1912] A.C. 716 HL 6–30B
Lloyd's Syndicate v X [2011] EWHC 2487 (Comm); [2012] 1 Lloyd's Rep. 123; [2011]
    Arb. L.R. 48 10–28
Lloydminster Credit Union v 324007 Alberta Ltd [2011] SKCA 93; (2011) 333 D.L.R.
    (4th) 699 17–15
Lloyds TSB Bank Plc v Markandan & Uddin (A Firm) [2012] EWCA Civ 65; [2012] 2 All
    E.R. 884; [2012] P.N.L.R. 20; (2012) 162 N.L.J. 328 . . . . 10–23, 10–119
LMS International Ltd v Styrene Packaging & Insulation Ltd [2005] EWHC 2065 (TCC);
    [2006] T.C.L.R. 6 20–162
LNS v Persons Unknown; sub nom. Terry v Persons Unknown [2010] EWHC 119 (QB);
    [2010] E.M.L.R. 16; [2010] 2 F.L.R. 1306; [2010] 1 F.C.R. 659; [2010] Fam. Law
    453; (2010) 107(7) L.S.G. 18 . . . . 27–39, 27–44, 27–47
Lockheed Martin Corp v Willis Group Ltd [2010] EWCA Civ 927; [2010] C.P. Rep. 44;
    [2010] P.N.L.R. 34 32–20
London and Birmingham Railway Ltd (t/a London Midland) v Associated Society of
    Locomotive Engineers and Firemen (ASLEF). See National Union of Rail, Maritime
    and Transport Workers v Serco Ltd (t/a Serco Docklands)
London Helicopters Ltd v Heliportugal LDA-INAC [2006] EWHC 108 (QB); [2006] 1 All
    E.R. (Comm) 595; [2006] 1 C.L.C. 297; [2006] I.L.Pr. 28 7–03
London Tara Hotel Ltd v Kensington Close Hotel Ltd [2011] EWCA Civ 1356; [2012] 2
    All E.R. 554; [2012] 1 P. & C.R. 13; [2012] 1 E.G.L.R. 33; [2012] 8 E.G. 100; [2011]
    48 E.G. 86 (C.S.); [2011] N.P.C. 119 19–38
London Trocadero Ltd v Family Leisure Holdings Ltd [2012] EWCA Civ 1037. 17–31
London Underground Ltd v Associated Society of Locomotive Engineers and Firemen
    [2011] EWHC 3506 (QB); [2012] I.R.L.R. 196 . . . . 5–85, 24–112, 24–147, 24–163
Lonmar Global Risks Ltd v West [2010] EWHC 2878; [2011] I.R.L.R. 138 24–35
Lord Ashcroft v Foley. See Foley v Lord Ashcroft
Lord Browne of Madingley v Associated Newspapers Ltd. See Browne v Associated
    Newspapers Ltd
Lord McAlpine of West Green v Bercow [2013] EWHC 1342 (QB) 22–08, 22–25
Louver-Lite Ltd v Harris Parts Ltd (t/a Harris Engineering) [2012] EWPCC 53 25–68
Lucas-Box v News Group Newspapers Ltd; Lucas-Box v Associated Newspapers Group
    Plc [1986] 1 W.L.R. 147; [1986] 1 All E.R. 177; (1986) 83 L.S.G. 441; (1986) 130
    S.J. 111 CA (Civ Div). 22–74
Lucasfilm Ltd v Ainsworth [2011] UKSC 39; [2012] 1 A.C. 208; [2011] 3 W.L.R. 487;
    [2011] 4 All E.R. 817; [2012] 1 All E.R. (Comm) 1011; [2011] Bus. L.R. 1211;
    [2011] E.C.D.R. 21; [2012] E.M.L.R. 3; [2011] F.S.R. 41; 7 A.L.R. Int'l 711; (2011)
    161 N.L.J. 1098. . . . . 7–19, 25–09, 25–54
Ludsin Overseas Ltd v Eco3 Capital Ltd; sub nom. Eco3 Capital Ltd v Ludsin Overseas
    Ltd [2013] EWCA Civ 413. 18–20
Lumley v Gye, 118 E.R. 1083; (1854) 3 El. & Bl. 114 QB. 24–95
Lumos Skincare Ltd v Sweet Squared Ltd [2013] EWCA Civ 590 26–17
M (Adult Patient) (Minimally Conscious State: Withdrawal of Treatment), Re; sub nom. W
    v M [2011] EWHC 2443 (Fam); [2012] 1 W.L.R. 1653; [2012] 1 All E.R. 1313;
    [2012] P.T.S.R. 1040; [2012] 1 F.L.R. 495; [2012] 1 F.C.R. 2; (2011) 14 C.C.L. Rep.
    689; [2011] Med. L.R. 584; (2011) 122 B.M.L.R. 67; [2011] Fam. Law 1330; (2011)
    108(39) L.S.G. 18; (2011) 156 N.L.J. 1368 . . . . 10–53, 10–61, 15–126
MacLennan v Hartford Europe Ltd [2012] EWHC 346 (QB). 2–36, 13–27
MacSalvors Plant Hire Ltd v Brush Transformers Ltd. See Jose v MacSalvors Plant Hire Ltd
Maga v Birmingham Roman Catholic Archdiocese Trustees; sub nom. Maga v Archbishop
    of Birmingham [2010] EWCA Civ 256; [2010] 1 W.L.R. 1441; [2010] P.T.S.R. 1618;
    (2010) 107(13) L.S.G. 15; (2010) 154(11) S.J.L.B. 28 . . . . 6–30A
Maguire v Harland & Wolff Plc [2005] EWCA Civ 1; [2005] P.I.Q.R. P21; (2005) 102(12)
    L.S.G. 26; (2005) 149 S.J.L.B. 144 . . . . 13–21A

Maharishi Foundation Ltd v Office for Harmonisation in the Internal Market (Trade Marks
    and Designs) (OHIM) (T–426/11) [2013] E.T.M.R. 22   25–76
Mahood v Irish Centre Housing Ltd [2011] Eq. L.R. 586 EAT. 6–12, 6–27
Maier v ASOS Plc [2012] EWHC 3456 (Ch); (2012) 156(46) S.J.L.B. 31.   26–17
Mainline Private Hire Ltd v Nolan [2011] EWCA Civ 189; [2011] C.T.L.C. 145   17–22
MAK v United Kingdom (45901/05); RK v United Kingdom (40146/06); sub nom. K v
    United Kingdom (45901/05) [2010] 2 F.L.R. 451; (2010) 51 E.H.R.R. 14; 28
    B.H.R.C. 762; (2010) 13 C.C.L. Rep. 241; [2010] Fam. Law 582.   8–84
Makro Zelfbedieningsgroothandel CV v Diesel SpA (C–324/08) [2010] Bus. L.R. 608;
    [2009] E.C.R. I–10019; [2010] E.T.M.R. 2   25–82
Makudi v Triesman [2013] EWHC 142 (QB)   22–94
Malcolm v Ministry of Justice [2011] EWCA Civ 1538   14–85,
                                                                                                 14–110
Malik v Fassenfelt [2013] EWCA Civ 798; [2013] 28 E.G. 84 (C.S.); (2013) 157(27)
    S.J.L.B. 31.   19–18
Maloco v Littlewoods Organisation Ltd; Smith v Littlewoods Organisation Ltd [1987]
    A.C. 241; [1987] 2 W.L.R. 480; [1987] 1 All E.R. 710; 1987 S.C. (H.L.) 37; 1987
    S.L.T. 425; 1987 S.C.L.R. 489; (1987) 84 L.S.G. 905; (1987) 137 N.L.J. 149; (1987)
    131 S.J. 226 HL.   13–04
Manchester Ship Canal Co Ltd v United Utilities Water Plc [2013] EWCA Civ 40; [2013]
    1 W.L.R. 2570; [2013] 2 All E.R. 642; [2013] Env. L.R. 20   19–31
Marcic v Thames Water Utilities Ltd; sub nom. Thames Water Utilities Ltd v Marcic
    [2003] UKHL 66; [2004] 2 A.C. 42; [2003] 3 W.L.R. 1603; [2004] 1 All E.R. 135;
    [2004] B.L.R. 1; 91 Con. L.R. 1; [2004] Env. L.R. 25; [2004] H.R.L.R. 10; [2004]
    U.K.H.R.R. 253; [2003] 50 E.G. 95 (C.S.); (2004) 101(4) L.S.G. 32; (2003) 153
    N.L.J. 1869; (2003) 147 S.J.L.B. 1429; [2003] N.P.C. 150   14–49
Marks & Spencer Plc v Interflora Inc. See Interflora Inc v Marks & Spencer Plc
Marks and Spencer Plc v Palmer. See Palmer v Marks and Spencer Plc
Marleasing SA v La Comercial Internacional de Alimentacion SA (C–106/89) [1990]
    E.C.R. I–4135; [1993] B.C.C. 421; [1992] 1 C.M.L.R. 305.   25–74
Martin v JRC Commercial Mortgages Plc [2012] EWCA Civ 63; [2012] P.N.L.R. 18   10–21
Mason v Levy Auto Parts of England Ltd [1967] 2 Q.B. 530; [1967] 2 W.L.R. 1384; [1967]
    2 All E.R. 62; [1967] 1 Lloyd's Rep. 372; (1967) 111 S.J. 234 Assizes (Winchester) . . .   20–162
Mason v Mills & Reeve. See Swain Mason v Mills & Reeve
Matania v National Provincial Bank Ltd [1936] 2 All E.R. 633..   20–73
Mayer v Hoar [2012] EWHC 1805 (QB); (2012) 156(28) S.J.L.B. 31   22–89
Mayor of London v Hall; sub nom. Hall v Mayor of London [2010] EWCA Civ 817; [2011]
    1 W.L.R. 504; [2011] Costs L.R. Online 13; (2010) 107(30) L.S.G. 12; [2010] N.P.C.
    83. . . . .   14–93A, 29–02
Mayor of London v Samede. See City of London Corp v Samede
McCabe v Royal Mail Group Plc, 2011 G.W.D. 15–375 Sh Ct.   13–57
McCarrick v Park Resorts Ltd [2012] EWHC B27 (QB) 12–27, 12–29
McCaughey's Application for Judicial Review, Re [2011] UKSC 20; [2012] 1 A.C. 725;
    [2011] 2 W.L.R. 1279; [2011] 3 All E.R. 607; [2011] N.I. 122; [2011] H.R.L.R. 25;
    [2011] U.K.H.R.R. 720; [2011] Inquest L.R. 22; (2011) 155(20) S.J.L.B. 35   14–75
McClaren v News Group Newspapers Ltd [2012] EWHC 2466 (QB); [2012] E.M.L.R. 33;
    (2012) 109(35) L.S.G. 20; (2012) 162 N.L.J. 1156   29–22
McCook v Lobo [2002] EWCA Civ 1760; [2003] I.C.R. 89.   13–35
McCoy v East Midlands SHA [2011] EWHC 38 (QB); [2011] Med. L.R. 103; (2011) 118
    B.M.L.R. 107   10–96
McDonagh v Commissioner of Police for the Metropolis, Times, December 28, 1989
    QBD   14–116
McElhatton v McFarland [2012] NIQB 114   13–35
McGhee v National Coal Board [1973] 1 W.L.R. 1; [1972] 3 All E.R. 1008; 1973 S.C.
    (H.L.) 37; 1973 S.L.T. 14; 13 K.I.R. 471; (1972) 116 S.J. 967 HL . . . .   2–58—2–68
McGlinchey v General Motors UK Ltd [2012] CSIH 91; 2013 G.W.D. 1–47 . . . .   11–41, 11–68
McKaskie v Cameron Unreported July 1, 2009 County Ct (Blackpool).   12–20
McKerr's Application for Judicial Review, Re; sub nom. McKerr, Re [2004] UKHL 12;
    [2004] 1 W.L.R. 807; [2004] 2 All E.R. 409; [2004] N.I. 212; [2004] H.R.L.R. 26;

[2004] U.K.H.R.R. 385; 17 B.H.R.C. 68; [2004] Lloyd's Rep. Med. 263; [2004]
Inquest L.R. 35; (2004) 101(13) L.S.G. 33; (2004) 148 S.J.L.B. 355 14–75
McLaughlin v Lambeth LBC [2010] EWHC 2726 (QB); [2011] E.M.L.R. 8; [2011]
H.R.L.R. 2; [2011] E.L.R. 57 22–35
McLeod v Crawford [2010] CSOH 101; 2010 S.L.T. 1035; 2011 S.C.L.R. 133; [2010]
P.N.L.R. 33; 2010 G.W.D. 29–609 10–111
McLeod v Rooney [2009] CSOH 158; 2010 S.L.T. 499; 2009 G.W.D. 40–684 24–73
McWilliams v Sir William Arrol & Co Ltd [1962] 1 W.L.R. 295; [1962] 1 All E.R. 623;
1962 S.C. (H.L.) 70; 1962 S.L.T. 121; (1962) 106 S.J. 218 HL 2–12
Meadow v General Medical Council; sub nom. General Medical Council v Meadow [2006]
EWCA Civ 1390; [2007] Q.B. 462; [2007] 2 W.L.R. 286; [2007] 1 All E.R. 1; [2007]
I.C.R. 701; [2007] 1 F.L.R. 1398; [2006] 3 F.C.R. 447; [2007] LS Law Medical 1;
(2006) 92 B.M.L.R. 51; [2007] Fam. Law 214; [2006] 44 E.G. 196 (C.S.); (2006)
103(43) L.S.G. 28; (2006) 156 N.L.J. 1686 16–73
Medeva BV v Comptroller General of Patents, Designs and Trade Marks [2012] EWCA
Civ 523; [2012] 3 C.M.L.R. 9; [2012] E.C.C. 21; [2012] R.P.C. 26 25–91
Medeva BV v Comptroller General of Patents, Designs and Trade Marks (C–322/10)
[2012] R.P.C. 25 25–91
Mellor v Partridge [2013] EWCA Civ 477 .... 18–34, 18–46
Merck & Co Inc v Primecrown Ltd (C–267/95); Beecham Group Plc v Europharm of
Worthing Ltd (C–268/95) [1996] E.C.R. I–6285; [1997] 1 C.M.L.R. 83; [1997]
F.S.R. 237 25–102
Merthyr Tydfil CBC v C [2010] EWHC 62 (QB); [2010] 1 F.L.R. 1640; [2010] 1 F.C.R.
441; [2010] P.I.Q.R. P9; [2010] Fam. Law 345 8–43
Metall Market OOO v Vitorio Shipping Co Ltd; Lehmann Timber, The; sub nom. Metall
Market OOO v Vitorio Shipping Ltd [2013] EWCA Civ 650; [2013] 2 All E.R.
(Comm) 585 .... 17–26, 17–71
Metroline Travel Ltd v Unite the Union [2012] EWHC 1778 (QB); [2012] I.R.L.R. 749;
(2012) 109(28) L.S.G. 19 .... 5–85, 24–152
MGN Ltd v United Kingdom (39401/04); sub nom. Mirror Group Newspapers Ltd v
United Kingdom (39401/04) [2011] 1 Costs L.O. 84; [2011] E.M.L.R. 20; (2011) 53
E.H.R.R. 5; 29 B.H.R.C. 686;................................. 22–04, 22–15, 27–48
Michael v Chief Constable of South Wales Police [2012] EWCA Civ 981; 2012] H.R.L.R.
30.. 8–56, 14–28, 14–72
Michael v Musgrove (t/a YNYS Ribs); Sea Eagle, The [2011] EWHC 1438 (Admlty);
[2012] Lloyd's Rep. 37 32–79
Midland Packaging Ltd v HW Accountants Ltd [2010] EWHC 1975 (QB); [2011] P.N.L.R.
1.. 10–207
Millar v Galashiels Gas Co Ltd. See Galashiels Gas Co Ltd v Millar
Miller v Associated Newspapers Ltd [2012] EWHC 3721 (QB) 22–76
Miller v Miller [2011] HCA 9; (2011) 275 A.L.R. 611 High Ct (Aus) 3–05, 3–11, 3–33
Milligan's Executors v Hewats [2013] CSOH 60; 2013 S.L.T. 758; [2013] P.N.L.R. 23;
2013 G.W.D. 16–345 10–08
Milton Keynes BC v Nulty; National Insurance & Guarantee Corp Ltd v Nulty [2013] EWCA
Civ 15; [2013] 1 W.L.R. 1183; [2013] B.L.R. 134; [2013] Lloyd's Rep. I.R. 243 ..... 2–07, 2–8
Minio-Paluello v Commissioner of Police of the Metropolis [2011] EWHC 3411
(QB) 15–52, 15–76
Ministry of Housing and Local Government v Sharp [1970] 2 Q.B. 223; [1970] 2 W.L.R.
802; [1970] 1 All E.R. 1009; 68 L.G.R. 187; (1970) 21 P. & C.R. 166; (1970) 114 S.J.
109 CA (Civ Div) 8–106
Misell v Essex CC, 93 L.G.R. 108 QBD..................................... 8–187
Mitchell v Glasgow City Council [2009] UKHL 11; [2009] 1 A.C. 874; [2009] 2 W.L.R.
481; [2009] 3 All E.R. 205; [2009] P.T.S.R. 778; 2009 S.C. (H.L.) 21; 2009 S.L.T. 247;
2009 S.C.L.R. 270; [2009] H.R.L.R. 18; [2009] H.L.R. 37; [2009] P.I.Q.R. P13; 2009
Hous. L.R. 2; (2009) 153(7) S.J.L.B. 33; [2009] N.P.C. 27; 2009 G.W.D. 7–122 14–54
Mobile Telesystems Finance SA v Nomihold Securities Inc [2011] EWCA Civ 1040;
[2012] 1 All E.R. (Comm) 223; [2012] Bus. L.R. 1166; [2012] 1 Lloyd's Rep. 6;
[2012] C.P. Rep. 1; [2011] 2 C.L.C. 856; [2011] Arb. L.R. 29; (2011) 108(35) L.S.G.
22; (2011) 161 N.L.J. 1214.. 29–44, 29–50

Monk v Cann Hall Primary School [2013] EWCA Civ 826 13–26
Moore v British Waterways Board [2013] EWCA Civ 73; [2013] 3 W.L.R. 43; [2013] 3 All
    E.R. 142; [2013] 2 P. & C.R. 7 . . . . 19–41, 19–75
Morgan v Ministry of Justice [2010] EWHC 2248 (QB) 5–03, 14–65, 14–70
Morris v CW Martin & Sons Ltd; sub nom. Morris v Martin [1966] 1 Q.B. 716; [1965] 3
    W.L.R. 276; [1965] 2 All E.R. 725; [1965] 2 Lloyd's Rep. 63; (1965) 109 S.J. 451 CA . . 6–30B
Morrison Sports Ltd v Scottish Power Plc; Pitchers v Scottish Power Plc; Singh v Scottish
    Power Plc [2010] UKSC 37; [2010] 1 W.L.R. 1934; 2011 S.C. (U.K.S.C.) 1; 2010
    S.L.T. 1027 9–15
Morrissey v McNicholas [2011] EWHC 2738 (QB) 22–201
Mortgage Express Ltd v Iqbal Hafeez Solicitors [2011] EWHC 3037 (Ch) 10–119
Mortgage Express v Sawali [2010] EWHC 3054 (Ch); [2011] P.N.L.R. 11; [2011] 1
    E.G.L.R. 58; [2011] 7 E.G. 98; [2010] N.P.C. 114 10–34
Mosley v United Kingdom (48009/08) [2012] E.M.L.R. 1; [2012] 1 F.C.R. 99; (2011) 53
    E.H.R.R. 30; 31 B.H.R.C. 409; (2011) 161 N.L.J. 703 ECtHR 27–38
Moteurs Leroy Somer v Société Dalkia France (C–285/08) [2009] E.C.R. I–4733 11–46
Moulton v Chief Constable of the West Midlands [2010] EWCA Civ 524 . . . . 16–37, 16–52, 16–53,
    16–54
Moyes v Lothian Health Board, 1990 S.L.T. 444 OH 2–14
Mulcaire v News Group Newspapers Ltd [2011] EWHC 3469 (Ch); [2012] Ch. 435;
    [2012] 2 W.L.R. 831; (2012) 109(3) L.S.G. 14 4–35
Mumford v Oxford, Worcester and Wolverhampton Railway Co, 156 E.R. 1107; (1856) 1
    Hurl. & N. 34 Ct Ex 20–66
Munro v Sturrock t/a Scotmaps [2012] CSIH 35; 2012 G.W.D. 15–312 11–09
Murdoch v Department for Work and Pensions [2010] EWHC 1988 (QB); [2011] P.T.S.R.
    D3 . . . . 8–19, 14–17, 14–48, 14–51A
Murdock v Scarisbrick Group Ltd [2011] EWHC 220 (QB) 12–28
Murfin v Campbell [2011] EWHC 1475 (Ch); [2011] P.N.L.R. 28 10–207
Murphy v Brentwood DC [1991] 1 A.C. 398; [1990] 3 W.L.R. 414; [1990] 2 All E.R. 908;
    [1990] 2 Lloyd's Rep. 467; 50 B.L.R. 1; 21 Con. L.R. 1; (1990) 22 H.L.R. 502; 89
    L.G.R. 24; (1991) 3 Admin. L.R. 37; (1990) 6 Const. L.J. 304; (1990) 154 L.G. Rev.
    1010; [1990] E.G. 105 (C.S.); (1990) 87(30) L.S.G. 15; (1990) 134 S.J. 1076 HL 8–128
Murphy v Culhane [1977] Q.B. 94; [1976] 3 W.L.R. 458; [1976] 3 All E.R. 533; (1976)
    120 S.J. 506 CA (Civ Div) 3–54
Musgrove v Pandelis [1919] 2 K.B. 43 CA 20–156
Mutua v Foreign and Commonwealth Office [2012] EWHC 2678 (QB); (2012) 162 N.L.J.
    1291 32–52
Nahome v Last Cawthra Feather [2010] EWHC 76 (Ch); [2010] P.N.L.R. 19 10–141
Naraji v Shelbourne [2011] EWHC 3298 (QB) 7–11, 31–23, 31–24
National Guild of Removers and Storers Ltd v Jones (t/a ATR Removals); National Guild
    of Removers and Storers Ltd v Mabberley (t/a Abbeymove and Clear & Store) [2012]
    EWCA Civ 216; [2012] 1 W.L.R. 2501 25–83
National Guild of Removers and Storers Ltd v Jones (t/a ATR removals) [2011] EWPCC 4 . . . 25–83
National Union of Rail, Maritime and Transport Workers v Serco Ltd (t/a Serco Docklands);
    Associated Society of Locomotive Engineers and Firemen (ASLEF) v London and
    Birmingham Railway Ltd (t/a London Midland); sub nom. London and Birmingham
    Railway Ltd (t/a London Midland) v Associated Society of Locomotive Engineers
    and Firemen (ASLEF) [2011] EWCA Civ 226; [2011] 3 All E.R. 913; [2011] I.C.R.
    848; [2011] I.R.L.R. 399; (2011) 108(11) L.S.G. 18 . . . . 24–112, 24–116, 24–145,
    24–147, 24–152, 24–163, 29–20
Nationwide Building Society v Davisons Solicitors; sub nom. Davisons Solicitors v
    Nationwide Building Society [2012] EWCA Civ 1626; [2013] 3 Costs L.O. 464;
    [2013] P.N.L.R. 12; [2013] 1 E.G.L.R. 73; [2013] 10 E.G. 148; [2013] W.T.L.R. 393;
    (2012) 156(48) S.J.L.B. 31 . . . . 10–21, 10–23, 10–119
Nayyar v Denton Wilde Sapte [2010] EWCA Civ 815 3–31
Network Rail Infrastructure Ltd v Conarken Group Ltd; Network Rail Infrastructure Ltd v
    Farrell Transport Ltd; sub nom. Conarken Group Ltd v Network Rail Infrastructure
    Ltd [2011] EWCA Civ 644; [2012] 1 All E.R. (Comm) 692; [2011] 2 C.L.C. 1; [2011]
    B.L.R. 462; 136 Con. L.R. 1; (2011) 108(24) L.S.G. 19 . . . . . . 8–132, 19–06, 20–184, 20–192

Neurim Pharmaceuticals (1991) Ltd v Comptroller-General of Patents (C–130/11)
[2013] R.P.C. 23 25–91
Newcastle International Airport Ltd v Eversheds LLP [2012] EWHC 2648 (Ch); [2013]
P.N.L.R. 5 10–134
Newsat Holdings Ltd v Zani [2006] EWHC 342 (Comm); [2006] 1 All E.R. (Comm) 607;
[2006] 1 Lloyd's Rep. 707 7–03
Newspaper Licensing Agency Ltd v Meltwater Holding BV [2011] EWCA Civ 890; [2012]
Bus. L.R. 53; [2012] R.P.C. 1 25–23
NHS Trust v Baby X [2012] EWHC 2188 (Fam); [2013] 1 F.L.R. 225; (2012) 127 B.M.L.R.
188; [2012] Fam. Law 1331 10–57
Nigeria v Ogbonna [2012] 1 W.L.R. 139; [2012] I.C.R. 32; [2011] Eq. L.R. 1060 EAT 5–29
Ningbo Wentai Sports Equipment Co Ltd v Wang [2012] EWPCC 51.................... 27–08
NML Capital Ltd v Argentina; sub nom. Argentina v NML Capital Ltd [2011] UKSC 31;
[2011] 2 A.C. 495; [2011] 3 W.L.R. 273; [2011] 4 All E.R. 1191; [2012] 1 All E.R.
(Comm) 1081; [2011] 2 Lloyd's Rep. 628; [2011] 2 C.L.C. 373; (2011) 155(27)
S.J.L.B. 39... 5–22
Noble v Owens; sub nom. Owens v Noble [2010] EWCA Civ 224; [2010] 1 W.L.R. 2491;
[2010] 3 All E.R. 830; [2010] C.P. Rep. 30; [2010] R.T.R. 22; [2010] P.I.Q.R. Q2;
(2010) 107(12) L.S.G. 25 31–16
Nokia Corp v Revenue and Customs Commissioners [2009] EWHC 1903 (Ch); [2009]
E.T.M.R. 59; [2010] F.S.R. 5; (2009) 32(8) I.P.D. 32054......................... 25–84
Nouri v Marvi Nouri v Marvi [2010] EWCA Civ 1107; [2011] C.P. Rep. 6; [2011] P.N.L.R.
7; [2010] 3 E.G.L.R. 79; [2010] 50 E.G. 64; [2010] 42 E.G. 105 (C.S.) 32–13
Ntuli v Donald; sub nom. Donald v Ntuli [2010] EWCA Civ 1276; [2011] 1 W.L.R. 294;
[2011] C.P. Rep. 13; [2011] E.M.L.R. 10 .... 27–37, 27–39,, 27–44, 27–47, 29–28A
Nulty v Milton Keynes BC. *See* Milton Keynes BC v Nulty
Numatic International Ltd v Qualtex (UK) Ltd [2010] EWHC 1237 (Ch); [2010] R.P.C. 25;
(2010) 107(24) L.S.G. 18 26–12
NWL Ltd v Woods (The Nawala) (No.2); NWL Ltd v Nelson and Laughton; Nawala, The
[1979] 1 W.L.R. 1294; [1979] 3 All E.R. 614; [1980] 1 Lloyd's Rep. 1; [1979] I.C.R.
867; [1979] I.R.L.R. 478; (1979) 123 S.J. 751 HL.............................. 24–163
O v Commissioner of Police of the Metropolis [2011] EWHC 1246 (QB); [2011] H.R.L.R.
29; [2011] U.K.H.R.R. 767..................................... 14–75, 14–79,
14–100
O'Leary International Ltd v Chief Constable of North Wales [2012] EWHC 1516 (Admin);
(2012) 176 J.P. 514; [2013] R.T.R. 14 17–47
OBG Ltd v Allan; Mainstream Properties Ltd v Young; Douglas v Hello! Ltd; sub nom.
OBG Ltd v Allen [2007] UKHL 21; [2008] 1 A.C. 1; [2007] 2 W.L.R. 920; [2007] 4
All E.R. 545; [2008] 1 All E.R. (Comm) 1; [2007] Bus. L.R. 1600; [2007] I.R.L.R.
608; [2007] E.M.L.R. 12; [2007] B.P.I.R. 746; (2007) 30(6) I.P.D. 30037; [2007] 19
E.G. 165 (C.S.); (2007) 151 S.J.L.B. 674; [2007] N.P.C. 54 .... 24–09, 24–15, 24–55, 24–70,
24–73, 24–95
Och-Ziff Management Europe Ltd v Och Capital LLP [2010] EWHC 2599 (Ch); [2011]
Bus. L.R. 632; [2011] E.C.C. 5; [2011] E.T.M.R. 1; [2011] F.S.R. 11 .... 25–15, 25–81,
26–15, 26–18
Ocular Sciences Ltd v Aspect Vision Care Ltd (No.2) [1997] R.P.C. 289; (1997) 20(3)
I.P.D. 20022 Ch D... 27–33
Oliver Brüstle v Greenpeace e.V. (C–34/10), [2012] All E.R. (EC) 809; [2012]
1 C.M.L.R. 41 .... 25—94
Olympic Delivery Authority v Persons Unknown [2012] EWHC 1012 (Ch)..... 14–93A, 20–30
OM (Nigeria) v Secretary of State for the Home Department [2011] EWCA Civ 909....... 15–135
Omega Proteins Ltd v Aspen Insurance UK Ltd [2010] EWHC 2280 (Comm); [2011] 1 All
E.R. (Comm) 313; [2010] 2 C.L.C. 370; [2011] Lloyd's Rep. I.R. 183; (2010) 107(37)
L.S.G. 17; (2010) 160 N.L.J. 1260 .... 11–21, 11–23
Ontario Store Fixtures v Mmmuffins [1989] 70 O.R. (2d) 42......................... 24–36
OOO v The Commissioner of Police for the Metropolis. *See* O v Commissioner of Police
of the Metropolis
OPQ v BJM [2011] EWHC 1059 (QB); [2011] E.M.L.R. 23 27–47
Opuz v Turkey (33401/02) (2010) 50 E.H.R.R. 28; 27 B.H.R.C. 159 ECtHR 14–70
Oracle America Inc v M-Tech Data Ltd. *See* Sun Microsystems Inc v M-Tech Data Ltd

Osman v United Kingdom (23452/94) [1999] 1 F.L.R. 193; (2000) 29 E.H.R.R. 245; 5
    B.H.R.C. 293; (1999) 1 L.G.L.R. 431; (1999) 11 Admin. L.R. 200; [2000] Inquest
    L.R. 101; [1999] Crim. L.R. 82; [1998] H.R.C.D. 966; [1999] Fam. Law 86; (1999)
    163 J.P.N. 297 ECtHR. 14–72, 14–79, 14–93
Owens v Brimmell [1977] Q.B. 859; [1977] 2 W.L.R. 943; [1976] 3 All E.R. 765; [1977]
    R.T.R. 82 QBD 3–84
P v National Association of School Masters Union of Women Teachers (NASUWT); sub
    nom. P v National Association of Schoolmasters Union of Women Teachers
    (NASUWT); P (FC), Re [2003] UKHL 8; [2003] 2 A.C. 663; [2003] 2 W.L.R. 545;
    [2003] 1 All E.R. 993; [2003] I.C.R. 386; [2003] I.R.L.R. 307; [2003] E.L.R. 357;
    (2003) 100(17) L.S.G. 27; (2003) 153 N.L.J. 350 . . . . 24–112, 24–145, 24–146, 24–147
Padden v Bevan Ashford (A Firm) [2013] EWCA Civ 824; (2013) 157(29) S.J.L.B. 31 10–134
Padden v Bevan Ashford Solicitors [2011] EWCA Civ 1616; [2012] 1 W.L.R. 1759; [2012]
    2 All E.R. 718; [2012] 2 Costs L.O. 223; [2012] 2 F.C.R. 264; [2012] P.N.L.R.
    14. . . . . 10–109, 10–133, 10–134
Page v Hewetts Solicitors [2012] EWCA Civ 805; [2012] C.P. Rep. 40; [2012] W.T.L.R.
    1427. 32–01
Painer v Standard Verlags GmbH (C–145/10) [2012] E.C.D.R. 6. 25–09
Palmer v Marks and Spencer Plc [2001] EWCA Civ 1528 13–54
Paramasivan v Wicks [2013] EWCA Civ 262 3–69
Paratus AMC Ltd v Countrywide Surveyors Ltd [2011] EWHC 3307 (Ch); [2012] P.N.L.R.
    12. . . . . 10–166, 10–178, 10–181
Parbulk II A/S v PT Humpuss Intermoda Transportasi TBK (The Mahakam); Mahakam,
    The [2011] EWHC 3143 (Comm); [2012] 2 All E.R. (Comm) 513; [2011] 2 C.L.C.
    988. 29–42
Parshall v Bryans; sub nom. Parshall v Hackney [2013] EWCA Civ 240; [2013] 3 W.L.R.
    605; [2013] 3 All E.R. 224; [2013] 15 E.G. 104 (C.S.); [2013] 2 P. & C.R. DG5
    [2013] EWCA Civ 240; [2013] 3 W.L.R. 605; [2013] 3 All E.R. 224; [2013] 15 E.G.
    104 (C.S.); [2013] 2 P. & C.R. DG5 . . . . 19–70, 19–75
Patchett v Swimming Pool & Allied Trades Association Ltd [2009] EWCA Civ 717; [2010]
    2 All E.R. (Comm) 138; [2009] Info. T.L.R. 185 8–106
Pearce v Ove Arup Partnership Ltd (Jurisdiction) [2000] Ch. 403; [2000] 3 W.L.R. 332;
    [1999] 1 All E.R. 769; [1999] I.L.Pr. 442; [1999] F.S.R. 525; (1999) 22(4) I.P.D.
    22041; (1999) 96(9) L.S.G. 31; [1999] N.P.C. 7 CA (Civ Div) 7–19
Pearson v United Kingdom (Admissibility) (40957/07) (2012) 54 E.H.R.R. SE11 ECtHR. . . . 14–75
Pell Frischmann Engineering Ltd v Bow Valley Iran Ltd [2009] UKPC 45; [2011] 1 W.L.R.
    2370; [2010] B.L.R. 73; [2011] Bus. L.R. D1 24–95
PepsiCo Inc v Grupo Promer Mon-Graphic SA (C–281/10 P); sub nom. PepsiCo Inc v
    Office for Harmonisation in the Internal Market (Trade Marks and Designs) (OHIM)
    (C–281/10 P) [2012] F.S.R. 5 25–63
Peterson v Merck Sharpe & Dohme (Aust) Pty Ltd [2010] FCA 180; (2010) 266 A.L.R. 1 . . . 11–31
Petrina v Romania (78060/01), October 14, 2008 14–87
Phee v Gordon [2013] CSIH 18; 2013 S.L.T. 439; 2013 Rep. L.R. 79; 2013 G.W.D.
    11–235. . . . . 8–145, 12–27, 12–29, 12–30
Phelps v Hillingdon LBC; Jarvis v Hampshire CC; G (A Child) v Bromley LBC; Anderton
    v Clwyd CC; sub nom. G (A Child), Re [2001] 2 A.C. 619; [2000] 3 W.L.R. 776;
    [2000] 4 All E.R. 504; [2000] 3 F.C.R. 102; (2001) 3 L.G.L.R. 5; [2000] B.L.G.R.
    651; [2000] Ed. C.R. 700; [2000] E.L.R. 499; (2000) 3 C.C.L. Rep. 156; (2000) 56
    B.M.L.R. 1; (2000) 150 N.L.J. 1198; (2000) 144 S.J.L.B. 241 HL 14–13
Phethean-Hubble v Coles [2012] EWCA Civ 349; [2012] R.T.R. 31 3–69
Phillips v Britannia Hygienic Laundry Co Ltd [1923] 2 K.B. 832 CA 9–15
Phillips v News Group Newspapers Ltd; Coogan v News Group Newspapers Ltd; Gray v
    News Group Newspapers Ltd; sub nom. Phillips v Mulcaire [2012] UKSC 28; [2013]
    1 A.C. 1; [2012] 3 W.L.R. 312; [2012] 4 All E.R. 207; [2012] 5 Costs L.O. 609;
    [2012] E.M.L.R. 31; [2013] F.S.R. 12 . . . . 24–90, 24–92,
                                                                                          27–04
Phimister v DM Hall LLP [2012] CSOH 169; 2013 S.L.T. 261; [2013] P.N.L.R. 6; 2013
    Rep. L.R. 34; 2012 G.W.D. 35–720 . . . . 10–163, 10–166
Pinchbeck v Craggy Island Ltd [2012] EWHC 2745 (QB) 8–160

Pitts v Hunt [1991] 1 Q.B. 24; [1990] 3 W.L.R. 542; [1990] 3 All E.R. 344; [1990] R.T.R. 290; (1990) 134 S.J. 834 CA (Civ Div) 3–18

Plato Films Ltd v Speidel; sub nom. Speidel v Plato Films Ltd; Speidel v Unity Theatre Society [1961] A.C. 1090; [1961] 2 W.L.R. 470; [1961] 1 All E.R. 876; (1961) 105 S.J. 230 HL 22–136

Plentyoffish Media Inc v Plenty More LLP [2011] EWHC 2568 (Ch); [2012] E.C.C. 15; [2011] Info. T.L.R. 75; [2012] R.P.C. 5 26–05

Pocket Kings Ltd v Safenames Ltd [2009] EWHC 2529 (Ch); [2010] Ch. 438; [2010] 2 W.L.R. 1110; [2010] 2 All E.R. (Comm) 631.................................. 5–27

POI v Lina [2011] EWHC 25 (QB)... 27–47

Poppleton v Trustees of the Portsmouth Youth Activities Committee; sub nom. Trustees of the Portsmouth Youth Activities Committee v Poppleton [2008] EWCA Civ 646; [2009] P.I.Q.R. P1; [2008] N.P.C. 65 8–160

Port of London Authority v Ashmore [2010] EWCA Civ 30; [2010] 1 All E.R. 1139; [2010] N.P.C. 14... 19–75

Portakabin Ltd v Primakabin BV (C–558/08) [2011] Bus. L.R. 1339; [2010] E.C.R. I–6963; [2011] C.E.C. 552; [2010] E.T.M.R. 52 25–81

Porubova v Russia (8237/03) [2009] E.C.H.R. 1477 27–41

Powell v United Kingdom (Admissibility) (45305/99) [2000] Inquest L.R. 19; (2000) 30 E.H.R.R. CD362 ECtHR... 14–73

Practice Guidance (HC: Interim Non-Disclosure Orders) [2012] 1 W.L.R. 1003; [2012] E.M.L.R. 5 .... 23–05, 27–47

Preskey v Sutcliffe Unreported February 18, 2013 County Court (Leeds).................. 21–15

Print N' Promotion (Canada) Ltd v Kovachis [2011] ONCA 23; (2011) 329 D.L.R. (4th) 421 CA (Ont)... 24–71

Pritchard v Teitelbaum [2011] EWHC 1063 (Ch); [2011] 2 E.G.L.R. 1; [2011] 30 E.G. 58; [2011] 18 E.G. 108 (C.S.); [2011] N.P.C. 43; [2011] 2 P. & C.R. DG18 19–72

Pro-Tec Covers Ltd v Specialised Covers Ltd Unreported October 18, 2011............... 25–59

Probert v Moore [2012] EWHC 2324 (QB) 3–72, 8–183

Protomed Ltd v Medication Systems Ltd [2012] EWHC 3726 (Ch).................... 25–83

Public Relations Consultants Association Ltd v Newspaper Licensing Agency Ltd [2013] UKSC 18; [2013] 2 All E.R. 852; [2013] 3 C.M.L.R. 11; [2013] E.C.D.R. 10; [2013] E.M.L.R. 21; [2013] R.P.C. 19 25–23

Punch v Sphere Time (T–68/10). See Sphere Time v Office for Harmonisation in the Internal Market (Trade Marks and Designs) (OHIM) (T–68/10)

Qadir v Associated Newspapers Ltd [2012] EWHC 2606 (QB); [2013] E.M.L.R. 15 22–146

Qantas Airways v Transport Workers Union of Australia [2011] FCA 470; (2011) 280 A.L.R. 503.............................. 24–15, 24–40, 24–55, 24–70, 24–73

QBE Management Services (UK) Ltd v Dymoke [2012] EWHC 80 (QB); [2012] I.R.L.R. 458; (2012) 162 N.L.J. 180.. 27–34

Qema v News Group Newspapers Ltd [2012] EWHC 1146 (QB) 16–50

Quinn v CC Automotive Group Ltd (t/a Carcraft) [2010] EWCA Civ 1412; [2011] 2 All E.R. (Comm) 584 6–50

R. (on the application of Abdi) v Secretary of State for the Home Department; Khalaf v Secretary of State for the Home Department; sub nom. Secretary of State for the Home Department v Abdi [2011] EWCA Civ 242; Times, March 11, 2011.......... 15135A

R. (on the application of Al-Skeini) v Secretary of State for Defence [2007] UKHL 26; [2008] 1 A.C. 153; [2007] 3 W.L.R. 33; [2007] 3 All E.R. 685; [2007] H.R.L.R. 31; [2007] U.K.H.R.R. 955; 22 B.H.R.C. 518; [2007] Inquest L.R. 168; (2007) 104(26) L.S.G. 34; (2007) 157 N.L.J. 894; (2007) 151 S.J.L.B. 809...................... 14–73

R. (on the application of AM (Angola)) v Secretary of State for the Home Department [2012] EWCA Civ 521 15–135

R. (on the application of Anam) v Secretary of State for the Home Department; sub nom. Anam v Secretary of State for the Home Department [2010] EWCA Civ 1140; [2011] A.C.D. 14 15–135

R. (on the application of Anam) v Secretary of State for the Home Department (No.2) [2012] EWHC 1770 (Admin)........................... 15–33, 15–135, 15–137

R. (on the application of Anand) v Revenue and Customs Commissioners [2012] EWHC 2989 (Admin); [2013] C.P. Rep. 2; [2013] Lloyd's Rep. F.C. 278; [2013] A.C.D.8 19–62

R. (on the application of AP) v HM Coroner for Worcestershire [2011] EWHC 1453
    (Admin); [2011] B.L.G.R. 952; [2011] Med. L.R. 397; [2011] Inquest L.R. 50; [2011]
    A.C.D. 100 .... 14–73, 14–74, 14–75
R. (on the application of Atapattu) v Secretary of State for the Home Department [2011]
    EWHC 1388 (Admin)... 14–48, 14–95,
                                                                                17–25, 17–48
R. (on the application of BA) v Secretary of State for the Home Department [2011] EWHC
    2748 (Admin) 15–135
R. (on the application of Bhatti) v Croydon Magistrates' Court; sub nom. Bhatti v Croydon
    Magistrates' Court [2010] EWHC 522 (Admin); [2011] 1 W.L.R. 948; [2010] 3 All
    E.R. 671; (2010) 174 J.P. 213; [2010] Lloyd's Rep. F.C. 522 19–61
R. (on the application of Bryant) v Commissioner of Police of the Metropolis [2011]
    EWHC 1314 (Admin); [2011] H.R.L.R. 27 27–37
R. (on the application of C) v Commissioner of Police of the Metropolis; sub nom. R. (on
    the application of J) v Commissioner of Police of the Metropolis [2012] EWHC 1681
    (Admin); [2012] 1 W.L.R. 3007; [2012] 4 All E.R. 510; [2012] H.R.L.R. 26; [2012]
    A.C.D. 103; (2012) 109(28) L.S.G. 21 14–86
R. (on the application of Catt) v Association of Chief Police Officers of England, Wales and
    Northern Ireland; R. (on the application of T) v Commissioner of Police of the
    Metropolis [2013] EWCA Civ 192; [2013] 3 All E.R. 583; [2013] H.R.L.R. 20........ 14–86
R. (on the application of Checkprice (UK) Ltd (In Administration)) v Revenue and Customs
    Commissioners; sub nom. Checkprice (UK) Ltd (In Administration) v Revenue and
    Customs Commissioners [2010] EWHC 682 (Admin); [2010] S.T.C. 1153; [2010]
    A.C.D. 67 .... 17–92, 17–107
R. (on the application of Coke-Wallis) v Institute of Chartered Accountants in England and
    Wales; sub nom. Coke-Wallis v Institute of Chartered Accountants of England and
    Wales [2011] UKSC 1; [2011] 2 A.C. 146; [2011] 2 W.L.R. 103; [2011] 2 All E.R. 1;
    [2011] I.C.R. 224; (2011) 108(5) L.S.G. 18 31–24
R. (on the application of Coleman) v Governor of Wayland Prison [2009] EWHC 1005
    (Admin); [2010] 1 Prison L.R. 231... 17–71
R. (on the application of Condliff) v North Staffordshire Primary Care Trust [2011] EWCA
    Civ 910; [2012] 1 All E.R. 689; [2012] P.T.S.R. 460; [2011] H.R.L.R. 38; (2011) 14
    C.C.L. Rep. 656; [2011] Med. L.R. 572; (2011) 121 B.M.L.R. 192; [2011] A.C.D.
    113; (2011) 155(30) S.J.L.B. 31 10–44
R. (on the application of Draga) v Secretary of State for the Home Department [2012]
    EWCA Civ 842.. 15–30, 15–135
R. (on the application of EH) v Secretary of State for the Home Department [2012] EWHC
    2569 (Admin) 15–135
R. (on the application of Equality and Human Rights Commission) v Prime Minister; R.
    (on the application of Al-Bazzouni) v Prime Minister; sub nom. Equality and Human
    Rights Commission v Prime Minister; Al-Bazzouni v Prime Minister [2011] EWHC
    2401 (Admin); [2012] 1 W.L.R. 1389; [2011] U.K.H.R.R. 1287.................... 15–53
R. (on the application of Faulkner) v Secretary of State for Justice. See R. (on the application
    of Sturnham) v Parole Board
R. (on the application of GC) v Commissioner of Police of the Metropolis; R. (on the
    application of C) v Commissioner of Police of the Metropolis [2011] UKSC 21;
    [2011] 1 W.L.R. 1230; [2011] 3 All E.R. 859; [2011] 2 Cr. App. R. 18; [2011]
    H.R.L.R. 26; [2011] U.K.H.R.R. 807; [2011] Crim. L.R. 964; (2011) 108(22) L.S.G.
    18; (2011) 155(20) S.J.L.B. 35 14–86
R. (on the application of Gujra) v Crown Prosecution Service [2012] UKSC 52; [2013] 1
    A.C. 484; [2012] 3 W.L.R. 1227; [2013] 1 All E.R. 612; [2013] 1 Cr. App. R. 12;
    [2013] Crim. L.R. 337.. 16–03
R. (on the application of Hussein) v Secretary of State for the Home Department. See R.
    (on the application of MH) v Secretary of State for the Home Department
R. (on the application of Infinis Plc) v Gas and Electricity Markets Authority; sub nom.
    Gas and Electricity Markets Authority v Infinis Plc [2013] EWCA Civ 70; [2013]
    J.P.L. 1037... 14–95
R. (on the application of James) v Secretary of State for Justice. See R. (on the application
    of Wells) v Parole Board

R. (on the application of Kambadzi) v Secretary of State for the Home Department; sub
    nom. SK (Zimbabwe) v Secretary of State for the Home Department; R. (on the
    application of SK (Zimbabwe)) v Secretary of State for the Home Department;
    Kambadzi v Secretary of State for the Home Department [2011] UKSC 23; [2011] 1
    W.L.R. 1299; [2011] 4 All E.R. 975; (2011) 108(23) L.S.G. 18.   15–135
R. (on the application of Kambadzi) v Secretary of State for the Home Department; sub
    nom. SK (Zimbabwe) v Secretary of State for the Home Department; R. (on the
    application of SK (Zimbabwe)) v Secretary of State for the Home Department;
    Kambadzi v Secretary of State for the Home Department [2008] EWCA Civ 1204;
    [2009] 1 W.L.R. 1527; [2009] 2 All E.R. 365.   15–135
R. (on the application of Kehoe) v Secretary of State for Work and Pensions; sub nom.
    Kehoe v Secretary of State for Work and Pensions; Secretary of State for Work and
    Pensions v Kehoe [2005] UKHL 48; [2006] 1 A.C. 42; [2005] 3 W.L.R. 252; [2005]
    4 All E.R. 905; [2005] 2 F.L.R. 1249; [2005] 2 F.C.R. 683; [2005] H.R.L.R. 30;
    [2006] U.K.H.R.R. 360; [2005] Fam. Law 850; (2005) 155 N.L.J. 1123; (2005) 149
    S.J.L.B. 921. . . . .   14–17, 14–51A
R. (on the application of Lamari) v Secretary of State for the Home Department [2012]
    EWHC 1630 (Admin).   15–135
R. (on the application of LE (Jamaica)) v Secretary of State for the Home Department;
    sub nom. LE (Jamaica) v Secretary of State for the Home Department [2012] EWCA
    Civ 597   15–135
R. (on the application of Lumba) v Secretary of State for the Home Department; R. (on the
    application of Mighty) v Secretary of State for the Home Department; sub nom. Abdi
    v Secretary of State for the Home Department; Ashori v Secretary of State for the
    Home Department; Madami v Secretary of State for the Home Department; Mighty
    v Secretary of State for the Home Department; Lumba v Secretary of State for the
    Home Department; R. (on the application of WL (Congo)) v Secretary of State for the
    Home Department; R. (on the application of KM (Jamaica)) v Secretary of State for
    the Home Department [2011] UKSC 12; [2012] 1 A.C. 245; [2011] 2 W.L.R. 671;
    [2011] 4 All E.R. 1; [2011] U.K.H.R.R. 437; (2011) 108(14) L.S.G. 20; (2011)
    155(12) S.J.L.B. 30. . . . .   1–12, 2–10, 15–33, 15–135, 15–137, 28–141, 28–142, 28–151
R. (on the application of MH) v Secretary of State for the Home Department [2010] EWCA
    Civ 1112   15–135
R. (on the application of Moos) v Commissioner of Police of the Metropolis [2012] EWCA
    Civ 12   15–64
R. (on the application of Moussaoui) v Secretary of State for the Home Department [2012]
    EWHC 126 (Admin); [2012] A.C.D. 55.   15–135
R. (on the application of Muqtaar) v Secretary of State for the Home Department; sub nom.
    Muqtaar v Secretary of State for the Home Department [2012] EWCA Civ 1270;
    [2013] 1 W.L.R. 649; [2013] A.C.D. 14. . . . .   15–135A
R. (on the application of Murad) v Secretary of State for the Home Department [2012]
    EWHC 1112 (Admin).   15–135
R. (on the application of Roberts) v Commissioner of Police of the Metropolis [2012]
    EWHC 1977 (Admin); [2012] H.R.L.R. 28; [2012] A.C.D. 104   15–62
R. (on the application of Sessay) v South London and Maudsley NHS Foundation Trust
    [2011] EWHC 2617 (QB); [2012] Q.B. 760; [2012] 2 W.L.R. 1071; [2012] P.T.S.R.
    742; [2012] Med. L.R. 123; [2012] M.H.L.R. 94.   15–100
R. (on the application of Smith) v Oxfordshire Assistant Deputy Coroner; Secretary of
    State for Defence v Smith; sub nom. R. (on the application of Smith) v Secretary of
    State for Defence [2010] UKSC 29; [2011] 1 A.C. 1; [2010] 3 W.L.R. 223; [2010] 3
    All E.R. 1067; [2010] H.R.L.R. 28; [2010] U.K.H.R.R. 1020; 29 B.H.R.C. 497;
    [2010] Inquest L.R. 119; (2010) 107(28) L.S.G. 17; (2010) 160 N.L.J. 973; (2010)
    154(26) S.J.L.B. 28. . . . .   5–13, 14–69A, 14–73, 14–75
R. (on the application of Sturnham) v Parole Board; R. (on the application of Faulkner) v
    Secretary of State for Justice; sub nom. R. (on the application of Sturnham) v
    Secretary of State for Justice [2013] UKSC 23; [2013] 2 W.L.R. 1157; [2013] 2 All
    E.R. 1013; [2013] H.R.L.R. 24; (2013) 157(18) S.J.L.B. 31 . . . .   14–81, 14–98, 14–99,
                                                                                       15–30, 15–141A, 28–01
R. (on the application of Truong Dia Diep) v Land Registry [2010] EWHC 3315 (Admin) . . .   19–75

R. (on the application of Ullah) v Special Adjudicator; Do v Immigration Appeal Tribunal; sub nom. Ullah (Ahsan) v Special Adjudicator; R. (on the application of Ullah (Ahsan)) v Secretary of State for the Home Department; Do v Secretary of State for the Home Department [2004] UKHL 26; [2004] 2 A.C. 323; [2004] 3 W.L.R. 23; [2004] 3 All E.R. 785; [2004] H.R.L.R. 33; [2004] U.K.H.R.R. 995; [2004] Imm. A.R. 419; [2004] I.N.L.R. 381; (2004) 101(28) L.S.G. 33; (2004) 154 N.L.J. 985; (2004) 148 S.J.L.B. 762 14–73

R. (on the application of Van der Pijl) v Kingston Crown Court; sub nom. Van der Pijl v Kingston Crown Court [2012] EWHC 3745 (Admin); [2013] 1 W.L.R. 2706; [2013] Lloyd's Rep. F.C. 287; [2013] A.C.D. 29 19–62

R. (on the application of Waxman) v Crown Prosecution Service [2012] EWHC 133 (Admin); (2012) 176 J.P. 121; [2012] A.C.D. 48; (2012) 109(7) L.S.G. 15. 14–100

R. (on the application of Wells) v Parole Board; R. (on the application of Walker) v Secretary of State for Justice; R. (on the application of Lee) v Secretary of State for Justice; R. (on the application of James) v Secretary of State for Justice; sub nom. Wells v Parole Board; Walker v Secretary of State for the Home Department; Secretary of State for Justice v Walker; Secretary of State for Justice v James (formerly Walker) [2009] UKHL 22; [2010] 1 A.C. 553; [2009] 2 W.L.R. 1149; [2009] 4 All E.R. 255; [2009] H.R.L.R. 23; [2009] U.K.H.R.R. 809; 26 B.H.R.C. 696; [2009] Prison L.R. 371 [2009] UKHL 22; [2010] 1 A.C. 553; [2009] 2 W.L.R. 1149; [2009] 4 All E.R. 255; [2009] H.R.L.R. 23; [2009] U.K.H.R.R. 809; 26 B.H.R.C. 696; [2009] Prison L.R. 371 15–30

R. (on the application of WL (Congo)) v Secretary of State for the Home Department. See R. (on the application of Lumba) v Secretary of State for the Home Department

R. (on the application of Wood) v Commissioner of Police of the Metropolis; sub nom. Wood v Commissioner of Police of the Metropolis [2009] EWCA Civ 414; [2010] 1 W.L.R. 123; [2009] 4 All E.R. 951; [2010] E.M.L.R. 1; [2009] H.R.L.R. 25; [2009] U.K.H.R.R. 1254; [2009] Po. L.R. 203; [2009] A.C.D. 75; (2009) 106(22) L.S.G. 24; (2009) 153(21) S.J.L.B. 30 27–39

R. v Beazley (Rosemary); R. v Beazley (Scott) [2013] EWCA Crim 567 25–84

R. v Ganyo (Molly); R. v Ganyo (Prize) [2011] EWCA Crim 2491; [2012] 1 Cr. App. R. (S.) 108; (2012) 176 J.P. 396. 15–140

R. v Gilham (Christopher Paul) [2009] EWCA Crim 2293; [2010] E.C.D.R. 5; [2010] Lloyd's Rep. F.C. 89; [2009] Info. T.L.R. 171; [2010] Crim. L.R. 407 25–23

R. v Henrys Solicitors [2012] EWCA Crim 1480; [2012] 6 Costs L.O. 858; [2012] P.N.L.R. 32. 10–121

R. v Kamran Hameed Ghori [2012] EWCA Crim 1115 25–84

R. v Morris (Daryl Howard) [2013] EWCA Crim 436; [2013] 2 Cr. App. R. 9; [2013] R.T.R. 22. 15–52

R. v Sones (John Richard) [2012] EWCA Crim 1377. 15–140

R. v SVS Solicitors [2012] EWCA Crim 319; [2012] 3 Costs L.R. 502; [2012] P.N.L.R. 21 10–121

Rabone v Pennine Care NHS Foundation Trust [2012] UKSC 2; [2012] 2 A.C. 72; [2012] 2 W.L.R. 381; [2012] 2 All E.R. 381; [2012] P.T.S.R. 497; [2012] H.R.L.R. 10; 33 B.H.R.C. 208; (2012) 15 C.C.L. Rep. 13; [2012] Med. L.R. 221; (2012) 124 B.M.L.R. 148; [2012] M.H.L.R. 66; (2012) 162 N.L.J. 261; (2012) 156(6) S.J.L.B. 31 . . . . . 1–79, 8–36, 10–78, 10–93, 10–104, 14–69, 14–70, 14–73, 14–93, 14–100, 28–01

Raiffeisen Zentralbank Osterreich AG v Royal Bank of Scotland Plc [2010] EWHC 1392 (Comm); [2011] 1 Lloyd's Rep. 123; [2011] Bus. L.R. D65 18–14

Ramroop v Ishmael; sub nom. Ramroop (also known as Sampson) v Ishmael [2010] UKPC 14. 19–11

Ramzan v Brookwide Ltd [2011] EWCA Civ 985; [2012] 1 All E.R. 903; [2012] 1 All E.R. (Comm) 979; [2011] 2 P. & C.R. 22; [2011] N.P.C. 95 . . . . 19–74A, 28–143, 28-

Rantsev v Cyprus (25965/04) (2010) 51 E.H.R.R. 1; 28 B.H.R.C. 313 14–79

RDC Promotions v Lawrence. See Coventry (t/a RDC Promotions) v Lawrence

Red Bull GmbH v Sun Mark Ltd [2012] EWHC 1929 (Ch). 25–81

Red Spider Technology v Omega Completions Technology [2010] EWHC 59 (Ch) 25–59

Redd Solicitors LLP v Red Legal Ltd [2012] EWPCC 54; [2013] E.T.M.R. 13. 25–79

Redwood Tree Services Ltd v Apsay (t/a Redwood Tree Surgeons) Unreported 26–18

Rees v Darlington Memorial Hospital NHS Trust [2003] UKHL 52; [2004] 1 A.C. 309;
    [2003] 3 W.L.R. 1091; [2003] 4 All E.R. 987; [2004] 1 F.L.R. 234; [2003] 3 F.C.R.
    289; [2004] P.I.Q.R. P14; [2004] Lloyd's Rep. Med. 1; (2004) 75 B.M.L.R. 69;
    [2004] Fam. Law 22; (2003) 153 N.L.J. 1599 10–85
Reeves v Commissioner of Police of the Metropolis [2000] 1 A.C. 360; [1999] 3 W.L.R.
    363; [1999] 3 All E.R. 897; (2000) 51 B.M.L.R. 155; [1999] Prison L.R. 99; (1999)
    96(31) L.S.G. 41; (1999) 143 S.J.L.B. 213 HL 3–54
Rehill v Rider Holdings Ltd [2012] EWCA Civ 628; [2013] R.T.R. 5 3–73
Reynolds v Strutt & Parker LLP [2011] EWHC 2263 (QB) 6–39
Reynolds v Times Newspapers Ltd [2001] 2 A.C. 127; [1999] 3 W.L.R. 1010; [1999] 4 All
    E.R. 609; [2000] E.M.L.R. 1; [2000] H.R.L.R. 134; 7 B.H.R.C. 289; (1999) 96(45)
    L.S.G. 34; (1999) 149 N.L.J. 1697; (1999) 143 S.J.L.B. 270... 22–04, 22–72, 22–136, 22–256
Reynolds v United Kingdom (2694/08) (2012) 55 E.H.R.R. 35 ECtHR.............. 1–79, 8–36,
                                                                        10–93, 14–73
Richards v Bromley LBC [2012] EWCA Civ 1476; [2013] E.L.R. 66................... 12–29
Richardson v Chief Constable of West Midlands [2011] EWHC 773 (QB); [2011] 2 Cr.
    App. R. 1; [2011] Crim. L.R. 903... 15–72
Rivella International AG v Office for Harmonisation in the Internal Market (Trade Marks
    and Designs) (OHIM) (T–170/11) [2013] E.T.M.R. 4 25–79
Roberts v Bank of Scotland [2013] EWCA Civ 882................................ 15–20
Roberts v Gill & Co [2010] UKSC 22; [2011] 1 A.C. 240; [2010] 2 W.L.R. 1227; [2010] 4
    All E.R. 367; [2010] P.N.L.R. 30; [2010] W.T.L.R. 1223; (2010) 154(20) S.J.L.B.
    36.. 32–20
Robins v Kordowski [2011] EWHC 981 (QB) 22–256
Robinson v PE Jones (Contractors) Ltd [2011] EWCA Civ 9; [2012] Q.B. 44; [2011] 3
    W.L.R. 815; [2011] B.L.R. 206; 134 Con. L.R. 26; [2011] 1 E.G.L.R. 111; (2011) 27
    Const. L.J. 145; [2011] C.I.L.L. 2972; [2011] 4 E.G. 100 (C.S.)............. 8–113, 8–122,
                                                                        8–126, 10–182
Robot Arenas Ltd v Waterfield [2010] EWHC 115 (QB) 17–72
Roder UK Ltd v West; sub nom. Roder UK Ltd v Titan Marquees Ltd [2011] EWCA Civ
    1126; [2012] Q.B. 752; [2012] 3 W.L.R. 469; [2012] 1 All E.R. 1305; [2012] 1 All
    E.R. (Comm) 659; (2011) 161 N.L.J. 1450; [2011] N.P.C. 101 18–53
Rothschild v Associated Newspapers Ltd [2011] EWHC 3462 (QB)..................... 22–03
Rothschild v Associated Newspapers Ltd [2013] EWCA Civ 197; [2013] E.M.L.R. 18 22–76,
                                                                            22–79
Rothwell v Chemical & Insulating Co Ltd. See Grieves v FT Everard & Sons Ltd
Rowley v Secretary of State for Work and Pensions; sub nom. R. (on the application of
    Rowley) v Secretary of State for Work and Pensions [2007] EWCA Civ 598; [2007]
    1 W.L.R. 2861; [2007] 2 F.L.R. 945; [2007] 3 F.C.R. 431; [2007] Fam. Law 896;
    (2007) 151 S.J.L.B. 856 .... 14–08, 14–17, 14–48, 14–51A
Royal Bank of Scotland Plc v Etridge (No.2); Barclays Bank Plc v Coleman; Barclays Bank
    Plc v Harris; Midland Bank Plc v Wallace; National Westminster Bank Plc v Gill;
    UCB Home Loans Corp Ltd v Moore; Bank of Scotland v Bennett; Kenyon-Brown v
    Desmond Banks & Co (Undue Influence) (No.2) [2001] UKHL 44; [2002] 2 A.C.
    773; [2001] 3 W.L.R. 1021; [2001] 4 All E.R. 449; [2001] 2 All E.R. (Comm) 1061;
    [2002] 1 Lloyd's Rep. 343; [2001] 2 F.L.R. 1364; [2001] 3 F.C.R. 481; [2002] H.L.R.
    4; [2001] Fam. Law 880; [2001] 43 E.G. 184 (C.S.); (2001) 151 N.L.J. 1538; [2001]
    N.P.C. 147; [2002] 1 P. & C.R. DG14;...................................... 10–134
Royal Bank of Scotland Plc v FAL Oil Co Ltd [2012] EWHC 3628 (Comm); [2013]
    1 Lloyd's Rep. 327 29–41
Royal Brunei Airlines Sdn Bhd v Tan; sub nom. Royal Brunei Airlines Sdn Bhd v Philip
    Tan Kok Ming [1995] 2 A.C. 378; [1995] 3 W.L.R. 64; [1995] 3 All E.R. 97; [1995]
    B.C.C. 899; (1995) 92(27) L.S.G. 33; (1995) 145 N.L.J. 888; [1995] 139 S.J.L.B.
    146; (1995) 70 P. & C.R. D12 PC.. 27–08
Rubenstein v HSBC Bank Plc [2012] EWCA Civ 1184; [2013] 1 All E.R. (Comm) 915; [2012]
    2 C.L.C. 747; [2013] P.N.L.R. 9; (2012) 156(35) S.J.L.B. 31 .... 2–175, 2–176, 2–177, 9–49
Ruddy v Chief Constable of Strathclyde [2012] UKSC 57; 2013 S.C. (U.K.S.C.) 126; 2013
    S.L.T. 119; 2013 S.C.L.R. 110; [2013] H.R.L.R. 10; 2013 Rep. L.R. 67; 2012 G.
    W.D. 40–779 14–79

Rugby Football Union v Cotton Traders Ltd [2002] EWHC 467 (Ch); [2002] E.T.M.R. 76 . . . 25–81
Rugby Football Union v Viagogo Ltd; sub nom. Rugby Football Union v Consolidated
    Information Services (formerly Viagogo Ltd) [2011] EWCA Civ 1585; [2012] 2
    C.M.L.R. 3; [2012] F.S.R. 11 . . . . 17–34, 17–128
Rylands v Fletcher; sub nom. Fletcher v Rylands (1868) L.R. 3 H.L. 330 HL 20–52, 20–54,
                                                                                    20–155, 20–156, 20–162
S (A Child) (Identification: Restrictions on Publication), Re; sub nom. S (A Child)
    (Identification: Restriction on Publication), Re [2004] UKHL 47; [2005] 1 A.C. 593;
    [2004] 3 W.L.R. 1129; [2004] 4 All E.R. 683; [2005] E.M.L.R. 2; [2005] 1 F.L.R.
    591; [2004] 3 F.C.R. 407; [2005] H.R.L.R. 5; [2005] U.K.H.R.R. 129; 17 B.H.R.C.
    646; [2005] Crim. L.R. 310; (2004) 154 N.L.J. 1654; (2004) 148 S.J.L.B. 1285 . . . . .   14–93A
S-C (Mental Patient: Habeas Corpus), Re [1996] Q.B. 599; [1996] 2 W.L.R. 146; [1996]
    1 All E.R. 532; [1996] 1 F.L.R. 548; [1996] 2 F.C.R. 692; (1996) 29 B.M.L.R. 138;
    [1996] Fam. Law 210 CA (Civ Div).   15–102
Sadcas Pty Ltd v Business & Professional Finance Pty Ltd [2011] NSWCA 267   17–21
Safeway Stores Ltd v Twigger [2010] EWCA Civ 1472; [2011] 2 All E.R. 841; [2011] Bus.
    L.R. 1629; [2011] 1 Lloyd's Rep. 462; [2011] 1 C.L.C. 80; [2011] U.K.C.L.R.
    339. . . . . 3–31, 3–31A
Saltri III Ltd v MD Mezzanine SA [2012] EWHC 1270 (Comm) 27–14
Samaan v Kentucky Fried Chicken Pty Ltd [2012] NSWSC 381 11–35
Samsung Electronics (UK) Ltd v Apple Inc [2012] EWCA Civ 1339; [2013] E.C.D.R. 2;
    [2013] E.M.L.R. 10; [2013] F.S.R. 9 . . . . 25–68, 25–69
Samsung Electronics (UK) Ltd v Apple Inc [2012] EWCA Civ 729; [2012] Bus. L.R. 1889;
    [2013] F.S.R. 8 . . . . 25–59, 25–69
Samuel Smith Old Brewery (Tadcaster) v Lee (t/a Cropton Brewery) [2011] EWHC 1879
    (Ch); [2012] F.S.R. 7; [2012] Bus. L.R. D97 . . . . 23–06, 25–81
Sanders v Snell [1998] HCA 64; (1998) 196 C.L.R. 329 24–70
Santander UK Plc v Keeper of the Registers of Scotland [2013] CSOH 24; 2013 S.L.T.
    362; 2013 G.W.D. 7–164 8–103
Santander UK Plc v RA Legal Solicitors [2013] EWHC 1380 (QB); [2013] P.N.L.R.
    24. . . . . 10–23, 10–146
Sar Petroleum Inc v Peace Hills Trust Co [2010] NBCA 22; (2010) 318 D.L.R. (4th)
    70. . . . . 24–14, 24–15, 24–18, 24–55
SAS Institute Inc v World Programming Ltd (C–406/10) [2013] Bus. L.R. 941; [2012] 3
    C.M.L.R. 4; [2012] E.C.D.R. 22; [2012] R.P.C. 31 25–07
SAS Institute Inc v World Programming Ltd [2013] EWHC 69 (Ch); [2013] R.P.C. 17 25–07
Saunders v Chief Constable of Sussex [2012] EWCA Civ 1197. 13–27
Savage v South Essex Partnership NHS Foundation Trust [2008] UKHL 74; [2009] 1 A.C.
    681; [2009] 2 W.L.R. 115; [2009] 1 All E.R. 1053; [2009] P.T.S.R. 469; [2009]
    H.R.L.R. 12; [2009] U.K.H.R.R. 480; 27 B.H.R.C. 57; (2009) 12 C.C.L. Rep. 125;
    [2009] LS Law Medical 40; (2009) 105 B.M.L.R. 180; [2008] Inquest L.R. 126;
    [2009] M.H.L.R. 41; (2009) 153(1) S.J.L.B. 34. . . . . 8–36, 14–70, 14–72, 14–100
Savill v Roberts, 88 E.R. 1267; (1703) 12 Mod. 208 KB 16–64
Sayce v TNT (UK) Ltd [2011] EWCA Civ 1583; [2012] 1 W.L.R. 1261; [2012] R.T.R. 22;
    [2012] Lloyd's Rep. I.R. 183; [2012] P.I.Q.R. P8. 28–9
Sayers v Chelwood (Deceased); sub nom. Sayers v Hunters [2012] EWCA Civ 1715;
    [2013] 1 W.L.R. 1695; [2013] 2 All E.R. 232; [2013] P.I.Q.R. P8; (2013) 157(1)
    S.J.L.B. 31. 32–55
Sayers v Hunters. See Sayers v Chelwood (Deceased)
Schering Chemicals Ltd v Falkman Ltd [1982] Q.B. 1; [1981] 2 W.L.R. 848; [1981] 2 All
    E.R. 321; (1981) 125 S.J. 342 CA (Civ Div) 27–10, 27–32
Schutz (UK) Ltd v Delta Containers Ltd [2011] EWHC 1712 (Ch) 25–81
Scott v Kennedys Law LLP [2011] EWHC 3808 (Ch) 10–141, 10–144, 10–152
Scott v Pedler [2003] FCA 650 24–73
Scout Association v Barnes [2010] EWCA Civ 1476 . . . . 1–13, 1–17, 8–160, 8–162, 8–163
Scullion v Bank of Scotland Plc (t/a Colleys) [2011] EWCA Civ 693; [2011] 1 W.L.R.
    3212; [2011] B.L.R. 449; [2011] H.L.R. 43; [2011] P.N.L.R. 27; [2011] 3 E.G.L.R.
    69; [2011] 37 E.G. 110; [2011] 25 E.G. 105 (C.S.); (2011) 155(25) S.J.L.B. 35;
    [2011] N.P.C. 62 . . . . 10–156, 10–157, 10–177, 10–178

Seager v Copydex Ltd (No.1) [1967] 1 W.L.R. 923; [1967] 2 All E.R. 415; 2 K.I.R. 828;
    [1967] F.S.R. 211; [1967] R.P.C. 349; (1967) 111 S.J. 335 CA (Civ Div) 27–20
Seal v United Kingdom (50330/07) (2012) 54 E.H.R.R. 6; [2011] M.H.L.R. 1 ECtHR 15–116
Sealed Air Ltd v Sharp Interpack Ltd [2013] EWPCC 23 25–68
Sear v Kingfisher Builders (A firm) (No.3) [2013] EWHC 21 (TCC) 18–07, 18–47
Secretary of State for the Home Department v AP [2010] UKSC 26; [2010] 1 W.L.R. 1652;
    [2010] 4 All E.R. 259; [2010] H.R.L.R. 26; [2010] U.K.H.R.R. 1014; (2010) 160
    N.L.J. 941 27–47
Sedleigh-Denfield v O'Callagan (Trustees for St Joseph's Society for Foreign Missions)
    [1940] A.C. 880; [1940] 3 All E.R. 349 HL 14–49, 20–193
Seeff v Ho [2011] EWCA Civ 186 19–46
Selwood v Durham CC [2012] EWCA Civ 979; [2012] P.I.Q.R. P20; [2012] Med. L.R.
    531; [2012] M.H.L.R. 373 . . . . 8–56, 14–54, 14–72
Shanks v Unilever Plc; sub nom. Unilever Plc v Shanks [2010] EWCA Civ 1283; [2011]
    R.P.C. 12; (2011) 117 B.M.L.R. 176 25–92
Sharma v Hunters [2011] EWHC 2546 (Fam); [2012] 2 Costs L.R. 237; [2012] P.N.L.R. 6;
    [2012] W.T.L.R. 259 10–120
Sharp v Top Flight Scaffolding Ltd [2013] EWHC 479 (QB) 13–64
Shelfer v City of London Electric Lighting Co (No.1); Meux's Brewery Co v City of
    London Electric Lighting Co [1895] 1 Ch. 287 CA 20–152
Shenzhen Taiden v OHIM—Bosch Security Systems (Communications Equipment)
    (T–153/08) June 22, 2010 25–68
Shepherd Construction Ltd v Pinsent Masons LLP [2012] EWHC 43 (TCC); [2012] B.L.R.
    213; 141 Con. L.R. 232; [2012] P.N.L.R. 31 . . . . 5–90A
Shevill v Presse Alliance SA (C–68/93) [1995] 2 A.C. 18; [1995] 2 W.L.R. 499; [1995] All
    E.R. (E.C.) 289; [1995] E.C.R. I–415; [1995] I.L.Pr. 267; [1995] E.M.L.R. 543 22–04
Shields v Chief Constable of Merseyside [2010] EWCA Civ 1281; *Times* March 3, 2011 15–75
Siemens Building Technologies FE Ltd v Supershield Ltd; sub nom. Supershield Ltd v
    Siemens Building Technologies FE Ltd [2010] EWCA Civ 7; [2010] 2 All E.R.
    (Comm) 1185; [2010] 1 Lloyd's Rep. 349; [2010] 1 C.L.C. 241; [2010] B.L.R. 145;
    129 Con. L.R. 52; [2010] N.P.C. 5 11–19
Sienkiewicz v Greif (UK) Ltd; Knowsley MBC v Willmore; sub nom. Costello (Deceased),
    Re; Willmore v Knowsley MBC [2011] UKSC 10; [2011] 2 A.C. 229; [2011] 2
    W.L.R. 523; [2011] 2 All E.R. 857; [2011] I.C.R. 391; [2011] P.I.Q.R. P11; (2011)
    119 B.M.L.R. 54; (2011) 108(12) L.S.G. 21; (2011) 155(10) S.J.L.B. 30 . . . . 2–27, 2–42,
                        2–58—2–68, 2–59, 2–62A, 2–64, 2–66, 4–06, 13–21A, 28–19
Silih v Slovenia (71463/01) (2009) 49 E.H.R.R. 37; [2009] Inquest L.R. 117 ECtHR 14–75
Simmons v Castle [2012] EWCA Civ 1288; [2013] 1 W.L.R. 1239; [2013] 1 All E.R. 334;
    [2013] C.P. Rep. 3; [2012] 6 Costs L.R. 1150; [2013] E.M.L.R. 4; [2013] P.I.Q.R. P2;
    [2013] Med. L.R. 4; (2012) 162 N.L.J. 1324; (2012) 156(39) S.J.L.B. 31 28–56
Simon v Helmot; sub nom. Helmot v Simon [2012] UKPC 5; [2012] Med. L.R. 394; (2012)
    126 B.M.L.R. 73 28–33
Simpson v Norfolk and Norwich University Hospital NHS Trust [2011] EWCA Civ 1149;
    [2012] Q.B. 640; [2012] 2 W.L.R. 873; [2012] 1 All E.R. 1423; [2012] 1 Costs L.O.
    9; [2012] P.I.Q.R. P2; (2012) 124 B.M.L.R. 1; (2011) 108(41) L.S.G. 24; (2011) 161
    N.L.J. 1451 5–64
Simpson v Savage, 140 E.R. 143; (1856) 1 C.B. N.S. 347 CCP 20–66
Singla v Stockler [2012] EWHC 1176 (Ch); [2012] B.P.I.R. 1061; (2012) 162 N.L.J. 713 . . . 10–129
SKA v CRH [2012] EWHC 766 (QB) 27–39, 27–47
Skov AEG v Bilka Lavprisvarehus A/S (C–402/03) [2006] E.C.R. I–199; [2006] 2
    C.M.L.R. 16 11–46
Smart v Forensic Science Service Ltd [2013] EWCA Civ 783 . . . . 10–41, 14–40, 16–72
Smeaton v Equifax Plc; sub nom. Equifax Plc v Smeaton [2013] EWCA Civ 108; [2013] 2
    All E.R. 959; [2013] B.P.I.R. 231 . . . . 5–46A, 8–99, 8–110
Smith v Chief Constable of Nottinghamshire [2012] EWCA Civ 161; [2012] R.T.R. 23 8–144
Smith v Chief Constable of Sussex. *See* Van Colle v Chief Constable of Hertfordshire
Smith v Dha [2013] EWHC 838 (QB) 22–01
Smith v Fordyce [2013] EWCA Civ 320 . . . . 8–173, 8–183
Smith v Hammond [2010] EWCA Civ 725; [2010] R.T.R. 30 8–178

Smith v Inco Ltd [2011] ONCA 628; (2011) 107 O.R. (3d) 321 CA (Ont). 20–08, 20–54
Smith v Jenkins [1970] HCA 2; (1970) 119 CLR 39. 3–05
Smith v Littlewoods Organisation Ltd. *See* Maloco v Littlewoods Organisation Ltd
Smith v Ministry of Defence; Allbutt v Ministry of Defence; Ellis v Ministry of Defence;
   Redpath v Ministry of Defence; sub nom. Ministry of Defence v Ellis; Ministry of
   Defence v Allbutt [2013] UKSC 41; [2013] 3 W.L.R. 69; [2013] H.R.L.R. 27. . . . 5–13, 8–20,
                                              9–10, 13–04, 14–13, 14–37, 14–38, 14–40, 14–69A, 14–70, 14–73
Smith v Youth Justice Board for England and Wales [2010] EWCA Civ 99. 2–120
Smithkline Beecham Ltd v GSKline Ltd [2011] EWHC 169 (Ch). 25–82, 26–04
Sobczak v DPP [2012] EWHC 1319 (Admin); (2012) 176 J.P. 575; [2013] Crim. L.R. 515;
   [2012] A.C.D. 73. 15–85
Societe des Produits Nestle SA v Cadbury UK Ltd [2012] EWHC 2637 (Ch); [2013]
   E.C.C. 5; [2013] E.T.M.R. 2; [2013] R.P.C. 14 25–74
South Australia Asset Management Corp v York Montague Ltd; Nykredit Mortgage Bank
   Plc v Edward Erdman Group Ltd; United Bank of Kuwait Plc v Prudential Property
   Services Ltd [1997] A.C. 191; [1996] 3 W.L.R. 87; [1996] 3 All E.R. 365; [1996] 5
   Bank. L.R. 211; [1996] C.L.C. 1179; 80 B.L.R. 1; 50 Con. L.R. 153; [1996] P.N.L.R.
   455; [1996] 2 E.G.L.R. 93; [1996] 27 E.G. 125; [1996] E.G. 107 (C.S.); (1996)
   93(32) L.S.G. 33; (1996) 146 N.L.J. 956; (1996) 140 S.J.L.B. 156; [1996] N.P.C. 100
   HL. 10–147, 10–177, 10–225
Southern Insulation (Medway) Ltd v How Engineering Services Ltd [2010] EWCA Civ
   999. 8–128
Spargo v North Essex DHA [1997] P.I.Q.R. P235; [1997] 8 Med. L.R. 125; (1997) 37
   B.M.L.R. 99; (1997) 94(15) L.S.G. 26; (1997) 141 S.J.L.B. 90 CA (Civ Div) 25–79
Spargo v North Essex District HA. 32–45
Specsavers International Healthcare Ltd v Asda Stores Ltd [2012] EWCA Civ 24; [2012]
   E.T.M.R. 17; [2012] F.S.R. 19 . . . . 25–15, 25–81
Spelman v Express Newspapers [2012] EWHC 355 (QB) 27–36, 27–44, 27–47, 27–48
Spencer v S Franses Ltd [2011] EWHC 1269 (QB) 17–26
Spencer v Wincanton Holdings Ltd (Wincanton Logistics Ltd) [2009] EWCA Civ 1404;
   [2010] P.I.Q.R. P8; (2010) 154(1) S.J.L.B. 29 2–120
Sphere Time v Office for Harmonisation in the Internal Market (Trade Marks and Designs)
   (OHIM) (T–68/10) [2011] E.C.D.R. 20 25–68
Spring v Guardian Assurance. 8–110
St John Poulton's Trustee in Bankruptcy v Ministry of Justice; sub nom. Trustee in
   Bankruptcy of St John Poulton v Ministry of Justice [2010] EWCA Civ 392; [2011]
   Ch. 1; [2010] 3 W.L.R. 1237; [2010] 4 All E.R. 600; [2010] B.P.I.R. 775; (2010)
   107(18) L.S.G. 15. . . . . 9–14, 9–18, 9–31, 9–42, 9–45, 14–56
St John Poulton's Trustee in Bankruptcy v Ministry of Justice; sub nom. Trustee in
   Bankruptcy of St John Poulton v Ministry of Justice [2010] EWCA Civ 392; [2011]
   Ch. 1; [2010] 3 W.L.R. 1237; [2010] 4 All E.R. 600; [2010] B.P.I.R. 775; (2010)
   107(18) L.S.G. 15. 8–99
Stadium Capital Holdings (No.2) Ltd v St Marylebone Property Co Plc [2011] EWHC
   2856 (Ch); [2012] 1 P. & C.R. 7; [2012] 1 E.G.L.R. 103; [2012] 4 E.G. 108 19–63
Stadium Capital Holdings v St Marylebone Properties Co Plc [2010] EWCA Civ 952. 19–46,
                                                                                                                     19–64, 28–152
Standard Chartered Bank v Pakistan National Shipping Corp (No.2); Standard Chartered
   Bank v Mehra [2002] UKHL 43; [2003] 1 A.C. 959; [2002] 3 W.L.R. 1547; [2003] 1
   All E.R. 173; [2002] 2 All E.R. (Comm) 931; [2003] 1 Lloyd's Rep. 227; [2002]
   B.C.C. 846; [2003] 1 B.C.L.C. 244; [2002] C.L.C. 1330; (2003) 100(1) L.S.G. 26;
   (2002) 146 S.J.L.B. 258 3–54
Stannard (t/a Wyvern Tyres) v Gore; sub nom. Gore v Stannard (t/a Wyvern Tyres) [2012]
   EWCA Civ 1248; [2013] 3 W.L.R. 623; [2013] 1 All E.R. 694; [2013] Env. L.R. 10;
   [2012] 3 E.G.L.R. 129; [2012] 42 E.G. 133 (C.S.). 20–155, 20–156, 20–159, 20–161,
                                                                                                                20–162, 20–163, 20–165
Stanton v Callaghan [2000] Q.B. 75; [1999] 2 W.L.R. 745; [1998] 4 All E.R. 961; [1999]
   C.P.L.R. 31; [1999] B.L.R. 172; (1999) 1 T.C.L.R. 50; 62 Con. L.R. 1; [1999]
   P.N.L.R. 116; [1998] 3 E.G.L.R. 165; (1999) 15 Const. L.J. 50; [1998] E.G. 115
   (C.S.); (1998) 95(28) L.S.G. 32; (1998) 95(33) L.S.G. 33; (1998) 148 N.L.J. 1355;
   (1998) 142 S.J.L.B. 220; [1998] N.P.C. 113 CA (Civ Div) 10–41

Starbucks (HK) Ltd v British Sky Broadcasting Group Plc [2012] EWHC 3074 (Ch);
    [2013] F.S.R. 29 . . . . 25–76, 26–05
Steedman v BBC [2001] EWCA Civ 1534; [2002] E.M.L.R. 17; (2001) 98(47) L.S.G. 17;
    (2001) 145 S.J.L.B. 260 22–197
Steven (Ex' of Thomson) v Hewats. *See* Milligan's Executors v Hewats
Steven v Hewats [2013] CSOH 61; 2013 S.L.T. 763; [2013] P.N.L.R. 22; 2013 Rep. L.R.
    90; 2013 G.W.D. 16–346 10–114
Stichting BDO v BDO Unibank Inc [2013] EWHC 418 (Ch); [2013] E.T.M.R. 31 25–82
Stiedl v Enyo Law LLP [2011] EWHC 2649 (Comm); [2012] P.N.L.R. 4 10–129
Stoddart v Perucca [2011] EWCA Civ 290 8–184
Stokes v Guest Keen & Nettlefold (Bolt & Nuts) Ltd [1968] 1 W.L.R. 1776; 5 K.I.R. 401;
    (1968) 112 S.J. 821 Assizes 13–21
Stovin v Wise [1996] A.C. 923; [1996] 3 W.L.R. 388; [1996] 3 All E.R. 801; [1996] R.T.R.
    354; (1996) 93(35) L.S.G. 33; (1996) 146 N.L.J. 1185; (1996) 140 S.J.L.B. 201
    HL 14–08, 14–57
Sturnham v Secretary of State for Justice. *See* R. (on the application of Sturnham) v Parole
    Board
Summers v Fairclough Homes Ltd; sub nom. Fairclough Homes Ltd v Summers [2012]
    UKSC 26; [2012] 1 W.L.R. 2004; [2012] 4 All E.R. 317; [2012] 4 Costs L.R. 760;
    [2013] Lloyd's Rep. I.R. 159; (2012) 162 N.L.J. 910; (2012) 156(26) S.J.L.B. 31 3–33
Sun Microsystems Inc v M-Tech Data Ltd; sub nom. Oracle America Inc v M-Tech Data
    Ltd [2010] EWCA Civ 997; [2011] 1 C.M.L.R. 43; [2011] E.C.C. 4; [2011] Eu. L.R.
    117; [2010] E.T.M.R. 64; [2010] Info. T.L.R. 315; [2011] F.S.R. 2 25–82
Sun Microsystems Inc v M-Tech Data Ltd; sub nom. Oracle America Inc v M-Tech Data
    Ltd [2012] UKSC 27; [2012] 1 W.L.R. 2026; [2012] 4 All E.R. 338; [2012] Bus. L.R.
    1631; [2012] 3 C.M.L.R. 28; [2012] E.C.C. 27; [2012] Eu. L.R. 727; [2012] E.T.M.R.
    43; [2013] F.S.R. 14 25–82
Supershield Ltd v Siemens Building Technologies FE Ltd. *See* Siemens Building
    Technologies FE Ltd v Supershield Ltd
Surtees v Kingston upon Thames RBC; Surtees v Hughes [1991] 2 F.L.R. 559; [1992]
    P.I.Q.R. P101; [1991] Fam. Law 426 CA (Civ Div) 8–51, 8–192
Sutherland v McConechy's Tyre Service Ltd [2012] CSOH 28; 2012 Rep. L.R. 46; 2012
    G.W.D. 10–195 13–63
Sutton v Syston Rugby Football Club Ltd [2011] EWCA Civ 1182 12–29
Swain Mason v Mills & Reeve [2012] EWCA Civ 498; [2012] S.T.C. 1760; [2012] 4 Costs
    L.O. 511; [2012] W.T.L.R. 1827; [2012] S.T.I. 1511 . . . . 10–128, 10–134, 10–138
Swan Housing Association Ltd v Gill [2012] EWHC 3129 (QB); [2013] 1 W.L.R. 1253;
    [2013] 1 E.G.L.R. 69; [2013] 5 E.G. 98; [2012] 46 E.G. 121 (C.S.); [2013] 1 P. &
    C.R. DG8 19–13
Swift v Secretary of State for Justice [2013] EWCA Civ 193; [2013] 2 F.C.R. 1; [2013]
    H.R.L.R. 21; [2013] P.I.Q.R. P14; (2013) 163(7555) N.L.J. 17 28–87
Swilas v Clyde Pumps Ltd, 2012 S.L.T. (Sh Ct) 146; 2011 G.W.D. 34–71 Sh Ct 13–48
Swinney v Chief Constable of Northumbria (No.1) [1997] Q.B. 464; [1996] 3 W.L.R.
    968; [1996] 3 All E.R. 449; [1996] P.N.L.R. 473; (1996) 146 N.L.J. 878 CA
    (Civ Div) 8–55, 14–30
Syed v DPP [2010] EWHC 81 (Admin); [2010] 1 Cr. App. R. 34; (2010) 174 J.P. 97; (2010)
    107(4) L.S.G. 14 . . . . 15–84, 15–122
Symbian Ltd v Comptroller General of Patents, Designs and Trademarks [2008] EWCA
    Civ 1066; [2009] Bus. L.R. 607; [2009] R.P.C. 1; (2008) 31(10) I.P.D. 31064; (2008)
    105(40) L.S.G. 17; (2008) 152(39) S.J.L.B. 30 25–94
Synthon BV v Merz Pharma GmbH & Co KGaA (C–195/09) [2012] R.P.C. 3 25–91
T (Adult: Refusal of Treatment), Re; sub nom. T (Consent to Medical Treatment) (Adult
    Patient), Re [1993] Fam. 95; [1992] 3 W.L.R. 782; [1992] 4 All E.R. 649; [1992] 2
    F.L.R. 458; [1992] 2 F.C.R. 861; [1992] 3 Med. L.R. 306; [1993] Fam. Law 27;
    (1992) 142 N.L.J. 1125 10–61
Taaffe v East of England Ambulance Service NHS Trust [2012] EWHC 1335 (QB); (2012)
    128 B.M.L.R. 71 . . . . 8–167, 10–68, 10–89
Tafa v Matsim Properties Ltd [2011] EWHC 1302 (QB) 12–04, 13–35
Tamiz v Google Inc [2013] EWCA Civ 68; [2013] 1 W.L.R. 2151; [2013] E.M.L.R. 14 . . . . 22–08, 22–67

Taylor v A Novo (UK) Ltd [2013] EWCA Civ 194; [2013] P.I.Q.R. P15; [2013] Med. L.R. 100. 8–72
Taylor v Diamond [2012] EWHC 2900 (Ch). 17–19
Taylor v Wincanton Group Ltd [2009] EWCA Civ 1581 13–54
Tchenguiz v Imerman; Imerman v Imerman; sub nom. Imerman v Tchenguiz [2010] EWCA Civ 908; [2011] Fam. 116; [2011] 2 W.L.R. 592; [2011] 1 All E.R. 555; [2010] 2 F.L.R. 814; [2010] 3 F.C.R. 371; [2010] Fam. Law 1177; (2010) 154(30) S.J.L.B. 32. . . . . 17–11, 27–16, 27–19, 27–39
Terrence Calix v Attorney General of Trinidad and Tobago. See Calix v Attorney General of Trinidad and Tobago
Tesla Motors Ltd v BBC [2013] EWCA Civ 152; (2013) 163 N.L.J. 290 23–16
Test Claimants in the FII Group Litigation v Revenue and Customs Commissioners; sub nom. Test Claimants in the Franked Investment Group Litigation v Inland Revenue Commissioners; Test Claimants in the Franked Investment Income Group Litigation v Revenue and Customs Commissioners [2012] UKSC 19; [2012] 2 A.C. 337; [2012] 2 W.L.R. 1149; [2012] 3 All E.R. 909; [2012] Bus. L.R. 1033; [2012] S.T.C. 1362; [2012] B.T.C. 312; [2012] S.T.I. 1707 9–48
Test Claimants in the FII Group Litigation v Revenue and Customs Commissioners; sub nom. Test Claimants in the Franked Investment Group Litigation v Inland Revenue Commissioners; Test Claimants in the Franked Investment Income Group Litigation v Revenue and Customs Commissioners [2012] UKSC 19; [2012] 2 A.C. 337; [2012] 2 W.L.R. 1149; [2012] 3 All E.R. 909; [2012] Bus. L.R. 1033; [2012] S.T.C. 1362; [2012] B.T.C. 312; [2012] S.T.I. 1707 32–23
Thames Valley Housing Association Ltd v Elegant Homes (Guernsey) Ltd [2011] EWHC 1288 (Ch); [2011] 22 E.G. 102 (C.S.); [2011] N.P.C. 54 4–12
Thomas v Curley [2013] EWCA Civ 117; [2013] Med. L.R. 141; (2013) 131 B.M.L.R. 111. 10–94
Thomas v Merthyr Tydfil Car Auction Ltd; Merthyr Tydfil Car Auction Ltd v Thomas [2013] EWCA Civ 815 20–13
Thomas v Warwickshire CC [2011] EWHC 772 (QB) 8–187
Thompson v Commissioner of Police of the Metropolis; Hsu v Commissioner of Police of the Metropolis [1998] Q.B. 498; [1997] 3 W.L.R. 403; [1997] 2 All E.R. 762; (1998) 10 Admin. L.R. 363; (1997) 147 N.L.J. 341 CA (Civ Div) 16–05
Thompson v Smiths Shiprepairers (North Shields) Ltd; Waggott v Swan Hunter Shipbuilders Ltd; Blacklock v Swan Hunter Shipbuilders Ltd; Nicholson v Smiths Shiprepairers (North Shields) Ltd; Gray v Smiths Shiprepairers (North Shields) Ltd; Mitchell v Vickers Armstrong Ltd [1984] Q.B. 405; [1984] 2 W.L.R. 522; [1984] 1 All E.R. 881; [1984] I.C.R. 236; [1984] I.R.L.R. 93; (1984) 81 L.S.G. 741; (1984) 128 S.J. 225 QBD 8–165, 13–21
Thomson v Deakin. See DC Thomson & Co Ltd v Deakin
Thomson v Scottish Ministers [2011] CSOH 90; 2011 S.L.T. 683; 2012 S.C.L.R. 19; 2011 G.W.D. 18–439 8–56
Thornton v Telegraph Media Group Ltd [2010] EWHC 1414 (QB); [2011] 1 W.L.R. 1985; [2010] E.M.L.R. 25. . . . . 5–88, 22–23
Thornton v Telegraph Media Group Ltd [2011] EWHC 159 (QB); [2011] E.M.L.R. 25. . . . 23–03, 23–04
Thornton v Telegraph Media Group Ltd [2011] EWHC 1884 (QB); [2012] E.M.L.R. 8 22–190
Thornton v Telegraph Media Group Ltd; sub nom. Telegraph Media Group Ltd v Thornton [2011] EWCA Civ 748; [2011] E.M.L.R. 29 22–03
Thorpe v Fellowes Solicitors LLP. See Hill v Fellowes Solicitors LLP
Threlfall v Hull City Council; sub nom. Threlfall v Kingston upon Hull City Council [2010] EWCA Civ 1147; [2011] I.C.R. 209; [2011] P.I.Q.R. P3; (2010) 107(42) L.S.G. 18. . . . . 13–36, 13–40, 13–54
Tilda Riceland Private Ltd v Office for Harmonisation in the Internal Market (Trade Marks and Designs) (OHIM) (T–304/09) [2012] E.T.M.R. 15 25–76
Tinseltime Ltd v Roberts [2011] EWHC 1199 (TCC); [2011] B.L.R. 515 . . . . 20–24, 20–63, 20–73, 20–163
Todd v Adams (t/a Trelawney Fishing Co) (The Maragetha Maria); Maragetha Maria, The; Margaretha Maria, The; sub nom. Todd v Adam [2002] EWCA Civ 509; [2002] 2 All E.R. (Comm) 97; [2002] 2 Lloyd's Rep. 293; [2002] C.L.C. 1050; (2002) 99(21) L.S.G. 32; (2002) 146 S.J.L.B. 118 9–15

Tolley v Carr [2010] EWHC 2191 (QB); [2011] R.T.R. 7. . . . . 3–78, 8–34
Tomlinson v Congleton BC [2003] UKHL 47; [2004] 1 A.C. 46; [2003] 3 W.L.R. 705; [2003]
    3 All E.R. 1122; [2004] P.I.Q.R. P8; [2003] 32 E.G. 68 (C.S.); (2003) 100(34) L.S.G.
    33; (2003) 153 N.L.J. 1238; (2003) 147 S.J.L.B. 937; [2003] N.P.C. 102. . . . . 8–160, 21–15
Toropdar v D [2009] EWHC 567 (QB); [2010] Lloyd's Rep. I.R. 358. 32–21
Town of Port Hedland v Hodder (No.2) [2012] WASCA 212. 3–70
Tree Savers International v Savoy (1991) 87 D.L.R. (4th) 202 CA (Alta) 24–94
Tresplain Investments Ltd v Office for Harmonisation in the Internal Market (Trade Marks
    and Designs) (OHIM) (C–76/11 P) [2012] E.T.M.R. 22 25–76
Trimingham v Associated Newspapers Ltd [2012] EWHC 1296 (QB); [2012] 4 All E.R.
    717; (2012) 109(25) L.S.G. 21 . . . . 15–20, 27–39, 27–41, 27–46
Tse Wai Chun Paul v Cheng; sub nom. Cheng v Tse Wai Chun Paul [2001] E.M.L.R. 31;
    10 B.H.R.C. 525; [2000] 3 H.K.L.R.D. 418 CFA (HK) 22–165
TTM v Hackney LBC; sub nom. R. (on the application of M) v Hackney LBC [2011]
    EWCA Civ 4; [2011] 1 W.L.R. 2873; [2011] 3 All E.R. 529; [2011] P.T.S.R. 1419;
    [2011] H.R.L.R. 14; [2011] U.K.H.R.R. 346; (2011) 14 C.C.L. Rep. 154; [2011]
    Med. L.R. 38; [2011] M.H.L.R. 171; [2011] A.C.D. 54. . . . . 15–102, 15–116
Turnbull v Warrener [2012] EWCA Civ 412; [2012] P.I.Q.R. P16; (2012) 156(14) S.J.L.B.
    31. . . . . 21–04, 21–05, 21–08
TUV v Person or Persons Unknown [2010] EWHC 853 (QB); [2010] E.M.L.R. 19; (2010)
    160 N.L.J. 619. 27–47
Tyburn Productions Ltd v Conan Doyle [1991] Ch. 75; [1990] 3 W.L.R. 167; [1990] 1 All
    E.R. 909; [1990] R.P.C. 185 Ch D 7–19
UCB Home Loans Corp Ltd v Soni [2013] EWCA Civ 62. 5–90
Unilever Plc v Gillette (UK) Ltd [1989] R.P.C. 583 CA (Civ Div). 27–08
Unilever Plc v Griffin [2010] EWHC 899 (Ch); [2010] F.S.R. 33 . . . . 25–27, 25–81
United Airlines Inc v United Airways Ltd [2011] EWHC 2411 (Ch) 25–83
United Closures and Plastics Ltd v Unite the Union [2011] CSOH 114; 2011 S.L.T. 1105;
    [2012] I.R.L.R. 29; 2011 G.W.D. 24–531. . . . . 24–147, 24–152, 24–163
United Marine Aggregates Ltd v GM Welding & Engineering Ltd [2013] EWCA Civ 516. 4–33
Uren v Corporate Leisure (UK) Ltd [2011] EWCA Civ 66; (2011) 108(7) L.S.G. 16; [2011]
    I.C.R. D11. . . . . 8–145, 8–162, 8–163, 13–06
Uren v Corporate Leisure (UK) Ltd [2013] EWHC 353 (QB) 8–145, 8–163, 13–06
Utopia Tableware Ltd v BBP Marketing Ltd [2013] EWPCC 15 25–69
Vaickuviene v J Sainsbury Plc [2012] CSOH 69; 2012 S.L.T. 849; 2012 G.W.D. 16–337. 13–08
Vaile v Havering LBC [2011] EWCA Civ 246; [2011] E.L.R. 274; (2011) 108(12)
    L.S.G. 20. . . . . 2–07, 13–14
Vakante v Addey and Stanhope School Governing Body; sub nom. Addey and Stanhope
    School v Vakante; V v Addet & Stanhope School [2004] EWCA Civ 1065; [2004] 4
    All E.R. 1056; [2005] 1 C.M.L.R. 3; [2005] I.C.R. 231; (2004) 101(36) L.S.G. 33 3–40
Valentine v Transport for London [2010] EWCA Civ 1358; [2011] B.L.R. 89; [2011]
    R.T.R. 24; [2011] P.I.Q.R. P7 . . . . 8–46, 8–187, 9–11, 20–193
Van Colle v Chief Constable of Hertfordshire; Smith v Chief Constable of Sussex; sub nom.
    Chief Constable of Hertfordshire v Van Colle [2008] UKHL 50; [2009] 1 A.C. 225;
    [2008] 3 W.L.R. 593; [2008] 3 All E.R. 977; [2009] 1 Cr. App. R. 12; [2008] H.R.L.R.
    44; [2008] U.K.H.R.R. 967; [2009] P.I.Q.R. P2; [2009] LS Law Medical 1; [2008]
    Inquest L.R. 176; [2008] Po. L.R. 151; (2008) 152(32) S.J.L.B. 31 . . . . . 14–28, 14–72, 14–79
Van Colle v United Kingdom (7678/09) (2013) 56 E.H.R.R. 23 ECtHR 14–72
Van der Pijl v Kingston Crown Court. See R. (on the application of Van der Pijl) v Kingston
    Crown Court
Varawa v Howard Smith Co Ltd (1911) 13 C.L.R. 35. . . . . 16–64A
Various Claimants v Catholic Child Welfare Society. See Various Claimants v Institute of
    the Brothers of the Christian Schools
Various Claimants v Institute of the Brothers of the Christian Schools; sub nom. Catholic
    Child Welfare Society v Various Claimants; Various Claimants v Catholic Child
    Welfare Society [2012] UKSC 56; [2013] 2 A.C. 1; [2012] 3 W.L.R. 1319; [2013] 1
    All E.R. 670; [2013] I.R.L.R. 219; [2013] E.L.R. 1; [2013] P.I.Q.R. P6; (2012) 162
    N.L.J. 1505; (2012) 156(45) S.J.L.B. 31 . . . . 5–87, 6–01,
                                                                                    6–09, 6–26

Vento v Chief Constable of West Yorkshire; sub nom. Chief Constable of West Yorkshire v
    Vento (No.2) [2002] EWCA Civ 1871; [2003] I.C.R. 318; [2003] I.R.L.R. 102;
    [2003] Po. L.R. 171; (2003) 100(10) L.S.G. 28; (2003) 147 S.J.L.B. 181 22–224,
                                                                                            27–46
Veolia ES Nottinghamshire Ltd v Nottinghamshire CC; sub nom. R. (on the application of
    Veolia ES Nottinghamshire Ltd) v Nottinghamshire CC [2010] EWCA Civ 1214;
    [2012] P.T.S.R. 185; [2011] Eu. L.R. 172; [2011] Env. L.R. 12; [2010] U.K.H.R.R.
    1317; [2011] B.L.G.R. 95; (2010) 107(44) L.S.G. 18 27–04
Vestergaard Frandsen S/A (now called MVF3 APS) v Bestnet Europe Ltd [2013] UKSC
    31; [2013] 1 W.L.R. 1556; [2013] I.C.R. 981; [2013] I.R.L.R. 654; [2013] E.M.L.R.
    24; (2013) 157(21) S.J.L.B. 31 . . . . 27–04, 27–05, 27–14, 27–15, 27–16,
                                                                              27–20, 27–32, 27–33
Viking Gas A/S v Kosan Gas A/S (formerly BP Gas A/S) (C–46/10) [2011] E.T.M.R.
    58. . . . . 25–81, 25–82
VL (A Child) v Oxfordshire CC [2010] EWHC 2091 (QB); [2010] 3 F.C.R. 63; [2010]
    P.I.Q.R. P20; (2010) 154(32) S.J.L.B. 29 . . . . 8–51, 8–55
Volkl GmbH & Co KG v Office for Harmonisation in the Internal Market (Trade Marks
    and Designs) (OHIM) (T–504/09) [2012] E.T.M.R. 21 25–79
Von Hannover v Germany (40660/08 and 60641/08) [2012] E.M.L.R. 16; (2012) 55
    E.H.R.R. 15; 32 B.H.R.C. 527 ECtHR. 27–38, 27–41
Von Hannover v Germany (59320/00) [2004] E.M.L.R. 21; (2005) 40 E.H.R.R. 1; 16
    B.H.R.C. 545. 27–44
VTB Capital Plc v Nutritek International Corp [2013] UKSC 5; [2013] 2 W.L.R. 398;
    [2013] 1 All E.R. 1296; [2013] 1 All E.R. (Comm) 1009; [2013] 1 Lloyd's Rep. 466;
    [2013] 1 B.C.L.C. 179; [2013] 1 C.L.C. 153 7–11
W v Essex CC [2001] 2 A.C. 592; [2000] 2 W.L.R. 601; [2000] 2 All E.R. 237; [2000] 1
    F.L.R. 657; [2000] 1 F.C.R. 568; [2000] B.L.G.R. 281; (2000) 53 B.M.L.R. 1; [2000]
    Fam. Law 476; (2000) 164 J.P.N. 464; (2000) 97(13) L.S.G. 44; (2000) 144 S.J.L.B.
    147 HL 8–43, 14–89
W v Home Office [1997] Imm. A.R. 302 CA (Civ Div) 14–48
W v M. See M (Adult Patient) (Minimally Conscious State: Withdrawal of Treatment), Re
W v Veolia Environmental Services (UK) Plc [2011] EWHC 2020 (QB); [2012] 1 All E.R.
    (Comm) 667; [2012] Lloyd's Rep. I.R. 419; [2011] C.T.L.C. 193. 28–10
Wagamama Ltd v City Centre Restaurants Plc [1997] Eu. L.R. 313; [1996] E.T.M.R. 23;
    [1995] F.S.R. 713 Ch D. 25–74
Wall v Mutuelle De Poitiers Assurances [2013] EWHC 53 (QB); [2013] 2 All E.R. 709;
    [2013] R.T.R. 18; [2013] I.L.Pr. 20; [2013] P.I.Q.R. P9. 7–15
Wallace v Glasgow City Council [2011] CSIH 57; 2011 Rep. L.R. 96; 2011 G.W.D.
    28–628. 13–51
Wallace v Kam [2013] HCA 19. . . . . 2–14, 2–17, 10–103
Wallbank v Wallbank Fox Designs Ltd. See Weddall v Barchester Healthcare Ltd
Walsh v Shanahan [2013] EWCA Civ 411; [2013] 2 P. & C.R. DG7 . . . . 27–04, 27–12
Waterson v Lloyd [2013] EWCA Civ 136; [2013] E.M.L.R. 17[2013] EWCA Civ 136;
    [2013] E.M.L.R. 17. 22–166
Watson Laidlaw & Co Ltd v Pott Cassels & Williamson (A Firm), 1914 S.C. (H.L.) 18;
    (1914) 1 S.L.T.130; (1914) 31 R.P.C. 104 HL 27–33
Watson v McEwan; Watson v Jones; sub nom. McEwan v Watson [1905] A.C. 480; (1905)
    7 F. (H.L.) 109; (1905) 13 S.L.T. 340 HL. 16–72
Watts v Bell & Scott WS [2007] CSOH 108; 2007 S.L.T. 665; [2007] P.N.L.R. 30; 2007
    G.W.D. 21–364 10–147
Webb Resolutions Ltd v E.Surv Ltd [2012] EWHC 3653 (TCC); [2013] P.N.L.R. 15;
    [2013] 1 E.G.L.R. 133 . . . . 10–163, 10–165,
                                                                                     10–166, 10–181
Webb v EMO Air Cargo (UK) Ltd (Reference to ECJ) [1993] 1 W.L.R. 49; [1992] 4 All
    E.R. 929; [1993] 1 C.M.L.R. 259; [1993] I.C.R. 175; [1993] I.R.L.R. 27; (1992) 142
    N.L.J. 1720; (1993) 137 S.J.L.B. 48. 25–74
Webster v Ridgeway Foundation School [2010] EWHC 157 (QB); [2010] E.L.R. 694. 8–198
Weddall v Barchester Healthcare Ltd; Wallbank v Wallbank Fox Designs Ltd [2012]
    EWCA Civ 25; [2012] I.R.L.R. 307. . . . . 6–29, 13–08

Wella Corp v Alberto-Culver Co [2011] EWHC 3558 (Ch); [2012] E.T.M.R. 24 25–76
White v Coventry City Council Unreported June 7, 2012 County Ct (Walsall) 13–54
White v Southampton University Hospitals NHS Trust [2011] EWHC 825 (QB); [2011]
    Med. L.R. 296; (2011) 120 B.M.L.R. 81 22–89
White v Withers LLP [2009] EWCA Civ 1122; [2010] 1 F.L.R. 859; [2009] 3 F.C.R. 435;
    [2010] Fam. Law 26 17–11
Whitehead v Trustees of the Chatsworth Settlement [2012] EWCA Civ 263; [2013] 1
    W.L.R. 251; [2012] I.C.R. 1154 . . . . 13–50A
Whittaker v Child Support Registrar [2010] FCA 43; (2010) 264 A.L.R. 473 24–55
Wicks v State Rail Authority of New South Wales [2010] HCA 22; (2010) 241 C.L.R. 60 8–74
Wilkinson v York City Council [2011] EWCA Civ 207; [2011] P.T.S.R. D39 . . . . 8–186, 9–11,
                                                                                                                20–192
Williams v Lishman Sidwell Campbell & Price Ltd [2010] EWCA Civ 418; [2010]
    P.N.L.R. 25; [2010] Pens. L.R. 227 32–24
Williams v University of Birmingham; sub nom. Williams (Deceased), Re [2011] EWCA
    Civ 1242; [2012] E.L.R. 47; [2012] P.I.Q.R. P4[2011] EWCA Civ 1242; [2012]
    E.L.R. 47; [2012] P.I.Q.R. P4 . . . . 2–50, 13–21A
Willis v Derwentside DC [2013] EWHC 738 (Ch); [2013] Env. L.R. 31 20–52
Willock v Corus UK Ltd [2013] EWCA Civ 519; [2013] P.I.Q.R. P21 . . . . 13–50B
Wilson v Exel UK Ltd (t/a Exel) [2010] CSIH 35; 2010 S.L.T. 671; 2010 S.C.L.R. 486;
    2010 Rep. L.R. 68; 2010 G.W.D. 18–365; 13–08
Wilson v Haden (t/a Clyne Farm Centre) [2013] EWHC 229 (QB) 12–29
Wilson v North Lanarkshire Council [2011] CSOH 178; 2011 G.W.D. 38–789. 13–59
Wink v Croatia Osiguranje DD [2013] EWHC 1118 (QB) 7–03, 7–04
Winn-Pope v ES Access Platforms Ltd; sub nom. Winn-Pope v CKD Galbraith LLP [2012]
    CSOH 87; 2012 S.L.T. 929; 2013 S.C.L.R. 1; 2012 Rep. L.R. 126; 2012 G.W.D.
    19–392. 13–35
Wintersteiger AG v Products 4U Sondermaschinenbau GmbH (C–523/10) [2013] Bus.
    L.R. 150; [2013] C.E.C. 15; [2012] E.T.M.R. 31; [2012] I.L.Pr. 23 7–03
Wood v Balfour [2011] NSWCA 382 18–06
Wood v Ministry of Defence [2011] EWCA Civ 792 5–11
Woodland v Swimming Teachers' Association; sub nom. Woodland v Essex CC [2012]
    EWCA Civ 239; [2012] B.L.G.R. 879; [2012] E.L.R. 327; [2012] P.I.Q.R. P12;
    [2012] Med. L.R. 419 . . . . 6–60, 8–197, 12–58
Woolley v Ultimate Products Ltd [2012] EWCA Civ 1038. . . . . 25–15, 26–05, 26–18
Wright (A Child) v Cambridge Medical Group (A Partnership) [2011] EWCA Civ 669;
    [2013] Q.B. 312; [2012] 3 W.L.R. 1124; [2011] Med. L.R. 496 . . . . 2–2, 10–98,
                                                                                                                12–116
WS Foster & Son Ltd v Brooks Brothers UK Ltd [2013] EWPCC 18 26–05
WXY v Gewanter [2012] EWHC 1601 (QB) 27–39, 27–46
WXY v Gewanter [2013] EWHC 589 (QB) 27–46
X (Baby) v An NHS Trust. *See* NHS Trust v Baby X
X (Minors) v Bedfordshire CC; M (A Minor) v Newham LBC; E (A Minor) v Dorset CC
    (Appeal); Christmas v Hampshire CC (Duty of Care); Keating v Bromley LBC
    (No.2) [1995] 2 A.C. 633; [1995] 3 W.L.R. 152; [1995] 3 All E.R. 353; [1995] 2
    F.L.R. 276; [1995] 3 F.C.R. 337; 94 L.G.R. 313; (1995) 7 Admin. L.R. 705; [1995]
    Fam. Law 537; (1996) 160 L.G. Rev. 123; (1996) 160 L.G. Rev. 103; (1995) 145
    N.L.J. 993 9–15
XA v YA [2010] EWHC 1983 (QB); [2011] P.I.Q.R. P1. . . . . 8–51, 8–192
XVW v Gravesend Grammar Schools for Girls [2012] EWHC 575 (QB); [2012] E.L.R.
    417. . . . . 6–25, 6–31,
                                                                                                                8–197
Yam Seng Pte Ltd v International Trade Corp Ltd [2013] EWHC 111 (QB); [2013] 1
    All E.R. (Comm) 1321; [2013] 1 Lloyd's Rep. 526; [2013] B.L.R. 147; 146 Con.
    L.R. 39 18–45
Yell Ltd v Giboin [2011] EWPCC 009 26–01
Yetkin v Mahmood; sub nom. Yetkin v Newham LBC [2010] EWCA Civ 776; [2011] Q.B.
    827; [2011] 2 W.L.R. 1073; [2011] P.T.S.R. 1295; [2010] R.T.R. 39 . . . . . 8–185, 8–187, 9–40,
                                                                                                        14–31, 14–51, 14–57, 20–193

Zarb v Parry [2011] EWCA Civ 1306; [2012] 1 W.L.R. 1240; [2012] 2 All E.R. 320; [2012]
    1 P. & C.R. 10; [2012] 1 E.G.L.R. 1; [2012] 3 E.G. 88; [2011] 47 E.G. 105 (C.S.);
    (2011) 161 N.L.J. 1633; (2011) 155(44) S.J.L.B. 31; [2011] N.P.C. 118 19–75
ZH v Commissioner of Police of the Metropolis; sub nom. Commissioner of Police of the
    Metropolis v ZH [2013] EWCA Civ 69; [2013] 3 All E.R. 113; [2013] H.R.L.R. 18;
    [2013] Eq. L.R. 363; (2013) 16 C.C.L. Rep. 109; [2013] P.I.Q.R. P11 . . . . 15–126, 15–137
Zurich Insurance Co Plc v Hayward [2011] EWCA Civ 641; [2011] C.P. Rep. 39. . . . . 18–03, 31–24

TABLE OF STATUTES

1825   Statute of Frauds Amendment Act
    (9 Geo. 4 c.14) 18–53

1925   Trustee Act (15 & 16 Geo. 5 c.19)–
    s.61 .... 10–23, 10–119

1925   Law of Property Act (15 & 16 Geo.
    5 c.20)–
    s.136 5–64

1934   Law Reform (Miscellaneous
    Provisions) Act (24 & 25
    Geo. 5 c.41). 14–69

1945   Law Reform (Contributory
    Negligence) Act (8 & 9 Geo.
    6 c.28) 3–54

1949   Registered Designs Act (12, 13 & 14
    Geo. 6 c.88). 25–63

1952   Prison Act (15 & 16 Geo. 6 & 1 Eliz.
    2 c.52)–
    s.42A 17–71

1952   Defamation Act (15 & 16 Geo. 6 & 1
    Eliz. 2 c.66)–
    s.5 22–04

1957   Occupiers' Liability Act (5 & 6 Eliz. 2
    c.31) 8–51, 12–04,
    12–07, 12–20
    s.2(5) 12–41

1961   Factories Act (9 & 10 Eliz. 2 c.34)–
    s.14 .... 13–32, 13–33
    s.29 .... 13–32, 13–33
    (1) 9–17

1967   Criminal Law Act (c.58)–
    s.3 15–52

1971   Animals Act (c.22)–
    s.2(2) 21–04, 21–15
    (a) 21–05, 21–08
    (b) 21–08
    s.5(1) 21–15
    (2) 3–105, 21–04,
    21–05, 21–15

1971   Immigration Act (c.77) 15–33,
    15–135
    Sch.2 para.17. 15–75

1972   Defective Premises Act
    (c.35) 12–83
    s.1 8–130
    (1) 8–130
    s.4 12–85

1972   European Communities
    Act (c.68) 25–04

1974   Health and Safety at Work etc. Act
    (c.37). 13–35
    s.47 .... 13–01A

1974   Consumer Credit Act (c.39) 8–110

1974   Rehabilitation of Offenders Act
    (c.53). 22–84

1976   Fatal Accidents Act
    (c.30) 10–93, 10–104, 28–87
    s.1A 1–79, 10–78,
    10–93, 10–104

1976   Race Relations Act (c.74). 6–27
    s.32 6–12

1977   Torts (Interference with Goods)
    Act (c.32) 17–19, 17–81
    s.12 17–19
    s.13 17–19

1977   Patents Act (c.37) 25–88
    s.4A 25–94
    ss.14–24 25–90
    s.41(2) 25–92
    s.44 25–102
    s.48 25–108
    s.48A 25–108
    s.48B 25–108
    s.60(5) 25–99
    (i) 25–99
    s.61(2) 25–103
    s.76A 25–94
    s.128B 25–91
    Sch.A2. 25–94
    Secion 3 25–94

1977   Criminal Law Act (c.45). 19–18

1977   Unfair Contract Terms
    Act (c.50) 10–18

1978   State Immunity Act
    (c.33). 5–27, 7–02

1978   Civil Liability (Contribution)
    Act (c.47) ..... 2–58—2–68, 3–75

1980   Limitation Act (c.58) 5–09
    s.3(2) 17–127
    s.14 5–09
    (1) 32–51
    s.15 19–70
    s.32A 22–197
    s.33 32–56
    (3)(a) 32–61
    s.38(1)(c) 32–23
    (2) 32–22
    (3) 32–22
    (4) 32–22

1980   Highways Act (c.66)–
    s.41 .... 8–186, 8–187, 9–11,
    20–192, 20–193
    (1A) 8–187
    s.58 .... 8–186, 9–11, 20–192
    (2) 8–186

	s.130	20–193
	(3)	20–193
1981	Senior Courts Act (c.54)–	
	s.51	10–120
	s.69	22–03
	(1)	22–04
	s.72(5)	27–04
1982	Civil Jurisdiction and	
	Judgments Act (c.27)–	
	ss.2–11.	7–02
	s.31	7–02
	(1)(a).	5–22
	(4)	5–22
	s.32	7–02
1983	Mental Health Act	
	(c.20). . . . 15–100, 15–102, 15–116	
	s.6(3)	15–102
	s.11(4) 15–102, 15–116	
	s.139(1)	15–116
1984	Occupiers' Liability	
	Act (c.3) 12–04, 12–20, 12–64	
1984	Dentists Act (c.24)–	
	s.27	27–29
1984	Police and Criminal Evidence Act	
	(c.60).	14–86
	s.15(6) 19–61, 19–62	
	s.16(5)	19–61
	s.17(1)(e).	15–84
	s.24(4)	15–49
	(5)	15–72
	s.32(1)	15–86
	(2)(b).	15–86
	s.63D	14–86
1985	Prosecution of Offences Act	
	(c.23).	16–03
1985	Sexual Offences Act (c.44).	20–03
1985	Housing Act (c.68)–	
	s.118	9–25
1987	Consumer Protection Act	
	(c.43).	11–46
	s.3(2)(c).	11–68
	s.4(1)(d).	11–68
1988	Copyright, Designs and Patents Act	
	(c.48). 25–04, 25–26, 25–55,	
	25–63, 25–88	
	Pt 1 . . . . 25–04, 25–05	
	s.1(1)(a).	25–23
	s.18A	25–19
	s.19	25–07
	ss.19–21	25–19
	s.35	25–76
	s.36	25–76
	s.36A	25–30
	ss.50A–50C.	25–07
	s.51	25–54
	(1)	25–54
	s.52	25–54
	s.90(2)	25–17
	ss.96–115.	25–30

	s.97A	25–34
	s.101A	25–33
	s.143(3)	25–61
	s.213(4)	25–55
	s.224	25–58
	s.226	25–59
	s.227	25–59
	s.228	25–59
	s.236	25–72
	s.237(1)	25–60
	s.249	25–61
	s.253	25–62
	s.287	27–05
	Sch.23(6).	25–61
1990	Town and Country Planning	
	Act (c.8)–	
	s.178	19–31
1990	Courts and Legal Services Act (c.41)–	
	s.58	22–04
1990	Environmental Protection Act (c.43)–	
	s.80	14–101
	s.82	14–101
1991	Water Industry Act (c.56)–	
	s.94	14–101
	s.106 . . . . . 9–09, 9–12, 20–77, 20–134	
1992	Trade Union and Labour Relations	
	(Consolidation) Act (c.52)–	
	s.219	24–116
	ss.226–235	24–145
	s.226A 5–85, 24–147	
	(2H)	24–147
	s.227(1)	24–147
	s.230	24–146
	(2)	24–147
	(2A)	24–147
	s.231	24–151
	s.232B 24–147, 24–153	
	s.234A	24–147
	(5C).	24–147
1994	Criminal Justice and Public Order	
	Act (c.33)–	
	s.60	15–62
1994	Trade Marks Act (c.26). 25–73,	
	25–74, 25–86	
	s.6A	25–79
	s.10(1)	25–83
	(2) 25–81, 25–83	
	(6)	25–82
	s.11(1)	25–83
	(2)	25–82
	(3)	25–82
	s.32	25–76
	s.47	25–79
	s.55(1)(b).	25–76
1995	Private International Law	
	(MiscellaneousProvisions)Act(c.42)–	
	s.11	7–15
1995	Disability Discrimination	
	Act (c.50)	15–137

1996	Defamation Act (c.31)–	2004	Patents Act (c.16) 25–88
	s.4(3) 22–190	2004	Employment Relations Act (c.24)–
1997	Protection from Harassment		s.24(1) 24–147
	Act (c.40) 5–89, 6–55, 27–36,	2005	Prevention of Terrorism
	27–46		Act (c.2) 15–89, 15–90
1997	Plant Varieties Act (c.66) 25–109	2005	Mental Capacity Act (c.9). 10–49,
1998	Data Protection		10–53, 10–61, 15–126, 32–21,
	Act (29) 8–110, 14–31, 22–84		32–22
1998	School Standards and Framework Act		s.1(6) 15–126
	(c.31) 14–08		s.2(1) 10–61
1998	Competition Act (c.41) 3–31		s.4A 10–61
1998	Human Rights Act (c.42) 1–79,		s.25(6) 10–53
	5–13, 10–93, 14–31, 14–38, 14–54,	2006	Compensation Act
	14–65, 14–69, 14–69A, 14–70,		(c.29) . . . . 2–58—2–68, 12–29
	14–75, 14–87, 14–93A, 14–96,		s.1 1–17
	14–98, 15–141A, 22–14, 22–23,		s.3 2–66
	24–145, 27–36, 28–87		(1) 2–66
	s.3 15–116	2008	Criminal Justice and Immigration
	ss.6–8 5–03		Act (c.4)–
	s.7 14–69		s.76 3–138
	s.8 . . . . 15–30, 15–141A	2008	Housing and Regeneration Act (c.17)–
	(4) 14–99		Sch.11 20–63
	s.12(3) 22–256	2010	Equality Act (c.15) 6–27
1999	Employment Relations Act (c.26)–		s.109 6–12
	Sch.3 para.9. 24–147		(4) 6–27
2000	Powers of Criminal Courts	2011	Terrorism Prevention and Investigation
	(Sentencing) Act (c.6)–		Measures Act (c.23)–
	ss.143–144 17–47		s.1 . . . . 15–89, 15–90
	s.144 17–47	2012	Consumer Insurance (Disclosure and
2000	Financial Services and Markets		Representations) Act (c.6). . 10–212
	Act (c.8) 9–13, 9–25, 29–28		Sch.2 para.2(b) 10–212
	s.74 9–25	2012	Protection of Freedoms Act (c.9)–
	s.91 9–25		s.1 14–86
	s.150(1) 9–49		s.54 17–135
	s.382 9–25		(2) 17–135
2000	Terrorism Act (c.11) 15–89	2012	Legal Aid, Sentencing and Punishment
	ss.41–43 15–89		of Offenders Act (c.10)–
	ss.44–46 15–84		s.44 22–04
	ss.44–47 15–89		(6) 28–56
	ss.47A–47C 15–89		s.148 3–138
2002	Land Registration Act (c.9) 19–13	2013	Prisons (Property) Act (c.11) . . . 17–71
	Sch.4 19–13	2013	Crime and Courts Act (c.22)–
	Sch.6 para.1(1) 19–13		s.43 3–138
	para.5(4)(c) 19–75	2013	Enterprise and Regulatory Reform Act
2002	Proceeds of Crime Act (c.29) . . . 25–84		(c.24) 25–04
2003	Criminal Justice Act (c.44)–		s.69 . . . . 13–01A
	s.329 15–134		s.74(2) 25–54
	(2) 15–134		Pt 6 25–04
	(3) 15–134		Sch.22 25–04
	(4)(a) 15–134	2013	Defamation Act (c.26) 22–04
	(b) 15–134		s.4(1) 22–04

TABLE OF STATUTORY INSTRUMENTS

1965 RulesoftheSupremeCourt(SI1965/1776)–
      Ord.113 r.7 19–72
1986 Insolvency Rules (SI 1986/
      1925). 14–56
      r.6.13 . . . . 8–99, 9–18
1989 Copyright (Industrial Process and
      Excluded Articles) (No.2)
      Order (SI 1989/1070) 25–54
1992 Manual Handling Operations
      Regulations (SI 1992/2793)–
      reg.4 13–59
      (1)(a). 13–58
1992 Personal Protective Equipment at
      Work Regulations (SI 1992/
      2966). 2–12, 13–36
      reg.4 13–36
1992 Workplace (Health, Safety and
      Welfare) Regulations
      (SI 1992/3004) 13–54
      reg.12 13–54
      reg.17 13–54
      (1) 13–54
      (2) 13–54
1992 Copyright (Computer Programs)
      Regulations (SI 1992/
      3233). 25–07
1996 Construction (Health, Safety and
      Welfare) Regulations (SI
      1996/1592) 12–04, 13–35
1998 Provision and Use of Work Equipment
      Regulations (SI 1998/2306)–
      reg.4 . . . . 13–46, 13–48
      reg.5 . . . . 13–48, 13–51, 13–63
      reg.12(1) 13–50A
      (2) 13–50A
      (a) 13–50A
      (b) 13–50A
      (3) 13–50A
      reg.15 13–51
      reg.17(2) 13–50B
1998 Civil Procedure Rules (SI 1998/
      3132)–
      r.26.11 22–03
      PD 6B para.3.9(a) 7–03, 7–04
      Pt 63 25–87
      Pt 63 PD 25–74
1999 Management of Health and Safety at
      Work Regulations (SI 1999/3242)–
      reg.3 . . . . 13–51, 13–54
      (1) 13–06

2003 Copyright and Related Rights
      Regulations (SI 2003/2498)–
      Pt 3 25–30
      reg.27 . . . . 25–30, 25–34
2004 Trade Marks (Proof of Use, etc.)
      Regulations (SI 2004/946) . . . 25–79
2004 Regulatory Reform (Patents) Order (SI
      2004/2357) 25–88
2005 Work at Height Regulations
      (SI 2005/735) 12–04, 13–35,
      13–52, 13–64
2006 Artist's Resale Right Regulations
      (SI 2006/346) 25–10
2006 Control of Asbestos Regulations
      (SI 2006/2739) 13–37
2007 Patents (Convention Countries) Order
      (SI 2007/276) 25–88
2007 Patents Rules (SI 2007/3291). . . 25–87
2007 Patents (Fees) Rules (SI 2007/
      3292). 25–87
2008 Copyright and Performances
      (Application to Other Countries)
      Order (SI 2008/677) 25–13,
      25–18
2009 Copyright and Performances
      (Application to Other Countries)
      (Amendment) Order (SI 2009/
      2745). 25–13, 25–18
2009 Patents (Convention Countries)
      (Amendment) Order (SI 2009/
      2746). 25–88
2010 Control of Artificial Optical Radiation
      at Work Regulations (SI 2010/
      1140). 13–37
2011 Terrorism Act 2000 (Remedial)
      Order (SI 2011/631) 15–84
      art.2 15–89
2011 CriminalProcedureRules(SI2011/1709)–
      r.34.3(2)(c) 10–121
2011 Artist's Resale Right (Amendment)
      Regulations (SI 2011/
      2873). 25–10
2012 Control of Asbestos Regulations
      (SI 2012/632) 13–37
2012 Health and Safety (Miscellaneous
      Revocations) Regulations
      (SI 2012/1537) 13–37
2013 Damages for Bereavement (Variation
      of Sum) (England and Wales)
      Order (SI 2013/510) 28–92

TABLE OF STATUTORY INSTRUMENTS

TABLE OF INTERNATIONAL TREATIES AND CONVENTIONS

Athens Convention Relating to the
Carriage of Passengers and their
Luggage by Sea (1974) 12–07
European Convention on Human
Rights (1950) 3–03, 15–89,
15–141A, 19–70
art.1 . . . . 14–38, 14–69A
art.2 . . . . . . 5–13, 8–36, 10–78, 10–93,
10–104, 14–28, 14–38, 14–54,
14–69, 14–70, 14–72, 14–73,
14–75, 14–79, 14–80
art.3 . . . . 14–75, 14–79, 14–80
art.4 . . . . 14–75, 14–79
art.5 14–80, 15–62, 15–64, 15–102,
15–116, 16–52
(1) 14–80, 14–81, 14–98, 15–30
(4) . . . 14–81, 14–98, 14–99, 15–30,
15–141A
art.6 . . . . 9–14, 13–03
art.8 . . . . 8–84, 10–44, 14–31, 14–51A,
14–87, 14–89, 14–100, 14–101,
22–14, 22–84, 22–119, 23–04,
27–37, 27–47, 28–87
(1) 14–86, 14–110
art.10 . . . . 14–87, 14–93A,
15–21, 22–15, 22–23,
27–39, 27–47, 27–48
(2) 14–87
art.11 . . . . 14–80, 14–93A, 15–21
(1) 24–145

art.13 14–73
art.34 14–69
Protocol 1 art.1 . . . . . . 13–03, 14–93A,
14–95
art.2 14–96
Protocol 4 art.2 14–80
European Patent Convention
(1973) 25–88
art.69 25–93
art.99 25–90
art.101 25–96
Lugano Convention on Jurisdiction and
the Enforcement of Judgments in
Civil and Commercial Matters
(1988) 7–02
art.5(3). 7–02, 7–02A
Paris Convention for the Protection of
Industrial Property (1967) . . . 25–88
Patent Cooperation Treaty
(1970) 25–88, 25–90
Treaty on the Functioning of the
European Union (TFEU)
art.101 25–92
art.102 . . . . 25–46, 25–102
art.267 25–91
art.288 25–74
Warsaw Convention for the Unification
of Certain Rules Relating to
International Carriage by
Air (1929) 12–07

CHAPTER 1

PRINCIPLES OF LIABILITY IN TORT

                                                                                          PARA.
1. The nature of tort liability 1–02
□ 2. The functions and development of tort liability 1–11
3. The framework of tort liability 1–23
    (a) Interests protected by the law of torts 1–25
       ■ (i) Personal interests 1–25
         (ii) Property interests 1–38
         (iii) Economic interests 1–42
         (iv) Loss of chance 1–44
         (v) Public interests 1–45
    (b) Nature of the injurer's conduct 1–49
         (i) Damage 1–50
         (ii) Causal distinctions 1–52
         (iii) Fault 1–55
    ■ (c) Impact of the Human Rights Act 1998 1–70

2. The Functions and Development of Tort Liability

Compensation or vindication of rights? Add: Note that there is a difference **1–12**
between saying that an award of damages can serve a vindicatory purpose, and the
claim that a special award of "vindicatory damages" should be made in circumstances where the claimant would otherwise be entitled only to nominal damages.
See *R. (on the application of WL (Congo)) v Secretary of State for the Home
Department* [2011] UKSC 12; [2012] 1 A.C. 245, where by a majority of the
Supreme Court it was held that claimants who had been falsely imprisoned by
reason of the defendant's breach of public law principles, but who had suffered no
loss because they would have been detained in any event if the defendant had
complied with her public law duty, were entitled to nominal damages only (cf. the
dissenting judgments of Lord Walker, Lord Hope and Baroness Hale on this point,
who would have awarded "vindicatory damages"). Lord Dyson doubted whether
vindicatory damages are ever justified as a remedy in tort (as opposed to a remedy
for the infringement of a constitutional right where there is a written constitution,
as in *Attorney General of Trinidad and Tobago v Ramanoop* [2005] UKPC 15;
[2006] 1 A.C. 328): "The implications of awarding vindicatory damages in the
present case would be far reaching. Undesirable uncertainty would result. If they
were awarded here, then they could in principle be awarded in any case involving
a battery or false imprisonment by an arm of the state. Indeed, why limit it to such
torts? And why limit it to torts committed by the state? I see no justification for
letting such an unruly horse loose on our law" (at [101]; see also Lord Collins at
[236]: "To make a separate award for vindicatory damages is to confuse the
purpose of damages awards with the nature of the award. A declaration, or an

award of nominal damages, may itself have a vindicatory purpose and effect. So too a conventional award of damages may serve a vindicatory purpose").

1–13   NOTE 47. Add: The deterrent effect as part of the purpose of potential tort liability is not often remarked upon by the courts, though in *Scout Association v Barnes* [2010] EWCA Civ 1476 at [34] Jackson L.J. (with whom Smith L.J. agreed, at [36]) noted that: "It is the function of the law of tort to deter negligent conduct and to compensate those who are the victims of such conduct." More commonly, the notion of deterrence features as part of the assessment of the potential negative effects of tort liability (e.g. as tending towards "defensive practice" on the part of certain public bodies if a duty of care was held to apply (see para.**8–20** of the Main Work), or as undermining socially desirable activities (see para.**1–17** of this Supplement)).

1–17   **Risk and autonomy.** Add: See also *Scout Association v Barnes* [2010] EWCA Civ 1476 at [34] Jackson L.J. (with whom Smith L.J. agreed, at [36]): "It is not the function of the law of tort to eliminate every iota of risk or to stamp out socially desirable activities: see generally Ch.11 'The standards of care in negligence law' in Owen (ed.), *The Philosophical Foundations of the Law of Tort* (Oxford: Clarendon Press, 1995). This principle is now enshrined in s.1 of the Compensation Act 2006. That provision was not in force at the time of the claimant's accident. However, the principle has always been part of the common law." For consideration of the Compensation Act 2006 s.1, see para.**8–162** of the Main Work and this Supplement.

3. THE FRAMEWORK OF TORT LIABILITY

(a) *Interests protected by the law of torts*

(i) *Personal interests*

1–27   **Physical security from injury.** NOTE 93. Add: In *AXA General Insurance Ltd v HM Advocate* [2011] UKSC 46; [2012] 1 A.C. 868 the Supreme Court held that the 2009 Act was not beyond the competence of the Scottish Parliament, nor was it subject to judicial review on the grounds of unreasonableness, irrationality and arbitrariness.

(c) *Impact of the Human Rights Act 1998*

1–79   Add: Note, however, that a claim under the Human Rights Act has the potential to provide a remedy in damages where the common law or other legislative provisions have declined to do so. See *Rabone v Pennine Care NHS Trust* [2012] UKSC 2; [2012] 2 A.C. 72 and *Reynolds v United Kingdom* (2694/08) (2012) 55 E.H.R.R. 35 providing damages for breach of art.2 in circumstances where the relatives of a deceased person would not have had a claim for bereavement damages under the Fatal Accidents Act 1976 s.1A: see paras **10–78, 10–93, 14–69**, and **14–73** of this Supplement.

CHAPTER 2

CAUSATION IN TORT: GENERAL PRINCIPLES

		PARA.
■ 1. Introduction	....	2–01
2. Factual causation	....	2–09
□ (a) The "but for" test	....	2–09
(b) The uncertainty of hypothetical human contact	....	2–12
■ (i) Claimant's hypothetical conduct	....	2–12
■ (ii) Claimant's response to advice about risks of medical treatment	....	2–14
(iii) Claimant's response to misrepresentation and deceit	....	2–19
■ (iv) Defendant's hypothetical conduct	....	2–21
(v) Third party's hypothetical conduct	....	2–23
(c) Scientific uncertainty about causal mechanisms	....	2–24
□ (i) Statistics and causation	....	2–27
□ (ii) Material contribution to the damage	....	2–29
■ (iii) Material contribution to the risk of damage	....	2–39
■ (iv) Multiple tortfeasors and contribution to the risk	....	2–44
□ (v) Statutory rule for mesothelioma	....	2–65
3. Loss of a chance	....	2–69
(a) Loss of a chance of financial benefit	....	2–70
(b) Loss of a chance of a better medical outcome	....	2–77
(i) The quantification argument	....	2–81
(ii) The loss of chance argument	....	2–83
(iii) Loss of chance of a better medical outcome after Gregg v Scott	....	2–87
4. Causation in law	....	2–91
(a) Successive sufficient causes	....	2–94
(i) Successive torts	....	2–95
(ii) Supervening non–tortious events	....	2–97
(b) Intervening acts	....	2–101
(i) Acts of nature	....	2–103
■ (ii) Intervening conduct of a third party	....	2–105
□ (iii) Intervening conduct of the claimant	....	2–119
(iv) Intervening conduct of the defendant	....	2–131
5. Remoteness of damage	....	2–133
(a) Remoteness and torts other than negligence	....	2–135
(i) Torts where questions of remoteness do not arise	....	2–135
(ii) Remoteness and trespass to the person	....	2–136
(iii) Remoteness and torts of strict liability	....	2–137
(iv) Remoteness and intended consequences	....	2–139
(b) Remoteness and liability in negligence for physical damage	....	2–141
(i) Foreseeability and directness	....	2–142
(ii) Manner of the occurrence	....	2–148
(iii) Type of damage	....	2–151
(iv) Extent of the damage	....	2–156
(v) Eggshell skulls	....	2–158
(vi) Claimant's impecuniosity	....	2–166
(c) Remoteness and liability in negligence for pure economic loss	....	2–170
□ (i) Conceptual issues	....	2–170
■ (ii) Impact of SAAMCO	....	2–175

1. INTRODUCTION

2–07 **The burden of proof.** After the second sentence, ending "of which he complains", insert Note 15a.

NOTE 15a. Although the burden of proof must be satisfied to the civil standard of proof, "on the balance of probability", it may be unwise to express this in percentage terms since it carries the danger of "pseudo-mathematics": "When judging whether a case for believing that an event was caused in a particular way is stronger than the case for not so believing, the process is not scientific (although it may obviously include evaluation of scientific evidence) and to express the probability of some event having happened in percentage terms is illusory": *Nulty v Milton Keynes BC* [2013] EWCA Civ 15; [2013] 1 W.L.R. 1183 at [35] per Toulson L.J.

NOTE 17. Add: Applied in *Vaile v Havering LBC* [2011] EWCA Civ 246; [2011] E.L.R. 274 at [32].

2–08 **Improbable theories and legitimate inferences.** NOTE 21. Add: In *Nulty v Milton Keynes BC* [2013] EWCA Civ 15; [2013] 1 W.L.R. 1183 counsel argued that if there is a closed list of possible causes, and if one possibility is more likely than the other, by definition that has a greater probability than 50 per cent; and that if there is a closed list of more than two possible causes, the court should ascribe a probability factor to them individually in order to determine whether one had a probability figure greater than 50 per cent. Toulson L.J. rejected the argument: "It is not only over-formulaic but it is intrinsically unsound" (at [37]). There is no rule of law that if possible causes A and B are very much less likely than possible cause C then possible cause C becomes the probable cause. The question is: "on an overall assessment of the evidence (i.e. on a preponderance of the evidence) whether the case for believing that the suggested event happened is more compelling than the case for not reaching that belief" (at [37]; and see also [42]).

2. FACTUAL CAUSATION

(a) *The "but for" test*

2–10 **"But for" test not always required: conversion.** Add: Note that for a tort that is actionable per se, such as trespass to the person, the claimant merely has to establish the requirements of the tort in order to establish liability and it is not a "defence" for a defendant to claim that he could have acted lawfully if in fact he had no lawful authority to do the act complained of. So, in the tort of false imprisonment where all that a claimant has to prove "is that he was directly and intentionally imprisoned by the defendant, whereupon the burden shifts to the defendant to show that there was lawful justification for doing so" (*R. (on the application of WL (Congo)) v Secretary of State for the Home Department* [2011] UKSC 12; [2012] 1 A.C. 245 at [65] per Lord Dyson), if the defendant acted unlawfully in detaining the claimant, it is no defence for the defendant to prove that he could have lawfully detained the claimant. This so called "causation test" has no place in the tort of false imprisonment, since "The fact that a person could have been lawfully detained says nothing on the question whether he was lawfully detained" (at [239] per Lord Kerr). On the other hand, the causation test is relevant if the claimant is seeking substantive, as opposed to nominal, damages. See further para.**15–135** of this Supplement.

(b) *The uncertainty of hypothetical human conduct*

(i) *Claimant's hypothetical conduct*

Causation depends on claimant's conduct. Add: In *Chief Constable of*   2–12
Hampshire v Taylor [2013] EWCA Civ 496 the defendant was found to have been in breach of the Personal Protective Equipment at Work Regulations 1992 in failing to provide thick gloves to a police officer instructed to dismantle a "cannabis factory" (see para.**13–36** of this Supplement). An issue arose as to who had the burden of proving that if gloves had been provided the claimant would have worn them and so avoided the injury that occurred. Elias L.J. (with whom Patten L.J agreed) commented, at [18], that "if [the claimant] had to discharge the burden, she failed to do so. Equally, if it was on the [defendant], he failed to discharge it". The trial judge had taken the view that the burden of proof lay with the defendant. Elias L.J., at [19], agreed: "this is a very firmly established principle and the judge was saying nothing novel. Once the employer is shown to be in breach of duty to provide equipment, the assumption is that it would have been used, because a reasonable employee would use it, unless the employer proves otherwise." His Lordship cited *McWilliams v Sir William Arrol* [1962] 1 W.L.R. 295 for this proposition (and the judgment of Longmore L.J. in *Ali Ghaith v Indesit Company UK Ltd* [2012] EWCA Civ 642 at [23]). *Sed quaere*: the result in *McWilliams v Sir William Arrol* did not turn on the burden of proof, since there was overwhelming evidence that the deceased would probably not have used a safety belt if the defendants had supplied one (see per Lord Devlin at 309). Viscount Kilmuir L.C. (with whom Lord Morris agreed) made it clear (at 299) that the burden of proving both breach of duty and causation lay with the claimant (both for the common law of negligence and breach of statutory duty). Lord Reid commented (at 306) that: "It has been suggested that the decision of this House in *Bonnington Castings Ltd v Wardlaw* lays down new law and increases the burden on pursuers. I do not think so. It states what has always been the law—a pursuer must prove his case. He must prove that the fault of the defender caused, or contributed to, the danger which he has suffered." His Lordship then considered what amounts to proof when there is no direct evidence because the victim is deceased and so unable to give evidence. In that situation the starting point is to make certain assumptions: "If general practice or a regulation requires that some safety appliance shall be provided, one would assume that it is of some use, and that a reasonable man would use it. And one would assume that the injured man was a reasonable man. So the initial onus on the pursuer to connect the failure to provide the appliance with the accident would normally be discharged merely by proving the circumstances which led to the accident, and it is only where the evidence throws doubt on either of these assumptions that any difficulty would arise. Normally it would be left to the defender to adduce evidence, if he could, to displace these assumptions." It might be said that in this situation, as with the principle of res ipsa loquitur (see para.**8–176** of the Main Work), there is an

evidential burden on the defendant to adduce evidence which displaces the initial inference that the breach of duty caused or materially contributed to the injury. But if the defendant does that, and (as rarely occurs in practice) the probabilities are equal, the claimant will fail on the basis that he has not discharged the burden of proving causation. It seems odd then, in a case where the claimant has had a full opportunity to establish causation on the evidence but has failed to discharge the burden of proof, to revert to the initial presumption that a "reasonable employee" would have used the equipment in order to establish causation.

2–13   **Negligent advice.** Add: In *Levicom International Holdings BV v Linklaters* [2010] EWCA Civ 494; [2010] P.N.L.R. 29, a case concerning negligent advice by a solicitor to a client about commencing proceedings, the Court of Appeal indicated that little will be needed in the way of evidence to establish causation, apparently on the basis that clients will usually accept the advice of their solicitors. Jacob L.J. (at [284]) commented: "When a solicitor gives advice that his client has a strong case to start litigation rather than settle and the client then does just that, the normal inference is that the advice is causative. Of course the inference is rebuttable—it may be possible to show that the client would have gone ahead willy-nilly. But that was certainly not shown on the evidence here. The judge should have approached the case on the basis that the evidential burden had shifted to [the defendant] to prove that its advice was not causative." Stanley Burnton L.J., agreeing with Jacob L.J., observed (at [261]) that: "one has to ask why a commercial company should seek expensive City solicitors' advice (and do so repeatedly) if they were not to act on it. I think that the evidence that a client did not act on advice in a case such as the present must be stronger than that which persuaded the judge." Lloyd L.J. also agreed (at [282]).

(ii) *Claimant's response to advice about risks of medical treatment*

2–14   **Negligent advice about the risks of medical treatment.** NOTE 39. Add: In *Wallace v Kam* [2013] HCA 19 the High Court of Australia held that where a patient is not warned about two distinct risks, and the patient would not have proceeded with the treatment had he been warned about both risks, but only one of those risks materialises and the evidence indicates that the patient *would* have proceeded with the treatment had he been warned about *that* risk, the claim fails on causation. The fact that the patient would have declined the treatment (and so avoided the risk which has in fact materialised) had he been informed about the risk that has not materialised is irrelevant. This is because: "the policy that underlies requiring the exercise of reasonable care and skill in the giving of that warning is neither to protect that right to choose nor to protect the patient from exposure to all unacceptable risks. The underlying policy is rather to protect the patient from the occurrence of physical injury the risk of which is unacceptable to the patient. It is appropriate that the scope of liability for breach of the duty reflect that underlying policy" (at [36]). The High Court considered that the position may have been different if there was a "risk of a single physical injury to which there are several contributing factors the combination of which operate to increase the risk of that physical injury occurring. To fail to warn the patient of one factor while informing the patient of another may in a particular case be to fail to warn the patient of the extent of the risk and thereby to expose the patient to a level of risk of the physical injury occurring that is unacceptable to the patient" (at [34], discussing the reasoning of Lord Caplan in *Moyes v Lothian Health Board* 1990 S.L.T. 444).

After the fourth sentence ending ". . . not exposure to risk per se" insert Note 48a. **2–17**
NOTE 48a. See *Wallace v Kam* [2013] HCA 19 at [9]: "However, consistent with the underlying purpose of the imposition of the duty to warn, the damage suffered by the patient that the common law makes compensable is not impairment of the patient's right to choose. Nor is the compensable damage exposure of the patient to an undisclosed risk. The compensable damage is, rather, limited to the occurrence and consequences of physical injury sustained by the patient as a result of the medical treatment that is carried out following the making by the patient of a choice to undergo the treatment" (citing this paragraph in the Main Work and M.A. Jones, *Medical Negligence*, 4th edn (London: Sweet & Maxwell 2008), para. 7–072).
NOTE 49. Add: See also *Wallace v Kam* [2013] HCA 19 at [20]: "The better analysis is that it is also a scenario in which a determination of factual causation should be made. Absent the negligent failure to warn, the treatment that in fact occurred would not have occurred when it did and the physical injury in fact sustained when the treatment occurred would not then have been sustained. The same treatment may well have occurred at some later time but (provided that the physical injury remained at all times a possible but improbable result of the treatment) the physical injury that was sustained when the treatment in fact occurred would not on the balance of probabilities have been sustained if the same treatment had occurred on some other occasion."

(iv) *Defendant's hypothetical conduct*

NOTE 64. Add: See *Wright (A Child) v Cambridge Medical Group* [2011] **2–21** EWCA Civ 669; [2013] Q.B. 312 per Lord Neuberger M.R. at [56]–[61] for discussion of the underlying rationale for this proposition. See further para.**2–116** Note 372 of this Supplement.

(c) *Scientific uncertainty about causal mechanisms*

(i) *Statistics and causation*

Add: See the extensive discussion in *Sienkiewicz v Greif (UK) Ltd* [2011] **2–27** UKSC 10; [2011] 2 A.C. 229 about the courts' use of statistical data from epidemiological studies, particularly in cases of "toxic torts". The Supreme Court was extremely cautious about the circumstances in which the use of epidemiological data to establish causation would be appropriate. Although epidemiological data may form an important element in the proof of causation, it had to be recognised that it deals with populations rather than individuals, and it would be inappropriate to reason from statistical data about causal effects within a population to a causal mechanism in an individual, unless there is something in the particular facts of the case which would enable the court to infer a causal link in relation to the individual claimant.

(ii) *Material contribution to the damage*

2–29—2–34   In *B v Ministry of Defence* [2010] EWCA Civ 1317; (2011) 117 B.M.L.R. 101 the claimants were former service personnel who alleged that they had been exposed to excessive ionising radiation during atmospheric nuclear tests carried out by the British Government in the Pacific between 1952 and 1958, and as a result had, many years later, developed various forms of cancer. The principal issue concerned limitation, but in considering the application of s.33 of the Limitation Act 1980 the court addressed the strength of the claimants' case on causation. Commenting on the defendants' submissions, the Court of Appeal noted (at [134]) that *Bonnington Castings Ltd v Wardlaw* amounted to a modification of the "but for" rule of causation because the claimant recovered damages for the harm caused by all the dust, not just the tortious component. If, as would probably be the case be nowadays, expert evidence had been called showing the effect of the different components the damages would probably have been apportioned (a view expressed by the Court of Appeal in *Holtby v Brigham Cowan (Hull) Ltd* [2000] 3 All E.R. 421; see para.**2–32** of the Main Work). The claimant would then have recovered damages only for the harm actually caused by the tort, and there would have been no need for modification of the "but for" rule. The modification of the "but for" rule is still available where the negligent and non–negligent causes have both contributed to the disease (as opposed to the risk of the disease) but it is not possible to apportion the harm caused. However: "This method of proving causation (by showing that the tort made a material contribution to the condition or disease) is only available where the severity of the disease is related to the amount of exposure; further exposure to the noxious substance in question is capable of making the condition worse" (at [134]). Since cancer is not a divisible condition (its severity does not depend on the extent of the exposure) the exposure to radiation had not made a material contribution to the disease, only to the risk that it might occur. The Court of Appeal accepted the defendants' submission (at [149]). With regard to cancer the claimants could not rely on *Bonnington Castings*, which applies "only where the disease or condition is 'divisible' so that an increased dose of the harmful agent worsens the disease . . . The tort did not increase the risk of harm; it increased the actual harm. Similarly in [*Bailey v Ministry of Defence* (see para.**2–30** of the Main Work)] the tort (a failure of medical care) increased the claimant's physical weakness. She would have been quite weak in any event as the result of a condition she had developed naturally. No one could say how great a contribution each had made to the overall weakness save that each was material. It was the overall weakness which led to the claimant's failure to protect her airway when she vomited with the result that she inhaled her vomit and suffered a cardiac arrest and brain damage. In those cases, the pneumoconiosis and the weakness were divisible conditions. Cancer is an indivisible condition; one either gets it or one does not. The condition is not worse because one has been exposed to a greater or smaller amount of the causative agent." (at [150]).

NOTE 86. Add: See Bailey, "Causation in negligence: what is a material contribution?" (2010) 30 L.S. 167 for extended discussion of the effect of *Bonnington Castings Ltd v Wardlaw*.

2–36   NOTE 115. Add: *MacLennan v Hartford Europe Ltd* [2012] EWHC 346 (QB) (claimant unable to establish any causal link between workplace stress and chronic fatigue syndrome; nor that her condition ought reasonably to have been foreseen by her employer, not least because, as a human resources manager, the claimant was aware of the need to inform her employer about stress and any perceived risks to her health but had not done so).

(iii) *Material contribution to the risk of damage*

Defendant's negligence more than doubles the risk. Add at the end of the paragraph: In *Sienkiewicz v Greif (UK) Ltd* [2011] UKSC 10; [2011] 2 A.C. 229 at [78] Lord Phillips agreed with Smith L.J.'s proposition: "as a matter of logic, if a defendant is responsible for a tortious exposure that has more than doubled the risk of the victim's disease, it follows on the balance of probability that he has caused the disease". However, the Supreme Court went on to hold that when applying the *Fairchild/Barker* test to causation it was not appropriate to apply such a statistical approach, so that it was not *necessary* when *Fairchild* applied for the claimant to prove that the defendant's breach of duty had more than doubled the risk. See para.**2–62A** of this Supplement. In *Sienkiewicz* Lord Phillips expanded on the circumstances in which the "doubles the risk" approach may or may not apply. There was "no scope for the application of the 'doubles the risk' test in cases where two agents have operated cumulatively and simultaneously in causing the onset of a disease. In such a case the rule in *Bonnington* applies. Where the disease is indivisible, such as lung cancer, a defendant who has tortiously contributed to the cause of the disease will be liable in full. Where the disease is divisible, such as asbestosis, the tortfeasor will be liable in respect of the share of the disease for which he is responsible" (at [90]). On the other hand: "Where the initiation of the disease is dose related, and there have been consecutive exposures to an agent or agents that cause the disease, one innocent and one tortious, the position will depend upon which exposure came first in time. Where it was the tortious exposure, it is axiomatic that this will have contributed to causing the disease, even if it is not the sole cause. Where the innocent exposure came first, there may be an issue as to whether this was sufficient to trigger the disease or whether the subsequent, tortious, exposure contributed to the cause. I can see no reason in principle why the 'doubles the risk' test should not be applied in such circumstances, but the court must be astute to see that the epidemiological evidence provides a really sound basis for determining the statistical probability of the cause or causes of the disease" (at [91]). Finally, where there were "competing alternative, rather than cumulative, potential causes of a disease or injury, such as in *Hotson*, I can see no reason in principle why epidemiological evidence should not be used to show that one of the causes was more than twice as likely as all the others put together to have caused the disease or injury" (at [93]).

In *Jones v Secretary of State for Energy and Climate Change* [2012] EWHC 2936 (QB) Swift J. used a "doubling of the risk" approach to the determination of causation of both lung and bladder cancers where the claimants had been exposed to carcinogenic fumes and dust.

(iv) *Multiple tortfeasors and contribution to the risk*

(3) Applying Fairchild

Limits to *Fairchild*. NOTE 160. Add: The test for breach of duty in a case of **2–50** mesothelioma is not whether the defendant exercised reasonable care to avoid

9

exposing the claimant to a material increase of the risk of developing mesothelioma, but whether the defendant exercised reasonable care to ensure that the claimant was not exposed to a foreseeable risk of asbestos-related injury (with the question of foreseeability to be judged by reference to the state of knowledge and practice at the time): *Williams v University of Birmingham* [2011] EWCA Civ 1242; [2012] P.I.Q.R P4 at [40]. See also *Asmussen v Filtrona United Kingdom Ltd* [2011] EWHC 1734 (QB); *Hill v John Barnsley & Sons Ltd* [2013] EWHC 520 (QB) and para.**13–21A** of this Supplement.

(4) Barker v Corus

2–58—2–68   Paragraphs **2–58—2–68** of the Main Work must now be read bearing in mind the effect of the decision of the Supreme Court in *Durham v BAI (Run Off) Ltd* [2012] UKSC 14; [2012] 1 W.L.R. 867 (also known as "the Trigger litigation"). In *Durham* the Supreme Court had to revisit the question of the combined effect of *Fairchild v Glenhaven Funeral Services Ltd, Barker v Corus UK Ltd* and s.3 of the Compensation Act 2006. The issue was whether employers' liability insurance policies responded to claims by former employees against their former employers in respect of negligent exposure to asbestos when the employees developed mesothelioma many years later. The answer to that question depended, in part, on whether the wording of the relevant insurance policies covered a situation where the exposure to asbestos occurred during the period of insurance but the injury to the employees manifested itself many years after the period of insurance, applying the principles of insurance law. However, it became apparent during argument before the Supreme Court that the answer also depended on the correct approach to causation in the claims by the employees against their former employers. If *Barker v Corus* had the effect that an employer was only liable to the extent that his negligence contributed to the risk that the employee would develop mesothelioma, and was not liable for causing the mesothelioma itself (which is the interpretation of *Barker* set out in paras **2–60** and **2–61** of the Main Work), then it was accepted that the insurance policies would not respond to the claims. If, on the other hand, the combined effect of *Fairchild* and *Barker* was that, for reasons of policy, the common law was prepared to accept a weak, or broad, view of the causal requirements in the case of asbestos-induced mesothelioma, but the defendant was nonetheless to be regarded as having *caused the mesothelioma* (as opposed to having contributed to *the risk* of the employee developing mesothelioma) the insurance policies would respond to the claims.

In a dissenting judgment Lord Phillips P.S.C. insisted that *Barker* created liability only in respect of the risk of the employee developing mesothelioma. His Lordship (at [117], [127]) said that his own statement in *Sienkiewicz v Greif (UK) Ltd* [2011] UKSC 10; [2011] 2 A.C. 229 at [70] that *Fairchild* and *Barker* "developed the common law by equating 'materially increasing the risk' with 'contributing to the cause' in specified and limited circumstances, which include ignorance of how causation in fact occurs" was a mistake. Rather, the combined effect of *Fairchild* and *Barker* was that defendants were to be held severally (and not jointly) liable in such cases, a result achieved by "holding that the liability of each defendant resulted from adding to the risk that the employee would contract mesothelioma. It did not result from an implication that each defendant had actually contributed to the cause of the disease" (at [124]). The *Fairchild* principle was not based on a legal fiction which deemed that each defendant had actually caused the mesothelioma; rather the creation of a material risk of mesothelioma was sufficient for liability. It would have been possible, said Lord Phillips, for the House of Lords in *Barker* to have "defined the special approach in *Fairchild* as one that treated contribution to risk as contribution to the causation of damage. The important fact is, however, that the majority did not do so. They were at pains to emphasise that the special approach was not based on the fiction that the defendants *had* contributed to causing the mesothelioma. Liability for a proportion of the mesothelioma resulted from contribution to the risk that mesothelioma would be caused and reflected the *possibility* that a defendant might have caused or contributed to the cause of the disease" (at [130]). The objective of the majority in *Barker*, said his Lordship, was to ensure that employers bore a fair share of responsibility for their wrongdoing, but it was unlikely that they gave consideration to the insurance implications of their decision. The only way of avoiding the conclusion that the insurance policies did not respond to the claims would be to hold that the majority in *Barker* were wrong and that the true basis of the *Fairchild* principle was "that contribution to risk should be deemed to be contribution to causation" (at [130]). However, his Lordship considered that it would be wrong to depart from the reasoning of the majority in *Barker* for the sole purpose of imposing liability on employers' liability insurers (at [137]).

Lord Mance J.S.C. (with whom Lord Kerr, Lord Clarke and Lord Dyson JJ.S.C. agreed) considered that the distinction said to have been drawn in *Barker* between materially contributing to increasing the risk of a disease and causing that disease was "elusive" (at [61]) and it was "over-simple" to describe the legal responsibility established in *Fairchild* and *Barker* as being liability "for the risk" (at [66]). If the cause of action were simply for the risk created by exposing someone to asbestos:

"then the risk would be the injury; damages would be recoverable for every exposure, without proof by the claimant of any (other) injury at all. That is emphatically not the law: see *Rothwell* and the statements in *Barker* itself, cited above. The cause of action exists because the defendant has previously exposed the victim to asbestos, because that exposure *may* have led to the mesothelioma, not because it did, and because mesothelioma has been suffered by the victim. As to the exposure, all that can be said (leaving aside the remote possibility that mesothelioma may develop idiopathically) is that *some* exposure to asbestos by someone, something or some event led to the mesothelioma. In the present state of scientific knowledge and understanding, there is nothing that enables one to know or suggest that the risk to which the defendant exposed the victim actually materialised. What materialised was at most a risk of the same kind to which someone, who may or may not have been the defendant, or something or some event had exposed the victim. The actual development of mesothelioma is an essential element of the cause of action. In ordinary language, the cause of action is 'for' or 'in respect of' the mesothelioma, and in ordinary language a defendant who exposes a victim of mesothelioma to asbestos is, under the rule in *Fairchild* and *Barker*, held responsible 'for' and 'in respect of' both that exposure and the mesothelioma" (at [65]).

His Lordship considered that it was "entirely natural" to view responsibility for the mesothelioma as being based on a "weak" or "broad" view of the "causal requirements" or "causal link". Moreover, there was "no magic about concepts such as causation or causal requirements, wherever they appear. They have the meanings assigned to them and understood in ordinary usage in their context. A logician might disagree with a reference to causation or a causal link in a particular context, but that is not the test of meaning . . . The present appeals concern the meanings we assign to the concept of causation, first in the context of considering employers' liability to their employees and then in considering the scope of employers' insurance cover with respect to such liability" (at [66]).

Lord Mance concluded that "for the purposes of the insurances" liability for mesothelioma following exposure to asbestos during an insurance period involved a "weak" or "broad" causal link sufficient for the disease to be regarded as "caused" within the insurance period. It was not accurate to treat the employer's liability as being either solely or strictly for the risk. The reality was that the "employer is being held responsible for the mesothelioma" (at [73]). For the purposes of the policies, said his Lordship, the negligent exposure of an employee to asbestos could "properly be described as having a sufficient causal link or being sufficiently causally connected with subsequently arising mesothelioma for the policies to respond. The concept of a disease being 'caused' during the policy period must be interpreted sufficiently flexibly to embrace the role assigned to exposure by the rule in *Fairchild* and *Barker*" (at [74]).

Lord Clarke (with whom Lord Dyson agreed) clearly had reservations as to whether *Barker* was correctly decided, commenting: "It seems to me that, whether the majority in *Barker* . . . were correct or not, there is no escape from the conclusion that, in all these cases, where it is not possible to show that the particular employer caused the claimant to suffer mesothelioma, the underlying question is who should be held responsible for causing the mesothelioma . . ." (at [83]). His Lordship took the view that the injury was the mesothelioma, not the risk of developing mesothelioma, but that "by creating the risk of mesothelioma in the future, the employer is *deemed to have caused* the mesothelioma, if it should develop in the future" (at [85] emphasis added).

The possible significance of Durham v BAI (Run Off) Ltd

(1) If Lord Phillips' interpretation had been accepted then the employers' liability insurance policies would not have responded to mesothelioma claims, which would have had a major impact on the ability of claimants to obtain compensation.

(2) The Compensation Act 2006 reversed the effect of *Barker* in relation to joint and several liability in respect of claims for asbestos-induced mesothelioma, so a return to the previous interpretation of *Fairchild* will not, in practice, make much difference to such claims.

(3) Where it will have a potential effect is in claims for other forms of harm (as e.g. in *McGhee v NCB*). Such claims are not affected by the Compensation Act 2006 but are governed by the common law, previously regarded as represented by *Barker* (see para.**2–68** of the Main Work). However, if the claim against the defendant is in respect of the negligent causation of

the claimant's damage, as opposed to the negligent creation of the risk of damage, a claimant who succeeds under the *Fairchild* principle will be entitled to damages which reflect the full loss attributable to the claimant's medical condition (subject to any contributory negligence). Defendants will be jointly and severally liable, so that a solvent/insured defendant will be liable for the full loss, but will have possible claims for contribution from other defendants under the Civil Liability (Contribution) Act 1978. This would be vindication of Lord Rodger's dissenting speech in *Barker* (see para.**2–61**, Note 189 of the Main Work).

(4)   The one possible caveat to this view is that the approach adopted by the majority in *Durham v BAI (Run Off) Ltd* may be limited to the interpretation of the applicability of liability insurance policies in order to make it clear that they respond to such claims (Lord Mance said more than once "for the purposes of the insurances"). That is of practical importance in the context of asbestos-induced mesothelioma, since it would be something of an anomaly if, Parliament having clearly rejected the House of Lords' view in *Barker* in relation to establishing defendants' joint and several liability, the *Barker* approach to "causation" was to be used to enable insurers to avoid meeting claims by employers and employees or former employees. A more glaring anomaly, however, would be if in non-mesothelioma cases the *Barker* approach continued to be applied to a *claimant* seeking to establish liability, but that if the claimant succeeded on that basis *Durham v BAI (Run Off) Ltd* were to be applied in order to ensure that the *liability insurer* had to indemnify the defendant (and hence compensate the claimant). This would involve applying different "liability rules" (on the same facts) to the claimant's claim against the defendant and then the defendant's claim for indemnity against the insurer. For this reason, it is suggested that *Durham v BAI (Run Off) Ltd* should not be limited to the interpretation of the applicability of liability insurance, but should be regarded as having, in effect if not explicitly, overruled *Barker*.

In commenting on *Barker*, Lord Phillips acknowledged the vigorous dissent of Lord Rodger in *Barker*, noting his observation that the majority in *Barker* were not so much reinterpreting as rewriting the key decisions in *McGhee v NCB* and *Fairchild*, and that the effect of *Barker* would be to maximise the inconsistencies in the law (see para.**2–61**, Note 189 of the Main Work). Lord Phillips expressed sympathy with Lord Rodger's observations (at [130]). There is more than a touch of irony in this, since without expressly overruling *Barker* the majority in *Durham v BAI (Run Off) Ltd* appear to have "rewritten" *Barker* so as to bring the *Fairchild* principle back to the position that many commentators considered had been established prior to *Barker v Corus*.

The Court of Appeal has now confirmed that, in the light of subsequent developments, the decision in *Barker* "has become past history": *International Energy Group Ltd v Zurich Insurance Plc UK* [2013] EWCA Civ 39; [2013] 3 All E.R. 395 at [13] per Toulson L.J. Lord Rodger's dissenting speech in *Barker* had been vindicated by Parliament in the Compensation Act 2006, and Lord Mance's judgment in *Durham v BAI (Run Off) Ltd* was "entirely consistent with Lord Rodger's dissenting judgment in *Barker* and indeed their approach was fundamentally identical" (at

[15] and [23]). Toulson L.J. pointed out that the interpretation of *Fairchild* adopted by the majority in *Barker* was inconsistent with the decision of their Lordships in *Rothwell v Chemical and Insulating Co Ltd* [2007] UKHL 39; [2008] 1 A.C. 281 (see para.**8–85** of the Main Work) that not even the emergence of pleural plaques "marking" the past exposure to asbestos constituted injury for the purpose of giving rise to a cause of action. Thus: "Under *Fairchild* the damage in respect of which a victim might sue was his contraction of mesothelioma; his wrongful exposure to asbestos in the course of his employment met the causal requirement for him to be entitled to hold the employer responsible in law for his illness" (at [28]). Aikens L.J. at [48], agreed: "It is now clear, from those majority judgments [in *Durham v BAI (Run Off) Ltd*], that when an employee has contracted mesothelioma as a result of being exposed to asbestos fibres or dust at work, his cause of action rests on the fact that he has contracted the disease. The mesothelioma itself is the damage and it is that damage which is the 'gist' of the cause of action of the employee against the employer. Or put the other way, the essence of the cause of action is not that the employee has been tortiously exposed to the risk of mesothelioma: see in particular Lord Mance's judgement at [52] and [72] and Lord Clarke of Stone-cum-Ebony's judgment at [77]." Maurice Kay L.J. agreed with both judgments.

2–59   **Effect of non-tortious exposures.** NOTE 185. Add: Lord Hoffmann's view was endorsed by the Supreme Court in *Sienkiewicz v Greif (UK) Ltd* [2011] UKSC 10; [2011] 2 A.C. 229, where the Court held that the *Fairchild* principle applied in a case of exposure to asbestos by a single defendant where the claimant had also been non-tortiously exposed to asbestos.

2–62   **Claims under the Fatal Accident Act 1976.** Note that if *Durham v BAI (Run Off) Ltd* [2012] UKSC 14; [2012] 1 W.L.R. 867 has the effect of overruling *Barker v Corus* the issues raised in this paragraph of the Main Work are no longer significant. See the discussion of *Durham* at para.**2–58** of this Supplement.

At the end of para.**2–62** insert new subheading: (v) *Exposure by single tort-feasor and contribution to the risk*
Insert new para.**2–62A**:

2–62A   **Exposure by a single tortfeasor.** In *Sienkiewicz v Greif (UK) Ltd* [2011] UKSC 10; [2011] 2 A.C. 229 the Supreme Court considered two conjoined appeals (*Sienkiewicz v Greif* and *Willmore v Knowsley MBC*) where individuals had developed mesothelioma (and subsequently died) having been exposed to asbestos by only one defendant, but where the evidence was that they had also been exposed to asbestos as a result of the background environmental risk. The defendants argued that in such circumstances the *Fairchild* principle did not apply and the claimant should have to prove causation on the basis that the defendants' tortious exposure of the deceased to asbestos had "more than doubled the risk" of the deceased developing mesothelioma from the background environmental risk. Neither claimant could do this, since in *Sienkiewicz* the evidence was that the tortious exposure had increased the risk attributable to the non-tortious environmental exposure by 18 per cent and in *Willmore* there was no evidence as to the precise increase in the risk. The Supreme Court rejected the defendants' argument. The claimants' problems in proving causation arose from the same "rock of uncertainty" that had been identified by Lord Bingham in *Fairchild*, and the same policy considerations applied (per Lord Rodger at [142]; see also per Lord Phillips at [103]). There was no justification for distinguishing cases involving multiple tortious exposures from cases of a single tortious exposure by applying a "doubles the risk" test of causation in the case asbestos-induced mesothelioma. For comment on *Sienkiewicz* see J. Stapleton, "Factual causation, mesothelioma and statistical validity" (2012) 128 L.Q.R. 221; S. Steel and D. Ibbetson, "More grief on uncertain causation in tort" [2011] C.L.J. 451.

After NOTE 199 in the text, add: In *Sienkiewicz v Greif (UK) Ltd* [2011] UKSC **2–64** 10; [2011] 2 A.C. 229 the Supreme Court rejected the defendants' argument that in order to constitute a *material* increase in the risk it must be shown that the defendant's tortious exposure of the claimant had more than doubled the environmental, non-tortious risk. The Supreme Court accepted that an increase in risk of developing mesothelioma as a result of exposure to asbestos of 18 per cent over the background risk constituted a material increase in the risk. If the exposure was de minimis then it would not constitute a material increase in the risk. However, Lord Phillips doubted whether it was possible to define, in quantitative terms, what amounts to de minimis for this purpose. This is a question for the judge on the particular facts of each case (at [108]).

NOTE 204. Add: See also *B v Ministry of Defence* [2010] EWCA Civ 1317; (2011) 117 B.M.L.R. 101 at [154] where the Court of Appeal said that there was: "no foreseeable possibility that the Supreme Court would be willing to extend the *Fairchild* exception so as to cover conditions such as we are here concerned with, which have multiple potential causes some of which have not even been identified. ... The inroad [into the normal rules of causation made by *Fairchild*] is slight and there were strong policy reasons for it. But the inroad applies only to cases where the cause of the condition is known. It does not apply where the cause is unknown. Here the causes of the claimants' conditions are not known. All that can be said in these cases is that radiation exposure is one of several possible causes." In the Supreme Court, Lord Phillips P.S.C. agreed with the Court of Appeal that there was no foreseeable possibility of the Supreme Court extending the principle in *Fairchild: B v Ministry of Defence* [2012] UKSC 9; [2013] 1 A.C. 78 at [157]. See also per Lord Brown J.S.C. at [75].

NOTE 208. Add: See now *Sienkiewicz v Greif (UK) Ltd* [2011] UKSC 10; [2011] 2 A.C. 229, where the Supreme Court held that in the case of asbestos-induced mesothelioma the principle of *Fairchild* applied, and a defendant would be liable, where the exposure of the claimant to asbestos had materially increased the risk. There is no requirement for the claimant to prove that the exposure had more than doubled the existing risk, even in a case involving a single defendant; and there is no requirement for a claimant to establish that the defendant had doubled an existing risk in order for the increase in risk to be classified as "a material increase".

Renumber the prior subheading "(v) *Statutory rule for mesothelioma*" to "(vi) **2–65** *Statutory rule for mesothelioma*"

Add: On appeal the Supreme Court dismissed the defendants' appeal, but for **2–66** reasons which differed from those of the Court of Appeal: *Sienkiewicz v Greif*

(UK) Ltd [2011] UKSC 10; [2011] 2 A.C. 229. The Supreme Court held that s.3 of the Compensation Act 2006 was not relevant to the outcome of the case, since all that the section did was hold that, in the case of asbestos-induced mesothelioma, if the common law reached the conclusion that liability was established applying whatever test of causation that the court considered was the correct test at common law, the defendant would be jointly and severally liable for the damage and not simply severally liable for contributing to the risk of damage. Thus, Lord Phillips commented (at [70]) that: "Section 3(1) does not state that the responsible person will be liable in tort if he has materially increased the risk of a victim of mesothelioma. It states that the section applies where the responsible person is liable in tort for materially increasing that risk. Whether and in what circumstances liability in tort attaches to one who has materially increased the risk of a victim contracting mesothelioma remains a question of common law. That law is presently contained in *Fairchild* and *Barker*." Lord Rodger put the matter succinctly (at [131]): "Section 3 was not concerned with prescribing the basis for defendants being held responsible for claimants' mesothelioma. Rather, its purpose was to reverse the decision of the House of Lords in *Barker*". See further para.**2–62A** of this Supplement.

4. Causation in Law

(b) *Intervening acts*

(ii) *Intervening conduct of a third party*

2–105   Add: In *Chubb Fire Ltd v Vicar of Spalding* [2010] EWCA Civ 981; [2010] 2 C.L.C. 277; [2010] N.P.C. 92 at [54]–[73] Aikens L.J. analysed a case of intervening acts (vandals setting off a fire extinguisher in a church; suppliers of the fire extinguisher had allegedly failed to advise the church about the respective cost of cleaning up the resultant mess associated with different types of extinguisher) drawing upon the four issues set out in what is now para.**2–105**. In broad terms, said his Lordship, the issue is now considered in terms of whether it is "fair" to hold the defendants responsible (citing Lord Bingham in *Corr v IBC Vehicles Ltd* [2008] UKHL 13; [2008] 1 A.C. 884 at [15]: "The rationale of the principle that a novus actus interveniens breaks the chain of causation is fairness"; see para.**2–129** of the Main Work). This, said Aikens L.J., at [64], involves a value judgment: "If 'remoteness of damage' and 'causation' are means of deciding who is to be responsible for things that have happened, then in all cases the ultimate question is: what is the extent of the loss for which a defendant ought fairly or reasonably or justly to be held liable." The answer, on the particular facts, was that it was unfair to hold the suppliers of the fire extinguisher liable for the actions of the vandals. Arden and Longmore L.JJ. agreed that the action failed on the basis that the church had not proved that it would have chosen a different option even if the correct advice had been given. They expressed no view on the question of intervening acts.

2–116   NOTE 372. Add: See further *Wright (A Child) v Cambridge Medical Group* [2011] EWCA Civ 669; [2013] Q.B. 312 where a general practitioner had negligently delayed referring the claimant to hospital by two days, and following negligent treatment by the hospital the patient developed a permanent disability in the hip. The general practitioner argued that the delay had not caused the loss because with appropriate treatment at the hospital the disability would have been avoided. The trial judge proceeded on the basis that even if the claimant had been referred promptly by the general practitioner it was probable that the hospital would have treated the claimant negligently on that hypothetical occasion also, so that the delay in referral had not caused the disability. The Court of Appeal held that, on the facts, the judge was not entitled to draw the inference that the hospital would probably have been negligent whenever the claimant had been referred, though Lord Neuberger M.R. went further, holding that this inference was not open to the judge as a matter of law. His Lordship derived this proposition from consideration of the statement of Lord Browne-Wilkinson in *Bolitho v City and Hackney Health Authority* [1998] A.C. 232 at 240 that a defendant cannot escape liability by saying that the damage would have occurred in any event because he would have committed some other breach of duty thereafter (see para.2–21 of the Main Work). Lord Neuberger M.R. suggested (at [58]) that one reason why this proposition is correct is that: "by committing the breach of duty, the doctor has prevented the patient from the opportunity of being treated appropriately, and had the patient had that opportunity, she would have had a claim for the same damage against the doctor for the very negligence upon which the doctor is relying to avoid liability. In other words, if a negligent doctor contends that the damage would have occurred anyway, because he would have committed a subsequent act of negligence, the patient can say that, if that argument is correct, it gets the doctor nowhere: as a result of his breach of duty, the doctor has deprived her of the right to claim for damages for the subsequent (if notional) act of negligence." The same reasoning applied where the hypothetical negligence was not that of the defendant, but of a third party such as a hospital, so that "in a case where a doctor has negligently failed to refer his patient to a hospital, and, as a consequence, she has lost the opportunity to be treated as she should have been by a hospital, the doctor cannot escape liability by establishing that the hospital would have negligently failed to treat the patient appropriately, even if he had promptly referred her. Even if the doctor established this, it would not enable him to escape liability, because, by negligently failing to refer the patient promptly, he deprived her of the opportunity to be treated properly by the hospital, and, if they had not treated her properly, that opportunity would be reflected by the fact that she would have been able to recover damages from them" (at [61]). Nor could it be said that the hospital's negligence had broken the chain of causation. The hospital's failure to treat the claimant properly "was not such an egregious event, in terms of the degree or unusualness of the negligence, or the period of time for which it lasted, to defeat or destroy the causative link between the defendants' negligence and the claimant's injury" (at [37] per Lord Neuberger M.R.). (Elias L.J. dissented as to the outcome on the basis that the claimant's permanent disability did not fall within the scope of the general practitioner's duty; sed quaere). For further comment see N. McBride and S. Steel, "Suing for the loss of a right to sue: why *Wright* is wrong" (2012) 28 P.N. 27; J. McQuater [2011] J.P.I.L. C172.

(iii) *Intervening conduct of the claimant*

2–120   Add: See also *Dalling v R J Heale & Co Ltd* [2011] EWCA Civ 365 where the defendants' negligence resulted in a head injury to the claimant producing "executive dysfunction", which, inter alia, changed his drinking habits markedly. Prior to the accident the claimant rarely drank to excess, but after the accident he frequently drank to excess because the head injury had reduced his ability to control his drinking. More than three years after the original accident the claimant fell whilst drunk and sustained a further head injury. The Court of Appeal accepted that the tort had impaired the claimant's ability to control his drinking so that the act of getting drunk was not a free and voluntary act. On that basis it was fair to hold the defendants partially responsible for the injuries attributable to the fall whilst the claimant was drunk (damages being reduced by one third for the claimant's contributory negligence).

In *Smith v Youth Justice Board for England and Wales* [2010] EWCA Civ 99 the claimant was a custody officer at a secure training centre. Together with two other officers, she was involved in the physical restraint of a 15-year-old boy who died as a consequence of the manner in which the procedure was used. She claimed damages for post-traumatic stress disorder on the basis that the defendants had negligently authorised the continuing use of a dangerous system of restraint. The Court of Appeal rejected the claim on the basis that, even if the defendants had been negligent to permit the continued use of the restraint technique, two things had intervened between that breach and the boy's death: unnecessary use of the technique in breach of the rules which rendered it an assault that the boy was entitled to resist; and excessive use by the officers' continuing with the hold in spite of the boy's manifestations of distress which were clear and were ignored. Responsibility for the boy's death (and its effect on the claimant's mental health) lay with the claimant (along with the other two officers): "It would be rightly regarded as unjust if she were to recover damages for its effect on her" (at [36] per Sedley L.J.). The claim thus failed, not on the ground of public policy (which had been rejected by the trial judge), but on the ground of causation. Sedley L.J. (repeating the views he had expressed in *Spencer v Wincanton Holdings Ltd* [2009] EWCA Civ 1404; [2010] P.I.Q.R. P8) held that the causal effects of an event will come to an end "when it becomes unfair to let it continue."

2–121   NOTE 389. Add: cf. *Dalling v R J Heale & Co Ltd* [2011] EWCA Civ 365 (see para.**2–120** of this Supplement).

5. REMOTENESS OF DAMAGE

(c) *Remoteness and liability in negligence for pure economic loss*

(ii) *Impact of SAAMCO*

2–175   **Non-recoverable economic loss.** NOTE 534. After the first sentence, ending "the position may have been different" Add: See *Rubenstein v HSBC Bank Plc* [2011] EWHC 2304 (QB); [2012] P.N.L.R. 7 at [106] per Judge Havelock-Allan Q.C., distinguishing *Andrews v Barnett Waddingham LLP (a firm)* on precisely this point (reversed on appeal, but not affecting this point: [2012] EWCA Civ 1184; [2013] P.N.L.R. 9).

Add at the end of the Note: See also *Haugesund Kommune v Depfa ACS Bank* [2011] EWCA Civ 33; [2011] 3 All E.R. 655 where the defendant solicitors were in breach of duty in failing to advise a lender that swap transactions entered into with Norwegian municipalities were invalid. The Court of Appeal held that, notwithstanding that the lender would not have entered into the transactions had it been informed of their invalidity, the lender was not entitled to recover losses attributable to the creditworthiness or impecuniosity of the municipalities or to the lender's inability to enforce a judgment against the municipalities from the solicitors because such losses fell outside the scope of the solicitors' duty, which was limited to advising on the validity of the transactions.

Recoverable loss At the end of the paragraph add: In *Rubenstein v HSBC Bank*   **2–176** *Plc* [2011] EWHC 2304 (QB); [2012] P.N.L.R. 7 the defendant bank had advised the claimant to invest in a particular investment fund, on the basis that it was equivalent to, and so as safe as, a cash deposit. The claimant lost a substantial sum following the collapse of Lehman Brothers in September 2008 which resulted in a loss of confidence in the financial markets, and a consequent reduction in the value of the fund. His Honour Judge Havelock-Allan Q.C., sitting as a High Court judge, held that the claimant's financial loss was too remote, because the "extraordinary and unprecedented financial turmoil which surrounded the collapse of Lehman Brothers" was not reasonably foreseeable by the defendants. The Court of Appeal overturned this ruling ([2012] EWCA Civ 1184; [2013] P.N.L.R. 9). Relating the scope of the defendants' duty to the issue of remoteness of the damage, Rix L.J. commented (at [115]): "[The defendants' financial adviser] misled his client, by omission and commission, into thinking that he had invested in something which was the same as cash. This is not, to my mind, a promising context in which to find that a loss suffered as a result of following a recommendation to enter into an unsuitable investment, when that loss came about because of the very factor which made the investment unsuitable (namely its inherent susceptibility to risk from market movements) was too remote to be recovered from the defaulting advising bank." The insolvency of Lehman Brothers may have been unforeseeable, but the claimant was not invested in Lehman Brothers. It was the collapse in the value of the market securities in which the claimant's money had been invested which caused the loss, "but such a loss was both foreseeable and foreseen" (at [117]). But in any event, the claimant had been advised that the investment into which he had put his money was the same as a cash deposit, which it was not: "It was the bank's duty to protect Mr Rubenstein from exposure to market forces when he made clear that he wanted an investment which was without any risk (and when the bank told him that his investment was the same as a cash deposit). It is wrong in such a context to say that when the risk from exposure to market forces arises, the bank is free of responsibility because the incidence of market loss was unexpected" (at [118]).

Loss attributable to negligent advice. At the end of the paragraph insert a new   **2–177** Note 541a:

NOTE 541a. "The key to the giving of advice is that the information is either accompanied by a comment or value judgment on the relevance of that information to the client's investment decision, or is itself the product of a process of selection involving a value judgment so that the information will tend to influence the decision of the recipient. In both these scenarios the information acquires the character of a recommendation": *Rubenstein v HSBC Bank Plc* [2011] EWHC 2304 (QB); [2012] P.N.L.R. 7at [81] per Judge Havelock-Allan Q.C. (The decision was reversed on appeal, but the issue of whether the defendants had given the claimant advice rather than information was not contested in the appeal: [2012] EWCA Civ 1184; [2013] P.N.L.R. 9).

CHAPTER 3

GENERAL DEFENCES

		PARA.
1.	Introduction	3–01
□ 2.	Claimant's wrongdoing (*ex turpi causa*).	3–02
□	(a) Conceptual foundation of *ex turpi causa*	3–04
	□ (i) Impossible to determine the standard of care	3–05
	(ii) Affront to the public conscience	3–06
	(iii) Claimant's reliance on his own illegality.	3–07
	■ (iv) The integrity of the legal system	3–11
	(v) Relationship to duty of care in negligence.	3–20
	■ (vi) Which test?.	3–22
	(b) Applying *ex turpi causa*	3–29
	■ (i) Seriousness of the claimant's conduct	3–30
	■ (ii) Connection with the claimant's injury	3–33
	■ (iii) Proportionality	3–36
	■ (iv) Illegality in the context of the employment relationship	3–38
	(v) Property rights	3–41
	(vi) Trespassers.	3–42
	(vii) Relationship to other defences	3–43
3.	Contributory negligence	3–44
	■ (a) Fault of the claimant	3–44
	(b) Contribution to damage.	3–45
	■ (c) Scope of contributory negligence	3–51
	■ (d) The standard of care	3–65
	(e) Doctrine of identification	3–79
	(f) Proof of contributory negligence	3–82
	□ (g) Apportionment	3–83
4.	Consent and assumption of risk	3–87
	(a) Consent	3–87
	□ (b) Volenti non fit injuria	3–91
	(i) Claimant's agreement.	3–93
	(ii) Agreement must be voluntary	3–98
	□ (iii) Claimant's knowledge	3–100
	□ (iv) Statutory defence of consent	3–105
	(v) Vehicle accidents	3–106
	■ (vi) Work accidents.	3–109
	(vii) Rescuers.	3–114
	(viii) Sport.	3–115
	(ix) Volenti and contributory negligence	3–117
5.	Exclusion of liability.	3–118
	(a) Unfair Contract Terms Act 1977.	3–119
	(b) Exclusions and third parties	3–124
6.	Miscellaneous defences	3–128
	(a) Necessity.	3–128
	■ (b) Self-defence	3–138
	(c) Authorisation.	3–142
	(d) Mistake	3–152
	(e) Inevitable accident	3–154
	(f) Limitation	3–156
	(g) Personal immunity	3–157

2. Claimant's Wrongdoing (Ex Turpi Causa)

3–03   **Ex turpi causa non oritur actio.** Add: In *Al Hassan-Daniel v Revenue and Customs Commissioners* [2010] EWCA Civ 1443; [2011] Q.B. 866 the Court of Appeal held that ex turpi causa does not apply to a claim for breach of a Convention right under the European Convention on Human Rights.

(a) *Conceptual foundation of ex turpi causa*

3–04   NOTE 19. Add: See also *Al Hassan–Daniel v Revenue and Customs Commissioners* [2010] EWCA Civ 1443; [2011] Q.B. 866 where the Court of Appeal, at [9], considered that ex turpi causa is not, strictly, a defence: "It makes simple sense that, if a claim is brought to enforce or secure the benefit of a criminal transaction, the courts should have nothing to do with it, even if it means that one party secures an illicit benefit. This is the basis of what we have called the criminality defence (though, since it is a point which the court itself will if necessary take, it is more correctly understood as a control on jurisdiction)." *Lexi Holdings Plc v DTZ Debenham Tie Leugn Ltd* [2010] EWHC 2290 (Ch) at [11] per Briggs J.: "In a clear case the court may have to take the point of its own motion".

(i) *Impossible to determine standard of care*

3–05   NOTE 21. Add: Note that in *Miller v Miller* [2011] HCA 9; (2011) 275 A.L.R. 611 the High Court of Australia concluded that the illegality defence did not depend on whether it was impossible to set a standard of care: "Setting a norm of behaviour as between criminals may be difficult, but it is not impossible" (at [54]). The issue was whether the court should set a standard of care in the particular case, and this was a question of policy.

NOTE 22. Add: The decisions of the High Court of Australia in *Jackson v Harrison* and *Smith v Jenkins* must now be considered in the light of *Miller v Miller* [2011] HCA 9; (2011) 275 A.L.R. 611, taking the view that it is not impossible to specify a standard of care as between "joy-riders"; the issue was whether it would be "incongruous" for the law to proscribe the claimant's conduct and yet allow recovery in negligence for damage suffered in the course of that unlawful conduct (on the facts of *Miller* the answer was "no" because the claimant had ceased to be a joint participant in the crime because she had asked to be let out of the vehicle before the accident in which she was injured occurred). See further para.**3–11** of this Supplement.

(iv) *The integrity of the legal system*

3–11   Add: In *Miller v Miller* [2011] HCA 9; (2011) 275 A.L.R. 611 at [16] the High Court of Australia held that the correct approach to the illegality defence looked to: "whether there is some relevant intersection between the law that made the plaintiff's conduct unlawful and the legal principles that determine whether the plaintiff should have a cause of action for negligence against the defendant. Ultimately, the question is: would it be incongruous for the law to proscribe the plaintiff's conduct and yet allow recovery in negligence for damage suffered in the course, or as a result, of that unlawful conduct? Other questions, such as whether denial of liability will deter wrongdoers or advantage some at the expense of others, are neither helpful nor relevant. And likewise, resort to notions of moral outrage or judicial indignation serves only to mask the proper identification of what is said to produce the response and why the response could be warranted." The question of whether permitting a claim to succeed would be "incongruous" expresses a similar idea to that of maintaining the integrity of the legal system. The High Court considered that in the case of a statutory offence the court should consider whether an award of damages would be inconsistent with the purposes of the statute (at [74]). In the case of the offence of illegally taking and using a motor vehicle, one of the purposes of proscribing the conduct was because of its association with reckless and dangerous driving (it was not simply a crime against property). The court concluded that the statutory purpose of a law proscribing dangerous or reckless driving was not consistent with one offender owing a co-offender a duty to take reasonable care: "The inconsistency or incongruity arises regardless of whether reckless or dangerous driving eventuates. It arises from the recognition that the purpose of the statute is to deter and punish using a vehicle in circumstances that often lead to reckless and dangerous driving" (at [101]).

Add: The distinction between illegal conduct that was the cause of the claim-   **3–18** ant's loss and illegal conduct which merely provided the occasion for which someone else caused the loss is illustrated by two recent cases. In *Delaney v Pickett* [2011] EWCA Civ 1532; [2012] 1 W.L.R. 2149 the Court of Appeal held that a claim by a passenger injured by the negligent driving of the defendant was not defeated by the ex turpi causa defence, notwithstanding that it was probable that both the defendant and the claimant were in possession of cannabis with intent to supply it at the time of the accident. The criminal behaviour was not causally linked to the claimant's damage. As Ward L.J. put it: "It is not a question of whether or not it is impossible to determine the appropriate standard of care. We are not concerned with the integrity of the legal system. We do not need to ask whether the claim would be an affront to the public conscience. There is no need for an analysis of the pleadings to establish whether or not the claimant is relying on his illegality to found his claim. It is not a question of the claimant profiting from his own wrongdoing. Here the crucial question is whether, on the one hand, the criminal activity merely gave occasion for the tortious act of the defendant to be committed or whether, even though the accident would never have happened had they not made the journey, which at some point involved their obtaining and/ or transporting drugs with the intention to supply, or on the other hand whether the immediate cause of the claimant's damage was the negligent driving. The answer to that question is in my judgment quite clear. Viewed as a matter of causation, the damage suffered by the claimant was not caused by his or their criminal activity. It was caused by the tortious act of the defendant in the negligent way in which he drove his motor car. In those circumstances the illegal acts are incidental and the claimant is entitled to recover his loss" (at [37]; see also per Tomlinson L.J. at [73]: "there was no relevant nexus between the illegality upon which the claimant was engaged and the tortious conduct of [the defendant] which gave rise to his injuries"). [Mr Delaney's success in his tort claim against Mr Pickett was a Pyrrhic victory, however, since the Court of Appeal went on to decide (Ward L.J. dissenting) that the claimant's illegal conduct was such that the Motor Insurers'

Bureau was entitled to exclude liability under cl.6(1)(e)(iii) of the MIB Agreement which permits the MIB to avoid liability where the claimant "knew or ought to have known that . . . the vehicle was being used in the course or furtherance of a crime"].

On the other hand, in *Joyce v O'Brien* [2012] EWHC 1324 (QB); [2012] P.I.Q.R. P18 the claimant was injured when he fell from the rear of a van being driven by the defendant. The parties had jointly stolen a set of ladders from a house and the ladders were too long to fit into the van with the rear doors closed, so the claimant was standing on the rear footplate holding onto the ladders and the van when he lost his grip. Cooke J. held that applying the causation test for ex turpi causa the claim must fail: "Speed was of the essence of the getaway and the claimant's actions were an essential part of the joint enterprise. His injuries were caused by a combination of the first defendants' driving at speed and his position on the back, which made that driving dangerous. What he was doing was so unusual as to be as causative of his injuries as the driving, both of which were part of the criminal activity in which they were both engaged" (at [37]). This decision was upheld on appeal ([2013] EWCA Civ 546). Elias L.J. (with whom Rafferty and Ryder L.JJ. agreed) indicated (at [27]) that the same causation principle should apply whether the criminal is acting alone or as part of a joint enterprise. The additional feature in a joint enterprise claim is that "the claimant may be denied recovery not merely where the injury results directly from his own criminal conduct, but also where it results from the action of a joint participator carried on in furtherance of the joint enterprise. In certain cases the injury will still be treated as having been caused by the claimant even though the direct cause of the injury was his co-defendant." For this purpose the "injury will be caused by, rather than occasioned by, the criminal activity of the claimant where the joint criminal illegality affects the standard of care which the claimant is reasonably entitled to expect from his partner in crime. This is consistent with the result in [*Ashton v Turner* [1981] Q.B. 137 and *Pitts v Hunt* [1991] 1 Q.B. 24], but it focuses on causation rather than duty" (at [28]). Elias L.J. said (at [29]) that the principle was: "where the character of the joint criminal enterprise is such that it is foreseeable that a party or parties may be subject to unusual or increased risks of harm as a consequence of the activities of the parties in pursuance of their criminal objectives, and the risk materialises, the injury can properly be said to be caused by the criminal act of the claimant even if it results from the negligent or intentional act of another party to the illegal enterprise. I do not suggest that this necessarily exhausts situations where the ex turpi principle applies in joint enterprise cases, but I would expect it to cater for the overwhelming majority of cases." For Elias L.J. this approach had the effect of re-casting the cases suggesting that when ex turpi causa applies to a joint enterprise case no duty of care is owed, to give effect to Lord Hoffmann's causation principle (from *Gray v Thames Trains Ltd*). On the facts in *Joyce v O'Brien* the claimant's own carelessness in taking the risk he did as part of his criminal offending was a cause of, and not merely the occasion of, his injury. There was "no sensible basis for asserting that the very act which naturally arises in a quick getaway, namely driving too fast for the nature of the road, takes the case outside the scope of the joint enterprise. Indeed, the accident which occurred was precisely the kind of accident which might have been foreseen as the result of the particular getaway arrangements even if the [defendant] had not been driving so dangerously" (at [46]).

(vi) *Which test?*

After the third sentence, ending ". . . a wider perception of the integrity of the   **3–26**
legal system" insert: Nonetheless the courts remain anxious to avoid giving the
impression that they have a discretion to refuse a claim based on the public
conscience. In *Les Laboratoires Servier v Apotex Inc* [2012] EWCA Civ 593;
[2013] Bus. L.R. 80 at [93] Laws L.J. commented: "Nor can the rule be founded
on a discretionary power to give effect to the public conscience. If it was, it would
be no more than a plea to how the merits struck the judge, and that would be too
fragile and amorphous a basis on which to secure the law's integrity."

(b) *Applying ex turpi causa*

(i) *Seriousness of claimant's conduct*

NOTE 99. Add: See also *Joyce v O'Brien* [2013] EWCA Civ 546 at [51]–[52]   **3–30**
per Elias L.J., para.**3–36** of this Supplement.

NOTE 106. Add: The Court of Appeal reversed the trial judge, not on the ques-   **3–31**
tion of the seriousness of a breach of the Competition Act 1998, but on the question of whether the liability of the claimant companies was primary or vicarious:
Safeway Stores Ltd v Twigger [2010] EWCA Civ 1472; [2011] 2 All E.R.841. It
was held that liability under the Act was direct and so the question of whether the
defendants "were the 'directing mind and will' of the companies does not come
into the matter" (at [25]). If the liability of the company was personal (rather than
merely vicarious) then there was no impediment to the application of ex turpi
causa (except, perhaps, in cases of strict liability where there has been no intention or negligence on the part of any person) (at [26]). Given that the companies
were personally liable to pay the penalties imposed under the Act, it would be
inconsistent with that liability for them to be able to recover those penalties in the
civil courts from the defendants (who were therefore granted summary judgment
on the basis that ex turpi applied).
   NOTE 107. An appeal on a different point was refused: *Nayyar v Denton Wilde
Sapte* [2010] EWCA Civ 815.
   At the end of para.**3–31** insert new para.**31A**.

Breach of civil law In *Les Laboratoires Servier v Apotex Inc* [2011] EWHC 730   **3–31A**
(Pat); [2011] R.P.C. 20 Arnold J. held that application of the ex turpi causa rule
was not limited to criminal conduct or tortious acts involving moral turpitude
amounting to dishonesty. The defendants sought compensation under a cross-
undertaking in damages given by the claimants when the claimants were granted
an interim injunction restraining the defendants from importing or marketing a
drug in the United Kingdom, allegedly in breach of patents in both Europe and
Canada. The European patent was subsequently held to be invalid, but in Canada
the courts held that the Canadian patent was valid and the defendants had infringed
it. The defendants alleged that they had lost profits because of the injunction. The
claimants argued that ex turpi causa applied and the defendants could not recover
damages for being prevented from selling a product whose manufacture infringed
a valid foreign patent. Arnold J. accepted the claimants' argument. *Safeway Stores*

Ltd v Twigger [2010] EWCA Civ 1472; [2011] 2 All E.R. 841 (see para.**3–31** of this Supplement) was "authority for the proposition that a quasi-criminal act committed intentionally or negligently is sufficiently serious to engage the *ex turpi causa* rule" (at [91]). The authorities did not require that in the case of a merely tortious act the rule only applied if the act involved dishonesty. There would be situations where the tort was not sufficiently serious to engage the rule, but that would depend on the facts of the case, and the "key factor in most cases is likely to be the claimant's state of knowledge at the time of committing the act in question. If the claimant knew the material facts, and particularly if he committed the act in question intentionally, then the rule is likely to apply" (at [93]). On appeal the Court of Appeal reversed Arnold J.'s decision: [2012] EWCA Civ 593; [2013] Bus. L.R. 80. Etherton L.J. accepted that the defendants' claim to damages involved relying on an unlawful act that was sufficiently causative of its claim to engage the illegality defence (because an essential element of the claim for loss of profit was the manufacturing of a drug that would have taken place unlawfully in Canada). Whether the defence should succeed depended on "intense analysis of the particular facts and of the proper application of the various policy considerations underlying the illegality principle so as to produce a just and proportionate response to the illegality. That is not the same as an unbridled discretion" (at [75]). On the facts there were five factors which pointed against application of the illegality defence (see [81]–[88]): (1) the illegality (the infringement of the Canadian patent) constituted a statutory wrong under Canadian law irrespective of the infringer's state of mind, and the defendants honestly and reasonably believed that the Canadian patent was invalid; (2) the grant of a patent confers a monopoly and enormous economic advantages on the patentee: "It not infrequently transpires, however, that patents are open to challenge and invalid, but it takes time to secure revocation of an invalid patent. The combination of those features can not only confer on the holder of an invalid patent huge but unjustified benefits but also be greatly to the disadvantage of society. It can stifle innovation and competition". The financial benefit to the claimants of the injunction was some £60 million in profit, largely at the expense of the NHS. This, combined with the strict liability nature of patent infringement, demonstrated why "the taking of a commercial risk by a competitor to the patentee by marketing a product in breach of the patent but reasonably believing and in good faith that the patent is invalid is low on the scale of culpability in terms of the illegality defence"; (3) sales of products in the United Kingdom which had been manufactured in Canada in breach of the Canadian patent were not unlawful under either Canadian or UK law; (4) the Canadian court was not willing to grant the claimants an interlocutory injunction restraining the manufacture and export in Canada of products in breach of the Canadian patent; and (5) the defendants had conceded that there should be deducted from the award of damages to the defendants an amount equal to what the Canadian court would have ordered the defendants to pay the claimants in Canada for infringement of the Canadian patent in manufacturing and exporting products for sale in the United Kingdom had there been no interlocutory injunctions preventing sales in the United Kingdom. This put the defendants in the position in which they would have been had there been no interlocutory injunctions in the United Kingdom and without offending comity with Canada. [Etherton L.J. had already accepted, at [69], that the illegality defence could apply where the relevant illegality was under foreign law, and "in such a case, an important policy consideration, and possibly the principal one, is comity, that is to say respect for the law and courts of other countries"]. Laws L.J. (at [94]) agreed that the court should take into account a wide range of considerations in order to ensure that the defence only applies where it is a "just and proportionate response to the illegality", and that the illegality defence does not arise where the unlawful act is "merely trivial or where the illegality is the result of an inadvertent breach of some law or regulation."

(ii) *Connection with claimant's injury*

Add: The "connection" of the illegality with the claimant's injury is essentially   **3–33** a causation test for the application of ex turpi causa which, since the decision of the House of Lords in *Gray v Thames Trains*, is now increasingly used by the courts as the crucial factor: see *Delaney v Pickett* [2011] EWCA Civ 1532; [2012] 1 W.L.R. 2149 and *Joyce v O'Brien* [2013] EWCA Civ 546, para.**3–18** of this Supplement.

NOTE 114. Add: See now *Miller v Miller* [2011] HCA 9; (2011) 275 A.L.R. 611 at [50]–[56], where the High Court of Australia took a different approach to the application of the illegality defence from that of *Jackson v Harrison* (see para.**3–11** of this Supplement), though not affecting the point in the text.

NOTE 117. Add: The fraudulent exaggeration of a claim is an abuse of process and the court has jurisdiction to strike out such a claim; but the power to strike out after a trial will be exercised only in very exceptional circumstances: *Summers v Fairclough Homes Ltd* [2012] UKSC 26; [2012] 1 W.L.R. 2004.

NOTE 118. Add: See also *Joyce v O'Brien* [2013] EWCA Civ 546, para.**3–18**   **3–34** of this Supplement.

(iii) *Proportionality*

Add: In *Joyce v O'Brien* [2012] EWHC 1324 (QB); [2012] P.I.Q.R. P18 at [37]   **3–36** Cooke J. rejected the claimant's argument that a principle of proportionality should apply to weigh the seriousness of the claimant's damage against the degree of criminality of the claimant: "I am unable to detect any such element in [*Gray v Thames Trains*] or [*Delaney v Pickett*], where causation was treated as the key . . . If the question is one of causation, there is no room for the operation of any considerations of the disproportionate injury suffered as against the heinousness of the crime committed." On appeal ([2013] EWCA Civ 546), in response to the claimant's argument that a principle of proportionality should apply and that it would not be offensive to the public to permit recovery where the criminal offence was of a relatively trivial nature, Elias L.J. accepted that there should be some flexibility in the operation of ex turpi causa: "The doctrine will not apply, for example, to minor traffic offences. I suspect that in most joint criminal liability cases at least, the nature and characteristics of the principal offence will in practice determine which acts of a co-conspirator will attract the application of the ex turpi doctrine, and for relatively trivial offences the range of such acts is likely to be very limited. Nonetheless, I recognise that there may be a problem in determining in certain cases whether the offence attracts the application of the doctrine or not" (at [51]). However, on the facts (para.**3–18** of this Supplement) Elias L.J. concluded that the claim was caught by the principle of ex turpi causa: "wherever the precise line is to be drawn, the theft of these ladders would fall clearly on the side where the doctrine applies. It is not merely an imprisonable offence but carries a seven year maximum sentence; it is not a strict liability offence which may be committed without any real moral culpability" (at [52]).

(iv) *Illegality in the context of the employment relationship*

3–40   **Collateral illegality.** NOTE 147. Note that. *Vakante v Addey and Stanhope School* was affirmed by the Court of Appeal: [2004] EWCA Civ 1065; [2004] 4 All E.R. 1056; [2005] I.C.R. 231. *Vakante* was followed by the Court of Appeal in *Allen v Hounga* [2012] EWCA Civ 609; [2012] I.R.L.R. 685 (claimant's entitlement to compensation for race discrimination barred on public policy grounds since the contract of employment was tainted with illegality because she knew she was not allowed to work in the United Kingdom). An appeal to the Supreme Court in *Allen v Hounga* is pending.

3. CONTRIBUTORY NEGLIGENCE

(a) *Fault of the claimant*

3–44   NOTE 165. Add: See also *Brumder v Motornet Service and Repairs Ltd* [2013] EWCA Civ 195; [2013] 3 All E.R. 412 at [4], where it was conceded that a finding of 100 per cent contributory negligence was wrong in principle.

(c) *Scope of contributory negligence*

3–52   **Breach of statutory duty** NOTE 205. Add: See also *Brumder v Motornet Service and Repairs Ltd* [2013] EWCA Civ 195; [2013] 3 All E.R. 412, discussed at para.**13–63** of this Supplement.

3–54   **Intentional injury to the person.** Add: This paragraph must now be read in light of the decision of the Court of Appeal in *Co–operative Group (CWS) Ltd v Pritchard* [2011] EWCA Civ 329; [2012] Q.B. 320 where it was held that contributory negligence could not be relied upon as a defence to an action in trespass to the person (specifically battery or assault). This was on the basis that the analysis of the meaning of the word "fault" in Law Reform (Contributory Negligence) Act 1945 undertaken by the House in *Standard Chartered Bank v Pakistan National Shipping Corp (No.2)* [2002] UKHL 43; [2003] 1 A.C. 959 and *Reeves v Commissioner of Police for the Metropolis* [2000] 1 A.C. 360 meant that, as applied to a claimant, fault could only be taken into account if his conduct gave rise to a defence of "contributory negligence" at common law before the passing of the Act (see the discussion at para.**3–60** of the Main Work). Since there was no case before the Act which held that contributory negligence constituted a defence to assault and battery the Act could not be relied on to reduce a claimant's damages for assault and battery. Aikens L.J. concluded, at [62], that:

"Insofar as there are cases since the 1945 Act that suggest that the Act can be used to reduce damages awarded for the torts of assault or battery in a case where it is found that the claimant was 'contributorily negligent' they are unsatisfactory and cannot stand with statements of principle made in two subsequent House of Lords decisions. . . . [T]he 1945 Act cannot, in principle, be used to reduce damages in cases where claims are based on assault and battery, despite the remarks in such cases as *Lane v Holloway* and *Murphy v Culhane*, which I would say are not binding on this court. Moreover, it seems to me that such a conclusion is in keeping with the purpose of the 1945 Act, as set out in section 1(1), which was to relieve claimants whose actions would previously have failed, not to reduce the damages which would have previously have been awarded to claimants."

Smith L.J. agreed with the analysis, whilst expressing the view that it was regrettable that the court could not apportion damages where the claimant has, by his misconduct, contributed to the occurrence of the incident. However, a change in the law would require the intervention of Parliament. For discussion of the case see J. Goudkamp, "Contributory negligence and trespass to the person" (2011) 127 L.Q.R. 519.

(d) *The standard of care*

At the end of the paragraph add: On the other hand, with older children there **3-69** may be no good reason to apply a different standard of care from that applied to an adult: see *Phethean-Hubble v Coles* [2012] EWCA Civ 349; [2012] R.T.R. 31 (16-year-old cyclist who turned from the pavement into the road in front of the defendant's car held to be 50 per cent contributorily negligent; the judge had not been justified in reducing an initial assessment of 50 per cent contributory negligence to 33 per cent by reason of the claimant's age).
NOTE 262. Add: *Paramasivan v Wicks* [2013] EWCA Civ 262 (13-year-old boy held 75 per cent contributorily negligent when he ran into the road without looking); *Jackson v Murray* [2012] CSIH 100; 2013 S.L.T. 153 (13-year-old 70 per cent contributorily negligent in crossing a rural two way road without looking from behind a school minibus).

Contributory negligence of disabled persons For consideration of whether a **3-70** claimant's mental and physical disabilities should be taken into account in assessing contributory negligence see *Town of Port Hedland v Hodder (No.2)* [2012] WASCA 212, where there was marked disagreement in the Western Australia Court of Appeal. The claimant, who was blind, deaf, intellectually disabled and suffered from cerebral palsy, dived into the shallow end of a swimming pool, struck his head on the bottom and was rendered quadriplegic. The pool had diving blocks at the shallow end which the trial judge found were an "invitation" to dive or jump. Martin C.J., in the minority on this point, considered (at [159]) that there was no logic or justice in a system of law which took a subjective view of the claimant when it came to causation (since the tortfeasor must take the victim as he is found) and assessing compensation, but proceeded on an entirely hypothetical and unreal basis to assess the question of whether the claimant has failed to take reasonable care for his or her own safety. Martin C.J. commented that "The harshness, injustice and unfairness" of an objective approach which ignored the claimant's various disabilities was manifest: "It assumes a miracle of biblical proportions and requires the court to assess the question of contributory negligence in some parallel universe in which the blind can see, the deaf can hear, the lame can walk or even run, and the cognitively impaired are somehow restored to full functionality" (at [156]). McLure P. considered that the claimant had not been contributorily negligent, applying an objective standard ("With the exception of children, the issue of negligent breach at common law by both a plaintiff and a defendant involves a judgment that the person ought to have behaved differently, not that they were capable of doing so": at [292]); whereas Murphy J.A. would have upheld the trial judge's assessment of 10 per cent contributory negligence.

3–72   NOTE 267. Add: cf. *Belka v Prosperini* [2011] EWCA Civ 623 (pedestrian's contributory negligence assessed at two-thirds where he took take a deliberate risk in running across the road in front of a vehicle which had the right of way). In *Probert v Moore* [2012] EWHC 2324 (QB) it was held that a 13-year-old claimant who was struck from behind by a vehicle when walking along a narrow country lane in the dark had not been contributorily negligent in failing to wear a high visibility jacket.
    NOTE 268. Add: *Lightfoot v Go-Ahead Group Plc* [2011] EWHC 89 (QB); [2011] R.T.R. 27—40 per cent reduction for contributory negligence in the case of a drunken pedestrian on the road.

3–73   NOTE 273. Add: See also *Rehill v Rider Holdings Ltd* [2012] EWCA Civ 628; [2013] R.T.R. 5—pedestrian who stepped onto a Pelican crossing against the red light, and into the path of a bus, held 50 per cent contributorily negligent.

3–75   NOTE 284. Add: See also *Hughes v Williams* [2013] EWCA Civ 455; [2013] P.I.Q.R. P17 (mother negligent in restraining three-year-old child on a booster seat, for which the child did not meet the height or age criteria, rather than a forward facing child seat with a 5-point harness; mother held liable to 25 per cent contribution under the Civil Liability (Contribution) Act 1978).

3–78   **Contributory negligence in rescue cases.** Add: In *Tolley v Carr* [2010] EWHC 2191 (QB); [2011] R.T.R. 7 the claimant was attempting to move a vehicle that had come to a halt in the outside lane of a motorway when he was struck by two other vehicles, suffering serious injuries. Hickinbottom J. rejected the defendants' contention that the claimant had been contributorily negligent. In *Baker v TE Hopkins & Sons Ltd* [1959] 1 W.L.R. 966 at 977 Morris L.J. had considered that a rescuer could be contributorily negligent: "If a rescuer acts with a wanton disregard of his own safety it might be that in some circumstances it might be held that an injury to him was not the result of the negligence that caused the situation of danger." Applying this "generous approach of the common law to those who imperil themselves in order to save others from risks arising from the negligence of others", Hickinbottom J. noted (at [23]) that: "The law appreciates that a rescuer may act—and may feel impelled to act—under the pressures of the moment, where delay may be considered vital to the safety of those he is considering protecting from risk. It is not appropriate to subject a rescuer's actions, or his subjective view of the risks involved to himself and/or to others, to fine scrutiny in the court room." Moreover, "exceptional bravery is not the same as foolhardiness" (at [47]).

(g) *Apportionment*

NOTE 318. Add: The fact that a standard reduction for contributory negligence **3–84** of 25 per cent will apply to the failure to wear a seatbelt (*Froom v Butcher* [1976] Q.B. 286) and a reduction of 20 per cent will normally apply to accepting a lift from a drunken driver (*Owens v Brimmell* [1977] Q.B. 859) does not mean that a claimant who both accepted a lift from a drunken driver and failed to wear a seatbelt will be subject to a 45 per cent deduction for contributory negligence: *Best v Smyth* [2010] EWHC 1541 (QB)—maximum reduction of 30 per cent on the facts.

4. CONSENT AND ASSUMPTION OF RISK

(b) *Volenti non fit injuria*

Assuming the risk of injury. NOTE 352. Add: See also *Geary v Wetherspoon* **3–92** Plc [2011] EWHC 1506 (QB); [2011] N.P.C. 60—claimant who fell whilst attempting to slide down a banister had voluntarily assumed the risk because she "freely chose to do something which she knew to be dangerous. . . . She knew that sliding down the banisters was not permitted, but she chose to do it anyway. She was therefore the author of her own misfortune. The defendant owed no duty to protect her from such an obvious and inherent risk. She made a genuine and informed choice and the risk that she chose to run materialised with tragic consequences", per Coulson J. at [46].

(iii) *Claimant's knowledge*

Knowledge of danger. NOTE 386. Add: *Geary v Wetherspoon Plc* [2011] **3–100** EWHC 1506 (QB); [2011] N.P.C. 60 (claimant who fell whilst attempting to slide down a banister had voluntarily assumed the risk).

(iv) *Statutory defence of consent*

For discussion of recent authorities applying s.5(2) of the Animals Act 1971 see **3–105** para.**21–15** of this Supplement.

(vi) *Work accidents*

NOTE 427. Add: See also *Brumder v Motornet Service and Repairs Ltd* [2013] **3–113** EWCA Civ 195; [2013] 3 All E.R. 412, discussed at para.**13–63** of this Supplement.

6. MISCELLANEOUS DEFENCES

(b) *Self-defence*

NOTE 530. Add: The Criminal Justice and Immigration Act 2008 s.76 is **3–138** amended by the Legal Aid, Sentencing Punishment of Offenders Act 2012 s.148 and the Crime and Courts Act 2013 s.43.

CHAPTER 4

JOINT LIABILITY AND CONTRIBUTION

		PARA.
	1. Introduction	4–01
■	2. Joint and several torts	4–02
□	3. Contribution	4–12
□	4. Apportionment	4–28
■	5. Indemnity	4–30

2. JOINT AND SEVERAL TORTS

Definition of joint tortfeasors. At the end of the paragraph add: Nor will there **4–03** be joint tortfeasance where A and B are acting jointly in a potentially tortious manner, but A alone causes injury to the claimant. Thus, where two drivers are racing one another at excessive speeds, and only one driver crashes (thereby causing injury to his passenger), the other driver—though also having driven recklessly—cannot be treated as a joint tortfeasor.[4a]

NOTE 4a. *Davis v Catto* [2011] CSIH 85; 2012 Rep. L.R. 40.

In the first sentence, just after the words "and his employer" add: (even if the **4–04** employer became insolvent before the time of the trial)[4b].

NOTE 4b. *Catanzano v Studio London Ltd* UKEAT/0487/11/DM.

After Note 5 in the text insert: Equally, a parent company and its subsidiary may be regarded as joint tortfeasors in respect of loss or injury sufferred by employees of the subsidiary *so long as* a supervisory duty is borne by the parent company.[5a]

NOTE 5a. *Chandler v Cape Plc* [2012] EWCA Civ 525; [2012] 1 W.L.R. 3111; [2012] 3 All E.R. 640. As Arden L.J. explained, at [80]: "[T]his case demonstrates that in appropriate circumstances the law may impose on a parent company responsibility for the health and safety of its subsidiary's employees. Those circumstances include a situation where, as in this case, (1) the business of the parent and subsidiary are in a relevant respect the same; (2) the parent has, or ought to have, superior knowledge on some relevant aspect of health and safety in the particular industry; (3) the subsidiary's system of work is unsafe as the parent company knew, or ought to have known; and (4) the parent knew or ought to have foreseen that the subsidiary or its employees would rely on its using that superior knowledge for the employees' protection." See also para.**13–04** of this Supplement.

After Note 9 add: However, it is important to appreciate that although mere facilitation of the commission of a tort will not suffice, a sufficient common design may nonetheless be held to exist where D1 makes a more than de minimis contribution to the commission of a tort by D2. As Beatson L.J. put it: "providing that the act furthering an undoubted common design is more than *de minimis*, I do not consider that there is a further hurdle requiring it to have been 'an essential part' of or of 'real significance' to the commission of the tort".[9a]

NOTE 9a. *Fish & Fish Ltd v Sea Shepherd UK* [2012] EWCA Civ 544 at [58]. See also *Football Dataco Ltd v Sportradar GmbH* [2013] EWCA Civ 27; [2013] E.C.C. 12 (where D1 had a website containing material that infringed the intellectual property rights of C and D1's purpose in placing the material on the website was to cause or procure acts which amounted to infringements of those rights by any users of the website).

At the end of the paragraph add: On the other hand, there will be joint tortfeasance where the completion of the tort requires distinct acts on the part of both tortfeasors. An example is that of reutilising material in which the claimant has database rights. In such a case the actual infringement committed by X (i.e. that of copying the database material) is combined with the independent act of another party, Y, who makes use of the copied information. So, where a German company copied information from the internet in which the claimant (based in the United Kingdom) had database rights, and the German company then worked in tandem with a UK—based company to make that information available in the United Kingdom via an alternative internet source from that controlled by the claimant, the German company and its UK collaborator could be regarded as joint tortfeasors.[18a]

NOTE 18a. *Football Dataco Ltd v Sportradar GmbH* [2010] EWHC 2911 (Ch); [2011] F.S.R. 10. (The Court of Appeal allowed the defendants' appeal in part, but not affecting this point: [2011] EWCA Civ 330; [2011] F.S.R. 20).

4–06   **Several tortfeasors causing different damage.** NOTE 29. Delete the whole Note and substitute: Importantly, s.3 does no more than impose joint and several liability in cases where liability exists for having caused a victim to contract mesothelioma by virtue of tortious exposure to asbestos. The section does not instantiate any free-standing liability rule. It simply makes clear that the liability, which must be established in accordance with existing principles tort law—such as, in this case, D having created a material increase in the risk of C contracting mesothelioma—is joint liability. Nor does it in any way reinforce, or disturb, the common law rule that a "material increase in risk" is a more than merely de minimis increase: *Sienkiewicz v Greif* [2011] UKSC 10; [2011] 2 A.C. 229. See further paras **2–42**, **2–62A** and **2–66** of this Supplement.

3. Contribution

4–12   **Contribution and indemnity between joint tortfeasors.** At the end of the paragraph add: The words in parenthesis can have special significance in the context of the tort of inducing breach of contract, for while the parties cannot be joint tortfeasors (because the contract breaker can only be liable for breach of contract in the absence of any conspiracy), the two parties are nonetheless jointly responsible for causing the same damage.[51a]

NOTE 51a. See, e.g. *Thames Valley Housing Association Ltd v Elegant Homes (Guernsey) Ltd* [2011] EWHC 1288 (Ch); [2011] N.P.C. 54.

Who may claim contribution. At the end of the paragraph add: But if D1   **4–13**
and D2 are jointly or concurrently liable for a tort created by virtue of anti-
discrimination legislation, claims in respect of contribution are almost certainly
only justiciable in the ordinary courts since an employment tribunal does not have
jurisdiction to determine such matters.[55a]

NOTE 55a. *Beresford v Sovereign House Estates Ltd* [2012] I.C.R. D9 (EAT)
at [12] per Underhill J.

"Same damage" may entail distinguishing damages from restitution.   **4–22**
NOTE 81. Add: See in similar vein *Jubilee Motor Policies Syndicate 1231 at
Lloyd's v Volvo Truck & Bus (Southern) Ltd* [2010] EWHC 3641 (QB).

4. APPORTIONMENT

Apportionment of damages. After Note 96 in the text insert the following: So   **4–28**
wide is this discretion that the court may even decline to allow a party from whom
a contribution is sought to be joined to the action, where it forms the view that "no
court would think it just and reasonable that [the party in question] should be
ordered to make a contribution".[96a]

NOTE 96a. *African Strategic Investment (Holdings) Ltd v Main* [2011] EWHC
2223 (Ch) at [47] per Bernard Livesey Q.C.

After Note 105 in the text insert the following: Conversely, where the causative   **4–29**
potency of both parties' acts is equal, but the moral blameworthiness of one
party's conduct is significantly greater than that of the other, the court will probably depart from an equal division of the damages.[105a]

NOTE 105a. *Furmedge v Chester-Le-Street DC* [2011] EWHC 1226 (QB).

5. INDEMNITY

Contractual indemnity or contribution in respect of liability for tort. Delete   **4–30**
existing NOTE 117.

At the end of the paragraph add: Yet if such clauses are intended, effectively, to
exonerate the plant owner from negligence liability, the usual contra proferentem
approach to interpreting the exculpatory contractual term will be adopted. So, in
one case involving plant/operator hire, the contract stipulated that the hirer was to
indemnify the plant owner in respect of "all claims by any person whatsoever for
injury to person or property caused by, or in connection with, the use of the plant
during the hire period". The operator was injured by virtue of negligence on the
part of the owner and no such indemnity could be claimed. If owners intended to
exonerate themselves from their own negligence, then they had to bring their
intentions to the notice of prospective hirers in very specific terms.[117]

NOTE 117. *Jose, MacSalvors Plant Hire Ltd v Brush Transformers Ltd* [2009]
EWCA Civ 1329; [2010] T.C.L.R. 2 at [17]–[18] per Ward L.J.

4–33   Just prior to the last sentence insert the following: On the other hand, this approach will not be taken where there exists a valid indemnity agreement within an insurance contract which the defendant is unable to invoke because he fails to meet the conditions set out in the insurance agreement.[121a]

NOTE 121a. In *United Marine Aggregates Ltd v GM Welding & Engineering Ltd* [2012] EWHC 779 (TCC) D had failed to remove from an area in which welding work had been conducted all combustible material as required by the "Burning and Welding Warranty" contained in D's insurance contract. As such, D was unable to rely on the contractual indemnity contained in the insurance contract. (Reversed on appeal in relation only to the question of recoverable costs: [2013] EWCA Civ 516).

4–34   At the end of the paragraph add the following: Where the indemnity agreement is between an employee and employer, the critical question will be whether crime could be said to be committed in a misguided discharge of the employee's contractual duties. In *Coulson v News Group Newspapers Ltd*,[123a] a newspaper editor sought to rely on an indemnity agreement with his employer in order to claim back the costs of defending criminal proceedings based on the editor's illicit payments to police officers and unlawful interception of private communications. It was held that he could do so. The Court of Appeal distinguished between criminal charges arising out of the allegedly criminal manner in which he had done his job as editor, and criminal charges associated with an act that had nothing whatever to do with the performance of his job. Their Lordships gave as an example of the former, the publication of material alleged to be in contempt of court. According to McCombe L.J., such criminal charges should be seen as "the very occupational hazards of editorship" and precisely the kind of thing for which the indemnity exists.[123b]

NOTE 125a. [2012] EWCA Civ 1547; [2013] I.R.L.R. 116.

NOTE 125b. [2012] EWCA Civ 1547; [2013] I.R.L.R. 116, at [48].

4–35   Replace the last sentence with the following: Equally, if one of two joint tortfeasors agrees to indemnify the other *after* the criminal event giving rise to civil liability, the agreement can be treated as valid, for the relevant rule of public policy applies only to indemnity agreements that are made *prior* to the commission of the criminal-cum-tortious act in question.[130a]

NOTE 130a. *Mulcaire v News Group Newspapers Ltd* [2011] EWHC 3469 (Ch); [2012] Ch. 435 at [43]–[45] per Sir Andrew Morritt.

After para.**4–38** insert a new para.**4–39** as follows:

4–39   **Indemnity: mesothelioma cases**
Two particular problems concerning indemnity are apt to arise in mesothelioma cases. The first occurs where the claimant was tortiously exposed to asbestos during the currency of a third party insurance contract held by the employer, but the disease does not become manifest until many years later by which time the defendant employer has changed insurer. The second problem centres on cases where the inhalation of the relevant asbestos dust occurs over a long period of time, only part of which was covered by the policy on the basis of which the employer now seeks to claim an indemnity. In both cases, the relevant insurer may

seek to deny liability to pay all or part of any indemnity sought. In *Durham v BAI (Run Off) Ltd*,[141] the insurance policy in question made the insurer liable to indemnify the employer in respect of illness contracted or sustained by an employee during the currency of the policy. However, the mesothelioma in this case did not manifest itself, nor was it actionable, until after the relevant insurance contract had ceased. Nonetheless, Lord Mance J.S.C. held that "for the purposes of the insurances, liability for mesothelioma following upon exposure to asbestos created during an insurance period involves a sufficient 'weak' or 'broad' causal link for the disease to be regarded as 'caused' within the insurance period".[142] On this footing, the insurer was held liable to pay the indemnity. In *International Energy Group Ltd v Zurich Insurance Plc UK*,[143] by contrast, the insurance policy in question had only been in place for 6 of the 27 years during which the relevant employee had been tortiously exposed to asbestos dust. The insurer argued that it was unfair that it should be expected to pay a full indemnity when it had only been paid an insurance premium for 6 of the 27 years during which there had been tortious exposure. The Court of Appeal was unsympathetic. Adopting the reasoning of Lord Mance J.S.C. in the *Durham* case, Toulson L.J. held that "there was a sufficient causal link between Mr Carré's exposure to asbestos during the years when IEG was insured by Zurich [for Zurich to be liable to pay the indemnity in full]".[144]

NOTE 141. [2012] UKSC 14; [2012] 1 W.L.R. 867.
NOTE 142. [2012] UKSC 14; [2012] 1 W.L.R. 867 at [73].
NOTE 143. [2013] EWCA Civ 39; [2013] P.I.Q.R. P10.
NOTE 144. [2013] EWCA Civ 39; [2013] P.I.Q.R. P10 at [38].

CHAPTER 5

CAPACITY AND PARTIES

		PARA.
1.	Introduction.	5–01
2.	The Crown	5–02
	□ (a) Crown Proceedings Act 1947	5–03
	■ (b) Armed forces	5–08
	(c) Judicial and prerogative powers	5–14
	(d) Acts of state	5–16
	□ (e) Other acts	5–18
3.	Postal services	5–23
4.	Foreign states and ambassadors	5–27
	□ (a) Foreign states	5–27
	(b) Ambassadors	5–38
5.	Visiting forces	5–42
■ 6.	Bankrupts	5–45
7.	Children	5–49
8.	Persons of unsound mind	5–59
9.	Husband and wife	5–62
■ 10.	Assignees	5–64
■ 11.	Corporations	5–70
■ 12.	Unincorporated associations and trade unions	5–79
■ 13.	Partners	5–89
14.	Joint claimants	5–91
15.	Judicial acts	5–93
	□ (a) General	5–93
	(b) Error of law	5–101
	(c) Error of fact	5–106
	(d) Knowledge	5–108
	(e) Remedies	5–110
16.	Statutory protection of justices	5–113
17.	Ministerial acts	5–117
18.	Constables	5–119

2. THE CROWN

(a) *Crown Proceedings Act 1947*

Crown immunity in tort. Immediately before the last sentence in the para- **5–03**
graph insert the following: On the other hand, where tortious liability cannot be
established personally on the part of, say, a secretary of state or prison governor,
there is no point pursuing an alternative remedy against the Crown (as a "public
authority" liable for the acts or omissions of any servant, agent or other person or
entity empowered to exercise public functions) for breach of a Convention right
under ss.6–8 of the Human Rights Act 1998. That no such action will lie was
made clear by Supperstone J. in *Morgan v Ministry of Defence* [2010] EWHC
2248 (QB) at [52]. In such circumstances, he explained, "the Crown cannot be the

only public authority, and therefore there must be some limit on the circumstances in which proceedings can be brought against the Crown as opposed to some other public authority."

(b) *Armed forces*

5–09   Replace the last sentence with the following: But this focus on the exposure to radiation, rather than on any given act of negligence, may well spawn problems of evidence for the purposes of the operation of the Limitation Act 1980. For example, in *B v Ministry of Defence*[27]—a case in which soldiers had been exposed to radiation by virtue of MOD thermonuclear testing in the South Pacific in the 1950s—the question of when the soldiers could be deemed to have acquired the requisite knowledge for the purposes of the 1980 Act was only finally resolved by the Supreme Court.[27a]

NOTE 27. [2012] UKSC 9; [2013] 1 A.C. 78.

NOTE 27a. The claims had originally been issued in 2005, on the basis of the soldiers' suspicion that they had tortiously been exposed to radiation. The claimants argued, however, that it was not until 2007, when they received an expert's report confirming the likelihood that their illness was attributable to radiation exposure, that they gained the requisite knowledge for the purposes of s.14 of the Limitation Act. The Supreme Court ruled that, although it was not logically impossible to issue a claim without *sufficient knowledge* for the purposes of s.14, on the facts of this case, the claimants did in fact possess the requisite knowledge more than three years before the issue of proceedings.

5–11   **Repeal of Armed Forces Exemption.** NOTE 32. Add the following: For an example of this exemption in operation, see *Wood v Ministry of Defence* [2011] EWCA Civ 792.

5–13   **Armed forces' duty of care.** At the end of the paragraph add: On the other hand, the Supreme Court has now made clear that an action based upon breach of art.2 of the European Convention on Human Rights may be available where a soldier's life is placed in extreme jeopardy otherwise than in "battle conditions".[36a] Furthermore, it has also been held by the Supreme Court in *Smith v Ministry of Defence* that art.2 applies extra-territorially so long as the state exercises control and authority over the soldier in question.[36b] Their Lordships also made clear in that case that the common law duty to provide safe equipment and a safe system of work does exist outside battle conditions[36c]; and that such conditions are to be judged as a question of fact.[36d]

NOTE 36a. *R. (on the application of Smith) v Oxfordshire Assistant Deputy Coroner* [2010] UKSC 29; [2011] 1 A.C. 1. On the other hand, it was also pointed out that unless he or she was on a UK military base, any British soldier on active service overseas would not have been within the jurisdiction of the United Kingdom for the purposes of the European Convention on Human Rights and could not, therefore, claim the benefit of the protections afforded by the Human Rights Act 1998. But see now *Smith v Ministry of Defence* and the discussion at paras **14–69A** and **14–73** of this Supplement.

NOTE 36b. [2013] UKSC 41; [2013] 3 W.L.R. 69 at [46] per Lord Hope J.S.C. (Lord Walker, Baroness Hale and Lord Kerr JJ.S.C. agreed). For further discussion of this case see paras **14–13, 14–38, 14–69A** and **14–73** of this Supplement.
NOTE 36c. [2013] UKSC 41; [2013] 3 W.L.R. 69 at [94]-[98].
NOTE 36d. [2013] UKSC 41; [2013] 3 W.L.R. 69 at [96].

(e) *Other acts*

Delete the final sentence of the paragraph and replace with the following: **5–22** However, before such recognition and enforcement can occur, two conditions must be satisfied. The first is that "the normal conditions for recognition and enforcement of judgments are fulfilled" and the second is that "the foreign State would not have been immune if the foreign proceedings had been brought in the United Kingdom".[61a]
NOTE 61a. *NML Capital Ltd v Argentina* [2011] UKSC 31; [2011] 2 A.C. 495 at [118] per Lord Collins (with whom Lord Walker agreed), interpreting Civil Jurisdiction and Judgments Act 1982 s.31(1)(a); (4). The same conclusion was reached by Lord Phillips (at [54]).

4. FOREIGN STATES AND AMBASSADORS

(a) *Foreign states*

State Immunity Act 1978. Immediately after Note 62 in the text add the **5–27** following: Importantly, individual states within the United States of America do not constitute states for the purposes of the State Immunity Act. Rather, they are to be regarded as mere "constituent territories" within the federal state of the United States of America.[62a]
NOTE 62a. *Pocket Kings Ltd v Safenames Ltd* [2009] EWHC 2529 (Ch); [2010] Ch.438.

Immunity in tort. In the sentence following Note 70, after the words "personal **5–29** injury", insert NOTE 70a.
NOTE 70a. For these purposes, personal injury can be construed so as to include psychiatric illness "if, but only if, it was consequent on a physical injury in the sense of some damage to the body as opposed to the mind'': *Nigeria v Ogbonna* [2012] 1 W.L.R. 139 at [14] per Underhill J. (EAT).

6. BANKRUPTS

After para. **5–46** insert new para. **5–46A** as follows:

Although there is no authority that confirms this, it seems that a bankrupt may, **5–46A** in certain circumstances, be able to invoke the tort of negligence to sue for purely economic losses (so far as such losses are recoverable under that tort). The matter was considered in *Smeaton v Equifax Plc*.[127a] In that case, the respondent was a bankrupt who had had a bankruptcy order against him rescinded in May 2002. The appellant, a credit reference agency, had not been notified of its rescission and it did not amend its records concerning the respondent. In July 2006 the respondent had his application for a business loan declined on the basis of "adverse data" on his credit file. The respondent then brought an action against the appellant alleging, inter alia, that his inability to secure the loan had resulted in a loss of projected profits for his new company. The respondent sought to base his claim on an assumed responsibility owed to all those whose personal data the appellant held. On the facts, the Court of Appeal held that no duty was owed. It would not, they said, be appropriate to conclude that a credit rating agency had assumed a responsibility to every member of the public simply by virtue of running that kind of business.[127b] Concerns about indeterminate liability also served to rule out the imposition of a duty of care on the basis of the *Caparo* test. In particular, the third limb of that test could not be satisfied since the prospect of indeterminate liability would place an unreasonable burden on the appellant to do what would be necessary in order to guarantee that its records would be fully up to date.[127c] Interestingly, however, what was *not* ruled out in this case was the notion that a bankrupt might *in principle* succeed in a negligence action for pure economic loss.

NOTE 127a. [2013] EWCA Civ 108; [2013] 2 All E.R. 959.

NOTE 127b. [2013] EWCA Civ 108; [2013] 2 All E.R. 959 at [74] per Tomlinson L.J.

NOTE 127c. [2013] EWCA Civ 108; [2013] 2 All E.R. 959 at [75] per Tomlinson L.J.

10. ASSIGNEES

5–64 **Assignees.** After Note 200 in the text insert the following: Although the extent to which causes of action in tort can be assigned is still less than fully settled, the Court of Appeal introduced some measure of clarification in *Simpson v Norfolk and Norwich University Hospital NHS Trust*.[200a] The appellant argued that a bare cause of action for personal injuries inflicted by virtue of the defendant's negligence was incapable of assignment. There, in deciding the case, the Court of Appeal stipulated as follows. First, a right to recover compensation for personal injury could not be assigned so long as it was an essentially personal chose in action. But as Moore-Bick L.J. pointed out, "the obligation to pay compensation, which arises by operation of law, is not one that is personal in the sense that it depends upon the identity of the claimant".[200b] As such it could be regarded as a chose in action—a species of property within the meaning of s.136 of the Law of Property Act 1925—and therefore assignable. Secondly, and by way of caveat, his Lordship went on to add that, on public policy grounds, the law would not recognise the assignment of a right to litigate if the person acquiring that right lacked sufficient interest, or if the assignment was only taken in order to enable the assignee to make a profit out of the litigation.[200c] Unfortunately, the Court of Appeal failed to offer absolute clarity here when it observed that perceptions of what is in the public interest change over time, thus rendering it uncertain just when exactly an assignment would be considered void for reasons of public policy. And in the very same paragraph of its judgment, the Court of Appeal also pointed out that it was not possible to state definitively what will amount to a sufficient interest in order to render the assignment valid.[200d]

NOTE 200a. [2011] EWCA Civ 1149; [2012] Q.B. 640.

NOTE 200b. [2011] EWCA Civ 1149; [2012] Q.B. 640 at [9].

NOTE 200c. [2011] EWCA Civ 1149; [2012] Q.B. 640 at [24].

NOTE 200d. [2011] EWCA Civ 1149; [2012] Q.B. 640 at [24].

11. CORPORATIONS

After para.**5–78** insert new para.**5–78A** as follows:

Liability of parent companies. If a parent company can be shown to be in **5–78A** breach of a personal duty owed to employees of a subsidiary company, that parent company may be held liable for a breach of that duty, even if the subsidiary company has ceased to exist. So, in one case in which it was held that the parent company was under an ongoing duty to provide health and safety advice to the employees of its subsidiary, the fact that its subsidiary had ceased to trade did not absolve the parent company of its joint and several liability towards the former employees.[254a]

NOTE 254a. *Chandler v Cape Plc* [2012] EWCA Civ 525; [2012] 1 W.L.R. 3111. See also paras **4–04** and **13–04** of this Supplement.

12. UNINCORPORATED ASSOCIATIONS AND TRADE UNIONS

Unincorporated associations. NOTE 259. Insert at the beginning of the Note: **5–79** For application of this rule, see *Astellas Pharma v Stop Huntingdon Animal Cruelty* [2011] EWCA Civ 752; (2011) 155(26) S.J.L.B. 27.

Trade unions: tort liability. After the sentence ending "were 'authorised or **5–85** endorsed' by the trade union", add the following: However, there is also a set of procedural requirements that must be met. These include giving the employer notice of the intention to put a strike ballot to union members and a requirement that the employer be told how many of its workforce are union members likely to be affected.[273a] Any failure to comply with these procedural requirements may ground an application by the employer for an interim injunction restraining the union from undertaking the proposed industrial action.[273b]

NOTE 273a Trade Union and Labour Relations Act 1992 s.226A.

NOTE 273b *Metroline Travel Ltd v Unite* [2012] EWHC 1778 (QB); [2012] I.R.L.R. 749.

Also, add to the end of the paragraph: On the other hand, where it is not the case that the conduct in question is clearly tortious, and it in fact seems likely that the defendant union will be able to establish a trade dispute defence, no such interim injunction will be granted.[276a]

NOTE 276a. *Balfour Beatty Engineering Services Ltd v Unite* [2012] EWHC 267 (QB); [2012] I.C.R. 822; *London Underground Ltd v Associated Society of Locomotive Engineers and Firemen* [2011] EWHC 3506 (QB); [2012] I.R.L.R. 196.

5–87   **Vicarious liability.** After the first sentence insert the following: So, for example, it is perfectly possible for an unincorporated association of lay brothers to be liable for the torts committed by brothers who perform teaching duties at a school. However, for such vicarious liability to be imposed, two hurdles had to be crossed. First, it had to be shown that the relationship between the defendant association and the brother actually perpetrating abuse was sufficiently akin to that of employer and employee. Secondly, it had to be shown that the defendants had placed the abuser in such a position not merely that the abuser could carry on the business of the defendant, but also in a manner which created or significantly increased the risk that the victim would suffer abuse.[277a]

NOTE 277a. *Catholic Child Welfare Society v The Institute of the Brothers of the Christian Schools* [2012] UKSC 56; [2012] 3 W.L.R. 1319. See further para.**6–01**.

5–88   **Defamation.** At the end of the paragraph add: On the other hand, it has been mooted obiter that there may be a variant tort—namely, "business defamation"— which is animated by the fact that defamatory claims made about the union have the capacity to "adversely affect the union's ability to keep its members or attract new ones or to maintain a convincing attitude towards employers".[281a] That the tort would be a variant of the traditional tort of defamation was thought explicable in terms of the fact that it neither reflects on the claimant's character or personal qualities (as would an ordinary claim for defamation), nor requires proof of malice (as would the tort of malicious falsehood). However, perhaps the safest conclusion is not that this case establishes a new tort of business defamation but merely that loss of reputation may mean something different from the norm where it is the business interest of a non-human claimant, rather than an individual's standing in the eyes of the community, that is at stake.

NOTE 281a. See *Thornton v Telegraph Media Group Ltd* [2010] EWHC 1414 (QB); [2011] 1 W.L.R. 1985 at [37] (quoting Lord Keith in *Derbyshire CC v Times Newspapers Ltd* [1993] A.C. 534 at 547).

13. Partners

5–89   After Note 283 in the text add the following: And although the Protection from Harassment Act 1997 makes reference to a person pursuing a course of conduct that amounts to harassment, it has been held that it is perfectly appropriate to regard a partnership as "a person" for the purposes of the civil action that that statute makes available.[283a]

NOTE 283a. *Iqbal v Dean Manson Solicitors* [2011] EWCA Civ 123; [2011] I.R.L.R. 428.

NOTE 282. Delete the sentence referring to *Dubai Aluminium Co Ltd v Salaam.*

Also, after Note 282 in the main text insert the following: The question of whether any given act has been done in the ordinary course of business is one of fact. Depending on the circumstances, even fraudulent conduct may sometimes be treated as having been done in this way.[282a] But if X has several businesses, and Y is a partner in only one or some of them, any fraudulent representation made by X under the auspices of a business venture that he runs alone will not result in liability on Y's part if Y is ignorant of, and in no way sanctions or agrees with the making of, the fraudulent representation. In such circumstances, the fact that X's fraudulent misrepresentation stated that Y was his partner will not suffice to bring Y within s.14 of the Partnership Act 1890 (which extends liability to a person "who knowingly suffers himself to be represented, as a partner in a particular firm").[282b]

NOTE 282a. *Dubai Aluminium Co Ltd v Salaam* [2002] UKHL 48; [2003] 2 A.C. 366.

NOTE 282b. *UCB Home Loans Corp Ltd v Soni* [2013] EWCA Civ 62.

After para.**5–90** insert new para.**5–90A**:

From time to time, partnerships—such as those formed by solicitors—may **5–90A** merge or otherwise reconstitute themselves (for example, as limited liability partneships). In such cases, the newly constituted partnership will not generally bear an ongoing commitment or duty to keep under review all previous advice proffered by the earlier partnership if at the time of the merger or reconstitution, the retainer was complete. As Akenhead J. explained in *Shepherd Construction v Pinsent Masons LLP*[287a]: "There is something commercially and professionally worrying if professional people are held responsible for reviewing all previous advice or indeed services provided. There is a difference to be drawn between a specific retainer or commission which imposes a continuing duty on a professional to keep earlier advice or services under review and some sort of obligation which requires the professional to review and revise previous advice given, or services provided, on commissions or retainers which are complete."

NOTE 287a. [2012] EWHC 43 (TCC); [2012] B.L.R. 213 at [31].

15. JUDICIAL ACTS

(a) *General*

Judicial acts. Replace the second sentence in the paragraph with the following: **5–94** So, for example, a disciplinary tribunal can be characterised as acting judicially,[298a] as can certain acts of subordinate officers of courts of justice, even though many of their duties are purely ministerial.

NOTE 298a. *Baxendale-Walker v Middleton* [2011] EWHC 998 (QB).

CHAPTER 6

VICARIOUS LIABILITY

	PARA.
■ 1. Introduction	6–01
2. Liability for employees.	6–04
(a) Relationship of employer and employee	6–04
■ (i) Control test	6–07
(ii) The organisation test	6–10
□ (iii) Multiple test	6–11
■ (b) Particular types of employment	6–17
□ 3. Liability of the employer	6–28
□ (a) Course of employment	6–29
■ (b) Examples	6–32
4. Independent contractors	6–56
(a) General	6–56
(b) Statutory non-delegable duties	6–58
□ (c) Common law non-delegable duties	6–60
(d) Casual or collateral negligence	6–72
5. Loan of chattel	6–74
6. Principal and agent	6–78
7. Ratification of torts	6–80
8. Limitations on liability	6–83

1. INTRODUCTION

Scope of chapter. Replace the third sentence as follows: While this classical **6–01** understanding of vicarious liability tends to relate simply to the commission of a common law tort by an employee, it is clear that vicarious liability is neither limited to the commission of common law torts, nor to the commission of torts by those who are employees in the strict sense.[1a]

NOTE 1a. According to Lord Phillips J.S.C. in *Various Claimants v Catholic Child Welfare Society* [2012] UKSC 56; [2012] 3 W.L.R. 1319, the question of whether D2 can be held vicariously liable for the torts of D1 involves a two-stage test. The first stage, he said (at [21]), involves considering "the relationship of D1 and D2 to see whether it is one that is capable of giving rise to vicarious liability". He later made clear (at [49]) that the way to determine whether it is so capable is by asking "whether the workman was working on behalf of an enterprise or on his own behalf and, if the former, how central the workman's activities were to the enterprise and whether these activities were integrated into the organisational structure of the enterprise". More specifically, his Lordship, endorsed (at [47]) the preparedness of the Court of Appeal in *JGE v Trustees of the Portsmouth Roman Catholic Diocesan Trust* [2012] EWCA Civ 938; [2013] 2 W.L.R. 958 to extend vicarious liability to those whose relationships were simply very much "akin to that between an employer and an employee".

2. LIABILITY FOR EMPLOYEES

(a) *Relationship of employer and employee*

(i) *Control test*

6–09   Change the heading as follows: **Limitations of the control test.**

Also, Replace the last sentence of the paragraph as follows: Recognising this, Lord Phillips has since set out a much more limited role for the control test in the modern era. In his view, "it is not realistic to look for a right to direct how an employee should perform his duties as a necessary element in the relationship between employer and employee . . . Thus the significance of control today is that the employer can direct what the employee does, not how he does it".[30a]

NOTE 30a. *Various Claimants v Catholic Child Welfare Society* [2012] UKSC 56; [2012] 3 W.L.R. 1319 at [36].

(iii) *Multiple test*

6–12   **No universal test.** Add to the first sentence of the paragraph the following: and regardless of whether an employer (or agency) would be adjudged to be vicariously liable for the discriminatory acts of an agency worker at common law, it may be necessary to take account of a statutory defence based on the employer having taken all reasonable steps to prevent the employee from doing the thing alleged or other similar things in the context of torts based on anti–discrimination legislation.[42a]

NOTE 42a. As Judge Serota QC explained in *Mahood v Irish Centre Housing Ltd* [2011] Eq. L.R. 586 (EAT): "even if a sufficient degree of control could be established over [the worker] . . . so as to render the respondent liable at common law in tort for his actions, such has no bearing on issues of liability under employment legislation relating to discrimination . . . if an Employment Tribunal is to find that an employer is liable for acts of discrimination by an agency worker it would need to . . . [show] that the person in question was acting either as an employee or agent . . . within the meaning of s.32 of the Race Relations Act [now section 109 of the Equality Act 2010]".

(b) *Particular types of employment*

6–25   **Dual Vicarious Liability.** Replace Note 102 with the following: In *XVW v Gravesend Grammar School for Girls* [2012] EWHC 575 (QB); [2012] E.L.R. 417 there was no formal contract of employment between the school and the man, casually engaged as a guide on a school trip, who committed several sexual assaults against pupils. Mackay J. warned at [46] that, "[b]ecause the doctrine [of vicarious liability] imposes strict liability . . . there is high authority for the proposition that, although it can apply to relationships other than that of employment or 'servant or agent' . . . it is a principle which has to be kept within bounds". See further para.**4–29**.

6–26   Retain the first sentence but replace the rest of the paragraph as follows. In that case, a marked preference was shown for May L.J.'s control-based test of dual vicarious liability,[104] just as it was in *Colour Quest Ltd v Total Downstream UK Plc*.[105] However, both this test and Rix L.J.'s integration test were used by Stanley-Burnton L.J. in *Biffa Waste Services Ltd v Maschinenfabrik Ernst Hese GmbH*[106] leaving the matter of which test ought to be used somewhat uncertain. Since then, the Supreme Court has expressly rejected May L.J.'s test for dual vicarious liability and come down firmly in favour of the integration test proffered by Rix L.J.[106a]

NOTE 104. [2006] EWCA Civ 8; [2006] P.I.Q.R. 17 at [83] per Hallet L.J.

NOTE 105. [2009] EWHC 540 (Comm); [2009] 2 Lloyd's Rep. 1 at [220] per Steel J. There was no appeal on this point in the Court of Appeal: [2010] EWCA Civ 180; [2010] 3 All E.R. 793.

NOTE 106. [2008] EWCA Civ 1257; [2009] Q.B. 725 (control at [55], integration at [58]).

NOTE 106a. *Various Claimants v Catholic Child Welfare Society* [2012] UKSC 56; [2012] 3 W.L.R. 1319.

Agency workers. At the end of the paragraph add: Also, where the agency **6–27** worker has acted contrary to the Equality Act 2010, a court will have to assess whether the worker in question acted as an employee or agent of the agency and whether the agency took all reasonable steps to prevent the worker from committing the act in question or anything of that description.[110a]

NOTE 110a. See Equality Act 2010 s.109(4); *Mahood v Irish Centre Housing Ltd* [2011] Eq. L.R. 586 (EAT), but applying the equivalent provision in the now repealed Race Relations Act 1976.

3. LIABILITY OF THE EMPLOYER

Liability of employer for torts of employee. After the sentence that follows **6–28** Note 112, insert Note 112a:

NOTE 112a. So, for example, in *Adams v Law Society* [2012] EWHC 980 (QB), Foskett J. recognised the possibility of an institution being held vicariously liable in respect of an employee's misfeasance in a public office, which tort requires the claimant to show malice or recklessness on the part of the public officer. On the other hand, he was careful to point out that, "if an institutional defendant such as the Law Society asserts that one of its employees was so outside the scope of his or her employment that vicarious liability is not accepted, then the cause of action in misfeasance in public office would have to be maintained against the individual": at [160]. He failed to elaborate on where an employee's acts would be "so outside the scope of his or her employment", but did suggest that "[i]n the normal course of events, the proceedings can be launched against the institution": at [161].

(a) *Course of employment*

Close connection test. Add to end of paragraph: Where, however, an employee **6–29** returns to his place of work, while drunk, in order to assault a fellow employee who is working a night shift there, there will not be a sufficiently close connection for vicarious liability to be imposed. As Pill L.J. said of the instant case: the assault in question "was an independent venture of [the employee's] own, separate and distinct from [his] employment as a Senior Health Assistant at a care home".[125a]

NOTE 125a. *Weddall v Barchester Healthcare Ltd* [2012] EWCA Civ 25; [2012] I.R.L.R. 307, at [45]; cf. *Wallbank v Wallbank Fox Designs Ltd* [2012] EWCA Civ 25; [2012] I.R.L.R. 307 (conjoined appeal with *Weddall*).

6–30   Delete the last sentence of the paragraph (after Note 126) and insert two new paras **6–30A** and **6–30B**:

6–30A   An example of this uncertainty at play can be observed in *Maga v Birmingham Roman Catholic Archdiocese Trustees* [2010] EWCA Civ 256; [2010] 1 W.L.R. 1441 a case one step removed from the facts of *Lister v Hesley Hall*. In *Maga*, the claimant (who suffered from learning difficulties) brought a claim against a Roman Catholic archdiocese in respect of the sexual abuse he suffered as a child at the hands of a Roman Catholic priest employed by the archdiocese. The claimant was not himself a Catholic but he had met the priest in the course of the latter's youth work at such events as church discos which were open to all young people. He had also done various odd jobs for the priest, including some in the presbytery where part of the sexual abuse occurred. The Court of Appeal found the archdiocese vicariously liable even though the claimant was not a Catholic parishioner and had nothing especially to do with the Church. They took the view that the priest's special responsibility for youth work among Catholics and non-Catholics (including his duty to evangelise the latter), and the development of his relationship with the claimant via the work done for him by the claimant (giving the priest an opportunity to be alone with the claimant), both arose from his employment by the archdiocese as a priest. Accordingly, the acts of sexual abuse were sufficiently closely connected to his employment by the archdiocese and, in turn, the latter could legitimately be held vicariously liable.

6–30B   Another case in which all the circumstances of the case made it fair and just to conclude that the tort committed had a sufficiently close connection with the employment contract was *Brink's Global Services v Igrox Ltd* [2010] EWCA Civ 1207; [2011] I.R.L.R. 343. There, an employee engaged to fumigate containers prior to their being shipped returned after work to one such container and stole several silver bars that were never recovered. Nonetheless, Moore–Bick L.J. noted that by virtue of his job, the thief, Renwick, "was authorised to enter the secure compound where the container was stored and . . . allowed to enter the container and thus have access to its contents". As such, it was held that there was a "sufficiently close connection between Renwick's theft of the silver and the purpose of his employment to make it fair and just that Igrox [his employer] should be held vicariously liable" (at [30]). In the light of this decision, it is somewhat easier to see how certain earlier cases—such as *Morris v CW Martin and Sons Ltd* [1966] 1 Q.B. 716 and *Lloyd v Grace Smith & Co Ltd* [1912] A.C. 716 (which have widely been thought to turn upon the defendant's breach of a non–delegable duty of care)[126a]—should have been presented in *Lister* as involving vicarious liability.

NOTE 126a. In the light of such confusion, Lord Nicholls deliberately left these two cases to one side in *Dubai Aluminium*: see [2002] UKHL 48; [2003] 2 A.C. 366 at [27]–[28].

Broad approach. After Note 131 in the text insert the following: That said, the **6–31** courts will not adopt an approach so broad that it brings within the compass of the vicarious liability principle liability for those who, although they enjoy a form of close connection with the employer, are not so closely connected to be in a relationship that is very much akin to that of employment. So, for example, while it might be possible to impose vicarious liability for sexual abuse perpetrated by a "houseparent" working in a children's home on the basis of the *Lister* close connection test, no such liability ought to be imposed in relation to sexual abuse perpetrated by the houseparent's son in the absence of him discharging any of the functions actually expected of his parents. In such circumstances, the son is not really acting as a surrogate for his parent, nor properly to be thought of as under the control of, or working on behalf of, the employer.[131a] However, the relationship between a Roman Catholic priest and a bishop is regarded as close enough in character to an employer–employee relationship so as to make it fair and just that the diocese should be held vicariously liable in respect of acts of child abuse perpetrated by the priest.[131b]

NOTE 131a. *EL v Children's Society* [2012] EWHC 365 (QB). See also, in very similar vein, *XVW v Gravesend Grammar School for Girls* [2012] EWHC 575; [2012] E.L.R. 417.

NOTE 131b. *E v English Province of Our Lady of Charity* [2012] EWCA Civ 938; [2013] 2 W.L.R. 958.

(b) *Examples*

Place of work. NOTE 161. Add to the end of the Note: In similar vein see **6–39** *Reynolds v Strutt & Parker LLP* [2011] EWHC 2263 (QB) (employee injured in a cycling accident at an activities event organised by his employer but in no sense related to his job).

At the end of the paragraph add: In such cases, the court is not entitled to expect **6–50** a fraud victim to make enquiries about the legitimacy of a transaction even if there are reasonable grounds for suspicion. All that matters is that the defendant's employee had actual or ostensible authority to act the way that he did and that the claimant was defrauded. As Gross L.J. explained in *Quinn v CC Automotive Group Ltd* [2010] EWCA Civ 1412; [2011] 2 All E.R. (Comm) 584 at [27], the fact that the victim was taken in by the employee's deceit was neither here nor there.

Employee's breach of statutory duty. NOTE 220. Replace the case there **6–55** cited with the following: *Iqbal v Dean Manson Solicitors* [2011] EWCA Civ 123; [2011] I.R.L.R. 428 at [63] per Rix L.J.

After the sentence that begins "On the other hand, their Lordships also stressed ..." insert in the text the following: Yet in this respect, it has been held that the fact that liability under the Protection from Harassment Act 1997 turns on a guilty mind of sorts is no objection to the imposition of vicarious liability on a corporate or unincorporated body.[221a] Nor is it an objection that the statute imposes liability on *a person* since corporate and unincorporated bodies fall within the definition of the "person" in the Interpretation Act 1978 for civil liability purposes.[221b]

NOTE 221a. *Iqbal v Dean Manson Solicitors* [2011] EWCA Civ 123; [2011] I.R.L.R. 428 at [63] per Rix L.J.

NOTE 221b. *Iqbal v Dean Manson Solicitors* [2011] EWCA Civ 123; [2011] I.R.L.R. 428 at [63] per Rix L.J.

4. INDEPENDENT CONTRACTORS

(c) *Common law non-delegable duties*

6–60 **Common law duty.** NOTE 242. Add: Applied in *Woodland v Swimming Teachers' Association* [2012] EWCA Civ 239; [2012] P.I.Q.R. P12 (it was not considered appropriate to impose a non-delegable duty of care on a local authority to ensure that reasonable care be taken of a pupil during a swimming lesson which had been arranged by the school, but actually provided by a third party).

CHAPTER 7

FOREIGN TORTS

		PARA.
1.	Introduction	7–01
■ 2.	Jurisdiction	7–02
■ 3.	Choice of law	7–05
□ 4.	Particular types of tort	7–18
5.	Limitation	7–22

2. JURISDICTION

Jurisdiction: Council Regulation and the Lugano Convention. Add to the 7–02
text of Note 3 the following: Note, too, that art. 5(3) "must be interpreted as
meaning that an action for a negative declaration seeking to establish the absence
of liability in tort, delict, or quasi-delict falls within the scope of that provision":
Folien Fischer AG v Ritrama SpA (C 133/11) [2013] Q.B. 523.

After Note 3 in the text add: And if, in an action that is brought principally
against D1 (domiciled in state A), it is prudent to add D2 (domiciled in state B) as
second defendant, such joining of D2 to the proceedings will be permissible
provided that "the claims are so closely connected that it is expedient to hear and
determine them together to avoid the risk of irreconcilable judgements resulting
from separate proceedings".[3a]

NOTE 3a. Council Regulation art.6(1). On the way in which the question of
whether there exists a risk of irreconcilable judgments should be determined, see
Alfa Laval Tumba AB v Separator Spares International Ltd [2012] EWCA Civ
1569 at [36] per Longmore L.J.

At the end of the paragraph add: In relation to the recognition and enforcement
of foreign judgments, matters are normally quite straightforward. First, in cases
involving the recognition and enforcement of a foreign judgment against a state,
so long as an exception to the general rule on state immunity can be made out in
accordance with the provisions of the State Immunity Act 1978 (see paras **5–27—
5–37**), a facility to enforce the foreign judgment is enshrined in s.31 of the Civil
Jurisdiction and Judgments Act 1982.[7a] Secondly, in relation to foreign judgments
against tortfeasors other than foreign states, s.32 of the same Act allows for recognition and enforcement of the judgement so long as the judgment in question was
not obtained in breach of an agreement to settle out of court.

NOTE 7a. Under this provision, two conditions must be satisfied: viz., the
judgment would be recognised and enforced if it had not been given against a
state; and the foreign court in question would have had jurisdiction in accordance
with rules corresponding to those applicable to state liability in the United
Kingdom as per ss.2–11 of the State Immunity Act 1978.

After para.**7–02** insert new para.**7–02A** as follows:

7–02A   **Actions for breach of confidence.** In *Innovia Films Ltd v Frito-Lay North America Inc*[7a] the key question concerned choice of law. And in order to determine the appropriate choice of law rules, a prior issue had to be resolved: namely, whether the action in question—which lay in respect of a breach of confidence—ought properly to be considered an action for tort or delict. Arnold J. began by noting that "IFL's claim is for breach of an equitable obligation of confidence". He then held that since "the Court of Appeal held that claims for breach of an equitable obligation of confidence did not arise in tort as a matter of English law in the context of considering whether they fell within Article 5(3) [in *Kitechnology BV v Unicor GmbH Plastmaschinen*[7b]] ... it follows that the applicable law must be determined in accordance with common law principles of conflicts of law".[7c] With respect, however, this reasoning seems to be a little out of touch with both the current state of English law in relation to actions for breach of confidence and the relevant words of art.5(3). On the first of these, there is a notable omission in Arnold J.'s judgment to consider the growing judicial support for the view that the action for breach of confidence has, since the *Kitechnology* case was decided, now acquired tortious status.[7d] Further, art.5(3) is not as narrow as Arnold J. portrays it to be. It does not refer simply to matters relating to "tort". It refers, instead, to matters relating to "tort, delict or quasi delict". It is therefore submitted that, although definitive confirmation of the tortious nature of an action for breach of confidence is yet to be supplied by the English courts, there is nonetheless a very strong argument that it qualifies as an action for "quasi-delict".

NOTE 7a. [2012] EWHC 790 (Pat); [2012] R.P.C. 24.

NOTE 7b. [1995] F.S.R. 765.

NOTE 7c. [2012] EWHC 790 (Pat); [2012] R.P.C. 24 at [101]–[102]. A similar analysis was deployed by the same judge in the course of distinguishing the action for breach of confidence from an action based on breach of contract in *Force India Formula One Team Ltd v 1 Malaysia Racing Team* [2012] EWHC 616 (Ch); [2012] R.P.C. 29.

NOTE 7d. For details, see para.**27–04**.

7–03   Replace the sentence in parenthesis following Note 10 as follows. (The same is true of negligent misstatements made in one country, but relied upon detrimentally by the claimant, in another.)[11]

NOTE 11. *Barclay-Watt v Alpha Panereti Public Ltd* Unreported November 23, 2012. On the other hand, it has also been held that the place where the harmful event occurs covers the place where the misstatement was made: *London Helicopters Ltd v Heliportugal LDA-INAC* [2006] EWHC 108 (QB); [2006] 1 All E.R. (Comm) 595; *Newstat Holdings Ltd v Zani* [2006] EWHC 342 (Comm); [2006] 1 All E.R. (Comm) 607.

After the sentence "When a libel is disseminated in several states, the claimant may be able to sue in each place where that libel is published", insert the following: Equally, it has been held by the European Court of Justice that where a trade mark is registered in Member State A, but infringed in Member State B, the courts of either state will be entitled to hear the case.[11a]

NOTE 11a. *Wintersteiger AG v Products 4U Sondermaschinenbau GmbH* (C-523/10) [2012] E.T.M.R. 31. The difficulties that arise in connection with the use of the internet to infringe the sui generis rights that exist with respect to electronic databases were considered by the ECJ in *Football Dataco Ltd v Sportradar GmbH* (C–173/11) [2013] 1 C.M.L.R. 29. There, data protected by such a right was uploaded from a database onto a computer in Member State A. It was later forwarded, upon request, to a website user in Member State B. It was held that in such circumstances, an infringement may be said to have occurred "at least, in Member State B, where there is evidence from which it may be concluded that the act discloses an intention on the part of the person performing the act to target members of the public in Member State B": at [47].

NOTE 14 add: Compare the interpretation of CPR PD 6B para.3.9(a) in cases falling beyond Regulation 44/2001 art.5(3) in *Wink v Croatia Osiguranje* [2013] EWHC 1118 (QB) (which does embrace a deterioration in the claimant's health after he has returned to his country of domicile for the purposes of determining whether C will be entitled to service out of the jurisdiction). See also para.7–04.

Jurisdiction: common law. NOTE 21. Add: See also *Wink v Croatia Osiguranje*   **7–04**
[2013] EWHC 1118 (QB) where "any damage flowing from the tort" was considered enough to meet the requirement of "damage . . . sustained within the jurisdiction" for the purposes of CPR PD 6B para.3.9(a).

Add to the end of the paragraph: However, since then, the European Court of Justice has suggested that "[g]iven that the impact which material placed online is liable to have on an individual's personality rights might best be assessed by the court of the place where the alleged victim has his centre of interests, the attribution of jurisdiction to that court corresponds to the objective of the sound administration of justice".[25a]

NOTE 25a. *eDate Advertising GmbH v X; Martinez v MGN Ltd* [2012] Q.B. 654.

3. CHOICE OF LAW

Immediately after the words "would be the applicable law under the general   **7–11**
rule" add Note 44a:

NOTE 44a. For an illustration of the kinds of connecting factors that the courts take into consideration in this context, see *Naraji v Shelbourne* [2011] EWHC 3298 (QB).

After the words, "the defendant was English and the incident occurred in England" add: Since then, the Supreme Court has confirmed that "the general rule should not be dislodged easily, lest it be emasculated".[45a]

NOTE 45a. *VTB Capital Plc v Nutritek International Corp* [2013] UKSC 5; [2013] 2 W.L.R. 398 at [205] per Lord Clarke J.S.C. In similar vein, see *Fiona Trust and Holding Corp v Skarga* [2013] EWCA Civ 275.

In the text replace the words "driving of one of the claimants" with: driving of one of the claimants' family: the husband of the first claimant, and father of the second and third claimants.

NOTE 55. Add: In similar vein, see *Cox v Ergo Versicherung AG* [2011] EWHC   **7–13**
2806 (QB); [2012] R.T.R. 11; aff'd [2012] EWCA Civ 1001.

7–14   **Rome II.** NOTE 58. Add: Although Rome II, in line with many European legislative instruments, draws a distinction between entry into force and the date from which the instrument becomes applicable, it has since been confirmed that the date from which its provisions are to apply is January 11, 2009: *Bacon v Nacional Suiza CIA Seguros y Reseguros SA* [2010] EWHC 2017 (QB); [2010] I.L.Pr. 46 at [61] per Tomlinson J.; *Homawoo v GMF Assurances SA* (C–412/10) [2012] I.L.Pr. 2.

7–15   Replace the second sentence in this way. As the provision states: "the law applicable to a non-contractual obligation arising out of a tort/delict shall be the law of the country in which the damage occurs irrespective of the country in which the event giving rise to the damage occurred and irrespective of the country or countries in which the indirect consequences of that event occur".[59a]

NOTE 59a. This choice of law rule does not extend, however, to the law governing matters of procedure and evidence. These are governed by the law of the forum: art.1(3); *Wall v Mutuelle De Poitiers Assurances* [2103] EWHC 53 (QB); [2013] 2 All E.R. 709.

Then, immediately afterwards, insert the following: As with questions relating to jurisdiction, difficulties can arise in relation to internet-based torts or delicts. Thus, in one case in which a Norwegian man made huge financial losses via an internet gambling service based in the United Kingdom, it was held that the losses were incurred in the United Kingdom. The reason for so finding was that the gambler bought virtual chips which he placed in a virtual wallet, and it was financial loss from this "English" virtual wallet that was regarded as being the "harmful event".[59b]

NOTE 59b. *Hillside (New Media) Ltd v Baasland* [2010] EWHC 3336 (Comm); [2010] 2 C.L.C. 986 at [30] per Andrew Smith J.

Replace the next sentence as follows: Just as with s.11, the general rule in art.4(1) of Rome II is susceptible to exceptions.

4. Particular Types of Tort

7–19   **Intellectual property rights.** Delete the words between ". . . has been added" and "In *Pearce v Ove*".

Also, replace the words following the ". . . requires no such registration." as follows: Since then, the Supreme Court has made clear that the English courts will have jurisdiction to determine a claim for infringement of a foreign copyright provided there is a basis for an in personam jurisdiction over the defendant. Their Lordships' reasoning proceeded along lines essentially similar to those in *Pearce*. Pointing out that Regulation 44/2001 art.22(4) only assigns exclusive jurisdiction in cases where there is a registration or validity issue, their Lordships were content to confer jurisdiction in relation to cases involving a breach of copyright given the absence of any such validity/registration issues.[74] The decision of the Court of Appeal was reversed, and the decision in *Tyburn Production Ltd* was overruled.[74a]

NOTE 74. at [105]–[109] per Lords Walker and Collins (combined judgment). Lady Hale, Lord Mance and Lord Phillips agreed.

NOTE 74a. *Lucasfilm Ltd v Ainsworth* [2011] UKSC 39; [2012] 1 A.C. 208 at [110] per Lords Walker and Collins.

Replace the first sentence of this paragraph as follows: Notwithstanding the 7–20 foregoing, one question that does remain open is whether a claim against a defendant *not* domiciled in a Regulation/Convention state, or in respect of rights arising or granted under the laws of such a state, can be brought in England.

CHAPTER 8

NEGLIGENCE

PARA.

1. The tort of negligence...8–01
2. Duty of care 8–05
   (a) The nature of the duty concept................................8–05
   ■ (b) The test for notional duty.................................8–12
   ■ (c) Claimant's status..8–29
   ■ (d) Defendant's status.......................................8–38
   □ (e) Omissions..8–46
       □ (i) Special relationship................................8–51
       □ (ii) Specific assumption of responsibility...............8–53
       ■ (iii) Specific responsibility for protection from third parties.....8–54
   (f) Psychiatric injury and distress..............................8–61
       (i) Primary victims......................................8–62
       ■ (ii) Secondary victims.................................8–67
       (iii) Psychiatric illness resulting from factors other than personal injury or
            imperilment..8–78
       □ (iv) Distress..8–84
   (g) Unwanted childbirth and loss of autonomy.....................8–86
   (h) Financial loss resulting from reliance or dependence............8–91
       ■ (i) The need for a special relationship..................8–92
       ■ (ii) Relevant factors..................................8–101
       □ (iii) Disclaimers.....................................8–121
   □ (i) Financial loss resulting from the acquisition of defective property.....8–125
   □ (j) Financial loss following damage to another's property..........8–131
3. Breach of duty 8–136
   (a) Introduction..8–136
   (b) The criteria of reasonableness...............................8–139
       ■ (i) Objectivity..8–139
       ■ (ii) Balancing cost and benefit.........................8–149
       ■ (iii) Common practice and expectations..................8–165
   ■ (c) Proof of carelessness....................................8–170
   (d) Particular instances of breach...............................8–177
       ■ (i) Road accidents....................................8–178
       □ (ii) Transport accidents...............................8–188
       ■ (iii) Care for children.................................8–192

2. DUTY OF CARE

(b) *The test for notional duty*

Legal policy. NOTE 76. Add: *Murdoch v Department for Work and Pensions* **8–19**
[2010] EWHC 1988 (QB).

Public policy. NOTE 85. Add: See also *Jones v Kaney* [2011] UKSC 13; [2011] **8–20**
2 A.C. 398, holding that the immunity formerly applied to expert witnesses in
respect of claims for negligence should be abolished (see paras **10–41** and **14–35**

of this Supplement). See further *Smith v Ministry of Defence* [2013] UKSC 41; [2013] 3 W.L.R. 69 apparently narrowing the scope of "combat immunity" (see para.**14–38** of this Supplement).

(c) *Claimant's status*

8–34   **Careless rescue.** Add: See *Tolley v Carr* [2010] EWHC 2191 (QB); [2011] R.T.R. 7 (considered at para.**3–78** of this Supplement).

8–36   **Suicide** Add: Note that in some cases of suicide art.2 of the European Convention on Human Rights will be engaged such that the relatives of the deceased may be entitled to damages from a public authority (such as the NHS) where there has been a culpable failure to prevent the suicide. See *Rabone v Pennine Care NHS Trust* [2012] UKSC 2; [2012] 2 A.C. 72 and *Reynolds v United Kingdom* (2694/08) (2012) 55 E.H.R.R. 35, discussed at paras **10–78**, **10–93**, **14–69**, and **14–73** of this Supplement. And see also *Savage v South Essex Partnership NHS Trust* [2008] UKHL 74; [2009] 1 A.C. 681, paras **10–93** and **14–73** of the Main Work.

(d) *Defendant's status*

8–40   **Vendors and lessors of premises.** In *Drysdale v Hedges* [2012] EWHC B20 (QB); [2012] 3 E.G.L.R. 105 Mr Leighton Williams QC applied *Cavalier v Pope* in holding that the defendant landlord owed no duty to a tenant in respect of an unguarded drop of eight feet which pre-existed the defendant's acquisition of the property.

8–43   Add: In *Merthyr Tydfil CBC v C* [2010] EWHC 62 (QB); [2010] P.I.Q.R. P9; [2010] 1 F.L.R. 1640 a mother reported to the NSPCC her concern that her two young children had been abused by an older neighbouring child. This complaint was passed to the local authority, which advised her to keep her children indoors. Two years later she reported similar concerns to the local authority. At a meeting the council wrongly denied that the claimant had ever reported the earlier incident, refused to get in touch with the NSPCC to check this, and allocated the same social worker to her family as was allocated to the abuser's family. C brought an action against the local authority in respect of alleged psychiatric harm that she suffered as a consequence. The defendants sought to strike out the claim on the basis that *D v East Berkshire NHS Trust* was authority for the proposition that a local authority could not owe a duty of care to the parent of a child who had been, or who was suspected of having been, abused, either because of the potential conflict of interest or because the parent was a "third party" whose claim was parasitic on the duty owed to the child. Hickinbottom J., distinguishing *D v East Berkshire*, rejected the argument that just because a local authority owe a duty of care to the child they can never owe a duty to the parents (citing *A v Essex CC* [2003] EWCA Civ 1848; [2004] 1 W.L.R. 1881; *Lambert v Cardiff CC* [2007] EWHC 869; [2007] 3 F.C.R. 148; (2007) 97 B.M.L.R. 101; and *W v Essex CC* [2001] 2 A.C. 592): "What *JD v East Berkshire* held was that the usual consonancy of interests between parents and children is displaced, as a matter of law, where the parent is suspected of abusing the child. It does not hold that, whenever there is any bare potential for some future conflict of interest between a child and his/her parents, then an authority is immune from owing any duty of care to the parents and from any negligence suit at the hands of the parents" (at [27]). Although, applying *D v East Berkshire*, a local authority did not owe a duty of care to those who are suspected of abusing the children, there was no general principle that, where a local authority owe a duty of care to a child, it cannot as a matter of law at the same time owe a duty of care to parents of that child. The fact that there was "some conceivable potential for such a conflict in the future is insufficient to make an authority immune from a suit in negligence at that hands of a parent" (at [36]). Nor, on the pleaded facts, was this a "third party" case. The mother's claim, said Hickinbottom J., was not parasitic on the duty owed by the local authority to her children. The duty which the claimant asserted was owed to her had a different basis and was of a different scope from that owed to her children. Moreover, the alleged failings of the authority were not of a policy nature; they were all failings which were "operational" in character.

NOTE 188. Add: See also *Desmond v Chief Constable of Nottinghamshire* [2011] EWCA Civ 3; [2011] 1 F.L.R. 1361 where the Court of Appeal held that no duty of care is owed by the police to a person applying for an enhanced criminal record certificate, even though errors in the information provided, affected the claimant's ability to obtain employment, partly on the basis that if such a duty were held to exist "there would be a plain conflict between the . . . putative duty to [the claimant] and the statutory purpose of protecting vulnerable young people" (at [49]).

(e) *Omissions*

The principle. Add: The distinction between a pure omission and a positive act **8–46** may, on occasion, be a subtle one. In *Valentine v Transport for London* [2010] EWCA Civ 1358; [2011] P.I.Q.R. P7 a motorcyclist died after skidding on an accumulation of surface grit on a sliver of tarmac at the edge of a road. The local authority undertook some cleaning operations on the road. An allegation that the local authority, in sweeping the road, had missed the sliver of tarmac was a claim based on a pure omission (in the absence of any duty upon the local authority to sweep the road) and so was struck out as disclosing no reasonable cause of action. However, it was a least arguable that in sweeping the road but not the sliver of tarmac the authority had created a trap, which was a positive act; alternatively it was arguable that in sweeping the road grit had been pushed onto the sliver of tarmac which would be a sin of commission rather than omission.

(i) *Special relationship*

Protective relationships. Add: In *Everett v Comojo (UK) Ltd (t/a Metropolitan)* **8–51** [2011] EWCA Civ 13; [2012] 1 W.L.R. 150 the Court of Appeal held that the management of a nightclub could owe a duty of care to customers in respect of an assault by a third party (another customer), applying the *Caparo* tripartite test (see para.**8–15** of the Main Work), on the basis of: (1) the control that the management exercises over entry to and removal from the premises; (2) the economic relationship between the management and customers; (3) the foreseeability of the risk that (in an environment where alcohol is consumed which can lead to loss of control and violence) one guest might assault another guest (though the foreseeable risk will vary with the nature of the premises); and (4) the fact that the relationship between management and customers already carried an established duty under the Occupiers Liability Act 1957 (Smith L.J. noted, at [33], that: "It would be surprising if management could be liable to a guest who tripped over a worn carpet and yet escape liability for injuries inflicted by a fellow guest who was a foreseeable danger—for example in that he had previously been excluded on account of his violent behaviour and who on this occasion had been allowed in carrying an offensive weapon"). The question of whether there has been a breach of this duty should be measured, said the court, by reference to the "common duty of care" imposed on occupiers by the Occupiers Liability Act 1957.

NOTE 214. Add: But there is no duty to warn passengers of hazards likely to be encountered after the journey has been completed merely because they are close to the passenger's destination: *Fernquest v City & County of Swansea* [2011] EWCA Civ 1712 (passenger slipped on ice on the pavement close to a bus stop, after he had alighted from a bus; defendants aware of icy pavement but not liable for failing to warn passenger).

NOTE 215. Add: But the duty to the child may not extend to protecting the child's financial interests, at least where the preservation of the family unit is at stake: *VL (A Child) v Oxfordshire CC* [2010] EWHC 2091 (QB); [2010] P.I.Q.R. P20 (see para.**8–55** of this Supplement). See also *XA v YA* [2010] EWHC 1983 (QB); [2011] P.I.Q.R. P1 (para.**8–192** of this Supplement)—the court should be slow to find a parent in breach of a duty of care owed to their children (citing comments of Sir Nicholas Browne Wilkinson in *Surtees v Kingston upon Thames RBC* [1991] 2 F.L.R. 559 at 583), particularly where such a duty could only have been discharged by the break-up of the family.

(ii) *Specific assumption of responsibility*

8–53   **Assumption of responsibility.** NOTE 222. Add: *Desmond v Chief Constable of Nottinghamshire* was reversed by the Court of Appeal: [2011] EWCA Civ 3; [2011] 1 F.L.R. 1361—no duty of care owed by the police to a person applying for an enhanced criminal record certificate, even though errors in the information provided affected the claimant's ability to obtain employment. There was no assumption of responsibility by the police beyond that required by the proper performance of the statutory duty to provide a certificate.

NOTE 226. Add: cf. *Geary v Wetherspoon Plc* [2011] EWHC 1506 (QB); [2011] N.P.C. 60—occupiers of premises had not assumed any specific responsibility to a customer who chose to slide down a banister and fell off; nor was there any evidence of specific reliance by the claimant on the defendant. The position might have been different "if the defendant had been organising banister-sliding competitions" (per Coulson J. at [60]).

(iii) *Specific responsibility for protection from third parties*

8–55   **Assumption of responsibility to claimant.** Add: Although, in the light of *Swinney v Chief Constable of the Northumbria Police*, the police may, on appropriate facts, undertake responsibility for the physical safety of an informant, the relationship of an informant to the police does not mean that they have undertaken responsibility to protect the informant from pure economic loss: *An Informer v Chief Constable* [2012] EWCA Civ 197; [2013] 2 W.L.R. 694. For comment see para.**14–30** of this Supplement.

NOTE 236. Add: But where the claim is in respect of pure economic loss (an alleged failure to apply for criminal injuries compensation on behalf of a minor) a local authority exercising parental responsibilities will not necessarily owe the child a duty of care: *VL (A Child) v Oxfordshire CC* [2010] EWHC 2091 (QB); [2010] P.I.Q.R. P20 (no duty to maximise the economic position of a child in care by allocating time and resources to a pursuit of all available financial claims in circumstances where the primary responsibility of the local authority was to rehabilitate the father [who had caused the child's injuries] into the family unit).

Assumption of responsibility by public authorities. See also *Thomson v Scottish Ministers* [2011] CSOH 90; 2011 S.L.T. 683—no duty of care owed by the Prison Service to a member of the public killed by a prisoner on short term leave, where risk to the general public, even if grave, was not enough to satisfy the requirement of proximity; there had to be a special risk of harm to the claimant that they did not share with other members of the public. See further *Furnell v Flaherty* [2013] EWHC 377 (QB) (para.**14–54** of this Supplement) (no duty owed by local authority or Health Protection Agency to defendant to notify outbreak of E.coli at defendant's petting farm, or to take steps to limit visitors' exposure to infection—mere knowledge on the part of the local authority or Health Protection Agency fell far short of giving rise to an assumption of responsibility). **8–56**

Add: On the other hand, there may be situations where the claimant is in a particularly close relationship with a public authority, such that no express assumption of responsibility is required to establish a duty of care. In *Selwood v Durham CC* [2012] EWCA Civ 979; [2012] P.I.Q.R. P20 the Court of Appeal held that it was at least arguable that two NHS Trusts had assumed responsibility to a social worker employed by a local authority who was attacked and seriously injured by a mental health patient. The social worker worked closely with the two NHS Trusts to provide integrated health and social care through a Community Mental Health Team (CMHT) and a Crisis Resolution Team (CRT). The working relationship between the three defendants (the Trusts and the local authority) was set out in a lengthy policy document governing working arrangements. The patient was known to have a history of violent behaviour and posed a risk of harm to others. Employees of the Trusts became aware that he had expressed his intention to kill the claimant if he saw her, but the claimant was not warned. Dame Janet Smith (with whom Rimer and Thorpe L.JJ. agreed) considered that it was possible to infer an assumption of responsibility from the circumstances, and in particular the close working relationship, "to do what was reasonable in the circumstances to reduce or avoid any foreseeable risk of harm to which an employee of a co-signatory was exposed in the course of their joint operations" (at [52]). Given that the defendants, in their capacity as employers, would owe a duty of care to their employees "notwithstanding that there may be a potential conflict of interest between that duty and the defendant's duties to the recipients of its core service users" it was not a big step to suggest that they could owe a duty of care in respect of the actions of a third party to someone in the claimant's position since "the force of some of the policy considerations which render a wider duty undesirable is much less than if the duty is said to be owed to the world at large" (at [53]).

NOTE 239. Add: *Michael v Chief Constable of South Wales* [2012] EWCA Civ 981; [2012] H.R.L.R. 30.

(f) *Psychiatric injury and distress*

(ii) *Secondary victims*

8–72 **Physical and temporal proximity.** Add: In *Taylor v A Novo (UK) Ltd* [2013] EWCA Civ 194; [2013] P.I.Q.R. P15; [2013] Med. L.R. 100 the issue was whether in order to qualify as a secondary victim the claimant had to have close physical and temporal proximity to the *initial accident* or to the physical consequences of the accident to the accident victim some time later. The claimant's mother was injured at work when a stack of racking boards was negligently tipped over on top of her. Three weeks later she suddenly and unexpectedly collapsed and died at home as a result of deep vein thrombosis and pulmonary emboli, which had been caused by the accident at work. The claimant did not witness the accident at work, but she did witness her mother's death and subsequently developed post traumatic stress disorder. The defendants conceded that the claimant satisfied all the criteria to qualify as a secondary victim, with the exception of the requirement that she either be present at the scene of the accident which caused the death or must have been involved in its immediate aftermath. The claimant argued that the relevant "event" to which she must be proximate in time and space was not the initial accident but her mother's collapse and death that was caused by it. The trial judge held that the claimant was a secondary victim, charactering the "operative event" as the mother's death: "She was present at the scene and witnessed it with her own senses. The fact that there was an earlier incident caused by the same negligent act is irrelevant. The fact that the second event would not have occurred but for the first adds nothing" (cited by Lord Dyson M.R. at [19]). The Court of Appeal disagreed and reversed the decision. Lord Dyson pointed out the different senses in which the word "proximity" is used: first as shorthand for the neighbour principle it describes the relationship between the parties which is necessary in order to found a duty of care owed by one to the other (at [26]). But in secondary victim cases, the word "proximity" is also used in a different sense to mean physical proximity in time and space to an event, and used in this sense it is one of the control mechanisms which limits the number of persons who can claim damages for psychiatric injury as secondary victims: "In a secondary victim case, physical proximity to the event is a necessary, but not sufficient, condition of legal proximity" (at [27]). The real issue was whether the claimant and the defendant were in a relationship of legal proximity. Lord Dyson did not accept that there were two events; there was a single accident or event which had two consequences, the first of which was injury to the claimant's mother's head and arm, and the second, three weeks later, was her death. To allow the claimant to recover as a secondary victim in such circumstances "would be to go too far" (at [29]). If the judge's approach were correct the claimant would be able to succeed even if her mother's death had occurred months and possibly years after the accident, which suggested that the concept of proximity to a secondary victim could not reasonably be stretched so far. On the other hand if her mother had died in the accident and the claimant had not witnessed the accident but had come on the scene shortly *after* the immediate aftermath she would not qualify as a secondary victim: "The idea that Ms Taylor could recover in the first situation but not in the others would strike the ordinary reasonable person as unreasonable and indeed incomprehensible. In this area of the law, the perception of the ordinary reasonable person matters. That is because where the boundaries of proximity are drawn in this difficult area should, so far as possible, reflect what the ordinary reasonable person would regard as acceptable" (at [30]). Moreover, the effect of finding the claimant to be a secondary victim would be to "extend the scope of liability to secondary victims considerably further than has been done hitherto. The courts have been astute for the policy reasons. . . to confine the right of action of secondary victims by means of strict control mechanisms. In my view, these same policy reasons militate against any further substantial extension. That should only be done by Parliament" (at [31]). For Lord Dyson, the paradigm secondary victim case is one involving an accident which (i) more or less immediately causes injury or death to a primary victim and (ii) is witnessed by the claimant: "In such a case, the relevant event is the accident. It is not a later consequence of the accident."

Sudden shock. NOTE 359. Add: See also *Wicks v State Rail Authority of New*   **8–74**
South Wales [2010] HCA 22; (2010) 241 C.L.R. 60 where, in the context of statutory rules limiting recovery for "mental harm" to certain claimants who "witnessed, at the scene, a person being killed, injured or put in peril", the High Court of Australia held that this was not necessarily limited to an event that may be measured in minutes. So, in a claim by two police officers who assisted at the scene of a rail disaster for several hours, the High Court held that the perils to which living passengers were subjected as a result of the defendants' negligence did not end when the carriages came to rest: "A person is put in peril when put at risk; the person remains in peril . . . until the person ceases to be at risk" (at [50]), which was when they had been rescued by being taken to a place of safety.

(iv) *Distress*

Distress. NOTE 397. Add: Though on the facts of this case the European Court   **8–84**
of Human Rights found that there had been a breach of the parent's art.8 rights: *MAK v United Kingdom* (45901/05) [2010] 2 F.L.R. 451; (2010) 51 E.H.R.R. 14.

Disease anxiety. NOTE 404. Add: In *AXA General Insurance Ltd v HM*   **8–85**
Advocate [2011] UKSC 46; [2012] 1 A.C. 868 the Supreme Court held that the 2009 Act was not beyond the competence of the Scottish Parliament, nor was it subject to judicial review on the grounds of unreasonableness, irrationality and arbitrariness.

(h) *Financial loss resulting from reliance or dependence*

(i) *The need for a special relationship*

NOTE 460. Add: See also *St John Poulton's Trustee in Bankruptcy v Ministry*   **8–99**
of Justice [2010] EWCA Civ 392; [2011] Ch. 1; [2010] 4 All E.R. 600—no common law duty on a court to send a notice of a bankruptcy petition, with a request that it be registered in the register of pending actions, to the Chief Land Registrar, in breach of the statutory duty imposed by the Insolvency Rules 1986

r.6.13. The defendant's only obligation to do anything at all arose out of the statutory provision, and in the absence of a claim for breach of statutory duty there was no basis for a claim in negligence (applying *Gorringe v Calderdale MBC* [2004] UKHL 15; [2004] 1 W.L.R. 1057 and *Customs and Excise Commissioners v Barclays Bank Plc* [2006] UKHL 28; [2007] 1 A.C. 181). See also *Smeaton v Equifax Plc* [2013] EWCA Civ 108; [2013] 2 All E.R. 959 applying similar reasoning in rejecting an argument for a duty of care to be owed by credit reference agencies to members of the public.

(ii) *Relevant factors*

8–103   **Purpose of service.** NOTE 472, Add: cf. *Santander UK Plc v Keeper of the Registers of Scotland* [2013] CSOH 24; 2013 S.L.T. 362 where it was held that the land registry in Scotland were not liable in negligence for losses sustained by a lender when a borrower fraudulently persuaded the land registry to accept a discharge of the borrower's mortgage, with the result that a later lender took priority on sale of the mortgaged property. Lord Boyd concluded that the pursuers had failed to establish that it was fair just and reasonable (under the third limb of the *Caparo* test) to impose a duty of care on the land registry (distinguishing *Ministry of Housing and Local Government v Sharp*). A large commercial banking enterprise takes a number of commercial risks when making a decision to lend money, one of which is as to the honesty of their customer. If a duty of care were imposed on the land registry, then it would be the public purse that would bear the loss and not the commercial enterprise that initially assumed the risk (at [107]). The loss had been caused by the criminal acts of the pursuers' customer and it was not fair, just and reasonable that the defendants should be liable for those criminal acts (at [109]).

8–106   **Knowledge of reliance.** NOTE 487. *Patchett v Swimming Pool & Allied Trades Association Ltd* [2009] EWCA Civ 717 is now reported at: [2010] 2 All E.R. (Comm) 138.

8–110   **Reasonable reliance or dependence.** NOTE 497. Add: See also *Gatt v Barclays Bank Plc* [2013] EWHC 2 (QB) at [34]–[35], where Judge Moloney Q.C. was prepared to apply *Spring v Guardian Assurance* to the provision of information by a bank to a credit reference agency, the duty being owed not solely to the customer about whom the reference was provided, but also the spouse of that customer where she was a joint account holder and co-director of a family business that was dependent on her husband's credit. The judge noted "the importance of credit rating in the modern world and the analogies (more than just semantic) between job references and credit references". The action failed on the facts. On the other hand, a credit reference agency does not owe a duty of care in negligence to members of the public about whom it collects data: *Smeaton v Equifax Plc* [2013] EWCA Civ 108; [2013] 2 All E.R. 959 (credit reference agency's responsibilities governed by the Data Protection Act 1998 and the Consumer Credit Act 1974; there was no scope for imposing a co-extensive duty in tort).

NOTE 498. Add: *Desmond v Chief Constable of Nottinghamshire* was reversed by the Court of Appeal: [2011] EWCA Civ 3; [2011] 1 F.L.R. 1361. There is no duty of care owed by the police to a person applying for an enhanced criminal record certificate, even though errors in the information provided affected the claimant's ability to obtain employment. There was no assumption of responsibility by the police beyond that required by the proper performance of the statutory duty to provide a certificate, and there was no sufficient relationship between the police and the claimant (distinguishing *Spring v Guardian Assurance*).

Contractual context. Add: In *Robinson v PE Jones (Contractors) Ltd* [2011]   8–113
EWCA Civ 9; [2012] Q.B. 44 at [80] Jackson L.J. summarised Lord Goff's analysis of the relationship between contractual and tortious duties in the following terms:

"(i)   When A assumes responsibility to B in the *Hedley Byrne* sense, A comes under a tortious duty to B, which may extend to protecting B against economic loss.

(ii)   The existence of a contract between A and B does not prevent such a duty from arising.

(iii)   In contracts of professional retainer, there is commonly an assumption of responsibility which generates a duty of care to protect the client against economic loss."

However, an ordinary building contract does not, in itself, give rise to an assumption of responsibility between the builder and the building owner, and (in the absence of physical injury to the owner or some other property) their relationship will be governed by the terms of the contract rather than the law of tort. Stanley Burnton L.J. added, at [92]:

"In my judgment, it must now be regarded as settled law that the builder/vendor of a building does not by reason of his contract to construct or to complete the building assume any liability in the tort of negligence in relation to defects in the building giving rise to purely economic loss. The same applies to a builder who is not the vendor, and to the seller or manufacturer of a chattel. The decision of the House of Lords in *Anns v Merton LBC*, like its earlier decision in *Junior Books Ltd v Veitchi Co. Ltd* [1983] 1 A.C. 520, must now be regarded as aberrant, indeed as heretical."

(iii) *Disclaimers*

Statutory control of disclaimers. NOTE 562. Add: In *Robinson v PE Jones*   8–122
(Contractors) Ltd [2011] EWCA Civ 9; [2012] Q.B. 44 the Court of Appeal upheld the trial judge's conclusion that clauses in a building contract limiting the building owner's remedies against a builder to a claim under the NHBC agreement (thereby excluding any liability in negligence) satisfied the test of reasonableness in the Unfair Contract Terms Act 1977.

(i) *Financial loss resulting from the acquisition of defective property*

Dangerous defects and economic loss. NOTE 578. Add: In *Robinson v PE*   8–126
Jones (Contractors) Ltd [2011] EWCA Civ 9; [2012] Q.B. 44 the Court of Appeal

upheld the decision that a builder had not assumed responsibility to the purchaser of a property simply by entering a contract to build the property. The existence of clauses in the contract that limited the builder's liability for building defects to the first two years, after which provision was made for the purchaser to claim for any defects under the NHBC scheme, made it clear that the builder had not undertaken any responsibility in tort to the purchaser. The Court of Appeal went further than this, however, indicating that beyond the realm of a professional's relationship with a client, it is highly unlikely that a contract will create concurrent liability in tort. Jackson L.J. noted that the relationship between the manufacturer of a product or the builder of a building and the immediate client is primarily governed by the contract between those two parties: "Absent any assumption of responsibility, there do not spring up between the parties duties of care co-extensive with their contractual obligations. The law of tort imposes a different and more limited duty upon the manufacturer or builder. That more limited duty is to take reasonable care to protect the client against suffering personal injury or damage to other property" (at [68]). There was nothing in the facts to suggest that the builder had assumed responsibility in the *Hedley Byrne* sense: "The parties entered into a normal contract whereby the defendant would complete the construction of a house for the claimant to an agreed specification and the claimant would pay the purchase price. The defendant's warranties of quality were set out and the claimant's remedies in the event of breach of warranty were also set out. The parties were not in a professional relationship whereby, for example, the claimant was paying the defendant to give advice or to prepare reports or plans upon which the claimant would act" (at [83]). See also the comments of Stanley Burnton L.J. at [92] (quoted at para.**8–113** of this Supplement).

8–128   **Damage to other property and the complex structure theory.** Add: The issue of what constitutes "other property" can be difficult to determine. In *Linklaters Business Services (formerly Hackwood Services Co) v Sir Robert McAlpine Ltd* [2010] EWHC 1145 (TCC); [2010] B.L.R. 537 sub-contractors fitted insulation material to steel pipework used for air conditioning. It was alleged that defects in the fitting of the insulation allowed water and air to penetrate the insulated pipework with the result that the steel rusted and corroded. The sub-contractors applied to strike out the contractors' claim for contribution on the basis that the sub-contractors owed no duty of care to the building owners (the lessees who had undertaken substantial renovation work to the building). The issue was whether the insulated steel pipework was one "thing" or, in the context that the pipework was part of an installation in an overall building, whether it was to be considered simply as an indivisible part of the whole building. Akenhead J., on the assumption that the corrosion and rusting was classified as physical damage to the steel pipework, refused to strike out the claim. This was an area of developing jurisprudence and there were too many factual uncertainties for summary judgment or for a striking out. His Lordship noted (at [27]) that *Murphy v Brentwood DC* and *D & F Estates v Church Commissioners* "do not specifically address the extent of any duty of care owed by a sub-contractor or supplier who provides an element of or within the building being constructed or developed, save that it is clear that the duty of care does not extend to cover the cost of replacement or repair, or the loss, of the element itself. . . . What has not been explored and examined in any great detail is the extent of the duty of care owed by those in the position of sub-contractors . . . and suppliers whose carelessness in and about providing the work, materials, services or equipment which are incorporated into a building or structure causes consequential damage to other elements of the building. The scope of this duty and where the dividing lines are remain to be explored jurisprudentially and in practice." The matter was not resolved on appeal, though the Court of Appeal commented that they were "issues which may require the attention of the Supreme Court in due course": *Southern Insulation (Medway) Ltd v How Engineering Services Ltd* [2010] EWCA Civ 999 at [10].

See further *Broster v Galliard Docklands Ltd* [2011] EWHC 1722 (TCC); [2011] B.L.R. 569; [2011] P.N.L.R. 34, where a row of six terraced houses had been designed and constructed with a common roof. In a very high wind the roof lifted and fell back damaging the roof and the houses, allegedly because roof joists had not been strapped to the walls. The second defendant, who had designed and constructed the terraced houses for the first defendant, argued that they were not liable to the purchasers because the damage to the roof and walls was to "the thing itself". Akenhead J., applying Lord Bridge's statement of principle in *Murphy v Brentwood DC*, agreed: "It would be wholly artificial to argue that the segment of the roof over each individual terraced unit was to be considered as separate from the whole roof or indeed that the roof as a whole was to be considered as separate from the walls of the units below. It follows that there is damage 'to the thing itself'. Put another way, the duty of care does not extend to protect the owners of the property from damage to the roof itself or to the units below caused by the dislodgement of the roof. The House of Lords in the context of negligence has repeatedly warned against an artificial sub-division of a building, no matter how large, into constituent elements and, whether or not the 'complex structure' theory still has a material part to play in the law of negligence relating to buildings and structures, it does not extend to a case such as this" (at [16]).

Statutory consequences. Add: See *Broster v Galliard Docklands Ltd* [2011] **8–129** EWHC 1722 (TCC); [2011] B.L.R. 569; [2011] P.N.L.R. 34 at [20]–[22].

Add: The duty owed under s.1 of the Defective Premises Act 1972 does not **8–130** apply to improvements to an existing dwelling-house: *Jenson v Faux* [2011] EWCA Civ 423; [2011] 1 W.L.R. 3038. It would apply to conversion of a property from, say, commercial use to a dwelling-house, and could apply where the work constituted the provision of a new dwelling where the "identity" of the property had been changed. The extent and cost of the works is not decisive in determining whether the identity of the property has changed: "There may be cases in which a small amount of work might be needed to create a separate one-floor dwelling which would thus fall within s.1 of the 1972 Act; but there can be very extensive works to a house or dwelling which will not make it a dwelling whose identity is 'wholly different' from before" (at [18] per Longmore L.J.).

NOTE 602. Add: In *Harrison v Shepherd Homes Ltd* [2011] EWHC 1811 (TCC); (2011) 27 Const. L.J. 709 Ramsey J. held that the duty under s.1(1) of the Defective Premises Act to "see that the work which he takes on is done in a workmanlike or, as the case may be, professional manner, with proper materials and so that as regards that work the dwelling will be fit for habitation when completed" is a single duty, so that the obligation to complete the work in a workmanlike manner and with proper materials is to be measured by reference to whether the dwelling is "fit for habitation"; they are not three distinct duties. His Lordship was clearly reluctant to accept this interpretation but concluded that he was bound by the decision of the Court of Appeal in *Alexander v Mercouris* [1979] 1 W.L.R. 1270. Ramsey J. went on to hold that significant defects in the foundations of the properties in question were "properly matters which could be said to give rise to a lack of fitness for habitation" (at [164]). (An appeal on the assessment of damages only in the case was dismissed: [2012] EWCA Civ 904; [2012] 3 E.G.L.R. 83).

(j) *Financial loss following damage to another's property*

8–132   NOTE 608. Add: See also *Network Rail Infrastructure Ltd v Conarken Group Ltd* [2010] EWHC 1852 (TCC); [2010] B.L.R. 601 where the defendants negligently damaged a bridge belonging to the claimants, and the issue was whether the claimants were entitled (in addition to the cost of repairs) to recover sums that they were required to pay to train operating companies as a result of delays to rail services whilst repairs were carried out. The payments were made under the terms of a complex contract between the claimants and train operating companies intended to compensate the train operating companies for, inter alia, the immediate and future loss of revenue due to delays in the rail service. Akenhead J. held that the claimants were entitled to recover the contractual payments, even though under the contractual formula for calculating the payments part of the sum was not directly related to lost income but included, e.g. sums related to incentive payments and estimates of lost future income as a result of passengers affected by delays choosing alternative means of transport in the future. The loss of use and revenue to the claimant was a reasonably foreseeable consequence of the negligence and it was not necessary for the precise loss or the machinery by which the loss was ascertainable to be foreseen or foreseeable. The fact that the contract provided a complex formula for determining the value or cost for the non-provision of the rail track was immaterial.

    The Court of Appeal upheld this decision ([2011] EWCA Civ 644; [2012] 1 All E.R. (Comm) 692), though with differing emphases as to the correct approach. Pill L.J., although agreeing with the outcome on the facts, considered that the contract did not necessarily bind the defendants to pay the contractual sums to the claimants: "It is not open to a party to dictate to the whole world the extent of tortious liability and what is reasonably foreseeable and not too remote in order to achieve what it regards as a satisfactory contract with a third party" (at [69]). It was "too simplistic in circumstances such as the present to say that because a kind of loss, financial loss, is reasonably foreseeable to one who causes physical damage, all financial loss agreed between the victim and a third party is reasonably foreseeable. Had there been no such contract, analysis of the headings under which the alleged loss is claimed, and the manner in which it is calculated, would be necessary. The existence of the contract does not, in my judgment, remove the need for such analysis" (at [78]). Moore-Bick L.J. took the view that the terms of the contract were similar to liquidated damages provisions commonly found in commercial contracts where the effects of delay or the interruption of performance are difficult to quantify financially. That meant that the clauses quantifying the loss "cannot be regarded as too remote on the grounds that it exceeds any reasonable assessment of the amount of loss actually caused by the loss of availability of the track" (at [98]). It followed that the way in which the payments had been calculated was irrelevant: "All that matters for present purposes is that they represent a genuine and reasonable attempt to assess the damage caused to the [train operating companies] by the closure of the lines and the consequent disruption to services" (at [99]). Jackson L.J. held that the loss of revenue was plainly foreseeable and the action "should be characterised as a simple claim for loss of income consequent upon damage to revenue earning property. This is a well established category of recoverable economic loss" (at [150]). In the absence of exceptional circumstance or some obviously unreasonable feature in the claimant's business arrangements it was not appropriate for the court "to explore in detail the build-up of any loss of revenue following damage to revenue generating property. It is sufficient for the claimant to prove that the loss of revenue has occurred" (at [153]).

3. BREACH OF DUTY

(b) *The criteria of reasonableness*

(i) *Objectivity*

Add: So in *Baker v Quantum Clothing Group* [2011] UKSC 17; [2011] 1 **8–142** W.L.R. 1003 the House of Lords held that a judge was entitled to conclude that employers who had greater knowledge than the average employer of the risks to employees of exposure to noise at work between 85dB(A)lepd and 90dB(A)lepd could be in breach of their duty, even though the knowledge of the average employer was based on a Government Code of Practice on occupational exposure to noise levels. Larger employers had the resources to look beyond the Code of Practice and reach their own conclusions about the nature and extent of the risks posed to their employees and "their appreciation that the Code limit [of 90dB(A) lepd] was no longer acceptable was sufficient to found liability" (at [104] per Lord Dyson). [Though note Lord Mance's view (at [25]) that this appears to penalise employers "who have a safety department and medical officers and take noise more seriously than the ordinary reasonable employer" since they are held liable, while others are not. In his Lordship's opinion that was "appropriate if extra resources or diligence lead to relevant fresh knowledge. But here they have led simply to the formation or inception of a different view to that generally accepted about what precautions to take. In such a case, the effect of the judge's approach is not to blame employers 'for not ploughing a lone furrow'; rather, it positively blames them for ploughing a lone furrow but not doing so deeply enough."].

Acting in an emergency. NOTE 656. Add: See also *Smith v Chief Constable of* **8–144** *Nottinghamshire Police* [2012] EWCA Civ 161; [2012] R.T.R. 23 (police vehicle responding to an emergency, with flashing blue lights, being driven at 40–50mph in a busy town centre on a Friday night hit pedestrian in the middle of the road; police driver held to have been negligent).

Sporting activity. NOTE 663. Add: See also *Phee v Gordon* [2013] CSIH 18; **8–145** 2013 S.L.T. 439—an amateur golfer does not act in the heat of competition in deciding to play a shot when other golfers are in the vicinity (defendant golfer held liable for golf ball striking claimant, having overestimated his own skill; he could have waited for the claimant to have moved).

NOTE 664. Add: Note that the Court of Appeal in *Uren v Corporate Leisure (UK) Ltd* [2011] EWCA Civ 66; [2011] I.C.R. D11, while not disagreeing with the comments of Field J. quoted in the Text, questioned whether the judge had reached the correct balance between the level of risk and the social utility of the game that the claimant had been participating in. Smith L.J. accepted that such balancing judgments were "very much a matter for the trial judge and this court will not interfere with such a judgment unless the judge has made a recognisable error or unless his conclusion is clearly wrong" (at [69]). Although Smith L.J. "would not have assessed the social value of this game in quite such glowing terms as did the judge" there was no error in the judge's approach. However, the claimant's appeal was allowed on the basis that the judge had taken an incorrect approach to the assessment of the degree of risk of serious injury. If the risk assessment was flawed that threw into question whether the appropriate balance between the degree of risk and the social value of the game had been reached. At the re-trial the defendants were held liable on the basis that the risk assessment was inadequate in failing to take into account the potential severity of the injury, even though the likelihood of it occurring was small; although the risk had to be balanced against the social value of the game being played it could have been eliminated by banning head-first diving into a shallow pool of water without significantly detracting from its social value: *Uren v Corporate Leisure (UK) Ltd* [2013] EWHC 353 (QB) (Foskett J. considered that a warning to participants of the dangers of diving would have been sufficient, but accepted the expert evidence that banning it was the appropriate response to the risk: at [204]–[208]). See also *Phee v Gordon* [2013] CSIH 18; 2013 S.L.T. 439 where a golf club was held jointly liable with a golfer for injury to the claimant caused by a stray golf ball because the club had not undertaken a risk assessment and had failed to place warning signs (club held 80 per cent responsible and golfer 20 per cent); *Corbett v Cumbria Kart Racing Club* [2013] EWHC 1362 (QB) (organisers of a motorcycle and sidecar race negligent in arrangement of safety barriers in that an ambulance was parked too close to the barriers; claimant left the track at speed, went through the barriers and collided with the ambulance). The position will be different where the accident was wholly unforeseeable: *Blair-Ford v CRS Adventures Ltd* [2012] EWHC 2360 (QB) ("freak accident" during "welly-wanging" event was not reasonably foreseeable and therefore, despite a "dynamic risk assessment" having been carried out, no steps were required to modify the method of throwing the welly, nor was there any need to provide specific warnings to the claimant).

(ii) *Balancing cost and benefit*

8–153   **Degree of likelihood of harm.** NOTE 702. Add: See also *Addis v Campbell* [2011] EWCA Civ 906.

8–158   **Occupiers.** Add: In considering what it is reasonable for the individual occupier to do to satisfy a "measured duty of care" the court must consider all the circumstances, including the claimants' right to recover the cost of remedial works from another defendant and the likelihood that the claimants were insured against damage to their properties by flooding: *Lambert v Barratt Homes Ltd* [2010] EWCA Civ 681; [2010] B.L.R. 527. This case concerned liability for the cost of remedial works to prevent flooding of the claimants' property. A local authority had sold a parcel of land to a developer who built houses on the land and in doing so blocked part of a drainage ditch and drain. Water accumulated on land retained by the local authority and occasionally flooded the claimants' properties. The Court of Appeal noted that a local authority could be expected to have access to funds far in excess of those available to the individual claimants, but the resources of the local authority were not the only issue: "it is well known that most local authorities are under a degree of financial pressure. Moreover their resources are held for public purposes and are not generally available for the benefit of private citizens" (at [22]). The fact that the claimants had a right to recover the whole of the cost of the remedial work from the developer was "a powerful factor to take into account when determining the current scope of [the local authority's] duty of care" (at [23]) and it was accordingly not fair, just or reasonable to impose on the authority a duty to carry out and pay for any part of the work. The authority's duty was limited to a duty to co-operate in a solution which involved the construction of suitable drainage and a catch pit on their retained land.

The utility of freedom to take risks. Add: The failure of a judge to refer to **8-160** Lord Hoffmann's analysis in *Tomlinson v Congleton BC* of the balancing exercise that has to be performed does not necessarily mean that there is an error of law, provided that the judge actually undertakes an assessment of balance between the social value of the activity giving rise to the risk and the cost of preventative measures: *Scout Association v Barnes* [2010] EWCA Civ 1476, where the defendants were found to be in breach of duty in respect of injury to 13-year-old scout sustained when playing a game called "Objects in the Dark" in which boys rushed to the centre of a hall to compete for possession of blocks when the lights were turned off. The judge considered that playing the game in the dark added to the risk of injury, but the only value it added was to increase the excitement of the game: "The darkness did not add any other social or educative value but it did significantly increase the risk of injury". Smith L.J. accepted that scouting activities are valuable to society and will often properly include an element of risk, but that could not mean that any scouting activity, however risky, is acceptable just because scouting is a good thing: "The social value of the particular activity must be taken into account in assessing whether the activity was reasonably safe" (at [46]). Smith L.J. accepted that "the law of tort must not interfere with activities just because they carry some risk. Of course, the law of tort must not stamp out socially desirable activities. But whether the social benefit of an activity is such that the degree of risk it entails is acceptable is a question of fact, degree and judgment, which must be decided on an individual basis and not by a broad brush approach" (at [49]). Jackson L.J dissented on the basis that he could not see how the increased risks from turning off the lights outweighed the social benefits of the activity. Ward L.J., though clearly hesitant about the outcome (see at [50]) agreed with Smith L.J. that the judge had engaged "in the *Tomlinson* task of balancing the social value of the activity giving rise to the risk and the cost of the preventative measures: more fun playing in the dark but more risk; less fun and less risk playing with the lights on. Is the benefit of added fun worth the added risk? He decided it was not worth it" (at [59]).

NOTE 732. Add: *Poppleton v Trustees of the Portsmouth Youth Activities Committee* [2008] EWCA Civ 646; [2009] P.I.Q.R. P1 was distinguished in *Pinchbeck v Craggy Island Ltd* [2012] EWHC 2745 (QB) where it was held that the defendants had assumed responsibility for the safety of the claimant who was injured in a fall whilst "bouldering", and therefore the defendants were under a duty to provide appropriate supervision and instruction.

8–162   Add: In *Uren v Corporate Leisure (UK) Ltd* [2011] EWCA Civ 66; [2011] I.C.R. D11 at [13] the Court of Appeal endorsed the view that s.1 of the Compensation Act 2006 adds nothing to the common law which "at least since *Tomlinson v Congleton Borough Council*, if not before" has required the court to take into account the matters set out in the section. See also *Scout Association v Barnes* [2010] EWCA Civ 1476 at [34] per Jackson L.J. (quoted at para.**1–17** of this Supplement).

8–163   **Balancing risk and utility.** Add: See also *Scout Association v Barnes* [2010] EWCA Civ 1476, discussed at para.**8–160** of this Supplement.

NOTE 740. Add: See further the decision of the Court of Appeal in *Uren v Corporate Leisure (UK) Ltd* [2011] EWCA Civ 66; [2011] I.C.R. D11 on the balance to be drawn between the degree of risk of injury and the social utility of a game; and the analysis of Foskett J. in *Uren v Corporate Leisure (UK) Ltd* [2013] EWHC 353 (QB). In *Blair-Ford v CRS Adventures Ltd* [2012] EWHC 2360 (QB) at [68] Globe J. commented that where there was no foreseeable real risk of injury "the social utility of the activity which gave rise to incident does not fall to be considered".

(iii) *Common practice and expectations*

8–165   **Common practice.** Add: In *Baker v Quantum Clothing Group* [2011] UKSC 17; [2011] 1 W.L.R. 1003 the Supreme Court held that a Government Code of Practice issued in 1972 on occupational exposure to noise levels between 85dB(A) lepd and 90dB(A)lepd set the standard for the reasonable and prudent employer without specialist knowledge until the late 1980s, so that the "average" employer was not in breach of duty in following the guidance. However, the Code of Practice did not provide an excuse to large employers with knowledge of the risks to some employees of exposure to noise levels between 85dB(A)lepd and 90dB(A) lepd, since they had come to the conclusion that the 90dB limit was no longer acceptable. Lord Dyson commented, at [101], that: "There is no rule of law that a relevant code of practice or other official or regulatory instrument necessarily sets the standard of care for the purpose of the tort of negligence. The classic statements by Swanwick J. in *Stokes* and Mustill J. in *Thompson v Smiths Shiprepairers (North Shields) Ltd* [1984] QB 405 . . . remain good law. What they say about the relevance of the reasonable and prudent employer following a 'recognised and general practice' applies equally to following a code of practice which sets out practice that is officially required or recommended. Thus to follow a relevant code of practice or regulatory instrument will often afford a defence to a claim in negligence. But there are circumstances where it does not do so. For example, it may be shown that the code of practice or regulatory instrument is compromised because the standards that it requires have been lowered as a result of heavy lobbying by interested parties; or because it covers a field in which apathy and fatalism has prevailed amongst workers, trade unions, employers and legislators (see per Mustill J. in *Thompson* at pp.419–420); or because the instrument has failed to keep abreast of the latest technology and scientific understanding. But no such circumstances exist here."

Logical scrutiny of practice: the *Bolitho* test. NOTE 769. Add: *Taaffe v East*   **8–167** *of England Ambulance Service NHS Trust* [2012] EWHC 1335 (QB); (2012) 128 B.M.L.R. 71 at [68]–[70]. By the same token, where the views of expert witnesses supportive of the defendant do stand up to logical analysis the inevitable conclusion will be that the defendant was not in breach of duty: *Carter v Ministry of Justice* [2010] EWCA Civ 694 at [22].

(c) *Proof of carelessness*

Burden of proof. NOTE 786. Add: But note that where the defendant is under   **8–170** a duty to measure noise levels in the workplace and negligently fails to do so the court will look more benevolently on the claimant's evidence that the noise levels were excessive: *Keefe v Isle of Man Steam Packet Co Ltd* [2010] EWCA Civ 683 at [19]: "Similarly a defendant who has, in breach of duty, made it difficult or impossible for a claimant to adduce relevant evidence must run the risk of adverse factual findings".

Occurrence cannot normally happen without negligence. NOTE 805. Add: **8–173** Though where the evidence indicates that the vehicle skidded on black ice which could not reasonably have been foreseen the inference of negligence may be rebutted: *Smith v Fordyce* [2013] EWCA Civ 320.

Procedural effect of res ipsa loquitur. NOTE 820. Add: However, proof by   **8–176** the defendant that there was a system in place to deal with the particular hazard (spillages in a restaurant) may not be sufficient to discharge the evidential burden when there was no direct evidence as to how long the liquid had been on the floor. In circumstances where there were many employees who could have given evidence but did not, the existence of a system to clean up spillages did not in itself give rise to the inference that the spillage must have occurred a very short time before the claimant fell: *Dawkins v Carnival Plc (t/a P&O Cruises)* [2011] EWCA Civ 1237; [2012] 1 Lloyd's Rep. 1. See also *Hassan v Gill* [2012] EWCA Civ 1291; [2013] P.I.Q.R. P1 (shopkeeper liable for injuries sustained by customer slipping on a grape in the absence of evidence from the defendant about the system for dealing with spillages).

(d) *Particular instances of breach*

(i) *Road accidents*

General principles. NOTE 830. Add: In *Smith v Hammond* [2010] EWCA Civ   **8–178** 725; [2010] R.T.R. 30 at [12] the Court of Appeal rejected, as a counsel of perfection, the claimant's contention that the defendant should have sounded his horn while he was also engaged in emergency braking, swerving in an attempt to avoid a collision and at the same time doing his best to maintain control of his vehicle.

NOTE 831. Add: Though note that in *Smith v Hammond* [2010] EWCA Civ 725; [2010] R.T.R. 30 the Court of Appeal criticised a trial judge who had rejected expert evidence about reaction times to the sound of a horn on the basis that in his own experience of driving "one reacts pretty instantaneously to the shock of a horn going off". Although the judge was not bound to accept the expert evidence, if he did reject it he had to give reasons other than simply saying that it did not accord with his own experience.

8–179   **Highway Code.** NOTE 833. Add: *Goad v Butcher* [2011] EWCA Civ 158.

8–183   **Pedestrian accidents.** NOTE 869. Add: But a skid on unforeseeable black ice will rebut an inference of negligence: *Smith v Fordyce* [2013] EWCA Civ 320.
NOTE 870. Add: *Probert v Moore* [2012] EWHC 2324 (QB).

8–184   **Animals.** NOTE 875. Add: See also *Stoddart v Perucca* [2011] EWCA Civ 290—motorist collided with a horse, the rider having attempted to cross a road at a trot without looking; motorist held 50 per cent responsible for the collision, even though the rider was considered to be significantly more at fault, taking into account the fact that the motorist was driving a car.

8–185   **Dangers on the road.** NOTE 886. Add: See also *Yetkin v Newham LBC* [2010] EWCA Civ 776; [2011] Q.B. 827—highway authority which planted shrubs in a central reservation which grew to such an extent as to obscure the view of pedestrians attempting to cross the road had created a foreseeable danger to users of the highway. The highway authority's liability extended both to careful and careless pedestrians, and it did not have to be established by the claimant that the authority had created a "trap".

8–186   **Responsibility of the highway authority for road maintenance.** Add: Section 58 requires an objective judgment based on the risk to users of the highway, and does not take account of the highway authority's resources: *Wilkinson v York City Council* [2011] EWCA Civ 207. Toulson L.J. commented (at [35]) on the effect of s.58(2): "The various matters, of course not exhaustive, to which the court is required to have particular regard in section 58(2) are all objective matters going to the condition of the highway and what the authority may reasonably have been expected to know about it. There is a good reason for this. The obligation to maintain highways in a structural condition which makes them free from foreseeable danger to traffic using the road in the ordinary way is an unqualified obligation of highway authorities of long standing. If Parliament had wanted to weaken that fundamental obligation, now contained in section 41, it would have done so. Section 58 had a different purpose. Section 58 was designed simply to afford a defence to a claim for damages brought against a highway authority which was able to demonstrate that it had done all that was reasonably necessary to make the road safe for users, not an authority which decided that it was preferable to allocate its resources in other directions because other needs were more pressing than doing what was reasonably required to make the roads safe."

Scope of the duty. Add: Section 41 of the Highways Act 1980 does not extend   **8–187**
to a duty to remove surface-lying material, obstructions or spillages, whether or not they result in danger to road users: *Valentine v Transport for London* [2010] EWCA Civ 1358; [2011] P.I.Q.R. P7 (no duty in respect of accident caused by gravel/loose debris on the highway, applying *Goodes v East Sussex CC* [2000] 1 W.L.R. 1356). The fact that s.41(1A) extended the duty to the removal of snow and ice (thus reversing the conclusion on the specific facts of *Goodes*) merely served to emphasise the general rule that a highway authority is not under a duty to remove other surface material such as spillages of oil, landslips, mud or the accumulation of grit. On the other hand, where an accidental spillage of concrete has hardened and bonded to the surface of the road the concrete has become part of the fabric of the road sufficient to bring it within s.41: *Thomas v Warwickshire CC* [2011] EWHC 772 (QB) at [74]. The fact that the accretion to the fabric of the road surface was accidental rather than deliberate was irrelevant.

NOTE 895. Add: Note that in *Misell v Essex CC* it was apparently conceded by the local authority that the failure to clear mud off the road could amount to a failure to maintain the highway in breach of s.41 of the Highways Act 1980 (it was "common ground that the drainage of the highway and the taking of physical steps on the highway to remove the mud or prevent its accumulation would be 'maintenance' "). This view may now have to be reconsidered in light of the decision in *Valentine v Transport for London* [2010] EWCA Civ 1358; [2011] P.I.Q.R. P7 (above).

NOTE 897. Add: Note that *Gorringe* cannot be treated as authority for the view that a highway authority's common law duty not negligently, by some positive act, to create a danger on the highway is owed only to reasonably careful, prudent road users; nor is it limited to a duty not to create a "trap" into which the user of highway has been enticed: *Yetkin v Newham LBC* [2010] EWCA Civ 776; [2011] Q.B. 827 (planting shrubs in a central reservation which obscured the view of pedestrians attempting to cross the road could constitute actionable negligence).

(ii) *Transport accidents*

Road transport. NOTE 928. Add: But not dangers encountered by a passenger   **8–190**
after alighting from the vehicle: *Fernquest v City & County of Swansea* [2011] EWCA Civ 1712 (see para.**8–51**, Note 214 of this Supplement).

(iii) *Care for children*

Parental duty to child. Add: See also *XA v YA* [2010] EWHC 1983 (QB);   **8–192**
[2011] P.I.Q.R. P1 where Thirlwall J. drew upon the reservations expressed in *Surtees* and *Barrett* to suggest that it was not fair, just and reasonable to impose a duty of care on a mother to protect a child of the family from physical assault by the child's father where the only means of discharging the duty would have been to break up the family unit by one means or another. The mother had also been the victim of domestic violence and was in a vulnerable psychological state. Thirlwall J. doubted "that the imposition of a common law duty of care would improve the lives of children within the home" and considered that it was "undesirable for the

ordinary civil courts to have to judge, retrospectively, the decisions of a mother about how best to ensure a secure upbringing for her children in the context of a claim for damages for negligence" (at [143]). These observations were obiter, since Thirlwall J. had already ruled that the child's claim was statute barred.

8–193　　　　NOTE 944, Add: See also *Cockbill v Riley* [2013] EWHC 656 (QB) (householder not liable for injuries sustained when 16-year-old belly-flopped or dived into a paddling pool at a party).

8–197　　　　**School responsibility.** Add at the end of the paragraph: A school does not owe a non-delegable duty of care to a pupil to ensure that third parties exercise reasonable care with respect to the pupil's safety: *Woodland v Swimming Teachers' Association* [2012] EWCA Civ 239; [2012] P.I.Q.R. P12 (claimant injured in the course of a swimming lesson arranged by the school but provided by a third party; school not liable for alleged negligence of independent contractors in supervising the claimant). See also *XVW v Gravesend Grammar Schools for Girls* [2012] EWHC 575 (QB); [2012] E.L.R. 417 (school not liable for rape of claimant pupils by a local man on a school trip to Belize).

8–198　　　　**Playing and bullying.** NOTE 975. *Webster v Ridgeway Foundation School* [2010] EWHC 157 (QB) is now reported at [2010] E.L.R. 694.

8–199　　　　**Sports supervision.** NOTE 982. Add: *Hammsersley-Gonsalves v Redcar and Cleveland BC* [2012] EWCA Civ 1135; [2012] E.L.R. 431 (claimant pupil struck by golf club swung by another pupil; teacher could not be expected to see every action of each of 22 boys and so held not negligent in supervising the group).

8–200　　　　**Educational development.** Add: A claim that a student failed to reach an appropriate level of educational achievement as a consequence of negligent teaching is potentially available, but the claimant must prove a breach of duty applying the *Bolam* test: *Abramova v Oxford Institute of Legal Practice* [2011] EWHC 613 (QB); [2011] E.L.R. 385. Such a claim would require expert evidence as to responsible educational practice.

CHAPTER 9

BREACH OF STATUTORY DUTY

			PARA.
1.	Introduction		9–01
■ 2.	Categorising breaches of statutory duty		9–05
■ 3.	Is the breach actionable?		9–11
	□ (a)	Duty imposed for the protection of a particular class of individuals	9–14
	■ (b)	Significance of the remedy provided by the statute	9–18
	□ (c)	Actions against public authorities	9–31
	□ (d)	Other factors in determining whether the breach is actionable	9–42
	□ (e)	Kind of damage sustained by the claimant	9–43
	□ (f)	Secondary legislation	9–45
	■ (g)	Breach of European legislation	9–46
	■ (h)	Proposals for reform	9–49
4.	Damage within the ambit of the statute		9–50
5.	The standard of liability		9–54
■ 6.	Causation		9–60
7.	Defences		9–63

2. CATEGORISING BREACHES OF STATUTORY DUTY

The principle that a mere failure to perform a statutory duty will not normally **9–09** give rise to a common law right to damages if the statute itself does not, on its true construction, give rise to an action for breach of statutory duty, was applied by the Court of Appeal in *Dwr Cymru Cyfyngedig (Welsh Water) v Barratt Homes Ltd* [2013] EWCA Civ 233; (2013) 147 Con. L.R. 1. The defendants had wrongfully denied access to their sewers contrary to the Water Industry Act 1991 s.106. The court held that breach of that section did not give rise to an action for damages for breach of statutory duty and that, in those circumstances, the aggrieved occupiers could not bring a claim for damages in nuisance since, in the absence of the statute, there could be no basis for such a common law claim. The claimants' only remedy was to seek an order compelling performance of the public law duty to permit access to the sewers: see *Barratt Homes Ltd v Dwr Cymru Cyfyngedig (Welsh Water)* [2009] UKSC 13; [2010] 1 All E.R. 965 (decided in earlier proceedings between the same parties).

The observations of Lord Hoffmann and Lord Scott in *Gorringe v Calderdale MBC*, on the difficulty of deriving a common law duty of care from the mere existence of a statutory duty, were relied upon by Turner J. in *Flaherty v Turner* [2013] EWHC 377 (QB). In this case an outbreak of E.Coli occurred at a visitor attraction for which the defendant public authorities had statutory health and safety responsibilities. A negligence claim based upon an alleged failure by the defendants to take a proactive role in the events surrounding the outbreak was struck out.

9–10   **Relationship between the parties.** In *Smith v The Ministry of Defence* [2013] UKSC 41; [2013] 3 W.L.R. 69 the Supreme Court held, by a majority, that the well-established common law duty of care owed by an employer to his employee enabled negligence actions to proceed against the Ministry of Defence in respect of service personnel killed or injured in Iraq due to the provision of allegedly defective equipment or inadequate training. Whether the duty had been *breached* could only be determined after a full trial which would need to investigate whether the considerations which bore upon the allegedly negligent decisions, including any relevant political or policy issues, were such as to render the imposition of liability not fair, just or reasonable.

3. IS THE BREACH ACTIONABLE?

9–11   **Express provision.** NOTE 37. In *Ali City of Bradford* [2010] EWCA Civ 1282; [2012] 1 W.L.R. 161 the Court of Appeal held that the Highways Act 1980 s.130, which requires a highway authority "to prevent, as far as possible, the stopping up or obstruction" of any highway for which they are responsible (subs.(3)), does *not* give rise to a civil action for breach of statutory duty. The scope of the duty to maintain the highway under s.41 of the Highways Act 1980 was examined in contrasting decisions of the Court of Appeal. In *Valentine v Transport for London* [2010] EWCA Civ 1358; [2011] P.I.Q.R. P7 an alleged failure to remove grit from the road surface did not give rise to liability under the section, whereas in *Wilkinson v York City Council* [2011] EWCA Civ 207 allowing a pothole to go unrepaired did so (an attempted s.58 defence of reasonable care was rejected in the latter case).

9–12   **Statute is silent.** The various presumptions or "indicators" were considered by the Court of Appeal in *Dwr Cymru Cyfyngedig (Welsh Water) v Barratt Homes Ltd* [2013] EWCA Civ 233; (2013) 147 Con. L.R. 1 in deciding whether contravention of s.106 of the Water Industry Act 1991 gave rise to an action for damages for breach of statutory duty. The court concluded that it did not do so, notwithstanding that the provision, which compels water companies to permit access to their sewers, was for the benefit of a limited class of persons and highly specific (rather than discretionary) in nature. The overall policy of the Act, and a comparison of the section with other provisions in the same statute, led the court to conclude that Parliament had not intended to provide an action for damages.

In *Digicel v Cable & Wireless* [2010] EWHC 774 (Ch) legislation was passed in various Caribbean jurisdictions to promote the entry of new operators into their telecommunications markets. The claimants, who were new operators, sought damages for breach of statutory duty from the defendants, the former monopoly provider of telecommunication services, on the ground that they had contravened the legislation by failing to facilitate the entry of the new operators. Morgan J. reviewed the English authorities on breach of statutory duty (the parties having agreed that they were applicable), and deduced 15 "principal matters" from them to be addressed in interpreting the legislation (see at [161] and Annex H). The various jurisdictions fell to be considered separately, although the conclusions of Morgan J. were broadly similar in each of them. In the case of one of the jurisdictions, St Lucia, he considered that the indicators against actionability were "very much stronger" than those in favour (see [2010] EWHC at [179]), and concluded that the legislation "was primarily passed in the public interest rather than for the benefit of telecommunications operators" (see [2010] EWHC 774 at [163]).

The "narrow" construction test The first sentence of this paragraph in the **9–13** Main Work was quoted with approval by Hamblen J. in *Brown v Innovations Plc* [2012] EWHC 1321 at [1273] (decided on the Financial Services Act 2000).

NOTE 44. Add See also *Brown v Innovations Plc* [2012] EWHC 1321 at [1273].

(a) *Duty imposed for the protection of a particular class of individuals*

Protection of a limited class of the public. The majority decision of the House **9–14** of Lords in *Cullen v Chief Constable of the Royal Ulster Constabulary*, that breach of a detained person's right to consult a solicitor does not give right to an action for damages for breach of statutory duty, must now be read in the light of the unanimous decision of a seven member Supreme Court in *Cadder (Peter) v HM Advocate* [2010] UKSC 43; [2010] 1 W.L.R. 2601, that the failure of Scottish criminal law to afford such a right to detained persons constitutes a breach of art.6 of the European Convention on Human Rights.

NOTE 50. *St Poulton's Trustee in Bankruptcy v Ministry of Justice* [2010] EWCA Civ 392 is now reported in [2011] Ch.1; [2010] 4 All E.R. 600. See also para.**9–18** below.

General public as a particular class. The dictum of Atkin L.J. in *Phillips v* **9–15** *Britannia Hygienic Laundry*, that in an appropriate case all members of the public may qualify as claimants for breach of a statutory duty, was criticised by Lord Rodger in *Morrison Sports Ltd v Scottish Power Plc* [2010] UKSC 37; [2010] 1 W.L.R. 1934. His Lordship referred with approval to the observations of Neuberger J., in *Todd v Adams and Chope (The "Margaretha Maria")* [2002] EWCA Civ 509; [2002] 2 Lloyd's Rep. 293 at [20], to the effect that the dictum "is inconsistent with the approach which is authoritatively laid down by the House of Lords in *X (Minors) v Bedfordshire County Council* and three other cases" (see [2010] UKSC 37 at [39]). It is nevertheless respectfully submitted that Atkin L.J.'s criticism of the notion of benefit of a specific class as a condition for liability in damages for breach of statutory duty retains much persuasive force. It is an inherently vague notion which seems to be giving effect to two objectives, which are admittedly important, but which would benefit from more explicit recognition and discussion. The first is the importance of limiting claimants to those within the risk of the danger envisaged by the statute, and the second is that of protecting statutory undertakers from huge potential liabilities (see Buckley, "Liability in Tort for Breach of Statutory Duty" (1984) 100 L.Q.R. 204, 210–214). Indeed Lord Rodger's own defence of the proposition "that one of the necessary preconditions of the existence of a private law cause of action is that the statutory duty in question was imposed for the protection of a limited class of the public" (see [2010] UKSC 37 at [40]) reflects the first of those objectives. One of the claims in the *Morrison* case was for the cost of weatherproofing a building which had become exposed as a result of the demolition of a neighbouring building following a fire caused by the defendants' alleged breach of the Electricity Supply Regulations 1988. In rejecting that particular claim Lord Rodger said: "On one view, [the claimants] can simply be regarded as members of the public who are averred to have suffered loss as a result of Scottish Power's breach of the 1988 Regulations. It seems extremely unlikely, however, that Parliament would ever have intended persons in that position to have a right of action for damages for breach of the 1988 Regulations" (see [2010] UKSC 37 at [40]). It is submitted, however, that the claim could have been dismissed more clearly and appropriately on the ground that the loss was not within the risk of the kind of harm envisaged by the Regulations (cf. *Gorris v Scott* (1874) L.R. 9 Exch. 125).

9–17   **Industrial safety legislation.** The relationship between the action for breach of statutory duty, in the context of industrial safety legislation, and common law negligence, was considered by the Supreme Court in *Baker v Quantum Clothing Group* [2011] UKSC 17; [2011] 1 W.L.R. 1003; [2011] I.C.R. 523. The claimants alleged that the levels of noise to which they had been exposed while working in the defendants' factories contravened s.29(1) of the Factories Act 1961, and also constituted negligence at common law. With scientific knowledge of the potential of noise to cause hearing damage increasing as the years went by, a critical issue was the date by which employers should have been aware of the risk so as to begin taking appropriate precautions. Section 29(1) of the 1961 Act requires that every workplace "shall, so far as is reasonably practicable, be made and kept safe for any person working there". The Court of Appeal held that the defendants had been in breach of the provision and were therefore liable to the claimants. The Court held that liability under the section was significantly more severe on defendants, and favourable to claimants, than common law negligence. By a 3 to 2 majority, however, the Supreme Court reversed the Court of Appeal and held that the defendants would not incur liability, either under the section or at common law, until a later date than that favoured by the Court of Appeal. The three Justices in the majority (Lords Mance, Dyson and Saville) considered that the criteria for liability under s.29(1), having regard to the proviso for reasonable practicability, were not significantly different from those for negligence at common law (apart from the burden of proof). Lord Dyson said (at [127]):

"I assume that the justification for saying that the statutory duty must differ from the common law duty is that the statutory provisions would otherwise be otiose. But there is no principle of law that a statutory obligation cannot be interpreted as being co–terminous with a common law duty. As Stephenson L.J. said in *Bux v Slough Metals Ltd* [1973] 1 W.L.R. 1358, 1369–1370: 'The statutory obligation may exceed the duty at common law or it may fall short of it or it may equal it'. Sometimes Parliament may decide that, in the interests of clarity and certainty, there is advantage in providing a detailed all-embracing set of rules. The merit in setting these out in a single authoritative document, such as a statute, is not undermined even if they do no more than reflect what the courts would be likely to decide when applying the common law."

Since, however, the two dissentients (Lords Kerr and Clarke) would have construed s.29(1) as imposing a stricter duty than the common law (see especially per Lord Clarke in [2011] UKSC 17 at [191] et seq.), the observations of the majority on the relationship between industrial safety legislation and the common law of negligence should perhaps be approached with caution when other statutory provisions fall to be construed.

(b) *Significance of the remedy provided by the statute*

No remedy provided by the statute. The already doubtful proposition that the   **9–18**
absence of a remedy in the statute creates a presumption in favour of an action in tort for breach of statutory duty (otherwise the statute would be a "pious aspiration") has been further weakened by the decision of the Court of Appeal in *St Poulton's Trustee in Bankruptcy v Ministry of Justice* [2010] EWCA Civ 392; [2011] Ch. 1; [2010] 4 All E.R. 600. In this case the court held that the Insolvency Rules 1986 r.6.13, intended to protect creditors in an insolvency, do not give rise to an action for breach of statutory duty in the event of failure by a court to comply with the requirement in the Rules to notify the Chief Land Registrar of the filing of a petition against the bankrupt; notwithstanding the absence of any sanction for breach of the Rules. The duty rested upon court officials and the absence of a sanction was therefore of little relevance since "Court officers and staff have, it may be assumed, every reason to carry out their duties efficiently, and no reason to fail to do so": see per Pill L.J. in [2010] EWCA Civ 392 at [104], see also per Lloyd L.J. at [42].

Cullen v Chief Constable of the Royal Ulster Constabulary must now be read   **9–24**
in the light of *Cadder (Peter) v HM Advocate* [2010] UKSC 43; [2010] 1 W.L.R. 2601 (see para.**9–14** above).

Alternative remedies. In *Hall v Cable and Wireless Plc* [2009] EWHC 1793   **9–25**
(Comm); [2010] 1 B.C.L.C. 95 the High Court held that breach of the listing rules made under s.74 of the Financial Services and Markets Act 2000 did not give rise to an action for damages for breach of statutory duty. The Act provides a complex scheme of different remedies for breach of the listing rules, including the power of the Financial Services Authority to impose a penalty (see s.91), and the power of the court to make restitution orders (see s.382). Moreover certain provisions of the Act are expressly made actionable at the suit of individuals, but these provisions do not apply to the rules in question. The court therefore concluded that the scheme of the Act "provided a clear indication that Parliament did not intend that a breach of the listing rules would give rise to a cause of action at the suit of a private person". To hold otherwise would "interfere with the scheme and modes of enforcement" laid down by the Act (see [2009] EWHC 1793 (Comm) at [16] per Teare J.). See also *Brown v Innovations Plc* [2012] EWHC 1321 at [1277] in which Hamblen J. followed Teare J. in a case also decided under the Financial Services and Markets Act 2000.

In *Francis v London Borough of Southwark* [2011] EWCA Civ 1418; [2012] H.L.R.16 the claimant sought damages for breach of statutory duty on the ground that, when he sought to exercise the statutorily conferred right to buy the council property in which he had formerly lived, that right had wrongfully been denied him and that, in consequence, he had lost the benefit of the discount on the purchase price which he would have enjoyed together with the benefit of compensation which he would have received when, as occurred subsequently, the property was demolished. The defendant Council had denied the claimant the right to buy on the ground that he was not a secure tenant and was therefore not qualified. A subsequent judicial decision had, however, established that in fact he *had* been a secure tenant. The Court of Appeal nevertheless held that his claim for damages would fail. Parliament had not intended, when conferring the right to buy in the Housing Act 1985 s.118, and associated procedural provisions, to create a right to damages for breach of statutory duty in the event of a failure to grant the right to buy to someone who was entitled to it. The Housing Act made its own provision for sanctions to enforce the landlord's obligation in the event of wrongful denial of the right to buy, which was considered to point against an action for damages. It was unfortunate that owing to the special circumstances of the instant case, including the demolition of the property, the sanctions expressly provided for did not assist the claimant as the law then stood. "However", observed Carnwath L.J., "the mere fact that in some circumstances the remedy created by the Act is not complete, is not a justification for reading into it words which are not there".

(c) *Actions against public authorities*

9–31   NOTE 132. *St Poulton's Trustee in Bankruptcy v Ministry of Justice* [2010] EWCA Civ 392 is now reported in [2011] Ch.1; [2010] 4 All E.R. 600. See also para.**9–18** above.

9–40   The importance of not allowing negligence claims based upon a duty of care at common law to become confused with those applying to claims sought to be derived from a statute, merely because the relationship between the parties happens to arise out of the exercise by a public authority of its statutory functions, was illustrated by *Yetkin v Newham LBC* [2010] EWCA Civ 776; [2011] Q.B. 827. The defendant highway authority had planted shrubs and bushes and plants in the central reservation of a busy highway. The claimant pedestrian was hit by a car while crossing the road. Although she had clearly been contributorily negligent, she sought to hold the highway authority liable, alleging that the bushes had obscured her view. The trial judge agreed that they had done so, but nevertheless exonerated the defendant authority from liability in reliance on observations in *Gorringe v Calderdale MBC* [2004] UKHL15; [2004] 1 W.L.R. 1057, dealing with the absence of a duty on highway authorities to protect road users from the consequences of their own carelessness. The Court of Appeal reversed the decision of the trial judge, however, holding that the *Gorringe* case was not in point. A decision dealing with the inability of a statutory power to give rise to a common law duty of care which did not otherwise exist, and with an omission to exercise that power therefore not giving rise to negligence liability, was not relevant to a situation in which the positive actions of a highway authority had given rise to ordinary negligence liability at common law by creating a new source of danger which had not previously existed.

The proposition that where acts claimed to be negligent are carried out within **9–41** the ambit of a statutory discretion that is not in itself a reason why no claim for negligence can be brought in respect of them was applied in unusual circumstances in *Connor v Surrey CC* [2010] EWCA Civ 286; [2011] Q.B. 429. See para.**14–08** of this Supplement. The claimant headmistress brought a claim for stress at work against her employer, the local education authority. She suffered a nervous breakdown following unjust allegations of racism made against her by present and former members of the school's governing body. She claimed successfully that the defendants should have used their statutory discretion to dissolve the governing body, which had become dysfunctional, and replace it with an interim executive board. The Court of Appeal rejected the contention that the authority's discretion whether or not to exercise its power in this way was not justiciable. The court emphasised that the claim was based on the common law duty of care owed by an employer to its employee, it was not a case in which an attempt was being made to derive the duty of care from the statute itself. Furthermore, on the facts of the case there was no conflict between the defendants' public and private law duties. From both perspectives the chaotic state of the governance of the school had called for intervention by the authority.

(d) *Other factors in determining whether the breach is actionable*

NOTE 164. *St Poulton's Trustee in Bankruptcy v Ministry of Justice* [2010] **9–42** EWCA Civ 392 is now reported in [2011] Ch.1; [2010] 4 All E.R. 600. See also para.**9–18** above.

(e) *Kind of damage sustained by the claimant*

Cullen v Chief Constable of the Royal Ulster Constabulary must now be read **9–44** in the light of *Cadder (Peter) v HM Advocate* [2010] UKSC 43; [2010] 1 W.L.R. 2601 (see para.**9–14** above).

(f) *Secondary legislation*

NOTE 181. *St Poulton's Trustee in Bankruptcy v Ministry of Justice* [2010] **9–45** EWCA Civ 392 is now reported in [2011] Ch.1; [2010] 4 All E.R. 600. See also para.**9–18** above.

(g) *Breach of European legislation*

In *AB v Home Office* [2012] EWHC 226; [2012] 4 All E.R. 276 the High Court **9–48** considered a claim for damages for breach of European legislation. The claimants, a citizen of the European Union and his co-habiting partner, a Bolivian citizen, sought compensation for financial losses they allegedly suffered as a result of delay and mishandling by the Home Office of the Bolivian citizen's immigration status as a resident. Mr Richard Salter QC (sitting as a Deputy Judge of the Queen's Bench Division) examined the facts of the case in the light of the three conditions for the conferring of a right to damages by European Community Law, but concluded that they were not satisfied. The applicable provisions of the relevant EC Directive (the "Citizens Directive") did not confer a right to a grant of residence but, in any event, the conduct of which the claimants complained was merely maladministration and could not constitute a "sufficiently serious" breach of Community law. The question posed by the third condition, which relates to causation, therefore did not arise.

NOTE 191. Add: *Test Claimants in the Franked Investment Group Litigation v Inland Revenue Commissioners* [2010] EWCA Civ 103; [2010] S.T.C. 1251; [2010] B.T.C. 265; reversed in part at [2012] UKSC 19; [2012] 2 A.C. 337.

(h) *Proposals for reform*

9–49   A prominent example of a statutory provision expressly designed to create new civil remedies is the Financial Services and Markets Act 2000 s.150(1). This provides that contravention of a defined type of delegated legislation promulgated by the Financial Services Authority will "be actionable at the suit of a private person who suffers loss as a result of the contravention subject to the defences and other incidents applying to actions for breach of statutory duty". In *Rubenstein v HSBC Bank Plc* [2012] EWCA Civ 1184; [2013] 1 All E.R. (Comm) 915 an investor who had been mis-sold an inappropriate product by the defendant bank was awarded substantial damages for, inter alia, breach of statutory duty pursuant to this section. The provision is a good illustration of the beneficial simplification which express statements of Parliamentary intention can facilitate.

In its report *Administrative Redress: Public Bodies and the Citizen*, Law Com No.232, published in 2010, the Law Commission abandoned a suggestion, which it had made earlier in a consultation paper, that the action for breach of statutory duty should be abolished "in most contexts" (see (2008) Law Com. CP 187 at para.4–105). In the consultation paper the Commission had noted the non-implementation of its 1969 proposal for the enactment of a general statutory presumption, and recommended instead the introduction of an entirely new, wider, remedy enabling individuals to obtain financial redress from public bodies if those bodies had been "seriously at fault" (see (2008) Law Com. CP 187 at para.4–95). Since, however, in its final report the Commission dropped the proposal for the new remedy, it followed that the suggestion that the existing remedy of breach of statutory duty should be abolished was also not proceeded with (see *Administrative Redress: Public Bodies and the Citizen*, Law Com No.232 paras 3–73—3–74).

7. DEFENCES

9–65   **Delegation of duty** NOTE 268 Add: See also *Brumder v Motornet* [2013] EWCA Civ 195; [2013] P.I.Q.R. P13 (on which see para.**13–63** of this Supplement).

CHAPTER 10

PROFESSIONAL LIABILITY

PARA.

1. General considerations 10–01
   ■ (a) Professional liability 10–01
   ■ (b) Professional negligence: exclusion of duty. 10–17
   ■ (c) Stricter liability 10–21
   (d) Breach of fiduciary duty 10–22
      ■ (i) Fiduciary duties generally 10–23
      ■ (ii) Remedies for breach of fiduciary duty. 10–30
   □ (e) Breach of confidence 10–34
   ■ (f) Immunity from suit 10–36
■ 2. Medicine and allied professions 10–44
   (a) Consent to treatment 10–46
      ■ (i) Adults. 10–48
      ■ (ii) Children 10–55
      ■ (iii) Persons suffering from mental incapacity 10–59
   ■ (b) Medical negligence 10–63
      (i) Diagnosis 10–69
      (ii) Treatment 10–70
      (iii) Failure to warn 10–73
      ■ (iv) Self-harm 10–77
      ■ (v) Antenatal injuries 10–79
      ■ (vi) Failed sterilisation 10–83
      ■ (vii) Liability of other medical and quasi-medical professionals 10–86
      ■ (viii) Hospitals and health authorities. 10–90
      ■ (ix) Proving negligence. 10–94
      ■ (x) Causation. 10–96
      ■ (xi) Damages. 10–104
3. Law 10–105
   (a) Immunities 10–106
   (b) Duties owed by lawyers 10–109
      ■ (i) Duties to clients 10–109
      ■ (ii) Duties to third parties. 10–112
      ■ (iii) Fiduciary and equitable duties 10–119
   □ (c) Wasted costs orders. 10–120
   ■ (d) What amounts to breach of duty 10–124
   (e) Specific duties. 10–133
      ■ (i) The duty to advise 10–133
      (ii) The duty to explain documents 10–136
      (iii) Duty to keep client informed 10–137
      □ (iv) Duty to take care in carrying through transaction 10–138
      □ (v) Duty to take care in conduct of litigation. 10–139
   □ (f) Damages 10–140
   ■ (g) Causation. 10–146
4. Surveyors 10–154
   (a) Duties owed 10–154
      (i) Duties to clients 10–154
      □ (ii) Duties to non-clients 10–155
      (iii) Exclusion of duty 10–159
   (b) Negligence 10–163
      ■ (i) General. 10–163

■ (ii) Valuation 10–166
   (iii) Failure to observe defects in property 10–168
   (iv) advice, etc. 10–171
 (c) Causation. 10–172
□ (d) Damages 10–174
5. Architects and consulting engineers 10–182
 (a) Duties 10–182
□ (i) Duties to clients 10–182
□ (ii) Duties to others 10–183
 (b) Breach of duty. 10–188
□ (i) Design and supervision 10–188
   (ii) Advice 10–190
□ (iii) Certification issues. 10–191
■ (c) Damages 10–192
6. Finance 10–195
 (a) Accountants and auditors 10–195
   (i) Duties to clients 10–196
■ (ii) Duties to others 10–197
 (b) Breach of duty. 10–200
   (i) Adult 10–201
□ (ii) Advice 10–204
   (iii) Conflict of interest 10–205
 (c) Causation. 10–206
□ (d) Damages 10–207
 (e) Accountants as receivers. 10–209
 (f) Stockbrokers 10–211
7. Insurance brokers 10–212
□ (a) Duties 10–212
   (i) Duties to clients 10–213
   (ii) Duties to others 10–214
 (b) Breach 10–216
   (i) Failure to arrange insurance as instructed 10–217
□ (ii) Failure to obtain insurance suitable for client 10–218
   (iii) Negligent advice 10–219
   (iv) Failure to provide full and correct information to insurer 10–220
□ (c) Damages 10–221
□ (d) Causation. 10–227
 (e) Contributory negligence 10–231

1. GENERAL CONSIDERATIONS

(a) *Professional liability*

10–03   NOTE 8. Add: Also relevant here is the practice of not generally holding a professional person liable in the absence of expert evidence that a practice is misguided. For a recent example see *Caribbean Steel Co Ltd v Price Waterhouse* [2013] UKPC 18; [2013] P.N.L.R. 27.

10–08   **Clients, patients and personal representatives.** NOTE 45. Add: See too *Steven (Ex'or of Thomson) v Hewats* [2013] CSOH 60; [2013] P.N.L.R. 23 (citing this footnote).

10–15   **Duty of care: personal liability of employed professional.** NOTE 81. Add: See too, for a further suggestion that personal liability of an employed person for negligent advice is very much the exception rather than the rule, *Challinor v Juliet Bellis & Co* [2013] EWHC 347 (Ch) at [719]–[742] (Hildyard J.).

Duties to clients and others: the impact of company law. Add: Again, it **10–16** has been held that the rule against reflexive loss will normally not apply where the claimant is a secured creditor of the company concerned and the claim is against a receiver for misfeasance: see *International Leisure Ltd v First National Trustee Co UK Ltd* [2012] EWHC 1971 (Ch); [2013] Ch. 346; [2012] P.N.L.R. 34.

(b) *Professional negligence: exclusion of duty*

General statutory limitations on exclusion. Add: On the effect of the Unfair **10–18** Contract Terms Act 1977, see *Dennard v PricewaterhouseCoopers LLP* [2010] EWHC 812 (Ch). Accountants negligently undervalued certain PFI projects on which clients of theirs wished to capitalise, thus reducing the amount for which their interest in the projects could be sold on. In fact damages were well under £1 million: but one issue which might have arisen was whether the Act invalidated a £1 million limitation clause contained in the contract with the client. Vos J., discussing the matter obiter, had no doubt that it did not. Even though there was an element of inequality of bargaining power—the defendants being one of the biggest accountancy firms in the world and the claimants a medium-sized business—the claimants, he observed at [226], "are not to be regarded as innocents abroad. They were entirely capable of protecting their own interests. They knew and understood that accountancy firms customarily limited their liability by clauses of this kind, but chose not to discuss or negotiate the limitation."

Excluding liability and preventing it arising. NOTE 107. Add: See too, for a **10–20** similar holding, *Avrora Fine Arts Investment Ltd v Christie, Manson & Woods Ltd* [2012] EWHC 2198 (Ch); [2012] P.N.L.R. 35.

(c) *Stricter liability*

Strict liabilities: services and goods. NOTE 109. Add: Nevertheless, such **10–21** agreement to be liable in the absence of negligence is not lightly inferred: see *Martin v JRC Commercial Mortgages Plc* [2012] EWCA Civ 63; [2012] P.N.L.R. 18 (despite *Platform Funding*, no promise by mortgage broker to obtain mortgage in any event, it being inherently unlikely that an absolute guarantee of results was ever intended). See too *Dhamija v Sunningdale Joineries Ltd* [2010] EWHC 2396 (TCC); [2011] P.N.L.R. 9 (refusal by Coulson J. to construe architects' certification duty as covering defects that were present, but which reasonable inspection would not reveal); and the important decision in *Nationwide Building Society v Davisons Solicitors* [2012] EWCA Civ 1626; [2013] P.N.L.R. 12 at [51]–[58] (Morritt C.: lender's solicitor's duty to advance monies against valid mortgage not a strict duty, so no breach of retainer if acted reasonably but was duped by clever mortgage fraudsters).

(d) *Breach of fiduciary duty*

(i) *Fiduciary duties generally*

10–23   **Incidence of fiduciary duties.** NOTE 125. Add: Note too *Lloyds TSB Bank Plc v Markandan & Uddin (A Firm)* [2012] EWCA Civ 65; [2012] 2 All E.R. 884. In a novel twist, solicitors who released mortgage funds without the necessary documentation, and thus rendered themselves liable for breach of trust, sought the aid of s.61 of the Trustee Act 1925 (which empowers the court to exonerate a trustee who "has acted honestly and reasonably, and ought fairly to be excused for the breach of trust"). They failed in this plea, having been at fault and thus put themselves outside the section. A further plea, that the discretion under s.61 allowed the court to take account of alleged contributory negligence by the claimant, was also smartly seen off. Rimer L.J. at [61], however, made an important converse point: although liability for breach of trust was on principle strict, solicitors who faced a liability of this type without having been at fault would be likely to have the s.61 discretion exercised in their favour and thus to be exonerated. See too, on the extent of liability, *Nationwide Building Society v Davisons Solicitors* [2012] EWCA Civ 1626; [2013] P.N.L.R. 12; *AIB Group (UK) Plc v Mark Redler & Co* [2013] EWCA Civ 45; [2013] P.N.L.R. 19, and *Santander UK Plc v RA Legal Solicitors (a firm)* [2013] EWHC 1380 (QB).

10–28   **Conflict of interest** NOTE 152. Add: See too, in the context of a professional engaged as an expert witness, *A Lloyd's Syndicate v X* [2011] EWHC 2487 (Comm); [2012] 1 Lloyd's Rep. 123.

(ii) *Remedies for breach of fiduciary duty*

10–33   NOTE 164. Add: See too, on the measure of recovery for breach of trust, *AIB Group (UK) Plc v Mark Redler & Co* [2013] EWCA Civ 45, [2013] P.N.L.R. 19.

(e) *Breach of confidence*

10–34   **The duty of confidence.** Add: A professional's duty of confidentiality may of course be excluded, in whole or in part, by agreement. For example, see *Mortgage Express v Sawali* [2010] EWHC 3054 (Ch); [2011] P.N.L.R. 11 (same solicitors acting for house purchasers and lenders: clients' common-form authorisation to solicitors to share files with lenders: when lenders later sued solicitors for negligence, no objection based on confidentiality to disclosure of entire files).

(f) *Immunities from suit*

10–41   **Litigation: testimony and connected matters.** Add: This paragraph must be read with enormous care since the decision in *Jones v Kaney* [2011] UKSC 13; [2011] 2 A.C. 398. While it seems clear that witnesses of fact retain complete immunity from suit in respect of testimony and related matters, expert witnesses no longer do, and may now be sued by those calling them, if through negligence they fail to show a sufficient degree of expertise or otherwise prejudice a client's case. In *Jones v Kaney* itself, a medical expert called by the claimant in personal injury litigation, having originally reported favourably, was alleged to have allowed herself later to be browbeaten by an opposing expert into damaging and entirely unjustified admissions, with the result that the payment in settlement was much reduced. Overruling a constant line of authority based on cases such as *Stanton v Callaghan* [2000] 1 Q.B. 75, the Supreme Court by a majority refused to strike a claim by the client for the lost recovery. The reasons were several. The immunity of someone appointed and paid to advance a client's interests, however apparently well-established, was anomalous (see [57] (Lord Phillips) and [110] (Lord Dyson)); and it was not clear that its removal would discourage potential expert witnesses from acting at all (see Lords Phillips, Collins and Dyson at [56], [83], [110]) or giving properly frank testimony (see Lords Phillips, Collins, Kerr and Dyson at [56], [83], [94], [118]). Nor was potential liability inconsistent with the expert witness's duty to the court, any more than it had been in respect of an advocate (see Lords Phillips and Dyson at [46]–[50] and [120]).

Nevertheless, two qualifications to the new rule of liability should be noted. First, Lord Collins noted at [72]–[73] that the result in *Jones* was limited to duties (a) in negligence, and (b) owed to the litigant in whose interest an expert witness acted. It had nothing to say about witness immunity outside the law of negligence (for example, in defamation); and should on no account be taken as condoning the creation of duties vis-à-vis parties other than the employing client. And secondly, at [60] Lord Phillips suggested, with great good sense, that in criminal cases a convicted defendant should be unable to sue his expert witness unless and until acquitted or cleared on appeal (as is already the case where he seeks to sue his advocate). See generally S. Carr and H. Evans, "The Removal of Immunity for Expert Witnesses" (2011) 27 P.N. 128.

The proposition that even after *Jones v Kaney* expert witnesses owe no duty to parties other than those employing them was accepted and reiterated by Supperstone J. in *Baxendale-Walker v Middleton* [2011] EWHC 998 (QB) at [128].

In *Smart v Forensic Science Service Ltd* [2013] EWCA Civ 783 it was held, following *Darker v Chief Constable of the West Midlands Police* [2001] 1 A.C. 435, that where evidence submitted to a forensic science laboratory was apparently tampered with, proceedings for breach of duty against the laboratory by a person wrongly convicted as a result should not be struck out.

2. MEDICINE AND ALLIED PROFESSIONS

Liability of medical practitioners to patients. NOTE 232. Add: See too E. **10-44** Cave, "Redress in the NHS" (2011) 27 P.N. 136.

NOTE 235. Add: See too *R (Condliff) v North Staffordshire Primary Care Trust* [2011] EWCA Civ 910; [2012] 1 All E.R. 689, seeing off a challenge under ECHR art.8 (privacy and family life) to a refusal by the NHS to fund costly treatment for gross obesity. Provided that determinations as to who would and would not be treated at the public charge were made on defensible clinical grounds, decisions as to funding were essentially a political matter not open to challenge under art.8.

10–45   **Liability to those other than patients.** Add: See too R. Mulheron, *Medical Negligence: Non-Patient and Third Party Claims* (Farnham: Ashgate Publishing Ltd, 2010).

NOTE 241. Add: See too *Less v Hussain* [2012] EWHC 3513 (QB); (2013) 130 B.M.L.R. 51 (no claim by father for psychiatric injury due to alleged negligent advice leading to continuation of pregnancy and stillbirth).

(a) *Consent to treatment*

(i) *Adults*

10–49   Add: It is now absolutely clear that the jurisdiction just described to intervene in the patient's best interests where there is no valid refusal of consent has survived the enactment of the Mental Capacity Act 2005: see *Re L (Vulnerable Adults with Capacity: Court's Jurisdiction)* [2012] EWCA Civ 253; [2013] Fam. 1.

10–53   **Advance directives.** Add: On advance directives, note *W v M* [2011] EWHC 2443 (Fam); [2012] 1 W.L.R. 1653 (patient in persistent vegetative state, but slightly conscious: evidence of previous informal conversations suggesting no desire to have life prolonged in such circumstances: such statements not valid advance directive, since not clear that they covered situation where subject conscious, and in addition not in writing as required by Mental Capacity Act 2005 s.25(6)). Importantly, Baker J. also stated at [6] that prior indications which, as here, did not satisfy the stringent requirements of the 2005 Act might have some significance, but carried comparatively little weight in deciding whether treatment was overall in the patient's best interests. In *A Local Authority v E* [2012] EWHC 1639 (COP); (2012) 127 B.M.L.R. 133 it was said that where there was some doubt as to the validity of an advance directive, treatment should be given.

(ii) *Children*

10–56   **Older children: refusal of treatment.** NOTE 315. Add: Note too S. Gilmore & J. Herring, "'No' is the Hardest Word: Consent and Children's Autonomy" (2011) 23 C.F.L.Q. 3, and E. Cave and J. Walbank, "Minors' capacity to refuse treatment" (2012) 20 Med. L. Rev. 423.

10–57   **Younger children.** NOTE 321. Add: See too *X (Baby) v An NHS Trust* [2012] EWHC 2188 (Fam); (2012) 127 B.M.L.R. 188.

(iii) *Persons suffering from mental incapacity*

10–61   **Non–detainable mentally incapacitated patients: the Mental Capacity Act 2005.** On the criteria to be applied in ordering compulsory treatment of those unable to make a decision, see *DH NHS Foundation Trust v PS* [2010] EWHC 1217 (Fam); [2010] 2 F.L.R. 1236, on which Mullender, "Involuntary medical treatment, incapacity, and respect" (2011) 127 L.Q.R. 167; and also *W v M* [2011] EWHC 2443 (Fam); [2012] 1 W.L.R. 1653 (patient in persistent vegetative state: nevertheless, no order allowing discontinuance of treatment since experience not overwhelmingly negative and some prospect of improvement in quality and enjoyment of life).

In certain cases detention measures under s.4A of the 2005 Act may fall foul of art.5 or art.8 of the ECHR, as happened in *Hillingdon LBC v Neary* [2011] EWHC 1377 (COP); [2011] 4 All E.R. 584 (detention of autistic patient in support unit without proper regard to whether better off there, or to his own clearly-expressed desire to be at home).

One further thing should also be noted. It is now clear that the jurisdiction under the Mental Capacity Act 2005 is in addition to, and does not replace, the earlier inherent jurisdiction at common law to intervene where a patient lacked the capacity to make a free choice or express a genuine consent: see *Re L (Vulnerable Adults with Capacity: Court's Jurisdiction)* [2012] EWCA Civ 253; [2013] Fam. 1. It is therefore apparent that there remains a possibility of a court making a declaration of lawfulness even if a patient is not technically incompetent under the 2005 Act. This may well be important where a patient's ability to decide is constrained, not by some "impairment of, or a disturbance in the functioning of, the mind or brain" (as required by s.2(1) of that Act) but by (for example) the undue influence of a third party. Thus the pre-Act case of *Re T (Adult: Refusal of Medical Treatment)* [1993] Fam. 95, sanctioning a blood transfusion to a patient who refused it only because she was acting under the overbearing influence of her mother, would doubtless be decided the same way today.

(b) *Medical negligence*

Negligence: The *Bolam* test and professional practice. Add: For other **10–67** straightforward examples of the *Bolam* test in practice, see *Buxton v Abertawe Bro Morgannwg University Local Health Board NHS Trust* [2010] EWHC 1187 (QB); (2010) 115 B.M.L.R. 62 (even though treatment had foreseeable side-effects, no liability for administering it, since could not be shown no practitioner would have acted as defendant did); also *Ecclestone v Medway NHS Foundation Trust* [2013] EWHC 790 (QB).

Add: For an application of *Bolitho* to paramedics, see *Taaffe v East of England* **10–68** *Ambulance Service NHS Trust* [2012] EWHC 1335 (QB); (2012) 128 B.M.L.R. 71 (failure by paramedics to infer cardiac problems from chest pains not defensible under *Bolam*).

NOTE 386. Add: See too Mulheron, "Trumping Bolam: a critical legal analysis of Bolitho's 'gloss'" [2010] C.L.J. 609.

(iv) *Self-harm*

Self-harm: vulnerable victims. Add: This paragraph must now be read with **10–78** much care, in the light of the Supreme Court's very important determination in *Rabone v Pennine Care NHS Trust* [2012] UKSC 2; [2012] 2 A.C. 72, reversing the Court of Appeal decision at [2010] EWCA Civ 698; [2011] Q.B. 1019. Liability for breach of art.2 ECHR may now apply in any case where a state organ such as a hospital fails to deal with imminent and clear threats to life, including self-harm, if the victim is "especially vulnerable by reason of their physical or mental condition" (Lord Dyson's words at [22]). There is no limit to those under state coercion, such as prisoners or formally detained mental patients (as the Court of Appeal had decided). Thus where a voluntary mental patient was given home leave despite suicidal indications and took the opportunity to do away with herself, there was found to have been a breach of art.2 in failing to detain and thus save her. With regard to liability, this result probably reflects the position at common law anyway. But the fact that art.2 is engaged remains important, since the ECHR jurisprudence peremptorily demands that where that article is in issue, bereavement damages be available to a larger class of a victim's relatives than provided for by s.1A of the Fatal Accidents Act 1976, with the bizarre result that to that extent the whole scheme of wrongful death liability now falls to be rewritten. Thus in *Rabone* itself the successful claimants were an adult victim's parents, who had no claim under s.1A. On this aspect of the case, see A. Tettenborn, "Wrongful Death, Human Rights and the Fatal Accidents Act" (2012) 128 L.Q.R. 327. For further comment see paras **14–69, 14–70** and **14–73** of this Supplement.

(v) *Antenatal injuries*

10–82   **Antenatal injury and "wrongful life".** NOTE 465. Add: See too R. Scott, "Reconsidering 'wrongful life' in England after thirty years: legislative mistakes and unjustifiable anomalies" [2013] C.L.J. 115.

(vi) *Failed sterilisation*

10–85   NOTE 486. Add: In *Less v Hussain* [2012] EWHC 3513 (QB); (2013) 130 B.M.L.R. 51 it was held that *Rees v Darlington* would not apply where, owing to bad advice, a pregnancy was continued and resulted in a stillbirth. In such a case damages fell to be awarded on normal principles.

(vii) *Liability of other medical and quasi-medical professionals*

10–89   **Other allied professions.** NOTE 508. Add: Also see *Taaffe v East of England Ambulance Service NHS Trust* [2012] EWHC 1335 (QB); (2012) 128 B.M.L.R. 71 (paramedics).

(viii) *Hospitals and health authorities*

10–93   **Hospitals and health authorities: negligence and the Human Rights Act 1998.** Add: This paragraph must now be read in the light of the Supreme Court's decision in *Rabone v Pennine Care NHS Trust* [2012] UKSC 2; [2012] 2 A.C. 72, reversing the Court of Appeal decision at [2010] EWCA Civ 698; [2011] Q.B. 1019. Potential liability for death based on a breach of art.2 ECHR is now much wider than was previously thought. It now seems that a state organ such as a hospital will be liable on this basis in any case where it culpably fails to deal with an imminent and clear threat to the life of a patient "especially vulnerable by reason of their physical or mental condition" (Lord Dyson's words at [22]). There is no limit to those under state coercion, such as prisoners or formally detained mental patients (as the Court of Appeal had decided in *Rabone*). *Rabone* itself involved the suicide of a voluntary mental patient who was given home leave despite clear indications of suicidal intent. This was held to have been a breach of art.2. Nor is this limited to suicide. In *Reynolds v United Kingdom* (2694/08) [2012] ECHR 437; (2012) 55 E.H.R.R. 35 a mental patient fell to his death from an insufficiently-reinforced institutional window. This again was held by the ECtHR to be a breach of art.2.

In fact cases of this sort would almost certainly involve liability at common law. But art.2 remains important, since the ECHR jurisprudence demands that the carefully—modulated scheme of liability for wrongful death under the Fatal Accidents Act 1976 be largely thrown over where there is a breach of art.2, and in particular requires—somewhat vaguely—that unquantified bereavement damages be available to any close relative of the victim, rather than to the limited class provided for by s.1A of the 1976 Act. Both *Rabone* and *Reynolds* involved parents of adults, who had no claim under s.1A of the 1976 Act. The award was £5,000 per parent in *Rabone* and €8,000 for a mother (the only claimant) in *Reynolds*.

(ix) *Proving negligence*

Generally. NOTE 540. Add: But res ipsa loquitur is not commonly invoked **10–94** with success in the medical context. See *Hussain v King Edward VII Hospital* [2012] EWHC 3441 (QB) at [11]–[12] (Eady J.); *Thomas v Curley* [2013] EWCA Civ 117; [2013] Med. L.R. 141 at [10] (Lloyd-Jones L.J.). Nevertheless even if res ipsa loquitur does not apply, the court may, as a matter of common sense, infer negligence from the occurrence of something that should not happen in a well-conducted procedure. See *Thomas v Curley* [2013] EWCA Civ 117; [2013] Med. L.R. 141 (injury during operation to body part remote from site of operation).

(x) *Causation*

General. Add: A similar case was *McCoy v East Midlands Strategic Health* **10–96** *Authority* [2011] EWHC 38 (QB); (2011) 118 B.M.L.R. 107 (failure by doctor to notice that CTG trace might indicate possibility of hypoxia and order a retest: but since retest concerned would have done no better, no liability). See too the Canadian decision in *Ediger v Johnston* (2011) 333 D.L.R. (4th) 633 (burden on claimant to show on a balance of probabilities that negligence contributed to injury) (reversed for other reasons in the Supreme Court of Canada: [2013] SCC 18; (2013) 356 D.L.R. (4th) 575).

Add: There have been further developments on the question: what happens **10–98** where a defendant negligently fails to refer a patient but then argues that even if referred the patient would have been negligently treated, so that the doctor's fault left the patient no worse off? Where both doctor and referee work for the same employer, it was accepted in *Bolitho* that this cannot insulate the employer: but what if the person to whom the patient should have been referred was independent? It was suggested in the text that in such a case the doctor could escape on causation grounds: but this view, though accepted by McKay J. at first instance, was rejected by the Court of Appeal in *Wright v Cambridge Medical Group* [2011] EWCA Civ 669; [2011] Med. L.R. 496. Doctors negligently failed to refer a little girl with a hip infection to a local hospital with sufficient promptness: the girl ended up disabled. The doctors led evidence that, even if the patient had been referred to the hospital on time, the hospital would not have treated her competently, and argued on that basis that their negligence had not caused any loss. As it happened this plea failed on the facts, and a majority of the Court of Appeal held that "but-for" causation could be inferred. However, all three members of the court accepted that as a matter of law it was not open to a doctor to escape liability merely on the basis that if he had not been negligent someone else would have negligently caused the same damage, and hence he personally had occasioned no loss. On the contrary: the doctor in such a case would be liable on the basis that he had deprived the claimant of the opportunity of proper treatment, and that was sufficient to create liability. Another way of justifying the same result might be to say that, if subsequent actual negligence by a third party is not necessarily sufficient to insulate a defendant from liability even if technically that defendant can say that the defendant would have been injured anyway, the same should go for subsequent hypothetical negligence.

10–103   **Causation: "failure to warn" cases.** Add: In Australia it has been held that where a surgeon negligently fails to warn of two risks A and B, and on the evidence the patient if properly warned would not have undergone the procedure, but would have accepted risk A had that been the only risk, then the patient cannot sue if risk A eventuates. See *Wallace v Kam* [2013] HCA 19.
NOTE 590. Add: See too *Wallace v Kam* [2013] HCA 19 at [20].

(xi) *Damages*

10–104   **Damages in medical negligence cases.** Add: On what amounts to compensable damage, see too the important decision of the Northern Ireland Court of Appeal in *A (A Minor) v A Health & Social Services Trust* [2011] NICA 28; [2012] N.I. 77 (action by IVF child for negligence causing it to be born a different colour from its parents struck out: no recoverable loss suffered). On which, see O. Buttler, "Remedying wrongs in IVF negligence: grasping the nettle?" (2011) 127 L.Q.R. 203 (on the first instance decision) and S. Sheldon, "Only skin deep? The harm of being born a different colour to one's parents" (2011) 19 Med. L. Rev. 657.
NOTE 597. Add: Note also that as a result of the Supreme Court's decision in *Rabone v Pennine Care NHS Trust* [2012] UKSC 2; [2012] 2 A.C. 72 the principles of the Fatal Accidents Act 1976 may have to be jettisoned whenever a death caused by medical or clinical negligence can also be categorised as a breach of art.2 of the ECHR, and in particular a fairly substantial award of bereavement damages made to any close relative of the deceased even if they are not within the categories enumerated in s.1A of the 1976 Act. See generally A. Tettenborn, "Wrongful Death, Human Rights and the Fatal Accidents Act" (2012) 128 L.Q.R. 327.

3. Law

(b) *Duties owed by lawyers*

(i) *Duties to clients*

10–109   **Duties owed to clients.** NOTE 631. Add: That the same duty is owed to a non-paying as to a paying client is emphasised by Lord Neuberger M.R. in *Padden v Bevan Ashford Solicitors* [2011] EWCA Civ 1616; [2012] 1 W.L.R. 1759 at [41] (inadequate advice to wife called upon to charge her property for husband's liability; fact that solicitors advised free of charge did not lighten onerous duty placed on them).

Duties to clients: trustees and personal representatives. NOTE 641. See too **10–111**
the Scots decision in *McLeod v Crawford* [2010] CSOH 101; [2010] P.N.L.R. 33;
2011 S.C.L.R. 133 (solicitors acting for client owe no duty to his dependants: so
no claim for negligence in settling claim by moribund claimant outright, rather
than provisionally, so as to protect his relatives' interest were he to die).

(ii) *Duties to third parties*

NOTE 667. Add: In the Scots decision in *Steven v Hewats* [2013] CSOH 61; **10–114**
2013 Rep. L.R. 90; [2013] P.N.L.R. 22 Lord Tyre granted proof before answer (i.e.
refused a strike-out) in a claim by a donee inter vivos in respect of misdrafting by
a solicitor which caused the gift to be chargeable to IHT. This must leave in some
doubt the proposition that *White v Jones* cannot extend to inter vivos transfers.
NOTE 669. Add: *Haugesund Kommune v Depfa ACS Bank* was reversed in the
Court of Appeal (see [2011] EWCA Civ 33; [2011] 3 All E.R. 655), but upheld on
this point.

Duties to third parties: other cases. NOTE 673. Add: For a recent reiteration **10–116**
of this principle, see the important decision in *Edenwest Ltd v CMS Cameron
McKenna (A Firm)* [2012] EWHC 1258 (Ch); [2013] B.C.C. 152 (even though
receivers appointed to company by creditor regarded for many purposes as the
company's agents, solicitors instructed by receivers to advise on disposal of
company's assets owe no duty to company).
NOTE 676. Add: Note: *Houlgate Investment Co Ltd v Biggart Baillie LLP*
[2009] CSOH 165; [2010] P.N.L.R. 13 was re-argued, with the same result, in
Houlgate Investment Co Ltd v Biggart Baillie LLP [2011] CSOH 160; [2012]
P.N.L.R. 2.

NOTE 683. Add: See too *Chen v Gu* [2011] NSWSC 1622. **10–118**

(iii) *Fiduciary and equitable duties*

Fiduciary and equitable liabilities. NOTE 689. Add: In *Mortgage Express* **10–119**
Ltd v Iqbal Hafeez Solicitors [2011] EWHC 3037 (Ch), solicitors released mortgage funds without receiving the necessary documentation to substantiate the
mortgage. It turned out that the transaction was a fraud, the *soi-disant* vendors'
solicitors bogus, and the security null. The solicitors were held in breach of trust
and thus liable for the mortgagees' loss (see too *Nationwide Building Society v
Davisons Solicitors* [2012] EWCA Civ 1626; [2013] P.N.L.R. 12). In *Lloyds TSB
Bank Plc v Markandan & Uddin (A Firm)* [2012] EWCA Civ 65; [2012] 2 All
E.R. 884, where much the same thing happened, the defendants were unsuccessful
in their attempt to invoke s.61 of the Trustee Act 1925 (which empowers the court
to exonerate a trustee who "has acted honestly and reasonably, and ought fairly to
be excused for the breach of trust") because they had been at fault. If they had
been blameless it might well have been different: see Rimer L.J. at [61]. In addition it was made clear that s.61 could not be prayed in aid to allow reduction of
compensation for contributory negligence on the part of the lenders. Nevertheless,
there will be liability under this head only in so far as monies are strictly proved
to have been disbursed without any authority to do so. In *AIB Group (UK) Plc v
Mark Redler & Co* [2013] EWCA Civ 45; [2013] P.N.L.R. 19, solicitors instructed

to release purchase money only after discharging two prior mortgages paid off the larger one but inadvertently failed to discharge the smaller, which stood at about £300,000. The lenders' security was depreciated as a result, being postponed to that liability. The lenders' claim in breach of trust for the whole of their loss on the transaction, amounting to some £2.4 million owing to the collapse of the market and the mortgagors' insolvency, was unsuccessful. There was technically a breach of trust in respect of the whole £300,000, but the only loss properly resulting from the breach was the value of the incumbrance not discharged.

(c) *Wasted costs orders*

10–120   **Liability under the Senior Courts Act 1981 s.51: "wasted costs orders".** Add: Paragraph 53.1 of the Costs Practice Direction provides that wasted costs orders can be made "at any stage in the proceedings up to and including the proceedings relating to the detailed assessment of costs". The time limit provided here is inflexible, and once detailed assessment has taken place the wasted costs jurisdiction falls away: *Sharma v Hunters (Wasted Costs)* [2011] EWHC 2546 (COP); [2012] P.N.L.R. 6.

10–121   Add: For what may attract a wasted costs order in connection with disclosure in litigation, see *CMCS Common Market Commercial Services AVV v Taylor (Wasted Costs)* [2011] EWHC 324 (Ch); [2011] P.N.L.R. 17 (improper for solicitors to allow client to redact disclosed documents without explaining circumstances to the other side: though in the event no loss held to have resulted, and hence no order was made). Similarly too in criminal litigation, where the defence fails to make disclosure of material required by the Criminal Procedure Rules, with a view to gaining an unfair advantage: see *R v SVS Solicitors (Wasted Costs)* [2012] EWCA Crim 319; [2012] P.N.L.R. 21 (failure to particularise objection to hearsay as required by Criminal Procedure Rules 2011 r.34.3(2)(c), resulting in the Crown unnecessarily flying in and accommodating witness from Australia).

NOTE 709. Add: So too with a solicitor making bookings for hearings which may clash if things go wrong: see *R. v Henrys Solicitors* [2012] EWCA Crim 1480; [2012] P.N.L.R. 32 (morning and afternoon appointments 50 miles apart).

(d) *What amounts to breach of duty*

10–126   Add: See too *Thorpe v Fellowes (A firm)* [2011] EWHC 61 (QB); [2011] P.N.L.R. 13 (solicitors sued for negligence in selling house for old lady allegedly incompetent to instruct them: action by her representatives dismissed, since even if client incompetent (which she had not been) solicitors had not been on notice of this fact, and had been under no general duty to check whether client competent).

NOTE 741. Add: See too Clarke J. in the Irish decision in *ACC Bank Plc v Johnston & Co* [2010] IEHC 236; [2010] 4 I.R. 605; [2011] P.N.L.R. 19 at [6.23]: "[T]he mere fact that a practice is universal does not, of itself, immunise the professional concerned from potential liability, if it is a practice which, on reasonable consideration, the professional concerned ought to have identified as giving rise to a significant risk." The practice there, which Clarke J. condemned, consisted in completing a very large land transaction not by paying the vendor, but paying the latter's solicitor against its mere undertaking to pay over the completion monies to the vendor.

NOTE 752. Add: See also *Mason v Mills & Reeve* [2011] EWHC 410 (Ch); **10–128** [2011] S.T.C. 1177, especially at [149] (tax advice by firm with specialist tax department: client entitled to advice of standard typical of such firms). The decision was upheld, save as to costs, in the Court of Appeal: see *Mason v Mills & Reeve* [2012] EWCA Civ 498; [2012] S.T.I. 1511.

Conflicts of interest. NOTE 758. Add: Note also that where a solicitor has **10–129** previously acted for A and B jointly, or has otherwise been permitted by a previous client A to share information with B, he will not normally be prevented from acting for B in subsequent litigation against A. See *Singla v Stockler* [2012] EWHC 1176 (Ch); [2012] B.P.I.R. 1061.

NOTE 759. Add: Note, however, *Stiedl v Enyo Law LLP* [2011] EWHC 2649 (Comm); [2012] P.N.L.R. 4 (where solicitor has not previously acted for claimant but comes across documents owing to mistaken disclosure, normally enough simply to prohibit solicitor from reading or using them).

Solicitor acting on counsel's advice. NOTE 782. Add: But see *Herrmann v* **10–132** *Withers LLP* [2012] EWHC 1492 (Ch); [2012] P.N.L.R. 28 (despite advice from eminent counsel that house purchaser would obtain right to use communal garden, negligent not to warn of chance that that advice might be wrong—as in the event it was).

(e) *Specific duties*

(i) *The duty to advise*

The duty to advise. Add: In a suitable case the duty to advise may include a **10–133** duty to warn about possible uncertainties, as where there is some doubt about the right of a purchaser of residential property in London to use a communal garden: see *Herrmann v Withers LLP* [2012] EWHC 1492 (Ch); [2012] P.N.L.R. 28.

NOTE 792. Add: *Haugesund Kommune v Depfa ACS Bank* was reversed by the Court of Appeal (see *Haugesund Kommune v Depfa ACS Bank* [2011] EWCA Civ 33; [2011] 3 All E.R. 655) on the question of the damages recoverable, but remains good law on this point.

NOTE 794. Add: See also *Padden v Bevan Ashford Solicitors* [2011] EWCA Civ 1616; [2012] 1 W.L.R. 1759.

Extent of duty to advise. Add: See too now *Inventors Friend Ltd v Leathes* **10–134** *Prior (A firm)* [2011] EWHC 711 (QB); [2011] P.N.L.R. 20 (distribution agreement: solicitors in breach by protecting distributor in event that licensor sold IP rights elsewhere, but not if licensor merely licensed them out: see especially [72]–[74]).

In cases where issues of undue influence or misrepresentation may arise, as where a wife is asked to charge her share of the matrimonial home for her husband's debts and required for that purpose to obtain independent advice (see *Royal Bank of Scotland Plc v Etridge (No.2)* [2001] UKHL 44; [2002] 2 A.C. 773), the duty on the solicitor is onerous. There must be advice in some detail on the nature of the transaction, and much care shown to ensure that the client is genuinely acting free from any undue influence. Anything short of that, such as bare or formulaic advice not to enter into the transaction at all, will not do: see *Padden v Bevan Ashford Solicitors* [2011] EWCA Civ 1616; [2012] 1 W.L.R. 1759. Furthermore, the client must be advised in some detail as to the risks involved: see *Padden v Bevan Ashford Solicitors (No.2)* [2013] EWCA Civ 824 (wife contemplated burdening her share of house to prevent husband's prosecution for fraud: solicitors ought to have advised that this was unlikely to avert criminal proceedings).

Where a solicitor is instructed by someone with the client's ostensible authority to set the bounds of the advice required, there is normally no duty to inquire further: see *Newcastle International Airport Ltd v Eversheds LLP* [2012] EWHC 2648 (Ch); [2013] P.N.L.R. 5 (lawyers instructed, in fact quite improperly, to draw up over-generous remuneration packages for senior executives: no liability for failure to query the point).

NOTE 799. Add: Also see *Mason v Mills & Reeve* [2012] EWCA Civ 498; [2012] S.T.I. 1511 (solicitors retained to advise on management buy-out of business not liable for failure to draw attention to IHT liability if seller died shortly afterwards, despite some evidence that they knew seller was in poor health).

(iv) *Duty to take care in carrying through transaction*

10–138 **Duty to take care in carrying out transaction.** Add: See too, for further emphasis on the duty to co-ordinate activities properly, *Mason v Mills & Reeve* [2011] EWHC 410 (Ch); [2011] S.T.C. 1177 at [150]. An appeal to the Court of Appeal was dismissed, save as to costs: see [2012] EWCA Civ 498; [2012] S.T.I. 1511.

(v) *Duty to take care in conduct of litigation*

10–139 **Conduct of litigation.** Add: On a similar basis, a lawyer is not normally required to take steps which, on the basis of a considered opinion, might unduly risk his client's chances. See *Boyle v Thompsons Solicitors* [2012] EWHC 36 (QB); [2012] P.N.L.R. 17 (not negligent for personal injury claimant's solicitors to fail to seek further report from apparently ambivalent expert: further report might itself be unfavourable, but would still have to be disclosed, with possible ill-effects on claimant's chances).

(f) *Damages*

10–140 **Need to prove loss.** Add: See now the decision in *Haugesund Kommune v Depfa ACS Bank* [2011] EWCA Civ 33; [2011] 3 All E.R. 655. Where banks lent money to Norwegian municipalities under unenforceable contracts of loan, but because of the unenforceability gained a right to the immediate return of the sums advanced on the basis of unjust enrichment, Rix L.J. at [86] doubted, obiter, whether any recoverable loss had been suffered. Although Gross L.J. was less sure and Peter Smith J. expressed no opinion, it is submitted that Rix L.J.'s view shows good sense and should be followed. It should not be open to a party to construct a wholly artificial loss, merely by arguing that money lent, while repayable, is now recoverable on a technically different basis from that originally contemplated.

NOTE 845. Add: *Haugesund Kommune v Depfa ACS Bank* was reversed in the Court of Appeal (see [2011] EWCA Civ 33; [2011] 3 All E.R. 655), but upheld on this point.

Measure of recovery. Add: See too *Nahome v Last Cawthra Feather* [2010]   **10–141**
EWHC 76 (Ch); [2010] P.N.L.R. 19 (where lease lost through negligent failure to renew, measure of damages is generally capital value of leasehold interest lost).

NOTE 847. Add: See too the decision of the Irish High Court in *Kelleher v O'Connor* [2010] IEHC 313; [2011] P.N.L.R. 3 (solicitors fail to warn of food hygiene problem in restaurant being bought by client: measure of damages is price, less actual value).

NOTE 850. Add: See too *Scott v Kennedys Law LLP* [2011] EWHC 3808 (Ch) (purchase of guest-house; buyer's solicitors fail to notice planning condition making transaction unviable; buyer later sold out at a loss; measure of damages capital loss on transaction).

For another case of consequential loss being recoverable, see *Joyce v Bowman*   **10–142**
Law Ltd [2010] EWHC 251 (Ch); [2010] P.N.L.R. 22 (negligent failure by purchaser's solicitors to embody in contract an option to buy extra land from vendors: although purchaser paid no more than land was worth and would-be option price approximated to market value, solicitors liable for loss of chance to make profit from redeveloping land subject to option).

Timing. NOTE 859. Add: See also *Scott v Kennedys Law LLP* [2011] EWHC   **10–144**
3808 (Ch) (purchase of business; negligent failure to notice planning condition making business unviable; claimant later sold out at a loss; measure of damages capital loss reckoned as at time of eventual resale). Also instructive is the Scottish decision in *Kirkton Investments Ltd v VMH LLP* [2011] CSOH 200; [2012] P.N.L.R. 11 (solicitors wrongly advise developer that it has the necessary right of access to neighbouring premises to allow it to erect vital flue; right in fact non-existent but could have been obtained at commencement of works for £75,000; after unsuccessful litigation neighbouring owner successfully held out for £324,000; solicitors liable for latter sum).

(g) *Causation*

Generally. Add: So too where solicitors acting for a mortgage lender commit   **10–146**
breaches of retainer in and about releasing mortgage funds to fraudsters, those breaches will not make them liable except to the extent that they caused the monies to be lost or frustrated their recovery from a third party: see, e.g. *Santander UK Plc v RA Legal Solicitors (a firm)* [2013] EWHC 1380 (QB). Nevertheless, although the burden of proof is always on principle on the claimant to prove that his lawyer's fault has caused him loss, the courts may on occasion be generous in

this respect. Thus note Jacob J. in *Levicom International Holdings BV v Linklaters* [2010] EWCA Civ 494; [2010] P.N.L.R. 29 at [284]: "When a solicitor gives advice that his client has a strong case to start litigation rather than settle and the client then does just that, the normal inference is that the advice is causative. Of course the inference is rebuttable—it may be possible to show that the client would have gone ahead willy-nilly. But that was certainly not shown on the evidence here. The judge should have approached the case on the basis that the evidential burden had shifted to Linklaters to prove that its advice was not causative."

10–147   Add: For another case where *SAAMCO* went to reduce the amount recoverable from lawyers, see *Haugesund Kommune v Depfa ACS Bank* [2011] EWCA Civ 33; [2011] 3 All E.R. 655 (misadvice by lawyers to lender about legal validity of loan: lawyer not liable to lender when failure to recover loan amount due not to legal unenforceability but simply to borrower's financial inability to pay).

NOTE 878. Add: For other examples of the same reasoning, see *Broker House Insurance Services Ltd v OJS Law* [2010] EWHC 3816 (Ch); [2011] P.N.L.R. 23 (neither solicitors' improper but effective registration of second mortgage, nor their omission to obtain permission from first mortgagee, makes them liable for borrower's later failure to repay through insolvency); also *AIB Group (UK) Plc v Mark Redler & Co* [2013] EWCA Civ 45; [2013] P.N.L.R. 19 at [10] (Patten L.J.) and the Irish decision in *KBC Bank Ireland Plc v BCM Hanby Wallace (A Firm)* [2012] IEHC 120; [2013] P.N.L.R. 7 (failure by lender's solicitor to make good security: liability limited to value of security not obtained).

NOTE 879. Add: Similar to *Watts* in reasoning is another Scottish case, *Kirkton Investments Ltd v VMH LLP* [2011] CSOH 200; [2012] P.N.L.R. 11 (solicitors' misadvice to property developer concerning access to neighbouring land causes delayed completion of urban development; solicitors liable for lost chance of making expected profits had development been completed on time).

10–148   NOTE 881. Add: See also the Irish case of *KBC Bank Ireland Plc v BCM Hanby Wallace (A Firm)* [2012] IEHC 120; [2013] P.N.L.R. 7 (liability for failure by lender's solicitor to make good security limited to value of security not obtained: but liability for failure to warn security unavailable was for entire loss suffered by lender when real estate values collapsed).

10–152   **Remoteness of damage.** Add: A similar decision is *Scott v Kennedys Law LLP* [2011] EWHC 3808 (Ch) (purchase of guest-house useless to claimant because of planning condition; claim for capital loss but not cancellation of holiday, this being unforeseeable). On the other hand, where a lawyer's bungle led to a property developer receiving payment late and deprived him of the opportunity to invest the money profitably in another project, a Scottish court refused to regard the claim as unarguable: *Henderson v Wotherspoon* [2013] CSOH 113; [2013] P.N.L.R. 28. *Sed quaere.*

10–153   **Contributory negligence.** NOTE 914. Add: But contributory negligence will not lightly be found where lender, having agreed a loan in principle, releases the funds despite later indications that all is not well: *KBC Bank Ireland Plc v BCM Hanby Wallace (A Firm)* [2012] IEHC 120; [2013] P.N.L.R. 7

4. SURVEYORS AND VALUERS

(a) *Duties owed*

(ii) *Duties to non-clients*

Liability to mortgagees and purchasers. Add: A potential difficulty with   **10–156**
liability to lenders and purchasers appeared in *Scullion v Bank of Scotland Plc (t/a Colleys)* [2010] EWHC 2253 (Ch); [2011] P.N.L.R. 5. Valuers acting for mortgagees of a "buy-to-let" property, but also owing a duty to the purchaser, negligently over-estimated the likely rental income that could be used to service the mortgage. Sued by the purchaser (who had fallen into arrears), the valuers sought to extract an undertaking to use the damages to pay off the arrears. The judge, however, while mindful of the defendants' predicament (since they faced potential liability to the mortgagees themselves), said that he had no power to impose any such condition: as between himself and a defendant, a claimant was entitled to do as he wished with any damages recovered. The decision itself was reversed in the Court of Appeal (see [2011] EWCA Civ 693; [2011] 1 W.L.R. 3212); but this point was not discussed.

Liability to mortgagors. Add: The above must now be read, however, in the   **10–157**
light of *Scullion v Bank of Scotland Plc (t/a Colleys)* [2011] EWCA Civ 693; [2011] 1 W.L.R. 3212, where the Court of Appeal declined to hold that a lender's valuer owed any duty to a "buy-to-let," as against a residential, purchaser. The reasons giver by Lord Neuberger M.R. (at [49]–[52]) were effectively threefold. Commercial investors were less deserving of protection than those seeking somewhere to live (see [49]); reliance on the lender's report, rather than on advice obtained independently, was a good deal less likely in practice ([50]); and the interests of lender and borrower were more disparate, with the former more concerned with capital, and the latter with rental, values.

(b) *Negligence*

(i) *General*

Breach of duty: general. Add: The terms of a surveyor's instructions will not   **10–163**
readily be construed as ousting a duty to follow proper professional practice. See *Webb Resolutions Ltd v E.Surv Ltd* [2012] EWHC 3653 (TCC); [2013] P.N.L.R. 15 (instructions from mortgage lender mandating professional standards but then requiring tick-box valuation and stating that further comments would be ignored: nevertheless, obligation to comment where necessary).
NOTE 960. Add: See too *Phimister v DM Hall LLP* [2012] CSOH 169; 2013 S.L.T. 261; [2013] P.N.L.R. 6 (valuer for mortgage purposes not expected to measure area of plot).

NOTE 968. Add: But the surveyor must take account of the limitations of such   **10–165**
comparable figures, for example where they do not necessarily represent actual prices paid: see *Webb Resolutions Ltd v E.Surv Ltd* [2012] EWHC 3653 (TCC); [2013] P.N.L.R. 15.

(ii) *Valuation*

10–166   **Breach of duty: valuation.** Where appropriate, a valuer must not surprisingly take proper account of the terms of any lease or other contract affecting the property concerned. Thus in *K/S Lincoln v CB Richard Ellis Hotels Ltd* [2010] EWHC 1156 (TCC); [2010] P.N.L.R. 31 valuers putting a value on freehold hotels subject to leases were held at fault when they failed adequately to factor in the effect of a term in the leases which in certain cases might cause the expected rent to be sharply reduced.

NOTE 971. Add: See too *Webb Resolutions Ltd v E.Surv Ltd* [2012] EWHC 3653 (TCC); [2013] P.N.L.R. 15 (failure to factor in proximity to house of railway and council estate).

NOTE 974. See too the Scots decision in *Phimister v DM Hall LLP* [2012] CSOH 169; 2013 S.L.T. 261; [2013] P.N.L.R. 6 (valuer for mortgage purposes accepted area of land as stated without measuring it, but valued it correctly: no liability where area rather less and land could accommodate fewer houses as a result).

10–167   **Valuation: the "bracket".** Add: On the measure of the "bracket", see too *Webb Resolutions Ltd v E.Surv Ltd* [2012] EWHC 3653 (TCC); [2013] P.N.L.R. 15 at [22]–[29] (Coulson J.).

NOTE 979. Add: See too, to the same effect, the decisions in *K/S Lincoln v CB Richard Ellis Hotels Ltd* [2010] EWHC 1156 (TCC); [2010] P.N.L.R. 31; *Paratus AMC Ltd v Countrywide Surveyors Ltd* [2011] EWHC 3307 (Ch); [2012] P.N.L.R. 12; and *Webb Resolutions Ltd v E.Surv Ltd* [2012] EWHC 3653 (TCC); [2013] P.N.L.R. 15 at [22]–[29] (Coulson J.). But this does not mean that an idle valuer desirous of agreeing the figure suggested by the client can simply add a figure representing the margin of error to what he thinks is the genuine figure: see *Webb Resolutions Ltd v E.Surv Ltd* [2012] EWHC 3653 (TCC); [2013] P.N.L.R. 15 above at [112]–[113].

(d) *Damages*

10–177   **Timing.** Add: See too the valuers' case of *Scullion v Bank of Scotland Plc (t/a Colleys)* [2010] EWHC 2253 (Ch); [2011] P.N.L.R. 5, where the "time of purchase" rule was applied, and indeed regarded as an aspect of *South Australia Asset Management v York Montague Ltd* [1997] A.C. 191. Thus the purchaser of a misvalued apartment was entitled only to the difference between price and true value at the time of purchase (which in the event was nil), and not to anything in respect of a subsequent drop in value, this latter being regarded as outside the scope of the valuer's duty. The case was reversed on other grounds (see [2011] EWCA Civ 693; [2011] 1 W.L.R. 3212), but this holding was apparently unaffected.

10–178   **Damages: mortgagees.** Add: It has been held that the fact that a loan has been securitised and passed on to a third party who bears the ultimate risk of non-payment does not prevent the original lender claiming in full from a negligent valuer: see *Paratus AMC Ltd v Countrywide Surveyors Ltd* [2011] EWHC 3307 (Ch); [2012] P.N.L.R. 12 at [54] ff.

NOTE 1039. Add: A similar conclusion has been reached (albeit obiter) with regard to rental, as against capital, values: see *Scullion v Bank of Scotland Plc (t/a Colleys)* [2011] EWCA Civ 693; [2011] 1 W.L.R. 3212 at [62]–[68] (Lord Neuberger M.R.).

NOTE 1043. Add: *Haugesund Kommune v Depfa ACS Bank* was reversed in   **10–179**
the Court of Appeal (see [2011] EWCA Civ 33; [2011] 3 All E.R. 655), but upheld on this point.

Contributory negligence. NOTE 1055. Add: See too *Paratus AMC Ltd v*   **10–181**
Countrywide Surveyors Ltd [2011] EWHC 3307 (Ch); [2012] P.N.L.R. 12, where it was said that a lender who lent on a 90 per cent LTV basis without making even fairly obvious checks on the borrower's status would have been 60 per cent contributorily negligent had the defendants been liable at all (which in the event they were not). H.H. Judge Keyser went on to say at [80] ff. however, that (following Phillips J. in *Banque Bruxelles Lambert SA v Eagle Star Insurance Co Ltd* [1994] 2 E.G.L.R. 108 at 137) it was inappropriate to categorise 90 per cent LTV lending in and of itself as amounting to contributory fault. Note also *Webb Resolutions Ltd v E.Surv Ltd* [2012] EWHC 3653 (TCC); [2013] P.N.L.R. 15 (85 per cent LTV not as such negligent: but 95 per cent was when combined with other failures to make rudimentary checks).

5. ARCHITECTS AND CONSULTING ENGINEERS

(a) *Duties*

(i) *Duties to clients*

Duties to clients. Add: In *Robinson v PE Jones (Contractors) Ltd* [2011]   **10–182**
EWCA Civ 9; [2012] Q.B. 44, the Court of Appeal held, after exhaustive analysis, that builders did not owe concurrent duties in tort to their clients (the issue having arisen in the context of limitation). But both Jackson L.J. (at [51] and [74]) and Stanley Burnton L.J. (at [93]) seemingly accepted that architects continued to owe concurrent duties by virtue of their undertaking of professional responsibility for their design. This leaves problematical the question of "design and build" contracts, where the same concern undertakes the duties of both design and construction. It is suggested that here, for better or worse, the courts are likely to take the view that the design and construction elements must be separated, with concurrent duties owed only in respect of the former.

(ii) *Duties to others*

Add: Another case illustrating and clarifying the need for damage to other prop-   **10–184**
erty is *Broster v Galliard Docklands Ltd* [2011] EWHC 1722 (TCC); [2011] P.N.L.R. 34. Developers arranged for the building of a terrace of town-houses which were then sold off to different purchasers. The whole terrace was later damaged in a high wind owing to alleged misfitment by the defendant design and

build contractors of a roof fitment on one property. A suit against the defendants by the owners of the other properties was dismissed. The entire terrace had been constructed as one single unit, and for the purposes of tort law this was damage to that unit. The fact that the unit had later been split into different ownerships, and that this subdivision had always been contemplated, was neither here nor there.

(b) *Breach of duty*

(i) *Design and supervision*

10–189   NOTE 1107. Add: See too *Cooperative Group Ltd v John Allen Associates Ltd* [2010] EWHC 2300 (TCC); (2012) 28 Const. L.J. 27 (architects entitled to rely on specialist advice obtained on the desirability of "vibro piling"—a method of providing foundational stability by repeatedly adding and consolidating rubble in a hole in otherwise yielding ground). But in the same case Ramsey J. made it clear that the mere fact that an architect acts on third party advice is not enough: he must act reasonably in doing so. Relevant considerations included (see [180]) whether the specialist was an appropriate one; whether it was reasonable to seek assistance from other professionals or other sources; whether there was information which should have led the professional to give a warning; how far the client might have a remedy in respect of the advice from the other specialist; and whether the defendant should have advised the client to seek advice elsewhere.

(iii) *Certification issues*

10–191   **Negligent certification.** Add: Note *Dhamija v Sunningdale Joineries Ltd* [2010] EWHC 2396 (TCC); [2011] P.N.L.R. 9, where Coulson J. unhesitatingly rejected suggestions that quantity surveyors charged with certifying that work had been properly done owed a strict duty to the building owner, so as to make them liable even in the absence of negligence if they passed work that was in fact defective. In that case the quantity surveyors had themselves relied on the architects' approval of the works: Coulson J. allowed the claim to proceed only on the basis of an allegation that they had somehow been at fault in so relying.

(c) *Damages*

10–192   **Damages.** NOTE 1121. Add: For remoteness in this context, see *John Grimes Partnership Ltd v Gubbins* [2013] EWCA Civ 37; [2013] P.N.L.R. 17 (on principle, consulting engineer liable for foreseeable loss, here loss in development value of land due to late provision of designs).

6. FINANCE

(a) *Accountants and auditors*

(ii) *Duties to others*

Accountants and auditors: duties to third parties. NOTE 1136. Add: And   **10–197**
note also *Arrowhead Capital Finance Ltd (In Liquidation) v KPMG LLP* [2012]
EWHC 1801 (Comm); [2012] P.N.L.R. 30 (failure to advise trader about measures against being caught up in VAT "missing trader" fraud: no liability to investor
in trader which lost its money when trader became insolvent as a result).

(b) *Breach of duty*

(ii) *Advice*

Advice. NOTE 1181. Add: See too, on the "bracket" for valuations, *Dennard v*   **10–204**
PricewaterhouseCoopers LLP [2010] EWHC 812 (Ch).

(d) *Damages*

Damages. Add: Where accountants bungle tax advice, the measure of damages   **10–207**
is on principle, as might be expected, any extra tax payable: see *Midland
Packaging Ltd v HW Accountants Ltd* [2010] EWHC 1975 (QB); [2011] P.N.L.R.
1 (advice on tax-efficient structuring of family holdings: recovery of extra corporation tax and IHT unnecessarily payable).
   In a suitable case, damages against accountants may be awarded on "loss of
chance" principles. See, e.g. *Dennard v PricewaterhouseCoopers LLP* [2010]
EWHC 812 (Ch) (undervaluation of PFI projects for clients wishing to capitalise
on them: damages based on loss of chance of getting larger sale price).
   As in the rest of the law of damages, subsequent events may be taken into
account as reducing a claimant's loss where it is just so to do. See, e.g. *Murfin v
Ford Campbell* [2011] EWHC 1475 (Ch); [2011] P.N.L.R. 28 (accountants' negligence deprives claimant of benefit of potential set-off against liability to third
party which at the time was likely to accrue: later events show that liability never
in fact accrued, so nothing for set-off to bite on: held, no loss).
   NOTE 1194. Add: Another case where no loss was shown is *Murfin v Ford
Campbell* [2011] EWHC 1475 (Ch); [2011] P.N.L.R. 28 (loss of potential set-off
against liability that in the event never accrued).

7. INSURANCE BROKERS

(a) *Duties*

General duty. Add: The statement above, that a broker acts as the agent of the   **10–212**
assured, will need to be qualified in respect of consumer insurance contracts as

and when the Consumer Insurance (Disclosure and Representations) Act 2012 comes into force. In particular, under Sch.2 para.2(b), where the underwriter gives the broker express authority to collect information from the assured, the broker will be deemed to act as the underwriter's agent and not the assured's. This will be highly significant in cases where brokers fail to pass on information to underwriters, since in such a situation the underwriter will no longer have the right to avoid for misrepresentation or non-disclosure. As a result a productive source of potential liability of brokers to the assured will disappear (no doubt to be replaced by an equally rich vein of litigation on brokers' liability to underwriters). It should be noted, however, that the Act only applies to consumer insurance contracts. Commercial insurance is unaffected.

(b) *Breach*

(ii) *Failure to obtain insurance suitable for client*

10–218   **Duty to obtain insurance suitable for the client's needs.** NOTE 1255. Add: For another case on the need to obtain reasonably indisputable cover, see *Ground Gilbey Ltd v Jardine Lloyd Thompson UK Ltd* [2011] EWHC 124 (Comm); [2011] P.N.L.R. 15.

(c) *Damages*

10–225   Add: On limitations based on *South Australia Asset Management v York Montague Ltd* [1997] A.C. 191, see too *Jones v Environcom Ltd* [2011] EWCA Civ 1152; [2012] P.N.L.R. 5. Property owners suffered a disastrous fire, for which insurers declined to pay more than a fraction of the loss on the basis that they had a strong case of non-disclosure and failure to take precautions required under the policy. The owners sought to recover for the effects of the fire itself from their brokers, arguing inter alia that the latter had negligently failed to advise on those precautions, and that had they been taken the fire would never have happened at all. Steel J. had no hesitation in rejecting this claim as outwith the scope of the defendants' duty, and the Court of Appeal agreed.

(d) *Causation*

10–227   **Causation.** Add: For another case where brokers' negligence was held to have caused no loss, see *Jones v Environcom Ltd* [2011] EWCA Civ 1152; [2012] P.N.L.R. 5. Underwriters refused to pay out in full for a fire, contending that they had a strong case for arguing that the assured had failed to take precautions required under the policy. The assured owners sued their brokers, arguing inter alia that the latter had negligently failed to advise on those precautions. Steel J. held the brokers at fault, but dismissed the claim on the basis that even if advised the owners would not have taken the precautions concerned, and that without them they were effectively uninsurable. The Court of Appeal dismissed an appeal by the owners.

Amounts received from the insurer. NOTE 1301. Add: *Haugesund Kommune* **10–228**
v Depfa ACS Bank was reversed in the Court of Appeal (see [2011] EWCA Civ
33; [2011] 3 All E.R. 655), but upheld on this point. See too *Ground Gilbey Ltd v
Jardine Lloyd Thompson UK Ltd* [2011] EWHC 124 (Comm); [2011] P.N.L.R.
15, especially at [109] (accepted that settlement might be attacked, but not where
it was "within the range of settlements which reasonable commercial people
might have made").

CHAPTER 11

PRODUCT LIABILITY AND CONSUMER PROTECTION

		PARA.
1.	Product liability in general	11–01
2.	Liability in contract	11–03
3.	Negligence	11–08
	☐ (a) Generally	11–08
	☐ (b) Damage	11–19
	(c) Liability	11–26
	(i) General	11–26
	(ii) Manufacturing and design defects	11–28
	☐ (iii) Failure to warn	11–30
	☐ (iv) Failure to recall defective products	11–34
	■ (d) Causation	11–35
	(e) Qualification of negligence liability	11–37
	(i) Probability of intermediate examination	11–37
	(ii) Default of the claimant	11–40
	■ (iii) Defect arose after product left defendant's hands	11–41
	(iv) Unexpected or misguided use	11–42
	(v) Abnormally sensitive claimants	11–43
	(vi) Exclusion of duty	11–44
4.	The Consumer Protection Act 1987 Pt I(a)	11–45
	■ (a) Generally	11–45
	(b) What is a "product"?	11–49
	(c) When is a product "defective"?	11–54
	■ (d) What defences are available?	11–66
	(e) Defendants	11–73
	(f) Claimants	11–80
	(g) Damage recoverable	11–81
	(h) Limitation	11–84
	(i) Miscellaneous matters	11–87
5.	Breach of statutory duty: the Consumer Protection Act 1987 Pt II	11–90

3. NEGLIGENCE

(a) *Generally*

Extent of the principle. Add: There equally seems no reasons why the principle in *Donoghue v Stevenson* should not extend to products, such as books, maps or computer disks, containing information which has been negligently compiled or provided and as a result causes danger to users or others. One Scottish case certainly proceeds on that assumption: see *Munro v Sturrock (t/a Scotmaps)* [2012] CSIH 35 (rally driver injured owing to alleged error in detailed guide to route; claim failed, but only—it seems—because the guide was held not misleading on the facts). **11–09**

(b) *Damage*

11–19   **For what damage?** Add: Even if a defendant is liable under *Donoghue v Stevenson* [1932] A.C. 562, he will be liable for damage only if there is a sufficient degree of likelihood to make it reasonably foreseeable. Nevertheless, this is a malleable criterion. If a product is intended to mitigate the effects of a particular emergency, even an extremely unlikely one, and because of negligent manufacture fails to do so, it seems the manufacturer will be liable. Cf. *Supershield Ltd v Siemens Building Technologies FE Ltd* [2010] EWCA Civ 7; [2010] 1 Lloyd's Rep. 349 (failure of anti-flooding device aimed at highly unlikely escape of water).

NOTE 91. Add: See too *Linklaters Business Services Ltd v Sir Robert McAlpine Ltd* [2010] EWHC 2931 (TCC); (2010) 133 Con. L.R. 211, especially at [115]–[119] (doubted whether sub-contracted assemblers of insulated piping liable in tort to building owners when defectiveness of insulation caused pipe to corrode: insulation and pipe were essentially one and the same thing).

11–21   **"Damage".** NOTE 107. Add: In the insurance decision in *Omega Proteins Ltd v Aspen Insurance UK Ltd* [2010] EWHC 2280 (Comm); [2011] 1 All E.R. (Comm) 313; [2010] 2 C.L.C. 370 it seems to have been accepted that rendering something unsalable might amount to damage even in the absence of physical lesion. Thus where sellers negligently supplied meat parts whose sale was forbidden by Euro-law and these parts were mixed with other meat, thus rendering the whole unsalable, the buyers were held to have a claim in tort, despite the lack of any indication that the meat supplied was actually toxic or tainted.

11–23   **"Other property": components fitted by owner.** NOTE 112. Add: But contrast Christopher Clarke J.'s decision in *Omega Proteins Ltd v Aspen Insurance UK Ltd* [2010] EWHC 2280 (Comm); [2011] 1 All E.R. (Comm) 313; [2010] 2 C.L.C. 370. Sellers sold illegal parts of cattle carcases which buyers mixed with other, lawful, parts and resold. The buyers as a result found themselves liable to their sub-buyers. It was held that the sellers would have been liable in tort to the buyers and thus that the buyers could claim against the sellers' insurers, despite the fact that the sellers' insurance excluded all but tortious third-party liability. Presumably the distinction with *Bacardi–Martini* (which was not mentioned) is that the buyers did not produce any new substance but simply mixed similar substances and thus contaminated their existing good meat product.

11–24   **"Other property": components fitted by manufacturer.** Add: See too *Linklaters Business Services Ltd v Sir Robert McAlpine Ltd* [2010] EWHC 2931 (TCC); (2010) 133 Con. L.R. 211, especially at [115]–[119] (suggesting that where sub-contracted assemblers of insulated piping alleged to have supplied defective insulation, insulation and pipe counted as essentially one and the same thing, thus negativing liability in tort).

(c) *Liability*

(iii) *Failure to warn*

The duty to warn. Add: *A & L Plumbing Ltd v Ridge Tool Co* [2009] 313 Sask.   **11–30**
R. 19 was upheld on appeal: see *A & L Plumbing Ltd v Ridge Tool Co* [2010] 350
Sask. R. 148.

Add: That non-manufacturers may themselves be under a duty to warn   **11–31**
was illustrated by the Alberta decision in *Hutton v General Motors of Canada Ltd*
[2010] ABQB 606; [2011] W.W.R. 284 (Canadian distribution branch of
General Motors under duty to warn Canadian user of defect in car, despite
car itself having been manufactured by the American parent company (in
Mexico)).
NOTE 151. Add: See too, for some scepticism on the applicability of the
"learned intermediary" defence, *Peterson v Merck Sharpe & Dohme (Aust) Pty
Ltd* [2010] FCA 180; (2010) 266 A.L.R. 1 at [796]–[798].

(iv) *Failure to recall defective products*

Duty to recall. Add: If recall takes place, it goes without saying that any correc-   **11–34**
tions or modifications made must be properly carried out. See *Hutton v General
Motors of Canada Ltd* [2010] ABQB 606; [2011] W.W.R. 284 (air-bags on cars
deployed when they should not; modification inadequate; liability).

(d) *Causation*

Causation. NOTE 163. Add: But courts may be prepared to infer causation   **11–35**
from fairly exiguous evidence. See e.g. *Samaan v Kentucky Fried Chicken Pty Ltd*
[2012] NSWSC 381 (salmonella poisoning: court inferred causation simply from
evidence that claimant had eaten at restaurant which regularly infringed hygiene
standards).

(e) *Qualification of negligence liability*

(iii) *Defect arose after product left defendant's hands*

Subsequently-appearing defects out of account. NOTE 188. Add: A simi-   **11–41**
larly generous attitude to claimants appears in *Divya v Toyo Tire & Rubber Co Ltd
(t/a Toyo Tires of Japan)* [2011] EWHC 1993 (QB) (high-speed tyre blow-out
otherwise unexplained: judge prepared to infer that there must have been a defect
in the tyre at the time of manufacture). But Scottish courts may be more cautious
here: see the broadly similar *McGlinchey v General Motors UK Ltd* [2012] CSIH
91, where the Inner House of the Court of Session, faced with an inexplicable
handbrake failure which injured a motorist, held that the judge had rightly declined
to draw from this the inference of a manufacturing defect and dismissed the claim
as a result.

4. The Consumer Protection Act 1987 Part I

(a) *Generally*

11–46   **The Consumer Protection Act 1987.** Add: Under art.13 the Directive "shall not affect any rights which an injured person may have according to the rules of the law of contractual or non-contractual liability or a special liability system" if those rights existed at the moment of notification. The extent to which the Directive should otherwise be regarded as pre-empting national laws in the same area is now clearer. Despite the wording of art.13, it does supplant any other strict (as against fault-based) tort liability in manufacturer or anyone else in the supply chain for personal injury or damage to domestic property, even if predating the Directive: see *Skov AEG v Bilka Lavprisvarehus A/S* (C402/03) [2006] E.C.R. I–199; [2006] 2 C.M.L.R. 16 and the decision of the French *Cour de Cassation* in *Cass Comm* May 26, 2010, 08–18545 (also reported as *Acte IARD (Société) v Ettax (Société)* [2010] E.C.C. 24). But it does not prevent such liability in respect of damage which it does not cover, such as harm to commercial property: see the ECJ decision in *Moteurs Leroy Somer v Société Dalkia France* (C–285/08) [2009] E.C.R. I–4733, duly applied by the *Cour de Cassation* in *Cass Comm* May 26, 2010, 07–11744 (also reported as *Dalkia France (Société) v Moteurs Leroy Somer (Société)* [2010] E.C.C. 32). Nor does it pre-empt the subjection of service providers to strict liability, even if that liability is premised on a defect in the equipment used. See *Centre hospitalier universitaire de Besançon v Dutrueux* (Case C-495/10) [2012] 2 C.M.L.R. 1 (claim by hospital patient in respect of overheating bed, based on French provisions making hospitals strictly liable for injuries caused by defects in equipment).

(d) *What defences are available?*

11–68   **Subsequent defects.** Add: Although s.4(1)(d) seems to say fairly explicitly that the defendant bears the burden of proving that the defect was not present when the product left his hands, in the Scottish decision in *McGlinchey v General Motors UK Ltd* [2011] CSOH 206; [2012] Rep. L.R. 20 this seems to have been overlooked. A parked car rolled back when the handbrake failed; the driver was injured as a result, and sued the manufacturers. It being unclear whether the handbrake had been defective at the time of manufacture, Lord Brailsford assoilzied the defenders, apparently relying on s.3(2)(c) of the 1987 Act (see at [13]). It is respectfully suggested that his decision is difficult to support on this point. The point did not arise on appeal at [2012] CSIH 91.

CHAPTER 12

OCCUPIERS' LIABILITY

		PARA.
1.	Liability of occupiers to visitors for condition of premises	12–01
2.	The Occupiers' Liability Act 1957	12–02
■	(a) Scope of the 1957 Act	12–03
■	(b) Who is an occupier?	12–08
□	(c) Who is a visitor?	12–14
■	(d) The common duty of care	12–23
	(e) Specific issues	12–32
□	(f) Defences	12–41
■	(g) Independent contractors	12–56
	(h) Damage covered by the 1957 Act	12–60
3.	Liability to trespassers	12–61
	(a) Introduction	12–61
□	(b) The duty of care under the 1984 Act	12–64
□	(c) Standard of care owed to trespassers	12–67
	(d) Defences	12–73
4.	Liability to other non-visitors on the defendant's premises	12–78
■ 5.	Liability of landlord	12–82
6.	Liability to persons not on the premises	12–87

2. The Occupiers' Liability Act 1957

(a) *Scope of the 1957 Act*

Add: See too *Everett v Comojo (UK) Ltd* [2011] EWCA Civ 13; [2012] 1 **12–04**
W.L.R. 150 (nightclub patron knifed: proprietor owed duty to protect him from
such murderous conduct, but not under the 1957 Act: on which, [2011] J.P.I.L.
C79). In the event the proprietor was held not to have been at fault. Similar in
conception is *Tafa v Matsim Properties Ltd* [2011] EWHC 1302 (QB) (employee
of irresponsible and insolvent contractor injured while working on building:
company which occupied building liable at common law for failure to take proper
care for his safety, together with employee responsible for health and safety; in
addition, latter employee liable as joint tortfeasor). In *Geary v Wetherspoon Plc*
[2011] EWHC 1506 (QB); [2011] N.P.C. 60 the obvious point was made that even
where there would not ordinarily be liability under the 1957 Act there might be a
specific assumption of responsibility. So although a high-class bar was not liable
when a tipsy patron suffered injury after sliding down nineteenth-century banisters, Coulson J. accepted (at [60]) that "if the defendant had been organising
banister-sliding competitions, there may well have been an assumption of responsibility," and hence the result might have been different.

NOTE 8. Add: See too *Hatcher v ASW Ltd* [2010] EWCA Civ 1325, a case
under the Occupier's Liability Act 1984 (child injured while climbing on

buildings in abandoned Cardiff steelworks equipped with formidable anti-trespasser defences: held, no danger *due to state of premises*).

NOTE 11. Add: In *Kmiecic v Isaacs* [2011] EWCA Civ 451; [2011] I.C.R. 1269 the Court of Appeal rebuffed an argument that certain health and safety legislation (there the Construction (Health, Safety and Welfare) Regulations 1996 and the Work at Height Regulations 2005) rendered a householder, as well as an employer, liable to employees doing work on his house on the basis that he was someone "who controls the way in which any construction work is carried out by a person at work." The mere fact that a Hampstead householder could (and did) decline to let a worker onto her garage roof through a bedroom window, thus causing him to use a dangerous ladder instead, did not (it was held) bring her within the relevant description. But any further involvement may make even a private householder liable under the Regulations, even if not at common law: cf. *Tafa v Matsim Properties Ltd* [2011] EWHC 1302 (QB), above.

12–07   **Fixed or movable structures.** NOTE 25. Add: Note, however, that claims by passengers on ships or aircraft may well be pre-empted by the relevant international conventions, notably the Athens Convention Relating to the Carriage of Passengers and their Luggage by Sea 1974 and the Warsaw Convention for the Unification of Certain Rules Relating to International Carriage by Air 1929 (as amended). Cf. *Adams v Thomson Holidays Ltd* [2009] EWHC 2559 (QB), and the Irish decision in *Hennessey v Aer Lingus Ltd* [2012] IEHC 124. Nevertheless in practice the duty is often much the same under the Athens Convention as under the 1957 Act: compare *Dawkins v Carnival Plc (t/a P&O Cruises)* [2011] EWCA Civ 1237; [2012] 1 Lloyd's Rep. 1.

(b) *Who is an occupier?*

12–09   **Owners, occupiers and licensees.** Add: And in Scotland it has been held that an owner who moves out during building works falls to be treated the same way: *Dawson v Page* [2012] CSOH 33; 2012 Rep. L.R. 56 (affirmed for other reasons: [2013] CSIH 24).

NOTE 34. Add: See too *Drysdale v Hedges* [2012] EWHC B20 (QB); [2012] 3 E.G.L.R. 105 (landlord not liable under Act for slippery step in front of tenanted house).

NOTE 35. Add: See too *Esdale v Dover DC* [2010] EWCA Civ 409 (lessor's liability for unevenness in concrete access path in housing estate).

12–10   **Other occupiers.** Add: The law on ad hoc occupiers was clarified in *Furmedge v Chester-Le-Street DC* [2011] EWHC 1226 (QB) (which at [141] cited paras **12–09—12–11** with approval). An inflatable interactive sculpture some 150ft sq, through which the public were invited to walk, was blown free from its moorings in a public park by a high wind. Several participants were injured, and two died. The company which had organised the placement, which had personnel on site, erected the showpiece, and controlled entry and egress, was held to be an occupier, and in the circumstances liable for the injuries on the basis that it had failed to obtain a proper risk assessment. The owner of the land, on the other hand, was said at [146] not to have been the occupier of the errant structure.

(c) *Who is a visitor?*

Limited permission. Add: The doctrine of limited permission was applied **12–17** with some strictness in order to disqualify an entirely undeserving claimant in *Harvey v Plymouth City Council* [2010] EWCA Civ 860; [2010] P.I.Q.R. P18 (non-descript piece of urban land next to precipice, licensed de facto for recreational use because local authority which owned it did nothing to stop that use: nevertheless, claimant not a lawful visitor when he used the land as a means of escape from a bilked taxi-driver, tripped, and fell down the drop).

NOTE 79. Add: For a literal application of the dictum in *The Carlgarth*, where a visitor did slide down the banisters, suffered injury, and duly failed in her claim, see *Geary v Wetherspoon Plc* [2011] EWHC 1506 (QB); [2011] N.P.C. 60.

Highway users. Add: Although a landowner escapes liability to people *on* a **12–20** path over his land, ironically he faces much more hazard as soon as they stray *off* it, since then he owes a duty under the 1984 Act, or if the straying is tolerated, under the 1957 Act. For an instance, see *McKaskie v Cameron* Unreported July 1, 2009 H.H. Judge Howarth, Blackpool County Court, (farmer liable under 1957 Act where cattle attacked and mauled walker who strayed off path to use a tolerated shortcut). The decision, not surprisingly, is a matter for concern in the farming community.

(d) *The common duty of care*

NOTE 108. Add: Doubts as to whether an occupier should be held liable for not **12–25** barring access to dangers *outside* his premises are reinforced (correctly, it is submitted) by *Armstrong v Keepmoat Homes Ltd* Unreported February 3, 2012 QBD (Newcastle District Registry). It was on this basis that occupiers of a grassed area separated by a hedge from a busy dual carriageway were exonerated when a child went through an obvious gap in the hedge into the path of a car on the road.

Examples of liability. NOTE 120. Add: See too *McCarrick v Park Resorts Ltd* **12–27** [2012] EWHC B27 (QB) (unguarded and deceptively shallow pool).

NOTE 123. Add: A fortiori where the third parties are there with the occupier's permission; e.g. *Phee v Gordon* [2013] CSIH 18; 2013 S.L.T. 439 (golf club liable to visitor struck by ball for lack of warning notice on course).

Examples of non-liability. Add: See too *Murdock v Scarisbrick Group Ltd* **12–28** [2011] EWHC 220 (QB) (not negligent for sauna floor to be slippery); *Clark v Bourne Leisure Ltd* [2011] EWCA Civ 753 (no negligence where disabled bar patron tried to steer wheelchair down a flight of stairs obvious as such to a casual glance, in the belief that they constituted a wheelchair ramp).

Factors in account. Add: Today a good deal of emphasis is placed, at least in **12–29** the case of business or governmental defendants, on the need for adequate systems or risk assessment procedures. If they are present, then even if an accident occurs despite them, there is unlikely to be liability; if absent, liability is correspondingly likely to follow. Typical is *Hufton v Somerset CC* [2011] EWCA Civ 789; [2011] E.L.R. 482. A 15-year-old pupil slipped on a puddle of water in a school hall. The judge exonerated the school on the basis that it had an adequate system in place for preventing such puddles forming. The Court of Appeal agreed: the fact that it had evidently failed to prevent this particular accident was largely discounted. Similarly the National Trust was exonerated in *Bowen v National Trust* [2011] EWHC 1992 (QB) when despite the carrying out of an impeccable risk-assessment exercise a tree branch on an amenity property fell, killing a child. Two recent cases on the other side of the line are *Furmedge v Chester-Le-Street DC* [2011] EWHC 1226 (QB) (occupiers of amusement equipment liable when it blew away with fatal results, partly because of inadequate risk assessment) and the Scottish *Phee v Gordon* [2013] CSIH 18; 2013 S.L.T. 439 (golfer struck by ball negligently mishit from another tee; owners of golf course 80 per cent liable, partly on basis of lack of proper formal assessment of danger).

NOTE 133. Add: See also *Hassan v Gill* [2012] EWCA Civ 1291; [2013] P.I.Q.R. P1 (slipping on grape at fruit stall: evidentiary burden not discharged by two-hourly sweep of area); *Dawkins v Carnival Plc (t/a P & O Cruises)* [2011] EWCA Civ 1237; [2012] 1 Lloyd's Rep. 1 (slippage on pool of liquid in popular walk-through location on cruise ship; inference drawn, in absence of clear evidence, that puddle had probably been there long enough to attract a duty to mop it up). With respect, this latter case seems a remarkably generous application of the res ipsa loquitur doctrine.

NOTE 134. Add: See too *Sutton v Syston Rugby Football Club Ltd* [2011] EWCA Civ 1182 (no need for minute inspection of rugby pitch for debris); also *Bowen v National Trust* [2011] EWHC 1992 (QB) and *Richards v London Borough of Bromley* [2012] EWCA Civ 1476; [2013] E.L.R. 66 (despite previous minor incident with allegedly dangerous door, school could wait until next holidays to remodel). A fortiori where removal of the danger would itself be unsafe: see *Hughes (A Minor) v Newry & Mourne District Council* [2012] NIQB 54 (child injured by firework abandoned in park: no liability in council for failure to remove, since operatives likely to be set upon by thugs who frequented park).

NOTE 137. Add: See too *Cockbill v Riley* [2013] EWHC 656 (QB) (private householder not expected to supervise pool at boisterous party too closely, or carry out risk assessment).

NOTE 138. Add: See also *Cowan v The Hopetoun House Preservation Trust* [2013] CSOH 9; 2013 Rep. L.R. 62 (no need to fence ha-ha at stately home, though duty to warn visitors at night).

NOTE 142. Add: See too *Corbett v Cumbria Kart Racing Club* [2013] EWHC 1362 (QB); also *McCarrick v Park Resorts Ltd* [2012] EWHC B27 (QB) (failure by pool owner to follow HSE guidance relevant); *Wilson v Haden (t/a Clyne Farm Centre)* [2013] EWHC 229 (QB) (relevance of British Standards to instructions given, and physical precautions provided, at assault course).

NOTE 143. Add: In *Sutton v Syston Rugby Football Club Ltd* [2011] EWCA Civ 1182 the Court of Appeal invoked the 2006 Act as one reason for not holding a rugby club liable for failing to inspect its pitch minutely before every match in case it might contain debris.

Obvious dangers and ordinary risks. NOTE 149. Add: See too Thirlwall J.'s   **12–30**
decision in *Grimes v Hawkins* [2011] EWHC 2004 (QB) (teenage visitor disabled
after misjudging dive into entirely ordinary domestic swimming pool; householder understandably held not liable). Nevertheless landowners are not always
exonerated for obvious risks; e.g. *Phee v Gordon* [2013] CSIH 18; 2013 S.L.T.
439 (golf club liable to player struck by ball on account of lack of warning
notice).

(f) *Defences*

Volenti non fit injuria. Add: The statutory defence under s.2(5) has been   **12–41**
confirmed to be "indistinguishable from the common law defence of *volenti*"—
see *Geary v Wetherspoon Plc* [2011] EWHC 1506 (QB); [2011] N.P.C. 60 at [36]
(Coulson J.).

(g) *Independent contractors*

NOTE 250. Add: An occupier may also be liable if he is party to the act   **12–57**
of an independent contractor creating a danger, or knows that work has created a
danger but does nothing about it. See *Alexander v Freshwater Properties Ltd*
[2012] EWCA Civ 1048 (landlord of apartment block allowing builder to
remove door handle from heavy entrance door, leaving door likely to trap unwary
fingers).
Add: Just as an occupier is not liable for the negligence of independent contrac-   **12–58**
tors, conversely it goes without saying that, barring exceptional circumstances, an
independent third party sending someone onto an occupier's land is not liable for
the occupier's own negligence: *Woodland v Swimming Teachers' Association*
[2012] EWCA Civ 239; [2012] P.I.Q.R. P12 (school arranging swimming at independent pool not liable for lifeguard's negligence).

3. LIABILITY TO TRESPASSERS

(b) *The duty of care under the 1984 Act*

Trespassers owed "such care as is reasonable". Add: See too *Hatcher v ASW*   **12–64**
Ltd [2010] EWCA Civ 1325 (child injured climbing on abandoned Cardiff steelworks notwithstanding presence of formidable anti-trespasser defences: held, no
liability, since no danger due to state of premises, and in any case presence not
reasonably foreseeable).

(c) *Standard of care owed to trespassers*

Obvious dangers. NOTE 315. Add: See too *Geary v Wetherspoon Plc* [2011]   **12–69**
EWHC 1506 (QB); [2011] N.P.C. 60 (patron of bar, after a few drinks, choosing
to slide down banisters and falling off, with disastrous results).

5. Liability of Landlord

12–83   **Landlord's liability at common law.** NOTE 379. Add: See also *Drysdale v Hedges* [2012] EWHC B20 (QB); [2012] 3 E.G.L.R. 105 (painting front steps with slippery paint, though no negligence on the facts).

NOTE 381. Add: The correctness of *Cavalier v Pope* with regard to defects not covered by the Defective Premises Act 1972 was accepted in *Drysdale v Hedges* [2012] EWHC B20 (QB); [2012] 3 E.G.L.R. 105 (front steps painted with slippery paint, and also precipitous drop into area next to them).

12–85   **Defective Premises Act 1972 s.4.** NOTE 394. Add: See also *Drysdale v Hedges* [2012] EWHC B20 (QB); [2012] 3 E.G.L.R. 105 (leaving slippery paint on front steps misguided, but not a matter relating to repair).

CHAPTER 13

EMPLOYERS' LIABILITY

		PARA.
■	1. Introduction.	13–01
	2. Liability for breach of personal duty of care	13–03
	■ (a) Nature of the employer's duty	13–03
	■ (b) Aspects of the employer's personal duty	13–07
	■ (c) Standard of care expected of an employer	13–19
■	3. Breach of statutory duty	13–30
	■ (a) Provision and Use of Work Equipment Regulations.	13–40
	■ (b) Workplace (Health, Safety and Welfare) Regulations	13–51
	□ (c) Manual Handling Operations Regulations	13–57
	(d) Control of Substances Hazardous to Health Regulations	13–60
■	4. Defences	13–61

1. INTRODUCTION

NOTE 1. After *Redgrave's Health and Safety*, delete "6th edn (2008)", and **13–01** replace with: 8th edn (2012)

After para.**13–01**, add a new para. **13–01A** as follows:

Major change in civil liability for breach of statutory duty, including liability **13–01A** under the many health and safety regulations, is signalled by the enactment of s.69 of the Enterprise and Regulatory Reform Act 2013, which received Royal Assent on April 24, 2013 but is not yet in force. Section 69 amends s.47 of the Health and Safety at Work Act 1974 so far as it relates to civil liability, and provides that breach of a duty imposed by a statutory instrument "containing health and safety regulations", or breach of a duty imposed by an existing statutory provision, shall not be actionable except so far as regulations under s.47 (as revised) so provide. In a Press Release from the Department for Business, innovation and Skills, the statutory revision was described by Business Minister Jo Swinson both as establishing "the principle that an employer should always have the opportunity, even where a strict duty applies, to defend themselves on the basis of having taken all reasonable steps to protect their employees", and as ensuring that a civil claim for breach of health and safety duties can only be brought where it can be proved that an employer has been negligent. Neither is achieved by the section alone but these statements indicate the likely content of regulations under the revised section. The legislative change will apply only to breaches of duty occurring after the commencement date of the section, and the law as it currently stands will continue to be of relevance to claims arising from earlier breaches of duty. Section 69 came into force on October 1, 2013: Enterprise and Regulatory Reform Act 2013 (Commencement No. 3, Transitional Provisions and Savings) Order 2013/2227.

2. LIABILITY FOR BREACH OF PERSONAL DUTY OF CARE

(a) *Nature of the employer's duty*

13–03   **Governed by the general principles.** NOTE 15. After "launched by some insurers on grounds of", delete the rest of the sentence and replace with: conflict with the European Convention and on common law grounds (the legislation was an unreasonable, irrational, and arbitrary exercise of legislative authority). The challenge failed before the Scottish courts ([2011] CSIH 31; 2011 S.L.T. 439), and also before the Supreme Court, where the Convention argument was based on art.1 Protocol 1, not on art.6: *Axa General Insurance Ltd, Petitioners* [2011] UKSC 46; [2012] 1 A.C. 868; 2011 S.L.T. 1061.

13–04   **Duty to employees.** Add to the end of the paragraph: The existence of a duty between employer and employee does not negate the potential for duties to be owed by other parties in respect of the worker's safety, on ordinary negligence principles. In its important decision in *Chandler v Cape Plc* [2012] EWCA Civ 525; [2012] 1 W.L.R. 3111, the Court of Appeal found that the parent company of a subsidiary which had employed the claimant owed a duty of care to the claimant in respect of his exposure to asbestos. The Court made clear that it was not concerned with "piercing the corporate veil", and that the duty was one owed by the defendant on application of ordinary negligence principles: "in appropriate circumstances the law may impose on a parent company responsibility for the health and safety of its subsidiary's employees". Those circumstances are not exhausted by the situation in this case ([80]), and the Court did not confine its remarks narrowly.

In *Cape* itself, it was conceded that the system of work in operation was defective. The subsidiary was no longer in existence, and its Employers' Liability insurance policy had in any event excluded liability for asbestosis, the condition suffered by the claimant, so that there was no possibility of direct recourse against an insurer. In finding that a duty had been owed, the Court of Appeal recognised that this was the first reported case in which a parent company was found to owe a duty to employees of another company within the group, though it noted that (as explained earlier in this paragraph) independent contractors had been held to owe duties to employees of the employer in some circumstances; and that it had been held to be arguable that a duty might be owed by a parent ([66]). In terms of the need for incremental development, the analogous line of cases was said to be the line of authority on the duty of a person to intervene to prevent damage to another (*Smith v Littlewoods Ltd* [1987] A.C. 241). Although the Court of Appeal approved the judge's finding that the duty here was, in terms of the *Caparo* approach, based upon an "assumption of responsibility", the Court was quick to point out that "assumption" in this context is a misnomer, and that "attachment" of responsibility "might be more accurate" (at [64]). The Court rejected an argument that the factors evidencing such an assumption (or attachment) must go beyond the "normal incidents of the relationship between a parent and subsidiary company". Although analysis of the factual context will be essential, the Court therefore emphasised that there need not be an unusual relationship between the parent and its subsidiary (and therefore no need to define what is the norm). Relevant circumstances justifying the existence of a duty and exemplified by this case were identified as: (1) that the businesses of the parent and subsidiary are in a relevant respect the same; (2) the parent has, or ought to have, superior knowledge on some relevant aspect of health and safety in the particular industry; (3) the subsidiary's system of work is unsafe as the parent company knew, or ought to have known; and (4) the parent knew or ought to have foreseen that the subsidiary or its employees would rely on its using that superior knowledge for the employees' protection (at [80]). Here, the subsidiary's unsafe working practice was inherited from the parent company. The factors set out in (1)–(4), however, do not exhaust the possibilities, and the case merely illustrates the way in which the requirements of *Caparo v Dickman* [1990] 2 A.C. 605 may be satisfied between a parent company, and the employee of a subsidiary.

NOTE 23. Add to the end of the note: The employer's duties to provide safe equipment and a safe system of work have been of particular importance in relation to the armed forces, where the extra-territorial application of the Human Rights Act was interpreted restrictively until the decision of the Supreme Court in *Smith v Ministry of Defence* [2013] UKSC 41; [2013] 3 W.L.R. 69: see further para.**14–38**.

Non-delegable duty. Add to the end of the paragraph: In *Uren v Corporate*   **13–06**
Leisure (UK) Ltd [2011] EWCA Civ 66; (2011) 108(7) L.S.G. 16; [2011] I.C.R. D11, the Court of Appeal suggested that the duty to conduct a risk assessment under reg.3(1) of the Management of Health and Safety at Work Regulations 1999 was closely related to the common law duty to take care for the safety of employees and was itself non-delegable. Although breach of the duty to conduct an appropriate risk assessment could not be directly causative of injury, it will be indirectly causative where a proper assessment would have led to a precaution being taken to remove a particular risk. In this case, the Royal Air Force as employer could not plausibly argue that it had effectively delegated the responsibility for risk assessment to a contractor organising a "Health and Fun Day", since no convincing risk assessment had been carried out by either party. The judge had given no convincing reason for his conclusion that the risk of spinal injury from diving head first into shallow water as part of a game was low, and a retrial with a different judge was required. At the retrial, Foskett J. held that a competent risk assessment would indeed have shown the dangers of participants entering the water head first, and the result would have been clear warnings and advice which would have prevented the injury: *Uren v Corporate Leisure* [2013] EWHC 353 (QB). See also para.**13–36** on the relationship between duties to conduct risk assessments and substantive duties to minimise or remove risks.

(b) *Aspects of the employer's personal duty*

Safe staff. Add to the end: Similar in some respects is *Vaickuviene v J Sainsbury*   **13–08**
Plc [2012] CSOH 69; 2012 S.L.T. 849, which was argued, however, in terms of vicarious liability for harassment of the deceased by a fellow employee who was known to hold extreme and racist views, and who eventually murdered the deceased, rather than in terms of the employer's personal or primary duty. On this basis, the case would not necessarily fail at proof, and could be distinguished from

authorities in which there was insufficient connection between violent acts and employment (particularly *Wilson v Exel UK Ltd* [2010] CSIH 35; 2010 S.L.T. 671). For example, the deceased had invoked the defendant's disciplinary procedures against the murderer, and the claim relied on an allegation of vicarious liability for harassment within the terms of the Protection from Harassment Act 1997. Vicarious liability lies outside the core concerns of this chapter. For further consideration of the boundary between violent acts committed between employees, and vicarious (rather than personal) liability on the part of the employer, see *Weddall v Barchester Healthcare Ltd*; *Wallbank v Wallbank Fox Designs Ltd* [2012] EWCA Civ 25; [2012] I.R.L.R. 307 (para.**6–29**).

13–13   **Distant places of work.** NOTE 94. Add to the end: See also *Berry v Ashtead Plant Hire Co Ltd* [2011] EWCA Civ 1304; [2012] P.I.Q.R. P6, where a claim by a very seriously injured claimant for an interim payment was rejected. The employer's duty in respect of places of work not occupied by them was too fact sensitive to be sure that one or other of the defendants (the identity of the "employer" being in dispute) would be liable. Neither did the applicable Regulations offer sufficient certainty in this instance.

13–14   **Safe system of work.** Add to the end of the paragraph: In *Vaile v London Borough of Havering* [2011] EWCA Civ 246; [2011] E.L.R. 274, the Court of Appeal found an education authority liable to a teacher who had been seriously injured in an attack by a 14-year-old pupil. The judge's findings of fact established sufficient failings to constitute a breach of the duty to provide a safe system of working, and this could be said to have continued for a lengthy period of time. Although the claimant could not identify what precise steps should have been taken in order to prevent the attack, this was the result of a failure to assess the risks posed by the pupil to the claimant in light of his behaviour, and on the balance of probability a proper risk assessment would have led to the identification of steps which would have avoided the injuries.

(c) *Standard of care expected of an employer*

13–21   **Sufficient knowledge.** Delete the final sentence of the paragraph, and move Note 143 to the end of the previous sentence. Add the following: On appeal to the Supreme Court, the employers' arguments were largely successful (*Baker v Quantum Clothing Group Ltd* [2011] UKSC 17; [2011] 1 W.L.R. 1003). The Court was sharply divided on the correct approach both to the common law duty, and to the statutory duty (as to which see further paras **13–30, 13–32** and **13–33**). The majority, Lords Mance, Dyson and Saville, considered that the correct approach to the common law duty was to take as a starting point the relevant Code of Practice, which required protection where there was exposure to decibel levels in excess of 90dB(A)lepd, but did not require protection against the slightly lower levels to which the claim related. Applying "classic statements" on the content of the employer's duty in *Stokes v Guest Keen and Nettlefold (Bolt & Nuts) Ltd* [1968] 1 W.L.R. 1776, and *Thompson v Smiths Shiprepairers (North Shields) Ltd* [1984] Q.B. 405, the majority held that a reasonable employer could "legitimately rely" upon the standards set by the Code of Practice (Lord Mance at [25]), unless certain exceptions applied, namely that the established practice was "clearly bad", or, if the situation is one where there is developing knowledge about the risks involved, if the employer has "greater than average knowledge of the risks" (at [23]). It is suggested that this is an unusually literal application of dicta from a lower court, particularly since the principles interpreted are simply the general principles of common law as they apply to employers. For the minority, both Lord Kerr and Lord Clarke argued that the existence of a Code which required protection of employees from noise above a certain threshold could not be considered to protect employers from a common law duty to protect their employees from a discoverable risk of harm at lower levels. The Code required action, and was not a blueprint for inaction (Lord Kerr at [148]). There remained an obligation on employers to remain abreast of information and not to remain passive where risks became known. Lord Kerr in particular argued that the Code itself made plain that its requirements did not eliminate risks. The dissenting opinions therefore emphasised the duty of employers to give positive thought to the risks posed to employees by their undertaking, irrespective of established practice. On the question of date of knowledge, a majority of the Court held that Meridian Ltd as a larger employer ought to have had earlier knowledge of the risk posed to employees by exposure to noise between 85dB(A) and 90dB(A) than smaller employers. Lord Mance was in a minority on this point. For other aspects of the case see paras **13–30, 13–32** and **13–33**.

Add a new para.**13–21A** as follows:

Application in cases of mesothelioma. The general approach to breach of   **13–21A** duty, as elaborated in *Baker v Quantum Clothing*, remains applicable to mesothelioma cases, notwithstanding the modification of the test for causation in such cases (*Fairchild v Glenhaven Funeral Services* [2002] UKHL 22; [2003] 1 A.C. 32; *Sienkiewicz v Greif* [2011] UKSC 10; [2011] 2 A.C. 229). In recent instances relating to relatively low levels of exposure, liability has been defeated on the basis that there has been no breach of duty either at common law, or in the case of those statutory duties interpreted as akin to negligence. In *Williams v University of Birmingham* [2011] EWCA Civ 1242; [2012] P.I.Q.R P4, the Court of Appeal held that a judge had wrongly identified the proper test in relation to breach of duty in mesothelioma cases (though understandably so, in the opinion of Patten L.J. at [81]). It is suggested that despite the comments of Patten L.J., it is correct and appropriate for the approach to breach of duty to remain independent of the revised test for causation, since the problems of uncertainty underlying the *Fairchild* approach affect the claimant's ability to show evidence of cause and effect (which exposure caused the harm, or did the risk created by the defendant's breach eventuate?), but do not create the same difficulties in relation to "reasonable precautions" (were adequate steps taken to protect from the risk?). Nevertheless, it is also suggested that the approach in *Baker* is capable of leading to a questionable emphasis on the received practice of employers in cases where exposure levels are relatively low. Note, for example, *Hill v John Barnsley & Sons Ltd* [2013] EWHC 520 (QB), where Bean J. at [31], drew attention to a potential conflict between some aspects of the approach in *Williams*, and established authorities such as *Maguire v Harland and Wolff* [2005] EWCA Civ 1; [2005] P.I.Q.R. P21. In *Hill* itself however, concentrations in the air were highly variable as the claimant was involved in the construction of a power station and the environment was not a static one, as in *Williams*. It was concluded that even if the defendant was correct to argue that HM Factory Inspectorate's Technical Data Note (TDN) 13, issued a year after the exposure in 1970, should be treated as expressing a safe level (a contention which was in any event in tension with the reasoning in *Maguire*), this level was exceeded in the particular case and breach of duty could be established.

In *Williams*, the trial judge had been mistaken because she appeared to ask simply whether the exposure of the deceased to asbestos while at the University of Birmingham had materially increased the risk of developing the disease, and had applied this question to issues of breach, rather than only causation. The Court of Appeal explained that "material increase in risk" is not the test for breach of duty. In the present case, the deceased had been exposed to asbestos dust during scientific experiments conducted in a tunnel while a student. The Court of Appeal identified the test for breach as requiring the court to ask whether the University ought reasonably to have foreseen the risk of contracting mesothelioma arising from undertaking the experiments in the tunnel, "to the extent that the University should (acting reasonably) have refused to allow the tests to be done there, or taken further precautions or at the least sought advice." (at [35]). Reasonable foresight of a risk had to be judged by reference to the reasonable employer of the time *both* in relation to the state of knowledge (what causal links were understood?), *and* in relation to whether that risk was to be seen as one to be avoided, or at least one on which advice should be taken. Aikens L.J. adopted (at [37]) the following statement of Simon J. in *Asmussen v Filtrona United Kingdom Ltd* [2011] EWHC 1734 (QB) at [55], also a case of mesothelioma, which he found applied to the university just as it did to the employer in that case:

"... the foreseeability of injury has to be tested against the standard of the well-informed employer who keeps abreast of the developing knowledge and applies [its] understanding without delay, and not by the standard of omniscient hindsight. An employer can rely upon a recognised and established practice to exonerate itself from liability in negligence for failing to take precautions unless (a) the practice is clearly bad practice, or (b) in the light of developing knowledge about the risks involved in some location or operation a particular employer acquired greater than average knowledge of the risks."

13–25   Add to end of paragraph: For a case where the employer's liability flowed from a failure to protect an employee from a campaign of personal vilification, see *Connor v Surrey CC* [2010] EWCA Civ 286; [2011] Q.B. 429, discussed in para.**14–08.** This was an extreme case in terms of the pressure on the claimant and it seems that in these circumstances too, knowledge of pre-existing vulnerability is not relevant: the harm is foreseeable in any event.

13–26   **Care in respect of known stress vulnerability.** Add to the end of the paragraph: In *Monk v Cann Hall Primary School* [2012] EWHC 3819 (QB), an admission of negligence was validly withdrawn and a claim struck out since it was held to depend upon the manner in which the claimant had been dismissed from her employment. Following *Johnson v Unisys Ltd* [2001] UKHL 13; [2003] 1 A.C. 518, damages could not be recovered at common law for the fact of or manner of dismissal. However, the Court of Appeal reversed the decision on the latter point.

The claimant would be allowed to amend her claim to distance the alleged negligence from the dismissal itself: *Monk v Cann Hall Primary School* [2013] EWCA Civ 826.

Causation. NOTE 177. Add at the end: See also *MacLennan v Hartford Europe*   **13–27**
Ltd [2012] EWHC 346 (QB), where a claimant failed to establish that her chronic fatigue syndrome was a result of workplace stress. She had not shown that she found her work particularly stressful; nor was there a proven causal link between stress, and chronic fatigue syndrome, either generally or in her particular case. The case would also have failed for lack of foreseeability on the part of her employer. Illustrating the difficulties facing claimants is *Saunders v Chief Constable of Sussex* [2012] EWCA Civ 1197: the Court of Appeal felt unable to disturb the judge's conclusion that even if relevant support had been available to the claimant on his return to work—which it was not—he would not have sought help nor acted differently. The difficulty facing the claimant in proving what would have been was noted.

Material contribution. NOTE 186. Add to the end of the Note: In *Brown v*   **13–28**
London Borough of Richmond Upon Thames [2012] EWCA Civ 1384 at [21], Treacy L.J. noted the apparent conflict between dicta in *Hatton* and *Dickins v O2 Plc*, and suggested that the point remained to be resolved, without mentioning the unanimity of the dicta in the latter case. In *Brown* itself, there was no appeal on the question of apportionment and the point therefore did not arise for discussion.

3. BREACH OF STATUTORY DUTY

Industrial safety legislation. After the first sentence, add: However, this entire   **13–30**
section must now be read subject to the far-reaching prospective change noted in para. **13–01A.**
At the end of the quotation from Smith L.J., ending with Note 194, delete the rest of the paragraph and replace it with the following: The Supreme Court in *Baker v Quantum Clothing Ltd* [2011] UKSC 17; [2011] 1 W.L.R. 1003 reversed the judgment of the Court of Appeal. Lord Mance, in the majority, said that the point did not need to be resolved given his approach to "safety" (see paras **13–32** and **13–33**), but stated that he considered the "gross disproportion" test to be an "unacceptable gloss" on the statutory wording (at [84]). He did not refer expressly to *Edwards v National Coal Board* [1949] 1 K.B. 704, but took the view that: "The criteria relevant to reasonable practicability must on any view largely reflect the criteria relevant to satisfaction of the common law duty of care. Both require consideration of the nature, gravity and imminence of the risk and its conse-quences, as well as of the nature and proportionality of the steps by which it might be addressed, and a balancing of the one against the other." Lord Mance rejected any assumption that the statutory duties must necessarily be intended to be stricter than the common law, arguing that the imposition of criminal liabilities implied that the duties should not be interpreted too broadly. It should be noted that Lord Dyson, also in the majority, did not comment on the "gross disproportion" test,

but referred to *Edwards v National Coal Board* [1949] 1 K.B. 704 as the leading authority on the meaning of "reasonably practicable" in industrial safety legislation. Since Lord Mance's comments on "gross disproportion" were not necessary to his decision, and he did not mention *Edwards* expressly, it is suggested that the authority of that decision is unaffected. There is some difficulty describing the gross disproportion test as a "gloss" on the statutory language given that the interpretation was well established long before the Factories Act 1961 was drafted.

13–32   **Safety and dangerousness.** Add to the end of the paragraph: However, the Supreme Court in *Baker v Quantum Clothing Group Ltd* [2011] UKSC 17; [2011] 1 W.L.R. 1003 held by a majority that "safety" is always dependent on ideas of foreseeability judged according to the standards of the time at which the risk was encountered; and that the authorities interpreting s.14 of the Factories Act 1961 (relating to "dangerous" equipment) are also of relevance to the interpretation of s.29 of the Factories Act 1961, which sets out a duty to keep the workplace "safe", so far as reasonably practicable. Section 14 however is not qualified by a provision that the dangers should be removed so far as reasonably practicable, and the minority thought this a pertinent reason why "safe" in s.29 should not necessarily be interpreted as the antonym of "dangerous" in s.14. It is suggested that reading "safe" and "dangerous" as simple "antonyms" in this way is to take them out of their statutory context and, in a sense, to give them invariable meanings of the sort which the majority said it was rejecting when it denied that s.29 referred to an absolute notion of safety.

13–33   **Safety.** After the sentence ending "thus avoiding liability", delete the rest of the paragraph, and replace it with the following: On appeal to the Supreme Court, the decision of the Court of Appeal was reversed and its approach to "safety" disapproved (*Baker v Quantum Clothing Group Ltd* [2011] UKSC 17; [2011] 1 W.L.R. 1003). *Larner v British Steel* was overruled, the majority concluding that the interpretation of "safety" should reflect reasonable foreseeability judged in accordance with the standards of the time, in line with cases interpreting s.14 of the same Act (see para.**13–32**). There was no such thing as an unchanging notion of "safety". Although it was not disputed that the burden of showing that it was not reasonably practicable to make the workplace "safe" lay with the employer, the employee must do more than show that an injury occurred and was likely with hindsight. The employee must also show that there was a reasonable foreseeability of harm and that the risk of harm was not acceptable, before the workplace could be shown not to have been "safe". Safety, according to the majority, was a matter of opinion. The minority rejected this view, emphasising that the section did not refer to reasonable safety, and arguing that a workplace which was believed (even reasonably) to be safe at the time of exposure was not thereby safe for the purposes of the statute. The question, rather, would be whether there were reasonably practicable steps that could have been taken in view of the knowledge existing at the time of exposure. In line with the approach of the Court of Appeal, the minority would therefore have dealt with issues of reasonableness largely in connection with "reasonable practicability", where the burden was on the employer. Lord Clarke, in the minority, emphasised that the purpose of the statutory duty was first and foremost to protect employees, not employers, and that a balance between these interests was established through the qualification that employers may show they have taken all steps that are "reasonably practicable". Lord Clarke proposed that s.29 was different from common law duties in that it was "results-oriented": there was a duty to achieve a particular result (that the workplace should be safe, not reasonably safe or believed to be safe); but the content of the duty was only to do what was reasonably practicable to this end.

It will be noted that the effect of applying the s.14 authorities on "dangerousness" to the s.29 duty is that claimants encounter more obstacles to a claim under s.29 than under s.14. First they must show that the workplace was not "safe" according to the standards of the time (effectively importing a foreseeability requirement), and the employer then has the opportunity to show that steps to make the workplace safe would not be reasonably practicable. The majority's approach therefore significantly increases the protection of employers where s.29 is concerned, even if Lord Mance's rejection of "gross disproportion" is not taken up.

Health and Safety at Work etc Act 1974. Add at the end of paragraph: Some   **13–35**
of the Regulations impose duties not only in respect of employees, but also in respect of persons at work and under a defendant's control. In *Kmiecic v Isaacs* [2011] EWCA Civ 451; [2011] P.I.Q.R. P13, the Court of Appeal emphasised that this did not mean that the Regulations impose duties on ordinary householders toward workers on their premises. Even if the householder controls access to the premises (in this instance, by barring access to a roof through a bedroom window), this does not mean that the householder controls the work, which determines whether a duty is owed under the Construction (Health, Safety and Welfare) Regulations 1996, and the Work at Height Regulations 2005. "Control" over construction work includes control over access and duties arise in respect of access; but this does not mean that controlling access is sufficient to show that an occupier exercises control over construction work. In any given case, whether or not an occupier exercises "control" over the work (thus owing duties under the Regulations) is a question of fact, as explained in *McCook v Lobo* [2002] EWCA Civ 1760; [2003] I.C.R. 89. It would be absurd to think that requiring anyone who asks for repair work to be done on their house to assume responsibility under the Regulations would improve the safety of workers, which was the rationale of the Framework Directive and Implementing Directive 92/57 of June 24, 1992. (For a similar result in a case argued in negligence, where an elderly couple owed no duty of care to a volunteer working on their house, see *McElhatton v McFarland* [2012] NIQB 114.) The reason for the claim against the householder in *Kmiecic* was that the employer had not insured his employee. Nor had the immediate employer in *Tafa v Matsim Properties Ltd* [2011] EWHC 1302 (QB), but here it was held that the second and third defendants did have sufficient control to come under the duties in the 1996 and 2005 Regulations. It was suggested that the nature of "control" in these two sets of Regulations was different, in that in order to owe a duty under the 1996 Regulations, the defendant must control the manner in which the work is carried out, whereas the 2005 Regulations impose a duty on anyone who controls the person conducting the work. It should be noted, however, that the latter Regulations only impose a duty to the extent of the control exercised. In any event, the defendants were held to owe both the duties in this case, where the immediate employer was considered plainly inappropriate to

take responsibility for safety in connection with the project. The need for control in relation to the risk was, by contrast, fatal to the pursuer's claim against surveyors in *Kenneth Winn-Pope v ES Access Platforms Ltd and CKD Galbraith LLP* [2012] CSOH 87; 2012 S.L.T. 929, also involving alleged breaches of the Work at Height Regulations 2005. The pursuer was the driver and operator of equipment hired to surveyors in order to enable them to inspect the roof of a building. He had unexpectedly chosen to follow one of the surveyors onto the roof, apparently in order to continue a conversation, when he suffered a fall. The surveyors were in control of the work, but it was concluded that this work was not intended to include the pursuer, who ought to have worn a harness which would have made it impossible for him to leave the raised basket. He had come onto the roof for his own purposes. The defendants therefore did not control the pursuer, and did not owe him the relevant duty.

A contrast is provided by *Ceva Logistics v Lynch* [2011] EWCA Civ 188; [2011] I.C.R. 746. Here, the owner and operator of a warehouse was held to be in breach of duty under the Workplace (Health, Safety and Welfare) Regulations 1992 to a visiting electrician who was not an employee, and who suffered injury on the premises. The defendant was not in control of the way in which the electrician carried out his electrical work, but was in control of operations within the warehouse and could make and enforce rules of conduct to assure the safety of those on site. As the electrician was injured when he was struck by a vehicle in the warehouse, the injury fell within the matters over which the defendant had control, and the defendant owed the relevant duties under the Regulations. The defendant ought to have ensured separation of pedestrians and vehicles within the warehouse. There was also a breach of the common law duty of care owed to independent contractors.

13–36   **Duty to conduct risk assessment.** Add to the end of paragraph (after the quotation from Smith L.J.): In *Threlfall v Kingston-upon-Hull City Council* [2010] EWCA Civ 1147; [2011] I.C.R. 209, Smith L.J. again emphasised the connection between a duty to conduct a risk assessment (on this occasion, in reg.6 of the Personal Protective Equipment at Work Regulations 1992 (SI 1992/2966)), and a duty to provide "suitable" equipment (reg.4 of the same Regulations). For equipment to be suitable in accordance with reg.4, it had to be at least appropriate for the risk and, as far as practicable, effective to prevent or adequately control the risk. The identification of risk is therefore essential to the judgment of suitability; and it was not open to the judge in this particular case to base his assessment of the suitability of equipment on an inadequate risk assessment by the employer. Here, the claimant had suffered lacerations to his hand from a concealed sharp object when clearing garden refuse. He had been supplied with ordinary gardening gloves which would not protect from such lacerations. Although the risk of such lacerations was not high, this did not mean that the gloves could be said to be suitable. Gloves which would protect against such lacerations were available from the same suppliers, albeit at greater cost. Smith L.J. said that an adequate risk assessment would have considered the risk of laceration from sharp objects, and the suitability of the equipment should be judged accordingly. In general terms, Smith L.J. described the difference made by the statutory duties introduced to the employment context over the last 20 years, with reference both to her own comments in *Allison* and those of Lord Walker in *Fytche v Wincanton Logistics*

Plc [2004] UKHL 31; [2004] I.C.R. 975, in terms of the duty to anticipate and guard against risks (at [35]):

"In many instances, a statutory duty to conduct . . . a risk assessment has been imposed. Such a requirement (whether statutory or not) has to a large extent taken the place of the old common law requirement that an employer had to consider (and take action against) those risks which could reasonably be foreseen. The modern requirement is that he should take positive thought for the risks arising arising from his operations."

A failure to undertake a risk assessment was not itself sufficient basis for liability. It still needed to be shown that the equipment was not suitable. But effectiveness was at the heart of suitability ([41]), and effectiveness was judged in relation to the avoidance of the risks that ought to have been identified. Given that an adequate risk assessment would have considered the risk of laceration, the equipment was not, in the circumstances, "suitable". The judge below had come close to adopting the common law standard, which was not the standard of the Regulations. See also the comments of the Court of Appeal on the relationship between risk assessment and the employer's non-delegable duty at common law (para.13–06). The Court of Appeal in *Chief Constable of Hampshire Police v Taylor* [2013] EWCA Civ 496 emphasised that the task on which an employee is engaged at the time of injury should not be subjected to such fine analysis that the risks against which protection is to be afforded are artificially limited in scope. This would be to undermine the protection of the Regulations (at [17]). Thus, where the claimant was engaged in dismantling a cannabis factory and gashed her hand attempting to open a window to alleviate the fumes inside the factory, it was established that she should have been supplied with thick gloves. She was expected to assist in dismantling the factory, which involved a range of tasks, and it was no answer that her injury was not caused by removal of the plants themselves. Equally, the burden remains on the employer to show that if suitable equipment had been supplied, the injury would still have occurred (at [18], referring to comments of Longmore L.J. in *Gaith v Indesit* [2012] EWCA Civ 642 (para.13–58), and describing as "a very established principle" (at [19]) the notion that once a breach of the duty to supply equipment is established, it is assumed that the equipment would have been used). See further para.2–12 of this Supplement on the causation issue.

Applying the structured approach in *Threlfall*, the decision of the Court of Appeal in *Blair v Chief Constable of Sussex Police* [2012] EWCA Civ 633 emphasises the significance both of the idea of "practicability", as distinct from common law negligence, and the location of the burden of proof on the employer. The claimant suffered a broken leg during off-road ("green lane") motorcycle training. He argued that the injury could and should have been prevented by providing him with stronger boots, such as those worn for motocross (but which made walking difficult). Applying the structured approach, the boots provided were plainly ineffective to prevent injury. Equally, it would have been possible to provide stronger boots for the purpose of off-road motorcycle training, which on the available evidence would probably have avoided the injury to the claimant's leg. Therefore, the employer needed to establish that the provision of such stronger boots would have been "impracticable". This had not been done, and since neither party sought a retrial, judgment was entered (it appears somewhat reluctantly) for the claimant. Longmore L.J. specifically pointed out that the question of whether provision of more effective equipment was "practicable" was not the same question as whether it would be "sensible", nor did questions of foreseeability enter into the matter. There had been a "sea-change" from "the old concepts of common law negligence".

13–37   NOTE 225. In the penultimate line, remove the word "and", and add to the end of the last sentence (before the full stop):; the Control of Artificial Optical Radiation at Work Regulations 2010 (SI 2010/1140); Health and Safety (Miscellaneous Revocations) Regulations 2012 (SI 2012/1537); and Control of Asbestos Regulations 2012 (SI 2012/632, which revoke and re-enact the Control of Asbestos Regulations 2006 (SI 2006/2739) to consolidate the Asbestos Regulations).

(a) Provision and Use of Work Equipment Regulations

13–40   **Work Equipment and the Coverage of the Regulations.** NOTE 239. Delete last sentence and preceding full stop, and replace with:, and *Threlfall v Kingston-upon-Hull City Council* [2010] EWCA Civ 1147; [2011] I.C.R. 209, para.**13–36.**

NOTE 240. Add to the end of the Note: See also the decision of the Court of Appeal in Northern Ireland in relation to an accident occurring during the harvesting of potatoes in Cumbria: *Hyndman v Brown and Bradley* [2012] NICA 3. The claimant had obtained judgment against the first respondent, who was his employer, on the basis of vicarious liability for the actions of a fellow employee; but it appears that the first respondent had no employers' liability insurance in place ([22]), and a claim against the second respondent was pursued. The first respondent had borrowed a harvester from the second respondent in order to complete his contract with the second respondent, his own harvester having broken down. The Court of Appeal decided that the second respondent did not have control of the harvester in the relevant sense at the time of the accident. It was appropriate for the work and well-maintained, and the second respondent knew that the first respondent was an experienced contractor. It had no control over the staff selected to operate the machinery and no control over how they operated it.

13–46   **Suitability of work equipment.** NOTE 266. Add to the end of the Note: See also the decision of the Court of Appeal in *Hide v Steeplechase Co (Cheltenham) Ltd* [2013] EWCA Civ 545, where a jockey was injured as his horse fell and he hit a post on the rail running around the track. The judge had been wrong to import the common law idea of "reasonable foreseeability" into the Regulations. Rather, a defendant could escape liability under reg.4 by showing the injury was caused by the particular types of event set out in art.5(4) of Directive 89/391: occurrences due to unforeseeable circumstances beyond his control; and occurrences due to exceptional events whose consequences were unavoidable. The claim should not have been dismissed on the basis that the way the claimant was injured was unusual.

Absolute duty in regulation 5. Add at the end of the paragraph: In *Johnstone* 　**13–48**
v AMEC Construction Ltd [2010] CSIH 57; 2011 S.C.L.R. 178; 2010 Rep. L.R.
96, the Inner House of the Court of Session accepted that the very fact that a
barrier fence failed to remain in position and was blown over by the wind meant
that it was not maintained in an efficient state, in efficient working order and in
good repair, as required by reg.5. The Court applied the dictum of Lord Reid in
Millar v Galashiels Gas Company [1949] A.C. 275, which it thought applicable
to reg.5:

> "If the duty is proper maintenance and maintenance is defined as maintenance
> in efficient working order, then, once it is established that the duty goes beyond
> a duty to exercise care, the fact that on a particular occasion the mechanism was
> not in working order shows that there had not been proper maintenance."

There was also a breach of reg.4 on the facts. The fence was treated as work
equipment which was used by the appellant, a security guard who was patrolling
the perimeter and was injured when he first tried to replace the fence, and then to
step over it. Similarly, perimeter gates were held to be "work equipment" so far as
a security guard was concerned in *Swilas v Clyde Pumps Ltd* 2011 GWD 34–714.
The fact that they were also part of the fabric of the premises was irrelevant (and
see *Hodgkinson v Renfrewshire Council* [2011] CSOH 142; 2011 G.W.D. 29–639,
where there was however no breach of reg.4).

NOTE 272. Delete the last sentence and replace it with the following: On the
general relationship between assessment of risks and duties under Health and Safety
Regulations to provide suitable equipment, training, and so on, see para.**13–36**.

After para **13–50**, add two new paras**13–50A** and **13–50B**:

Protection against specified hazards. Regulation 12(1) imposes a duty on 　**13–50A**
employers to take measures to ensure that exposure of a person using work equipment to risk arising from a list of specified hazards is either prevented or, where
that is not reasonably practicable, adequately controlled. The required measures
are defined in reg.12(2) as measures "other than" the provision of protective
personal equipment, instruction, training and supervision "so far as is reasonably
practicable" (reg.12(2)(a)). Regulation 12(2)(b) requires that this will, where
appropriate, include measures to minimise the effects of hazard as well as to
reduce the likelihood of its occurring. This distinctive wording was considered by
the Court of Appeal in *Whitehead v Trustees of the Chatsworth Settlement* [2012]
EWCA Civ 263; [2013] 1 W.L.R. 251. A gamekeeper, disregarding what he knew
to be safe practice, attempted to cross a stile without removing live ammunition
from his rifle. The stile crumbled and the rifle discharged two bullets into his leg.
The danger from the gun was accepted to fall into the listed hazards in reg.12(3)
(specifically, "the unintended or premature discharge of any article . . . which . . .
is produced, used or stored in [the work equipment]", reg.12(3)(b)). The Court
decided that the wording of reg.12(1) ("to take measures" to prevent or adequately
control) meant that in the case both of prevention, and of control, reasonable practicability was relevant. This was because the nature of the required measures was
defined in reg.12(2). The meaning of reg.12(2) was that measures intended to
safeguard the user from risk may include, but must not be limited to, provision of

protective equipment, training, instruction, supervision and so on, so far as it was reasonably practicable to take additional measures. Although the duty can extend to injury caused by the claimant's own misuse of equipment, in this instance the claimant was working alone and appropriate training and instruction had been issued. There were no further protective measures that were reasonably practicable either to prevent or control the hazard. The employer was, therefore, not in breach of the duty.

13–50B   **Nature of risk to health and safety.** In *Willock v Corus (UK) Ltd* [2013] EWCA Civ 519, the Court of Appeal held that the risks to health and safety which must be avoided so far as reasonably practicable in the positioning of controls according to reg.17 were not confined to dangers associated with people coming into contact with dangerous machinery. Regulation 17(2), which requires employers to ensure so far as reasonably practicable that no control for work equipment is in a position where any person operating the control is exposed to a risk to his health or safety, was broad enough to apply to back pain if it arose from the positioning of the controls.

(b) *Workplace (Health, Safety and Welfare) Regulations*

13–51   NOTE 279. Add to the end of the Note: See also *Brown v East Lothian Council* [2013] CSOH 62; 2013 S.L.T. 721: a fitness instructor's claim failed, as she had not shown that premises she had hired for a fitness class were made available to her "as a place of work", rather than as a place where she (as a self-employed person) was working; and *Howarth v Cummins Ltd* Unreported June 1, 2012 County Court (Bristol): delivery driver who fell on premises when he got out of his van to ask directions not owed a duty under the Regulations.

After NOTE 279 in the text, add: However, they do apply to independent contractors working on premises provided the duty in question relates to matters within the control of the defendant: *Ceva Logistics Ltd v Lynch* [2011] EWCA Civ 188; [2011] I.C.R. 746, discussed at para.**13–35.**

After the sentence (seven lines from end of the paragraph) ending "strictly liable for the breach" add: By contrast in *Caerphilly CBC v Button* [2010] EWCA Civ 1311; [2011] I.C.R. D3, the Court of Appeal considered that reg.5 was not easily applicable to a case where an employee was injured tripping over a kerb placed on a loose slope in a car park at work. The case did not involve "equipment, devices and systems", which were the main concern of reg.5, and it would be artificial to say that the kerb was not in an "efficient state". The case was dealt with under reg.12, and as a claim in negligence at common law.

Add to the end of the paragraph: Equipment does not fail to be in an efficient state, or in efficient working order, if it is used for a purpose for which it is not designed or provided: in *Wallace v Glasgow City Council* [2011] CSIH 57; 2011 Rep. L.R. 96, there was no breach of reg.5 when a toilet bowl toppled while the pursuer was standing on it in order to open a window and ventilate the room. There was, however, a breach of reg.15, which provides that windows, skylights and ventilators which are capable of being opened shall not be likely to be opened in a way which exposes the person opening it to a risk to their health and safety, taken together with the duty to conduct risk assessments set out in reg.3 of the

Management of Health and Safety at Work Regulations 1999 (SI 1999/3242). A pole should have been readily available for use by those seeking to open the window. Damages, however, were reduced by 50 per cent because this was not a case of momentary inattention but a deliberate act which was acknowledged to be dangerous.

Add at the end of the paragraph: Note also the Work at Height Regulations **13–52** 2005, which came into force on April 6, 2005, and were interpreted by the Court of Appeal in *Bhatt v Fountain Motors Ltd* [2010] EWCA Civ 863; [2010] P.I.Q.R. P17. The Regulations are directed at eliminating the risks involved in working at height if reasonably practicable to carry out the work otherwise than at height, and minimising those risks which cannot be avoided in this way. See further paras **13–35** and **13–64.**

Add to the end of the paragraph: See also *Gillie v Scottish Borders Council* **13–53** [2013] CSOH 76; 2013 Rep. L.R. 86: a school janitor slipped and fell on stairs, probably because of petroleum jelly left by students as a practical joke on their final day. The probability of this was low and it was not reasonably practicable for the school to ensure that the stair was kept free of the substance.

At the end of the paragraph, add: In *Marks and Spencer Plc v Palmer* [2001] **13–54** EWCA Civ 1528, Waller L.J. emphasised that the correct approach to the question of whether a traffic route was "suitable" was to ask whether, by reference to the factors arising before the accident took place and not with the benefit of hindsight, the route was suitable. "Suitability" required a qualitative assessment. In *Taylor v Wincanton Group Ltd* [2009] EWCA Civ 1581, Waller L.J. accepted that this may be much the same as making a risk assessment, the approach taken by Smith L.J. in *Allison v London Underground* [2008] EWCA Civ 71; [2008] I.C.R. 719 (para.**13–36**). On the other hand, Smith L.J. in *Threlfall v Kingston-upon-Hull City Council* [2010] EWCA Civ 1147; [2011] I.C.R. 209 has distinguished between different sets of Regulations in relation to whether they require a "qualitative" judgment as to suitability, concluding that the Personal Protective Equipment at Work Regulations, which were in issue in that case, included clear detail on how suitability was to be judged, and therefore did not require a qualitative judgment of the same sort once a relevant risk had been identified (para.**13–36**). In *Caerphilly CBC v Button* [2010] EWCA Civ 1311; [2011] I.C.R. D3 (para.**13–51**), which like *Marks and Spencer v Palmer* was concerned with reg.12 of the Workplace (Health, Safety and Welfare) Regulations 1992, Pill L.J. concluded that on the particular facts of that case, the question of whether a traffic route was "suitable" raised essentially the same issues as the question whether there had been a breach of a duty at common law, in contrast with the clear distinction between the Regulations and the common law duty drawn by Smith L.J. in *Threlfall*. In this particular instance, the traffic route was not suitable and the employers fell below the standard expected of them. However it should be noted that Richards L.J., agreeing in the result, nevertheless referred to the "strict" nature of the duties under the 1992 Regulations. Compare *White v Coventry City Council* Unreported June 7, 2012 County Court (Walsall), where the route chosen by the claimant was prohibited and was not considered a "traffic route" for the purposes of reg.12. An illustrative case involving breach of reg.17 (concerned with the organisation of traffic routes, so that they are sufficient for the persons or vehicles using them) is *Hook v Eatons Solicitors* Unreported July 17, 2012 County Court (Leeds). The claimant fell downstairs when stepping back to open a door on a tiny landing. Only a small misjudgement was needed for the accident to occur, and there was no contributory negligence. The workplace fell within reg.17(5) and liability was subject to what was "reasonably practicable". Here there had been no risk assessment and there were breaches of the Management of Health and Safety at Work Regulations 1999 reg.3, and of the Workplace (Health, Safety and Welfare) Regulations 1992 reg.17(1) and (2).

13–56   After the sentence ending "the regularity of the occurrence", add: *Ellis* was applied in *Cheung v Zhu* [2011] EWHC 2913 (QB). Here the claimant was a counter assistant in the defendant's fish and chip shop, and slipped on wet ceramic tiles. As in *Ellis*, the tiles became slippery with sufficient frequency for the floor to be described as unsuitable within the terms of the Regulations.

(c) *Manual Handling Operations Regulations*

13–57   NOTE 303. At the end add: In *McCabe v Royal Mail Group Plc* 2011 GWD 15–375, it was suggested that the duties in the Regulations were not designed to place responsibility for every possible medical risk which might affect their employees, and were more reasonably directed towards prevention of lumbar and limb injuries.

13–58   **Distinct duties.** At the end of the paragraph, add: Similarly, see the decision of the Court of Appeal in *Gaith v Indesit Co UK Ltd* [2012] EWCA Civ 642. The claimant had exacerbated a back injury during a stock take which involved lifting heavy items over the course of several hours. There had been no risk assessment relating to stock taking. The judge's approach, which was to conclude that the absence of a risk assessment had on the balance of probabilities made no difference, was inadequate. The correct approach was set out in *Egan*: in the absence of a risk assessment, the employer must still show that the relevant risk had been reduced to the lowest level reasonably practicable in accordance with reg.4(1)(a)(ii), and the burden in this respect was on the employer. The employer faced a more severe difficulty in the absence of a risk assessment, since such an assessment would have set out the risk to be reduced. In this instance there was no reduction for contributory negligence, as this was inappropriate to a case of "momentary inattention" of this sort.

13–59   After Note 310 in the text, add: Although an absence of refresher training, where this is reasonably practicable, is capable of constituting a breach of reg.4 (failure to take appropriate steps to reduce the risks to the lowest level reasonably practicable), it must still be shown that the absence of refresher training caused the injury. In other words, there needs to be evidence to show that the training would lead the claimant to alter their practice, and that it would have avoided the particular injury in the particular circumstances: *Costa v Imperial London Hotels Ltd* [2012] EWCA Civ 672 (on the evidence before the court, refresher training would not have prevented a chamber maid from suffering a back and neck injury).

Add to the end of the paragraph: This is also the case if the evidence suggests that the injury suffered is genetically predetermined and not the result of handling operations: see for example *Wilson v Lanarkshire Council* [2011] CSOH 178.

4. DEFENCES

Defendant's breach of duty coextensive with that of the claimant. After the **13–63** sentence ending "provided the claimant was the sole cause of his own loss.", add a new Note 328A:

NOTE 328A. An example in connection with the employer's duty to provide a safe system of work at common law is *Sutherland v McConechy's Tyre Service Ltd* [2012] CSOH 28; 2012 Rep. L.R. 46. S was a manager at a tyre fitting depot, and the reason that the employer's safety system was not in operation at the premises in which S worked was solely that S had not put it into effect: he had failed to implement what he knew to be proper practice. Had there been liability, contributory negligence would have been assessed at 80 per cent.

At the end of the paragraph, add: In the difficult case of *Brumder v Motornet Service and Repairs Ltd and Aviva Insurance* [2013] EWCA Civ 195; [2013] 3 All E.R. 412, the defence in *Ginty* and *Boyle v Kodak* was extended by the Court of Appeal to a case where the claimant was the sole director and shareholder of the defendant, and had breached a different duty (namely, a duty of care owed to the company) from the duty whose breach was the basis of his action. The defendant company was in breach of its absolute duty under the Provision and Use of Work Equipment Regulations 1998 reg.5, when the compressor in a raised hydraulic ramp failed. The claimant lost a finger attempting to descend from the ramp. It was found that the claimant, as sole director, had not given any consideration to health and safety and had not conducted a risk assessment nor sought to ensure that statutory obligations were met. The Court of Appeal rejected the judge's finding of 100 per cent contributory negligence as contrary to principle. However, it extended the defence in *Boyle* and *Ginty* to this situation. It is suggested that this extension of a defence which was previously understood to be tightly confined could pose some difficulties, since the claimant's breaches of duty in this instance were different in kind from the defendant's breach of absolute duty under reg.5. So, for example, it was suggested that the company would be able to recover its losses from the claimant if he should succeed in his action, so that the result would be circuitous actions (at [49], [51]). This argument was also used in *Ginty*. But where the duties breached by the parties are different in kind it is difficult to be certain that this would be the case. For example, was the claimant's failure causative of the defendant's breach of duty, or would the ramp have failed even if a risk assessment had been carried out? In a short concurring judgment, Longmore L.J. based his agreement more directly on the policies which he identified as underlying absolute duties, most particularly the aim of encouraging high standards of compliance (at [62]). It is open to question whether leaving an individual director without compensation for personal injury is an ideal means of encouraging compliance. In any event, the decision plainly extends the defence beyond cases where the breaches of duty are "coextensive".

13–64   **Contributory negligence.** Add to the end of the paragraph: Similarly in *Bhatt v Fountain Motors Ltd* [2010] EWCA Civ 863; [2010] P.I.Q.R. P17, where breaches of the Work at Height Regulations 2005 had exposed an employee to unnecessary risk of injury, it was appropriate to start with the regulations and their breach and not with the conduct of the claimant. An employee's failure to follow prescribed procedure when doing work he should not have been asked to do at all could not be said to be the whole cause of the accident, as the defendants argued, though in this case, it did go to contributory negligence. In *Sharp v Top Flight Scaffolding* [2013] EWHC 479 (QB), the approach in *Bhatt* was applied to breaches of the same regulations, where work at height was necessary but the defendants had failed to ensure that the claimant was properly trained or supervised. However, the claimant's decisions to construct scaffolding without ladders for egress, and to descend the outside of the scaffolding despite the obvious dangers, were taken deliberately and consciously, and contributory negligence was assessed at 60 per cent.

CHAPTER 14

PUBLIC SERVICE LIABILITY

		PARA.
1.	Introduction.	14–01
2.	Negligence liability.	14–02
	□ (a) Justiciability	14–03
	■ (b) Fair just and reasonable	14–09
	□ (i) Child welfare	14–16
	(ii) Educational welfare	14–24
	■ (iii) Police services	14–25
	(iv) Rescue services	14–32
	□ (v) Participants in legal proceedings	14–33
	■ (vi) Armed forces	14–37
	■ (vii) Immunities	14–39
	(c) Proximity.	14–41
	(i) Regulatory agencies.	14–42
	(ii) Custodial agencies	14–43
	(iii) Police	14–44
	(d) Omissions	14–45
	□ (i) Statutory powers and duties	14–46
	■ (ii) Common law basis for duty	14–51
	□ (e) Standard of care	14–61
	(i) Ambit of discretion	14–62
	(ii) Resources	14–63
□ 3.	Liability under the Human Rights Act 1998.	14–64
	(a) Article 6 and common law liability	14–66
	■ (b) Public authority liability under the Human Rights Act 1998	14–69
	■ (c) Damages under the Human Rights Act 1998	14–97
4.	Misfeasance in public office	14–102
	■ (a) Nature of the tort.	14–102
	□ (b) Scope of the tort	14–113
5.	Conclusion	14–118

2. NEGLIGENCE LIABILITY

(a) *Justiciability*

Ambit of discretion. At the end of the paragraph add: This analysis is consistent **14–08** with observations of Laws L.J. in *Connor v Surrey CC* [2010] EWCA Civ 286; [2011] Q.B. 328, concerning justiciability. Summarising the impact of the leading authorities (at [103]), Laws L.J. proposed that where pure decisions of policy are in issue, courts "will not ascribe a duty of care to the policy-maker. So much is owed to the authority of Parliament and in that sense to the rule of law". However, "if a decision, albeit a choice of policy, is so unreasonable that it cannot be said to have been taken under the statute, it will (for the purposes of the tort of negligence) lose the protection of the statute". In such cases, a duty of care "along *Caparo* lines" must still be established.

However, Laws L.J. went on to suggest, at [104]–[105], that *Connor* itself did not fall within these principles gleaned from existing authorities, because it was a case where a duty of care arose "independently of the relevant statute". The defendant was the employer of the claimant and thus owed the recognised duty of an employer to take reasonable care to protect the employee from personal injury, including personal injury in the form of psychiatric harm, as here. This was a case where the alleged breach of this recognised private law duty lay, in part, in a failure to exercise the defendant's discretion, in particular by removing a "dysfunctional" Board of Governors and replacing it with an interim executive board pursuant to powers under the School Standards and Framework Act 1998. There was a second alleged breach—accepted by two members of the Court of Appeal to amount to negligence—in that the defendants responded to "outrageous" criticisms of the claimant not by supporting her, but by establishing an inquiry into the allegations made. Laws L.J. suggested that this was a case where a duty was clearly owed, and the issue was as to the duty's scope. He concluded that a party who owes a private law duty "may be required to fulfil his pre-existing duty by the exercise of a public law discretion", but only to the extent that this is consistent "with the duty-ower's full performance of his public law obligations" (at [107]). This should be interpreted to mean that there was "no inconsistency" between the private law aim and the public purpose (at [108]). The other members of the Court of Appeal agreed with Laws L.J. that this was a case where a duty of care at private law was owed and breached by the defendant, but did not expressly agree with his detailed reasoning. Agreeing in the result, Sedley L.J. pointed out that all employers owe duties to their employees and that these frequently coexist with other duties (for example to shareholders and regulators) which may pull in different directions (at [119]). Admittedly this could create more complex problems for public authority employers. In this case, Surrey County Council had "the unenviable task of responding in an equitable fashion to an inequitable campaign designed to capture a secular state school for a particular faith which happened to be that of a majority of the families whose children attended the school" (at [120]). The Council had compromised with this move, instead of protecting "the head, the staff, and the school", and the critical point was that to do so would have been consistent both with public law functions and with private law obligations (at [121]). Private and public law functions did not pull against one another. Along the same lines, Thomas L.J. described the council's response as an "abdication of responsibility" by those who were charged with protecting the interests of educating school children in Surrey—clearly a wide enough idea to encompass public functions. This case illustrates that failure to exercise a statutory power can be a breach of a private law duty, provided that duty is justified in the usual way and there is no contradiction between the private and public law obligations owed. The distinction drawn by Laws L.J. between questions as to the existence of a duty and questions as to the scope of a duty may prove hard to maintain, but this is a very different case from (for example) *Rowley v Secretary of State for Work and Pensions* [2007] EWCA Civ 598; [2007] 1 W.L.R. 2861 (para.**14–17**), where the existence of a statutory duty and performance of the duty were the sole grounds on which a duty of care at private law was said to exist. It is also distinct from *Stovin v Wise* [1996] A.C. 923 (para.**14–46**) since the duty does not arise out of a statutory power. Rather, a recognised common law duty is breached, in this case, by a failure to exercise a statutory power. Had there been no such power, the authority would have been unable to defend the claimant by replacing the Board of Governors, and could not have been held liable for not doing so (see also *Geddis v Bann Reservoir Proprietors* (1878) 3 App. Cas. 430, although this was a case of negligent exercise of a power, rather than negligence consisting in failure to exercise a power). More broadly, this case hints that there might remain a category of cases where English courts see private law as capable of reinforcing the performance of public functions rather than undermining them. At least, this was not a case where the courts should "stay off the field" (Laws L.J. at [106]).

(b) *Fair, just and reasonable*

Greater emphasis on duty. Add to the end of the paragraph: *Barrett* and   **14–13**
Phelps were both cited by the Court of Appeal in *Smith v Ministry of Defence* [2012] EWCA Civ 1365; [2013] 2 W.L.R. 27, where claims in negligence were not struck out. Here the Court of Appeal took the view that the policy issues raised by the Ministry of Defence were, for the most part, best considered in terms of breach of duty (and the remaining issues, which were appropriately seen as duty questions, should not be determined in the absence of evidence). Citation of *Phelps* and *Barrett* has been considered surprising: J. Morgan, "Negligence: Into Battle" (2013) 72 C.L.J. 14, and the emphasis on breach may appear to contradict the general position described in this paragraph. Moses L.J. argued that the duties argued for in this case were not *novel* duties. Rather, they were well-established duties owed by the Ministry of Defence as an employer to its employees. This, he said, was the "fatal flaw" in the Ministry of Defence argument (at [45]): they sought to use the presence of policy arguments to deny a *recognised* duty. On this view, the established, restrictive approach to duties of care where there are policy issues is to be confined to novel duties. On appeal to the Supreme Court (*Smith v Ministry of Defence* [2013] UKSC 41; [2013] 3 W.L.R. 69), Lord Hope, who delivered the judgment of the majority, appears to have adopted a similar position, but the boundaries between duty questions and breach questions were much less clearly drawn. In the minority, Lord Mance drew upon cases which were not concerned with employment relationships, suggesting in effect that the situation was indeed a novel one, since it concerned the extent of a duty to protect personnel under conditions where the enemy is seeking to kill them. See further discussion in para.**14–38**.

Application of the fairness test. In the sentence beginning "Only the policy   **14–15**
protection of . . ." after "witnesses" insert "of fact".
After the end of this sentence ("remains untouched"), add: The immunity from negligence actions in particular of expert witnesses has been removed by the Supreme Court in *Jones v Kaney* [2011] UKSC 13; [2011] 2 A.C. 398 (see further para.**14–35**). The immunity remains in place for actions other than negligence (see para.**16–72**).
In the next sentence beginning "Balancing the less restrictive . . .", replace "remained" with "remain".

(i) *Child welfare*

14–17 **Child welfare and child support.** At the end of the paragraph add: It has become increasingly clear that the reasoning applied in *Rowley* and *Kehoe* is of much wider application than the child support context. This is illustrated by *Murdoch v Department for Work and Pensions* [2010] EWHC 1988 (QB). Here Walker J. ruled, applying *Rowley*, that an action in negligence would be inconsistent with the statutory scheme relating to the payment of incapacity benefit and income support. This was because the statute made plain the intended finality of determination of entitlement under the Act. Following *Customs and Excise Commissioners v Barclays Bank Plc* [2006] UKHL 28; [2007] 1 A.C. 181, there was also no duty of care in any event. There was no assumption of responsibility simply through action to discharge a statutory duty; there was no special proximity; any such development would be more than incremental; and it would not be "fair, just and reasonable" to offer a remedy where alternative remedies existed. As to this last point, to the extent that the complaints did not depend on questioning decisions made under statute, but only on failures to pay the money which had been determined to be due to the claimant, a simple action to recover the debt in the County Court was already available. A negligence action added undue complexity. For individuals in the position of the claimant, who had to borrow money on very disadvantageous terms, a key question is whether this alternative remedy is apt to cover his full losses. As to the availability of other, albeit lesser remedies see also *Home Office v Mohammed* [2011] EWCA Civ 351; [2011] 1 W.L.R. 2862 (paras **14–48** and **14–51**).

(iii) *Police services*

14–28 Eight lines from the end of the paragraph, after "alternative remedy in domestic law.", add a new sentence: The potential significance of the alternative remedy founded on art.2 is illustrated by *Michael v Chief Constable of South Wales Police* [2012] EWCA Civ 981; [2012] H.R.L.R. 30, a case which bears some comparison with *Smith*. The claims concerned the murder of a woman after she had placed a 999 call to police. A claim in negligence was struck out as clearly falling within the ambit of the decision in *Hill*; but a claim based on art.2 was, by a majority, allowed to proceed to trial. See further para.**14–72**.

14–30 **Assumption of responsibility by the police** Add to the end of the paragraph: In *An Informer v A Chief Constable* [2012] EWCA Civ 197; [2013] Q.B. 579, the Court of Appeal declined to apply the reasoning in *Swinney* to a failure to protect the economic interests of the claimant informer or "Covert Human Intelligence Source" (CHIS). The claimant had himself become a suspect in the course of the investigation in relation to which he was providing information to the police, with the consequence that a restraint order was secured preventing him from disposing of assets. The claimant alleged negligence in, amongst other things, failing to inform investigators that he was a CHIS. This information would have been relevant to the court's decision as to the necessity for the order to be made. Members of the Court of Appeal gave a range of different reasons for deciding that the case fell within the *Hill* principle. Toulson L.J. considered that the duty to protect the welfare of informers, as illustrated in *Swinney*, did not extend to protection of financial welfare and could not justify recovery of economic losses (at [82]).

Arden L.J. focused on the particular facts. She accepted that the investigation into C's activities had to take place without intervention from his "handlers" so that the independence and integrity of the process was not compromised. In the circumstances, the "public policy underpinning the investigations immunity" (the *Hill* principle) displaced the assumption of responsibility on the part of the police where financial harm to the CHIS was concerned (at [129]). Pill L.J. was clearly less satisfied with the outcome of the case and considered that the recognised duty to C arising out of proximity of the relationship was capable of extending beyond physical welfare. However, he was "prepared to find" that the failure to notify investigators of the claimant's status as a CHIS was not a breach of the extended duty owed to him. He emphasised that the *Hill* principle did not give carte blanche to the police to "treat courts and CHISs as they please in order to satisfy operational requirements" (at [193]), and indicated that future failures may not be interpreted in the same manner, given that awareness would now be raised that the welfare of the informant needed to be more fully assured.

NOTE 132. Delete the current reference and add: [2011] EWCA Civ 3; [2011] **14–31** 1 F.L.R. 1361; [2011] Fam. Law 358.

In the first sentence of the paragraph replace "concluded that" with "accepted that in principle".

Delete the sentence beginning "Wyn Williams J. declined to strike out an action", and replace it with: The Court of Appeal concluded that the action should be struck out as disclosing no arguable duty of care. The Court of Appeal considered it possible that the case fell outside the "core principle" in *Hill*. But this would not suffice, and it still needed to be established that a duty of care was owed in the particular context of the case. Here, the fact that the officers concerned were performing statutory duties appears to have persuaded the Court of Appeal that a voluntary assumption of responsibility would need to be shown even outside the ambit of *Hill* because, if the policy of the statute is not to create a statutory liability to pay compensation, this same policy should "ordinarily exclude" a common law duty of care (at [39]). There would need to be compelling circumstances, such as the undertaking of responsibilities (or carrying out of acts), to make it fair and reasonable to impose the duty.

After the sentence ending "was considered", delete the final sentence, and replace it with: In this instance, there could not be said to be an assumption of responsibility because the defendant acted under statutory duty. The officer concerned "does not assume a responsibility which the statute has not obliged him to undertake", and "There is nothing beyond the existence of the statutory duty from which a common law duty of care might be discerned" (at [48], *Yetkin v Newham LBC* [2010] EWCA Civ 776; [2011] Q.B. 827 distinguished as it involved positive actions, pursuant to powers rather than duties). As in the case of omissions liability, for an assumption of responsibility to be a sufficient basis for a duty of care in the context of statutory duties the duty must be voluntarily assumed, which means that it is not identical to a duty imposed by statute (para.**14–56**; see also by way of contrast the discussion of duties arising out of an employment relationship, at para.**14–08**). It was also treated as relevant that the claimant might have other remedies, albeit of a different type. This included the potential for a Human Rights Act remedy for interference with art.8 rights, a claim for which was still continuing in *Desmond* itself (and now see *Desmond v Foreman*

[2012] EWHC 1900 (QB), where Tugendhat J. held that the claimant had a real prospect of succeeding in an argument based on art.8 ECHR and the Data Protection Act 1998).

(v) *Participants in Legal Proceedings*

14–35   **Judges, witness and parties.** In the second line, after "witness" insert "of fact".

After NOTE 147 in the text, replace "Witnesses" with: "Prior to *Jones v Kaney* [2011] UKSC 13; [2011] 2 A.C. 398, all witnesses"

In the same sentence, replace "have immunity" with "had immunity".

In the following sentence, beginning "The basis of this immunity is", replace "is" with "was".

At the end of this sentence, ending "fearlessly.", insert the following: The immunity of expert witness has been removed by the Supreme Court in *Jones v Kaney* [2011] UKSC 13; [2011] 2 A.C. 398. While expert witnesses presumably continue to enjoy other immunities in common with other participants in legal proceedings (see further para.**16–72**), expressly so in relation to defamation (see for example Lord Phillips at [62]), the restrictive requirements associated with establishing a duty of care in negligence appear to have persuaded the majority of the Supreme Court that no difficulty would be created by withdrawal of the negligence immunity in particular. Where duties of care are established the role of expert witness is much more akin to the role of an advocate rather than the role of a witness of fact. Presumably, where this is not the case, no duty of care will be owed on ordinary principles. Lord Collins, who joined the majority in the decision, would have preferred to maintain an immunity properly so-called for hostile witnesses (at [73]). The dissenting judges, Lord Hope and Baroness Hale, thought the issues raised, and particularly the precise boundaries of the area of potential liability of expert witnesses, were not easily resolved by a court and would have preferred to see exploration by the Law Commission (at [173], [190]). The present position is uncertain to the extent that the ambit of the duty of care is uncertain. It is suggested that immunities in torts other than negligence should be seen as unaffected by the decision since the underlying reasons for the general immunity apply to expert witnesses as to any other participant in legal proceedings. Equally, the "core immunity" continues to protect participants in legal proceedings, including counsel, outside the ambit of the duties recognised in *Hall v Simons* (para.**14–34**) and *Jones v Kaney: A and B v Chief Constable of Hampshire Constabulary* [2012] EWHC 1517 (QB). See further para.**10–41** of this Supplement.

(vi) *Armed forces*

14–37   **Armed forces** Add to the end of Note 164: That no application had been made by the Secretary of State to reinstate the immunity for the purposes of engagement in Afghanistan and Iraq was considered by Moses L.J. to support the Court of Appeal's decision not to strike out the claims in *Smith v Ministry of Defence* [2012] EWCA Civ 1365; [2013] 2 W.L.R. 27 (para.**14–38**). The Secretary of State, he argued, had not considered the availability of tort actions outside the limits of combat immunity to be undesirable or harmful to the interests of personnel in these circumstances. No similar argument featured in the decision of the majority of the Supreme Court.

Add at the end of the paragraph: The Supreme Court has now ruled on the **14–38** nature and extent of combat immunity at common law in *Smith v Ministry of Defence* [2013] UKSC 41; [2013] 3 W.L.R. 69. The Human Rights Act aspects of the decision are considered in paras **14–69A** (jurisdictional extent, and art.1) and **14–73** (right to life, art.2). In respect of the claims at common law, counsel for the Ministry of Defence had advanced arguments based both on combat immunity, and on the application of the general "fair, just and reasonable" test derived from *Caparo Industries v Dickman*. Lord Hope, with whom Lord Walker, Lady Hale and Lord Kerr agreed, accepted that combat immunity is "best thought of as a rule" (at [83]). However, he interpreted this rule narrowly. It is suggested that he took as the paradigm of combat immunity those decisions made in the heat of battle: such decisions could not fairly be questioned in litigation. At first instance, Owen J. had interpreted combat immunity as not confined to cases involving "the presence of the enemy", and ruled that the immunity applied to all "active operations" in which service personnel are exposed to attack, or a threat of attack. This extended to decisions taken in the planning of the operations in which injury was sustained, though not to the planning and preparation for possible future operations, and it was on this basis not all of the common law claims had been struck out. Lord Hope, however, considered the judgment of Owen J. to amount to an unjustified "extension" of the immunity, as it could apply to decisions "taken far away in place and time" from the active operations themselves (at [89]). Lord Hope described the rule as "a particular application of what is fair, just and reasonable". Nevertheless, it operated like a rule, and should be approached in a restricted way. Lord Hope thought of combat immunity as an exceptional defence available to governments and individuals who cause damage, injury or death "in the course of actual or imminent armed conflict", and amounting to an exception to the principle in *Entick v Carrington* that the executive cannot simply rely on the interests of the state as a justification for the commission of wrongs (at [90]). The doctrine should be narrowly construed (at [92]), and more generally, any extension of an existing immunity needs to be carefully justified (at [94]). Although counsel had argued that, beyond the extent of the immunity, public policy reasons existed which would justify the non-existence of a duty of care, it is suggested that surprisingly little argument was devoted to this possibility by Lord Hope for the majority. Rather, Lord Hope took the view that any further questions about the existence of a duty could not be determined without hearing evidence. Further, Lord Hope appeared to argue that questions of breach would be particularly significant in controlling the operation of negligence outside the area of combat immunity, suggesting that courts must pay attention to the context in which decisions were reached in deciding whether or not the duty has been breached, and that duties must not be "unrealistic or excessively burdensome" (at [99]). At the same time, he described what amounts to a fair, just and reasonable outcome in terms of a "balance", which could not be struck in a general way and must reflect a factual enquiry. This approach appears to run counter to the general preference for resolving questions of policy at the duty stage, outlined in para.**14–13**.

The significance of this approach can be illustrated by way of contrast with the dissenting judgments of Lords Mance and Carnwath. Lord Mance in particular stressed the importance of asking *what duty was owed* in relation to a death in active operations. Lord Hope, by contrast, emphasised the unassailable nature of *decisions* made in the course of active operations as the core of combat immunity, which was itself a limited exception to the rule that the interests of the state do not take priority over individual rights. Lord Hope was reluctant to extend the area of "no duty" beyond this zone. Lord Mance proposed a larger area of "non-justiciability", which reflected the idea that the interests of military personnel were necessarily subordinate to the attainment of military objectives (at [122]); and the need (for this reason) to avoid litigation both after, and during, active engagement with an enemy. Both dissenting judges referred to decisions such as *Van Colle* and *Brooks* in which duties of care were denied not because decisions were made "in the heat of the moment", but for policy reasons. Their point was that Lord Hope's majority judgment appears to give little weight to the presence of policy factors in relation to decisions taken in advance of active engagement, and is unusual among recent decisions of the highest courts in preferring to leave balancing questions to the tribunal of fact (see further para.**14–13**). It is suggested that this is because of the way that combat immunity was identified by the majority with decisions unassailable because of battle or combat conditions, rather than as part of a continuum of policy questions underpinned by the subordination of interests ordinarily protected by private law to other objectives in the context of war. This subordination is not unlimited, but the majority judgments supply little information about how to approach duties outside the range of decisions taken in the course of active operations, to which "combat immunity" must now be said most centrally to apply.

It is plain from Lord Hope's judgment that the context in which decisions are made will continue to affect judgments as to breach. An example is *Birch v Ministry of Defence* [2013] EWCA Civ 676, where the defendant was held liable for severe personal injuries suffered by a marine serving in Afghanistan who lost control of a Land Rover while driving down a mountain track. The accident was the result of driver error rather than mechanical defect. The claimant was not qualified to drive the vehicle, and should not have been allowed to do so. Although the case fell outside the limits of combat immunity, so that the action could proceed, it would seem that the conditions were nevertheless pertinent to the decision not to make a deduction for contributory negligence. The claimant had selflessly volunteered to drive the vehicle and his superior officer knew that he was not qualified to do so. The claimant could not be held to blame in the circumstances.

(vii) *Immunities*

14–40   Add to the end of the paragraph: In the decision of the Supreme Court in *Smith v Ministry of Defence* [2013] UKSC 41; [2013] 3 W.L.R. 69 (para.**14–38**), and of the Court of Appeal in *Smart v Forensic Science Services* [2013] EWCA Civ 783 (para.**16–72**), reference was made to the exceptional nature of immunities, underlining that any advance in such immunities should be made cautiously and that the application of an immunity must be clearly justified.

(d) *Omissions*

(vii) *Statutory powers and duties*

14–48   **Irrationality.** NOTE 210. At the end add the following: It was distinguished by Walker J. in *Murdoch v Department for Work and Pensions* [2010] EWHC 1988 (QB) on the basis that it dealt with an entirely different statutory scheme and did not raise a claim to broadly defined liability for maladministration. In the more closely analogous case of *Home Office v Mohammed* [2011] EWCA Civ 351; [2011] 1 W.L.R. 2862, Sedley L.J. questioned Keith J.'s attempt to distinguish the authority of *W v Home Office* [1997] Imm. A.R. 302, a decision of the Court of Appeal. The reasoning underlying *W v Home Office* was said to be the same as the reasoning underlying *Rowley v Secretary of State for Work and Pensions* [2007] EWCA Civ 598; [2007] 1 W.L.R. 2861: see further para.**14–51**. In *R. (on the application of Atapattu) v the Secretary of State for the Home Department* [2011] EWHC 1388 (Admin), it was said that as a consequence of *Mohammed*, the decision of Keith. could not safely be relied upon. The reluctance of the courts to create liability for "negligent detention" is further underlined by the decision in *Jama v Ministry of Justice* [2012] EWHC 533 (QB), where Jonathan Parker J. relied on both *W v Home Office* and *Mohammed*, concluding that "claims of this nature under current law" are "doomed to fail" (at [63]).

Statutory duty. At the end of the paragraph add: In *Ali v The City of Bradford* **14–49** *Metropolitan DC* [2010] EWCA Civ 1282; [2012] 1 W.L.R. 161, the Court of Appeal relied upon the reasoning in *Gorringe* and concluded that the Highways Act 1980 s.130 did not create express obligations to remove obstructions and was concerned with the rights of the public at large. It gave rise to no civil action for damages on the part of a pedestrian who fell and was injured descending steps which were unsafe due to debris. Positive duties to act may arise in nuisance, and in *Ali* the claimant argued, presumably in order to avoid the effect of *Gorringe*, that such a duty had been breached. The Court of Appeal held that there was also no room for a nuisance action in this instance. Applying the reasoning in *Marcic v Thames Water* [2003] UKHL 66; [2004] 2 A.C. 42, and particularly its interpretation of the measured duty to abate nuisances under *Sedleigh-Denfield v O'Callaghan* [1940] A.C. 880, the Court concluded that "for the courts to impose such a liability through the law of nuisance would be to use a blunt instrument to interfere with a carefully regulated statutory scheme and would usurp the proper role of Parliament" (at [39]).

(ii) *Common law basis for duty*

Common law basis for a duty. NOTE 221. Add at the end: In *Yetkin v* **14–51** *Mahmood* [2010] EWCA Civ 776; [2011] 2 Q.B. 827, the Court of Appeal concluded that *Gorringe* did not affect the liability of highway authorities for positive acts creating a danger (para.**14–57**). In *Connor v Surrey CC* [2010] EWCA Civ 286; [2011] Q.B. 429 (see further para.**14–08**), failure to exercise a discretion in order to protect an employee was held to amount to a breach of a negligence duty owed to that employee. That was a case where the kind of duty owed was well established (to take reasonable care for the safety of an employee). The significance of the case was that it confirmed that such a duty may be breached by failure to exercise a statutory power.

At the end of the paragraph (after NOTE 225) insert a new para. **14–51A**:

Although the existence of a statutory duty or power does not mean that no **14–51A** private law duty can arise, this must be read in the light of a growing body of case law suggesting that in the context of a "statutory scheme" designed to benefit groups of people including potential claimants, then no private law duty will arise unless it is compatible with that scheme. Thus the existence of the statutory duty will not in itself create an assumption of responsibility (para.**14–53**), nor proximity with an individual claimant, but more generally, remedies at private law may not be considered compatible with the statutory scheme. What amounts to incompatibility is a difficult question but the availability of other means of redress (even if not as generous as private law remedies), or statutory provisions intended to achieve finality in decision-making, are indications that the private law duty is inappropriate. Key cases in these respects are *Rowley v Secretary of State for Work and Pensions* [2007] EWCA Civ 598; [2007] 1 W.L.R. 2861, and *R. (on the application of Kehoe) v Secretary of State for Work and Pensions* [2005] UKHL 48; [2006] 1 A.C. 42, but the influence of this reasoning is much broader. For example in *Murdoch v Department for Work and Pensions* [2010] EWHC 1988 (QB), some aspects of the claim were considered to be inappropriate subject-matter for a private law duty because they amounted to questioning "protected decisions" (that is, decisions where the statute concerned showed an intention that the decisions made pursuant to it were to be final); other elements did not give rise to a duty of care because there was an available action for recovery of debts in the County Court, and the addition of a negligence action would add undesirable complexity. In *Home Office v Mohammed* [2011] EWCA Civ 351; [2011] 1 W.L.R. 2862, the complaints (that permanent leave to remain had not been granted when, as a matter of formal policy, it should have been) fell within the Parliamentary Ombudsman's remit and this may lead to a recommendation of compensation. This was one factor which persuaded the Court of Appeal that it was not a suitable case in which to allow for incremental development at the margins of the law. Having said that, a claim based on inconsistency with art.8 rights was held to be arguable in this instance and that claim too offered the possibility of an appropriate remedy.

14–54   **Specific assumption** Add to the end of the paragraph: A contrary conclusion was reached by the Court of Appeal in *Selwood v Durham CC* [2012] EWCA Civ 979; [2012] P.I.Q.R. P20, a decision not to allow the striking out of claims in negligence and under the Human Rights Act. A social worker was attacked by a mental patient, and brought actions against her employer (Durham County Council) and two NHS Trusts. As in *Mitchell*, threats had been made to attack the claimant, who was involved in family proceedings involving the patient's two children. These threats were not communicated to the claimant. The Court of Appeal thought it arguable that a duty was owed by the Trusts to the claimant under these circumstances. Foreseeability and proximity were established and the issue was whether the duty was "fair, just and reasonable". Smith L.J. argued that it is possible to infer an assumption of responsibility from circumstances, and that such an assumption might be inferred in this case from the working arrangements and applicable protocols: it was possible that an assumption of responsibility to the employee of a co-signatory in the working arrangements, to do what was reasonable to minimise risks, would be inferred if all the facts were explored (at [52]). Significantly, the Court of Appeal in this case also suggested that policy reasons could militate in favour of a duty of care even in the absence of an assumption of responsibility. The claimant was not a member of the general public, but one of a limited class of employees of one partner in the working arrangements (at

[53]). The claimant in *Mitchell* was also not one of the general public but a tenant of the defendant authority; this argument therefore depends on recognising different relationships as raising different issues. Further, protection of social workers undertaking difficult and dangerous work was a policy objective positively worth pursuing (at [54]). This departs from the general inclination of the courts in approaching duties in this context, but is arguably consistent with the applicable principles. In particular, the duty claimed is a "private law" duty arising from a relationship which is close to being one of employment: the claimant is the employee of a partner organisation in a defined working arrangement. In summary, the Court concluded that the special position of the claimant ought to have been considered, and the claim was not hopeless. An art.2 claim was also not struck out, as the relevant questions were fact-sensitive: was there a "real and immediate threat"? See further para.**14–71**. A contrasting and more typical case is *Furnell v Flaherty* [2013] EWHC 377 (QB). The defendant owner of a petting farm where there had been a serious outbreak of E.coli admitted liability to the claimant twins who had fallen gravely ill, but brought contribution proceedings against the Health Protection Agency and local authority, arguing that there had been failures to act upon their knowledge of the outbreak. The contribution claim was struck out. The Agency and local authority had assumed no responsibility to members of the public and there was no "proximate engagement" with those likely to be affected by conditions at the farm. The third parties were acting primarily for the public good and not in the private interests of the affected individuals and knowledge of the outbreak did not mean that they assumed responsibility. The defendant however owed a clear private law duty to the claimants as her visitors.

Voluntary assumption. At the end of the paragraph add: A further illustration   **14–56**
of the point is *St John Poulton's Trustee in Bankruptcy v Ministry of Justice* [2010] EWCA Civ 392; [2011] Ch.1. Here the Court of Appeal found that the duty of the court under the Insolvency Rules 1986, to send notice of a bankruptcy petition to the Chief Land Registrar, did not give rise to a private right of action. The argument that a duty of care at common law nevertheless arose fell foul of the principle in *Gorringe v Calderdale MBC* [2004] UKHL 15; [2004] 1 W.L.R. 1057 (para.**14–49**), and clearly could not succeed. An attempt to argue that responsibility for the claimant's interests was assumed by the court also failed because the duty arose through the operation of the rule and not through anything said or done by the court or its officers. This was no more voluntary than the position of the bank served with a freezing order in *Customs and Excise Commissioners v Barclays Bank Plc* [2006] UKHL 28; [2007] 1 A.C. 181.

Responsibility following creation of danger. After Note 237 in the text add: **14–57**
Similarly in *Yetkin v Mahmood* [2010] EWCA Civ 776; [2011] 2 Q.B. 827, the Court of Appeal concluded that the approach taken in *Stovin v Wise* [1996] A.C. 923 and *Gorringe v Calderdale MBC* [2004] UKHL 15; [2004] 1 W.L.R. 1057 did not affect the liability of highway authorities for positive acts creating a danger (here, the planting of shrubs in a central reservation, obscuring the claimant pedestrian's view of the road). Where there were positive steps taken which created a danger, claimants did not need to show that the negligence had created a "trap" for them, nor was a claimant who was herself negligent deprived of the protection of the ordinary duty of care. Comments of Lords Hoffmann and Brown

in *Gorringe* which might have given this impression were of no relevance to cases where the alleged breach consisted in positive creation of a danger. Here, a pedestrian who stepped out from a central reservation before the lights had changed was owed a duty. There was a reduction in damages of 75 per cent to reflect her contributory negligence.

(e) *Standard of care*

14–61   **General.** After Note 258 in the text add: For a further illustration in relation to teaching, albeit not in the context of an education authority, see *Abramova v Oxford Institute of Legal Practice* [2011] EWHC 613 (QB); [2011] E.L.R. 385. The claimant, who had failed her Law Society examinations at the defendant's Institute, failed to show that the practice of self-marking mock examination papers constituted negligence in light of the *Bolam* test. Though the practice had been criticised by the Law Society's assessors, there was no challenge to the defendant's argument that it was supported by academic research and kept its processes under review.

3. LIABILITY UNDER THE HUMAN RIGHTS ACT 1998

14–65   **Public authorities.** Line 5, after Note 274 in the text, add: It is not possible to bring an action against the state under the Human Rights Act. Although the Crown can be a "public authority" for the purposes of the Act, it cannot be held liable on the basis that there has been a breach of Convention rights in circumstances where no other liable public authority can be identified: *Morgan v Ministry of Justice* [2010] EWHC 2248 (QB).

(b) *Public authority liability under the Human Rights Act 1998*

14–69   **General position.** After "may include a monetary award" add: If the claimant has secured a remedy in tort, whether in court or through settlement of a tort action, this may mean that the claimant does not qualify as a "victim" of a violation of Convention rights, as is required by s.7, modelled on art.34 ECHR. However, caution is needed in determining the effect of any settlement. In *Rabone v Pennine Care NHS Trust* [2012] UKSC 2; [2012] 2 A.C. 72, the Supreme Court considered the Strasbourg jurisprudence on the influence of domestic remedies, finding that it was not easy to extract a clear statement of principle, and that a "broad approach" to the meaning of a settlement, in particular, needed to be taken. For a claimant to be deprived of the status of victim through acceptance of a settlement, the remedy achieved must be concerned with matters which form the basis of his or her Convention claim, and must afford "effective redress" for any Convention breach, including an acceptance that the right has been violated. In *Rabone* itself, the Court of Appeal had found that the claimants were not "victims" because negligence had been admitted and liability agreed ([2010] EWCA Civ 698; [2011] Q.B. 1019). The Supreme Court agreed that the Trust's admission of negligence was, in effect, a sufficient admission in respect of the violation of the positive duty to protect life under art.2, since this violation itself took the form of negligence (see paras **14–71–14–74**). However, it did not agree that the settlement of a claim under the Law Reform (Miscellaneous Provisions) Act 1934 in this case provided adequate redress for the violation of art.2. This was in part because the settlement of the claim under the 1934 Act was at a lower level than the Court of Appeal found would be appropriate under the Human Rights Act 1998, had liability under that Act been established (a sum accepted by the Supreme Court as appropriate), but partly also because compensation under the 1934 Act does not purport to compensate for non-pecuniary loss to relatives in the form of bereavement. The claimants here were the parents of an adult child, and therefore did not qualify for such damages under domestic law. In comparison with other decisions of the English courts in relation to Human Rights Act remedies, this places greater emphasis on compensation and monetary awards, perhaps because of the particular "tort-like" context of the positive operational duty as it is continuing to emerge. See further para.**14–73**.

At the end of the paragraph, insert a new para.**14–69A**:

Jurisdictional extent of the Human Rights Act: art. 1. Article 1 of the   **14–69A**
Convention provides that contracting states will secure the rights and freedoms defined in the Convention "to everyone within their jurisdiction". Prior to *Al-Skeini v UK* (55721/07) (2011) 53 E.H.R.R. 18, it was thought that the application of the Convention was essentially territorial, with defined exceptions. In *R. (on the application of Smith) v Oxfordshire Assistant Deputy Coroner* [2010] UKSC 29; [2011] 1 A.C. 1, the majority of the Supreme Court also interpreted the Strasbourg jurisprudence existing at that time as stating that the rights and freedoms in the Convention could not be divided and tailored to particular circumstances. In both respects, the decision of the Grand Chamber in *Al-Skeini* has had a significant impact on this understanding, as was carefully explained in the judgment of Lord Hope (with the agreement on this point of all members of the Supreme Court) in *Smith v Ministry of Defence* [2013] UKSC 41; [2013] 3 W.L.R. 69. In particular, three points were made by Lord Hope in relation to the current interpretation of art.1. In *Smith* itself, these points together led the Supreme Court to conclude that the state's armed forces overseas are capable of being within its jurisdiction for the purposes of art.1. First, the Strasbourg Court in *Al-Skeini* formulated a general principle with respect to state authority and control, designed to ensure that domestic courts would apply the general principle. The principle could therefore apply to circumstances which the Strasbourg Court itself had not considered, rather than simply explaining a range of exceptional situations. Secondly, the extent of the Convention is not necessarily "essentially territorial". Rather, the general principle is concerned with circumstances where the state had "authority and control" over the individuals concerned. Thirdly, the Grand Chamber departed from its earlier statements that the package of rights in the Convention is indivisible. As a consequence, the court when considering an alleged breach of a Convention right need not concern itself with the question whether the state is in a position to guarantee other Convention rights to that individual under the circumstances (at [49]). The decision in *R. (on the application of Smith) v Oxford Assistant Deputy Coroner* was therefore departed from. Whilst unanimous on this point, members of the Supreme Court were divided on the question of how art.2 applied to the claims in hand: para.**14–73**.

14–70   **Article 2 Right to life.** Line 11, after "procedures for protecting life", add: An example of breach of this general duty is to be found in *Opuz v Turkey* (2010) 50 E.H.R.R. 28, where it was found that the legislative framework in force in Turkey fell short of the requirement for an effective system for the prosecution and punishment of offenders of domestic violence.

At the end of the paragraph, add: Indeed, in *Rabone v Pennine Care NHS Trust* [2012] UKSC 2; [2012] 2 A.C. 72, it was suggested by Lord Mance that under the operational duty to protect life, the European Court of Human Rights "began to develop its own Convention rules of, in effect, tortious responsibility" (at [121]). This created "the difficult line to be drawn between direct Convention rights and national tort law" such as the case in hand. The existence of this specific, difficult line was identified again by Lord Mance, in dissent, in *Smith v Ministry of Defence* [2013] UKSC 41; [2013] 3 W.L.R. 69.

A significant difference between the two lies in the range of parties who may be offered compensation or redress in relation to a death, as *Rabone* itself exemplifies (para.**14–69**). As with all claims under the Human Rights Act, the claimant must be a "victim" of the violation, and this is determined by reference to Strasbourg jurisprudence. In *Morgan v Ministry of Justice* [2010] EWHC 2248 (QB), a fiancée of the deceased was accepted to be a victim, and it was suggested that if she had not been engaged to the deceased, whether or not she was a victim would depend on the facts of the case. *Savage v South Essex Partnership NHS Foundation Trust* [2010] EWHC 865 (QB); [2010] P.I.Q.R. P14; [2010] Med. L.R. 292 further illustrates that "victim" status is not connected to domestic law categories but considered on the facts of the case. Here, the claimant was held to be a victim. In light of ECHR authorities, relevant factors were that "S was her mother to whom she was close", and that "much of her final illness centred around a deluded but sincere concern for the safety of the claimant" (at [94]).

14–72   Four lines from the end of the paragraph, after the sentence ending "invariable.", add: In *Van Colle v UK* (2013) 56 E.H.R.R. 23, the European Court of Human Rights also concluded that there had been no violation of art.2, applying the test in *Osman*. It could not be said that the facts involved "higher risk factors" than in *Osman* itself. Two members of the Court, though concurring in the result, implied that *Osman* set too demanding a test and should be revisited.

At the end of the paragraph, add: The demanding nature of the test set out in *Osman v UK* was also noted by the Court of Appeal in *Michael v Chief Constable of South Wales* [2012] EWCA Civ 981; [2012] H.R.L.R. 30, where the claim was allowed to proceed to trial despite some doubts as to whether its chances of success were strong. Longmore L.J. suggested that the proper occasion on which to assess the facts was a trial and that the claim could not be said to be hopeless. Richards L.J. thought it a marginal case but agreed that doubts should be resolved at trial; while Davis L.J. would have struck out the claim on the basis that it was considerably less strong than the claim in *Osman* itself, where the European Court of Human Rights had found no violation of the positive duty under art.2. A claim under art.2 was also not struck out in *Selwood v Durham CC* [2012] EWCA Civ 979; [2012] P.I.Q.R. P20, where the issues were said to be fact sensitive and therefore suitable for trial. The Court of Appeal in the latter case rightly noted that the authorities on the approach to art.2 in respect of risks to voluntarily detained patients were not determinative of a case where a voluntarily detained patient posed a threat to the life of another party. In *Savage v South Essex Partnership NHS Foundation Trust* [2010] EWHC 865 (QB); [2010] P.I.Q.R. P14; [2010] Med. L.R. 292, the approach of the House of Lords in *Savage* and *Van Colle* was taken to provide helpful guidance to a lower court applying the Strasbourg jurisprudence. The general method however was to apply the approach of the Strasbourg court, described by Mackay J. as: "to set out the facts of the case fairly fully, . . . state the test and then simply state its finding that violation of the article is or is not established". As with other claims based on Convention rights, if a breach of art.2 is shown then there is no need to prove causation in the English law sense: loss of substantial chance of survival is sufficient (at [82]). Indeed, art.2 may be violated where the person at risk survives.

NOTE 300a. Before "where Mackay J.", add:; [2010] Med. L.R. 292   **14–73**
Add to the end of the Note: The judge awarded a declaration, and damages of £10,000. See further paras **14–72** and **14–100**.

Delete the final sentence of the paragraph, and replace it with the following: In *Rabone v Pennine Care NHS Trust* [2012] UKSC 2; [2012] 2 A.C. 72, the Supreme Court reversed a decision of the Court of Appeal and found that the operational duty to protect life was owed to a psychiatric patient who was not formally detained. The vulnerability of the patient played a significant role in the decision; and in this instance, the reality of the patient's situation was not markedly different from that of a detained patient: given the control exercised by the defendant over the deceased, the difference between her situation and that of a detained patient was "one of form, not of substance" (at [34]). In taking this route, the Supreme Court was extending the positive operational duty further than any decision of the Strasbourg Court at this date. Lord Brown, however, was at pains to point out that this was not a reversal of the general approach taken by the House of Lords and later the Supreme Court, most notably in *R. (on the application of Ullah) v Special Adjudicator* [2004] UKHL 26; [2004] 2 A.C. 323, namely that the English courts should offer no greater protection of Convention rights through the HRA than was offered by the Strasbourg Court. Rather, this was a case where the Strasbourg Court had yet to rule on the relevant issues in the particular form in which they arose. Lord Dyson concluded, indeed, that the European Court of Human Rights would hold that the operational duty existed in this case. Several of the judges referred to the developing nature of the positive operational duty under art.2, and its gradual extension since it was first recognised in *Osman v United Kingdom*. Nevertheless, it remains the case that in the "generality of cases" involving medical negligence, there is no operational duty under art.2 (at [33]). It is increasingly difficult to be certain of where the boundary between *Powell* type cases, governed by negligence law principles, and *Osman* or *Rabone* type cases will lie, given rejection by the Supreme Court of a bright line based on formal detention in this case. Subsequently, in *Reynolds v United Kingdom* (2694/08) (2012) 55 E.H.R.R. 35, the European Court of Human Rights not surprisingly found a violation of art.13, in conjunction with art.2, where the applicant's domestic claim in relation to the death of her son while in the care of a NHS Trust had been struck out. There was little discussion of the applicable principles, other than by reference to the Supreme Court's decision in *Rabone*.

In *R. (on the application of AP, MP) v HM Coroner for the County of Worcestershire* [2011] EWHC 1453 (Admin); [2011] Med. L.R. 397, the Court of Appeal's decision in *Rabone* was considered by Hickinbottom J., concluding that the art.2 positive operational duty is not owed in all cases where there is a "real and imminent risk" of death, but only where some "additional element" is present. Apart from cases where the police ought to have been aware of such a risk to an individual, "the required additional element has been confined to cases in which the state has effective, entire and non-voluntary control over an individual". This may mean detention in prison or in hospital, or the claimant may be a conscripted soldier. No such obligation, it was concluded, has been found where there is an element of agreement to the control (at [86]). This conclusion must be qualified following the Supreme Court's decision in *Rabone*. Prior to its decision in *Rabone*, the Supreme Court considered the application of art.2, and particularly implied positive duties, to military personnel on active service in *R. (on the application of Smith) v Oxfordshire Assistant Deputy Coroner* [2010] UKSC 29; [2011] 1 A.C. 1. The Supreme Court reiterated its earlier position that military personnel are outside the jurisdiction of the European Convention on Human Rights when serving overseas, unless the alleged breaches occur within a military base: *R. (on the application of Al–Skeini) v Secretary of State for Defence* [2007] UKHL 26; [2008] 1 A.C. 153. This was thought to reflect the essentially territorial nature of the Convention and was based on the European Court of Human Rights' approach to art.1 ECHR. It was recognised by English courts that the position might be clarified by the Grand Chamber in *Al-Skeini: Al-Skeini v UK* (55721/07) and *Al-Jedda v UK* (27021/08) (see *Smith v Ministry of Defence* [2011] EWHC 1676 (QB); [2011] H.R.L.R. 35 at [28]), and this has indeed been the case. In *Al-Skeini v UK* (2011) 53 E.H.R.R. 18, the Grand Chamber held unanimously that the deceased relatives of the applicants, Iraqi civilians who had been shot and killed during operations in Iraq, had fallen within the jurisdiction of the United Kingdom. There had been a breach of the procedural obligation under art.2 to carry out an effective investigation into the deaths of the relatives of five of the applicants, and compensation in respect of non-pecuniary damage was awarded. The relationship between the decisions of the Supreme Court in *R. (Smith) v Oxfordshire Assistant Deputy Coroner*, and of the Grand Chamber in *Al-Skeini v UK*, was resolved in *Smith v Ministry of Defence* [2013] UKSC 41; [2013] 3 W.L.R. 69, where the Supreme Court departed from its earlier decision in *R. (Smith)* on this point: see further para. **14–69A**. In *R. (Smith)* itself, it was accepted however that if the jurisdiction issue were to be resolved in favour of the claimant (as it was accepted would be the case, for example, where a death occurred within a military base), it would become arguable that there had been substantive breach of art.2 rights where the deceased died from hyperthermia. The deceased here was not a conscript, and the Court of Appeal had been incorrect to treat volunteer personnel in the same way as conscripts: there was no analogy with those in the custody of the state (at [103]). However, there were cases where the death of service personnel may indicate a "systemic or operational failing" on the part of the state, and in these circumstances art.2 may be violated.

Smith v Ministry of Defence was occupied not with the procedural obligation, but with one or other variation of the substantive obligation to protect life. The majority identified the need to ensure that the positive obligations imposed on the state in connection with the planning for and conduct of military operations in situations of armed conflict are not disproportionate or unrealistic (at [76]); and identified decisions that were essentially political in nature, or which were taken in the course of armed conflict, as unsuitable for review through an action under the Human Rights Act. However, the claims under art.2 should not be struck out: as with the claims in negligence, it would not be clear until hearing the evidence whether the positive obligation to take preventative operational measures had been breached. Lord Mance, in dissent, preferred to begin with the common law and particularly with the position (as he saw it) that no duty of care was owed in these circumstances. Strasbourg had not extended its jurisprudence in relation to positive operational duties under art.2 to circumstances analogous to this, and it would be wrong for the domestic courts to advance the jurisprudence in this way. Lord Mance's concerns are summarised at [143]: "It should be for the Strasbourg court to decide whether it will review the procurement and training policy of the British army over recent decades in the context of claims under art.2". The particular, tort-like quality of actions in relation to the operational duty under art.2 lies behind these concerns.

At the end of the paragraph add: Similarly in *R. (on the application of AP, MP)*   **14–74** *v HM Coroner for the County of Worcestershire* [2011] EWHC 1453 (Admin); [2011] Med. L.R. 397, a local authority providing community care services pursuant to statutory duties did not thereby assume responsibility for the safety of the people it provided with welfare services. Any such duty fell to the police, and in this instance no such duty had been breached.

Duties to investigate derived from art.2. Delete the last two sentences in the   **14–75** paragraph. Add the following: In *R. (on the application of Smith) v Oxfordshire Assistant Deputy Coroner* [2010] UKSC 29; [2011] 1 A.C. 1, the Supreme Court decided that the death of a soldier in combat did not raise a prima facie case for saying that there had been a breach on the part of the army of his art.2 rights. (On the jurisdictional question raised by this case, and later departure from the conclusion in this case on that issue, see paras **14–69A**; **14–73**). Here, however, the deceased had died of hyperthermia whilst at an army base in Iraq. It was at least possible that there had been a failure in the system that should have protected soldiers from the risk of high temperatures while serving in Iraq, so it was arguable that there was a breach of substantive obligations under art.2 through systemic failure. This was a case where the procedural requirement for a convention-compliant investigation was applicable, even though the deceased was not a conscript—in other words, there was an element of choice in his employment. The apparent contrast with recent decisions in a medical context, where an element of voluntariness in the patient's presence in hospital appears to operate decisively against the presence of a positive operational duty (para.**14–73**), is explained by the potential presence of systemic failure. On this basis an investigation into the death of personnel on a military base ought to take all reasonable steps to find out, as art.2 requires, what caused the death; and to identify what defects in the system brought it about, and any other factors that may be relevant. The European Court of Human Rights, and the English courts, have distinguished between "legal" questions and "political" questions. The art.2 investigative duty relates only to the former.

In *R. (on the application of AP, MP) v HM Coroner for the County of Worcestershire* [2011] EWHC 1453 (Admin); [2011] Med. L.R. 397, the principles applicable to duties to investigate under art.2 were reviewed in a case where the claimants argued that the coroner should be required to reopen an inquest into the death of their son. No duty to investigate arises unless there is a suspected breach of substantive obligations under art.2. Where there is such a breach (or suspected breach), then in order to determine whether sufficient investigation has been carried out, the totality of the investigations available (including both criminal and civil proceedings, including proceedings in tort) should be considered. In this instance, not only was there no substantive breach of art.2 duties, but the available investigations were sufficient to satisfy the requirements of the Convention. Further issues relating to the nature of duties to investigate breaches of Convention rights were considered in *OOO v The Commissioner of Police for the Metropolis* [2011] EWHC 1246 (QB); [2011] U.K.H.R.R. 767. This was a claim based on arts 3 (inhuman and degrading treatment) and 4 (slavery and servitude). However, arts 2, 3 and 4 were said to give rise to similar issues in respect of positive duties: see further para.**14–79**. Following the ground-breaking decision of the Grand Chamber of the European Court of Human Rights in *Silih v Slovenia* (2009) 49 E.H.R.R. 1, holding that the investigative obligation is not ancillary to a particular death but may arise subsequent to that death, the impact of *McKerr* in respect of the investigative obligation has been fundamentally altered. The UK Supreme Court has now accepted that although the Human Rights Act 1998 does not have retrospective effect (the conclusion reached in *McKerr*), states are nevertheless under a free-standing and autonomous international law obligation to ensure that any investigation into a death satisfies the procedural requirements of art.2. This obligation applies to investigation of deaths occurring before the commencement of the HRA, just as it applied in *Silih v Slovenia* to investigation of deaths arising before the relevant state had accepted individual rights of petition to the Strasbourg Court: *Re McCaughey* [2011] UKSC 20; [2012] 1 A.C. 725. Here, where a decision had been reached after commencement of the HRA, to investigate a death which had occurred before commencement of the HRA, it was appropriate for the Court to issue a declaration that the coroner was obliged to conduct the inquest in a way which satisfied the state's procedural obligation under art.2. The content of the investigative obligation associated with art.2 has been further clarified by the European Court of Human Rights in *Pearson v United Kingdom* (2012) 54 E.H.R.R. SE11. The duty has both investigative and accountability objectives. On the facts of that particular case, where the deceased had died some time after release from custody and where the allegation was effectively of carelessness on the part of the police and others, the pre-HRA style of inquest was capable of fulfilling the investigative element of the duty. It was also held that the accountability objective could be satisfied by the availability of a civil negligence claim. Notwithstanding the known limits to negligence actions in relation to public authorities including the police, the Court considered that there remains sufficient scope for such an action to arise in a case where a "special relationship" is found to exist. The existence of exceptions to the *Hill* principle, limited though they may be, is therefore also significant in the context of the investigative duty under art.2. Equally, the Court considered that the availability of disciplinary measures was also relevant to satisfaction of the accountability objective. The claim was therefore inadmissible.

14–79   Delete heading "**Conditions of detention**" and replace with "**Positive duty to investigate**".

At the end of the paragraph add: Further consideration was given to the duty to investigate, and particularly to its scope, in *OOO v The Commissioner of Police for the Metropolis* [2011] EWHC 1246 (QB); [2011] U.K.H.R.R 767. This was a claim brought by the victims of trafficking, in respect of art.3, and also art.4 (right not to be placed in slavery or servitude). The claimants were brought illegally to the United Kingdom from Nigeria and forced to work without pay. They were also subjected to regular violence. It was accepted that there had been breaches of their rights under arts 3 and 4 on the part of the traffickers. In an action against the police, Wyn Williams J. upheld their claim that there had been breaches of the positive duty to investigate, and awarded a declaration and damages under s.8 accordingly. In determining the scope of the duty to investigate, he considered the common law could not assist because, for policy reasons, no positive duties to investigate could be said to exist in the law of England and Wales. It was apparent from the decision of the House of Lords in *Van Colle v Chief Constable of Hertfordshire* [2008] UKHL 50; [2009] 1 A.C. 225 that duties to protect Convention rights were to be considered according to Strasbourg principles and not by attention to common law, and the policy reasons which lay behind the limitations to common law could not be said to be applicable to actions for violation of Convention rights. Since *Osman v UK* was concerned with the preventive duty under art.2 rather than the duty to investigate events that had already occurred, the leading authority was *Rantsev v Cyprus* (25965/04) (2010) 51 E.H.R.R. 1. The reasoning in *Rantsev* was equally applicable to arts 3 and 4. Important principles which emerged from this were that the existence of a duty does not depend on a complaint from the victim or a next of kin, and is triggered when a credible allegation of an infringement of the rights has been made to the police; that the duty may arise even where no victim is identified by name, though this will be a relevant factor; and that the duty to investigate carries with it a duty to investigate promptly and/or with reasonable expedition (at [152], [162]–[164]). There was no basis for suggesting that a failure to investigate is a breach only where the failure is "egregious".

In *Ruddy v Chief Constable of Strathclyde* [2012] UKSC 57; 2013 S.C. (UKSC) 126; [2013] H.R.L.R. 10, the Supreme Court considered and rejected procedural objections to a damages claim based on violations of art.3 both in relation to an alleged assault by police officers, and in relation to an alleged failure to investigate. The courts below in Scotland had rejected the claims as irrelevant, on the basis that they involved a disguised attempt to challenge decisions through a claim for damages, whereas a judicial review action would be the appropriate course. The Supreme Court drew attention to the fact that the allegations were all of completed acts or failures to act. The applicant was not seeking to have decisions corrected, but was seeking just satisfaction for breach of art.3 rights (at [15]).

Article 5 right to liberty and security. Delete the last sentence of the paragraph **14–80** and add: On March 15, 2012, the Grand Chamber of the European Court of Human Rights handed down its important judgment in *Austin v United Kingdom* (39692/09) (2012) 55 E.H.R.R. 14; [2012] Crim. L.R. 544. By a majority, the Grand Chamber concluded that there had been no violation of art.5(1). The reasoning of the majority was generally compatible with the analysis of the House of Lords in *Austin v Commissioner of Police of the Metropolis* [2009] UKHL 5; [2009] 1 A.C. 564. The majority emphasised that the Convention must be read as a whole and interpreted so as to promote internal consistency and harmony between its provisions. It referred to the existence of other provisions offering qualified protection to freedom of movement (art.2, Protocol 4, which has not been ratified by the United Kingdom), where public order reasons may justify restrictions; and to freedom of assembly (art.11), where the Court has held that restrictions may be justified for the prevention of disorder or crime, or in order to protect the rights and freedoms of others. Equally, it was noted that arts 2 and 3 imply positive obligations on the authorities to take preventive operational measures to protect individuals at risk of serious harm. The underlying principle of art.5, on the other hand, was said to be the protection of the individual from arbitrariness, and the "fundamental" right involved was "protection of the individual against arbitrary interference by the State with his or her liberty" (at [60]). Where restrictions on movement did not follow the "paradigm" of confinement in a cell, the court could address the specific context and circumstances of the restrictions. Applying these principles to the specific circumstances of this case, there was no reason to depart from the finding of Tugendhat J. that the cordon represented the least intrusive and most effective means of averting a real risk of serious injury to people within the crowd. Since the police had consistently attempted to initiate a safe release of individuals beginning five minutes after the initial cordon was completed, in each case being prevented by disorder within the crowd from effecting a safe release, the court could not identify at what point "restriction on movement" could be said to have become a deprivation of liberty. On the "exceptional" facts of the case, there was no deprivation of liberty within the terms of art.5(1). The three dissenting judges took the view that the majority had allowed a legitimate public interest to justify a restriction of liberty despite the absence of any such potential justification from the terms of art.5 itself. By contrast, the emphasis of the majority was, like that of the domestic courts, on interpreting the reach of art.5 in the context of the Convention as a whole. The majority reached the important conclusion that the fundamental nature of the art.5 right was a reason not to interpret its reach too broadly.

14–81   Add to the end of the paragraph: Note also the success of a number of claims before domestic courts in respect of art.5(4) ECHR, which specifies a right for those arrested or detained to have the lawfulness of their detention "decided speedily by a court", and release ordered if the detention is unlawful. Article 5(4) may be violated by delayed reviews by the Parole Board, even where release would not have been ordered. Equally, art.5(1) may clearly be breached in circumstances which fall short of a false imprisonment, where an applicant has been deprived of "conditional liberty" through delay in the hearing. Significant questions have surrounded the approach to awarding damages in such cases given the general reluctance to create tort-like remedies in respect of maladministration, and the Supreme Court in *R. (on the application of Faulkner) v Secretary of State for Justice; R. (on the application of Sturnham) v Parole Board* [2013] UKSC 23; [2013] 2 W.L.R. 1157 has provided guidance: see further para.**14–98**.

14–85   **Article 8 Right to respect for private and family life.** After the first sentence, ending "a wide range of different circumstances", add: In *Malcolm v Secretary of State for Justice* [2011] EWCA Civ 1538, Richards L.J. referred to the breadth and "elusiveness" of art.8 and identified "how difficult it can sometimes be to determine whether a particular situation falls within it or not" (at [26]), concluding however that even accepting that enjoyment of exercise in the open air is capable of constituting an interest protected by art.8, no right on the part of a prisoner to enjoy a full hour's such exercise each day could be derived from the article (see also para.**14–110**).

At the end of the sentence concluding "pursuant to a blanket and indiscriminate   **14–86**
policy", add a new Note 333A as follows: Note 333A In *R. (on the application of
GC) v Commissioner of Police for the Metropolis* [2011] UKSC 21, [2011] 1
W.L.R. 1230, the Supreme Court declared that, in light of the European Court's
decision, retention of the claimants' data was an unjustified interference with
art.8(1) ECHR. By a majority, the governing legislation itself was not declared
incompatible with the Convention. Rather, it was concluded that the legislation
allowed scope for a policy which was less far-reaching than the existing guidelines. The present guidelines were therefore declared unlawful. See also *R. (on
the application of C) v Commissioner of Police of the Metropolis* [2012] EWHC
1681 (Admin); [2012] 1 W.L.R. 3007. Subsequently, Parliament has enacted
legislation incorporating a more limited scheme of retention (though this is not
yet in force): Protection of Freedoms Act 2012 s.1, inserting a new s.63D on
destruction of fingerprints and DNA profiles into the Police and Criminal Evidence
Act 1984.

At the end of para.**14–86** add: A different conclusion was initially reached,
applying the reasoning in *Wood*, in *Catt v Association of Chief Police Officers*
[2012] EWHC 1471 (Admin); [2012] H.R.L.R. 23. The claimant had a long
history of political protest and at first instance it was held that, given the public
nature of this, there was no reasonable expectation of privacy in relation to the
intelligence reports overtly compiled and retained by the defendant. This was
reversed on appeal. Even in these circumstances, the retention of the material
must be proportionate: *R. (on the application of Catt) v The Association of Chief
Police Officers of England, Wales and Northern Ireland* [2013] EWCA Civ 192;
[2013] H.R.L.R. 20.

At the end of the paragraph add: Particular concerns have surrounded orders to   **14–87**
maintain anonymity and confidentiality in legal proceedings, and although these
do not themselves involve actions for damages under the Human Rights Act the
interpretation of the balance between arts 8 and 10 ECHR is itself of significance
to common law actions modelled on protection of these rights. *In re Guardian
News and Media Ltd* [2010] UKSC 1; [2010] 2 A.C. 697 concerned the anonymity
of individuals who were subject to freezing orders while prosecutions were
in progress. Lord Rodger began his judgment by quoting the "provocative" words
of counsel for the newspapers, aimed at the recent prevalence of anonymity:
"Your first term docket reads like alphabet soup" (at [1]). The Supreme Court
emphasised that in reporting litigation art.8 and art.10 were both in play, and reiterated that neither had presumptive priority. However, the court also drew attention to the decision of the European Court in *Petrina v Romania* (78060/01,
October 14, 2008), and particularly its assertion (at [40]) that in cases where
publication raises a matter "of general interest", art.10(2) "scarcely leaves any
room for restrictions on freedom of expression" (*Guardian News* at [51]).
Weighing the considerations for and against anonymity, Lord Rodger suggested
that a more open attitude was consistent with the idea that parties are innocent of
criminal offences until found guilty, while concealing the identities of the parties
subject to the orders was "actually helping to foster an impression that the mere
making of the orders justifies sinister conclusions about these individuals". The
anonymity orders were discharged on the basis of a "powerful general, public
interest" in identifying the parties.

14–89   **Erratum.** The reference to *W v Essex CC* in line 11 on p.963 should be replaced with a reference to *A v Essex CC*. The reference for this case, which should appear in both Notes 345 and 346, is [2008] EWCA Civ 364; [2008] H.R.L.R. 31.

After "sufficiently severe to engage art.3", add: The art.8 point was not considered by the Supreme Court in dismissing an appeal from this decision ([2010] UKSC 33; [2011] 1 A.C. 280; para.**14–96**).

14–93   Add at end of sentence: Arguably, the decision in *Rabone v Pennine Care NHS Trust* [2012] UKSC 2; [2012] 2 A.C. 72 shows the beginnings of such a change, in the specific context of the operational duty to protect life (which was also the subject matter of *Osman v UK* itself): see paras **14–67, 14–73**.

After para.**14–93**, insert a new para.**14–93A**:

14–93A   **Article 10, Freedom of expression; Article 11, Freedom of assembly.** Articles 10 and 11 have recently come into contact with the law of tort in relation to actions brought by public authorities, and aimed at using tort remedies against protestors occupying public land and interfering with the rights of the public. In these cases, Convention rights have been raised by protestors in defence against domestic law remedies. They are not, therefore, actions under the Human Rights Act 1998, but show the breadth of the relevance of Convention rights in determining common law rights and duties. The proper approach to such arguments was outlined by the Court of Appeal in *Mayor of London v Samede* [2012] EWCA Civ 160; [2012] 2 All E.R. 1039, where the Mayor had applied for an order to evict those taking part in a camp at St Paul's Churchyard in London, and earlier in *Mayor of London v Hall* [2010] EWCA Civ 817; [2011] 1 W.L.R. 504. It was accepted that the arts 10 and 11 rights of the protestors are engaged in these instances; but it was also relevant that the actions of the protestors interfered with the rights of others, including substantial interferences with public rights of way, and with the rights of those wishing to worship. The court noted in *Samede* that it was very difficult to see how the arts 10 and 11 rights of the protestors "could ever prevail against the will of the landowner, when they are continuously and exclusively occupying public land, breaching not just the owner's property rights and certain statutory provisions, but significantly interfering with the public and Convention rights of others, and causing other problems (connected with health, nuisance, and the like), particularly . . . where the occupation has already continued for months, and is likely to continue indefinitely" (at [49]). While the value of the protestors' cause is irrelevant, the level of disruption caused is significant. The approach in *Samede* clearly involves weighing the protestors' rights against the rights and interests of others, and general public concerns (such as health) are also relevant. The approach has been applied in *Islington LBC v Jones* [2012] EWHC 1537 (QB), justifying an order to evict occupiers from a public square on the basis of interferences with the rights of the local authority and of the public; and in *Olympic Delivery Authority v Persons Unknown* [2012] EWHC 1012 (Ch) to prevent protestors from entering a site intended for use in the 2012 Olympics and disrupting work. In the latter case, Arnold J. applied the approach in *Re S (A Child)* [2004] UKHL; [2005] 1 A.C. 593, suggesting that neither the contractors rights under art.1 Protocol 1 (para.**14–95**), nor the protestors' rights under arts 10 and 11, took precedence, so that a proportionality approach must be applied to the restriction of each.

First Protocol, art.1 Right to peaceful enjoyment of possessions. At the end **14–95** of the paragraph add: It has been held that deprivation of one's passport does not amount to a violation of art.1 Protocol 1. The fact that a passport is a tangible object is not sufficient to constitute it as a "possession", and its significance or essence is that it represents an intangible privilege or entitlement, which was not "marketable": *R. (on the application of Atapattu) v Secretary of State for the Home Department* [2011] EWHC 1388 (Admin). A claim under art.8 also failed. Nevertheless, a claim at common law for conversion was successful, indicating that some possessions may be protected by conversion though not suitable for protection under art.1 Protocol 1. However, a legitimate expectation based on a judicial ruling or statutory provision is capable of protection under art.1 Protocol 1. In *The Gas and Electricity Markets Authority v Infinis Plc* [2013] EWCA Civ 70, the respondents were deprived of a pecuniary benefit when they were refused accreditation for Renewables Obligations Certificates under two Orders in respect of their electricity generating stations. Moreover, as the damage suffered was pecuniary and could be clearly calculated, "just satisfaction" required that it should be fully compensated.

First Protocol, art.2 Right to education. At the end of the paragraph add: The **14–96** Supreme Court has dismissed an appeal from the Court of Appeal's decision in respect of the claim based on art.2 Protocol 1 ([2010] UKSC 33; [2011] 1 A.C. 280). The court was, however, divided on a number of significant issues. On the appellant's key argument that exclusion from state education at school for a period of 18 months was capable of amounting to a violation of art.2 of the first Protocol, a majority of the court (Baroness Hale and Lord Kerr dissenting) agreed that this was not the case. The suggestion that there was any difference in approach between Lord Bingham and Lord Hoffmann in the *Lord Grey* case was rejected, and it was underlined that it was not only "systemic failure" in the education system which could amount to a violation of the right. However, there would not be a violation of the right simply because a state failed to cater "for the special needs of a small, if significant, portion of the population which is unable to profit from mainstream education" (Lord Phillips at [75]). Rather, the article "guarantees fair and non-discriminatory access for [a child with special needs] to the limited resources actually available to deal with his special needs". Thus the appellant's primary contention, that there was a positive obligation on the state to make provision for children with special needs, in these circumstances at enormous cost, was rejected. Equally, the appellant could not rely on a breach of domestic law as constituting a violation of the art.2 right: this was established by the *Lord Grey School* case.

A majority of the court (Lord Phillips and Kerr, and Baroness Hale) also considered a further argument however, and concluded that there was an arguable case that during the 18 months during which the appellant was excluded from school, he did not in fact have access to the educational resources that were, or might have been made, available. Essentially, he did not receive any education at all. Lord Kerr drew attention to the particular impact of such a failure on a child with such severe disabilities. Lord Clarke and Lord Brown dissented on this point. However, both Lord Phillips and Lord Kerr nevertheless concluded that the existence of an arguable case did not justify an extension of time to bring the claim outside the one year limitation period applied to claims under the Human Rights Act 1998.

The issues that arose would turn on the facts of the individual case, and would not be matters of principle; nor was it likely that substantial damages would be awarded. The claim, though arguable, was time barred. Baroness Hale dissented on this point, suggesting that the determination of the issues would offer guidance to education authorities in similar cases notwithstanding the preoccupation with the particular facts. Baroness Hale also doubted whether the earlier possibility of a judicial review action was a sufficient reason for not allowing an extension of time under a Human Rights Act claim, since bringing an action for judicial review, rather than seeking to negotiate a solution, was not necessarily the natural response for people in the position of the claimant's family.

(c) *Damages under the Human Rights Act 1998*

14–98   Add to the end of the paragraph: Two recent decisions of the Court of Appeal showed that the proper approach to damages in art.5(4) cases remained to be fully settled. The Supreme Court has now considered the applicable principles in relation to joined appeals on both cases. *R. (on the application of Faulkner) v Secretary of State for Justice* [2011] EWCA Civ 349; [2011] H.R.L.R. 23, was recognised by the Court of Appeal to be a likely "benchmark" decision capable of guiding the approach in subsequent cases. A Court of Appeal consisting of Sedley, Hooper and Wilson L.JJ. made an award of £10,000 to a prisoner who, for a period of 10 months, had been improperly denied access to the Parole Board which would, in all probability, have ordered his release. He had therefore been deprived of "conditional liberty" within the context of a lawful custodial sentence. The Court of Appeal found that such conditional liberty, while not the same as the liberty of an innocent person protected by the tort of false imprisonment, was nevertheless a thing of significant value, so that damages for deprivation of it should not generally be "insubstantial" (at [18]). Equally, the court thought it proper for the award to be sufficient to "operate on the mind" of the defendant, particularly where it was a public authority capable of repeating its mistakes—a clear deterrence objective. On the other hand, no separate award would be made for stress and anxiety, as these were designed to be aspects of a custodial sentence, and awarding a separate amount for these would amount to "double-counting". The Court noted considerable variation in the approach to such cases in Strasbourg as well as the lack of either articulated principles or a "discernible tariff", and proposed that more modest awards were the more recent trend. In *Sturnham v Secretary of State for Justice* [2012] EWCA Civ 452; [2012] 3 W.L.R. 476, a differently constituted Court of Appeal (Laws, McFarlane and Patten L.JJ.) awarded no damages to a life prisoner whose hearing by the Parole Board had been delayed in violation of art.5(4). In this instance, the Parole Board would not have ordered his release, and thus there was no deprivation of conditional liberty. On the subject of damages, the Court reversed the decision of Mitting J. to award the sum of £300 for stress and anxiety. Laws L.J., giving the judgment of the court, proposed that in an art.5(4) delay case, "the Convention right will be vindicated and just satisfaction ordinarily achieved by a declaration", since the focus of the Convention was on protection of the right rather than compensation of the claimant. However, if the violation involves an "outcome" for the claimant "in the nature of a trespass to the person" (essentially, deprivation of liberty), just satisfaction is likely to require an award of damages. Where the outcome is stress or anxiety and no more, there generally will not be an award of damages other than where there is a special feature of the case which materially aggravates the claimant's suffering. The decision in *Faulkner* was not discussed.

The two cases were distinguishable in that *Faulkner* involved a deprivation of conditional liberty while *Sturnham* did not. However, the award in *Faulkner* appeared high in light of the discussion in *Sturnham*, and it was plain that the applicable principles were not entirely clear. In *R. (on the application of Faulkner) v Secretary of State for Justice; R. (on the application of Sturnham) v Parole Board* [2013] UKSC 23; [2013] 2 W.L.R. 1157, the Supreme Court underlined that neither case involved a deprivation of liberty sufficient to amount to a false imprisonment nor to a violation of art.5(1). Both were cases of delay amounting to violations of art.5(4). They were to be distinguished from the case of *James v United Kingdom* (25119/09) (2012) 56 E.H.R.R. 12, where the European Court of Human Rights found a violation of art.5(1). That was because in *James v United Kingdom*, the claimants did not have access to relevant courses, without which they had no opportunity to show that they no longer posed a risk to the public. In that case, since the justification for detention after the expiry of a "tariff" period was protection of the public, it followed that the conditions of detention must allow a real opportunity for rehabilitation. That did not apply in the instant cases (at [22]).

In addition to important statements of principle in relation to the extraction of principles from Strasbourg case law in general (considered in para.**14–100**), the Court identified the principles applicable to art.5(4) cases arising from delay in review of detention. The conclusions were summarised at [13]. In particular, where it is established on the balance of probabilities that a violation of art.5.4 has resulted in the detention of a prisoner beyond the date when he would otherwise be released, damages should "ordinarily be awarded" for the resultant detention. Pecuniary losses shown to have been caused by prolongation of detention should be compensated "in full". The fact of recall to prison after release should not ordinarily be taken into account in assessing damages. There should be no award for loss of chance of release, nor any adjustment for the degree of probability of release. Where it is not established that an earlier hearing would have resulted in earlier release, there is a strong but not irrebuttable presumption that delay in violation of art.5.4 has caused feelings of frustration and anxiety. Where this is the case, the finding of a violation would not ordinarily constitute sufficient just satisfaction, and an award of damages "on a modest scale" should also be made. No award should be made where the delay was such that any resultant frustration and anxiety were insufficiently severe to warrant it. Where there is a delay of over three months, however, this is unlikely to be the case. Applying these conclusions to the two appeals, an award of damages was plainly justified in the *Faulkner* case, but it had been set at too high a level, and was reduced to £6,500. In the *Sturnham* case, where delay in the hearing had not led to a delay in release, the Court of Appeal had been wrong to refuse to award damages for frustration and anxiety, and the judge's award of £300 was reinstated. Lord Carnwath J.S.C. would have been prepared to accept that refusing to make an award of damages in relation to a delay of six months was consistent with the Strasbourg jurisprudence. However, he did not dissent from Lord Reed's approval of the award, nor from his statement of principles (at [127]). It should be noted that the quantum of the award in *Sturnham* did not fall to be considered by the Supreme Court, since leave to appeal on the question of quantum had been refused and the Court did not consider it necessary in order to do justice in the appeal. However, the Court made plain that awards for frustration and anxiety in cases of delay are invariably "modest" (at [67]); Lord Reed referred to the award of £300 as "reasonable in the circumstances of this case" (at [97]); and Lord Carnwath would have considered it compatible with Strasbourg case law not to make an award at all. There are clear indications, therefore, that the quantum of the award was considered acceptable.

14-99   **Assessment of damages** Add to the end of the paragraph: Indeed in *R. (on the application of Faulkner) v Secretary of State for Justice; R. (on the application of Sturnham) v Parole Board* [2013] UKSC 23; [2013] 2 W.L.R. 1157, Lord Reed J.S.C. suggested that the term "principles" in s.8(4) was to be understood "in a broad sense", not to be "confined to articulated statements of principle". Not only were statements of general principle on the part of the Strasbourg court uncommon, they should not be taken at face value (at [31]). At the present stage of development of the damages remedy, courts should be guided "primarily by any clear and consistent practice of the European court" (at [39]). In an important statement, Lord Reed, with whom Lords Neuberger, Mance and Kerr agreed, proposed however that the remedy under s.8 will in due course become "naturalised", emphasising a number of important differences between the role of an international court, and of a domestic court, when assessing damages. Thus, "over time, and as the practice of the European court comes increasingly to be absorbed into our own law through judgments such as this, the remedy should become naturalised. . . . we should have confidence in our own case law under section 8 once it has developed sufficiently, and not be perpetually looking to the case law of an international court as our primary source" (at [29]; see also [39], referring to the current "stage" in development of the remedy). For the time being, however, courts will need to assess damages in the light of Strasbourg practice. Lord Reed set out guidance as to the approach to be taken by parties when citing Strasbourg case law in order to direct courts to the underlying principles which the cases are said to express. Notably, that would not, according to Lord Reed, be necessary in cases relating to art.5.4, "which should take the present judgment as its starting point" (at [100]). In other words, principles will over time be identified and extracted from the case law in relation to particular articles of the Convention. The guidance, provided in paras [101]–[103], requires parties to prepare a table of authorities including identification of the particular violations which were established; the damages awarded; summaries of the appellants' and respondents' contentions in relation to the case; and a further chronological table of the authorities. The objective is for counsel to assist courts as much as possible in identifying those "principles" as to the relevant award of damages which can be extracted from the potential "blizzard of authorities" (at [103]) generated by Strasbourg cases. But in time, the first point of reference will increasingly be domestic decisions articulating the principles to be extracted from Strasbourg awards.

14-100   In line 16, after the sentence ending "£8,000", add: In *R. (on the application of Waxman) v Crown Prosecution Service* [2012] EWHC 133 (Admin), Moore-Bick L.J. awarded £3,500 in relation to a failure to prosecute an individual who was harassing the claimant, thus violating the claimant's art.8 rights. This was a less severe case than some of those considered by the European Court of Human Rights, in which applicants had been left vulnerable to serious physical abuse through failures to prosecute; but the failure did substantially affect the claimant's well-being. Reference to the quantum awarded in Strasbourg is now routine and the Supreme Court has offered general guidance on the preparation of argument as to quantum in light of the mass of available authorities (see para.**14–99**). In *Savage v South Essex Partnership NHS Foundation Trust* [2010] EWHC 865 (QB); [2010] P.I.Q.R. P14; [2010] Med. L.R. 292, Mackay J. said that it was hard to discern the principles on which Strasbourg awards were determined, but was referred to a table of awards made by the European Court of Human Rights. Taking into account that there had already been a full inquest into the death, he awarded £10,000, stating that this could only be "a symbolic acknowledgement that the defendant ought properly to give her some compensation to reflect her loss" (at [100]). That award was discussed without dispute by the Supreme Court in *Rabone v Pennine Care NHS Trust* [2012] UKSC 2; [2012] 2 A.C. 72. Here, the Court of Appeal's proposed award of £5,000 to each of the bereaved parents (had it found a violation) was not the subject of an appeal. Lord Dyson thought there was force in the argument that it was too low, but in the absence of an appeal by the claimants on quantum, the award was approved. Relevant factors in determining such an award in the context of breach of the operational duty to protect life included the closeness of family ties, and the serious nature of the breach in this instance. In *OOO v The Commissioner of Police for the Metropolis* [2011] EWHC 1246 (QB); [2011] U.K.H.R.R. 767, Wyn Williams J. identified substantial distress and frustration to be recognised by the European Court of Human Rights as justifying an award of damages for failure to investigate. In assessing damages, he took into account that the violation was in respect of failure to investigate rather than perpetration of the inhuman treatment, and referred to the restricted period of time during which the failure could be said to have extended the suffering of the claimants. This allowed him to position the case relative to others determined in Strasbourg, and he awarded £5,000 to each claimant.

At the end of the paragraph, add: Applying these principles, Ramsey J.   **14–101** concluded at the trial of the actions that although there had been violations of the art.8 rights of the claimants, no damages under the HRA were "necessary" to afford just satisfaction (*Dobson v Thames Water Utilities Ltd* [2011] EWHC 3253 (TCC); (2011) 140 Con. L.R. 135) in addition to the awards made for amenity nuisance. In the case of those without a proprietary interest living in family homes, all the circumstances of the case were to be taken into account. These circumstances included the award of damages in nuisance to those with proprietary interests, which would reflect the actual impact of the nuisance on the amenity of those living in the property. Even where the claimant was not a family member and/or not a minor, so that there was no guarantee that they would receive a share of the damages, it was not established that the award of damages was "necessary". This reflected the fact that "the principal objective of the Convention is to declare any infringement and put a stop to it", and that "the interests of an individual, rather than the wider public, are only part of the matters for consideration" (at [1099]). Other relevant circumstances in this case included the fact that the court made declarations in respect of violations of art.8 rights, and that remedies were available under ss.80 and 82 of the Environmental Protection Act 1990 by abatement notices and by way of a complaint to OFWAT under s.94 of the Water Industry Act 1991.

4. MISFEASANCE IN PUBLIC OFFICE

(a) *Nature of the tort*

14–110   Add: In *Iqbal v Prison Officers Association* [2009] EWCA Civ 1312; [2010] Q.B. 732, a claim in false imprisonment against a trade union whose members had undertaken an unlawful one day strike failed on the basis that the trade union was not directly responsible for the additional imprisonment of the claimant which resulted, nor did it intend it. The claimant had been confined to his cell as a consequence of the strike. Lord Neuberger M.R. suggested that claims involving additional periods of confinement due to the inaction of prison officers would be better confined to misfeasance in a public office, and therefore to cases where the inaction was "deliberate or dishonest". In *Malcolm v Ministry of Justice* [2010] EWHC 3389 (QB), this was taken to mean that in cases of loss of residual liberty (in this case, a reduction in time in the open air from 60 to 30 minutes each day), misfeasance provided a safety net to deal with the "most extreme" cases of bad faith and abuse of power. In this case, the inaction was not unlawful, so that there could be no action in misfeasance. But in any event the claimant had failed to show the required bad faith. An appeal based solely on violation of art.8 ECHR was dismissed by the Court of Appeal: *Malcolm v Secretary of State for Justice* [2011] EWCA Civ 1538. There was no basis on which to say that art.8(1) entitled prisoners to a full hour's exercise daily in the open air, where 30 minutes had in fact been provided.

(b) *Scope of the tort*

14–113   **Public officer.** After Note 443 in the text, add: However, it has been said that the ordinary approach is to bring an action against the institution or body as a whole on the basis that it will be vicariously liable for the misfeasance of its officers, rather than proceeding directly against individuals. This is for the protection of individuals going about their public duty, who should be the direct subject of a claim only where "absolutely necessary": *Adams v The Law Society of England and Wales* [2012] EWHC 980 (QB) at [160]–[162].

14–114   **Officers with law enforcement responsibility.**

(a) *Police officers*

Replace the full stop before Note 448 with a comma and add (after the note): and in *Amin v Imran Khan & Partners* [2011] EWHC 2958 (QB), a failure to add a claim for misfeasance based on untargeted malice was (amongst other failings) held to be in breach of the defendant solicitor's duty of care. The claimants' son was a young offender of Asian origin who had been killed by his cellmate—who was known to be racist and dangerous—while in detention. The failure to plead misfeasance was said to have weakened the claimants' bargaining position in seeking a settlement.

Vicarious liability. Add to the end of the sentence: Note also *Adams v The Law* **14–115**
Society of England and Wales [2012] EWHC 980 (QB), where it was said that vicarious liability would be the norm, and that it was for defendant institutions to raise the argument that the individual officer is acting outside the scope of his or her employment (see also para.**14–113**).

Improper exercise of power. At the end of the paragraph add: Consistently **14–116**
with this observation, in *Baxendale-Walker v Middleton* [2011] EWHC 998 (QB), claims in misfeasance in public office were among those struck out on the basis (inter alia) of immunities on the part of various of the nine defendants. The absolute privilege or immunity held to apply to the disciplinary tribunals involved was therefore treated as extending to the tort of misfeasance in public office; as did the witness immunity enjoyed by the eighth and ninth defendants (the Chairman of the Panel of the Solicitors Disciplinary Tribunal, and the Panel itself).

NOTE 461. Add at the end: In *Clifford v Chief Constable of the Hertfordshire Constabulary* [2011] EWHC 815 (QB) (see also paras **16–04** and **16–54**), a successful action in malicious prosecution, Mackay J. said briefly that he also considered that there was a misfeasance, but added no separate damages to reflect this (at [65]). He did not comment on the doubts expressed in *McDonagh* about the exclusivity of malicious prosecution.

CHAPTER 15

TRESPASS TO THE PERSON

	PARA.
1. Introduction.	15–01
2. Battery.	15–09
3. Assault.	15–12
4. Intentional infliction of injury.	15–14
(a) Liability based on defendant's intention to cause harm	15–14
(b) Harassment: common law.	15–18
■ (c) Protection from Harassment Act 1997	15–19
5. False imprisonment.	15–23
(a) What constitutes false imprisonment?	15–23
■ (b) Continuation of imprisonment	15–29
□ (c) Limitations on police detention: Police and Criminal Evidence Act 1984	15–31
(d) Imprisonment in unauthorised places or conditions	15–36
(e) Limitations on police detention: conditions of detention	15–39
■ (f) Responsibility for imprisonment committed through the instrumentality of officers of justice	15–41
■ 6. Defences to trespass to the person	15–49
(a) Self-defence	15–51
■ (b) Preventing crime	15–52
■ (c) Preventing a breach of the peace	15–54
(d) Lawful arrest.	15–65
■ (i) When is arrest justified?.	15–65
■ (ii) Duties when making an arrest	15–74
(iii) Duty after arrest complete	15–78
■ (e) Police powers of stop and search	15–84
■ (f) Anti-terrorism legislation	15–89
(g) Assisting an officer of the law	15–91
□ (h) Consent by the claimant	15–93
■ (i) Confinement and treatment for mental disorder under the Mental Health Act 1983	15–100
(j) Treatment and care of patients lacking mental capacity (other than under the Mental Health Act 1983)	15–118
□ (i) Common law	15–118
■ (ii) Mental Capacity Act 2005	15–123
(k) Parental or other authority	15–128
(l) Authority of shipmaster or commander of an aircraft	15–132
□ (m) Previous criminal proceedings	15–134
■ (n) Detention of persons prior to deportation	15–135
(o) Strip searches	15–136
■ 7. Damages	15–137

4. INTENTIONAL INFLICTION OF INJURY

(c) *Protection from Harassment Act 1997*

15–19   NOTE 87. Add: Importantly, the question of what the defendant knows or ought to know is confined only to the matter of what amounts to harassment. By contrast, the defendant need not know, or be able to foresee, the kind of harm which results from the harassment: *Jones v Ruth* [2011] EWCA Civ 804; [2012] 1 W.L.R. 1495 at [32] per Patten L.J.

NOTE 91. Add: See, e.g. *AMP v Persons Unknown* [2011] EWHC 3454 (TCC); [2011] Info. T.L.R. 25 at [44]–[45] per Ramsey J.

Also, after Note 92 insert the following sentence: Equally, the court must take into account the prospects of *future* harassment, regardless of any past conduct amounting to harassment, before granting an injunction, since an injunction will only be granted where the need for it exists *as of the date of the hearing*.[92a]

NOTE 92a. *APW v WPA* [2012] EWHC 3151 (QB).

15–20   After Note 96 in the text add: Thus, where a newspaper publishes a series of articles concerning a press officer who has had an affair with a prominent MP, it will not amount to harassment to publish those articles since "discussion or criticism of sexual relations which arose within a pre-existing professional relationship, or of sexual relationships which involved the deception of a spouse, or a civil partner, or others with a right not to be deceived, were matters which a reasonable person would not think was conduct amounting to harassment and would think was reasonable, unless there were some other circumstances which made it unreasonable".[96a]

NOTE 96a. *Trimmingham v Associated Newspapers Ltd* [2012] EWHC 1296 (QB); [2012] 4 All E.R. 717 at [262] per Tugendhat J.

NOTE 98. Add: The issue is whether the course of conduct, looked, at as a whole, is harassing not whether the incidents individually could be regarded as harassing. The Act "is intended to render actionable conduct which might not be alarming if committed once, but becomes alarming by virtue of being repeated": *Iqbal v Dean Manson Solicitors* [2011] EWCA Civ 123; [2011] I.R.L.R. 428 per Rix L.J. (three letters attacking claimant's professional integrity capable of constituting harassment: "A professional man's integrity is the lifeblood of his vocation. If it is deliberately and wrongly attacked, whether out of personal self-interest or malice, a potential claim lies under the Act").

NOTE 102. Add: Similarly, hundreds of automatic calls from a call centre to a bank customer have been held to amount to harassment: *Roberts v Bank of Scotland* [2013] EWCA Civ 882.

NOTE 104. Add: It is clear, however, that whilst only an individual can be a victim of harassment, a perpetrator can be a corporate body (see *Kosar v Bank of Scotland Plc (t/a Halifax)* [2011] EWHC 1050 (Admin); [2011] B.C.C. 500) or an unincorporated body, such as a partnership (see *Iqbal v Dean Manson Solicitors* [2011] EWCA Civ 123; [2011] I.R.L.R. 428—at least for the purposes of civil liability).

15–21   Replace the sentence that precedes Note 106 as follows. There is no guidance in the Act as to what constitutes reasonable conduct. However, the Supreme Court has made clear that, "[b]efore an alleged harasser can be said to have had the purpose of preventing or detecting crime. . . he must have thought rationally about the material suggesting the possibility of criminality and formed the view that the conduct said to constitute harassment was appropriate for the purpose of preventing or detecting it".[105a] In addition, it has also been said that the Act was not intended to be used to prevent individuals from exercising a right to protest about issues of public interest and the courts will resist attempts to interpret the defence widely.[106]

NOTE 105a. *Hayes v Willoughby* [2013] UKSC 17; [2013] 1 W.L.R. 935 at [15] per Lord Sumption J.S.C.

NOTE 106. Thus, a claim under the Act will fail if its success "would amount to a disproportionate interference with freedom of expression including the expression of protest": *EDO MBM Technology Ltd v Axworthy* [2005] EWHC 2490 (QB) at [26] per Walker J.

Also, add to the end of paragraph the following: Nor is it inappropriate to grant an injunction under the Act where the conduct in question takes the form of repeated, threatening protests made by animal rights activists who seek to legitimate their action on the basis of their art.10 and art.11 rights to freedom of expression and peaceful assembly. So long as the conduct complained of falls within the statutory definition of harassment, it can be restrained by injunction on account of this being "proportionate to the legitimate aim of preventing crime and disorder".[108a]

NOTE 108a. *Harlan Laboratories UK Ltd v Stop Huntingdon Animal Cruelty* [2012] EWHC 3408 (QB) at [70] per Lang J.

At the end of the paragraph add: In *Dowson v Chief Constable of Northumbria* [2010] EWHC 2612 (QB) at [142] Simon J. offered a summary of what must be proved in order for a claim in harassment to succeed:

"(1) There must be conduct which occurs on at least two occasions,

(2) which is targeted at the claimant,

(3) which is calculated in an objective sense to cause alarm or distress, and

(4) which is objectively judged to be oppressive and unacceptable.

(5) What is oppressive and unacceptable may depend on the social or working context in which the conduct occurs.

(6) A line is to be drawn between conduct which is unattractive and unreasonable, and conduct which has been described in various ways: 'torment' of the victim, 'of an order which would sustain criminal liability'."

5. FALSE IMPRISONMENT

(b) *Continuation of imprisonment*

Replace the last two sentences of the paragraph as follows. Provided an individual is in custody under an order of the court—as was the case in *Quinland*—the governor is not liable for false imprisonment since he will have had no option but to obey the warrant.   **15–30**

Then add to the end of the paragraph the following: The same is true where a prisoner serving an indeterminate sentence for the protection of the public has his detention prolonged by virtue of a delay by the Parole Board in reviewing his case following the expiry of his tariff. Because such a prisoner remains lawfully incarcerated by statute until the Board gives a direction for his release, he cannot sue for false imprisonment.[141a]

NOTE 141a. *R. (on the application of Sturnham) v Parole Board* [2013] UKSC 23; [2013] 2 W.L.R. 1157 at [13] per Lord Reed J.S.C. In similar vein see *R. (on the application of James) v Secretary of State for Justice (Parole Board intervening)* [2009] UKHL 22; [2010] 1 A.C. 553; *R. (on the application of Draga) v Secretary of State for the Home Department* [2012] EWCA Civ 842 (artificial termination of refugee status by Home Secretary inadequate basis for continued detention). Note also that in *Sturnham's* case three further things were made clear. The first was that such detention does not constitute a violation of art.5(1) of the European Convention on Human Rights (despite being in contravention of art.5(4)). Secondly, in view of the art.5(4) violation, it was said that damages under s.8 of the 1998 Act would be payable in respect of the delay where it could be established that an earlier review by the Parole Board would have resulted in an earlier release. Finally, it was said that, even in a case where it could not be shown that an earlier release would have been ordered, a modest sum of s.8 damages should be paid in any case where the prisoner suffered sufficiently severe frustration and anxiety about the prospect of release. See also paras **14–98, 14–99** and **15–151A** of this Supplement.

(c) *Limitations on police detention: Police and Criminal Evidence Act 1984*

15–33   **Review of detention.** NOTE 152. Add: See also *R. (on the application of WL (Congo)) v Secretary of State for the Home Department* [2011] UKSC 12; [2012] 1 A.C. 245 where, in the different context of the detention of foreign nationals pending deportation under the Immigration Act 1971, a majority of the Supreme Court held that a "causation test" does not apply to the tort of false imprisonment. The fact that the defendant *could* have acted lawfully to detain the claimant is not a basis on which liability can be avoided if the defendant has in fact acted unlawfully in detaining the claimant. But in such circumstances, the claimant will only receive nominal damages: see *R. (on the application of Anam) v Secretary of State for the Home Department (No.2)* [2012] EWHC 1770 (Admin). See further para.**15–135** of this Supplement.

(f) *Responsibility for imprisonment committed through the instrumentality of officers of justice*

15–42   **Ministerial and judicial proceedings.** Add to the end of the paragraph the following: Equally, where a defendant is granted bail, is unable to provide the surety and thus remanded in custody, "although a judicial act precludes liability in false imprisonment, it does not relieve the prosecutor of liability in false imprisonment . . . for the damage caused by his setting the prosecution in motion".[175a]

NOTE 175a. *Terrence Calix v Attorney General of Trinidad and Tobago* [2013] UKPC 15 at [23] per Lord Kerr.

6. DEFENCES TO TRESPASS TO THE PERSON

Add to Note 203 the following: It has been suggested at first instance that a   **15–49**
reasonable (albeit mistaken) belief on the part of the arresting officer that the
force used was necessary (as required by the Police and Criminal Evidence Act
1984 s.24(4)) will defeat a claim in battery by the arrested person: *Alleyne v
Commissioner of Police of the Metropolis* [2012] EWHC 3955 (QB) at [130]–
[135] per Seys-Llewellyn Q.C.

(b) *Preventing crime*

After the words "right to use force in the prevention of crime and the apprehen-   **15–52**
sion of offenders" insert the following: If invoked as a defence to the commission
of a crime, a mere honest belief that a crime is being committed is sufficient to
entitle a defendant to rely on the defence under s.3.[209a] Whether the defence will
succeed then depends on whether the defendant used only reasonable force.[209b] It
is unclear, when s.3 is invoked as a defence to the commission of a tort, whether
the defendant's belief that a crime was being committed must be *both* honest and
reasonable. This is certainly the case in when the defence of self-defence is relied
on in the civil law (although for the criminal law a mere honest belief suffices).[209c]

NOTE 209a. *R. v Morris* [2013] EWCA Crim 436; [2013] R.T.R. 22 at [19] per
Leveson L.J. (s.3 relied on in relation to the offence of dangerous driving).

NOTE 209b. *R. v Morris* [2013] EWCA Crim 436; [2013] R.T.R. 22 at [20].

NOTE 209c. It is submitted that s.3, when invoked in connection with the
commission of a tort, ought to require an honest *and* reasonable belief by analogy
with the decision and reasoning in *Ashley v Chief Constable of Sussex Police*
[2008] UKHL 25; [2008] 1 A.C. 962. See further para.**30–03** of the Main Work.

Also after Note 210 in the text insert: Thus, for example, the power to use reasonable force applies not only to the execution of a lawful arrest, but also to the removal
of persons who are attempting to prevent or inhibit the execution of a lawful arrest.[210a]

NOTE 210a. See *Minio-Paluello v Metropolitan Police Commissioner* [2011]
EWHC 3411 (QB) (note, however, in this case that the police officer concerned
committed a battery by virtue of the fact that the force used was neither reasonable
nor proportionate: at [68] per Eder J.).

Reasonable force. After Note 214 in the text add: On the other hand, the use of   **15–53**
hooding during a forcible arrest will always amount to the use of unreasonable
force since "it is likely to pose a risk to the detainee's physical or mental health by
virtue of the force".[214a]

NOTE 214a. *R. (on the application of Equality and Human Rights Commission)
v Prime Minister* [2011] EWHC 2401 (Admin); [2011] 1 W.L.R. 1389 at [83] per
Sir Anthony May.

(c) *Preventing a breach of the peace*

Add to Note 260 the following: For the application of s.60 in this context (and   **15–62**
for confirmation that it is not irreconcilable with the right to liberty afforded by

art.5 of the European Convention on Human Rights) see *R. (on the application of Roberts) v Commissioner of Police of the Metropolis* [2012] EWHC 1977 (Admin); [2012] H.R.L.R. 28.

15–64   **Mass detention of a crowd.** Add: In *Austin v United Kingdom* (39692/09) [2012] Crim. L.R. 544 the European Court of Human Rights held that the practice of containing a crowd behind a police cordon did not involve a breach of art.5 of the ECHR provided that it was unavoidable and necessary in order to avert a real risk of serious injury or damage. See also *R. (on the application of Moos) v Commissioner of Police of the Metropolis* [2012] EWCA Civ 12; *Castle v Commissioner of Police of the Metropolis* [2011] EWHC 2317 (Admin); [2012] 1 All E.R. 953.

(d) *Lawful arrest*

(i) *When is arrest justified?*

15–67   **Arrest by a constable.** NOTE 277. Add: The fact that the arrest must be necessary impliedly requires a police officer to consider measures short of arrest for "if he does not do so he is open to challenge". On the other hand, "[t]o require of a policeman that he pass through particular thought processes each time he considers an arrest, and in all circumstances no matter what urgency or danger . . . is to impose an unrealistic and unattainable burden": *Hayes v Chief Constable of Merseyside Police* [2011] EWCA Civ 911; [2012] 1 W.L.R. 517 at [40]. See also *Hanningfield v Chief Constable of Essex* [2013] EWHC 243.

15–69   **Reasonable grounds for suspicion.** Add to the end of the paragraph: Indeed, the Court of Appeal has stated explicitly that "the threshold for the existence of 'reasonable grounds' for suspicion is low, meaning that the amount of material that is known to the arresting officer in order to found 'reasonable grounds' for suspicion may be small, even sparse".[287a]
   NOTE 287a. *Alanov v Chief Constable of Sussex* [2012] EWCA Civ 234 at [25] per Aikens L.J.

15–72   **Acting on reasonable suspicion.** At the end of the paragraph add: Similarly, a police officer must both consider whether it is necessary to arrest and have grounds, as set out in s.24(5) of the Police and Criminal Evidence Act 1984, for believing that it is necessary to do so at the time of the arrest: *Richardson v Chief Constable of West Midlands* [2011] EWHC 773 (QB); [2011] 2 Cr. App. R. 1 (claimant arrested despite having voluntarily attended two police stations for interview and being calm and compliant, on the basis that he might interrupt the interview and leave the police station; arrest held to be unlawful in the absence of any evidential basis for a belief that the claimant would interrupt his interview; the defendant's argument would lead to the conclusion "that all voluntary attenders at the police station would have to be arrested if questioning was to be undertaken" without consideration of the circumstances of the particular case).

(ii) *Duties when making an arrest*

15–75   **Duty to inform of the grounds for arrest.** NOTE 314. Add: The duty to provide reasons under this section also applies to those arrests conducted in accordance with the Immigration Act 1971 Sch.2 para.17: *FS (Afghanistan) v Secretary of State for the Home Department* [2011] EWHC 1858 (QB).

NOTE 318. Add: So if a police officer informed a man who was wanted for murder that he was arresting him for murder, but by reason of diminished responsibility he was convicted of manslaughter, this would not render the arrest unlawful: *Shields v Chief Constable of Merseyside* [2010] EWCA Civ 1281; *The Times* March 3, 2011 at [23] per Toulson L.J.

A reasonable explanation. After the first sentence add: NOTE 319a. *Minio-   **15–76** Paluello v Commissioner of Police for the Metropolis* [2011] EWHC 3411 (QB).

Other factors. NOTE 324. Add: See also *Cumberbatch v Crown Prosecution   **15–77** Service; Ali v Department of Public Prosecutions* [2009] EWHC 3353 (Admin); [2010] M.H.L.R. 9.

(e) *Police powers of stop and search*

NOTE 349. Add: On the Terrorism Act 2000 ss.44–46 see the Terrorism Act   **15–84** 2000 (Remedial) Order (SI 2011/631) (see para.**15–89**, n.380 of this Supplement).

NOTE 350. Add: See further *Syed v DPP* [2010] EWHC 81 (Admin); [2010] 1 Cr. App. R. 34; (2010) 174 J.P. 97—power of entry under s.17(1)(e) of the Police and Criminal Evidence Act 1984 (for the purpose of "saving life or limb or preventing serious damage to property") requires a serious matter—"that what had happened in the premises, or what might happen in the premises, would involve some serious injury to an individual therein" (at [11])—and so entry without permission will not be lawful where there is merely "a concern for the welfare of someone within the premises".

Conditions for exercise of power. NOTE 358. Replace the existing case with   **15–85** the following: *Sobczak v Director of Public Prosecutions* [2012] EWHC 1319 (Admin);[2013] Crim. L.R. 515.

Search after arrest. In the second sentence, change the opening words to: **15–86** Section 32(1) provides.

Also, after the words ". . . is so restricted" insert the following:

NOTE 360a. Although complementary to the power contained in s.32(1), there is no requirement for the purposes of s.32(2)(b) that the arrestee be reasonably perceived to be a danger to himself or others: *Hanningfield v Chief Constable of Essex* [2013] EWHC 243 (QB).

(f) *Anti-terrorism legislation*

NOTE 376. The Prevention of Terrorism Act 2005 is repealed by the Terrorism   **15–89** Prevention and Investigation Measures Act 2011 s.1

NOTE 380. Add: The Terrorism Act 2000 (Remedial) Order (SI 2011/631) art.2 provides that the Terrorism Act 2000 is to have effect as if ss.44–47 were repealed. The Order inserts new ss.47A–47C providing more circumscribed stop and search powers which are intended to comply with the European Convention on Human

Rights, following the ruling in *Gillan v United Kingdom* (2010) 50 E.H.R.R. 45; 28 B.H.R.C. 420. Sections 41–43 of the Terrorism Act 2000 are not affected by the Order.

15–90 Note that the Prevention of Terrorism Act 2005 is repealed by the Terrorism Prevention and Investigation Measures Act 2011 s.1. The Act creates a new regime of terrorism prevention and investigation measures.

(h) *Consent by the claimant*

15–94 **The limits of consent.** Add: Consent may be express or implied, but caution must be exercised when seeking to imply consent. So, although consent to physical contact within the rules of the game may be implied for participants in a sport where contact is to be expected, an employee working at a school for children with special needs, including children with behavioural problems, does not impliedly consent to the use of violence against him by pupils: *H v Crown Prosecution Service* [2010] EWHC 1374 (Admin); [2012] Q.B. 257.

(i) *Confinement and treatment for mental disorder under the Mental Health Act 1983*

15–100 **Detention under the Mental Health Act 1983.** After the second sentence, insert the following: It constitutes the sole ground on which mentally incapacitated persons may be compulsorily admitted to hospital for the purpose of assessment and treatment. The common law doctrine of necessity cannot be used as an alternative.[427a]

NOTE 427a. *R. (on the application of Sessay) v South London and Maudsley NHS Foundation Trust* [2011] EWHC 2617 (QB); [2012] Q.B. 760.

15–102 **Procedural safeguards.** For the words "approved social worker" in this paragraph substitute "approved mental health professional".

NOTE 440. Add: See also *TTM v Hackney LBC* [2011] EWCA Civ 4; [2011] 1 W.L.R. 2873, where an approved mental health professional applied under the Mental Health Act 1983 to detain the claimant believing, incorrectly, that the nearest relative had withdrawn his objection to the application. On an application for judicial review, it was held that the judge should have found the local authority to be vicariously liable both at common law and under art.5 of the European Convention on Human Rights, since s.11(4) of the 1983 Act rendered the application unlawful, notwithstanding that the approved mental health professional had acted in good faith, and notwithstanding that the NHS Trust which in fact detained the claimant acted lawfully by virtue of s.6(3) in detaining the claimant on the basis of an application that "appears to be duly made". As Toulson L.J. noted (at [36]): "Lawfulness or unlawfulness is an attribute of the conduct of the defendant which caused the claimant's loss of liberty." Applying Sir Thomas Bingham M.R.'s approach in *Re S-C (Mental Patient: Habeas Corpus)* the claimant's "detention was unlawful, notwithstanding that the hospital had lawful authority to detain him, in as much as it was the direct consequence of an unlawful application by the AMHP, and the fact that the hospital managers, for their part, acted lawfully did not cure that underlying unlawfulness" (at [56]; see also at [59]). For the same reasons, the local authority had contravened the claimant's art.5 Convention rights, and the argument that the approved mental health professional had not contravened art.5 because the hospital had acted lawfully in detaining the claimant was "a back to front argument, reminiscent of the world of Alice Through The Looking-glass" (at [62]). It was a hallmark of a constitutional democracy, said Toulson L.J., that "in matters affecting individual liberty the law is strictly applied" (at [100]).

Protection against civil or criminal proceedings. NOTE 486. After the **15–116** second sentence (ending "with a view to obtaining leave.") add: In *Seal v United Kingdom* (50330/07) (2012) 54 E.H.R.R. 6; [2011] M.H.L.R. 1 the European Court of Human Rights held that the requirement to obtain leave under s.139(2) did not involve a breach of the claimant's right of access to the court under art.6 ECHR.

After Note 486 in the text add: For these purposes, "The threshold under s.139 is a low one".[486a]

NOTE 486a. *DD v Durham CC, Middlesbrough City Council* [2013] EWCA Civ 96 at [23] per Sir John Thomas P. Although his actual decision on the question of whether leave should be granted in the instant case was reversed by the Court of Appeal, Eady J., at first instance, said more elaborately of the low threshold that, "the test is whether there is a realistic prospect of success (i.e. one that is other than merely fanciful": [2012] EWHC 1053 (QB); [2012] Med. L.R. 34 at [1].

Also add at the end of the paragraph: The decision of the Court of Appeal in *TTM v Hackney LBC* [2011] EWCA Civ 4; [2011] 1 W.L.R. 2873 appears to have significant implications for the continued usefulness of s.139(1) of the Mental Health Act 1983 as a protection to defendants. In judicial review proceedings, a local authority was held to be vicariously liable both at common law and for breach of the claimant's art.5 rights under the European Convention on Human Rights for the action of an approved mental health professional who made an invalid application to detain the claimant under the Mental Health Act 1983, in breach of s.11(4) of the Act (see para.**15–102**, n.440 of this Supplement). This was notwithstanding that it was common ground that the approved mental health professional had acted in good faith (an argument that she had acted without reasonable care was not ruled upon). It is clear that counsel for the Secretary of State for Health sought to avoid a declaration that s.139(1) was incompatible with art.5, and therefore submitted that if a breach of art.5 was found to have occurred s.139(1) should be read down, by virtue of s.3 of the Human Rights Act 1998, so as to enable the claimant to recover compensation for the breach. In view of the fact that neither counsel for the local authority nor counsel for the Health Secretary disputed the claimant's argument that s.139(1) could be read down, Toulson L.J. (with whom May and Jackson L.JJ. agreed) was "happy to proceed on the basis that it is open to the court to read s.139(1) in that way without further consideration of the matter." The implication is that in any case where the defendant's conduct amounts to a breach of the claimant's Convention rights (and many factual situations will also involve a parallel breach of the claimant's common law rights, as in *TTM v Hackney LBC* itself) s.139(1) will no longer provide a defence. Whether on another occasion, where the defendant sought more robustly to rely on s.139(1), the court would be so ready to read down the provision remains to be seen.

(j) *Treatment and care of patients lacking mental capacity (other than under the Mental Health Act 1983)*

(i) *Common law*

15–122   NOTE 510. Add: But this must involve "serious injury" and not merely "a concern for the welfare of someone within the premises": *Syed v DPP* [2010] EWHC 81 (Admin); [2010] 1 Cr. App. R. 34; (2010) 174 J.P. 97 (see para.**15–84**, Note 350 of this Supplement).

(ii) *Mental Capacity Act 2005*

15–126   **Medical treatment of mentally incapacitated adults.** NOTE 528. Add: and the decision as to what constitutes a patient's best interests is to be determined by the court rather than the patient and her relatives. A balance sheet approach—that is, systematically comparing the various pros and cons of treatment—is to be adopted: *W v M* [2011] EWHC 2443 (Fam); [2012] 1 W.L.R. 1653.

After Note 530 in the text insert the following: So, when police officers restrained an autistic child with a strong aversion to being touched, the officers' honest belief that it was in the child's best interests to be so restrained was not regarded as a reasonable belief (as required by the statute) where it had been practicable and appropriate to consult the boy's carers before performing such restraint. (It was also held necessary, under s.1(6) of the Act, for the police officers to have considered whether there was a less restrictive way of handling the matter before acting in the way that they did).[530a]

NOTE 530a. *ZH v Commissioner of Police for the Metropolis* [2012] EWHC 604 (QB); [2012] Eq. L.R. 425; affd [2013] EWCA Civ 69; [2013] 3 All E.R. 113.

(m) *Previous criminal proceedings*

15–134   Add: Section 329 of the Criminal Justice Act 2003 introduced a defence to a claim for trespass to the person where the claimant has been convicted of an imprisonable offence committed on the same occasion as the alleged trespass to the person. The defence applies where the defendant did the act amounting to trespass to the claimant's person only because: (a) he believed that the claimant: (i) was about to commit an offence; (ii) was in the course of committing an offence; or (iii) had committed an offence immediately beforehand; and (b) he believed that the act was necessary to: (i) defend himself or another person; (ii) protect or recover property; (iii) prevent the commission or continuation of an offence; or (iv) apprehend, or secure the conviction of, the claimant after he had committed an offence; or was necessary to assist in achieving any of those things (s.329(4)(a) and (5)). In addition the defendant's act must not have been grossly disproportionate in all the circumstances (s.329(4)(b)). In addition, there is a requirement that in such cases a claimant obtain the permission of the court to bring civil proceedings (s.329(2) and (3)). This requirement is procedural not mandatory. Proceedings brought without permission are not null and void, and the defect can be cured on application to the court: *Adorian v Commissioner of Police of the Metropolis* [2009] EWCA Civ 18; [2009] 1 W.L.R. 1859.

(n) *Detention of persons prior to deportation*

Detention of persons prior to deportation. This paragraph should now be   **15–135**
read in the light of the decision of the Supreme Court in *R. (on the application of*
WL (Congo)) v Secretary of State for the Home Department [2011] UKSC 12;
[2012] 1 A.C. 245. The claimants were foreign nationals who had been detained,
after completing sentences of imprisonment for various offences, pending deportation under the Immigration Act 1971. The claimants alleged that they had
been unlawfully detained between April 2006 and September 2008 because,
although the Home Office had a published policy on the circumstances in which
detention would be used, the Secretary of State had applied an unpublished policy
involving almost blanket detention of all foreign national prisoners pending
deportation. The claimants sought judicial review and damages for false imprisonment on the basis that the unpublished policy was unlawful in that it involved a
breach of public law and that their detention under that policy was therefore also
unlawful. The defendants argued, inter alia, that the claimants would have been
detained even if the decision to detain had been made in accordance with the
published policy. The Court of Appeal held that the unpublished policy had been
unlawful because it operated as a blanket policy, but that it had not rendered
the claimants' detention unlawful because it had not been the cause of the detention since they would have been detained in any event if the published policy had
been applied. The Supreme Court, by a majority, agreed that the unpublished
policy was unlawful and therefore the claimants' detention between April 2006
and September 2008 had been an unlawful exercise of the Secretary of State's
power to detain. That rendered the claimants' detention tortious, since false
imprisonment is actionable per se. Once the claimant proves that he was directly
and intentionally imprisoned by the defendant the burden is on the defendant to
demonstrate that he had lawful authority to detain. In this case the Secretary of
State through breach of her public law duty had no lawful authority to detain the
claimants, and so the breach gave rise to an action for false imprisonment
(although not every breach of public law would be sufficient to give rise to a
cause of action in false imprisonment: public law errors that do not bear upon the
decision to detain will not found a claim, per Lord Dyson at [68]). Moreover, it
was no defence to false imprisonment to prove that a lawful decision to detain
the claimants could and would have been made. Lord Dyson, at [62], observed:
"The introduction of a causation test in the tort of false imprisonment is contrary
to principle both as a matter of the law of trespass to the person and as a matter of
administrative law. Neither body of law recognises any defence of causation so
as to render lawful what is in fact an unlawful authority to detain, by reference to
how the executive could and *would have* acted if it had acted lawfully, as opposed
to how it *did in fact* act. The causation test entails the surprising proposition
that the detention of a person pursuant to a decision which is vitiated by a public
law error is nevertheless to be regarded as having been lawfully authorised
because a decision to detain could have been made which was not so vitiated. In
my view, the law of false imprisonment does not permit history to be rewritten in
this way" (original emphasis). The "causation test" shifted "the focus of the
tort on to the question of how the defendant *would* have acted on the hypothesis
of a lawful self-direction, rather than on the claimant's right not *in fact* to be

unlawfully detained. There is no warrant for this" (at [66]; see also per Lord Hope at [175]; per Lord Collins at [221]; per Lord Kerr at [239]).

However, a different majority of the Supreme Court held that the causation test was relevant to the question of whether the claimants should be awarded substantive, as opposed to nominal, damages for the false imprisonment. Since the claimants were entitled to be placed in the position that they would have been in had the tort not been committed, and if the Secretary of State had applied the published policy the claimants would still have been detained, they had suffered no loss or damage from the false imprisonment and were entitled only to nominal damages to reflect the fact that they had been the victim of a tort. Similar reasoning in relation to an award of nominal damages was deployed in *R. (on the application of Anam) v Secretary of State for the Home Department (No. 2)* [2012] EWHC 1770 (Admin) where proper account of a medical report had not been taken, but where continued detention could nonetheless have been justified. In similar vein, see also *OM (Nigeria) v Secretary of State for the Home Department* [2011] EWCA Civ 909 and *R. (on the application of Moussaoui) v Secretary of State for the Home Department* [2012] EWHC 126 (Admin); [2012] A.C.D. 55. (See further para.1–12 of this Supplement).

NOTE 560. Add: The decision of the Court of Appeal in *R. (on the application of SK (Zimbabwe)) v Secretary of State for the Home Department* was reversed by the Supreme Court: *Kambadzi v Secretary of State for the Home Department* [2011] UKSC 23; [2011] 1 W.L.R. 1299, applying *R. (on the application of WL (Congo)) v Secretary of State for the Home Department* [2011] UKSC 12; [2012] 1 A.C. 245. The failure to conduct reviews in accordance with the Secretary of State's published policy rendered the claimant's continued detention unlawful, notwithstanding that he may have been lawfully detained if the Secretary of State had reviewed his detention in accordance with the published policy. Accordingly the claimant had been falsely imprisoned. In similar vein see *R. (on the application of EH) v Secretary of State for the Home Department* [2012] EWHC 2569 (Admin). Cf. *R. (on the application of BA) v Secretary of State for the Home Department* [2011] EWHC 2748 (Admin).

NOTE 561. Add: *R. (on the application of Hussein) v Secretary of State for the Home Department* was affirmed by the Court of Appeal: *R. (on the application of MH) v Secretary of State for the Home Department* [2010] EWCA Civ 1112.

NOTE 562. Add: *Anam v Secretary of State for the Home Department* [2009] EWHC 2496 (Admin); [2010] A.C.D. 31 was affirmed by the Court of Appeal: *R. (on the application of Anam) v Secretary of State for the Home Department* [2010] EWCA Civ 1140; [2011] A.C.D. 14. See also *R. (on the application of AM (Angola)) v Secretary of State for the Home Department* [2012] EWCA Civ 521.

Add to the end of the paragraph the following: Also, he cannot issue a cessation order—bringing to an end a detainee's refugee status—as a mere device in order to give the semblance of legitimacy to a deportation order (which in turn would legitimate the detention).[562a] And a claim for false imprisonment will similarly be available where the Secretary of State unreasonably prolongs a detention in the face of either serious mental health problems caused to the detainee by virtue of the detention where no immediate prospect of resolving the deportation issue exists,[562b] or where there is a telling absence of any real chance of effecting a deportation.[562c]

NOTE 562a. In *R. (on the application of Draga) v Secretary of State for the Home Department* [2012] EWCA Civ 842, Sullivan L.J. opined at [71]: "I have no doubt that reliance upon a 'device' to maintain a deportation order without which continued detention could not lawfully be authorised is a public law error in the decision making process which renders the continued detention unlawful."

NOTE 562b. *R. (on the application of Lamari) v Secretary of State for the Home Department* [2012] EWHC 1630 (Admin). Cf. *R. (on the application of LE (Jamaica)) v Secretary of State for the Home Department* [2012] EWCA Civ 597 (the detainee's schizophrenia was capable of being satisfactorily managed within detention) and *R. (on the application of Moussaoui) v Secretary of State for the Home Department* [2012] EWHC 126 (Admin); [2012] A.C.D. 55 (the detainee's mental health was merely one, non-determinative consideration along with his conviction for many prior thefts).

NOTE 562c. *R. (on the application of Murad) v Secretary of State for the Home Department* [2012] EWHC 1112 (Admin).

After para.**15–135** insert new para.**15–135A**:

One particular problem that has troubled the courts in recent years is whether a **15–135A** potential deportee can continue to be detained where the legality of such deportation is under review by the European Court of Human Rights. In *R. (on the application of Muqtaar) v Secretary of State for the Home Department*[562d] a Somali National had been detained pending deportation, but at that time the European Court of Human Rights was still considering the legality of deportation in an analogous case. The Strasbourg court issued a direction (known as a r.39 indication) that the deportation should not take place until it had resolved that other case. Pending the resolution of that case, the Somali immigrant remained imprisoned. In the instant case, the detainee argued that he should have been released. The Court of Appeal held otherwise. According to their Lordships, when the r.39 indication was received, there had been a realistic prospect that the Strasbourg proceedings would be resolved within a reasonable period of time. Equally, it had not been apparent that the Strasbourg Court's resolution of the other case would prevent the prisoner's deportation.[562e] Accordingly, his continued detention was lawful (there being no requirement that the Secretary of State be able to identify a timescale within which removal could be effected). Equally, since the Secretary of State had a number of similar cases to consider, it was not unlawful for her to continue to detain the Somali national in this case even after the Strasbourg Court had decided (in the other case) that such deportations would be contrary to the Convention.[562f]

NOTE 562d. [2012] EWCA Civ 1270; [2013] 1 W.L.R. 649.

NOTE 562e. Cf. *R. (on the application of Abdi) v Secretary of State for the Home Department* [2011] EWCA Civ 242.

NOTE 562f. *R. (on the application of Abdi) v Secretary of State for the Home Department* [2011] EWCA Civ 242 at [36]–[39] per Richards L.J.

7. DAMAGES

Damages in trespass. After Note 565 in the text, add: However, where a **15–137** claimant has been detained unlawfully as a consequence of a breach by the defendant of public law principles, and so has been falsely imprisoned, if the claimant could, on the facts, have been lawfully detained by the defendant complying with the relevant public law principles he will be entitled to nominal damages only, since he has suffered no loss or damage as a result of the defendant's unlawful exercise of the power to detain: *R. (on the application of WL (Congo)) v Secretary of State for the Home Department* [2011] UKSC 12; [2012] 1 A.C. 245. In similar vein, see *R. (on the application of Anam) v Secretary of State for the Home Department (No. 2)* [2012] EWHC 1770 (Admin). See also para.**15–135** of this Supplement.

Add to the end of the paragraph: However, where the claimant is disabled and receives an award of damages for injury to feelings under the Disability Discrimination Act 1995, "the risk of overlap is such that an award of aggravated damages is inappropriate".[570a]

NOTE 570a. *ZH v Commissioner of Police for the Metropolis* [2012] EWHC 604 (QB); [2012] Eq. L.R. 425 at [156] per Sir Robert Nelson (quantum of damages not challenged when unsuccessfully appealed: see [2013] EWCA Civ 69; [2013] 3 All E.R. 113).

15–140   **Compensation by the criminal courts.** NOTE 581. Add: See also *R. v Sones* [2012] EWCA Crim 1377 at [13] per Hedley J.

NOTE 582. Add: The fact that it will take the defendant many years to make the payment required by the compensation order will not be a reason not to make such an order: see *R. v Ganyo* [2011] EWCA Crim 2491; [2012] 1 Cr. App. R. (S.) 108.

15–141   **Criminal injuries compensation.** NOTE 588. Add: See also Begley, "The Criminal Injuries Compensation Scheme" [2011] J.P.I.L. 54.

After para.**15–141** insert new para.**15–141A**:

15–141A   **Damages for related human rights breaches.** As noted at various points in this chapter, there is considerable overlap between the various torts involving trespass to the person and the European Convention on Human Rights. But cases involving detention by state authorities are worthy of special note from the perspective of damages since it is possible that the tort of false imprisonment may not have been committed, even though there has been a violation of the art.5(4) right to a speedy review of the continuing need for a prisoner's detention. Such was the case in *R. (on the application of Sturnham) v Parole Board.*[589] In that case, a prisoner was serving an indeterminate sentence. His imprisonment was prolonged because of the delay on the part of the Parole Board in reviewing his case following the expiry of his tariff. Since his incarceration remained grounded in law until such time as the Board reviewed his case and sanctioned his release, he was unable to sue on the basis of either the tort of false imprisonment or under the Human Rights Act 1998 in respect of a violation of his art.5(1) right to liberty. On the other hand, there was a violation of his art.5(4) right to a speedy review of his case. In respect of such delays, the Supreme Court held that, where, on the balance of probabilities the prisoner would have enjoyed an earlier release but for the delay, he should be awarded compensatory damages. As to quantum in such cases, Lord Reed J.S.C. said that "the most reliable guidance as to the quantum of awards under section 8 will . . . be awards made by the European Court [of Human

Rights] in comparable cases brought by applicants from the UK or other countries with a similar cost of living".[590] Modest damages were also said to be payable in cases where, even though it could not be shown that an earlier review would have resulted in an earlier release, the breach of art.5(4) had demonstrably or presumptively caused the prisoner to suffer feelings of frustration and anxiety about his continued detention.[591]

NOTE 589. [2013] UKSC 23; [2013] 2 W.L.R. 1157. See further paras **14–98** and **14–99** of this Supplement.

NOTE 590. [2013] UKSC 23; [2013] 2 W.L.R. 1157. at [39].

NOTE 591. [2013] UKSC 23; [2013] 2 W.L.R. 1157. at [13].

CHAPTER 16

MALICIOUS PROSECUTION

		PARA.
■	1. Introduction.	16–01
■	2. Kinds of damage caused	16–04
■	3. Malicious prosecution.	16–09
	■ (a) Prosecution	16–10
	■ (b) Determination of prosecution	16–28
	(c) Reasonable and probable cause	16–30
	(i) Role of judge and jury	16–34
	□ (ii) Factors relevant to reasonable and probable cause	16–37
	□ (d) Malice	16–52
	(e) Courts-martial and foreign courts	16–58
	4. Malicious proceedings in bankruptcy and liquidation	16–60
■	5. Abuse of civil process.	16–62
■	6. Vexatious use of process	16–69

1. Introduction

Malicious institution of proceedings. NOTE 2. Add at the end: The Court of   **16–01**
Appeal in *Desmond* reversed the first instance decision on the basis that there was
no assumption of responsibility ([2011] EWCA Civ 3; [2011] 1 F.L.R. 1361;
[2011] Fam. Law 358; see para.**14–31**), but the claim nevertheless illustrates the
nature and extent of damage that may be suffered by a claimant who is wrongly
suspected of committing a crime.

In the text after Note 3 add: However, a majority of the Privy Council in
Crawford Adjusters v Sagicor General Insurance (Cayman) Ltd [2013] UKPC 17,
an appeal from the Cayman Islands, has chosen to depart from this clearly stated
position. Although not binding on courts in England and Wales, the decision was
clearly intended to express the position in England and Wales. On the other hand,
there were two substantial dissenting judgments. If followed in future cases, the
decision will considerably broaden the situations in which the tort of malicious
prosecution may be pursued, by opening up its application to civil cases. Since
modern prosecution practice has tended to diminish the significance of the tort in
relation to criminal proceedings, this would be a significant reversal in the fortunes
of this tort. The greater likelihood in practice of being subject to malicious civil,
rather than criminal proceedings was considered paradoxical by Lord Wilson (at
[68]). Presumably, Lord Wilson meant that the tort was unavailable where it is
most likely to be needed. There is however another way of looking at this issue,
which is that its availability in civil cases may give rise to a more significant risk
to civil claimants than it has to criminal complainants, particularly where defendants have superior financial resources. It may particularly be noted that procedural
changes in prosecution practice, which have played a large role in making the tort
increasingly rare in criminal proceedings, operate to protect those involved in

prosecuting criminal cases, including complainants, from subsequent civil actions. It is suggested that the policy issues raised by the dissenting judges are therefore real and significant. The decision is discussed in paras **16–04**; **16–06**; **16–62**; **16–64**.

16–03   **The Prosecution of Offences Act 1985.** NOTE 13. At the end add: Since 2009, the policy applied by the CPS has been to take over and discontinue prosecutions unless the evidence suggests that it is more likely than not that the defendant will be convicted, in line with the general evidential sufficiency test laid down in the Code for Crown Prosecutors. In *R. (on the application of Gujra) v Crown Prosecution Service* [2012] UKSC 52; [2013] 1 A.C. 484, a claimant's application for judicial review of a decision to discontinue private prosecutions on this basis was dismissed by the Supreme Court, on the basis that the policy did not frustrate the purpose of the right to bring a private prosecution, as retained by the legislation.

NOTE 16. After "EWCA Civ 1259", delete "see para" and add:, and at trial damages were awarded, see para.**16–05**.

2. KINDS OF DAMAGE CAUSED

16–04   **Nature of damage caused.** At the end of the paragraph, add: Two points should be made about the treatment of this famous dictum by the majority of the Privy Council in *Crawford Adjusters v Sagicor General Insurance (Cayman) Ltd* [2013] UKPC 17. First, Lord Wilson and Baroness Hale regarded the existence of the relevant forms of damage, together with malice, not merely as essential *requirements* of the action, but as themselves defining a "wrong" which would require a remedy unless principled reasons could be given to the contrary. Secondly, the majority considered that it was incorrect to read the statement as restricting the forms of damage that were recoverable, and it should not be read as though it was a statute. In particular, a wider range of economic losses was held to be recoverable than the statement itself has been taken to permit. It will be appreciated that these two conclusions in combination have the potential to expand the range of the tort of malicious prosecution considerably. See further, in relation to the tort of abuse of civil process, para.**16–64**.

16–05   At the end of the paragraph add: The Privy Council, in an appeal from the Court of Appeal of the Republic of Trinidad and Tobago, has emphasised that good character and social status are not to be confused: *Calix v Attorney General of Trinidad and Tobago* [2013] UKPC 15, at [14]. The claimant was "unconventional" or, in the view of the trial judge, "an odd man", who chose to live alone in squalid and unsanitary conditions and to survive by scavenging scrap metal, despite a reasonable level of education. The trial judge worked on the basis that, taking this into account, "his reputation and social standing did not amount to much". The Privy Council emphasised however that the claimant had no previous convictions and that he was therefore of "good character". The seriousness of the charge against him would have had a serious impact on his reputation independent of his social standing and should have been reflected in the award. While compensation is rightly adjusted to reflect the anguish caused by reputational damage, those who are more stoical should not be denied appropriate relief: to this extent, "reputation has an objective value" (at [10]). The judge and Court of Appeal had also erred in relation to the impact on the claimant of his loss of liberty. It was wrong to suggest, given the conditions inside the remand prison, that they were not much worse than the claimant's home; besides, this was freely chosen. Because of these and other errors of principle, and because the award was in any case palpably too low in contrast to other awards in the same jurisdiction, the award of damages was quashed and the case returned to the Court of Appeal for a new assessment of damages. In *Clifford v Chief Constable of Hertfordshire Police* [2011] EWHC 815 (QB) (see also para.**16–54**), the claimant was awarded the sum of £20,000, of which £10,000 were compensatory damages in relation to psychiatric damage in the form of depression suffered by the claimant as a consequence of the prosecution. Applying the principles and guidance on quantum set out in *Thompson v Commissioner of Police of the Metropolis*, a further compensatory sum of £10,000 was awarded in respect of the distress and non-psychiatric hurt and injury to feelings. The judge noted the "destructive effect" of the charges on his own feelings of self-worth, his relationships with business associates and family, and the element of social stigma including the threat of inclusion on the sex offenders' register. No aggravated or exemplary damages were included in the award.

Add to the end of the paragraph: This is, however, precisely the extension   **16–06** preferred by the majority of the Privy Council in *Crawford Adjusters v Sagicor General Insurance (Cayman) Ltd* [2013] UKPC 17. Lord Steyn's remarks on civil proceedings were treated as obiter dicta despite the fact that the House had heard exhaustive argument on the subject; but it was also suggested that the factors which justified his conclusion no longer applied. In particular, the conduct of civil litigation and award of costs neither fully protected claimants' reputation nor could genuinely be said to remove harm to the victim of malicious civil proceedings today. Lord Wilson explored historic materials which in his view demonstrated that there had not been a hard and fast line between the action for malicious prosecution of civil and criminal proceedings. Baroness Hale added that the boundaries of the tort should make sense in the modern world, proposing that malice together with relevant damage provided the relevant justification. While negligence has not been expanded to cover new types of wrongful harm arising in the course of litigation (referring, in particular, to *Jain v Trent SHA* [2009] UKHL 4; [2009] 1 A.C. 853), Baroness Hale was of the view that the element of malice made a sufficient difference: the law in this area could justifiably be extended, where negligence had been restricted by reference to policy concerns. There is room to doubt, however, that the wrongfulness associated with malice is necessarily sufficient answer to the policy concerns noted by Baroness Hale herself. Lord Kerr emphasised that there was no clear boundary between civil and criminal proceedings in that both involve a "public function". However, it was clear that Lord Kerr considered the application of malicious prosecution to civil proceedings to be an extension of the law, while Lord Wilson described it as a return to an earlier, "principled" position. It is suggested that the application of malicious prosecution to civil proceedings can rightly be called an extension of the modern tort, irrespective of the earliest position. Safeguards for individuals in the civil justice system will need to be carefully considered if the path preferred by the majority is to be followed.

16-08   **Abuse of process.** Add to the end of the paragraph: Evidently, the approach of the majority in *Crawford Adjusters v Sagicor General Insurance (Cayman) Ltd* [2013] UKPC 17 would absorb these instances into the general tort of malicious prosecution. The Privy Council did not, however, suggest enlargement to the tort of abuse of civil process: see further para.**16-62** and following paragraphs.

3. MALICIOUS PROSECUTION

16-09   **Essentials of the tort of malicious prosecution.** NOTE 37. Add to the beginning of the Note: The approach of the majority of the Privy Council in *Crawford Adjusters v Sagicor General Insurance (Cayman) Ltd* [2013] UKPC 17 departed from this statement of the first essential element of the tort, holding that where loss is caused and the remaining elements are established, the tort applies also to civil proceedings.

(a) *Prosecution*

16-10   **Prosecution on a criminal charge.** Add to the end of the paragraph: The Privy Council in *Crawford Adjusters v Sagicor General Insurance (Cayman) Ltd* [2013] UKPC 17 considered that civil proceedings may also have a sufficient reputational effect, since the bringing of civil proceedings is now a matter of public record.

(b) *Determination of prosecution*

16-29   **Determination need not be conclusive.** The law in Australia is consistent with the position stated in this and the preceding paragraph. In *Beckett v New South Wales* [2013] HCA 17, the High Court of Australia has confirmed that proof of the claimant's innocence plays no part in the civil action for malicious prosecution. The four criteria are as set out in para.**16-09**, and these make no reference to the innocence of the claimant. While the irrelevance of evidence as to the claimant's innocence had been accepted in *Commonwealth Life Assurance Society Ltd v Smith* (1938) 59 C.L.R. 527; [1938] HCA 2, the High Court had there allowed an exception where a prosecution had been discontinued by a direction from the Director of Public Prosecutions, that no further action be taken against the person. The exception was derived from the case of *Davis v Gell* (1924) 35 C.L.R. 275; [1924] HCA 56. In *Beckett*, the High Court determined that there is no exception, and that *Davis* should not be followed. It was not desirable for the claimant, or the defendant, to bring evidence as to the claimant's innocence or guilt in such an action. Evidence as to whether there is reasonable and probable cause (the third criterion, discussed below) is limited to issues which would have been known, or reasonably understood, by the defendants at the time of the prosecution. Given the requirements of malice and lack of reasonable and probable cause, there was no risk that a finding in favour of a claimant would "scandalise the administration of justice" (at [51]). The purpose of the requirement that the prosecution ended favourably to the claimant is to avoid re-litigation.

(c) *Reasonable and probable cause*

(ii) *Factors relevant to reasonable and probable cause*

What is reasonable and probable cause. After the quotation from *Hicks v* **16–37**
Faulkner ending "the crime imputed", add to the beginning of the next paragraph:
In *Moulton v Chief Constable of the West Midlands* [2010] EWCA Civ 524, this
test was taken to require a finding as to the subjective state of mind of the police
officer responsible, and an objective consideration of the adequacy of evidence. If
the evidence contains inconsistencies, this does not necessarily signify absence of
reasonable and probable cause. Here the officers had an honest belief in the truth
of the allegations, and the evidence taken as a whole gave reasonable grounds for
this belief. On the other hand, in an earlier case a [delete "A"]

Guilt of claimant. Add to the end of the paragraph: In *Qema v News Group* **16–50**
Newspapers Ltd [2012] EWHC 1146 (QB), where the claimant's conviction had
been quashed, the claimant did not deny the commission of criminal acts, but
argued that the prosecution was lacking in "reasonable and probable cause"
because of the role of the defendants' employee in the instigation of those acts. Mr
Mahmood was employed as investigations editor of the defendant former newspaper, and was otherwise known in that context as the 'Fake Sheikh'. On the facts
as proposed by the claimant and assumed for the purposes of the striking out question, Mr Mahmood had initiated a "sting" in which, with the help of an associate,
he had instigated commission of the offences by the claimant, and had then given
evidence to the police. The claimant had pleaded guilty to the offences at trial and
served a term of imprisonment, but later succeeded in having the conviction
reviewed and quashed, in light of other cases in which prosecutions had been
discontinued because of concerns about the role of Mr Mahmood and his associate. The claim for malicious prosecution was struck out on the basis that the
claimant had no prospect of showing lack of reasonable and probable cause.
Where, as here, a witness not only has an honest belief in the guilt of the claimant,
but knows them to have committed a criminal offence, the fact that the prosecution may for other reasons not be justified is irrelevant to the determination of
"reasonable and probable cause" as against that witness. Such issues are questions
for the prosecuting authorities. The insufficiency of adverse motive to the question of "reasonable and probable cause" was further underlined.

(d) *Malice*

Improper motives. Add at the end of the paragraph: In *Moulton v Chief* **16–52**
Constable of the West Midlands [2010] EWCA Civ 524, the Court of Appeal
rejected a suggestion that the test for malice should be lowered to reflect the
requirements of art.5 ECHR. Article 5 allowed for arrest and detention on reasonable suspicion. This was a low threshold consistent with the components of the
tort of malicious prosecution. The standard of malice required that the prosecutor
acted from a motive other than a legitimate desire to bring the accused to justice.

NOTE 226. Add:; *Moulton v Chief Constable of the West Midlands* [2010] **16–53**
EWCA Civ 524 at [44].

16–54   At the end of the paragraph add: Having said that, if police officers have communicated a change in evidence to the CPS and the prosecution has not been discontinued speedily, this is a CPS decision, and it does not mean that the police officers involved can be said to have continued a prosecution without reasonable and proper cause: *Moulton v Chief Constable of the West Midlands* [2010] EWCA Civ 524. Here, there was criticism both of the investigation itself and of delay in discontinuing the prosecution, but the difference between the requirements of negligence (which is not available on such facts in this jurisdiction) and of malicious prosecution was underlined.

At trial, the claim of malicious prosecution in *Clifford v Chief Constable of Hertfordshire Police* was held to be made out, and damages were awarded ([2011] EWHC 815 (QB) Mackay J.). The police officer preparing the charges had no reasonable and probable cause, either based on his own belief or judged according to the standards of a reasonable prosecutor, to charge the claimant with possession offences. Furthermore, the charges had been brought for an improper reason, namely to "bolster" a different charge being brought against the claimant. In this particular case, the officer had in his possession sufficient information to alert him to the fact that the images of child pornography found on the claimant's computer were in temporary files and that this was consistent with them being unsolicited. He did not alert the CPS to the meaning of the evidence, of which he was aware, and had offered no reasons for this. The judge concluded that the officer "must have made a decision to conceal that which he knew at the time of charging from the CPS".

5. Abuse of Civil Process

16–62   **Abuse of civil process.** At the beginning of the paragraph, delete the word "The" and replace with: "Prior to the decision of the Privy Council in *Crawford Adjusters v Sagicor General Insurance (Cayman) Ltd* [2013] UKPC 17, it was thought that the".

After Note 255, delete "makes" and replace with "made". At the end of the paragraph, add: In *Crawford Adjusters*, the majority declined to follow the conclusions of the House of Lords, and treated Lord Steyn's remarks as mere obiter dicta, even though full argument on the question of malicious civil proceedings had been heard. The practical reasons set out by Lord Steyn were considered unconvincing. Instead, it was thought that the treatment of the claimant amounted to a wrong, and that this required a remedy unless there were convincing and principled reasons to the contrary. Thus the possibility of a broad action for malicious civil prosecution is in theory reopened, and may develop in English law. The Privy Council clearly understood the action for abuse of civil process to be a separate tort, and interpreted it restrictively. This section deals with the separate tort of abuse of civil process.

16–64   Add a new title: **Scope of the Tort**
After the quotation from the Court of Appeal amend the text as follows: Delete the first sentence beginning "The Court continues" and replace with: "Apart from the first proposition above, which was dealt with in relation to malicious prosecution in para.**16–06**, the other remarks of the Court of Appeal just cited are

consistent with the decision of the Privy Council in *Crawford Adjusters*." At the start of the second sentence, remove "The Court considered however, that" and replace with: "However, in *Fladgate Fielder*, the Court of Appeal also considered that". At the end of the paragraph, add: "These comments are inconsistent with the approach of Lord Wilson in the decision of the Privy Council in *Crawford Adjusters v Sagicor General Insurance (Cayman) Ltd* [2013] UKPC 17. Lord Wilson took the view that neither the tort of malicious prosecution, nor the tort of abuse of process, was limited strictly to the heads of damage described by Holt C.J. in *Savill v Roberts* and described in **para.16–04**. In particular, both torts were capable of extending to economic losses suffered by the claimant as a consequence of civil proceedings".

At the end of the paragraph insert a new para.**16–64A**:

Improper Purpose. The Privy Council in *Crawford Adjusters v Sagicor*   **16–64A**
General Insurance (Cayman) Ltd [2013] UKPC 17 sought to clarify the nature of the relevant improper purpose in relation to a claim for abuse of process. Lord Sumption referred to the idea of civil proceedings which are "merely a stalking horse to coerce the defendant in some way entirely outside the ambit of the legal claim upon which the court is asked to adjudicate" (*Varawa v Howard Smith Co Ltd* (1911) 13 C.L.R. 35 at 91, Isaacs J.). It was unanimously agreed that the tort was not made out on the facts of *Crawford Adjusters* itself. Although the defendant's employee plainly intended to ruin the claimant, he wanted to do so through victory in the civil action. That purpose was therefore not collateral to the actions brought. In *JSC BTA Bank v Ablyazov* [2011] EWHC 1136 (Comm); [2011] 1 W.L.R. 2996, Teare J. suggested that existing authorities did not fully determine how to approach a case where the motives of the party putting a civil claim in process were "mixed". Here the Bank, which was insolvent and controlled by the state of Kazakhstan, brought actions for repayment of sums of money from its former chairman. He denied the claims and applied for the actions to be stayed on the basis of abuse of process, arguing that the President of Kazakhstan had brought the actions in order to eliminate a political opponent. Teare J. dismissed the application, concluding that there was no arguable abuse of process. Even if one of the motives for the claim could be shown to be the desire to eliminate a political opponent, the Bank also had a legitimate motive, namely to recover losses for the benefit of the bank and its creditors. His preferred view of the law was that in a case of mixed motives, there was no abuse of process provided one of the purposes is legitimate (at [22]). This was, he suggested, in line with comments of Bridge L.J. in *Goldsmith v Sperrings* [1977] 1 W.L.R. 478, although Bridge L.J. had not needed to determine the point. On this basis, there was no arguable claim against the Bank, for one of their purposes was "certainly legitimate" (at [52]). This approach was doubted by Lord Wilson in *Crawford Adjusters* ([65]). Lord Wilson suggested that Teare J. failed to emphasise the importance of the *predominant* motive: it would be too easy for a clamant with a predominantly improper purpose to point to a legitimate purpose, however slight. Teare J. also considered the position if he was wrong on this point, and if proceedings will be an abuse of process where there are mixed purposes and the "predominant purpose" is "sufficiently collateral to be illegitimate". On this basis too, he concluded that there was no arguable case that the claims were brought in abuse of process. The harm to

Mr Ablyazov should the actions succeed would be a consequence of the success of those actions and the likely remedies. These would harm his reputation and facilitate expropriation of his assets, and only in this way would a political opponent be eliminated (at [53]). As Simon Brown L.J. said in *Broxton v McClelland* [1995] E.M.L.R. 485, "a plaintiff is entitled to seek the defendant's financial ruin if that will be the consequence of prosecuting the legitimate claim". On this basis also, the likely consequences could not be an illegitimate purpose, as they were simply a natural consequence of the action succeeding.

6. Vexatious Use of Process

16–72   **No civil action for perjury.** After the fourth sentence, ending "to bypass the operation of rules of witness immunity" add: Where actions in negligence are concerned, important exceptions have been created to this general immunity from civil actions on the part of advocates and, most recently, expert witnesses: *Jones v Kaney* [2011] UKSC 13; [2011] 2 A.C. 398. The lower hurdle posed by the need only to show negligence rather than malice was treated by the majority as balanced by the need to show that the defendant owed the claimant a duty of care, which in the case of negligent misstatement is generally seen as an assumed duty (*Jones v Kaney* at [18]). In *Jones v Kaney*, expert witnesses were treated by the Supreme Court as more analogous in this respect to advocates (and other professionals generally) rather than to witnesses of fact. See further paras **10–41** and **14–35** of this Supplement.

Add to the end of the paragraph: For these reasons, in *Smart v Forensic Science Services* [2013] EWCA Civ 783 the Court of Appeal declined to strike out a claim in deceit and negligence brought against the forensic science service, where there was evidence suggesting that records in relation to forensic services had been changed, and no convincing explanation for this change, which wrongly incriminated the claimant. The claimant pleaded guilty to possession of live ammunition since a forensic report suggested that a bullet taken from his premises was live. Since the relevant offence was one of strict liability, his plea was inevitable in reliance on the forensic report. The Court pointed out that changing the report was, in its effect on the claimant, equivalent to planting evidence in the claimant's home. Since the plea of deceit was to proceed, there were no convincing policy reasons for maintaining an immunity in relation to the claim in negligence, since evidence in respect of what had occurred would need to be tried; and the negligence claim would therefore not be struck out. The clear implication is that immunities must in all circumstances be justified, and are to be seen as exceptional. See further para.**14–40**.

NOTE 303. After the reference to *Watson v M'Ewan* add: *Watson v M'Ewan* was treated by the majority of the Supreme Court in *Jones v Kaney* [2011] UKSC 13; [2011] 2 A.C. 398 as concerned primarily with slander rather than negligence.

16–73   Add to the end of the paragraph: The correctness of *Meadow v GMC* was not questioned before the Supreme Court in *Jones v Kaney* [2011] UKSC 13; [2011] 2 A.C. 398. The decision was however discussed without disapproval and the Supreme Court by its decision further limited the immunity enjoyed by an expert witness, to exclude actions in negligence.

CHAPTER 17

WRONGFUL INTERFERENCE WITH GOODS

		PARA.
1.	Introduction.	17–01
2.	Conversion	17–06
	□ (a) Forms of conversion	17–07
	□ (i) Conversion by taking or receiving property	17–09
	■ (ii) Conversion by transfer of property	17–15
	(iii) Conversion by loss: the case of the bailee	17–20
	□ (iv) Conversion by wrongful but effective sale	17–21
	■ (v) Conversion by keeping or refusal to return	17–22
	(vi) Conversion by destruction or misuse	17–29
	■ (vii) Conversion by wrongful denial of access	17–31
	■ (b) Subject matter of conversion	17–34
	(c) Persons entitled to sue.	17–43
	■ (i) Generally	17–43
	■ (ii) Title by mere possession	17–48
	(iii) Title to sue by virtue of immediate right to possession	17–60
	(d) Position of defendant	17–68
	(i) Co-owners	17–68
	(ii) Conversion wrongful unless excused.	17–71
	□ (iii) Defendant's ignorance of claimant's right generally no defence	17–72
	(iv) Exceptional cases where ignorance of claimant's title a defence	17–74
	□ (e) Multiple claims: jus tertii, estoppel and double liability.	17–81
	(i) *Jus tertii*: joinder of competing claimants	17–83
	(ii) Joinder of concurrent actions	17–84
	(iii) Double liability	17–85
3.	Remedies for conversion.	17–87
	(a) Orders for delivery	17–88
	□ (i) Judgment for specific delivery.	17–88
	(ii) Judgment for delivery or damages at defendant's option	17–90
	(iii) Interloctury orders for delivery up.	17–91
	(b) Damages	17–92
	□ (i) General rule: value of the goods	17–92
	□ (ii) Damages beyond value of goods: special damages	17–105
	□ (iii) Nature of claimant's interest	17–112
	(iv) Return of chattel.	17–122
	□ (v) Successive conversions and satisfaction	17–125
	(vi) Contributory negligence.	17–126
	■ (vii) Limitations of actions	17–127
4.	Trespass to goods	17–128
	■ (a) The nature of trespass to goods.	17–128
	(b) Subject matter of trespass to goods.	17–130
	(c) The claimant's interest	17–133
	(d) Remedies for trespass to goods.	17–134
	■ (e) Defences	17–135
5.	Negligence resulting in damage to goods.	17–141
6.	Reversionary injury.	17–144
7.	Wrongful interference by other torts.	17–146
	(a) Other torts generally	17–146
	(b) Rescous and pound breach	17–147
	(c) Replevin	17–148

2. CONVERSION

(a) *Forms of conversion*

17–07   **Forms of conversion.** NOTE 27. Add: See too the very careful judgment of Allsop P. in the New South Wales Court of Appeal case of *Bunnings Group Ltd v CHEP Australia Ltd* [2011] NSWCA 342, where his Honour says of conversion at [124]: "The essential elements, or basic features, involve an intentional act or dealing with goods inconsistent with or repugnant to the rights of the owner, including possession and any right to possession. Such an act or dealing will amount to such an infringement of the possessory or proprietary rights of the owner if it is an intended act of dominion or assertion of rights over the goods".

(i) *Conversion by taking or receiving property*

17–11   **Taking and using goods.** Add: The whole question of liability for temporary detention or use of another's chattel was exhaustively discussed in New South Wales in *Bunnings Group Ltd v CHEP Australia Ltd* [2011] NSWCA 342, concerning the allegedly unauthorised use of the plaintiff's pallets. The issue had to be approached with one eye to commercial common sense; and, said Allsop P., to amount to conversion the use had to be "an interference with the property which would not, as against the true owner, be justified, or at least excused, in one who came lawfully into the possession of the goods" (at [149]). Hence, on the facts in that case the defendants were justified in retaining pallets on which goods had been delivered for a reasonable time pending unpacking, but thereafter were potentially liable in conversion for any further use.

NOTE 46. Add: For careful discussion, and ultimate acceptance, of the proposition that unauthorised borrowing or joy-riding may be conversion, see the New South Wales decision in *Bunnings Group Ltd v CHEP Australia Ltd* [2011] NSWCA 342 at [138] (Allsop P.).

NOTE 50. Add: The suggestion made here, that the possible admissibility of evidence should not be capable of legitimating what is otherwise a clear wrong in obtaining it (following Ward L.J. in *White v Withers LLP* [2009] EWCA Civ 1122; [2009] 3 F.C.R. 435 and deprecating contrary suggestions of Wilson and Sedley L.JJ. in the same case) has now been trenchantly vindicated. See *Imerman v Tchenguiz* [2010] EWCA Civ 908; [2011] Fam. 116 at [36]–[53]; also [116]–[117].

(ii) *Conversion by transfer of property*

17–15   **Conversion by delivery.** Add: If the claimant has consented to the disposal this clearly bars an action in conversion. It has been held that this applies equally where the claimant has authorised a possessor to dispose of goods on the basis that the proceeds are to be paid over to him: even if they are not so accounted for, no action in conversion lies. See the Canadian decision in *Lloydminster Credit Union v 324007 Alberta Ltd* [2011] SKCA 93; (2011) 333 D.L.R. (4th) 699.

17–19   **Sale in emergency or where bailor disappears.** NOTE 89. Add: In *Taylor v Diamond* [2012] EWHC 2900 (Ch) at [106] Norris J. thought it subject to serious doubt whether an involuntary bailee could take advantage of the power of sale in the 1977 Act. It is worth noting, however, that ss.12 and 13 of the Act refer simply to a "bailee." There seems no warrant to read this down so as to exclude an involuntary bailee, particularly where the effect would be the perverse one of treating a person who had goods thrust upon him willy-nilly less favourably than one who agreed to look after them.

(iv) *Conversion by wrongful but effective sale*

Conversion by wrongful but effective sale. NOTE 95. Add: So also with a **17–21** purported lease without actual delivery: see *Sadcas Pty Ltd v Business & Professional Finance Pty Ltd* [2011] NSWCA 267 (equipment left in commercial premises).

(v) *Conversion by keeping or refusal to return*

Conversion by keeping: demand and refusal. NOTE 99. Add: See too **17–22** *Mainline Private Hire Ltd v Nolan* [2011] EWCA Civ 189; [2011] C.T.L.C. 145, where it was held enough for the defendant to have possession of a car through a bailee. In the same case there is a suggestion (see [35]) that the bailee himself did not have possession for the purposes of conversion since his possession was not claimed to be exclusive: *sed quaere*.

Refusal must be unconditional. NOTE 115. Add: The doubts expressed here **17–25** as to whether inaction was capable of amounting to a refusal were vindicated in *R. (on the application of Atapattu) v Home Secretary* [2011] EWHC 1388 (Admin). There the Home Office were held to have unconditionally refused to return a foreign visitor's passport by stonewalling the visitor's demands for it. The present footnote formed a large part of the basis for the judge's decision at [60]–[92] that there was no reason why, in appropriate circumstances, refusal should not be inferred from mere inaction, and that the present case was a suitable one in which to draw that inference.

Delay in complying with demand. Add: The defendant's right to make **17–26** enquiries was discussed in *Spencer v S Franses Ltd* [2011] EWHC 1269 (QB). Antique tapestries were demanded from the defendant, with whom they had been deposited for valuation and attribution, in 2005: formal demand, on which the claim was based, was made in 2009. Thirlwall J. held that in the circumstances the demand of 2005 had given the defendant ample time to enquire, and he was not entitled to any more in 2009. (In fact the claim failed on the basis that the defendant had a valid possessory lien, which amounted to a good defence to any possession claim). Thirlwall J. added at [295] that a bailee had a right to make enquiries similar to that of any other possessor, at least where he had actual notice that his bailor's title might not be watertight. In the same case, the defendant was subject to an injunction from an American court (admittedly unenforceable in England) preventing him from giving up the tapestry. At [306]–[312] his Lordship left it open whether a defendant in such a position was entitled to a reasonable opportunity to try to discharge a foreign court order.

NOTE 120. Add: Compare, however, *The Lehmann Timber* [2013] EWCA Civ 650 at [49] (complications arising out of attempt to separate out part of cargo).

(vii) *Conversion by wrongful denial of access*

17–31   **Conversion by denial of the benefit of goods.** Add: See too another aircraft case, *Blue Sky One Ltd v Blue Airways LLC* [2009] EWHC 3314 (Comm) (change of registration apparently accepted as amounting to conversion). In *London Trocadero Ltd v Family Leisure Holdings Ltd* [2012] EWCA Civ 1037 Davis L.J. regarded it as conversion for a landowner to refuse access to the lessor of equipment left there by a bankrupt lessee to take it away. At [36]–[40] the statement of the law in paras **17–31** and **17–32** of the present work was approved.

(b) *Subject-matter of conversion*

17–34   **General.** Add: In *Rugby Football Union v Viagogo Ltd* [2011] EWHC 764 (QB); [2011] N.P.C. 37 (upheld on other grounds: [2011] EWCA Civ 1585; [2012] F.S.R. 11) Tugendhat J. at [46] had not the slightest hesitation in rejecting the suggestion that there could be no conversion of things of negligible value (in this case the paper on which tickets of admission to sporting events were printed).

17–35   **Tangible and intangible property.** Add: See too S. Green, "Theft and conversion – tangibly different?" (2012) 128 L.Q.R. 564. However, even though intangible property cannot be converted, there is it would appear a cause of action at common law for its value, available against anyone obtaining it other than as a good faith purchaser without knowledge or notice of the claimant's title: see *Armstrong DLW GmbH v Winnington Networks Ltd* [2012] EWHC 10 (Ch); [2013] Ch. 156 (a case concerning EUAs, a form of EU-sponsored permit to pollute). It is not clear whether this can be regarded as a liability in tort, though in *Armstrong*, above, it was seemingly held to lie against a defendant who had disposed of the intangible concerned.

17–41   **Dead bodies.** NOTE 185. Add: Note too, for a sceptical look at whether property rights are appropriate in the case of body parts, J. Wall, "The legal status of body parts: a framework" (2011) 31 O.J.L.S. 783.

17–42   **Human tissue.** NOTE 200. Add: Australian authority is to similar effect, allowing representatives of a deceased person a claim to stored sperm. See *Bazley v Wesley Monash IVF Pty Ltd* [2010] QSC 118; [2011] 2 Qd R. 207; *Re Edwards* [2011] NSWSC 478; (2011) 4 A.S.T.L.R. 392. The former case was decided on the basis that the sperm was owned by the deceased when alive and so passed on death; the latter on the basis of a discretion vested in the court to accord rights to the representative. See generally L. Skene, "Property Interests in Human Bodily Material" (2012) 20 Med. L. Rev. 227.

(c) *Persons entitled to sue*

(i) *Generally*

17–44   **Claimant must have possession or immediate right to possession.** NOTE 205. Add: Similarly, a claimant cannot sue for conversion of goods which it is clear he has abandoned. See the Canadian decision in *Dean v Kotsopoulos* [2012]

ONCA 143 (restaurant fittings left on premises, though no abandonment found on the facts).

Right to possession where return illegal or contrary to public policy. Add: **17–47**
It is not impermissible, or contrary to the policy of ss.143–144 of the Powers of Criminal Courts (Sentencing) Act 2000, to bring an action in conversion in respect of property forfeited by a court from a criminal other than the owner, even though s.144 of the 2000 Act provides the true owner with a summary remedy. This is important because the remedy under s.144 excludes a claim by an owner who cannot show non-connivance in the offence, whereas the cause of action at common law does not. See *O'Leary International Ltd v Chief Constable of North Wales Police* [2012] EWHC 1516 (Admin); [2013] R.T.R. 14 (claim by foreign hauliers in respect of lorries forfeited for tachograph offences by those driving them).

NOTE 220. Add: That return would not be ordered where it would indirectly assist in or encourage a crime was confirmed by Thomas P. in *Chief Constable of Merseyside v Owens* [2012] EWHC 1515 (Admin) at [30] (a case actually on the Police (Property) Act 1897, but it was accepted that nothing turned on this). But in the same case the limitations of the defence were pointed out. Hence, police were not entitled to refuse to return a CCTV video taken by, and seized from, the victim of an arson attack merely because they reasonably thought he might use it to identify and take revenge on the arsonist. To do that they would have had to show that he intended to do so. Any contrary holding would, it was pointed out at [29], condone an unjustified power of executive confiscation with no statutory warrant.

(ii) *Title by mere possession*

The rights of the possessor. NOTE 223. Add: See, for another neat example,   **17–48**
R. (on the application of Atapattu) v Home Secretary [2011] EWHC 1388 (Admin) (claim by Sri Lankan visitor for unjustified detention of his passport: nothing to the point that passport technically the property of the Sri Lankan Government, provided claimant in possession when deprived).

(d) *Position of defendant*

(ii) *Conversion wrongful unless excused*

Add: In *The Lehmann Timber* [2013] EWCA Civ 650 at [49], Sir Bernard Rix   **17–71**
thought that practical difficulties of letting a claimant have his goods (here, problems of separating out 9 per cent of a cargo of steel coils) might be a defence to an action in conversion. *Sed quaere.*

NOTE 319. Add: *R. (on the application of Coleman) v Governor of Wayland Prison* [2009] EWHC 1005 (Admin) has now—perhaps predictably—been reversed as from February 28, 2013 by the Prisons (Property) Act 2013, which inserts a new s.42A into the Prison Act 1952 allowing destruction of contraband items.

(iii) *Defendant's ignorance of claimant's right generally no defence*

17–72   **Defendant's ignorance of claimant's right generally irrelevant.** Add: In the difficult case of *Robot Arenas Ltd v Waterfield* [2010] EWHC 115 (QB) buyers of a property found it full of what they reasonably saw as useless abandoned junk and disposed of the latter. It then turned out that the apparent junk was composed of film scenery of interest and arguable value. They were held not liable for conversion, on the basis that a person who destroyed something of which, having if necessary made enquiries, he reasonably believed himself to be the owner was not liable for conversion. With respect, and despite the tentative support of *Palmer on Bailment*, 3rd edn, at 6–020, this seems difficult to justify. It would draw an entirely anomalous distinction between conversion by destruction and conversion by alienation (where liability admittedly exists independently of fault); and however desirable it may be to limit the strict liability currently applying to convertors, the creation of yet further anomalies in the tort cannot be an acceptable solution.

NOTE 323. Add: Strict liability applies equally to use; but as Allsop P. pointed out in *Bunnings Group Ltd v CHEP Australia Ltd* [2011] NSWCA 342 at [125], the defendant may escape on the basis that there must be an intended "exercise of such dominion as is repugnant to the rights of the owner." If there is not—for example, a defendant is merely making a use of some commercial commodity such as pallets which would be justified whether or not they belonged to another— there is no conversion to start with.

(e) *Multiple claims: jus tertii, estoppel and double liability*

17–81   **Former position at common law.** In a recent illustration of the position at common law (and one which seems unaffected by the 1977 Act), Beatson J. decided in *Blue Sky One Ltd v Mahan Air* [2010] EWHC 631 (Comm) at [98]– [99] that a mortgagor of aircraft was entitled to full damages for deprivation by a third party without reference to the mortgagee's rights or any obligation he might be under to discharge the mortgage. Only if the action was against the mortgagee himself would credit have to be given for the mortgagee's interest.

3. Remedies for Conversion

(a) *Orders for delivery*

(i) *Judgment for specific delivery*

17–88   **Judgment for specific delivery and consequential damages.** Add: In *Blue Sky One Ltd v Blue Airways LLC* [2009] EWHC 3314 (Comm), Beatson J. accepted the existence of a category of goods that, while not absolutely unique, were "commercially unique" in the sense that obtaining substitutes would be difficult or the attendant delay would cause the claimant's business to be seriously interrupted. While he considered that the goods involved there (jumbo jets) could be commercially unique, he found that no undue prejudice would be suffered by the claimants (who held them largely with a view to leasing) and hence refused to order delivery (see [314]–[316]).

(b) *Damages*

(i) *General rule: value of the goods*

Damages for deprivation of goods. NOTE 420. Add: See too *Checkprice*   **17–92**
(UK) Ltd (in administration) v Revenue & Customs Commissioners [2010] EWHC
682 (Admin); [2010] S.T.C. 1153 at [56] per Sales J.

NOTE 421. Add: For a statement that departures from the value of the goods as
the measure of damages, while permissible, are rare, see *Blue Sky One Ltd v
Mahan Air* [2010] EWHC 631 (Comm) at [114] per Beatson J.

Presumption of value against wrongdoer? NOTE 456. Add: Similarly, see   **17–98**
the Canadian decision in *Bangle v Lafreniere* [2012] BCSC 256 at [39], where
Sewell J. in the British Columbia Supreme Court said that the "maximum value"
presumption applied "only in situations in which the wrongful conduct of the
defendant makes it impracticable for the plaintiff to value the loss."

Particular forms of property: title-deeds. Add: The suggestion in the text,   **17–104**
that damages for conversion of title-deeds today are not reckoned by the value of
the land, was accepted in *Chen v Gu* [2011] NSWSC 1622 at [141]–[154].

(ii) *Damages beyond value of goods: special damages*

Consequential damage if not too remote. NOTE 487. Add: For another   **17–107**
example, see *Aziz v Lim* [2012] EWHC 915 (QB) at [117] (diamonds wrongfully
sold, ending up in the hands of Swiss buyers: owner can claim cost of seeking out,
and attempting to recover possession of, diamonds in Geneva).

NOTE 493. Add: See too *Checkprice (UK) Ltd (in administration) v Revenue
& Customs Commissioners* [2010] EWHC 682 (Admin); [2010] S.T.C. 1153
(seizure of liquor: alleged lost profits from late return too remote).

NOTE 503. Add: The question whether use damages could be obtained against   **17–109**
a defendant who merely kept, rather than used, a chattel was left open by Allsop
P. in the New South Wales decision in *Bunnings Group Ltd v CHEP Australia Ltd*
[2011] NSWCA 342 at [175]–[179]. But his Honour (with whom Macfarlan J.A.
agreed) seems to have inclined to the view that use was not necessary, since he
categorised use damages as compensatory and not restitutionary. By contrast,
Giles J.A. in the minority preferred the view that such damages had a restitutionary basis.

(iii) *Nature of claimant's interest*

The unpaid seller in possession. Add: It is now clear that the decision in   **17–114**
Chinery v Viall (1860) 5 H. & N. 288 applies only where, by virtue of the conversion, the defendant loses the right to claim from the claimant (as the unpaid seller
did in that case). If that right is retained, the claimant for his part remains able to
claim in full from the convertor, even if the goods were obtained on credit from
the latter. See *Blue Sky One Ltd v Mahan Air* [2010] EWHC 631 (Comm) at [101]
ff. Aircraft were converted by a defendant who had in effect lent money to the
claimants to buy them. The claimants were held entitled to recover in full.

17–115   **The claimant with limited proprietary interest.** Add: The statement in the text, that a claimant with a limited interest such as a mortgagor can claim only to the extent of his interest, must now be qualified. It applies only where, as in cases such as *Brierly v Kendall* (1852) 17 Q.B. 937, the defendant is himself the mortgagee or someone who himself has an interest in the goods. Where the defendant is a third party with no interest the claimant recovers in full. See *Blue Sky One Ltd v Mahan Air* [2010] EWHC 631 (Comm), especially at [98]–[99], holding that a mortgagor of aircraft could recover in full from a third party converter without reference to the fact that its own interest was burdened with that of a mortgagor.

(v) *Successive conversions and satisfaction*

17–125   NOTE 556. Add: This may cause problems where a claimant sues A for tortiously disposing of his property, but is still negotiating with the ultimate acquirer B with a view to getting it back *in specie*. If A pays a damages award, the claimant's rights against B will ipso facto drop away. In *Aziz v Lim* [2012] EWHC 915 (QB), where there were proceedings against both A, who had wrongfully sold diamonds, and B, who was in possession of them in Switzerland, Hildyard J. avoided this problem by staying the assessment of damages payable by A until the conclusion of the Swiss proceedings against B. See at [117].

(vii) *Limitation of actions*

17–127   NOTE 563. Add: But it seems that the effect of s.3(2) is limited to the goods originally converted, and does not apply to new goods made or emanating from those goods. See the Australian decision in *Grant v YYH Holdings Pty Ltd* [2012] NSWCA 360, interpreting analogous New South Wales legislative provisions (where rare-breed ewes converted, six-year limitation extinguished title to those beasts, but not to their progeny born less than six years before action brought).

4. TRESPASS TO GOODS

(a) *The nature of trespass to goods*

17–128   **The nature of trespass to goods.** NOTE 567. Add: Similarly, in *Rugby Football Union v Viagogo Ltd* [2011] EWHC 764 (QB); [2011] N.P.C. 37 (upheld on other grounds, [2011] EWCA Civ 1585; [2012] F.S.R. 11), Tugendhat J. suggested at [10] that boarding a bus with neither a ticket nor the intent to buy one would be a trespass to goods.

NOTE 569. Add: See also *Fish & Fish Ltd v Sea Shepherd UK* [2013] EWCA Civ 544 (participation in the deliberate cutting of nets and fish cages).

(e) *Defences*

17–135   **Consent and self-help.** Add: On wheel-clamping, note s.54 of the Protection of Freedoms Act 2012 (in force from October 1, 2012), which makes it a criminal offence without lawful authority to immobilise a vehicle on private land with a view to preventing its removal by the owner. Whether this would affect civil liability is unclear: but the rather odd statement in s.54(2) that legally-binding consent by the owner is not a lawful excuse suggests that it does not, since otherwise the reference to legally-binding consent would be otiose. It is equally unclear whether the provision criminalises clamping on the basis, not of a notice, but of the common law right of distress damage feasant. The better view is that it does not. Although the section states expressly that consent by the owner is not to be a defence, it does require the clamping to have been done without lawful authority, and says nothing about other defences, which presumably remain applicable.

CHAPTER 18

DECEIT

		PARA.
□	1. Introduction.	18–01
	2. Requirements	18–05
	■ (a) Representation.	18–05
	(b) State of mind.	18–19
	■ (i) The belief of the defendant	18–19
	□ (ii) State of mind: vicarious liability	18–26
	(c) Representation intended to be acted on by the claimant.	18–30
	■ (d) Claimant must have been influenced by the misrepresentation	18–34
■	3. Damages	18–39
	4. Defences	18–49
■	5. Misrepresentation as to credit of third persons.	18–52
	6. Statutory liability for misstatements in a prospectus	18–54
	7. The action for fraud arising out of bribery	18–55

1. INTRODUCTION

Deceit and other liability for misrepresentation. NOTE 5. Add: See too **18–02** *Haringey LBC v Hines* [2010] EWCA Civ 1111; [2011] H.L.R. 6, especially at [39] (finding of fraud against tenant who exercised right to buy as a result of a misrepresentation overturned because allegation not put squarely to defendant).

Ambit of liability. Add: See too *Zurich Insurance Co Plc v Hayward* [2011] **18–03** EWCA Civ 641; [2011] C.P. Rep. 39, where the Court of Appeal refused to strike out a claim by an insurance company to recover a payout made to a claimant who was later alleged to have been deliberately malingering, despite the fact that the settlement had been embodied in a Tomlin order and was thus, to some extent, an order of the court.

2. REQUIREMENTS

(a) *Representation*

Misrepresentation required for liability. Add: However, see the view **18–05** expressed by Stadlen J. in *IG Index Plc v Colley* [2013] EWHC 478 (QB) at [746]–[763] that there may be liability for fraud without deceit, for example where fraudsters with the help of an insider are enabled to place false bets with a spread-betting company. *Sed quaere.*

NOTE 24. Add: Compare the Scots decision in *Frank Houlgate Investment Co Ltd v Biggart Baillie LLP* [2013] CSOH 80; [2013] P.N.L.R. 25 (solicitor unwittingly helping fraudster under duty to take steps to warn victim when fraud discovered, and otherwise will become accessory to the fraud). But this extended liability may depend on the peculiarities of Scots law.

18–06   **Misrepresentation and non-disclosure.** In *Wood v Balfour* [2011] NSWCA 382, a case of the sale of a house with hidden defects, a majority of the New South Wales Court of Appeal seems to have supported a departure from the established English position and the abandonment of any need for a positive representation: see Giles J.A. at [6] (with whom Meagher J.A. agreed). Macfarlan J.A. at [50] suggested that the act of marketing a house of itself could count as a representation that there were no defects of which the seller knew, which (one suspects) in practice comes to much the same thing. In the event no guilty knowledge was proved in the seller, so the point was, as matters turned out, moot.

18–07   **Half-truths.** Add: Where a person gives an apparently independent recommendation of a tradesman without disclosing a close relationship that makes the recommendation far from independent, this may amount to deceit: see *Sear v Kingfisher Builders (A firm) (No. 3)* [2013] EWHC 21 (TCC) at [6]–[7].
    NOTE 31. Add: Similarly, see *Mellor v Partridge* [2013] EWCA Civ 477 (reference to art dealer's "impeccable reputation" omitting to mention Getty Museum's allegation against him of passing off of non-genuine artworks).

18–08   **Active conduct or concealment.** Add: The question of when a representation might be implied was given a fairly expansive answer by Flaux J. in *Lindsay v O'Loughnane* [2010] EWHC 529 (QB); [2012] B.C.C. 153. The claimant had on a number of occasions successfully changed substantial sums of money into euros with X, a firm of foreign exchange dealers, on the basis of their standard terms, which included a term that his monies would be segregated until the Euros were provided. On a later occasion, however, X was in terminal difficulties and had begun using all new payments to satisfy old creditors. A sum of £565,000 sent for exchange by the claimant was not segregated but paid to other creditors of X, and the claimant in due course lost it when X collapsed. Flaux J. upheld a personal action in deceit against the controller of X, who had booked the order. He was prepared to hold that by so doing, the defendant had implicitly represented that the company was trading "properly and legitimately" (see [100]–[104], [119]); and that he also impliedly stated that he believed the terms and conditions requiring segregation would be observed (see [107]).

18–11   **Misrepresentation: promises and statements of intention.** NOTE 47. Add: See too *Al Khudairi v Abbey Brokers Ltd* [2010] EWHC 1486 (Ch); [2010] P.N.L.R. 32 (claimants' money deposited with company, misused and lost: statements by company controller as to how claimants' money would be handled held to amount to deceit on proof of lack of intent so to handle it, thus allowing personal claim).

18–14   Add: In *Raiffeisen Zentralbank Österreich AG v Royal Bank of Scotland Plc* [2010] EWHC 1392 (Comm); [2011] 1 Lloyd's Rep 123 at [86] Christopher Clarke J. made the obvious point that a representor "may qualify what might otherwise have been an outright statement of fact by saying that it is only a statement of belief, that it may not be accurate, that he has not verified its accuracy or completeness, or that it is not to be relied on." See too Hamblen J. in *Cassa di Risparmio della Repubblica di San Marino SpA v Barclays Bank Ltd* [2011] EWHC 484 (Comm); [2011] 1 C.L.C. 701 at [222]. But this will not, it is suggested, exonerate the representor if he actually knows the suggestion to be untrue, since the expression of an opinion of itself comports a belief that it is correct.

(b) *State of mind*

(i) *The belief of the defendant*

Motive irrelevant. NOTE 91. Add: Note too *Ludsin Overseas Ltd v Eco3*   **18–20**
Capital Ltd [2013] EWCA Civ 413 at [77]–[78] (Jackson L.J.).

(ii) *State of mind: vicarious liability*

Partners. Add: On the liabilities of partners, see too *Goldberg v Miltiadous*   **18–29**
[2010] EWHC 450 (QB) (accountancy firm whose business included giving investment advice: partners liable for fraud of partner who, apparently in course of partnership business, duped investor into investing in doubtful Cyprus real estate companies).

(d) *Claimant must have been influenced by the misrepresentation*

The claimant must have been influenced by the misrepresentation. Add: **18–34**
See *Mellor v Partridge* [2013] EWCA Civ 477 at [20], where the statement of the law in this paragraph was approved.

3. Damages

Timing. Add: Just as the fact that a claimant is "locked in" may cause damages   **18–44**
to be reckoned at a date later than the purchase of property, conversely in other situations this may lead to their being quantified at an earlier time. In *Butler-Creagh v Hersham* [2011] EWHC 2525 (QB) a purchaser was duped into buying an ex-conventicle in Oxfordshire for a great deal more than it was worth. Damages were computed as at the time of exchange of contracts in December 2008, not completion in April 2010 (by which time real estate values had appreciated noticeably, thus narrowing the difference between the sum paid and the value received). This was because it was at the former time that the claimant had become irrevocably committed.

Causation. NOTE 191. Add: See *Yam Seng Pte Ltd v International Trade*   **18–45**
Corporation Ltd [2013] EWHC 111 (QB); [2013] 1 All E.R. (Comm) 1321 at [209]–[217], where Leggatt J., citing this footnote with approval, doubted whether it was in fact the case that would-be losses suffered by the claimant did fall to be disregarded, and suggested that the authorities said to support it could be explained on other grounds.

18–46 **Consequential losses.** NOTE 193. Add: See too *Butler-Creagh v Hersham* [2011] EWHC 2525 (QB) (claimant duped into buying property for more than value: claim for additional expenditure such as stamp duty and maintenance costs); *Mellor v Partridge* [2013] EWCA Civ 477 at [45] (due diligence efforts by buyer duped into buying business to find the truth).

18–47 **Remoteness.** NOTE 204. Add: See also *Sear v Kingfisher Builders (A firm) (No. 3)* [2013] EWHC 21 (TCC) at [32]–[33] (Ramsey J).

5. MISREPRESENTATION AS TO CREDIT OF THIRD PERSON

18–53 Add: In the important decision in *Roder UK Ltd v West* [2011] EWCA Civ 1126; [2012] Q.B. 752, the Court of Appeal significantly limited the ambit of the 1828 Act. Their Lordships construed the phrase "to the intent or purpose that such other person may obtain credit, money or goods" as meaning "to the intent that such other person may obtain money or goods upon credit." Thus where directors of a company fraudulently (but orally) persuaded a creditor to hold off with an assurance that payment would be made from the future sale of certain company assets, it was held that the Act did not afford a defence. The company had received credit, in the form of the non-pursuit of a debt, as a result of the misrepresentation; but it had obtained neither money nor goods, and as a result the Act did not apply.

On signature for the purpose of the 1828 Act, see too *Lindsay v O'Loughnane* [2010] EWHC 529 (QB); [2012] B.C.C. 153 at [95], where Flaux J. gave a useful guide to the status of emails. "In a modern context," he said, "the section will clearly be satisfied if the representation is contained in an email, provided that the email includes a written indication of who is sending the email. It seems that it is not enough that the email comes from a person's email address without his having 'signed' it in the sense of either including an electronic signature or concluding words such as 'regards' accompanied by the typed name of the sender of the email . . .".

NOTE 234. Add: But note *Lindsay v O'Loughnane* [2010] EWHC 529 (QB); [2012] B.C.C. 153, where a fraudulent statement by the controller of a company in difficulties that certain funds in fact misused had been mislaid through its bankers' incompetence was held not covered by the section: the statement went to the managerial competence of the company, not to its creditworthiness. No doubt this holding, like that in *Roder UK Ltd v West* above, stems from a wish to confine s.6—which ex hypothesi is apt to provide a technical shield to undeserving fraudsters—as narrowly as possible.

CHAPTER 19

TRESPASS TO LAND AND DISPOSSESION

			PARA.
□	1.	The nature of trespass...	19–01
■	2.	Who may sue for trespass.......................................	19–10
	3.	Trespass by relation	19–26
	4.	Justification of trespass..	19–29
		■ (a) Licence to enter by law...................................	19–30
		■ (b) Justification under right of way and easement	19–37
		(c) Justification under customary rights...........................	19–43
		□ (d) Justification by licence	19–45
		(e) Justification by necessity	19–56
		■ (f) Police powers of entry	19–57
	5.	Measure of damages...	19–63
		■ (a) General	19–63
		■ (b) Exemplary damages	19–69
■	6.	Action for the recovery of land..................................	19–71
	7.	Statutes of limitation..	19–76
	8.	Waste..	19–92

1. THE NATURE OF TRESPASS

Examples of trespass. In the sentence following Note 6 in the text, replace the words "driving a nail into" with the words: "fixing air conditioning equipment onto".
    NOTE 7. Replace the citations in this Note with: *Eaton Mansions (Westminster) Ltd v Stinger Compania de Inversion SA* [2011] EWCA Civ 607; [2011] H.L.R. 42.

19–01

Intention or negligence in the defendant. After the first sentence insert the following: Put otherwise, "a negligent incursion on to and damage of a claimant's land or property can in law be a trespass".[26a]
    NOTE 26a. *Network Rail Infrastructure Ltd v Conarken Group Ltd* [2010] EWHC 1852 (TCC); [2010] B.L.R. 601 (affirmed in relation to the negligence issue also raised: [2011] EWCA Civ 644; [2011] B.L.R. 462).

19–06

2. WHO MAY SUE FOR TRESPASS

Concurrent possession. Replace the first sentence in the paragraph with: For the purposes of the tort of trespass to land, and for the purposes of possession, land, and its subsoil and superstructures may be divided in horizontal layers, as with apartment flats.[45a]
    NOTE 45a. *Ramroop v Ishmael* [2010] UKPC 14.

19–11

19–13   **Evidence of possession.** NOTE 64. Remove the reference to the first instance decision in the *Land Registry* case and leave only the reference to the Court of Appeal decision.

Immediately after Note 68 in the text insert the following: What is also of significance in this context is the facility within the Land Registration Act 2002[68a] whereby a squatter may, after 10 years adverse possession, apply to be registered as the legal proprietor of the land in question.[68b] That said, if the squatter only secures such registration by virtue of a fraudulent application, or an application based on an innocent but erroneous claim about having satisfied the adverse possession requirements, then that registration is liable to rectification so that the register is restored to its former state once again recording the original proprietor's title.[68c]

NOTE 68a. Sch.6 para.1(1).

NOTE 68b. Note that it is for the Land Registry, not the County Court, to decide in the first instance whether adverse possession has been acquired: *Swan Housing Association Ltd v Gill* [2012] EWHC 3129 (QB); [2013] 1 W.L.R. 1253 at [15] per Eady J.

NOTE 68c. *Baxter v Mannion* [2011] EWCA Civ 120; [2011] 1 W.L.R. 1594. As to the power more broadly to rectify errors on the register, see Land Registration Act 2002 Sch.4.

19–15   **De facto possession.** NOTE 80. Add: For these purposes, there is no fixed notion of an appropriate degree of control. Each case needs to be adjudged "bearing in mind the nature of the land": *Greenmanor Ltd v Laurence Pilford* [2012] EWCA Civ 756 at [27] per Etherton L.J; cf. *Chambers v Havering LBC* [2011] EWCA Civ 1576; [2012] 1 P. & C.R. 17.

19–18   **Self-help by rightful owner.** In the fifth sentence replace the words "and for this purpose the law sanctions a resort to force" with the following: but it is unlikely that the landowner may use force to this end.[93a]

Also, add to the end of the paragraph the following: One matter that requires clarification is whether art.8 of the European Convention on Human Rights has any bearing on applications by *private landowners* for possession orders. The courts that issue such orders are public authorities for the purposes of the Convention. Equally, squatters' living conditions, and therefore their private lives, will inevitably be affected by the grant of a possession order. In *Malik v Fassenfelt*,[94a] it was simply assumed on appeal that the first instance judge had been right to decide that art.8 was relevant. Accordingly, Lord Toulson, in the majority, was content to note that "I do not think that it would be right in these circumstances to decide whether the judge was correct about the availability of article 8 as a potential defence to the claim [for a possession order]".[94b] Lloyd L.J. said likewise, "the point was not taken before us, we had no submissions on it, and it does not seem to me that we ought to enter upon it so as to venture a view as to whether the judge was right or wrong".[94c]

NOTE 93a. In *Malik v Fassenfelt* [2013] EWCA Civ 798; [2013] 28 E.G. 84 (CS) at [25] Sir Alan Ward noted, obiter, that "the landowner has the remedy of self-help but the Criminal Law Act 1977 has prevented the use of force to evict an occupier". As such, "[h]is opportunity to obtain immediate relief by resorting to self-help may be curtailed if the squatters refuse to leave without a fight."

NOTE 94a. [2013] EWCA Civ 798; [2013] 28 E.G. 84 (CS).

NOTE 94b. [2013] EWCA Civ 798; [2013] 28 E.G. 84 (CS) at [42].

NOTE 94c. [2013] EWCA Civ 798; [2013] 28 E.G. 84 (CS) at [51]. Sir Alan Ward, in the minority, supplied a fully reasoned but nonetheless obiter account of why he thought the first instance judge had been right to say that art.8 was a relevant factor in such cases.

4. JUSTIFICATION OF TRESPASS

(a) *Licence to enter by law*

Modern statutes. In NOTE 152, add: Followed in *Manchester Ship Canal Co*   **19–31** *Ltd v United Utilities Water Plc* [2013] EWCA Civ 40; [2013] 2 All E.R. 642.

Also, at end of the paragraph add: By contrast, there is no abuse of statutory power where a local authority enters land under s.178 of the Town and Country Planning Act 1990 in order to ensure compliance with an enforcement notice issued in connection with an unauthorised use of land.[153a]

NOTE 153a. *Challinor v Staffordshire CC* [2011] EWCA Civ 90.

(b) *Justification under right of way and easement*

Private way. NOTE 180. Add: See further *London Tara Hotel Ltd v Kensington*   **19–38** *Close Hotel Ltd* [2011] EWCA Civ 1356; [2012] 2 All E.R. 554.

Water. NOTE 195. Add: The same rules apply to tidal stretches of canals: see   **19–41** *Moore v British Waterways Board* [2013] EWCA Civ 73; [2013] 3 W.L.R. 43.

(d) *Justification by licence*

Extent and construction of licence. Replace the first sentence of the para-   **19–46** graph with the following: It is important to appreciate that the defendant's presence on the claimant's land, or his encroachment onto his neighbour's buildings or fixtures, is only justified to the extent granted by the licence.[224a]

NOTE 224a. See, e.g. *Seeff v Ho* [2011] EWCA Civ 186.

NOTE 227. Add to the end of the Note: (revsd on quantum of damages payable: [2010] EWCA Civ 952).

(f) *Police powers of entry*

Search warrants. After Note 310 in the text add the following: Moreover, it   **19–61** seems arguable that a warrant procured out of malice will not be valid.[310a] Nor will a search be lawful if the copy of the warrant the officer concerned is obliged to give to the occupier[310b] fails to specify all those particulars specified by s.15(6) of the 1984 Act. Accordingly, in one case in which the copies did not on their face set out the details of the premises to be searched, the entry was judged to be unlawful.[310c]

NOTE 310a. See *Fitzpatrick v Commissioner of Police of the Metropolis* [2012] EWHC 12 (Admin); [2012] Lloyd's Rep. F.C. 361 at [144], per Globe J.

NOTE 310b. Police and Criminal Evidence Act 1984, s.16(5).

NOTE 310c. R. *(on the application of Bhatti) v Croydon Magistrates' Court* [2010] EWHC 522 (Admin); [2011] 1 W.L.R. 948. The fact that the relevant addresses were in fact handwritten onto an accompanying document stated by the defendant to be a "schedule" to the warrant was of no avail. It was the copy of the warrant itself which the statute required to contain this information.

19–62   NOTE 312. At the start of the Note insert the following: If there is a dispute about whether there has been compliance with these requirements, the onus is on the police officer to show on the balance of probabilities that he identified himself and that he produced the warrant: *Alleyne v Commissioner of Police of the Metropolis* [2012] EWHC 3955 (QB) at [96].

NOTE 313. Replace the first sentence as follows: Accordingly, searches conducted under warrants that are drawn too widely—i.e. those that do not stipulate precisely the matters specified in s.15(6)—are unlawful: see *Van der Pijl v Kingston Crown Court* [2012] EWHC 3745; [2013] Lloyd's Rep. F.C. 287. The same is true of searches under warrant conducted by tax inspectors: *R. (on the application of Anand) v Revenue and Customs Commissioners* [2012] EWHC 2989 (Admin); [2013] C.P. Rep. 2.

5. MEASURE OF DAMAGES

(a) *General*

19–63   Replace the sentence beginning, "For example, in one first instance case", as follows: According to a string of recent cases, one method of quantifying the damages is by reference to a hypothetical negotiation between C and D. In such cases, the damages are fixed in accordance with the price D would have had to pay to do the acts complained of had he negotiated with C for permission to do them.

NOTE 316. Replace the text in this NOTE *after* the reference to the *Elmbridge* case as follows: See also, *Enfield LBC v Outdoor Plus Ltd* [2012] EWCA Civ 608; [2012] C.P. Rep. 35; *Stadium Capital Holdings (No.2) Ltd v St Marylebone Property Co Plc* [2011] EWHC 2856 (Ch); [2012] 4 E.G. 108; *Eaton Mansions (Westminster) Ltd v Stinger Compania de Inversion SA* [2012] EWHC 3354 (Ch); [2012] 49 E.G. 66 (C.S.).

After Note 316 in the text, add: Just this approach was taken by the Supreme Court in *Bocardo SA v Star Energy UK Onshore Ltd*.[316a] There, the defendants had drilled (without permission) through the sub-strata of the claimant's land in the context of their oil extraction operations. They were again required to pay damages based on the hypothetical contract that the defendants would have negotiated with the claimant. But in assessing this amount, account had to be taken of the background statutory scheme which, in the case of oil extraction, meant the defendants were operating according to a government licence. For this reason it had to be assumed that the claimant's compensation would have been negotiated "on the usual basis *in compulsory acquisition cases*".[316b]

NOTE 316a. [2010] UKSC 35; [2011] 1 A.C. 80.

NOTE 316b. [2010] UKSC 35; [2011] 1 A.C. 80 at [91] per Lord Brown (emphasis added).

(i) Trespass productive of benefit to the defendant without damage to the claimant. At the end of the paragraph add: Finally, where the trespass takes the form of an incursion into the airspace above the claimant's land by an advertising hoarding fixed to a structure on the defendant's land, the measure of damages is a complicated matter. In one case, the first instance judge suggested that the damages should equate to the totality of the earnings generated by adverts placed on the hoarding. But on appeal, the Court of Appeal held that the first instance judge had erred in making such a simplistic calculation.[322a] Various plausible factors and alternative bases of calculation were mooted by their Lordships. These included the expenses incurred by the defendant, the charging of a reasonable fee for the use of the airspace, and restitution of *part* of the profits generated by the adverts (bearing in mind the fact that only *part* of the hoarding was in the claimant's airspace). Ultimately, the Court of Appeal merely set aside the decision on damages reached by the first instance judge and the matter of quantum was remitted for determination at a later date.   **19–64**

NOTE 322a. *Stadium Capital Holdings v St Marylebone Properties Co Plc* [2010] EWCA Civ 952.

(b) *Exemplary and aggravated damages*

After Note 338 insert the following: Whichever way the defendant seeks to profit, it is clear that his behaviour must be "sufficiently outrageous to merit punishment".[338a]   **19–69**

NOTE 338a. *Eaton Mansions (Westminster) Ltd v Stinger Compania de Inversion SA* [2012] EWHC 3354 (Ch); [2012] 49 E.G. 66 (C.S.) at [76] per Bartley Jones Q.C.

Also, in the sentence that ends with Note 339, insert after the word "dignity" the following footnote:

NOTE 338b. Note, however, that such damages are not available where the claimant is a corporation on the basis that inanimate corporations are incapable of suffering feelings of injured pride: ibid., at [74] per Bartley Jones Q.C.

6. ACTION FOR THE RECOVERY OF LAND

Recovery of land. After Note 344 insert the following: However, an application by A to have the Land Register corrected so as to record A having sole title (instead of, erroneously, both A and B having title) will "not be an action for the recovery of land within the meaning of s.15 of the [Limitation Act 1980]".[344a]   **19–70**

NOTE 344a. *Parshall v Bryans* [2013] EWCA Civ 240; [2013] 3 All E.R. 224 at [59] per David Donaldson Q.C.

After the words "Proof that the claimant was in possession before the defendant", insert the following Note.

NOTE 345a. Add: For these purposes, a local authority is deemed to have possession of a public highway so that a possession order can be obtained against protestors who have taken possession of the highway and have thereby caused a public nuisance; for in such circumstances, the protestors will have exceeded their limited right to protest under the European Convention on Human Rights: *City of London Corp v Samede* [2012] EWHC 34 (QB); (2012) 109(5) L.S.G. 21.

19–72   **Estoppel between landlord and tenant.** At the end of the paragraph add: Also, as a procedural matter, it is noteworthy that where a lessee seeks to eject a freeholder who has granted the lease but refuses to vacate the premises, by virtue of an order for possession, the lessee does so as against a trespasser and, in accordance with RSC Ord.113 r.7, does not require the court's permission to issue the writ of possession.[360a]

NOTE 360a. *Pritchard v Teitelbaum* [2011] EWHC 1063 (Ch); [2011] N.P.C. 43.

19–74   Immediately after para.**19–74**, insert a new para.**19–74A**:

19–74A   Sometimes, however, the property in question may have been permanently appropriated by the defendant. Such was the case in *Ramzan v Brookwide Ltd*.[376a] There, a first floor store room belonging to property X (an Indian restaurant) was actually located above property Y. Initially, while property X was owned by the claimant's father, the store room could only be accessed via property X. But, while still under the father's ownership, certain construction work was later done whereby the store room had been permanently subsumed within Y and the store room was now only accessible via that property. This permanent appropriation of the store room meant that the upper floor of property X could no longer be used as a function room since access to a fire escape had been lost. Shortly thereafter, the claimant acquired ownership of property X. The question that arose on these complex facts was what measure of damages the claimant would be entitled to. The Court of Appeal held the claimant's "only claim would be that the trespass had prevented him from re-establishing the earlier use of the first floor as a function room" and since "[t]hat would take some time [estimated to be about six months] . . . some deduction should be made for this so that the profits are calculated from 23 November 2001 [being six months later than the date on which the claimant acquired the property]".[376b] On top of this, the Court of Appeal also made clear that no claim for mesne profits (based on the notional letting value of the store room) would lie since there was never any prospect of *both* using the store room in conjunction with the restaurant (as a store room and fire escape) *and* letting it out to some or third party. Thus, the claimant had to make an election between the two heads of loss as they were alternative not cumulative claims; and this the claimant had done.[376c] Finally, it was noted that the misappropriation of the store room had a continuing effect on the life of the claimant which justified an award of exemplary damages.[376d]

NOTE 376a. [2011] EWCA Civ 985; [2012] 1 All E.R. 903.

NOTE 376b. [2011] EWCA Civ 985; [2012] 1 All E.R. 903 at [41] per Arden L.J

NOTE 376c. [2011] EWCA Civ 985; [2012] 1 All E.R. 903 at [67] per Arden L.J

NOTE 376d. [2011] EWCA Civ 985; [2012] 1 All E.R. 903 at [80] per Arden L.J.

7. STATUTES OF LIMITATION

Adverse possession and licensed possession. In the first sentence, after the **19–75** words "...fails to challenge a squatter" insert the following: (or other adverse possessor)[377a].

NOTE 377a. It is possible to enter into adverse possession without being a squatter. For example, one might acquire title to an unregistered stretch of a tidal river bed: see *Port of London Authority v Ashmore* [2010] EWCA Civ 30; [2010] 1 All E.R. 1139 (acknowledged to be correct in *Moore v British Waterways Board* [2013] EWCA Civ 73; [2013] 3 W.L.R. 43 at [57] per Lewison L.J.).

After the first sentence insert the following: Also, in order to interrupt the adverse possession, the paper title owner must, in a meaningful way, bring the adverse possessor's possession to an end.[377b]

NOTE 377b. *Zarb v Parry* [2011] EWCA Civ 1306; [2012] 1 W.L.R. 1240.

After the second sentence in the paragraph insert: However, where there is no evidence as to who is the paper title owner of land, the Land Registry will be entitled to register the applicant squatter's possessory, not absolute, title based on his or her adverse possession.[377c]

NOTE 377c. *R. (on the application of Truong Dia Diep) v Land Registry* [2010] EWHC 3315 (Admin).

In Note 383, add the following: However, where there has been a mistaken registration of both A and B as the registered owners of land, it is impossible for either party to enter into adverse possession vis-à-vis the other since anyone with registered title cannot possibly be in adverse possession relative to another. Adverse possession as between A and B only becomes possible after the mistake in the Register has been rectified and the disputed land is removed from A or B's title: see *Parshall v Bryans* [2013] EWCA Civ 240; [2013] 3 All E.R. 224.

At the end of the paragraph add the following: Since then, it has been further clarified that in order to satisfy the statutory requirement of having reasonable belief that the disputed land was actually owned by the person in adverse possession,[383a] such belief is to be judged according to what the person in adverse possession believed *personally* rather than what it was (or would have been) reasonable for the solicitors acting on his behalf to believe.[383b] So far as factual possession is concerned, the person claiming adverse possession will satisfy this requirement if he is able to provide evidence of his user of the land.[338c]

NOTE 383a. Land Registration Act 2002 Sch.6 para.5(4)(c).

NOTE 383b. *IAM Group Plc v Chowdrey* [2012] EWCA Civ 505; [2012] 2 P. & C.R. 13 at [27] per Etherington L.J.

NOTE 383c. *Akhtar v Brewster* [2012] EWHC 3521 (Ch).

CHAPTER 20

NUISANCE AND *RYLANDS V FLETCHER*

			PARA.
1.	The nature of nuisance		20–01
□	(a)	Role of nuisance	20–01
	(b)	Scope of private nuisance	20–06
	□ *(i)	Nuisance by encroachment or damage	20–07
	■ (ii)	Nuisance by interference with enjoyment	20–09
	(iii)	Nuisance by keeping animals	20–18
	(iv)	Natural nuisances	20–20
	■ (v)	Wrong to occupiers	20–24
	■ (vi)	Necessity for damage	20–26
2.	Nuisance and the standard of duty		20–31
	(a)	The problem	20–31
	(b)	Foreseeability and fault	20–35
	(c)	Nature of defendant's conduct	20–39
3.	The rule in *Rylands v Fletcher*		20–44
*	(a)	Status of *Rylands rule*	20–44
■	(b)	Activities subject to the *Rylands* rule	20–48
	(c)	Scope of liability	20–56
	(i)	Parties	20–56
	(ii)	Types of damage	20–58
	(iii)	Remoteness	20–60
	(iv)	Escape	20–61
	(v)	Exceptions to the rule of strict liability	20–62
□ 4.	Who can sue for nuisance?		20–63
5.	Who can be sued for nuisance?		20–70
□	(a)	Wrongdoer	20–70
■ *(b)	Occupier		20–75
	(c)	Landlord and tenant	20–78
6.	Defences to an action for nuisance		20–85
□	(a)	Prescriptive right to commit nuisance	20–85
■	(b)	Authorisation by statute	20–87
	(c)	Act of God	20–93
□	(d)	Act of a trespasser	20–94
	(e)	Act of a third party as a defence to the rule	20–96
		in *Rylands v Fletcher*	
	(f)	Ignorance of the nuisance	20–99
	(g)	Contributory negligence	20–102
	(h)	Consent of claimant as a defence to *Rylands v Fletcher*	20–104
	(i)	Necessity as a defence to *Rylands v Fletcher*	20–105
■	(j)	Ineffectual defences	20–106
7.	Particular types of nuisance		20–113
	(a)	Nuisance to water rights	20–113
	(i)	Taking water	20–114
	(ii)	Interference with flow	20–116
	□ *(iii)	Pollution	20–118
	(iv)	Underground and artificial water flow	20–120
	(b)	Liability in respect of damage caused by escaping water	20–124
	(i)	Common law	20–124
	(ii)	Statutory undertakers	20–132
	■*(iii)	Sewers and drains	20–133

- ■ (iv) Storage and piping 20–135
- (c) Withdrawal of support 20–139
- ■ (d) Nuisance to light 20–147
- (e) Fire 20–155
  - ■ (i) Common law 20–155
  - ■ *(ii) Statutory exemption for fires accidentally beginning . 20–156
  - ■ (iii) Responsibility for fire 20–163
  - (iv) Claimants 20–166
- (f) Gas 20–168
- (g) Electricity 20–173
- (h) Explosives 20–174
- (i) Poisonous waste 20–176
- (j) Nuclear installations 20–177
- 8. Obstruction of the highway 20–180
  - (a) Right of access 20–180
  - (b) Public nuisance by obstruction of highway 20–181
    - □ (i) Special damage 20–181
    - (ii) Obstruction 20–185
  - □ (c) Non-repair of highway 20–191

1. THE NATURE OF NUISANCE

(a) *Role of nuisance*

20–03   **Public nuisance.** In *DPP v Fearon* [2010] EWHC 340 (Admin); [2010] 2 Cr. App. R. 22 a divisional court of the Queen's Bench division emphasised "the importance of establishing the *public* nature of public nuisance" (see [2010] EWHC 340 at [8] per Elias L.J., italics supplied). The court accordingly held that a single attempt by a man to solicit a woman for sex could not constitute a public nuisance. The case also highlighted the importance of not allowing the open-ended concept of public nuisance to circumvent specific limitations on the scope of the statutory criminal law (the Sexual Offences Act 1985 requires such conduct to be "persistent" for the imposition of liability).

(b) *Scope of private nuisance*

(i) *Nuisance by encroachment or damage*

20–08   The Ontario Court of Appeal in *Smith v Inco Ltd* [2011] ONCA 628; (2011) 107 O.R. (3d) 321 held that a reduction in property values unaccompanied by actual physical damage, but caused by unjustified fears by the public about the possible health consequences of emissions from the defendants' refinery, did not constitute an actionable nuisance.

(ii) *Nuisance by interference with enjoyment*

20–10   **Question of degree.** In *Barr v Biffa Waste Services* [2012] EWCA Civ 312; [2013] Q.B. 455 the claimants contended that odours emanating from the defendant's waste-tipping site constituted a common law nuisance. The Court of Appeal reversed the court below (see [2011] EWHC 1003), which had found for the defendants. Carnwath L.J. observed that the case was "governed by conventional principles of the law of nuisance, which are well-settled" (see [2012] EWCA Civ at [36]). His Lordship also referred to this paragraph in the twentieth edition of this work when he continued: "There is no absolute standard; it is a question of degree whether the interference is sufficiently serious to constitute a nuisance. That is to be decided by reference to all the circumstances of the case". The Court of Appeal disapproved the approach of the trial judge who had considered that the odours could not constitute a nuisance unless they crossed a "threshold", of his imposition, which involved persistence on average of more than one day per week per year. The Court of Appeal considered that this approach was unsupported by authority, and that by "adopting such a threshold, the judge deprived at least some of the claimants of their right to have their individual cases assessed on their merits" (see [2012] EWCA Civ 312 at [46]).

NOTE 55. Add: See also *Hirose Electrical UK Ltd v Peak Ingredients Ltd* [2011] EWCA Civ 987; [2011] Env. L.R. 34.

Character of neighbourhood. In *Thomas v Merthyr Tydfil Car Auction Ltd* **20–13** [2013] EWCA Civ 815 claimants who lived near the defendants' business were able to recover damages for nuisance by noise notwithstanding that they lived in an area where "there were business uses and busy roads nearby".

Relevance of planning permission. This paragraph now needs to be read in the **20–14** light of the decision of the Court of Appeal in *RDC Promotions v Lawrence* [2012] EWCA Civ 26; [2012] 1 W.L.R. 2127. In this case the claimants contended that noise from a motor-racing stadium constituted a nuisance. The Court of Appeal, reversing the trial judge, held that the claim would fail. Jackson L.J. reviewed the authorities on planning permission changing the nature of a locality for the purposes of nuisance, and held that the permission granted for the stadium, which had been in existence for many years, had had the effect of changing the nature of the formerly rural locality in the instant case, thus enabling the defendants to succeed. In particular, Jackson L.J. referred with approval to the decision of the High Court in *Gillingham BC v Medway (Chatham) Dock Co Ltd* [1993] Q.B. 343, which has sometimes been doubted, saying that he agreed "both with the decision and with the reasoning on which it [was] based" (see *RDC Promotions v Lawrence* [2012] EWCA Civ at [58]). His Lordship went on to summarise the law as follows (at [65]):

"i)   A planning authority by the grant of planning permission cannot authorise the commission of a nuisance

ii)   Nevertheless the grant of planning permission followed by the implementation of such permission may change the character of a locality

iii) It is a question of fact in every case whether the grant of planning permission followed by steps to implement such permission do have the effect of changing the character of the locality.

iv) If the character of a locality is changed as a consequence of planning permission having been granted and implemented, then:

a)   the question whether particular activities in that locality constitute a nuisance must be decided against the background of its changed character;

b)   one consequence may be that otherwise offensive activities in that locality cease to constitute a nuisance."

It is to be noted that Jackson L.J., with whom Lewison and Mummery L.JJ. agreed, did not suggest that any of the cases in which the *Gillingham* decision has been distinguished were wrongly decided. Nevertheless, his emphasis upon the (albeit well-established) proposition that change of locality by planning permission is "a question of fact in every case" could be significant: see the obiter comment upon Jackson L.J.'s judgment by Carnwath L.J. in the contemporaneous case of *Barr v Biffa Waste Services* [2012] EWCA Civ 312; [2013] Q.B. 455 at [85]. If the approach in *RDC Promotions v Lawrence* is followed, it is therefore possible that the courts will be rather more prepared than before to find in favour of defendants on the ground that planning permission has changed the nature of the locality. (It should be noted that on July 26, 2012 the Supreme Court gave leave to appeal in the *RDC Promotions* case.)

(v)　*Wrong to occupiers*

20–24　　**Nuisance primarily a wrong to occupiers of land.** NOTE 123. Add: See also *Tinseltime Ltd v Roberts* [2011] EWHC 1199 (TCC); [2011] B.L.R. 515 (successful claim by licensee entitled to exclusive possession).

20–25　　**Continuing nuisances.** Add: The nature of the duty for a continuing nuisance caused by encroaching tree roots is necessarily highly fact-specific. The reasonableness of the defendants' action or inaction will depend, at least in part, upon the extent of the parties' knowledge of the degree of risk which existed at any particular time; a question which may itself be difficult to resolve. In determining the differing degrees of the parties' responsibility in *Berent v Family Mosaic Housing Association* [2011] EWHC 1353 (TCC) Judge Wilcox observed, at [101], that: "An attempt by the Arboriculturist Association to develop a computerised model capable of assessing the future risk of subsequent damage to buildings was abandoned because it was demonstrated as being impossible to predict. The study involved eminent mathematicians, computer experts and arboriculturists". The detailed findings of Judge Wilcox in this case were subsequently confirmed by the Court of Appeal (see [2012] EWCA Civ 961; [2012] B.L.R. 488) without affecting this observation.

(vi)　*Necessity for damage*

20–29　　**Intangible loss.** At the trial of the action in *Dobson v Thames Water Utilities* [2011] EWHC 3253 (TCC); (2011) 140 Con. L.R. 135 Ramsey J. held that liability to individual family members had been established under art.8 of the European Convention for the Protection of Human Rights but that, in the circumstances, including the fact that damages for nuisance had been awarded to the property owners, awards of damages to the individual family members were not necessary to achieve "just satisfaction", and so no damages were awarded for breach of the Convention.

NOTE 149. Add: Although the multiplicand will therefore usually be much more modest, the multiplicand/multiplier *method* of assessing general damages for personal injury can nevertheless be conveniently deployed in nuisance cases where there was a loss of amenity (see *Anslow v Norton Aluminium Ltd* [2012] EWHC 2610 at [474]).

20–30　　**Source of the interference.** In *Dwr Cymru Cyfyngedig (Welsh Water) v Barratt Homes Ltd* [2013] EWCA Civ 233; (2013) 147 Con. L.R. 1 Lloyd-Jones L.J.

observed, obiter, (at [57]) that "nuisance does not require a use by the defendant of *its* land" (original emphasis).

NOTE 153. Add: See also *Olympic Delivery Authority v Persons Unknown* [2012] EWHC 1012 (Ch).

3. THE RULE IN *RYLANDS V FLETCHER*

(b) *Activities subject to the Rylands rule*

Natural user of land The proposition that mining is a natural user of land which cannot give rise to liability under the rule in *Rylands v Fletcher* was applied in *Willis v Derwentside DC* [2013] EWHC 738 (see per Briggs J. at [45]–[46] referring to this paragraph). **20–52**

Different approach after *Cambridge Water.* Add: In *Smith v Inco Ltd* [2011] ONCA 628; (2011) 107 O.R. (3d) 321 the Ontario Court of Appeal held that a nickel refinery, which had emitted nickel particles for many years, did *not* constitute a non-natural use of land for the purposes of the rule in *Rylands v Fletcher*. **20–54**

4. WHO CAN SUE FOR NUISANCE?

Occupiers and residents. In *Austin v Mayor and Burgesses of the London Borough of Southwark* [2010] UKSC 28; [2011] 1 A.C. 355; [2010] 4 All E.R. 16 Lady Hale, with the agreement of other members of the court, carried out a detailed review of the anomalous status of "tolerated trespasser" (see [2010] UKSC at [44]–[56]). This status enabled a tenant whose tenancy had been terminated by a possession order to sue the landlord for nuisance, if the order had been suspended. Her Ladyship pointed out that the effect of detailed modifications to the previous legislation, contained in Sch.11 of the Housing and Regeneration Act 2008, is that the peculiar circumstances which gave rise to the status will not arise in the future; and existing "tolerated trespassers" have been given "a new tenancy which is in most respects the same as the tenancy they would otherwise still have had" (per Lady Hale at [55]. One possible remaining situation which could still have given rise to difficulty, where the "tolerated trespasser" died pending the final outcome of the proceedings, was resolved by the actual decision of the Supreme Court itself in the instant case. As far as the law of nuisance is concerned, the effect would appear to be that while the confused terminology of "tolerated trespasser" will disappear the claimants who would formerly have needed to invoke that status will still be able to sue in nuisance but on a more regular basis. **20–63**

NOTE 304. Add: For subsequent proceedings see *Dobson v Thames Water Utilities* [2011] EWHC 3253 (TCC); (2011) 140 Con. L.R. 135. (See also para.**20–29** of this Supplement).

NOTE 305. Add: *Tinseltime Ltd v Roberts* [2011] EWHC 1199 (TCC); [2011] B.L.R. 515.

20–65   **Reversioner.** In *John Smith & Co (Edinburgh) Ltd v Hill* [2010] EWHC 1016; [2010] 2 B.C.L.C. 556 the High Court examined the principles governing actions for nuisance brought by reversioners. Although the case involved unsuccessful proceedings for summary judgment, so that no final conclusion was reached, Briggs J. held that it was arguable that the orthodox view of the scope of the reversioner's rights may be too narrow. The tenants of the claimant landlords had declined to pay rent alleging that scaffolding which had been left around the premises demised had not only interfered with their enjoyment (which would not normally have justified refusal to pay rent) but had also, in view of the particular chain of leases involved in the case, constituted a breach of the landlord's own covenant of quiet enjoyment. The landlord therefore sought damages from those responsible for leaving the scaffolding in place on the ground that it constituted a nuisance which injured the reversion in as much as it had justified the tenants in refusing to pay rent. Briggs J. held that, although the scaffolding would not normally have constituted an injury to the reversion, since the tenant would himself have had to sue those responsible while continuing to pay rent to the landlord, it was arguable that an exception should be made if the nuisance justified the tenant in refusing to pay rent since that constituted an irrecoverable loss to the reversion. On the other hand it was also arguable that the circumstances of the case in question were so unusual that making an exception, in favour of the reversioner, to the general rule would not be justifiable see ([2010] EWHC 1016 at [31]). There were also factual uncertainties involved, and the issues were therefore not appropriate for resolution in summary proceedings.

NOTE 315. In *John Smith & Co (Edinburgh) Ltd v Hill* [2010] EWHC 1016; [2010] 2 B.C.L.C. 556 at [29] Briggs J. considered that the reasoning in *Bell v Midland Railway Company* (1861) 10 C.B. (NS) 287 provided support for the view that reversioners could sue for nuisance in a wider range of circumstances than those envisaged by the orthodox formulation of the law.

20–66   **Temporary nuisances.** In *John Smith & Co (Edinburgh) Ltd v Hill* [2010] EWHC 1016; [2010] 2 B.C.L.C. 556 (for the facts see para.**20–65** above) Briggs J. said (at [30]): "In my judgment it is at least well arguable that the supposed rule that a reversioner may not sue on a temporary nuisance is no more than a logical consequence, when applied to typical facts, of the true principle, which is that a reversioner may not sue in relation to a nuisance unless it causes injury to his reversion. If that is the true principle, then there may be unusual fact situations (such as that which occurred in the *Midland Railway* case) in which a temporary nuisance does injure the reversion, and it is at least well arguable that the assumed facts in the present case would also constitute a permissible exception".

NOTES 318 and 319. In *John Smith & Co (Edinburgh) Ltd v Hill* [2010] EWHC 1016 (Ch); [2010] 2 B.C.L.C. 556 Briggs J. considered the three cases cited in these two notes (i.e. *Mumford v Oxford, Worcester etc Ry* (1856) 1 H. & N. 34, *Simpson v Savage* (1856) 1 C.B. (NS) 347, and *Cooper v Crabtree* (1882) 20 Ch. D. 589). His Lordship pointed out that those cases involved nuisances by third parties unconnected to the reversioner and may therefore be distinguishable in cases in which, by providing the tenant with a right to redress against the landlord, a "temporary" nuisance could be said to damage the reversion (see [2010] EWHC 1016 (Ch) at [27]).

5. WHO CAN BE SUED FOR NUISANCE

(a) *Wrongdoer*

Scope of the principle. Add: In *Tinseltime Ltd v Roberts* [2011] EWHC 1199   **20–73**
(TCC); [2011] B.L.R. 515 Judge Stephen Davies emphasised the narrowness of
the principle which can sometimes render an occupier under a non-delegable duty
for nuisance. In particular, exceptional situations such as that in *Matania v
National Provincial Bank*, which *do* still give rise to a non-delegable duty, need to
be distinguished from the proposition that "ultra-hazardous" or "special risk" situations will give rise to a non-delegable duty: a proposition now effectively
discredited (see *Biffa Waste Service Ltd v Maschinenfabrik Ernst Hese GmbH*
[2008] EWCA Civ 1257; [2009] Q.B. 725 and para.**20–163** below). Situations of
the *former* type include those in which, as in *Matania*, work is carried out at a
point where two properties are divided and there is a danger that the claimant's
enjoyment of his property will be adversely affected by the defendant's work on
his own, adjoining, property. Judge Stephen Davies said (see [2011] EWHC 1199
at [49]): "The rationale for the dividing structures exception is separate and
distinct from the rationale for the special risks exception, and the dividing structure exception is particularly applicable to nuisance because it involves cases of
interference with easements or activities of a similar nature."

(b) *Occupier*

Statutory undertakers. In *Dwr Cymru Cyfyngedig (Welsh Water) v Barratt*   **20–77**
Homes Ltd [2013] EWCA Civ 233; (2013) 147 Con. L.R. 1 the Court of Appeal
held that a water company in breach of its statutory obligation to permit access to
its sewers under s.106 of the Water Industry Act 1991 will not thereby incur
liability for nuisance. The section does not create a right of action for breach of
statutory duty (see paras **9–09** and **9–12** of this Supplement) and could not provide
the basis for a claim in nuisance which did not exist at common law.
 In the trial of the action in *Dobson v Thames Water Utilities* [2011] EWHC
3253 (TCC); (2011) 140 Con. L.R. 135 liability for nuisance at common law was
imposed upon the defendant statutory undertakers. Their negligent operational
failures in relation to their sewage treatment works had resulted in odours causing
significant personal discomfort.

6. DEFENCES TO AN ACTION FOR NUISANCE

(a) *Prescriptive right to commit nuisance*

Prescriptive right to commit nuisance. This paragraph should now be read in   **20–85**
the light of the observations of the Court of Appeal in *RDC Promotions v Lawrence*
[2012] EWCA Civ 26; [2012] 1 W.L.R. 2127 in which the Court disapproved a
statement of the trial judge. Judge Richard Seymour QC, sitting as a Judge of the
High Court, had referred to this paragraph, and the difficulty of satisfying the

requirements for a prescriptive right in cases of nuisance by noise. He had gone on to conclude that he was "satisfied, on principle, that the law does not recognise an easement of noise, or an easement only exercisable between certain times of the day or on a limited number of occasions in the year" (see [2011] EWHC 360 (QB) at [223] sub nom *Lawrence v Fen Tigers Ltd*). In the Court of Appeal Lewison L.J., after referring to earlier cases, said that he had "no doubt that the law will recognise an easement exercisable between certain times of day" and could "see no reason in principle why an easement exercisable during certain times of the year is incapable of creation" (see *RDC Promotions v Lawrence* [2012] EWCA Civ 26; [2012] 1 W.L.R. 2127 at [88]). On the question of nuisance by noise Lewison L.J. agreed that "there is no reported case in which an easement to transmit sound waves has been acquired by prescription" (at [91]). But His Lordship, with whom Jackson and Mummery L.JJ. agreed, noted that there are several reported cases in which such claims have been made, and went on to express himself as follows: "The principal problem in such cases has been to establish what level of noise has been created over the whole of the period of prescription, so as to entitle the putative dominant owner to continue to transmit sound waves (i.e. to make a noise) at the same level that exists at the end of the prescriptive period. Whether this is a real problem of definition must, in my judgment, wait for another day and another case in which it really matters. What I cannot agree with is the judge's uncompromising statement that the law will not recognise an easement to transmit sound waves. In this area of the law, as in so many, 'never' is a word that it is better not to use."

(b) *Authorisation by statute*

20–87   **Authorisation of nuisance by statute.** In *Barr v Biffa Waste Services* [2012] EWCA Civ 312; [2013] Q.B. 455 the Court of Appeal, affirming the court below on this point (see [2011] EWHC 1003 (TCC); [2011] 4 All E.R. 1065), held that a commercial waste disposal company, which was under no statutory obligation to undertake its activities, could not rely on the defence of statutory authority notwithstanding that it was subject to an extensive and complex system of statutory regulation, including detailed conditional permits. It was "clear from the cases (notably *Allen v Gulf Oil Refining Ltd* [1981] A.C. 1001), [that] Biffa did not have statutory immunity, express or implied. The cross-appeal on this point [was] hopeless" (see *Barr v Biffa Waste Services* at [2012] EWCA Civ 312; [2013] Q.B. 455 at [94] per Carwath L.J.). Moreover, the Court of Appeal also held, forcefully *reversing* the court below, that the defendants could not rely on the complex regulatory regime to which they were subject as providing an indirect route whereby they could escape liability for nuisance. The trial judge, Coulson J., had held that the "cascade of legislation" under which the company operated was highly relevant to the existence of any possible liability for common law nuisance. He took the view that, provided the company complied with all the conditions imposed upon it by the regulatory scheme, and was not negligent, its user of land would be "reasonable" and that the emission of odours from the site would therefore not constitute a common law nuisance. The common law should be adapted to "march in step with" the legislation (see [2011] EWHC 1003 (TCC); [2011] 4 All E.R.1065 at [304] and [342]–[360]). The Court of Appeal considered that this approach was misconceived. Carnwath L.J. said (see [2012] EWCA Civ 312; [2013] Q.B. 455 at [94]): "The common law of nuisance has co-existed with statutory controls, albeit less sophisticated, since the 19th century. There is no principle that the common law should 'march with' a statutory scheme covering similar subject-matter. Short of express or implied statutory authority to commit a nuisance . . ., there is no basis, in principle or authority, for using such a statutory scheme to cut down private law rights."

Statutory powers saving liability for nuisance. NOTE 428. Add (For subse-   **20–90** quent proceedings see *Dobson v Thames Water Utilities* [2011] EWHC 3253 (TCC); (2011) 140 Con. L.R. 135 in which liability for an odour nuisance caused by negligence was imposed).

(d) *Act of a trespasser*

Continuance. In *Lambert v Barratt Homes Ltd* [2010] EWCA Civ 681 (now   **20–95** reported at [2010] B.L.R. 527; (2010) 131 Con. L.R. 29; [2011] H.L.R. 1; [2010] 2 E.G.L.R. 59; [2010] 33 E.G. 72) the Court of Appeal emphasised that where an occupier is held responsible for continuance of a nuisance caused by a third party, such as a trespasser, or an act of nature, the "measured duty of care" which rests upon it will depend upon the particular circumstances of the case and the scope of the duty will need to be indicated, at least in broad terms, by any court which deals with the matter. In the instant case flooding emanated from land occupied by Rochdale BC, but caused by the building activities of Barratts who had formerly occupied adjacent land. The trial judge in effect held that the council could be liable for the full cost of the necessary relief works notwithstanding that they had not been at fault in what had occurred and that the claimants, whose land had been flooded, had a good cause of action against Barratts. The Court of Appeal held that the judge's approach had been erroneous. Although the council was under a duty it was along the lines of an obligation actively to assist in finding a solution to the problem which caused the flooding, and cooperating in its implementation, rather than in bearing its full cost.

(j) *Ineffectual defences*

Public interest. NOTE 507. Add *Barr v Biffa Waste Services* [2012] EWCA   **20–107** Civ 312; [2013] Q.B. 455 at [31] and [86]–[88].

7. PARTICULAR TYPES OF NUISANCE

(a) *Nuisance to water rights*

(iii) *Pollution*

Sewage. In *Dobson v Thames Water Utilities* [2011] EWHC 3253 (TCC);   **20–119** (2011) 140 Con. L.R. 135 liability in damages for an odour nuisance caused by the negligent operation of their sewage treatment works was imposed upon the defendants. Injunctive relief was, however, considered to be inappropriate in the particular circumstances.

(b) *Liability in respect of damage caused by escaping water*

(iii) *Sewers and drains*

20–134   **Statutory provisions.** In *Dwr Cymru Cyfyngedig (Welsh Water) v Barratt Homes Ltd* [2013] EWCA Civ 233; (2013) 147 Con. L.R. 1 the Court of Appeal held that s.106 of the Water Industry Act 1991, which obliges water companies to permit access to its sewers, does not give rise to a claim for damages, either in nuisance or for breach of statutory duty, if the company fails to comply with it. The occupier wrongfully denied access can, however, obtain redress in public law by an application to the court to compel access: see *Barratt Homes Ltd v Dwr Cymru Cyfyngedig (Welsh Water)* [2009] UKSC 13; [2010] 1 All E.R. 965 (decided in earlier proceedings between the same parties).

NOTE 622. Add: (For subsequent proceedings see *Dobson v Thames Water Utilities* [2011] EWHC 3253 (TCC); (2011) 140 Con. L.R. 135 in which liability at common law for an odour nuisance was imposed).

(iv) *Storage and piping*

20–136   **Negligence in relation to cisterns.** NOTE 630 Add: *Gavin v Community Housing Association Ltd* [2013] EWCA Civ 580.

(d) *Nuisance to light*

20–147   **Right to light** The Law Commission is currently undertaking a study of the right to light. See Consultation Paper No. 210 (February 2013).

20–152   **Injunction and damages.** In *HKRUK II (CHC) Ltd v Heaney* [2010] EWHC 2245 (Ch); [2010] 3 E.G.L.R. 15 the High Court (H.H. Judge Langan QC) emphasised that a servient owner seeking to resist an injunction for interference with the dominant owner's right to light must satisfy *all* four of the criteria set out in *Shelfer v City of London Electronic Lighting Co* [1894] 1 Ch. 287. If he fails on any one of them an injunction will normally be awarded. Thus in *Heaney's* case itself an injunction was awarded because, although the case was regarded as close to the borderline, the injury to the rights of the dominant owner could not be considered as small. The case is also of interest in that, unusually, the proceedings were commenced by the servient owner which sought a declaration that it was not liable to the defendant. It claimed, inter alia, that the dominant owner's apparent reluctance to commence proceedings on its own account was a factor which the court should consider when deciding whether it would be oppressive to grant an injunction. Although an injunction was granted, H.H. Judge Langan did indicate, obiter, that had he decided otherwise this factor would have been relevant to his determination of the outcome of the hypothetical negotiation between the parties, used to arrive at an appropriate figure for the award of damages. The defendant's "seeming reluctance to commence proceedings made it unlikely that he would have pushed unduly hard in negotiations" (see [2010] EWHC 2245 (Ch) at [93]).

(e) *Fire*

(i) *Common law*

Danger from fire. In *Gore v Stannard (t/a Wyvern Tyres)* [2012] EWCA **20–155** Civ 1248; [2013] 1 All E.R. 694 the Court of Appeal subjected the application of the rule in *Rylands v Fletcher* to fire cases to an extensive and far-reaching examination, and concluded that its scope in that context is significantly narrower than interpretations of the rule in previous cases appeared to suggest. An electrical fire started on the defendant's premises, without fault on his part, and ignited a stock of several thousand tyres which he kept as part of his business. The resulting conflagration destroyed the claimant's neighbouring premises. The trial judge held the defendant liable under the rule in *Rylands v Fletcher* but the Court of Appeal reversed his decision. Tyres are difficult to set alight, even though once ignited they are capable of burning fiercely; moreover their storage on the defendant's premises did not represent a "non-natural" use of land. These findings would have been sufficient to negate liability under the rule as conventionally understood in cases involving fire. This required inherently inflammable material, stored in the course of a non-natural use of land, to catch fire and the fire to spread. But the Court went on to disapprove this interpretation and apparently to hold that *Rylands v Fletcher* liability should only be imposed in fire cases when the defendant, in the course of non-natural user, had deliberately introduced on to his land, or ignited, the fire itself; which then spread to neighbouring land. In practice this would seem to reduce the scope for liability under the rule in fire cases to vanishing point since it is not easy to envisage circumstances in which a fire thus commenced could spread to neighbouring land without any negligence on the defendant's part. Nevertheless the fact that the rule has not been formally abrogated in this context means that claimants continue to enjoy the potential advantage of not having actually to prove negligence, which could be beneficial if the evidence necessary to do so has been lost in the fire.

NOTE 709. After the reference to *Johnson v BJW Property Developments Ltd* add: This review must, however, now be read in the light of the decision of the Court of Appeal in *Gore v Stannard (t/a Wyvern Tyres)* [2012] EWCA Civ 1248; [2013] 1 All E.R. 694.

(ii) *Statutory exemption for fires accidentally beginning*

Fires Prevention (Metropolis) Act 1774. The applicability of the Act to fire **20–156** cases coming within the rule in *Rylands v Fletcher* was considered at length in *Gore v Stannard (t/a Wyvern Tyres)* [2012] EWCA Civ 1248; [2013] 1 All E.R. 694. The Court of Appeal was divided on the question whether the words "accidentally begin" have the effect of protecting defendants in *Rylands v Fletcher* fire cases from liability. Lewison L.J. took the view that they do have this effect, and that only cases involving negligence should be outside the protection of the Act (see [2012] EWCA Civ 1248; [2013] 1 All E.R. 694 at [89]–[96] and [147]–[170]). Etherton L.J. expressed a forceful opinion to the opposite effect, upholding the orthodox view that fires falling within *Rylands v Fletcher* are outside the protection of the Act and can therefore give rise to liability (see [2012] EWCA Civ 1248; [2013] 1 All E.R. 694 at [69]–[72]). Ward L.J. in effect took the same

view as Etherton L.J. so that the existing law on this point, laid down in the difficult decision of the Court of Appeal in *Musgrove v Pandelis* [1919] 2 K.B. 43,
remains unchanged.

20–159   **Accidental fire continued by negligence.** NOTE 725. At the end of this note
add: For discussion of *Goldman v Hargrave* see *Gore v Stannard (t/a Wyvern Tyres)*
[2012] EWCA Civ 1248; [2013] 1 All E.R. 694 at [156]–[159] per Lewison L.J.

20–161   **Fire in domestic grate.** The judgment of Lord Goddard C.J. in *Sochacki v Sas*
was quoted from with approval by Lewison L.J. in *Gore v Stannard (t/a Wyvern
Tyres)*: see [2012] EWCA Civ 1248; [2013] 1 All E.R. 694 at [151].

20–162   **"Dangerous thing".** In *Gore v Stannard (t/a Wyvern Tyres* [2012] EWCA Civ
1248; [2013] 1 All E.R. 694 the Court of Appeal confirmed (Lewison L.J.
dissenting on this point) that a fire within the rule in *Rylands v Fletcher* does not
begin accidentally for the purposes of s.86 of the Fire Prevention (Metropolis) Act
1774 (see para.**20–156** above). The decisions in *Mason v Levy Auto Parts of
England Ltd* and *LMS International Ltd v Styrene Packaging & Insulation Ltd*
would, however, now apparently be decided differently in view of the reformula-
tion of the scope of *Rylands v Fletcher* liability for fire in *Gore v Stannard (t/a
Wyvern Tyres* [2012] EWCA Civ 1248; [2013] 1 All E.R. 694. This seems to
require the defendant to have been responsible for introducing the fire itself on to
his or her land, in the course of a "non-natural" use, prior to its escape to the land
of the claimant (see para.**20–155** above).

(iii) *Responsibility for fire*

20–163   **Vicarious liability for operations involving the creation of fire.** It has
long been clear that the creation of fire is one of the exceptional situations in
which an employer will be liable for the negligence of his independent contractor:
see *Gore v Stannard (t/a Wyvern Tyres)* [2012] EWCA Civ 1248; [2013] 1 All
E.R. 694 at [34]–[35] per Ward L.J. and [155] per Lewison L.J., and the
cases there cited by both Lord Justices. (*Biffa Waste Service Ltd v Mashinenefabrik
Ernst Hese GmbH*, referred to in this paragraph of the text, was a case in
which vicarious liability was not imposed because the employers were entitled
to assume that appropriate precautions would be taken to ensure that no fire
would arise).

In *Tinseltime Ltd v Roberts* [2011] EWHC 1199 (TCC); [2011] B.L.R. 515
Judge Stephen Davies rejected a submission that the decision in *Biffa Waste
Service Ltd v Maschinenfabrik Ernst Hese GmbH* was confined to *negligence*
leaving the extent of liability in *nuisance* untouched. The *Biffa Waste*
decision, which in effect repudiates the proposition that there is a special
category of "ultra-hazardous" activities which will subject occupiers to a non-
delegable duty, therefore applies equally to both torts (see [2011] EWHC 1199
(TCC) at [49]).

20–165   **Liability of occupier.** NOTE 755. Add: See also *Gore v Stannard (t/a Wyvern
Tyres)* [2012] EWCA Civ 1248; [2013] 1 All E.R. 694 at [156]–[159] per Lewison
L.J.

8. OBSTRUCTION OF THE HIGHWAY

(b) *Public nuisance by obstruction of highway*

(i) *Special damage*

Prospective customers. NOTE 846. Add: Cf. *Network Rail Infrastructure Ltd v Conarken Group Ltd* [2011] EWCA Civ 644; [2011] B.L.R. 462 in which the Court of Appeal considered the extent to which economic losses caused by physical damage to railway infrastructure could be recovered in negligence. The defendants' vehicle collided with the claimant's railway bridge rendering the railway unusable. In addition to the cost of repairs the claimants were able to recover the financial losses they incurred due to their contractual obligations to train operating companies to provide infrastructure. See further para.**8–132** of this Supplement.   **20–184**

(c) *Non-repair of highway*

Circumstances relating to the statutory duty. In *Wilkinson v York City Council* [2011] EWCA Civ 207 the Court of Appeal rejected a highway authority's defence under s.58 of the Highways Act 1980 for a claim for failure to maintain the highway under s.41 of the same Act. The claimant had fallen from her bicycle when it ran into a pothole. The defendant authority had a regime for inspecting the road in question every twelve months. But the Court of Appeal upheld the finding of the trial judge that, in the circumstances, that was too infrequent.   **20–192**

NOTE 886. Add: Cf. *Network Rail Infrastructure Ltd v Conarken Group Ltd* [2011] EWCA Civ 644; [2011] B.L.R. 462 (see para.**20–184** above).

Standard of care. Passages in the House of Lords' judgments in *Gorringe v Calderdale MBC* [2004] UKHL 15; [2004] 1 W.L.R 1057 have been prayed in aid in two recent cases: in one by a claimant seeking to impose liability upon a highway authority, and in the other by a highway authority seeking to resist the imposition of liability. In neither case, however, did the attempted invocation of the passages in question have the desired effect: the claimant failing in the first case and the defendant authority doing so in the second. In *Ali City of Bradford* [2010] EWCA Civ 1282; [2012] 1 W.L.R. 161 the claimant suffered injury when she slipped on steps on a footpath which had become "covered with a considerable amount of mud, overgrown vegetation and all sorts of rubbish" (see [2010] EWCA Civ 1282 at [4]). She sued the local authority alleging breach of statutory duty under s.130 of the Highways Act 1980 and public nuisance at common law. Section 130 of the Highways Act requires an authority "to prevent, as far as possible, the stopping up or obstruction" of any highway for which they are responsible" (subs.(3)). The Court of Appeal held that s.130 imposed only public law duties and did not confer any private right of action. The common law nuisance claim also failed. The claimant had sought to rely on a dictum of Lord Scott in *Gorringe v Calderdale MBC* apparently suggesting that the private law nuisance principles expounded in *Sedleigh-Denfield v O'Callaghan* [1940] A.C.   **20–193**

880 might provide a basis for the imposition of liability upon highway authorities (see [2004] UKHL 15 at [51]), but the Court of Appeal was unpersuaded. The dictum was clearly obiter and to "compare the relationship between neighbouring private landowners with the relationship between a highway authority and users of the highway [was] not to compare like with like" (per Toulson L.J. in [2010] EWCA Civ 1282 at [37]). Longmore L.J. observed that "the duty to remove obstructions has never existed at common law" (see [2010] EWCA Civ 1282 at [44]). But in *Ali* Toulson L.J. also said: "I should stress that we are not here concerned with a nuisance which was created by the highway authority. There has never been any suggestion that a highway authority would not be liable at common law for a nuisance which it created" (at [39]). The importance of the principle in this observation is vividly illustrated by the other recent decision of the Court of Appeal in which *Gorringe v Calderdale MBC* was considered. In *Yetkin v Newham LBC* [2010] EWCA Civ 776; [2011] Q.B. 827 the defendant highway authority had planted shrubs and bushes and plants in the central reservation of a busy highway. The claimant pedestrian was hit by a car while crossing the road. Although she had clearly been contributorily negligent she claimed that the highway authority was also culpable, alleging that the bushes had obscured her view. The trial judge agreed that they had done so, but nevertheless exonerated the defendant authority from liability in reliance on certain observations in the *Gorringe* case dealing with the absence of a duty to protect road users from the consequences of their own carelessness. The Court of Appeal reversed the decision of the judge, however, pointing out that he had taken the *Gorringe* passages out of context. Observations dealing with the inability of a statutory power to give rise to a common law duty of care which did not otherwise exist, and with an omission to exercise that power therefore not giving rise to negligence liability, were not relevant to a situation in which the positive actions of a highway authority had created a new source of danger which had not previously existed. The actual decision in *Gorringe v Calderdale MBC* was applied in *Valentine v Transport for London* [2010] EWCA Civ 1358; [2011] P.I.Q.R. P7 in which an alleged failure to remove grit from the road surface did not give rise to liability against a highway authority under s.41 of the Highways Act. At the same time, however, a claim for common law negligence against the local authority for the area, which undertook street cleaning, was allowed to proceed. The claimant's husband had been killed when his motor cycle skidded on gravel and debris at the side of the road. It was alleged that the way in which the street cleaning had been carried out had created a trap by pushing debris against the kerb thereby making the road more dangerous than it otherwise would have been.

CHAPTER 21

ANIMALS

		PARA.
■	1. Liability for animals	21–01
	2. The Animals Act 1971	21–03
■	(a) Strict liability for animals under section 2	21–03
	(b) Strict liability for dogs under section 3.......................	21–16
	(c) Strict liability for straying livestock under section 4	21–17
	3. Liabilities for animals on the highway	21–22
□	4. Common law liabilities..	21–24

1. LIABILITY FOR ANIMALS

Common law and statute. NOTE 1. Delete: "is P.North, *The Modern Law of* **21–01** *Animals* (1972)' ", and replace with: is now P. North, *Civil Liability for Animals* (Oxford: Oxford University Press, 2012) (effectively a second edition of P. North, *The Modern Law of Animals* (1972)). For a review of the influences on the process of legal reform, exploring the reasons why the current law remains so complex, see R. Bagshaw, "The Animals Act 1971" in T.T. Arvind and J. Steele (eds), *Tort Law and the Legislature: Common Law, Statute and the Dynamics of Legal Change* (Oxford: Hart Publishing, 2013).

Other statutory provisions. NOTE 8. Replace: "*The Modern Law of Animals* **21–02** (1972)", with: *Civil Liability for Animals* (2012).

2. THE ANIMALS ACT 1971

(a) *Strict liability for animals under s.2*

Liability for animals of a non-dangerous species. At the end of the para- **21–04** graph, add: Subsequent courts have also commented adversely on the drafting of s.2(2). It has recently been described as "oracular and opaque" (*Goldsmith v Patchcott* [2012] EWCA Civ 183; [2012] P.I.Q.R. P11 at [31]), and "grotesque" (*Turnbull v Warrener* [2012] EWCA Civ 412; [2012] P.I.Q.R. P16 at [4]). In *Turnbull v Warrener* the Court of Appeal has gone further and expressed doubts about the direction in which interpretation of the subsection has developed, suggesting that the resulting extension of strict liability has undermined the intentions behind the statute. In both of these cases, the Court of Appeal has interpreted the defence in s.5(2) broadly. In *Turnbull*, this was done with the express intention of balancing the wide liability created by the subsection (at [55]).

21–05   **Section 2(2)(a) Likelihood of damage or its severity.** Add to the end of the paragraph: For the most part, subsequent courts have found the test in s.2(2)(a) to be easily satisfied. Indeed in *Goldsmith v Patchett* [2012] EWCA Civ 183; [2012] P.I.Q.R. P11, a case where the claimant suffered serious injury through being thrown from a horse, Jackson L.J. expressly said that s.2(2)(a) "will only eliminate a small number of cases". He added that "[m]ost animal-related damage which someone wishes to sue about" would fall into one of the categories in the subsection (at [33]). By contrast, the meaning of s.2(2)(a) was raised as a significant issue in *Turnbull v Warrener* [2012] EWCA Civ 412; [2012] P.I.Q.R. P16, and the Court was divided on the proper approach to take. Maurice Kay L.J. was of the view—consistent with *Smith v Ainger* and intervening authorities such as *Freeman v Higher Park Farm* [2008] EWCA Civ 1185; [2009] P.I.Q.R. P6—that there was no need to show that severe injury was statistically probable in order to fall within s.2(2)(a). Where a rider is thrown from a horse, as in this instance, severe injury was "reasonably to be expected". Lewison L.J., by contrast, was prepared to say that authorities such as *Freeman* were, in respect of s.2(2)(a), decisions of fact rather than principle, and that the statute had never been intended to apply to an "ordinary riding accident". It was not, in his view, self-evident that a rider who falls from a rearing horse (or a cantering horse) "is likely to suffer severe injury", because many such accidents occur without severe injury being suffered, and was prepared to uphold the judge's decision that the test in s.2(2)(a) was not fulfilled. Since Stanley Burnton L.J. agreed with the reasoning of Lewison L.J. on this point, the likelihood is that a range of accidents treated in recent years as clearly within s.2, and particularly riding accidents, will in future be questioned much more closely. It is suggested however that there is clearly no need to demonstrate statistical likelihood for the terms of s.2(2)(a) to be satisfied. All three judges in *Turnbull v Warrener* agreed, in any event, that the claim failed because it fell within the defence in s.5(2) (see para.**21–15**).

21–07   Add to the end of the paragraph: This reasoning is considerably less comfortable in cases where the claimant has willingly participated in an activity with full knowledge of the usual risks inherent in it. Being bound by *Mirvahedy*, the Court of Appeal has recently turned toward restricting liability in such cases by means of the defence of assumption of risk (see further para.**21–15**).

21–08   Add at end of paragraph: Even so, the Court of Appeal in *Goldsmith v Patchcott* [2012] EWCA Civ 183; [2012] P.I.Q.R. P11 accepted the truth of Lord Nicholls' observation in *Mirvahedy* that in most cases where s.2(2)(a) was satisfied, s.2(2)(b) would also be satisfied. This being the case, Jackson L.J. declared that he was not sure what purpose was served by s.2(2)(b). In *Turnbull v Warrener* [2012] EWCA Civ 412; [2012] P.I.Q.R. P16, while concluding with express reluctance that the case (of a horse resisting control when first cantering with a bitless bridle) fell within the terms of s.2(2)(b), two members of the Court of Appeal described the subsection as having been virtually "emasculated" by its drafting. The remaining judge, Stanley Burnton L.J., appears to have been prepared to find, rather, that the case did not fall within the terms of s.2(2)(b), thereby giving the subsection more substance.

21–15   **Defences.** In sub-para.(a), remove the words "Volenti non fit injuria", and replace with "Voluntary assumption of risk".

At the end of sub-para.(a), add the following: There are clear signs that the defence in s.5(2) will be more broadly interpreted as courts express unease with the breadth of strict liability under s.2(2). In both *Goldsmith v Patchcott* [2012] EWCA Civ 183; [2012] P.I.Q.R. P11, and *Turnbull v Warrener* [2012] EWCA Civ 412; [2012] P.I.Q.R. P16, the Court of Appeal found that the claimants, who were experienced horsewomen, had accepted the risks ordinarily associated with horses, even to the extent that these satisfied s.2(2)(a) and (b). In both instances, as in *Freeman v Higher Park Farm* [2008] EWCA Civ 1185; [2009] P.I.Q.R. P6, the Court of Appeal emphasised that the defence is not to be imbued with the intricacies of "volenti non fit injuria" at common law—thus escaping also the limitations of the common law defence. Rather, all that needs to be shown was said to be that: (1) the claimant fully appreciated the risk; and (2) they exposed themselves to it. It is not necessary that the claimant could foresee the "precise degree of energy with which the animal will engage in its characteristic behaviour" (*Goldsmith*, at [50]). Thus, it remains true that the defence will not defeat a claimant who was unaware of a dangerous propensity or characteristic of the animal which was known to the keeper, where that characteristic caused the harm. An example of this is *Flack v Hudson* [2001] Q.B. 698, where the horse's keeper, but not the claimant's wife, knew that the horse had a tendency to be frightened by agricultural machinery. But *Flack* has been distinguished in more recent cases, where the dangerous characteristic is one common to horses generally in particular circumstances, and is considered to be within the claimant's knowledge. The claimants' experience with the animals has been a significant factor in these cases. So also is the voluntary nature of the exposure to the risk. In *Turnbull v Warrener*, this "realistic application" of s.5(2) was expressly related by Lewison L.J. to the issues motivating the House of Lords' decision in *Tomlinson v Congleton BC* [2003] UKHL 47; [2004] 1 A.C. 46 (see para.**8–160** of the Main Work), and he took the view that the claimant's fall should be seen as merely the result of "one of the risks inherent in riding horses" (at [55]–[56]). To similar effect is the first instance decision in *Bodey v Hall* [2011] EWHC 2162 (QB); [2012] P.I.Q.R. P1, where the claimant was tipped out of a trap in which she was riding as a groom: the risk associated with the accident did not go beyond those of which the claimant would have been aware. These decisions therefore link certain claims under the Animals Act—where the claimant is participating in a leisure activity with an understanding of the ordinary risks—with other recent decisions regarding voluntarily assumed risks associated with leisure activities. In *Preskey v Sutcliffe* Unreported February 18, 2013 County Court (Leeds), Judge Belcher found that a claimant who had chosen to restrain a boxer dog had thereby voluntarily accepted the risk that the dog might feel threatened. He had exposed himself to the risk of being bitten by the dog and the defendants had the benefit of the statutory defences under both s.5(1) and (2).

At the end of sub-para.(b), add: *Preskey v Sutcliffe* (above, sub-para.(a)), is a case where the damage was found to be wholly the fault of the claimant, who had elected to restrain a dog from following its owner, despite the owner's requests to release the dog.

4. Common Law Liabilities

NOTE 111. Add: See also *Addis v Campbell* [2011] EWCA Civ 906.   **21–26**

CHAPTER 22

DEFAMATION

		PARA.
■	1. Generally	22–01
	(a) Jurisdiction	22–02
■	(b) Trial by jury	22–03
■	(c) Reform: Defamation Act 1996 And Civil Procedure	22–04
	Rules 1998	
	(i) Defamation Act 1996	22–05
	(ii) Civil Procedure Rules 1998	22–06
■	(d) Internet and email	22–08
□	(e) Human Rights Act	22–10
	2. Basis of liability	22–16
	3. What is defamatory?	22–23
■	(a) The test	22–23
■	(b) Examples	22–26
□	(c) Construction of language used	22–37
	(i) Language defamatory on the face	22–40
	(ii) Ambiguous language	22–42
	(iii) Language innocent on the face	22–43
	(d) Innuendo	22–45
	(e) Judge and jury	22–49
	4. Slander	22–53
	(a) Imputing a criminal offence	22–54
	(b) Imputing disease	22–55
	(c) Imputing unchastity to a woman	22–56
	(d) Slander on a person in his profession, trade or employment	22–57
	(e) Slander causing special damage	22–60
■	5. Publication	22–61
■	6. Defence	22–72
	(a) Justification	22–73
■	(i) Meaning to be proved true	22–74
■	(ii) Facts to be proved substantially true	22–79
□	(iii) Rehabilitation of Offenders Act 1974	22–84
	(b) Absolute privilege	22–86
■	(i) Judicial proceedings	22–88
■	(ii) Parliamentary proceedings	22–94
	(iii) Official communications	22–99
	(c) Qualified privilege	22–106
	(i) Principles	22–106
■	(ii) Grounds of qualified privilege	22–117
■	(d) Fair comment	22–164
■	(i) Comment not fact	22–166
■	(ii) Sufficient factual basis	22–167
	(iii) Fairness	22–168
	(iv) Public interest	22–170
	(v) Malice	22–176
	(vi) Procedure	22–177
	(e) Secondary responsibility: section 1 of the Defamation	22–179
	Act 1996	
	(f) Offers to make amends: section 2 of the Defamation	22–181
	Act 1996	

(i)	Statutory basis		22–181
(ii)	Offer of amends		22–182
(iii)	Acceptance of offer and damages		22–185
□ (iv)	Disqualification		22–190
(v)	Relationship with other defences		22–192
(vi)	Rejection		22–194
(vii)	Joint liability		22–195
(g)	Miscellaneous defences		22–196
□ (i)	Limitation		22–196
(ii)	Consent to publication		22–198
(iii)	Accord and satisfaction		22–200
□ (iv)	Abuse of process		22–201
7.	Malice		22–202
(a)	General		22–202
■ (b)	Examples of malice		22–207
8.	Repetition		22–216
9.	Damages		22–223
■ (a)	General		22–223
□ (b)	Purpose of damages		22–226
(c)	Exemplary damages		22–231
(d)	Actual and special damage		22–234
(e)	Mitigation of damages		22–237
(i)	Partial justification		22–238
□ (ii)	Background context		22–239
■ (iii)	Conduct and reputation of claimant		22–241
(iv)	Other publications		22–243
(v)	Apology		22–245
(vi)	Publication in good faith		22–246
(f)	Excessive damages		22–247
(g)	Non-jury awards		22–251
(h)	Costs		22–253
□ 10.	Injunction		22–256

1. GENERALLY

22–01 **Action for defamation** Add to NOTE 1: The death of the claimant abates the action, even if the claim is in progress and a hearing has taken place. In *Smith v Dha* [2013] EWHC 838 (QB) the court had reserved judgment following a hearing in a defamation claim, and the claimant died before judgment was handed down. The judge decided that the action had abated and in those circumstances it was not appropriate to hand down judgment from the previous hearing.

(b) *Trial by jury*

22–03 **Trial by jury.** Add: On the court's discretion to try a case without a jury, see *Fiddes v Channel 4 Television Corp* [2010] EWCA Civ 730; [2010] 1 W.L.R. 2245 and *Boyle v MGN Ltd* [2012] EWHC 2700 (QB). Notwithstanding the right to trial by jury conferred by s.69 of the Senior Courts Act 1981, in order to exercise that right, it is necessary for a party to make an application under CPR r.26.11 for trial by jury within 28 days of service of the Defence, failing which the right is lost and mode of trial will be a matter for the judge's discretion. See *Cook v Telegraph Media Group Ltd* [2011] EWHC 763 (QB), *Thornton v Telegraph*

Media Group Ltd [2011] EWCA Civ 748; [2011] E.M.L.R. 29 and *Rothschild v Associated Newspapers Ltd* [2011] EWHC 3462 (QB).

(c) *Reform: Defamation Act 1996 and Civil Procedure Rules 1998*

Reforms. In April 2013 the Defamation Act 2013 was enacted into law, with **22–04** the intention of redressing the balance of the law in favour of freedom of speech. As of July 2013, the Act is not yet in force and detailed consideration will be given in the next Supplement, when it is anticipated that it will be in force. The main features of the Act are as follows:

(i) There is a reversal of the presumption in favour of trial by jury, by virtue of s.69(1) of the Senior Courts Act 1981. The presumption now works the other way, so that trial by jury must be justified in accordance with a series of criteria including that such a trial would be in the public interest or the interests of justice.

(ii) A new public interest defence, which abolishes the common law defence of responsible journalism as set out in *Reynolds v Times Newspapers Ltd* [2001] 2 A.C. 127. The provision aims to greatly simplify the defence, now requiring the defendant merely to show that—

   (a) the statement complained of was, or formed part of, a statement on a matter of public interest; and
   (b) the defendant reasonably believed that publishing the statement complained of was in the public interest.

   Earlier drafts of the defence altered the factors set out by Lord Nicholls in *Reynolds* so as to seek to make the defence more straightforward for the media to apply. They also required the courts to take into account compliance with any relevant Code (e.g. the Press Complaints Commission Code). In its final form, the provision merely requires that all the circumstances of the case should be taken into account. Although the common law *Reynolds* defence is abolished, it is anticipated that the courts will continue to take into account the various factors laid down by Lord Nicholls in considering all the circumstances of the case. Accordingly, the case law on the *Reynolds* defence may still be of relevance in future. See e.g. *Hunt v Times Newspapers Ltd (No.2)* [2013] EWHC 1868 (QB) in which Silber J. commented (at [181]–[183]) that the elements of the *Reynolds* defence are "reflected but not reproduced" in s.4(1) of the new Act.

(iii) A defence of "truth", replacing the common law defence of justification. The defence succeeds if the defendant can show that the allegations are true or substantially true in either the meaning contended for by the claimant or a less serious meaning that the words are found to bear. Where a publication contains more than one meaning or allegation, the defence does not fail if any meaning or allegation not shown to be true does not materially injure the claimant's reputation having regard to the truth of the remaining allegations. This simplifies the common law defence, and includes the partial justification provision under s.5 of the Defamation Act 1952.

(iv) A defence of "honest opinion", replacing the common law defence of "fair comment" or "honest comment". This is intended to simplify the law of comment, and again make it more straightforward. The defence would succeed if there were one or more facts or otherwise privileged material on which an honest person could hold the opinion expressed. There is no concept of "malice" defeating a defence of honest opinion, although the defence fails if it is shown that the maker did not in fact hold the opinion expressed.

(v) Wider scope is given to report-based absolute and qualified privilege, extending the ambit of absolute privilege to reports of court proceedings around the world (whereas it was previously limited to reports of UK courts, the European Court of Justice, the European Court of Human Rights and international tribunals set up by the Security Council of the United Nations). Qualified privilege is also extended to "summaries" in addition to copies or extracts of material produced by a range of bodies which includes more international bodies or organisations.

(vi) The "multiple publication" (or *Duke of Brunswick*) rule, which entitled a claimant to bring an action more than one year after the original publication where the publication had been repeated (*Duke of Brunswick v Harmer* (1849) 14 Q.B. 185) is abolished. The "single publication rule" will apply to repeat publication of the same material by the same publisher, and prevent such an action being brought after the limitation period has expired in respect of the original publication (the limitation period being one year). This will mean that it will not be possible to bring an action over archive internet articles which are deemed under the *Duke of Brunswick* rule to be republished every day that they are accessible online.

(vii) There are new provisions aimed at dealing with "libel tourism", which require that an action against a person not domiciled in the United Kingdom or another Member State of the European Union should not be brought unless the court is satisfied that, of all the places where the statement complained of has been published, England and Wales is clearly the most appropriate forum for the action. The provision does not deal with the perceived problem of foreign claimants "forum shopping" and suing in England and Wales, and does not deal with European based claimants or defendants, since to do so would fall foul of the Brussels and Lugano Conventions and the *Shevill* case (*Shevill v Press Alliance SA* (C-68/93) [1995] 2 A.C. 18).

(viii) Further provisions deal with secondary responsibility, making it more difficult to bring actions against Internet Service Providers or the broadcasters of live programmes; bodies corporate suing (they are required to demonstrate that they are likely to suffer substantial financial loss as a result of the publication); and a threshold requirement for defamation claims proposing that a statement is not defamatory unless the publication has caused or is likely to cause "serious harm to the reputation of the claimant".

The Act does not address the rules on the recoverability of costs in defamation cases, and it is anticipated that new rules of court will be enacted to bring to an end or significantly limit the conditional fee (or "no win no fee") costs regime, which currently allows for successful litigants to claim success fee uplifts of up to 100 per cent of the costs claimed. The European Court of Human Rights has ruled that such success fees are a disproportionate interference with the right to freedom of expression: *MGN Ltd v United Kingdom* (39401/04) (2011) 53 E.H.R.R. 5. One such amendment to the rules of court governing the recoverability of success fees is the amendment of s.58 of the Courts and Legal Services Act 1990 (by virtue of s.44 of the Legal Aid, Sentencing and Punishment of Offenders Act 2012), under which the recoverability of success fees from losing parties is abolished and such fees are to be payable out of, and limited by reference to, the damages recovered by the claimant. The provisions, which came into force in April 2013, are currently not applicable to defamation claims. It is anticipated that they will be modified for the purposes of defamation claims to take account of concerns expressed by commentators regarding the lack of access to justice for impecunious defamation litigants if such measures were to be implemented for defamation claims.

At the end of para.**22–04** add new para.**22–04A**:

Reforms—Leveson Inquiry. Throughout late 2011 and 2012 Leveson L.J. conducted a detailed review of English media regulation, in light of the voicemail interception (or "phone hacking") scandal concerning News International, the publishers of *The Sun, The Times, Sunday Times* as well as the now defunct *News of the World*. The Leveson Report was published on November 29, 2012. He recommended fundamental changes to the system of self-regulation that had hitherto operated under the Press Complaints Commission. Leveson L.J. recommended self-regulation of the media to be bolstered by statutory underpinning, the imposition of fines for serious breaches of the regulatory code by publishers, as well as a more robust arbitration procedure for defamation claims. Parliament has come under significant pressure to enact Leveson L.J.'s findings, but has so far failed to reach a consensus on the way in which to do so. There has been much resistance, for example, to the proposal of statutory underpinning, which has been widely criticised as a fundamental attack on the independence of the media from interference by Parliament. The latest proposals include the use of a Royal Charter to provide a softer form of legislative "underpinning". However as of July 2013 there continues to be deadlock between the media and various campaigning groups on the detail of the future regulator.   **22–04A**

(e) *Internet and email*

The impact of the internet and email. In *Tamiz v Google Inc* [2012] EWHC 449 (QB); [2012] E.M.L.R. 24 it was held at first instance that Google, as the provider of *Blogger.com*, an internet platform for blogging, is not a publisher of defamatory content contained within individual blogs, on the basis that Google took no positive step in the process of continuing the accessibility of the offending material, irrespective of whether it had been notified of a complainant's objection. However, while the Court of Appeal ([2013] EWCA Civ 68; [2013] 1 W.L.R. 2151) upheld the judge's overall finding that the claim should be struck out, it disagreed on the important point of principle concerning the responsibility of Google for   **22–08**

blogs hosted on its platform. The Court of Appeal concluded that the judge had been wrong to regard Google's role as purely passive and to attach the significance he did to the absence of any positive steps by them in relation to continued publication of the comments. Google facilitated publication of the blogs, and once it had been notified of a complaint, it could be considered to be a secondary publisher, and therefore potentially liable for defamatory content continuing to be published on the blog after being notified by a complainant. The Court of Appeal observed that the provision of a platform for the creation of blogs was equivalent to the provision of a large notice board. Google provided tools to enable the blogger to design the layout of his part of the notice board, made the notice board available on terms of its own choice and could readily remove or block access to any notice that did not comply with those terms. In those circumstances, if Google allowed defamatory material to remain after it had been notified of a complaint, it might be inferred to have associated itself with, or to have made itself responsible for, the continued presence of the material and thereby to have become a publisher of the material. Such an inference could be drawn after Google had had a reasonable time in which to remove the comments. See also *Davison v Habeeb* [2011] EWHC 3031 (QB); [2012] 3 C.M.L.R. 6, the reasoning of which was approved of in *Tamiz* (above).

At the end of para.**22–08** add new para.**22–08A**:

22–08A Impact of social media. A growing number of cases have been brought which are the subject of discussions on social media platforms such as Facebook and Twitter. See e.g. *Lord McAlpine of West Green v Bercow* [2013] EWHC 1342 (QB) in which the defendant published on twitter: *"Why is Lord McAlpine trending? *Innocent face*"* The claimant brought proceedings for libel against the defendant in relation to the publication of the tweet to the defendant's 56,000 followers. After a preliminary ruling on defamatory meaning, in which the High Court concluded that the words were defamatory, the case settled with the defendant paying undisclosed damages to the claimant. See also *Cairns v Modi* [2012] EWCA Civ 1382; [2013] 1 W.L.R. 1015 (discussed at para.**22–224** below) where an allegation of match fixing made on Twitter and in an article published on the internet resulted in a damages award of £90,000 for the claimant.

(e) *Human Rights Act*

22–14   **Article 8.** Add: In *Clift v Slough BC* [2010] EWCA Civ 1484; [2011] 1 W.L.R. 1774 the Court of Appeal accepted that the act of a local authority in including a person on its violent persons register and emailing that information to various other departments was disproportionate and in breach of the individual's rights under art.8 of the Convention. As a result, the local authority did not therefore have a defence of qualified privilege. The Court of Appeal recognised that the right to reputation is an aspect of the right to a private life protected under art.8, and that in cases involving public authorities, following the enactment of the Human Rights Act 1998 defences such as qualified privilege could only be applied in compliance with the art.8 right under the Convention.

22–15   **Article 10.** Add: In *MGN Ltd v United Kingdom* (39401/04) (2011) 53 E.H.R.R. 5 the European Court of Human Rights was asked to consider whether the imposition of a 100 per cent uplift on the costs claimed by Naomi Campbell's lawyers following her win in her privacy case against MGN in the House of Lords was compatible with art.10 of the Convention. The uplift was a "success fee" claimed by the lawyers because they had represented Ms Campbell on a "no win, no fee" or conditional fee basis. The court ruled unanimously that the imposition of a success fee at 100 per cent (i.e. double the base costs) was incompatible with art.10, being a disproportionate infringement of the newspaper's right to freedom of expression. The case confirmed the view of the committee set up by Jackson L.J. to review costs in media publication cases that success fees at 100 per cent should play no part in such disputes, and heralds the end of the conditional fee regime in its current form. The regime is due to be the subject of new rules of court concerning the funding of such cases which are due to come into force within the next year.

3. What is Defamatory?

(a) *The test*

The test. In *Thornton v Telegraph Media Group Ltd* [2010] EWHC 1414 (QB); **22–23**
[2011] 1 W.L.R. 1985 Tugendhat J. considered the test for whether words are defamatory, and undertook a thorough review and analysis of the test. He drew a distinction between personal defamation—imputations as to the character or attributes of an individual—and business or professional defamation: where the imputation is as to an attribute of an individual, a corporation or similar body, and that imputation is with regard to the way the profession or business is conducted. He acknowledged that the various varieties are not mutually exclusive. With regard to personal defamation, he considered that this could be further sub-divided into three sub-categories: imputations as to what is sinful, mischievous or illegal; imputations that are not voluntary, or the result of the claimant's conscious act or choice, but rather a misfortune such as a disease; and imputations that ridicule the claimant. In relation to professional defamation, he recognised two sub-categories, namely imputations as to a person's goods or services being below the required standard and thus likely to cause adverse consequences to customers, and those allegations which could prevent investors from providing financial support, or dealing with the business or professional. The judge also identified that any definition of defamatory imputations must contain a threshold of seriousness, in that it should exclude trivial claims. This was required by the development of the law recognised in *Dow Jones & Co Inc v Jameel* [2005] EWCA Civ 75; [2005] Q.B. 946 as arising from the passing of the Human Rights Act 1998: regard for art.10 of the European Convention on Human Rights and the principle of proportionality both required it.

Language not defamatory on its face See also *Lord McAlpine of West Green v* **22–25**
Bercow [2013] EWHC 1342 (QB) in which an apparently innocuous question posted on Twitter was found to be defamatory to certain readers who would have been aware of specific facts. The tweet was: "*Why is Lord McAlpine trending? *innocent face*"*. The judge observed that the tweet was not a publication to the world at large, such as a daily newspaper or broadcast. It was a publication on Twitter and the hypothetical reader must be taken to be a reasonable representative of users of Twitter who followed the defendant. The circumstances which would be

known to such readers were that there was extensive speculation regarding the identity of an unnamed "senior Tory politician" who was said to be guilty of child abuse. The claimant would have been known to have been a senior conservative politician. The court concluded that the words "innocent face" would be regarded as insincere and ironical, giving rise to the defamatory imputation that the claimant was the abuser. The case subsequently settled with the claimant receiving damages.

(b) *Examples*

22–27   **Imputation of non-blameworthy conduct** In *John v Times Newspapers Ltd* [2012] EWHC 2751 (QB) the defendant newspaper was sued for defamation over an allegation that the claimant was involved in tax avoidance. The article featured the creator of a tax avoidance scheme, and mentioned that he happened to be the former accountant of the claimant, the well-known singer Elton John. The claimant contended that the reasonable reader would infer that he was implicated in immoral tax avoidance measures himself. The court ruled that the article was not defamatory of the claimant: references to him were fleeting and it was clear that any association between him and his former accountant had been in the past. Accordingly, even if there was an inference that the claimant had been involved in such a scheme, there was nothing on which the reasonable reader could base such an inference, and therefore to draw such a conclusion would be unreasonable. The claim was therefore struck out.

22–30   **Criminal association.** See also *Cruddas v Times Newspapers Ltd* [2013] EWCA Civ 748 in which the claimant, the former co-treasurer of the Conservative Party, brought proceedings over an article which he contended meant that he had, in exchange for cash donations to the party, corruptly offered for sale the opportunity to influence governmental policy and gain unfair advantage through secret meetings with ministers. The High Court was asked to determine meaning as a preliminary issue. It concluded that the meaning of the articles was indeed one of corruption, and that the words denoted commission of a criminal offence. The Court of Appeal disagreed. The use of the word "corruptly" in the article did not necessarily connote that a criminal offence had been committed. The defamatory meaning alleged by the claimant was to be treated as the most injurious meaning the words were capable of bearing and the judge should ask, first, whether the natural and ordinary meaning of the words was that alleged in the statement of claim and, second, if not, what less injurious defamatory meaning did they bear. Applying those principles, the newspaper was not alleging that the claimant was criminally corrupt in offering access to ministers for cash, but rather that his conduct was inappropriate and wrong. Although that could indicate corruption to some readers, the article did not explicitly or implicitly allege the commission of any criminal offence. The court observed that it is an important aspect of libel law that it should be open to a defendant to justify a lesser defamatory meaning than that alleged. Accordingly an order striking out a defence of justification on the basis of the lesser meaning was reversed.

22–32   **Imputation of insanity or disease.** In *Ibrahim v Swansea University* [2012] EWHC 290 (QB) the judge held that allegations that the claimant had "suffered with mental health difficulties" or from "chronic fatigue syndrome and anxiety" were not capable of being defamatory, since no reasonable person would nowadays think the worse of someone who had suffered from either condition. The claim was accordingly struck out.

Corporations. Even if the words complained of by a corporation are arguably **22–35** defamatory, the courts will scrutinise any claim and question whether any real and substantial tort has been committed. In *Euromoney Institutional Investor Plc v Aviation News Ltd* [2013] EWHC 1505 (QB) the court concluded that an emailed advertisement referring to the corporate claimant "fleecing" its customers was capable of bearing the defamatory meaning that the company had unfairly overcharged its customers, but no real or substantial tort had been committed since the measure of any likely recoverable damages for defamation was not worth the expenditure in costs and resources that would be involved in trying the case.

NOTE 178. Add: See also *McLaughlin v Lambeth LBC* [2010] EWHC 2726 (QB); [2011] E.M.L.R. 8, where the court refused to strike out a claim by the current and former head teachers of a school in the Lambeth local authority. The claimants sued for defamation after being accused (inter alia) of mistreating and failing to give proper supervision to newly qualified teachers. The defendants sought to strike out the action on the basis that the claim was an abuse of process, since it was an unlawful attempt to circumvent the rule in *Derbyshire CC v Times Newspapers Ltd* [1993] A.C. 534, which prevents governmental bodies from suing for defamation. However, the judge refused the application. In *Derbyshire* the House of Lords drew a distinction between governmental bodies and individuals employed by them: the right to sue of any individual carrying on the day to day functions of the governmental authority was not limited by the *Derbyshire* decision, provided they were referred to (or identifiable) from the publication.

(c) *Construction of language used*

Construction of language. Add: In *Dee v Telegraph Media Group Ltd* [2010] **22–39** EWHC 924 (QB); [2010] E.M.L.R. 20 Sharp J. ruled that in relation to newspaper articles on the same subject spread over a number of pages, the ordinary reasonable reader was to be taken to have turned over the pages and read what he was directed to on the continuation pages. In this case, the front page article was a limited one, commonly used to invite readers to view the inside "full story". It contained a clear cross-reference to the inside story and told readers where to find it. Accordingly, notwithstanding the article on the inside pages being a separate one, it was obvious to readers that the front page story was not the full story, and a defamatory imputation contained in the first article was to be read in the context of the second, since the two articles should be taken together.

5. PUBLICATION

Authorised repetition. NOTE 348. Add: See also *Baturina v Times Newspapers* **22–65** *Ltd* [2011] EWCA Civ 308; [2011] 1 W.L.R. 1526.

NOTE 348a. Add: See also *Baturina v Times Newspapers Ltd* [2011] EWCA Civ 308; [2011] 1 W.L.R. 1526.

22–67   **Intention or negligence.** As to the liability of internet platforms for the publication of blogging websites on their platforms, see *Tamiz v Google Inc* [2013] EWCA Civ 68; [2013] 1 W.L.R. 2151 and *Davison v Habeeb* [2011] EWHC 3031 (QB) (at para.**22–08** above).

6. DEFENCES

22–72   **Defences** It is increasingly common for the defences of justification, *Reynolds* and honest comment to be raised together. For a successful application of all three defences see *El Naschie v Macmillan Publishers Plc* [2012] EWHC 1809 (QB). For a successful application of *Reynolds* and justification, see *Hunt v Times Newspapers Ltd (No.2)* [2013] EWHC 1868 (QB).

(a) *Justification*

(i) *Meaning to be proved true*

22–74   **The meaning that must be proved to be true.** NOTE 381. On the requirement to plead specific and non-ambiguous allegations in the *Lucas-Box* meaning and particulars of justification, see *Lord Ashcroft v Foley* [2012] EWCA Civ 423; [2012] E.M.L.R. 25.

22–76   **"Grounds to suspect" meanings.** For a rare example of a "reasonable grounds to suspect" defence succeeding at trial, see *Rothschild v Associated Newspapers* [2012] EWHC 177 (QB). The Court of Appeal upheld the High Court ruling: [2013] EWCA Civ 197; [2013] E.M.L.R. 18. For another example of an unsuccessful defence on this basis, see *Miller v Associated Newspapers Ltd* [2012] EWHC 3721 (QB).

(ii) *Facts to be proved substantially true*

22–79   **Facts alleged must be substantially true.** See *Rothschild v Associated Newspapers* [2012] EWHC 177 (QB), upheld in the Court of Appeal: [2013] EWCA Civ 197; [2013] E.M.L.R. 18.

(iii) *Rehabilitation of Offenders Act 1974*

22–84   **The Rehabilitation of Offenders Act 1974.** In *KJO v XIM* [2011] EWHC 1768 (QB) Eady J. considered (obiter) what would be required to succeed in a claim for defamation based on the malicious disclosure of a spent conviction. Such a case in malice would generally be based not on the proposition that the defendant knew the allegations concerning the claimant to be false, but on the contrary, while knowing the words to be true, published them with the dominant motive of injuring the claimant's reputation. This was the alternative ground for advancing malice canvassed by Lord Diplock in *Horrocks v Lowe* [1975] A.C.

135. The judge described this as "almost untrodden territory", while not ruling out on the facts of the case that the claimant might succeed in establishing that motive. The judge also considered whether disclosure of a spent conviction could amount to an infringement of the right to privacy under art.8 of the European Convention on Human Rights and Fundamental Freedoms, or a breach of the principles of the Data Protection Act 1998. He refused to give summary judgment on those grounds, but observed that such a disclosure could arguably amount to a breach of confidentiality.

(b) *Absolute privilege*

(i) *Judicial proceedings*

Judicial proceedings. NOTE 433. See also *Iqbal v Mansoor* [2013] EWCA **22–88** Civ 149; [2013] C.P. Rep. 27.

NOTE 434. Add: See also *White v Southampton University Hospitals NHS Trust* [2011] EWHC 825 (QB); [2011] Med. L.R. 296 which has found that the General Medical Council's Fitness to Practise Directorate is a quasi-judicial body; a letter sent by a medical director to the General Medical Council raising concerns about a doctor's probity and conduct was protected by absolute privilege. See also *Mayer v Hoar* [2012] EWHC 1805 (QB), where an action for libel based on words that had been used in a letter written by a barrister in response to a request for comment by the Bar Standards Board was struck out as the communication was protected by absolute privilege.

Relevancy In *Iqbal v Mansoor* [2013] EWCA Civ 149; [2013] C.P. Rep. 27 the **22–92** Court of Appeal confirmed that witness statements made in the course of legal proceedings are prima facie protected by absolute privilege and it is not enough for the defamatory allegations to be irrelevant to the matter in hand for it to fall outside the privilege; it has to have no reference at all to the subject-matter of the proceedings.

Parliamentary proceedings. In *Makudi v Triesman* [2013] EWHC 142 (QB) **22–94** the court held that evidence of corrupt practices in regard to the bid for the 2018 World Cup given by a Member of Parliament to a select committee was covered by absolute privilege, whereas discussions the MP held with counsel appointed by the Football Association, and counsel's subsequent reports, were covered by qualified privilege.

(c) *Qualified privilege*

(ii) *Grounds of qualified privilege*

(1) Duty and interest

Interest of person to whom communication addressed. See also *Clift v* **22–119** *Slough BC* [2010] EWCA Civ 1484; [2011] 1 W.L.R. 1774, on the impact of art.8 of the European Convention on Human Rights in respect of actions against local authorities. In that case a local authority published the name of the claimant on a violent person's register. The claimant sued and the local authority pleaded a defence of qualified privilege, since it contended that those who received the communication (being officers, employees and some third party organisations who provided services on behalf of the local authority) had a duty or interest in receiving the information. The Court of Appeal agreed with the trial judge that the local authority lost the defence of qualified privilege because its disclosure of defamatory information to certain departments was disproportionate and could not be justified under art.8; accordingly the defence of qualified privilege was not available. Ill-considered and indiscriminate disclosure of defamatory information was bound to be disproportionate and the local authority should have verified the information and limited its disclosure to those that truly needed to know it or who were reasonably thought to be at risk from the individual. The court balanced the duty of the local authority to warn employees of the risks posed by the claimant as against their duty to protect her reputation and concluded that in the case of certain classes of employee who were unlikely to come into contact with the claimant, the duty to protect the claimant's reputation outweighed the duty to warn of any risk.

NOTE 592. Add: *Clift v Slough BC* approved in the Court of Appeal [2010] EWCA Civ 1484; [2011] 1 W.L.R. 1774.

22–129   **Existing relationships.** *Kearns v General Council of the Bar* was applied in *Cambridge v Makin* [2012] EWCA Civ 85; [2012] E.M.L.R. 19, where the defence of qualified privilege failed and the defendant was found to be malicious.

(2) Media communications

22–136   **Development of the *Reynolds* defence.** In *Flood v Times Newspapers Ltd* [2010] EWCA Civ 804; [2011] 1 W.L.R. 153 the Court of Appeal overruled the decision of Tugendhat J. on a preliminary issue regarding whether *The Times* was entitled to rely on the *Reynolds* qualified privilege defence in relation to an article concerning the claimant. The first instance decision had been the first case in which a national newspaper had successfully relied on the *Reynolds* defence. The victory was short-lived. The claimant, a Detective Sergeant with the Metropolitan Police, was alleged to have been paid for information about extradition requests concerning Russian oligarchs. Investigative journalists believed that a police investigation into the claimant may not have been conducted properly, and approached the claimant for comment. An article was published in *The Times* concerning a subsequent police investigation, prompted by the journalists' enquiries. The newspaper raised defences of *Reynolds* and justification. On the *Reynolds* defence, the Court of Appeal found that, following *Jameel v Wall Street Journal* [2006] UKHL 44; [2007] 1 A.C. 359, there are now three requirements for a *Reynolds* defence to be mounted: (a) the article as a whole must be on a matter of public interest; (b) the inclusion of the defamatory allegations should be part of the story and make a real contribution to it; and (c) the steps taken to gather and publish the information must be "responsible" and "fair". The Court of Appeal concluded that the inclusion of the claimant's name in the story was not warranted, and the steps taken to investigate the story were not to be classed as responsible or fair journalism. The Master of the Rolls observed that it would rarely be "justifiable reportage" to report that an unidentified informant had provided information which, if true, may incriminate a claimant. He concluded, at [63], that it would be "tipping the scales too far in favour of the media to hold that not only the name of the claimant, but the details of the allegations against him, can normally be published as part of a story free of any right in the claimant to sue for defamation just because the general subject matter of the story is in the public interest." The Master of the Rolls was satisfied that the "steps taken to verify the information" were such that the journalists did not seem to have done much to satisfy themselves that the allegations were true. They were "unsubstantiated unchecked accusations, from an unknown source, coupled with speculation." The Court of Appeal registered its distaste with a claim to *Reynolds* privilege in relation to allegations which were the subject of an investigation. The Master of the Rolls commented, at [104]:

"In my view responsible journalism requires a recognition of the importance of ensuring that persons against whom serious allegations of crime or professional misconduct are made are not forced to respond to them before an investigation has been properly carried out and charges have been made. It is very easy for allegations of impropriety or criminal conduct to be made, to the police, professional bodies and others who may have a duty to investigate their truth, out of malice, an excess of zeal or simple misunderstanding. If the details of such allegations are made public, they are capable of causing a great deal of harm to the individual concerned, since many people are inclined to assume that there is 'no smoke without fire'. Moreover, there is a serious risk that once the allegations have been published the person against whom they are made will feel obliged to respond to them publicly, thereby depriving himself of the safeguard of the ordinary process and risking a measure of trial by press."

The Master of the Rolls concluded by drawing a distinction between the present case, in which the allegations were published in detail in the article (with the claimant being identified and claims made about his conduct giving rise to the investigation) and the publication of the simple fact that a complaint has been made against him, without any details being given, or publication of the mere fact that a person has been charged with a criminal offence. The court also concluded that it was not for editors to determine whether the inclusion of the defamatory allegations was in the public interest. What was for editorial judgment was the tone or the manner in which the story sought to attract the attention and interest of readers. Whether or not the allegations were in the public interest was a question for the court.

Flood went to the Supreme Court (*Flood v Times Newspapers Ltd* [2012] UKSC 11; [2012] 2 A.C. 273) which allowed the defendant's appeal in relation to the publication of the allegations prior to the claimant being cleared of wrongdoing. The Supreme Court held that it was in the public interest that both the accusation against the claimant and most of the facts that supported it were published. There was a public interest both in the fact of police corruption and in the nature of that corruption. The motivation of the newspaper's journalist for publishing the accusation was also relevant. The journalist doubted whether the police were exercising due diligence in investigating the allegation, and this constituted a legitimate aim of publishing, and it was in the public interest that any investigation was carried out promptly. Overruling the Court of Appeal, the Supreme Court observed that naming the claimant did not conflict with the test of responsible journalism, or the public interest. The claimant would have been identified by other members of his unit, and failing to name him would cast suspicion on other members of the unit. An appeal in relation to the newspaper's failure to remove the allegations from its website when the claimant was later cleared of corruption was adjourned to a later date.

In *Hunt v Times Newspapers (No.1)* [2012] EWHC 110 (QB) the court applied the Supreme Court decision in *Flood* and concluded that although the subject matter of the article was of legitimate public interest (namely allegations of criminal behaviour), the mere existence of "allegations" or "rumours" could not found a *Reynolds* defence. The judge set out 11 principles that he extracted from the Supreme Court decision in *Flood*, when assessing the public interest justification for publishing allegations under the protection of *Reynolds*:

"i) The development of *Reynolds* privilege reflected a perception by the House of Lords that at that time English law had not adequately catered for the protection of the right of freedom of expression as contained in Article 10 of the European Convention on Human Rights and Fundamental Freedoms. (For a recent discussion of this theme, see A Mullis and A Scott, *The swing of the pendulum*, NILQ 63(1), 25–56.)

ii) There is a duty of verification imposed upon a responsible journalist which will be assessed in the circumstances of the case. Each case must turn on its own facts.

iii) This involves a 'spectrum' and will depend on the extent to which the defamatory allegations are adopted or endorsed by the publisher.

iv) A journalist in making the decision whether to publish will need to have regard to the full range of meanings that a reasonable reader could attribute to the article.

v) The duty of verification will be correspondingly more onerous the more serious the allegations. (No doubt, though, it is still necessary to have some regard to Lord Denning's warning in *Plato Films Ltd v Speidel* [1961] A.C. 1090 as to rumour being a 'lying jade'.)

vi) Verification involves a subjective and an objective element. The journalist must believe in the truth of the defamatory allegation and that must be a reasonable belief to hold.

vii) In a case such as the present, where there is a 'Chase Level 1' meaning, the journalist will have to satisfy himself on reasonable grounds that the relevant claimant is guilty of the defamatory 'charge'.

viii) The starting point in considering whether a publication was in the public interest will be to ask whether the subject-matter of the publication is itself a matter of public interest.

ix) At the next stage, when deciding to what extent the defamatory allegations about the individual claimant were appropriate to be included in the coverage of the subject-matter, allowance has to be made for editorial judgment.

x)   'Reportage' provides an example of circumstances in which the public interest may well justify publication of defamatory inferences without there being imposed on the journalist a duty to verify the truth of the inferences—at least where the inference relates to grounds for suspicion rather than a firm conclusion of guilt. Such circumstances may include the fact that there are police investigations on foot or that someone has been arrested.

xi) There is apparently a distinction to be drawn between the 'objective' aim of a publication and the 'subjective motives of the journalist' for publishing it. Ordinarily, the subjective motives of the journalist will be irrelevant to the issue of whether the publication is in the public interest."

Following a trial before Simon J., the *Reynolds* and justification defences in *Hunt* succeeded. See *Hunt v Times Newspapers Ltd (No.2)* [2013] EWHC 1868 (QB).

Verification and sources. For a successful application of the *Reynolds* defence,   **22–140**
see *El-Naschie v Macmillan Publishers Ltd* [2012] EWHC 1809 (QB). The court will carry out a detailed analysis of the research and sources used to verify the allegations, on examining a defence of *Reynolds*. The court will expect to see internal email correspondence between those responsible for authoring and editing the defamatory allegations, to ensure they have been properly verified.

Reports of legal proceedings. See generally *Qadir v Associated Newspapers*   **22–146**
Ltd [2012] EWHC 2606 (QB); [2013] E.M.L.R. 15 where a newspaper published two articles about court proceedings, in one article referring to the particulars of claim which accused the claimant of being involved in an alleged dishonest business deal, and in another reporting on a sentencing hearing in a criminal fraud claim. In the first, the defendant did not report that the claimant disputed the claim or the contents of his defence, which had been filed five weeks before the newspaper article was published. The court held that this was not fair or accurate and that there was no public interest in publishing false information; namely that the claimant had "declined to comment", which was untrue. In the second article, which alleged that the claimant had been "intimately involved" in "Britain's biggest mortgage fraud", those comments had been made during a sentencing hearing by counsel, but the judge had rebuked counsel, stating that he could not determine the complicity of others. The judge's comments had not been reported by the newspaper. The court held that the report of the sentencing hearing was not a fair and accurate report of those proceedings. The omission of the judge's comments seriously unbalanced the report, to the extent that the defendant could not rely upon the privilege, whether absolute or qualified.

(d) *Fair (now honest) comment*

Honest comment—basic elements. Add: In *Joseph v Spiller* [2010] UKSC 53;   **22–165**
[2011] 1 A.C. 852 the Supreme Court recommended that the defence of fair

comment be renamed "honest comment". The court ruled that it was not a prerequisite of the defence of honest comment that the readers should be in a position to evaluate the comment for themselves, as suggested by Lord Nicholls in *Tse Wai Chun Paul v Cheng* [2001] E.M.L.R. 31. In modern times, with the amount of information on the internet, it would often be impossible for readers to evaluate defamatory comments without detailed information about the facts which had given rise to the comments. The proposition that the comment must identify the matters on which it is based with sufficient particularity to enable the reader to judge for himself whether it was well founded was wrong. What was required was that the comment identified at least in general terms, the facts on which it was based.

(i) *Comment not fact*

22–166   **Fact or comment.** Add: In *Cook v Telegraph Media Group Ltd* [2011] EWHC 763 (QB) the court concluded that the allegation that the claimant was a "low value MP" was unarguably a comment rather than a statement of fact. Also, an allegation that the claimant set out to exploit or abuse the expenses system for MPs was capable of being fact or comment. See also *Cook v Telegraph Media Group Ltd* [2011] EWHC 1134 (QB). Political speech is more likely to be categorised as comment, following the Strasbourg jurisprudence. See *Waterson v Lloyd* [2013] EWCA Civ 136; [2013] E.M.L.R. 17.

NOTE 793. *British Chiropractic Association v Singh* [2010] EWCA Civ 350 is now reported at [2011] 1 W.L.R. 133.

(ii) *Sufficient factual basis*

After para.**22–167** add a new para.**22–167A**:

22–167A   **A sufficient factual basis.** Add: In *Cook v Telegraph Media Group Ltd* [2011] EWHC 763 (QB), the court also decided that where relevant facts were omitted from an article, this did not necessarily lead to a conclusion that the facts were not truly stated in the article, but rather might be relevant to the issue of honest belief.

See also *Lait v Evening Standard Ltd* [2010] EWHC 3239 (QB) (affirmed [2011] EWCA Civ 859; [2011] 1 W.L.R. 2973). The claimant sued over an article that suggested that, because she (a former Member of Parliament) had put her name to a letter published in *The Times* newspaper that sought to defend the much criticised old system under which MPs had claimed expenses, she "risked the ire of some". A basic fact in the article was wrong: the claimant was accused of having had to pay back £25,000 in expenses, although it was another MP that the newspaper had intended to refer to. Nevertheless, the defendant argued that the allegation was an honest comment since it could be based merely on the fact that, as an MP who had claimed under the old expenses system, it was inappropriate for her to seek to defend the old system. The claimant contended that such an argument was unreasonable—no reasonable person could be angry simply because the claimant had put her name to the letter. However, the court ruled that the inclusion of the false allegation concerning the £25,000 claim did not preclude the defendant from succeeding in a defence of fair comment provided that the comment was "fair" in relation to the facts that had been accurately stated. Reasonableness was not the test. The comment defence was available because the claimant, by having taken advantage of the flawed expenses system, had "forfeited the right to be heeded" on the topic of expenses. That was an opinion that could be honestly held, and the defence succeeded.

(f) *Offers to make amends: s.2 of the Defamation Act 1996*

(iv) *Disqualification*

The test for disqualification. Add: In *Thornton v Telegraph Media Group Ltd* **22–190** [2011] EWHC 1884 (QB); [2012] E.M.L.R. 8, Tugendhat J. accepted that the defence of an Offer of Amends under s.4(3) of the Defamation Act 1996 was defeated by a successful plea of malice. The claimant sued for defamation following the claim of a book reviewer that the claimant had (in her book) dishonestly claimed to have interviewed the reviewer herself for the book, when she had not. Tugendhat J. concluded that the reviewer knew these allegations to be false or was recklessly indifferent to the veracity of the allegation. The judge also concluded that the malice finding justified an award of aggravated damages, as did the manner in which the newspaper dealt with the complaint, which was high-handed and offensive. In addition, the claimant endured an upsetting and sustained cross-examination. An award of £65,000 damages was made.

(g) *Miscellaneous defences*

(i) *Limitation*

The discretion to extend. Add: In *Brady v Norman* [2011] EWCA Civ 107; **22–197** [2011] E.M.L.R. 16 the Court of Appeal confirmed that, when considering the discretion to disapply the one year limitation period for defamation actions under s.32A of the Limitation Act 1980, it was proper to take into account the respective prejudice to the parties which would be caused by a decision to disapply, or to refuse to disapply, the limitation period. The President accepted that, as noted in *Steedman v BBC* [2001] EWCA Civ 1534; [2002] E.M.L.R. 17, in a libel action, a direction under s.32A was always highly prejudicial to the defendant. In such a claim, brought to protect one's reputation, this ought to be pursued with vigour, given the ephemeral nature of most media publications.

(iv) *Abuse of process*

Abuse of process. A claim may also be struck out as an abuse of process where **22–201** there is a delay in bringing the matter to trial. See *Adelson v Anderson* [2011] EWHC 2497 (QB) where proceedings were struck out after the claimant delayed seven years in pursuing the claim and failed to comply with court orders. The court inferred that he no longer sought vindication and that there was no basis for ordering an injunction since the defendants had shown no indication of repeating the allegations of which he complained. For an example of a case that was allowed to proceed notwithstanding delays of a year, see *Morrissey v McNicholas* [2011] EWHC 2738 (QB).

7. MALICE

(b) *Examples of malice*

22–209 **Strong language not always evidence of malice.** Add: See also *Khader v Aziz* [2010] EWCA Civ 716; [2010] 1 W.L.R. 2673, where a malice claim based on "grossly exaggerated language" was struck out, since there was no evidence that the defendant did not believe the publication to be true or was indifferent to its truth or falsity.

22–210 **Knowledge of falsity of charge.** Add: See also *Cambridge v Makin* [2011] EWHC 12 (QB), affirmed by the Court of Appeal: [2012] EWCA Civ 85; [2012] E.M.L.R. 19 a rare case of a finding of malice based on the contention that the defendant did not honestly believe the allegations to be true or was reckless or indifferent to their truth or falsity.

9. DAMAGES

(a) *General*

22–224 **Principles of damages awards in defamation.** In *Al-Amoudi v Kifle* [2011] EWHC 2037 (QB) the court was required to assess damages in a claim by an Ethiopian businessman brought against the publisher of a website that covered news about Ethiopia. The judge awarded £175,000 damages in respect of allegations that the claimant had married off his under-age daughter to a Saudi royal as a symbol of his friendship to the royal family, had pursued his daughter to make her fear for her life, was probably responsible for the murder of his daughter's lover and the mutilation of his body, and that there were reasonable grounds for suspecting him of having knowingly funded terrorism. The judge found that it was difficult to imagine more serious allegations. The article was also likely to have been seen by several thousand people within the jurisdiction, largely among Ethiopians living in England. The behaviour of the defendant towards the claimant in response to his complaint added further insult, since he asserted the truth of the allegations. The judge observed that while in general a reasoned judgment could provide some vindication, in this case that was limited, since it followed after judgment was entered in default and the focus of the court was on the assessment of damages. Given that the decision was not contested on the merits, and the defendant's continued assertion of the libels' truth, the effect on damages of any vindication in the judgment would be marginal.

In *Cairns v Modi* and *KC v MGN Ltd* [2012] EWCA Civ 1382; [2013] 1 W.L.R. 1015 the Court of Appeal was required to review the damages awards in two separate actions for libel. In *Cairns* the claimant was a well-known international cricketer who brought proceedings against the ex-chairman of the Indian Premier League after he published a message on Twitter and an article which alleged that the claimant was involved in match-fixing. A defence of justification failed at trial and the judge awarded the claimant £15,000 to reflect one aspect of aggravation, namely the conduct of the defendant's former counsel during the trial. The total sum awarded was £90,000. In the other case, MGN was sued for libel by the father of "Baby P", a child who died in its mother's care. The defendant newspaper published an article in which it alleged that the claimant was a sex offender who had been convicted of raping a 14-year-old girl. The allegation was completely untrue. The newspaper apologised promptly and made an unqualified offer of amends. The judge assessed compensation by identifying a starting point of £150,000 and reducing it by 50 per cent to take account of all the mitigating factors. In *Cairns* it was contended that the sum awarded was disproportionate and excessive due to the narrow scope of the original publication and the reduced need for vindication by virtue of a reasoned judgment which dealt with the falsity of the allegations. It was also contended that the judge should have adopted a more analytical reasoning process, similar to that in *Vento v Chief Constable of West Yorkshire* [2002] EWCA Civ 1871; [2003] I.C.R. 318, and should have given a more detailed breakdown of the award. In the *MGN* case the newspaper argued that the judge had not given sufficient consideration to the fact that the claimant was anonymous throughout the time the allegations complained of circulated, and indeed throughout the trial. The Court of Appeal accepted that in the *Cairns* case only a small number of people would have read the original message on Twitter, but also recognised that as a consequence of modern technology, defamatory allegations could "percolate" more widely and more quickly than ever before. The court rejected the principle that damages should always be less following a trial by a judge alone than after the verdict of a jury, on the basis that the judge would provide a reasoned judgment which, if favourable to the claimant, would vindicate him. The court considered that most lay observers would be unlikely to read a detailed judgment and would be more interested to find out what sum the court, whether judge or jury, had awarded the claimant. In circumstances where the claimant had been subject to a serious attack on his reputation during the trial, the court considered that such a person would only be convinced by an award of some magnitude. The principles in *Vento* in which the court identified three broad bands of compensation for injury to feelings in the context of sex and race discrimination in the employment field, were not applicable in defamation cases. The process of determining compensation in defamation cases was well established, and adopting an analytical approach would give rise to practical difficulties. The Court of Appeal concluded that the sum awarded in *Cairns* was appropriate and proportionate. In respect of *KC v MGN*, the court found that the judge had attached too much importance to the large circulation and readership figures for the newspaper. In fact the circulation would have been very limited in the way it impacted on K's reputation, due to his anonymity. The court considered the appropriate starting point to be £100,000, which would be reduced by 50 per cent to allow for the offer of amends procedure. Accordingly the judge's award of £75,000 was reduced to £50,000.

(b) *Purpose of damages*

The purpose of awards in defamation. NOTE 997. On the capability of a **22–226** reasoned judgment to provide vindication, see also *Al-Amoudi v Kifle* [2011] EWHC 2037 (QB) (para.**22–224** above).

22–230 **State of mind of defendant material.** Add: See also *Henry v News Group Newspapers Ltd* [2011] EWHC 1058 (QB) where the judge observed that in a claim for aggravated damages, the state of mind of the defendant is relevant only insofar as it is known to the claimant. It is not relevant to enquire as to what is going on behind the scenes or what might have been in the minds of journalists when they prepared the story, except to the extent that such conduct affected the harm sustained by the claimant. In this case, the claimant was confined to pleading her case on aggravated damages with reference only to her perception of the defendant's journalists' conduct and the impact that had on her feelings.

(e) *Mitigation of damages*

(ii) *Background context*

22–240 **Admissibility of *Burstein* evidence.** Add: In *Hunt v Evening Standard Ltd* [2011] EWHC 272 (QB) Tugendhat J. refused to strike out a claim of general bad reputation in respect of the claimant, who was alleged to have such a reputation "for being the head of an organised crime group and for violent, criminal behaviour." The decision to allow such evidence was in part based on the fact that the claimant had in his particulars of claim made the allegation that he had a good reputation, which permitted the defence to challenge such a claim. This was also in line with the liberal approach proposed by the Court of Appeal in *Burstein v Times Newspapers Ltd* [2001] 1 W.L.R. 579.

(iii) *Conduct and reputation of claimant*

22–241 In *Joseph v Spiller* [2012] EWHC 2958 (QB) the court awarded nominal damages to members of a band who brought a defamation claim against their former promoter and booking company. This was because, notwithstanding their being successful on liability, it was proved at trial that one of claimants had attempted to deceive the court by fabricating part of a claim for special damages. The judge concluded that since the reputations of all the claimants were intertwined, they all suffered damage to their reputations by virtue of the fabrication, which gave rise to the nominal damages award.

22–242 **Bad reputation of claimant.** *Goody v Odhams Press* was applied in *King v Grundon* [2012] EWHC 2719 (QB), Sharp J. where the claimant's previous convictions for conspiracy to unlawfully detain and possession of a firearm was such that he had no reputation to protect or vindicate in the current proceedings. The proceedings served no useful purpose and were accordingly an abuse of process.

10. INJUNCTION

22–256 **Injunction.** Add: In *Robins v Kordowski* [2011] EWHC 981 (QB) the High Court granted an interim injunction with regard to defamatory allegations published about a solicitor. In addressing the rule in *Bonnard v Perryman* the court concluded that the words complained of were unarguably defamatory and there were no grounds for concluding that the statements might have been true. They were published by the defendant without any personal knowledge of their truth. The words "It is of my honest opinion" did not turn statements of fact into comment for the purposes of a defence of comment, and the defendant was not entitled to such a defence since he had no knowledge of the underlying facts. Nor was there any prospect of a defence of qualified privilege succeeding, in light of the defendant seeking to charge a removal fee in order to take down the publication from his website. That was not responsible journalism, and in any event, no steps were taken to verify the information prior to publication, there had been no urgency to publish and no comment had been sought from the claimant. Other *Reynolds* criteria were not made out. The court had regard to s.12(3) of the Human Rights Act 1998 and concluded that it was likely that a permanent injunction would be obtained at trial. In considering the balance of convenience, it was significant that the claimant maintained that the website entries were affecting the claimant's standing in the local community; there was also evidence that damages would be an inadequate remedy since the defendant lacked funds. Accordingly, an injunction was a practical necessity.

CHAPTER 23

MALICIOUS FALSEHOOD

		PARA.
■	1. Malicious falsehood	23–01
■	2. Essentials of the action	23–09
	(a) Published falsehoods	23–11
□	(b) Malice	23–12
■	(c) Damage	23–16
■	3. Rival traders	23–18

1. MALICIOUS FALSEHOOD

Malicious Falsehood and defamation compared. There is an appeal to the **23–03** Supreme Court outstanding in *Ajinomoto Sweetners Europe SAS v Asda Stores Ltd* [2010] EWCA Civ 609; [2011] Q.B. 497.

In *Cruddas v Calvert* [2013] EWCA Civ 748, the difference between the single meaning rule in defamation and the multiple meaning rule in malicious falsehood was discussed ([31]–[33]). With regard to malicious falsehood, Longmore L.J. stated at [30] that ". . . the duty of the judge at trial is to indicate the reasonably available meanings, decide if a substantial number of persons would reasonably have understood the words to have such a meaning and then decide, in respect of a meaning which is in fact false and damaging, whether the author was actuated by malice". In *Thornton v Telegraph* [2011] EWHC 159 (QB); [2011] E.M.L.R. 25 Tugendhat J. held that a defence of honest comment did not apply to the tort of malicious falsehood.

NOTE 16. With regard to absolute privilege and malicious falsehood see *Apison v Dilnot* [2011] EWHC 869 (QB) Tugendhat J. where statements made as part of a complaint to the Bar Standards Board were protected by absolute privilege.

Malicious falsehood and freedom of speech. In *Thornton v Telegraph* [2011] **23–04** EWHC 159 (QB); [2011] E.M.L.R. 25 Tugendhat J. at [34] noted that ". . . some malicious falsehood claims also involve art.8 rights, although less frequently than in defamation claims".

Interim injunctions. Note the *Practice Guidance (HC Interim Non-Disclosure* **23–05** *Orders)* [2012] 1 W.L.R. 1003 with regard to applications for interim non-disclosure orders in civil proceedings to restrain the publication of information. Such applications may be in respect inter alia of a threatened malicious falsehood (see further para.**27–47**, below).

"Threats" actions. For consideration of the "person aggrieved" see *Samuel* **23–06** *Smith Old Brewery (Tadcaster) v Lee* [2011] EWHC 1879 (Ch); [2012] F.S.R. 7, Arnold J.

2. ESSENTIALS OF THE ACTION

23–10   **Essentials of the action.** Add: *Euromoney v Aviation News* [2013] EWHC 1505 (QB) Tugendhat J.; a statement of opinion cannot be a falsehood for the purposes of a claim in malicious falsehood. See also *Cruddas v Calvert* [2013] EWHC 1096 (QB), Nicol J. The claimant sought permission inter alia to amend the particulars of claim in a malicious falsehood action to include an amendment that the defendant's intention in publishing the relevant articles was also to harm a third party (the Prime Minister). Held, though the authorities were not decisive, there are decisions which assume that the intention must be to injure the claimant (see [16]) and the other elements of the tort (that the publication must concern the claimant's economic interests and have caused him economic harm) must clearly relate to the claimant. The court was not prepared to make the novel extension suggested by the claimant. The court also rejected the analogy made by the claimant to the criminal law concept of "transferred malice". Further the court had to be particularly careful where novel extensions of the law impinged on areas of political debate (see *Horrocks v Lowe* [1975] A.C. 135).

(b) *Malice*

23–13   **The problem of definition.** *Khader v Aziz* [2010] EWCA Civ 716; [2010] 1 W.L.R. 2673: the concept of malice (in the context of qualified privilege and defamation) was discussed by Sir Anthony May (President, QB). He noted at [20]: "... grossly exaggerated language may be evidence of malice. However it is necessary that the evidence should raise the probability of malice, and be more consistent with its existence than its non-existence" (see also [29]). Part of Eady J.'s judgment in the lower court (for which see the Main Work) was referred to at [10].

(c) *Damage*

23–16   **Where no proof of special damage required.** Add: *Tesla Motors Ltd v BBC* [2013] EWCA Civ 152 (appeal to amend particulars of claim inter alia to reinstate malicious falsehood claim against defendant). Moore-Bick L.J. noted that since the claim was for general damages it was unnecessary for the claimant to identify the amount of pecuniary loss which it is said the falsehoods were calculated to cause. "All that is required in order to make the nature of the case clear is identification of the nature of the loss and the mechanism by which it is likely to be sustained" (at [37]). This, however, was a case in which the prospects of satisfying the court that the loss likely to be caused by the actionable falsehoods was significant was so small that in reality no substantial tort had been committed.

23–17   **Where proof of special damage required.** Add: *Citation Plc v Ellis Whittam Ltd* [2013] EWCA Civ 155. Application for a permanent injunction struck out where no reasonable risk of repetition of the alleged malicious falsehood. The falsehood had been made by the defendant's employee to a prospective client: the defendant had subsequently issued written instructions to all their sales staff not to make any such statements about the claimant trade rival.

3. Rival Traders

Comparative advertising. Add: *Euromoney v Aviation News* [2013] EWHC **23–18** 1505 (QB) Tugendhat J. at [105]: ". . . the claim about copying is not one that a reasonable man could take seriously in this case. The claim to be first is one that advertisers constantly make".

Trade Marks Act 1994. NOTE 125. Add: *Kingspan Group Plc v Rockwool Ltd* **23–21** [2011] EWHC 250 (Ch) Kitchin J.: comparative advertisement infringed TMA 1994 but no liability for malicious falsehood.

CHAPTER 24

ECONOMIC TORTS

			PARA.
☐	1.	General	24–01
☐	2.	Procuring a breach of contract	24–14
■		(a) Knowledge and intention	24–15
		(b) Breach	24–20
		(i) Breach of an existing contract	24–20
		(ii) Employment contracts and related issues	24–24
		☐ (iii) Bare interference without breach	24–26
		(iv) Breach of other obligations	24–27
		(c) The wrongful procurement	24–34
		☐ (i) Direct inducement	24–35
		(ii) Indirect procurement	24–45
		(d) Damage	24–51
		(e) Remedies	24–52
☐		(f) Defence of justification	24–55
☐	3.	Intimidation	24–57
■		(a) The threat	24–59
☐		(b) Unlawful act or means	24–61
		(c) Submission to threat	24–66
☐		(d) "Two party" and "three party" intimidation	24–67
		(e) Justification	24–69
■	4.	Unlawful interference	24–70
☐		(a) Intention	24–71
■		(b) Unlawful means	24–72
		(c) Related statutory torts	24–89
	5.	Conspiracy	24–90
■		(a) General	24–90
☐		(b) Unlawful means conspiracy	24–95
		■ (i) Intention	24–96
		■ (ii) Unlawful means	24–98
■		(c) Conspiracy to injure	24–104
	6.	Trade disputes	24–112
☐		(a) General	24–112
		(b) Trade disputes and procuring breach of contract	24–118
		(c) Trade disputes and intimidation	24–122
		(d) Specific limitations on the protection against liability	24–124
		(e) Dismissals and immunities	24–133
		(f) Trade disputes and conspiracy	24–137
		(g) Trade disputes and unlawful means	24–140
■		(h) Trade disputes and ballots	24–145
		(i) The statutory right of action	24–155
		(j) Picketing and trade disputes	24–156
☐		(k) Contemplation or furtherance of a trade dispute	24–161
		(i) The dispute	24–166
		(ii) Parties	24–167
		(iii) The content	24–169
		☐ (iv) Contemplation or furtherance	24–176

1. General

24–02   NOTE 12. Add: cf. the cautionary note sounded by the Manitoba Court of Appeal in *Johnson v BFI Canada Inc* [2010] MBCA 101; (2011) 326 D.L.R. (4th) 497 at [101] that the courts should be slow to expand the economic torts in cases where both parties had legitimate and competing interests. Inducing breach of contract and the unlawful interference tort were strictly limited in purpose and effect in a commercial world where much competitive activity was not only legal but encouraged as part of competitive behaviour that benefitted the economy.

24–09   **Interference.** NOTE 49. Add: cf. *Johnson v BFI Canada Inc* [2010] MBCA 101; (2011) 326 D.L.R. (4th) 497 at [40] and [45] where it was held that it would be wrong to decide the case on any basis other than that on which it was argued, which in that case was inducing breach of contract; the liability on which the trial judge had based his decision, "interference with economic or contractual relations" was a separate and admittedly broader tort per *OBG Ltd v Allan* [2007] UKHL 21; [2008] 1 A.C.1.

2. Procuring a Breach of Contract

24–14   NOTE 76. Add: cf. the analysis of the tort in terms of eight "essential elements" in *Sar Petroleum Inc v Peace Hills Trust Co* [2010] NBCA 22; (2010) 318 D.L.R. (4th) 70 at [39]–[78].

(a) *Knowledge and intention*

24–15   NOTE 78. Add: cf. *Qantas Airways v Transport Workers Union of Australia* [2011] FCA 470; (2011) 280 A.L.R. 503 at [442]–[444] noting the view that although the requirement of knowledge was sometimes expressed as separate, it was in fact an aspect of intention; sufficient knowledge meant sufficient to ground an intention to interfere with contractual rights: *Allstate Life Insurance Co v Australia and New Zealand Banking Group Ltd* (1995) 130 A.L.R. 469. On the facts in the *Qantas Airways* case the claim failed because none of the actions by the defendant union officials in response to Qantas' decision to outsource its baggage handling operations at Australian airports were intended to have the result that any Qantas workers would breach their contracts of employment.
    NOTE 79. Add: The claimant must show that the breach of contract was an end in itself or the means to an end: *OBG Ltd v Allan* [2007] UKHL 21; [2008] 1 A.C. 1 per Lord Hoffmann at [42]–[43]; see too *Sar Petroleum Inc v Peace Hills Trust Co* [2010] NBCA 22; (2010) 318 D.L.R. (4th) 70 NBCA at [51]–[55] where it was said that the Supreme Court of Canada's decision in *Jones v Fabbi* [1973] S.C.R. 42 was to the same effect.
    NOTE 83. Add: However, it has been accepted that an honest belief by the defendant that the outcomes sought by him would not involve any breach of contract was inconsistent with an intention to induce breach of contract even

if that belief was mistaken in law, muddleheaded or illogical: *OBG Ltd v Allan* [2007] UKHL 21; [2008] 1 A.C. 1 per Lord Nicholls at [202]; *1044807 Alberta Ltd v Brae Centre Ltd* [2008] ABCA 397; (2008) 302 D.L.R. (4th) 252 (Alberta CA) at [29]. See too *Sar Petroleum Inc v Peace Hills Trust Co* [2010] NBCA 22; (2010) 318 D.L.R. (4th) 70 at [47]–[50] citing the decision in *Mainstream Properties Ltd v Young*, one of the cases decided by the House of Lords in *OBG Ltd v Allan* [2007] UKHL 21; [2008] 1 A.C. 1, where the defendant financier honestly believed that two employees of the claimant company would not be breaking their employment contracts in pursuing a development opportunity themselves rather than trying to secure it for their employer.

NOTE 85. Add: See too the stricter approach in *Diver v Loktronic Industries Ltd* [2012] NZCA 131; [2012] 2 N.Z.L.R. 131 (NZCA) where after extensive citation from the English case law it was held that since this was an intentional tort a subjective rather than an objective inquiry was required to establish whether the defendant had sufficient knowledge of the contract. Where actual knowledge was not proved it had to be shown that the defendant had a suspicion of sufficient strength that a contract existed and made a deliberate choice not to make inquiries. It was not sufficient that the existence of a contract must have been obvious. On the facts the defendants' knowledge that there were long term relationships between Loktronic and two other companies was insufficient since a contract might not have been the only conceivable way in which the parties could have conducted business and accordingly a third party's stated belief that he was not aware of a contract or accepted assurances that there was none was more believable.

NOTE 96. Add: In *Qantas Airways v Transport Workers Union of Australia* **24-17** [2011] FCA 470; (2011) 280 A.L.R. 503 at [445] it was said that one aspect of intention was that the defendant's conduct must "in some real sense be aimed at the contract".

Recklessness. NOTE 101. Add: See too *Sar Petroleum Inc v Peace Hills Trust* **24-18** *Company* [2010] NBCA 22; (2010) 318 D.L.R. (4th) 70 at [45].

NOTE 106. Add: In *Led Technologies Pty Ltd v Roadvision Pty Ltd* [2012] FCA **24-19** 3; (2012) 287 A.L.R. 1 at [54] it was said that while reckless indifference might suffice, bearing in mind that this was an intentional tort, it was close to wilful blindness and would be negated by an honest belief, even one exhibiting a high degree of credulity as in *British Industrial Plastics Ltd v Ferguson* [1940] 1 All E.R. 479. Sufficient recklessness would only be established if the facts showed affirmatively that the alleged tortfeasor faced with knowledge of a prospect of breach proceeded not caring whether or not a breach would occur.

(b) *Breach*

(iii) *Bare interference without breach*

NOTE 143. Add: Frustration of the contract is not sufficient: *Alleslev-Krofchak* **24-26** *v Valcom Ltd* [2010] ONCA 557; (2010) 322 D.L.R. (4th) 193 Ont CA at [92].

(c) *The wrongful procurement*

(i) *Direct inducement*

24–35 NOTE 192. Add: cf. *Lonmar Global Risks Ltd v West* [2010] EWHC 2878; [2011] I.R.L.R. 138 at [220]: "As a matter of law I am sure that even silence in certain circumstances can be persuasive in encouraging breach of contract and can intend to do so".

24–36 NOTE 198. Add: In *Ontario Store Fixtures v Mmmuffins* [1989] 70 O.R. (2d) 42 it was said that there had to be separate identities of interest in this situation to give rise to a claim for inducing breach of contract as well as a claim for breach of contract; see too *1044807 Alberta Ltd v Brae Centre Ltd* [2008] ABCA 397; (2008) 302 D.L.R. (4th) 252 (Alberta CA) at [21]–[25] where it was said that there was general agreement that a director acting bona fide within the scope of his authority and in the best interests of the company would not be personally liable in tort for inducing a breach of contract by the company; something more had to be proved to establish liability as for example where directors acted in their own interests in making payments from the company to themselves for the purpose of defeating the plaintiff's claim in *Gainers Inc v Pocklington Holdings Inc* [2000] ABCA 307; (2000) 194 D.L.R. (4th) 109 (Alberta CA).

24–40 **Information and advice.** NOTE 215. Add: cf. *Qantas Airways v Transport Workers Union of Australia* [2011] FCA 470; (2011) 280 A.L.R. 503 at [438].
     NOTE 219. Add: In *Qantas Airways v Transport Workers Union of Australia* [2011] FCA 470; (2011) 280 A.L.R. 503 at [447]–[450] Moore J. said that it was tolerably clear that Finkelstein J. was there adopting Evershed M.R.'s distinction between persuasion and advice, in *Thomson v Deakin*; the dichotomy between advice, which appeared to be a fairly broad concept, and persuasion or procuration was, per Moore J. relevant to an assessment of whether any of the defendant union officials had committed the tort.

(f) *Defence of justification*

24–55 NOTE 296. Add: In *Whittaker v Child Support Registrar* [2010] FCA 43; (2010) 264 A.L.R. 473 it was held that where the defendants acted with statutory authority this provided a "short answer" to a claim for interference with contractual relations. On statutory authority as a defence to tort liability see paras **3–144—3–146** of the Main Work.
     NOTE 304. Insert in line 3 after "Stuart-Smith L.J. at 233).": In *Sar Petroleum Inc v Peace Hills Trust Co* [2010] NBCA 22; (2010) 318 D.L.R. (4th) 70 NBCA at [73] it was suggested that the defence of justification as applied in *Hill* had been incorporated into the test of intention as articulated in *OBG Ltd v Allan* [2007] UKHL 21; [2008] 1 A.C. 1 where the defendant acted for what the law considered a proper purpose, such as protecting its existing contractual or proprietary rights with a third party, the requisite intention for liability for procuring a breach of contract would be lacking. See too *Qantas Airways v Transport Workers Union of Australia* [2011] FCA 470; (2011) 280 A.L.R.503 at [454]–[458]: the essence of

the defence was that the conduct of the defendant involved the assertion of a greater right.

NOTE 309. Insert in line 8 after "justification": cf. *1044807 Alberta Ltd v Brae Centre Ltd* [2008] ABCA 397; (2008) 302 D.L.R. (4th) 252 (Alberta CA) at [33]–[38], where it was held that since a director was under a duty to act with a view to the best interests of the company the defence of justification might apply where those interests were best served by breaking the company's contractual commitments; even where this was not in fact the case, a director would only be liable for inducing breach of contract where there was affirmative proof that the dominating purpose of his acts was depriving the plaintiff of the benefits of the contract. cf. *Johnson v BFI Canada Inc* [2010] MBCA 101; (2011) 326 D.L.R. (4th) 497 (Manitoba CA) where having cited Canadian texts to the effect that the defence was not susceptible of precise or predictable guidelines, it was noted that action taken to protect the equal or superior rights of the defendant had been regarded as sufficient justification in *Hill v First National Finance Corporation* [1989] 1 W.L.R. 225 CA, and *Sar Petroleum Inc v Peace Hills Trust Co* [2010] NBCA 22; (2010) 318 D.L.R. (4th) 70 (NBCA). It was therefore held that action taken by defendants in good faith in pursuit of their own economic interests in accordance with existing contractual rights—on the facts in *Johnson* offering new contractual terms to a third party before the existing contract between them had expired but after the third party had entered into a new contract with the plaintiff—fell within the scope of the defence.

3. INTIMIDATION

The tort of intimidation. NOTE 316. Insert in line 2 after "of the tort":, cited   **24-57**
with approval by Longmore L.J. in *Berezovsky v Abramovich* [2011] EWCA Civ 153; [2011] 1 W.L.R. 2290 at [5].

(a) *The threat*

NOTE 334. Insert in line 3 after "(1983) 46 M.L.R. 229.": In *Berezovsky v*   **24-59**
Abramovich [2011] EWCA Civ 153; [2011] 1 W.L.R. 2290 at [81]–[83], having stated that a threat could be implied as well as express, depending on the context, Longmore L.J. added that it was sufficient for the claimant to allege that the defendant threatened that some act, such as (on the facts) expropriation would occur since this carried the implication that the defendant would do what he could to ensure that this would happen if the claimant did not comply with his wishes—on the facts by disposing of his interests in a particular company at a supposed undervalue.

NOTE 336. Add: cf. *Great Canadian Railtour Co v Teamsters Local 31* [2012] BCCA 238; (2012) 350 D.L.R. (4th) 364 where in the absence of any such legislation but where the defendant union had accepted that harassing conduct by pickets could form part of the tort of intimidation, it was held that an injunction could restrain not only conduct which amounted to the tort but also conduct which formed part of or contributed to the commission of that tort.

(b) *Unlawful act*

24–61   NOTE 350. Add: In the light of this very clear line of authority, the parties' agreement in *Berezovsky v Abramovich* [2011] EWCA Civ 153; [2011] 1 W.L.R. 2290 at [5] that "for the purposes of these interlocutory proceedings it is arguable that the means to be used need not necessarily be unlawful if they can be categorised as 'illegitimate'" seems to be inconsistent with clearly established authority.

(d) *"Two party" and "Three party" intimidation*

24–67   NOTE 392. Add: In *Berezovsky v Abramovich* [2011] EWCA Civ 153; [2011] 1 W.L.R. 2290 both the outline of the essential ingredients of the tort at [5] and discussion of the adequacy of the claimant's pleadings at [80]–[86] clearly contemplated the possibility of liability in the "two party" form of the tort.

NOTE 393. Add: cf. *Kolmar Group AG v Traxpo Enterprises Pvt Ltd* [2010] EWHC 113 (Comm); [2010] 2 Lloyds Rep. 653 where the definition and ingredients of this tort in the 19th edition of this work were cited with approval at [119] and on the facts the claimants were held to be entitled to succeed on the basis of claims for either restitution of sums paid under economic duress or damages for intimidation; see [118] and [121]. On economic duress see too *Burin Peninsula Community Development Corp v Grandy* [2010] NLCA 69; (2011) 327 D.L.R. (4th) 752.

4. UNLAWFUL INTERFERENCE

24–70   **Unlawful interference with economic and other interests.** Add at end of paragraph: The defence of justification which applies to the tort of procuring breach of contract is "not usually regarded as a defence to this tort".[410a] It is however included as the last item in the "general model for the essential tenets of the unlawful means tort" in *A.I. Enterprises Ltd v Bram Enterprises Ltd* [2012] NBCA 33; (2012) 350 D.L.R. (4th) 601. The other items, which it was conceded might need refinement over time, required the claimant to establish: (1) the existence of a valid business relationship with a third party; (2) that the defendant knew or ought to have known of this relationship; (3) that the defendant's conduct prevented formation of a contract or its performance in circumstances in which there was no breach of an existing contract; (4) the defendant's conduct qualified as unlawful means or warranted exceptional treatment; (5) the unlawful means were not directly actionable by the claimant; (6) the defendant intended to cause the claimant harm; and (7) the defendant's conduct was the proximate cause of the claimant's loss.[410b]

NOTE 405. Add: In *Future Investments SA v Federation Internationale De Football Association* [2010] EWHC 1019 (Ch) where part of the claim was for "causing harm by unlawful means" Floyd J. stated the law at [19]–[25] in the same terms as Lord Hoffmann in *OBG Ltd v Allan*. In *Qantas Airways v Transport Workers Union of Australia* [2011] FCA 470; (2011) 280 A.L.R. 503 at [425] and [426] Moore J. concluded that since the High Court in *Sanders v Snell* [1998] HCA 64; (1998) 196 C.L.R. 329 at [35]–[36] had found it unnecessary to decide whether this tort should be recognised in Australia, it had yet to be declared part of Australian law. By contrast in *A.I. Enterprises Ltd v Bram Enterprises Ltd* [2012] NBCA 33; (2012) 350 D.L.R. (4th) 601 it was said at [44] and [45] that while the Canadian Supreme Court had "yet to wade into the debate surrounding the proper tenets of the intentional torts . . . [i]t is an understatement to acknowledge that Canadian courts have relied heavily on the English jurisprudence."

NOTE 409. Add: On the distinction between an award of damages in this tort and an award for defamation arising out of the same events see *AlleslevKrofchak v Valcom* [2010] ONCA 557; (2010) 322 D.L.R. (4th) 193 (Ont CA) at [92].

NOTE 410a. *Johnson v BFI Canada Inc* [2010] MBCA 101; (2011) 326 D.L.R. (4th) 497 (Manitoba CA) at [55].

NOTE 410b. *A.I. Enterprises Ltd v Bram Enterprises Ltd* [2012] NBCA 33; (2012) 350 D.L.R. (4th) 601 at [56].

(a) *Intention*

NOTE 418. Add: cf. *Print N' Promotion (Canada) Ltd v Kovachis* [2011] **24–71** ONCA 23; (2011) 329 D.L.R. (4th) 421 (Ont CA) where the landlord's termination of the head lease because of the tenant's failure to pay the rent was not actionable in tort by a sub-tenant who was thereby prevented from using a wall of the premises for advertising purposes as an "intentional interference with contractual relations and economic interests", inter alia because no intention to injure the sub-tenant was established.

NOTE 419. Insert "owners" after "abattoir" at end of line 2.

(b) *Unlawful means*

NOTE 425. Add: cf. *McLeod v Rooney* [2009] CSOH 158; 2010 S.L.T. 499 at **24–73** [18] where Lord Glennie concluded from an extensive review of the speeches in *OBG Ltd v Allan* that "the essential aspect [of the tort] is that the loss is caused to the claimant through a third party on whom the defender unlawfully acted. That is the control mechanism. The inquiry focuses on the nature of the disruption as between the third party and the claimant rather than the causative link between the defender's wrong and the claimant's loss." Thus where Rooney, the general manager of V Ltd withdrew an offer of extra investment in the company and advised its sole supplier, REL, of V Ltd's financial difficulties, causing REL to submit invoices for outstanding payments and thereby forced the pursuers, the majority shareholders, to accept his offer for their shares, after which REL's invoices were cancelled, their claim in this tort failed since, if proved, it would have been for loss caused to the pursuers directly and not through the company as a third party.

NOTE 426. Insert in line 13 after "independently actionable by the plaintiff": In *Alleslev-Krofchak v Valcom Ltd* [2010] ONCA 557; (2010) 322 D.L.R. (4th) 193 at [60] the Ontario Court of Appeal concluded that "it is now clear that to qualify as 'unlawful means' the defendant's actions (i) cannot be actionable directly by the plaintiff and (ii) must be directed at a third party who becomes the vehicle through which harm is caused to the plaintiff" preferring the majority opinion of Lord Hoffmann to that of Lord Nicholls in *OBG Ltd v Allan* [2007] UKHL 21; [2008] 1

A.C. 1. The court noted, however, that among aspects of unlawful means that remained to be defined were whether the requirement of actionability by a third party was subject to any qualifications. On the facts in that case it was held that action by the defendants against ARINC, an American company through which the first plaintiff was providing her services was actionable as an unlawful means conspiracy by ARINC after the House of Lords decision in the *Total Network* case [2008] UKHL 19; [2008] 1 A.C. 1174 (see para.**24–100**) and this conspiracy could constitute unlawful means for the purposes of her claim in the unlawful interference tort. A different approach was taken by the New Brunswick Court of Appeal in *A.I. Enterprises Ltd v Bram Enterprises Ltd* [2012] NBCA 33; (2012) 350 D.L.R. (4th) 601; taking into consideration the case law in the Ontario Court of Appeal and the House of Lords' broader interpretation of unlawful conduct in the context of the tort of conspiracy in the *Total Network* case, it was held that the independent actionability requirement should be flexible and allow for exceptions which were principled and did not attract the criticism of ad hoc decision making: at [5] and [80]–[81]. Thus on the facts the conduct of one of the brothers in a family involved in real estate leasing—instituting arbitration proceedings and registering documents encumbering title to property which prevented its sale for two years until it was agreed to sell it to him for a lower price than earlier offers which had been received—was held to satisfy the requirement of unlawful means on the basis that his action was akin to the tort of abuse of process.

Although the existence of this tort in Australian law has yet to be finally decided (see Note 405 above), in *Qantas Airways v Transport Workers Union of Australia* [2011] FCA 470; (2011) 280 A.L.R. 503 at [428] it was said that if the tort did exist, acts that were only ultra vires or void would not be sufficient to constitute unlawful means; an act which was unlawful in the sense of prohibited by law was required, following *Scott v Pedler* [2003] FCA 650.

5. Conspiracy

(a) *General*

24–90   **The nature of conspiracy.** NOTE 487. Add: *Baxendale-Walker v Middleton* [2011] EWHC 998 at [59] and [60].

NOTE 491. Add: *Gray v News Group Newspapers Ltd* [2012] UKSC 28; [2013] 1 A.C. 1 at [43]–[45] per Lord Walker; the offence of conspiracy was complete when the agreement had been made and the conspirators could be prosecuted even though no performance had taken place.

24–92   **The combination.** NOTE 502. Add: cf. *Gray v News Group Newspapers Ltd* [2012] UKSC 28; [2013] 1 A.C. 1 at [44] where Lord Walker said that the crime of conspiracy "involved an agreement, express or implied".

24–93   NOTE 510. Add: In *The Dolphina* [2011] SGHC 273; [2012] 1 Lloyd's Rep. 304, on the basis that the purpose of the tort of conspiracy "seems to lie in the law's concern to prevent harmful combinations": *Revenue & Customs Commissioners v Total Network SL* [2008] UKHL 19; [2008] 1 A.C. 1174 per

Lord Hope at [44] and Lord Walker at [77], it was held at [254]–[256] that for this purpose a company should be identified with the person or persons who could cause it to combine with others so as to harm the plaintiff, which in the first instance would be its board of directors. On the facts the defendant company's knowledge was held to include knowledge which one of its directors gained as a director of another company.

NOTE 514. Add: *The Dolphina* [2011] SGHC 273; [2012] 1 Lloyd's Rep. 304 **24–94** at [265]. "A conspirator need not know all the details of the plot so long as he is aware of the common objective and what his role in bringing it about involves" at [282].

NOTE 517. Add: cf. *The Dolphina* [2011] SGHC 273; [2012] 1 Lloyd's Rep. 304 at [264] where it was said that in unlawful means conspiracy the requirements of "combination" and "unlawful act" though in theory discrete often had to be considered together because direct evidence of a combination was unlikely to be forthcoming and therefore proof of the combination was "usually gathered from the unlawful acts committed" which were "often sufficient . . . to justify the inference that their commission was the product of concert between the alleged conspirators."

NOTE 518. Substitute for last entry in Note beginning *"Tree Savers International"* as follows: However, the view of some commentators that unlawful means conspiracy was only a form of secondary civil liability for unlawful means which were themselves an actionable civil wrong was rejected by the House of Lords in *Revenue & Customs Commissioners v Total Network SL* [2008] UKHL 19; [2008] A.C. 1174 per Lord Walker at [101]–[104], Lord Mance at [116] and Lord Neuberger at [225]; see too *The Dolphina* [2011] SGHC 273; [2012] 1 Lloyd's Rep. 304 at [270]. On the overlap of liability for conspiracy and inducing breach of contract see *Tree Savers International v Savoy* (1991) 87 D.L.R. (4th) 202 (Alta. CA) at 206–207.

(b) *Unlawful means conspiracy*

After "damage" in line 3 add Note 518a: **24–95**

NOTE 518a. *Baxendale-Walker v Middleton* [2011] EWHC 998 at [60]. cf. *Pell Frischmann Engineering Ltd v Bow Valley Iran Ltd* [2009] UKPC 45; [2011] 1 W.L.R. 2370 where the Privy Council upheld the Jersey courts' decisions dismissing a claim for unlawful means conspiracy by one party to an intended joint venture against two others on the ground, inter alia, that there was no intention on the part of either of those companies to cause loss: at [55] per Lord Walker who cited Lord Hoffmann in *OBG Ltd v Allan* [2007] UKHL 21; [2008] 1 A.C. 1 at [62] in support of his reasoning on this point, although Lord Hoffmann was there referring to the *Lumley v Gye* and unlawful interference/causing loss by unlawful means torts rather than unlawful means conspiracy.

(i) *Intention*

NOTE 524. Add: See too *The Dolphina* [2011] SGHC 273; [2012] 1 Lloyd's **24–97** Rep. 304 at [279] where this was said to be consistent with the test of intention in the unlawful interference/causing loss by unlawful means tort.

(ii) *Unlawful means*

24–98   NOTE 532. Add: cf. *The Dolphina* [2011] SGHC 273; [2012] 1 Lloyd's Rep. 304 at [269] where it was held, on the basis of the provision in the Singapore Interpretation Act that where the context required "act" could mean "omission", that notwithstanding the authorities which referred to the requirement for an "overt act" in order to establish an unlawful means conspiracy, unlawful means could be effected by an omission.

24–100   NOTE 542. Add: cf. the discussion of Canadian case law on the scope of unlawful means in this form of the tort of conspiracy in the judgment of the Ontario Court of Appeal in *Agribrands Purina Canada Inc v Kasamekas* [2011] ONCA 460; (2011) 334 D.L.R. (4th) 714 at [27]–[38], where it was said that reliance on what had been held to be unlawful means in the tort of intentional interference with economic relations did not recognise that these two economic torts evolved separately and each had developed its own concept of unlawful conduct, citing Lord Walker in *Revenue & Customs Commissioners v Total Network SL* [2008] UKHL 19; [2008] 1 A.C. 1174 at [100] in support. The court concluded at [38] that "what is required therefore to meet the 'unlawful conduct' element of the conspiracy tort is that the defendants engage in concert in acts that are wrong in law, whether actionable in private law or not". Cf. para.**24–98** above.

(c) *Conspiracy to injure*

24–105   **Legitimate and illegitimate objects.** NOTE 570. Add: cf. *The Dolphina* [2011] SGHC 273; [2012] 1 Lloyd's Rep. 304 at [210]: predominant purpose of damaging the plaintiff bank not made out where purpose of one of the defendants was to secure payment due under a contract with one of the bank's customers.

6. TRADE DISPUTES

(a) *General*

24–112   **Trade disputes and the economic torts.** Add note 615a to "social policies" at the end of the paragraph.
NOTE 615a. For a concise account of this context see Elias L.J. in *London & Birmingham Railway Ltd v ASLEF* [2011] EWCA Civ 226; [2011] I.C.R. 848 at [2]–[9] concluding with a rejection of the claimant employers' submission in that case that the legislation should be construed strictly against the defendant unions since they were seeking to take advantage of an immunity, and an endorsement of Lord Bingham's approach in *P v NASUWT* [2003] I.C.R. 386 at [7] that the legislation should be given a "likely and workable construction". This approach was also expressly adopted in *London Underground Ltd v ASLEF* [2011] EWHC 3506 (QB); [2012] I.R.L.R. 196 per Eder J. at [14] and *Balfour Beatty Engineering Services Ltd v Unite* [2012] EWHC 267 (QB); [2012] I.C.R. 822 per Eady J. at [8].

24–116   NOTE 652. Add: In *London & Birmingham Railway Ltd v ASLEF* [2011] EWCA Civ 226; [2011] I.C.R. 848 the Court of Appeal rejected a submission that since unions were seeking to take advantage of an immunity from common law liability the legislative protection in TULRCA s.219 should be strictly construed against them. "The statutory immunities are simply the form which the law in this country takes to carve out the ability for unions to take lawful strike action", per Elias L.J. at [9].

NOTE 653. Add: cf. Lord Judge C.J. in *British Airways Plc v Unite* [2010] EWCA Civ 669; [2010] I.C.R. 1316 at [14] cautioning against reading a judgment on an appeal against an interlocutory order as a final judgment in the litigation.

(h) *Trade disputes and ballots*

NOTE 831. Add: For a concise up to date summary see Elias L.J. in *London &* **24–145** *Birmingham Railway Ltd v ASLEF* [2011] EWCA Civ 226; [2011] I.C.R. 848 at [15]–[30].

Amend text to Note 841 to read: (viii) the period of effectiveness of the ballot.

NOTE 841. Substitute for the opening words "See Simpson (1993) 22 I.L.J. 297" the following: On the correct judicial approach to construction of the statutory provisions on industrial action ballots in TULRCA ss.226–235 see *P v NASUWT* [2003] UKHL 8; [2003] 2 A.C. 663 per Lord Bingham at [7]: "The House must attempt to give the provisions a likely and workable construction." See too Elias L.J. in *London & Birmingham Railway Ltd v ASLEF* [2011] EWCA Civ 226; [2011] I.C.R. 848 at [9]: "the legislation should simply be construed in the normal way without presumptions one way or the other" with Lord Bingham's "likely and workable construction" as the starting point. In *Balfour Beatty Engineering Services Ltd v Unite* [2012] EWHC 267 (QB); [2012] I.C.R. 822 at [8] Eady J. added to these two approaches recognition "since the advent of the Human Rights Act 1998 at least that it is appropriate to construe the relevant statutory provisions in a way that is compatible with rights enshrined under the European Convention on Human Rights and Fundamental Freedoms ... the approach adopted at Strasbourg has been to recognise the right to strike as part and parcel of the right to freedom of association conferred under Article 11(1)."

Postal Ballots. NOTE 844. Add: In *Balfour Beatty Engineering Services Ltd v* **24–146** *UNITE* [2012] EWHC 267 (QB); [2012] I.C.R. 822 at [12] Eady J. cited Lord Walker in *P v NASUWT* [2003] UKHL 8; [2003] 2 A.C. 663 at [65]: "it is a fact of life that no trade union of any size can keep completely full and accurate records of the names and addresses of its ever-changing body of members, still less their current places of work, trade categories and pay grades" as highlighting the need to make due allowance for these realities in deciding whether the union had conducted the ballot in accordance with s.230.

Entitlement to vote. Replace the first two sentences of the Text (on lines 1–7) **24–147** and Note 846 with the following:

As amended in 2004, s.227(1) provides that entitlement to vote must be accorded equally to all those members who it is reasonable for the union to believe at the time of the ballot will be induced by the union to take part in the action, and to no others.[845a] This has been held to entitle a union to ballot workers who were not being induced by the union to take industrial action on a particular day but whom the union believed would be induced cto take part in the industrial action."845b After the 1999 and 2004 amendments the court may excuse failure to comply with the rule about entitlement (as well as a failure to comply with the posting rules) if the failures are accidental and unlikely to affect the result.846

NOTE 845a. Thus where the union issued ballot papers to members who were shortly to leave employment with the employer, having accepted voluntary redundancy, it was held that the union had not satisfied this requirement: *British Airways Plc v Unite* [2009] EWHC 3541 (QB); [2010] I.R.L.R. 423. It was also held on these facts that the union could not establish a reasonable belief that they were entitled to vote so as to fall within the "small accidental failures" disregard in s.232B: see text to Note 846. In *Re United Closures & Plastics Ltd* [2011] CSOH 114; 2011 S.L.T. 1105 at [49]–[52] the court rejected a submission that a ballot on industrial action in a dispute over changes to working conditions had to be limited to workers who would be directly affected by these changes; ss.226A(2H) and 234A(5C), which define the "persons concerned" for the purposes of notices of an industrial action ballot, and industrial action after a ballot in which the majority supported industrial action, refer respectively to those employees whom the union "reasonably believes" will be entitled to vote (s.226A) and induced by the union to take industrial action (s.234A).

NOTE 845b. *London Underground Ltd v ASLEF* [2011] EWHC 3506 (QB); [2012] I.R.L.R. 196 at [47] where Eder J. emphasised that s.227(1) referred to members who would be induced to "take part" and not "take". Thus a ballot of drivers in a dispute over working on Boxing Day was not invalid because it was not limited to members who had been rostered to work on Boxing Day (whose identity was not, in any event, known at the time when the ballot papers were sent out because the rosters for Boxing Day had not then been posted); moreover the union was considering calling for industrial action not only on Boxing Day but on other days in the New Year.

NOTE 846. TULRCA 1992 s.232B inserted by ERA 1999 Sch.3 para.9 and amended by ERA 2004 s.24(1). See *Balfour Beatty Engineering Services Ltd v Unite* [2012] EWHC 267 (QB); [2012] I.C.R. 822 at [18] where it was noted that since the duty was to provide those entitled to vote with a voting paper sent by post and a convenient opportunity to vote by post "so far as is reasonably practicable" the disregard of small accidental failures by the union in s.232B was an additional qualification to this duty on the union. It may be noted that before the 2004 amendment, it had been held that the reference to s.230(2A) in s.232B was an error for s.230(2B): *P v NASUWT* [2001] EWCA Civ 652; [2001] I.C.R. 1241 at [62]; [2003] UKHL 8; [2003] 2 A.C. 663. In *London & Birmingham Railway Ltd v ASLEF* [2011] EWCA Civ 226; [2011] I.C.R. 848, Elias L.J. cited the reasoning of the House of Lords in *P v NASUWT* in support of his conclusion that the accidental erroneous inclusion of two members who worked for another employer in the list of those entitled to vote was an error falling within the provision on entitlement to vote in s.230(2) so that the union could rely on the small accidental failures disregard in s.232B.

NOTE 849. Add: In *London & Birmingham Railway Ltd v ASLEF* [2011] EWCA Civ 226; [2011] I.C.R. 848 at [78]–[87] Elias L.J. concluded that the de minimis principle in the *British Railways Board v NUR* case still applied. It was consistent with the reasoning of Lord Bingham in *P v NASUWT* [2003] UKHL 8; [2003] 2 A.C. 663 and also Smith L.J.'s judgment in *British Airways Plc v Unite*

[2010] EWCA Civ 669; [2010] I.C.R. 1316 that "substantial compliance" was sufficient in relation to the duty in s.231 to inform members of the result of the ballot. See too *Re United Closures & Plastics Ltd* [2011] CSOH 114; 2011 S.L.T 1105 at [15].

Content of the ballot paper. NOTE 886. Add: In *British Airways Plc v Unite* [2010] EWCA Civ 669; [2010] I.C.R. 1316 the Court of Appeal, by a majority, held that this section did not require a separate report of the result to be sent to each member personally. Communication by electronic means to a membership that was highly computer literate and used the internet as part of their employment on a daily basis, supported by union notice boards and news sheets was sufficient to satisfy the requirements of s.231. **24–151**

Notices to employers. Add Note 887a to "employers" in line 5: **24–152**
NOTE 887a. In *London & Birmingham Railway Ltd v ASLEF* [2011] EWCA Civ 226; [2011] I.C.R. 848 at [118]–[120] Elias L.J. rejected the judge's finding that the purpose of the obligation to provide notices was to enable the employer to decide whether to take legal proceedings or not. Nor was it necessary for the union to explain "who did what and when" in compiling the figures or to explain a discrepancy with figures provided in earlier ballots, though it might be wise for the union to respond to a request for the latter.
Add Note 887b to "workplace" in line 9:
NOTE 887b. The union is also required to provide an explanation of how these figures were arrived at. In *London & Birmingham Railway Ltd v ASLEF* [2011] EWCA Civ 226; [2011] I.C.R. 848 Elias L.J. concluded at [92] that consistently with para.16 of the Code of Practice (see Note 841) this required the union to state the sources of its data and identify any potential weaknesses in its records highlighting any potential inaccuracies of which it was aware; "the duty on the union is not an onerous one" at [95].
NOTE 888. Add: In *EDF Energy Powerlink Ltd v RMT* [2009] EWHC 2852 (QB); [2010] I.R.L.R.114, the union's notice stating that it intended to ballot "members employed by the company as shift tester staff and categorised in our database as engineer technicians employed at the Tufnell Park workplace" was held to be inadequate since it failed to identify with sufficient particularity the "categories" of employee covered. The fact that a union might not record information about its members in these terms while potentially "highly material" was not "necessarily always decisive". Cf. *London & Birmingham Railway Ltd v ASLEF* [2011] EWCA Civ 226; [2011] I.C.R. 848 where at [60]–[77] after a review of the legislative history Elias L.J. rejected the employers' submission based on the *EDF* case that the union was required to take steps to obtain the information from its members. Both the limitation of the duty by reference to information in possession of the union and the fact that unions would normally have this information available supported limiting the duty to provide figures from information actually held by the union at the time they were provided. This approach was followed in *Re United Closures & Plastics Ltd* [2011] CSOH 114; 2011 S.L.T. 1105 at [46] and [47]. Cf. *Metroline Travel Ltd v Unite* [2012] EWHC 1778 (QB); [2102] I.R.L.R. 749 where the ballot notices to the three claimant companies stated the union's intention to ballot drivers and engineering grades working on Transport for London contracts, and the subsequent strike notice added that this included

both those working directly on these contracts or indirectly as engineers servicing vehicles and those working on Transport for London routes on overtime; both notices were held to fail to satisfy the statutory requirements because the employers could not readily deduce from them the information to which they were entitled: the total numbers to be balloted and called out on strike and the numbers in each category of worker and at each workplace.

24–153   Insert at the beginning of the paragraph:

Accidental failures in compliance. In addition to the small accidental failures disregard in s.232B noted above,[896a] there are other limits on the effects of non-compliance with the prescriptive details of these provisions.
NOTE 896a. See para.**24–147** above.

(k) *Contemplation or furtherance of a trade dispute*

24–163   NOTE 977. Insert in line 2 after "Lord Diplock": *London & Birmingham Railway Ltd v ASLEF* [2011] EWCA Civ 226; [2011] I.C.R. 848 at [10]–[14] per Elias L.J.

NOTE 982. Insert at the end of the first sentence in line 4 after "at 1307": See *United Closures & Plastics Ltd* [2011] CSOH 114; 2011 S.L.T. 1105 at [41]–[44] where it was accepted by the petitioner that the correct approach to the balance of convenience was that described by Elias L.J. in *London & Birmingham Railway Ltd v ASLEF* [2011] EWCA Civ 226; [2011] I.C.R. 848 at [10]–[12] and Lord Fraser's opinion in *NWL Ltd v Woods* [1979] 1 W.L.R. 1294 at 1309–1311.

NOTE 983. Add: In *Balfour Beatty Engineering Services Ltd v Unite* [2012] EWHC 267 (QB); [2012] I.C.R. 822 at [3]–[4], having noted that it was not easy to form a judgment on the outcome of a case on the basis of partial or incomplete evidence, Eady J. cited the Court of Appeal decision in *London & Birmingham Railway Ltd v ASLEF* [2011] EWCA Civ 226; [2011] I.C.R. 848 per Elias L.J. at [13] in support of his conclusion that while a defendant trade union's establishing the likelihood of it having a trade dispute defence did not conclude the interim injunction issue in its favour, it would be exceptional for a court having reached that conclusion to grant relief. No applicant in the position of the claimant employer in that case could "expect to succeed in obtaining interlocutory relief merely by showing: (i) that there is a serious issue to be tried; (ii) the balance of convenience lies in its favour; and (iii) that it is likely otherwise to suffer harm which cannot be adequately compensated for in damages."

NOTE 985. Add: The importance of adopting an approach which does not deprive a union's members of an "effective right to withhold their labour" was expressly recognised in *British Airways Plc v Unite* [2010] EWCA Civ 669; [2010] I.C.R. 1316 per Smith L.J. at [109] and [153] and *London Underground Ltd v ASLEF* [2011] EWHC 3506 (QB); [2012] I.R.L.R. 196 per Eder J. at [10]–[12].

(iv) *Contemplation or furtherance*

24–177   NOTE 1073. Add: cf. s.13 of the Irish Industrial Relations Act 1990 which uses the wording "in the reasonable belief that the act was done in contemplation or furtherance of a trade dispute" to qualify similar statutory defences in Irish law and was described in *Dublin City Council v Technical Engineering and Electrical Union* 2010 IEHC 289; [2010] 4 I.R. 667 at [48] as a *via media* between the subjective test of furtherance upheld by the majority of the House of Lords in the *McShane* case and the objective test adopted in Lord Wilberforce's dissenting speech in that case and by Lord Denning in *Associated Newspaper Group Ltd v Wade* [1979] I.C.R. 664 CA.

CHAPTER 25

STATUTORY INTELLECTUAL PROPERTY RIGHTS

		PARA.
■	1. Introduction.	25–01
	2. Copyright and related rights	25–04
■	(a) Scope of section	25–04
■	(b) Authorship and ownership	25–13
■	(c) Infringement of copyright.	25–19
□	(d) Remedies for infringement of copyright.	25–33
■	3. Moral rights.	25–39
□	4. Competition and control of licensing	25–46
■	5. Performers' rights	25–47
■	6. Design right.	25–53
■	7. Registered designs	25–63
	8. Registered trade marks	25–73
■	(a) Introduction.	25–73
■	(b) Registration.	25–76
■	(c) Infringement of trade mark	25–81
■	(d) Proceedings.	25–83
	9. Patents.	25–87
■	(a) Introduction.	25–87
■	(b) Validity	25–94
■	(c) Infringement	25–98
■	(d) Special regimes	25–108

1. INTRODUCTION

Intellectual Property. NOTE 1. Second sentence. Delete and substitute: **25–01**
For a full account of these rights see Garnett, Davies and Harbottle, *Copinger and Skone James on Copyright*, 16th edn (London: Sweet and Maxwell, 2010) and first and second supplements 2012 and 2013; Laddie, Prescott and Vitoria, *The Modern Law of Copyright and Designs*, 4th edn (London: Butterworths, 2011); Arnold, *Performers' Rights*, 4th edn (London: Sweet and Maxwell, 2008); and Davies and Garnett, *Moral Rights* (London: Sweet and Maxwell, 2010).

NOTE 2. Add: On patent law, see *CIPA Guide to the Patents Acts*, 7th edn (London: Sweet and Maxwell, 2011) and *Terrell on the Law of Patents*, 17th edn (London, Sweet and Maxwell, 2011).

NOTE 5. Add: See also *Gurry on Breach of Confidence-the Protection of Confidential Information*, 2nd edn (Oxford: Oxford University Press, 2012).

European Influence on Intellectual Property Rights. Second sentence. **25–03**
Delete and substitute: Copyright has been the subject of approximation of national laws by means of a series of Directives; however, to date, there is no European Union-wide copyright code to replace national laws.

Fifth sentence. Delete and substitute: Until very recently, there has been no European Union instrument governing patent law, although certain related rights, such as Supplementary Protection certificates, are governed by EU law.

Add new paragraph: Following an agreement reached in December 2012 by the European Parliament and 25 EU Member States (all Member States except Italy and Spain) concluding more than 30 years of negotiations, a patent package consisting of two Regulations and an international Agreement were adopted early in 2013, laying the foundations for the creation of unitary patent protection in the European Union. The Regulations implement enhanced co-operation in the area of unitary patent protection and the applicable translation requirements for such protection respectively. The Regulations entered into force on January 20, 2013. Unitary patents will be granted and administered by the existing European Patent Office (EPO). The third instrument, the Agreement on a Unified Patent Court, which will have exclusive jurisdiction relating to litigation concerning unitary patents, was signed by all Member States except Poland and Spain on February 19, 2013. Once the system is in force, the court will also have jurisdiction for existing and future traditional European bundle patents granted by the EPO to nationals of all EPO Member States including EU Member States. These three instruments will apply once the international Agreement enters into force following ratification by 13 contracting states, including France, Germany and the United Kingdom.[12a] The new patent regime will allow patent protection to be obtained for the 25 EU Member States on the basis of a single application to the European Patent Office (EPO).

NOTE 10. Delete and substitute: The Directives taken together represent EU legislation on copyright and make up the so-called "acquis communautaire". They are: Council Directive 87/54/EC of December 16, 1986, on the legal protection of topographies of semiconductor products; Council Directive 91/250/EEC of May 14, 1991, on the Legal Protection of Computer Programs (repealed and replaced by a new codified text by means of Directive 2009/24/EC with effect from April 23, 2009); Council Directive 92/100/EEC of November 19, 1992, on Rental Right and Lending Right and Certain Rights Related to Copyright in the Field of Intellectual Property (repealed and replaced by a new codified text by means of Directive 2006/115/EC with effect from January 16, 2007); Council Directive 93/83/EEC of September 27, 1993, on the Coordination of Certain Rules Concerning Copyright Applicable to Satellite Broadcasting and Cable Transmission; Council Directive 93/98/EEC of October 29, 1993, Harmonising the Term of Protection of Copyright and Certain Related Rights (repealed and replaced by a new codified text by means of Directive 2006/116/EC with effect from January 16, 2007 and Directive 2011/77/EU of the European Parliament and of the Council of September 27, 2011); Directive 96/9/EC of March 11, 1996, on the Legal Protection of Databases; Directive 2001/29/EC of May 22, 2001, on the Harmonisation of Certain Aspects of Copyright and Related Rights in the Information Society; Directive 2001/29/EC of September 27, 2001, on the Resale Right for the benefit of the author of an original work of art (droit de suite); Directive 2004/48/EC of April 24, 2004, on the Enforcement of Intellectual Property Rights; and Directive 2012/28/EU of the European Parliament and the Council of October 25, 2012 on certain permitted uses of orphan works.

NOTE 11. Delete and substitute: Nevertheless, by virtue of the implementation of the EU Copyright Directives in national law, the case law of the Court of Justice of the European Union (CJEU) arising from questions referred to it concerning the interpretation of the Directives is having an increasing impact on the harmonisation process. Since the First Supplement to the Main Work was completed in August 2011, the CJEU has handed down no less than 24 judgments in copyright cases. Moreover, the creation of an EU copyright title, by means of an EU copyright law, was recommended by the "Monti report" published in May 2010 ("A new strategy for the single market: at the service of Europe's economy and society", Report to the President of the European Commission by Mario Monti, May 9, 2010). The creation of a European Copyright Code was also taken up in a European Commission document, "A Single Market for Intellectual Property Rights", (COM (2011) 287 final, Brussels, May 24, 2011).

NOTE 12a. Regulation (EU) No. 1257/2012 of the European Parliament and of the Council of December 17, 2012, implementing enhanced cooperation in the area of the creation of unitary patent protection; Council regulation (EU) No. 1260/2012 of December 17, 2012, implementing enhanced cooperation in the area of the creation of unitary patent protection with regard to the applicable translation arrangements. The Agreement on a Unified Patent Court (UPC), signed on February 19, 2013. This instrument is an international agreement concluded outside the EU institutional framework.

NOTE 14. Delete and substitute: All Member States of the European Union are contracting states to the EPC, but the EPC also has 11 additional contracting states: Albania, Croatia, Iceland, Liechtenstein, Monaco, Norway, Former Yugoslav Republic of Macedonia, Serbia, San Marino, Switzerland and Turkey.

2. COPYRIGHT AND RELATED RIGHTS

(a) *Scope of section*

Copyright, Designs and Patents Act 1988. Second sentence. Delete and substitute: Under Pt 1 of the Copyright Act 1988 the owner of the copyright in a copyright work has the exclusive right to do and to prohibit others from doing certain acts in relation to the work, which are referred to in the Act as "the acts restricted by the copyright". These acts are the following: copying the work; issuing copies of the work to the public; renting or lending the work to the public; performing, showing or playing the work in public; communicating the work to the public, including the broadcasting of the work and the making available to the public of the work by electronic transmission in such a way that members of the public may access it from a place and at a time individually chosen by them, and making an adaptation of the work or doing any of the above in relation to an adaptation. **25–04**

Second paragraph. First sentence. Delete and substitute: Copyright is a proprietary right, giving the owner of the right the right to do and to authorise others to do the acts restricted by the copyright.

NOTE 18. Add: Further reform of the CDPA 1988 remains under consideration and over the past few years a series of reports and studies have been commissioned by the UK Government of which the most important have been: the *Gowers Review of Intellectual Property* (HM Treasury Report, December 2006) and the Hargreaves report, an independent report entitled *Digital Opportunity, A Review of Intellectual Property and Growth* by Professor Ian Hargreaves published in May 2011. The Government's response to the Hargreaves report was published on August 3, 2011 and on December 14, 2011 it launched a consultation seeking views on the Government's proposals for implementing a number of Hargreaves' recommendations relating to copyright. The consultation closed on March 21, 2012 and on July 2, 2012, the Government published a policy statement on modernising copyright. Meanwhile, the Enterprise and Regulatory Reform Act 2013 received Royal Assent on April 23, 2013. Part 6 of the Act and Sch. 22 thereof contain a number of amendments to the Copyright Act 1988 inter alia to allow the introduction of systems for the licensing of orphan works, and the authorisation of voluntary collective licensing schemes by means of regulation rather than primary legislation. The licensing of copyright and performers rights and the regulation of licensing bodies are also addressed. The Act also makes provision for the implementation of EU Directive 2011/77/EU under the European Communities Act which increases the term of protection of sound recordings and performances to 70 years.

NOTE 25. Second sentence. Delete and substitute: See the discussion in Laddie, Prescott and Vitoria, *The Modern Law of Copyright and Designs*, 4th edn (London: Butterworths, 2011); see also *Copinger and Skone James on Copyright*, 16th edn (London: Sweet & Maxwell, 2010), paras 2–06 and 3–18.

25–05   **Subjects of copyright.** First sentence. Delete and substitute: Copyright is given by Pt 1 of the Copyright Act 1988 to "works" of various types: original literary, dramatic, musical and artistic works, sound recordings, films, broadcasts and the typo-graphical arrangement of published editions.

25–07   **Literary and dramatic works.** First sentence. Delete and substitute: Literary works include written tables or compilations and computer programs (including preparatory design material for a computer program).

Penultimate sentence. Delete and substitute: Acts restricted by the copyright in such works include copying; reproduction in any material form; issue to the public; performance in public; communication to the public including the broadcasting of the work and the making available of the work by electronic transmission in such a way that members of the public may access it from a place and at a time individually chosen by them; making an adaptation of the work or doing any of the above in relation to an adaptation (e.g. a translation, or conversion to a dramatic work or a cartoon strip).

NOTE 32. Add new penultimate sentence: See, however, *Infopaq International A/S v Danske Dagblades Forening* (Case C-5/08) [2009] E.C.D.R. 16 ECJ where the CJEU held that 11 words could be a protected work provided they are the expression of the intellectual creation of their author.

NOTE 34. Penultimate sentence. Add at the end: A number of questions on this issue were referred in August 2010 to the CJEU in *SAS Institute Inc v World Programming Ltd* [2010] EWHC 1829 (Ch); [2011] R.P.C. 1. The CJEU held that neither the functionality of a computer program nor the programming language nor the format of data files used in a computer program in order to exploit certain of its functions constitute a form of expression of that program and as such are not protected by copyright (C-406/10, Judgment of May 2, 2012, point 1 [2012] E.C.D.R. 22). Meanwhile, the CJEU held that the Software Directive

(91/250) gives protection to the expression in any form of a computer program, such as the source code and the object code, which permits reproduction in different computer languages (see *Bezpecnosti softwarová asociace* C-393/09 [2011] E.C.D.R. 3 at [35]). For the subsequent decision of the UK High Court dated January 25, 2013, see *SAS Institute Inc and World programming Ltd* [2013] EWHC 69 (Ch).

Last sentence. Delete and substitute: See also CDPA 1988 ss.50A–50C (sections introduced by the Copyright (Computer Programs) Regulations 1992 (SI 1992/3233) in implementation of Council Directive 91/259/EEC of May 14, 1991, on the legal protection of computer programs) which provide special defences to infringement of copyright in the case of making back-up copies, decompilation for certain purposes and other acts permitted to lawful users of the program. In C-406/10, the CJEU held that under art.5(3) of the Directive the lawful user may observe, study or test the functioning of the program so as to determine the ideas and principles which underlie any element of the program (point 2 of the judgment).

NOTE 42. Delete and substitute: CDPA 1988 s.19. This includes performance, or showing or playing a work in public. As to performance in public, see e.g. *Harms (Inc) v Martans Club* [1927] 1 Ch. 526.

NOTE 43. Add at end: As to the definition of communication to the public, see *ITV Broadcasting Ltd v TV Catch Up Ltd* (C-607/11) [2013] 3 C.M.L.R. 1 Judgment of March 7, 2013, where the CJEU held that the concept "communication to the public" within the meaning of Directive 2001/29/EC of May 22, 2001, on copyright and related rights in the information society must be interpreted broadly and thus in this case as meaning that it covers a retransmission of the works included in a terrestrial television broadcast, where the retransmission is made by an organisation other than the original broadcaster. It is irrelevant whether the retransmission is of a profit-making nature or not and whether it is made by an organisation which is acting in direct competition with the original broadcaster.

Database rights. Last sentence. Delete and substitute. It should be noted that   **25–08** in addition to the sui generis database right, copyright may subsist in databases which, by reason of the selection or arrangement of their contents, constitute the author's own intellectual creation.

NOTE 47. Delete and substitute: Extended discussion is beyond the scope of this work. See the judgment of the CJEU in the case of *British Horseracing Board Ltd v William Hill Organisation Ltd* (C-203/02) [2005] 1 C.M.L.R. 15; [2005] R.P.C. 13 and *Copinger and Skone James on Copyright*, 16th edn (2010), ch.18 and supplements 2012 and 2013. With regard to what amounts to a "substantial part" of a database see judgments of the CJEU C-304/07 of October 9, 2008 (*Directmedia Publishing GmbH v Albert-Ludwigs-Universität Freiburg* [2008] C.C.C. I-1565) and C-545/07 of March 5, 2009 (*Apis-Hristovich EOOD* [2009] E.C.R. I-1627) and most recently the decision of the Court of Appeal in *Football Dataco Ltd v Stan James Plc* [2013] EWCA Civ 27; [2013] 2 C.M.L.R. 36, where it was held that, in relation to a database, the test of "substantial part" "depends on the scale of investment in obtaining verification of presentation of what was extracted. Even if only a small part is taken it can be qualitatively a substantial part if it represents significant investment" (at [84]). See also *Football Dataco Ltd v Sportradar GMBH* (C-173/11) [2013] 1 C.M.L.R. 29 where the CJEU held, in reply to a reference from the Court of Appeal, that art.7 of the Database Directive must be interpreted as meaning that the sending by one person, by means of a web server located in Member State A, of data previously uploaded by that person from a database protected by the sui generis right under that directive to the computer of another person located in Member State B, at that person's request, for the purpose of storage in that computer's memory and display on its screen, constitutes an act of re-utilisation of the data by the person sending it. That act takes place, at least, in Member State B, where there is evidence from which it may be concluded that the act discloses an intention on the part of the person performing the act to target members of the public in Member State B; such intention is for the national court to assess.

NOTE 48. Add: No other criteria shall be applied to determine their eligibility for that protection. In December 2010, in *Football Dataco Ltd v Yahoo! UK Ltd* [2010] EWCA Civ 1380; [2011] E.C.D.R. 9, the Court of Appeal referred to the CJEU questions relating to the type of skill and labour required for copyright protection in databases under art.3 of the Database Directive. The CJEU held that a database is protected by copyright provided that the selection or arrangement of the data which it contains amounts to an original expression of the creative freedom of its author, which is a matter for the national court to decide. Intellectual effort, significant labour and skill of creating the data cannot justify protection if they do not express any originality in the selection or arrangement of the data (C-604/10, judgment of March 1, 2012, [2012] E.C.D.R. 10).

25–09   **Musical works and artistic works.** NOTE 53. Add: With regard to the originality required by a portrait photograph under Council Directive 93/98/EEC of October 29, 1993 (the Term Directive) see judgment of December 1, 2011 in *Eva Maria Painer v Standard VerlagsGmbH et al* (C-145/10) [2012] E.C.D.R. 6.

NOTE 54. Add: In *Lucasfilm Ltd v Ainsworth* [2009] EWCA Civ 1328; [2010] Ch. 503, the Court of Appeal upheld a decision which held that armour and helmets used in a science fiction film were not "sculpture" or "works of artistic craftsmanship" because their purpose was functional and they were not created primarily for their visual appeal. The decision was subsequently upheld on this point by the Supreme Court: [2011] UKSC 39; [2012] 1 A.C. 208.

NOTE 56. Last sentence. Delete and substitute: This Directive was repealed and replaced by a new codified text by means of Directive 2006/116/EC with effect from January 16, 2007 ([2006] OJ L372/12) as amended by Directive 2011/77/EU of the European Parliament and of the Council of September 27, 2011.

25–10   **Artist's resale right.** Second and third sentences. Delete and substitute: When the right was first introduced, it only applied to living artists in the United Kingdom as the Government postponed the application of the resale right to sales of deceased artists until January 1, 2012. With effect from that date, artist's heirs and beneficiaries are now entitled to a resale royalty when a deceased artist's work is sold through an auction house, gallery or dealer.

NOTE 59. Delete and substitute: The Artist's Resale Right Regulations 2006 (SI 2006/346) as amended by the Artist's Resale Right (Amendment) Regulations 2011 (SI 2011/2873). For further details of the scope and application of this right, see *Copinger and Skone James on Copyright*, 16th edn (2010), ch.20 and supplements 2012 and 2013, and Stokes, *Art and Copyright* (Oxford: Hart Publishing, 2012). In *Fundación Gala-Salvador Dali Visual, Entidad de Gestión de Artistas Plásticos (VEGAP) v Société des auteurs dans les arts graphiques et plastiques (ADAGP)* (C-518/08) [2010] E.C.D.R. 13; [2011] F.S.R. 4 the CJEU handed down a judgment on the subject of the persons entitled to receive royalties after the death of the artist, holding that only the artist's legal heirs may benefit, to the exclusion of testamentary legatees.

Sound recordings and films. NOTE 61. Last sentence. Delete and substitute: **25–11** Note that a new EU Directive to extend the term of protection for performers and sound recordings to 70 years was adopted in September 2011 (Directive 2011/77/EU of the European Parliament and of the Council of September 27, 2011 amending Directive 2006/116/EC on the term of protection of copyright and certain related rights). The Directive has not been implemented to date in the United Kingdom. Member States must comply with the Directive by November 1, 2013 (art.2).

Broadcasts and cable programmes. Whole paragraph. Delete and substitute: **25–12** **Broadcasts.** A broadcast is an electronic transmission of visual images, sounds or other information which is transmitted for simultaneous reception by members of the public and is capable of being lawfully received by them, or is transmitted at a time determined solely by the person making the transmission for presentation to members of the public, and which is not an internet transmission. However, an internet transmission is a broadcast if it is a transmission taking place simultaneously on the internet and by other means, a concurrent transmission of a live event, or a transmission of recorded moving images or sounds forming part of a programme service offered by the person responsible for making the transmission, being a service in which programmes are transmitted at scheduled times determined by that person. Period of copyright: 50 years from end of calendar year in which the broadcast was made. Acts restricted: as for films. NOTE 68. Delete.

(b) *Authorship and ownership*

Qualifications for protection. NOTE 70. Insert after first sentence: The United   **25–13** Kingdom is party to a number of international treaties and conventions in the field of copyright and related rights and extends protection to the nationals of the other contracting states to such conventions, see *Copinger and Skone James on Copyright*, 16th edn (2010), ch.23.

Last sentence. Delete and substitute: See the Copyright and Performances (Application to Other Countries) Order 2008 (SI 2008/677) as amended by the Copyright and Performances (Application to Other Countries) (Amendment) Order 2009 (SI 2009/2745).

Originality. NOTE 73. Add at end: With regard to the concept of originality   **25–14** under the EU Copyright Directives as interpreted by the CJEU and the potential impact on UK law, see *Copinger and Skone James on Copyright*, 16th edn (2010), para.**3–128** and supplements 2012 and 2013. See also para.**25–23**, below.

25–16   **Ownership of copyright.** First paragraph. Last sentence, sub-paras (b) (c) and (d). Delete and substitute:

    (b) *Sound recordings.* In the case of a sound recording, the author is taken to be the producer.

    (c) *Films.* In the case of a film, the author is taken to be the producer and the principal director.

    (d) *Broadcasts.* In the case of a broadcast, the person making the broadcast is taken to be the author or in the case of a broadcast which relays another broadcast by reception and immediate re-transmission, the person making that other broadcast is the author.

    (e) *Typographical arrangements.* In the case of a typographical arrangement of a published edition, the publisher is taken to be the author.

25–17   **Assignment and disposition of copyright.** NOTE 83. Add: See also *Crosstown Music Co 1 LLC v Rive Droite Music Ltd* [2010] EWCA Civ 1222; [2012] Ch. 68 where the Court of Appeal held that a provision in an assignment of copyright allowing automatic reverter of the rights to the assignor on a future event, namely an unremedied material breach of contract by the assignee, was a valid partial assignment within CDPA s.90(2).

25–18   **Foreign works.** NOTE 86. First sentence. Delete and substitute: See para.**25–13**, and the Copyright and Performances (Application to Other Countries) Order 2008 (SI 2008/677) as amended by the Copyright and Performances (Application to Other Countries) (Amendment) Order 2009 (SI 2009/2745).

(c) *Infringement of copyright*

25–19   **Infringement of copyright.** NOTE 89. Third sentence. Delete and substitute: Infringement includes unauthorised rental and lending (s18A), performance, showing or playing a work in public, communicating the work to the public (including making a work available to the public by electronic transmission in such a way that members of the public may access it from a place and at a time individually chosen by them) and making an adaptation of a work (ss.19–21).

25–21   **Dealing with infringing copies and other secondary infringements.** Last sentence. Delete and substitute: It is similarly infringed by transmitting over a telecommunications system (otherwise than by communication to the public), knowing or having reason to believe that infringing copies of the work will be made by means of the reception of the transmission in the United Kingdom or elsewhere.

25–22   **Causal derivation and substantial similarity—copying a substantial part.** NOTE 98. Add at end: and see *Copinger and Skone James on Copyright*, 16th edn (2010), para.7–32.

25–23   Penultimate sentence. Delete and substitute: The CJEU held in *Infopaq International A/S v Danske Dagblades Forening* (C-05/8) [2009] E.C.D.R. 16;

[2010] F.S.R. 20 that the reproduction of an extract of a protected literary work, which comprised 11 consecutive words thereof, constituted reproduction within the meaning of art.2(a) of EU Copyright Directive 2001/29/EC (the so-called Information Society Directive), if that extract contained an element of the work which, as such, expresses the author's own intellectual creation; the court then stated that it is for the national court to make this determination.[110A]

NOTE 110. Delete and substitute: Judgment of the CJEU in case C-05/8 [2009] E.C.D.R. 16; [2010] F.S.R. 20 (*Infopaq I*). More recently, in joined cases *Football Association Premier League Limited v QC Leisure* and *Karen Murphy v Media Protection Services Ltd* C-403/08 and C-429/08 ([2012] 1 C.M.L.R. 29; [2012] C.E.C. 242; [2012] E.C.D.R. 1 the CJEU has further interpreted the meaning of reproduction under the Infosoc Directive holding that the reproduction right extends to transient fragments of the works within the memory of a satellite decoder and on a television screen, provided that those fragments contain elements which are the expression of the authors' own intellectual creation, and the unit composed of the fragments reproduced simultaneously must be examined in order to determine whether it contains such elements. See also *R. v Gilham* [2009] EWCA Crim 2293; [2010] E.C.D.R. 5, where it was held that a transient copy of an image constitutes substantial copying.

Add: NOTE 110A. In *Newspaper Licensing Agency Ltd v Meltwater Holding BV* [2011] EWCA Civ 890; [2012] R.P.C. 1, the Court of Appeal upheld the decision of the court of first instance in which *Infopaq I* was interpreted as meaning that no distinction was to be made between part of an [newspaper] article and the whole, provided that the part contained elements which were the expression of the intellectual creation of the author. There was no reference to "substantial part" in the Infosoc Directive and the CJEU had made it clear that originality rather than substantiality was the test to be applied to the part extracted. The Court of Appeal held that under s.1(1)(a) of the CDPA 1988, a headline had to be both "original" and "literary" in order to constitute an independent literary work and that the decision in *Infopaq I* had not qualified that test. The Supreme Court has referred questions to the CJEU on other aspects of the case ([2013] UKSC 18; [2013] 2 All E.R. 852).

Burlesques, parody, etc. NOTE 122. Add at the end: However, the Hargreaves **25–26** report (see para.**25–04**, Note 18 of this Supplement) recommended that parody and pastiche be made permitted acts under the CDPA 1988 (see below, para.**25–27**). Meanwhile the Government has announced its intention to introduce a fair dealing exception for parody, caricature and pastiche (HM Government *Modernising Copyright: a modern, robust and flexible framework,* (December 20, 2012)); the IPO published draft legislation for a new exception for parody for consultation on June 7, 2013.

Exceptions to infringement: permitted acts and fair dealing. NOTE 124. **25–27** The Government has announced its intention to make changes to copyright exceptions to make them more relevant to the digital world. It outlined the changes in *Modernising Copyright* (cf. NOTE 122, above) and on June 7, 2013, the IPO published proposals for new exceptions for private copying, parody, quotation and public administration.

NOTE 125. Add at end: and *Unilever Plc v Griffin* [2010] EWHC 899 (Ch); [2010] F.S.R. 33.

25–28   **Making of temporary copies.** NOTE 127. Add: See point 6 of the judgment of the CJEU in joined cases *Football Association Premier League Ltd v QC Leisure* and *Karen Murphy v Media Protection Services Ltd* (C-403/08 and C-429/08) [2012] 1 C.M.L.R. 29; [2012] C.E.C. 242; [2012] E.C.D.R. 1. See also the judgment of the CJEU in *Infopaq International A/S v Danske Dagblades Forening (Infopaq II)* (C–302/10 January 17, 2012) where it was emphasised that the exception for temporary copies must be interpreted strictly because it is a derogation from the general principle that the right holder shall authorise any reproduction of a protected work. Thus acts of reproduction carried out during a "data capture" process must fulfil the condition that they do not have an independent economic significance; it must not "enable the generation of an additional profit" for the user or lead to "a modification of" the work.

25–30   **UK statutory defences.** First paragraph and second paragraph, lines 1–5. Delete and substitute: The statutory defences are as follows:

(a)   fair dealing with a literary, dramatic, musical or artistic work or the typographical arrangement of a published edition for the purposes of research for a non-commercial purpose or for the purposes of criticism or review (of that or another work or of a performance of a work) provided that it is accompanied by a sufficient acknowledgement;

(b)   fair dealing with a work (other than a photograph) for the purpose of criticism, review and news reporting, provided that the work has been made available to the public.

Other exceptions include the following:

- incidental inclusion of copyright material in an artistic work, sound recording, film or broadcast;

- use for purposes of instruction or examination;

- the inclusion of a short passage in an educational anthology consisting mainly of non-copyright works;

NOTE 133. Add: Lending of copies by educational establishments is also permitted (CDPA 1988 s.36A). See Note 124, above.

(d)   *Remedies for infringement of copyright*

At the end of the sub-heading add new Note 152A:
NOTE 152A. Remedies for infringement of copyright are set out in CDPA 1988, ch.VI ss.96–115 as amended by the Copyright and Related Rights Regulations 2003 (SI 2003/2498) reg.27, with effect from October 31, 2003. For savings and transitional provisions, see Pt 3 of the Regulations.

25–33   **Civil remedies.** Insert after second sentence: Certain infringements are actionable by a non-exclusive licensee.[154a]

Add: NOTE 154a. CDPA 1988 s.101A inserted by the Copyright and Related Rights Regulations 2003 (SI 2003/2498) reg.27, with effect from October 31, 2003.

Injunction. Add at the end: The High Court has power to grant an injunction **25–34** against a service provider, where the service provider has actual knowledge of another person using their service to infringe copyright.[172a]
NOTE 172a. CDPA 1988 s.97A inserted by the Copyright and Related Rights Regulations 2003 (SI 2003/2498) reg.27, with effect from October 31, 2003.

Damages or account of profits. NOTE 176. Second sentence. Delete and **25–35** substitute: The court will not require certainty of proof and will often adopt the maxim *omnia praesumuntur contra spoliatorem* ("all things are presumed against a wrongdoer"): see *Infabrics Ltd v Jaytax Ltd* [1985] F.S.R. 75.

3. Moral Rights

The nature of moral rights. NOTE 194. Third sentence. Delete and substitute: **25–39** For more in-depth discussions of moral rights, see: Garnett, Davies and Harbottle, *Copinger and Skone James on Copyright*, 16th edn (2010), ch.11 and supplements 2012 and 2013 thereto; Ricketson and Ginsburg, *International Copyright and Neighbouring Rights, The Berne Convention and Beyond*, 2nd edn (Oxford: Oxford University Press, 2006); Adeney, *The Moral Rights of Authors and Performers—An International and Comparative Analysis* (Oxford: Oxford University Press, 2006); Davies and Garnett, *Moral Rights* (London: Sweet and Maxwell, 2010).

Right to be identified as author or director. NOTE 208. Delete second **25–40** sentence.

4. Competition and Control of Licensing

Copyright Tribunal—control of licensing and competition. Penultimate **25–46** sentence. Delete and substitute: Refusals to grant licences under a copyright can, in very special circumstances, be contrary to competition law, especially applying art.102 of the Treaty on the Functioning of the European Union (TFEU).
NOTE 237. Delete and substitute: See, for example, *Copinger and Skone James on Copyright*, 16th edn (2010), ch.28 and supplements 2012 and 2013 thereto.

5. Performers' Rights

Performers' rights. NOTE 254. Second sentence. Delete and substitute: Note **25–48** that a new EU Directive to extend the term of protection for performers and sound recordings to 70 years was adopted in September 2011 (Directive 2011/77/EU of the European Parliament and of the Council of September 27, 2011 amending Directive 2006/116/EC on the term of protection of copyright and certain related rights). The Directive has not been implemented to date in the United Kingdom. Member States must comply with the Directive by November 1, 2013 (art.2).

25–52   **Performers' moral rights.** NOTE 272. Add at the end: For a full account of these rights see *Copinger and Skone James on Copyright*, 16th edn (2010), ch.11 and supplement 2012 and 2013 thereto, and Davies & Garnett, *Moral Rights* (2010), Pt II.

6. DESIGN RIGHT

25–53   **Forms of design right protection—UK and Community.** Fifth sentence. Delete and substitute: In essence, the unregistered Community design has the same scope of protection and requirements for subsistence (other than registration) as registered Community designs but with a term of only three years commencing when it is first made available to the public within the Community.

25–54   **Removal of copyright protection for industrial designs.** Fourth sentence. Delete and substitute: "Design" is defined in para.**25–56**.

Fifth sentence. Delete and substitute: It is also not an infringement of copyright to deal in articles which do not themselves infringe by reason of the exception created by s.51(1) of the 1988 Act.

Add at the end: Section 52 of the 1988 Act significantly restricts the copyright protection afforded to artistic works that have been industrially exploited by or with the licence of the copyright owner by making copies of the work by an industrial process and then marketing such copies in the United Kingdom or elsewhere. Where such manufacture and marketing occurs, then after the expiry of 25 years from the end of the calendar year in which such articles were first marketed the work may be freely copied (i.e. without infringing) by making articles of any description or doing anything for that purpose, or doing anything with such articles. As to the meaning of "industrial process", and for certain articles excluded from the operation of s.52, see the Copyright (Industrial Process and Excluded Articles) (No.2) Order 1989 (SI 1989/1070).

NOTE 286. Add at the end: The scope of s.51 was considered in *Lucasfilm Ltd v Ainsworth* [2009] EWCA Civ 1328; [2010] Ch. 503, in which the Court of Appeal held that the helmets and armour forming part of the "Storm Trooper" costumes in the *Star Wars* films were neither sculptures nor works of artistic craftsmanship, and hence did not qualify as artistic works which would be excluded from the operation of s.51. The decision has been upheld on this point by the Supreme Court: [2011] UKSC 39; [2012] 1 A.C. 208. Moreover, the decision of the Court of Justice of the European Union in *Flos SpA v Semeraro Casa e Famiglia SpA* (C-168/09) [2011] E.C.D.R. 8; [2011] R.P.C. 10 has cast real doubt on whether ss.51 and 52 of the 1988 Act are compatible with Community law governing the term of copyright protection (see Council Directive 93/98/EEC–the Term Directive) and the requirement for "cumulation" of copyright and design right stipulated by art.17 of Council Directive 98/71/EC (the Designs

Directive). Article 10 of the Term Directive requires a harmonised term of protection of 70 years post death of author, while art.17 of the Designs Directive allows Member States to set the extent of, and subsistence conditions for, copyright protection. The CJEU held that art.17 does not extend to giving Member States a discretion to override the term of copyright protection, and it was clear that such copyright protection had to be conferred for the full term. However, it should be noted that the *Flos* decision probably only concerns registered design rights (as to which see para.**25–63** et seq.). Following these developments, and at least partly as a result of lobbying by interested parties, the UK Government has introduced a proposal to repeal s.52 of the 1988 Act; the repeal is now enacted as s.74(2) of the Enterprise and Regulatory Reform Act 2013, but with effect from a date yet to be appointed (as at June 2013).

Design Right At the end of the first sentence Add NOTE 290a: **25–55**
NOTE 290a Note that significant amendments to the scheme of the 1988 Act have been proposed as part of the Intellectual Property Bill 2013–14, which as at June 18, 2013 had passed the committee stage in the House of Lords. The Bill proposes, inter alia: removing "any aspect of" from the definition of design; modifying the ownership criteria in relation to commissioned works; modifying the qualification criteria; and adding exceptions to design right infringement, covering private acts, experiments, teaching, and certain uses on ships and aircraft. It is also proposed to insert the words "in a qualifying country" after the word "commonplace" in s.213(4).

Qualification. NOTE 302. Add at the end: The burden of proof is on the party   **25–57**
asserting the commission to prove that fact: *Bruhn Newtech Ltd v Datanetex Ltd* [2012] EWPCC 17.

Term of design right. First sentence. Delete and substitute: The right expires   **25–58**
15 years from the end of the calendar year in which the design is first recorded in a design document or an article was first made to the design, but if articles are made available for sale or hire by or with the licence of the design right owner anywhere in the world within five years of the end of that year, the right expires 10 years from the end of the year in which that first occurred.
Last sentence. Delete and substitute: Any assignment of the right must, to be effective, be in writing signed by or on behalf of the assignor. Design right may pass under a will or by operation of law.
NOTE 304: Last sentence should refer to s.224.

Design right infringement—remedies. First sentence. Delete and substitute: **25–59**
A design right is infringed by any unlicensed person who, for commercial purposes: makes an article substantially to that design; makes a design document recording it for the purpose of enabling such articles to be made; or imports into the United Kingdom infringing articles, has them in his possession or trades in them, when he knows or has reason to believe that they are infringing articles.[305]
Add at the end: It is also possible to apply to the courts for a declaration that a particular product does not infringe: see, e.g. *Samsung Electronics (UK) Ltd v Apple Inc* [2012] EWHC 889 (Ch) and [2012] EWCA Civ 729.
NOTE 305. Initial reference. Delete and substitute: CDPA 1988 ss.226 and 227.

Add at the end: See also *Red Spider Technology v Omega Completions Technology* [2010] EWHC 59 (Ch). Infringement of UK unregistered design has recently been considered in *Pro-Tec Covers Ltd v Specialised Covers Ltd* unreported October 18, 2011 Patents County Court (caravan towing covers; not infringed); *Ifejika v Ifejika* [2010] EWPCC 31; [2012] F.S.R. 6 (lens cleaning devices; infringed); and *Albert Packaging Ltd v Nampak Cartons & Healthcare* [2011] EWPCC 15; [2011] F.S.R. 32 (tortilla wrap cartons; not infringed). As to the meaning of "infringing article" see s.228.

NOTE 306. Add at the end: In *Albert Packaging Ltd v Nampak Cartons & Healthcare* [2011] EWPCC 15; [2011] F.S.R. 32 it was held that the similarities between the design and the alleged infringement were due to common derivation from an independent source. For the significance of copying in the context of an application for summary judgment, see *Dahlia Fashion Co Ltd v Broadcast Session Ltd* [2012] EWPCC 23.

25–60   **Compulsory licences.** NOTE 314. Last sentence. Delete and substitute: The Secretary of State may, by order, exclude certain designs from the operation of s.237(1). There are, in addition, wide powers to use design rights for the services of the Crown, which includes the NHS.

25–61   **Jurisdiction of the Comptroller and the court.** Add at the end: It is worth noting that the Patents County Court has jurisdiction over unregistered design right disputes, and seems to be attracting a significant number of such cases (at least as measured by the number of decisions the court is producing). This may reflect the fact that the PCC is arguably better suited than the High Court to determining what are often lower-value disputes requiring a straightforward, pragmatic approach.

NOTE 320. Add at the end: There are pending amendments to s.249 CDPA 1988 under s.143(3) and Sch.23(6) of the Tribunals, Courts and Enforcement Act 2007, but these have not yet been given effect.

25–62   **Groundless threats of legal proceedings.** NOTE 322. Add at the end: For examples of cases involving s.253, see *Landor & Hawa International Ltd v Azure Designs Ltd* [2006] EWCA Civ 1285; [2007] F.S.R. 9, and *Grimme Landmaschinenfabrik GmbH & Co KG v Scott* [2009] EWHC 2691(Pat); [2010] F.S.R. 11.

7. Registered Designs

25–63   **Registered designs.** First sentence. Delete and substitute: United Kingdom rights in registered designs are obtained by registration under the Registered Designs Act 1949 (RDA 1949) (as variously amended).

End of the first sentence. Add NOTE 322A: Note that the Intellectual Property Bill 2013–14 proposes significant changes to the RDA 1949 and to the CDPA 1988 in relation to registered designs. These include exceptions to infringement, ownership of designs and applications for registration, and rights of prior use. There is also a proposed criminal offence of "copying etc. of a design in course of business".

Third sentence. Delete and substitute: The RDA 1949 has now been heavily amended to harmonise UK registered designs with EU law; thus the validity and infringement characteristics of UK registered design rights apply also to registered EU designs, albeit that they have EU-wide protection.

Sentence after Note 324. Delete and substitute: Individual character is assessed by the overall impression produced by the design on the notional "informed user"; in assessing individual character, the degree of freedom of the designer shall be taken into consideration.

NOTE 323. Add at the end: Regulation 6/2002/EC art.4. Note that art.4 states that in relation to designs applied to or incorporated in a product which becomes a component part in a complex product, that design is only to be considered new or of individual character if it remains visible during normal use by the end user, and to the extent that the visible parts of that product are new and have individual character. See, e.g. *Kwang Yang Motor Co Ltd v OHIM* [2012] E.C.D.R. 2 General Court. Prior art can include products which have a similar appearance to the registered design but which were designed for a different purpose: *Gimex International Groupe Import Export v Chill Bag Co Ltd* [2012] EWPCC 31; [2012] E.C.D.R. 25.

NOTE 324. Add at the end: Regulation 6/2002/EC art.5.

NOTE 325. Add at the end: Regulation 6/2002/EC arts 6(1) and 6(2). The question of design freedom, and possible differences between UK law and EU law on this point, were considered by Arnold J. in *Dyson Ltd v Vax Ltd* [2010] EWHC 1923 (Pat); [2010] F.S.R. 39; aff'd [2011] EWCA Civ 1206; [2012] F.S.R. 4. In general, the higher the degree of technical specification the designer has to work to, the lower the level of design freedom. In *Grupo Promer Mon Graphic v OHIM—PepsiCo* (T-9/07) [2010] E.C.D.R. 7 the General Court said that similarities in features where there is greater design freedom will be of greatest significance, especially where those features are visible. PepsiCo appealed to the CJEU on three points; the appeal was dismissed by the Court of Justice case C-281/10, [2012] F.S.R. 5. The Court of Justice also opined on the definition of the informed user: it said that the notional informed user lies somewhere between the average user and the sectoral expert.

NOTE 329. Add at the end: Regulation 6/2002/EC art.12.

Exceptions. NOTE 330. Add at the end: Regulation 6/2002/ECart.8(1). See **25–64** also the dicta of Arnold J. in *Dyson Ltd v Vax Ltd* [2010] EWHC 1923 (Pat); [2010] F.S.R. 39, in which it was said that the test was whether the designer could have been influenced by anything other than purely functional considerations, applying the decision in *Lindner Recyclingtech GmbH v Franssons Verkstader AB* [2010] E.C.D.R. 1. *Dyson* was upheld by the Court of Appeal: [2011] EWCA Civ 1206; [2012] F.S.R. 4. The Court of Appeal also discussed the relevance and application of the degree of design freedom enjoyed by the designer.

NOTE 331. Add at the end: Regulation 6/2002/EC art.8(2). See for example *Camatic Pty Ltd v Bluecube Ltd* [2012] E.C.D.R. 12, in which a Community registered design was held invalid under the must-fit exception.

Proprietorship. NOTE 332. Add at the end: A dispute over ownership resulted **25–65** in cancellation of the registration in *Ifejika v Ifejika* [2010] EWPCC 31; [2012] F.S.R. 6.

25–66   **Registration.** Add at the end: The Register may also be searched online electronically by product type or registration number at the UKIPO website *http://www.ipo.gov.uk/pro–types/pro–design.htm*. [Accessed September 1, 2013].

25–68   **Infringement of registered design rights.** NOTE 338. Add at the end: See *Dyson v Vax* at first instance, [2010] EWHC 1923 (Pat); [2010] F.S.R. 39, and in the Court of Appeal: [2011] EWCA Civ 1206; [2012] F.S.R. 4. See also the decisions of the General Court in *Shenzhen Taiden v OHIM—Bosch Security Systems (Communications Equipment)* (T-153/08) June 22, 2010, which concerned telephone sets for making conference calls; *Grupo Promer Mon Graphic v OHIM–PepsiCo* (T-9/07) [2010] E.C.D.R. 7, which was about the design of a type of flat, disc-like toy known as a "pog"; and *Punch v Sphere Time* (T-68/10) [2011] E.C.D.R. 20 concerning watches on lanyards.

In *Sealed Air Ltd v Sharp Interpack Ltd* [2013] EWPCC 23 the court held that there was no infringement despite many visual similarities, since the great majority of these were a result of functional or conventional elements. Contrast *Louver-Lite Ltd v Harris Parts Ltd (t/a Harris Engineering)* [2012] EWPCC 53 (headrails for blinds), where a narrow scope of protection was nonetheless infringed as a result of the virtual identity of the defendant's design. In *Samsung Electronics (UK) Ltd v Apple Inc* [2012] EWHC 1882 (Pat); [2013] E.C.D.R. 1, the alleged infringement (a tablet computer) was found to lack the understated and extreme simplicity of the claimant's design.

Where the alleged infringement is a later registered design, the proprietor of the earlier registration may bring infringement proceedings without first having to seek a declaration of invalidity: *Celaya Emparanza y Galdos Internacional SA (Cegasa) v Proyectos Integrales de Balizameiento SL* (C-488/10) [2012] E.C.D.R. 17.

25–69   **Remedies.** Add at the end: Injunctive relief in respect of Community registered designs can be far-reaching—for example, a Community-wide injunction was obtained by Apple Inc against Samsung Electronics in the Düsseldorf District Court in Germany in August 2011, in respect of tablet computers said to infringe Apple's iPad registered design.

For an example of an interim injunction see *Utopia Tableware Ltd v BBP Marketing Ltd* [2013] EWPCC 15. The court can order publication of judgment where it is necessary to dispel commercial uncertainty caused by the defendant's actions—*Samsung Electronics (UK) Ltd v Apple Inc* [2012] EWCA Civ 1339; [2013] F.S.R. 9.

Article 91 of Regulation 6/2002 requires a stay of proceedings in most design disputes where the validity of the design in question is already in issue before another community design court. Where the claim is for a declaration of non-infringement and the counterclaim is for infringement, only the counterclaim need be stayed: *Samsung Electronics (UK) Ltd v Apple Inc* [2012] EWCA Civ 729; [2013] F.S.R. 8.

There is a defence available under art.110 of Regulation 6/2002, which excludes protection for designs which constitute a component part of a complex product used for the purpose of the repair of that complex product so as to restore its original appearance. The limitations of that defence were explored in great detail by Arnold J. in *Bayerische Motoren Werke AG v Round & Metal Ltd* [2012]

EWHC 2099 (Pat); [2013] F.S.R. 18, in which the defendant's replica alloy wheels were found to infringe and could not rely on the defence.

Rectification of register. NOTE 339. Add at the end: For an example of an ownership dispute, see the Court of Appeal decision in *Ifejika v Ifejika* [2010] EWCA Civ 563; [2010] F.S.R. 29.   **25–70**

Groundless threats of legal proceedings. NOTE 340. Add at the end: See also para.**25–62** above and s.236 CDPA 1988 in relation to unregistered design right.   **25–72**

8. REGISTERED TRADE MARKS

(a) *Introduction*

Trade mark infringement and passing off. First sentence. Delete and substitute: In addition to the common law right to prevent passing off, it is possible, by registering a trade mark under the provisions of the Trade Marks Act 1994, to obtain statutory rights to prevent others using in the course of trade the same mark or a mark confusingly similar to it (subject to certain conditions about the identity or similarity of the goods or services in question).   **25–73**
NOTE 341. Delete and substitute: For passing off, see ch.26

The Trade Marks Act 1994. NOTE 342. Delete and substitute: See Mellor et al., *Kerly's Law of Trade Marks and Trade Names*, 15th edn (London: Sweet & Maxwell, 2011), and Morcom et al., *The Modern Law of Trade Marks*, 2nd edn (London: Butterworth, 2008). There is only scope in this work to provide a short outline of the law and reference to the leading cases. Note that there is a parallel system of Community trade marks established by Council Regulation 40/94/EEC (codified by Council Regulation (EC) 207/2009) to which similar principles apply thanks to harmonising Council Directive 89/104/EEC (as codified by Directive 2008/95/EC). Such trade marks have effect throughout the Community, and may be obtained by application to the Office for the Harmonization of the Internal Market (OHIM) in Alicante, Spain. The OHIM website is helpful: *http://oami. europa.eu*. Further discussion of this and international applications are beyond the scope of this work. For procedure generally, see Trade Marks Rules 2008; CPR Part 63 PD—Intellectual Property Claims; and the website of the UK Intellectual Property Office: *http://www.ipo.gov.uk* [Accessed September 2013].   **25–74**
NOTE 344. Add at end: ("the Directive").
NOTE 346. Delete and substitute: The UK courts are required to interpret provisions of national law, whether introduced to implement the Directive or not, in the light of the wording and purpose of the Directive in order to achieve the result referred to in the third paragraph of what is now art.288 of the Treaty on the Functioning of the European Union, if it is possible to do so (*Marleasing SA v La Comercial Internacional de Alimentación SA* (C-106/89), [1992] 1 C.M.L.R. 305; *Webb v EMO Cargo (UK) Ltd* [1993] 1 W.L.R. 49; [1993] 1 C.M.L.R. 259). *Hansard* is of limited value in interpreting the Act: *British Sugar Plc v James Robertson Son Ltd* [1996] R.P.C. 281. See also *Wagamama Ltd v City Centre*

Restaurants Plc [1995] F.S.R. 713. In *Budejovicky Budvar Narodni Podnik v Anheuser-Busch Inc* [2009] EWCA Civ 1022; [2010] R.P.C. 7, Jacob L.J. stated: "Although the Judge below used the provisions of the UK Trade Marks Act 1994, it is common ground that those provisions not only are intended to implement the Directive but have the same meaning. Unfortunately the draftsman of the Act got the idea that it would be helpful in implementing the Directive to use different language. It is not. Quite the opposite. At best it wastes everyone's time trying to relate the section to the provision of the Directive which it is implementing. At worse it positively misleads. So, as I think should be the standard practice at all levels, I will use just the language of the Directive."

25–75   **The meaning of "trade mark".** NOTE 351. Add at the end: A chocolate company was entitled to register a shade of purple as a trade mark, since single colours are capable of being signs within the meaning of art.2 of Directive 2008/95/EC: *Societe Des Produits Nestle SA v Cadbury UK Ltd* [2012] EWHC 2637 (Ch); [2013] E.T.M.R. 2.

(b) *Registration*

25–76   **Registration of trade marks and applications for registration of trade marks.** NOTE 352. Delete and substitute: TMA 1994 s.32, which sets out the requirements of an application. The website of the UK Intellectual Property Office is helpful: *http://www.ipo.gov.uk/pro-tm.htm* [Accessed September 1, 2013]. There are provisions in the Act concerning claims to priority from applications for protection of a trade mark in a Convention country and other overseas applications (CDPA 1988 ss.35 and 36). As to the meaning of "Convention country", see TMA 1994 s.55(1)(b).

NOTE 353. Add at the end: The CJEU has held that applicants must identify the goods and services for which the protection of a trade mark is sought with sufficient clarity and precision to enable the competent authorities and economic operators to determine the extent of the protection conferred by the trade mark: *Chartered Institute of Patent Attorneys v Registrar of Trade Marks* (C-307/10) [2013] R.P.C. 11 Grand Chamber.

(a) *Distinctiveness*

NOTE 354. After the third sentence add: See also *32 Red Plc v WHG (International) Ltd* [2011] EWHC 62 (Ch); [2011] E.T.M.R. 21, upheld on appeal: [2012] EWCA Civ 19; [2012] E.T.M.R. 14.

Add at the end: For an example of lack of distinctive character see *Wella Corp v Alberto-Culver Co* [2011] EWHC 3558 (Ch); [2012] E.T.M.R. 24. In *JW Spear & Sons Ltd v Zynga Inc* [2012] EWHC 3345 (Ch); [2013] F.S.R. 28 the claimant's "tile mark" was found to encompass an infinite number of permutations and combinations of letters and numbers on a tile, and was held to lack distinctive character. The mark NOW TV in *Starbucks (HK) Ltd v British Sky Broadcasting Group Plc* [2012] EWHC 3074 (Ch); [2013] F.S.R. 29 was held to be either a characteristic of the television service in question, or else devoid of distinctive character. See also PHOTOS.COM held to lack distinctive character in *Getty Images (US) Inc v OHIM* (T-338/11) [2013] E.T.M.R.19 General Court. The mark

MEDITATION TRANSCENDANTALE was refused on similar grounds in *Maharishi Foundation Ltd v OHIM* (T-426/11) [2013] E.T.M.R. 22 General Court.

NOTE 355. Add at the end: The CJEU has ruled that the exclusion for descriptiveness applies to a word mark which comprises the juxtaposition of a descriptive word combination plus a letter sequence which is not in itself descriptive, but which the public will readily perceive as being an abbreviation consisting simply of the first letters of the word combination—see *Alfred Strigl* (Joined cases C-90/11 and C-91/11). The marks in question were "Multi Markets Fund MMF" and "NAI—der Natur-Aktien-Index". In *Fine & Country Ltd v Okotoks Ltd* [2013] EWCA Civ 672 the mark FINE AND COUNTRY was held to be not merely laudatory or descriptive.

NOTE 356. Final sentence: Reference should be to *Koninklijke* rather than *Koninklije*. Add at the end: The shape of a product which gives substantial value to a product cannot be registered as a trade mark even where, prior to the application for registration, it "acquired attractiveness as a result of its recognition as a distinctive sign following advertising campaigns presenting the specific characteristics of the product in question": *Benetton Group SpA v G-Star International BV* (371/06) [2008] E.T.M.R. 5 ECJ (CJEU). In relation to the technical result exclusion, see *Lego Juris A/S v Office for Harmonisation in the Internal Market (Trade Marks and Designs) (OHIM)* (C-48/09 P) [2010] E.T.M.R. 63 CJEU (Grand Chamber) September 14, 2010.

(b) *Other restrictions on registration*

NOTE 360. Penultimate sentence. Delete and substitute: This principle was applied by Henderson J. in *32Red Plc v WHG (International) Ltd* [2011] EWHC 62 (Ch); [2011] E.T.M.R. 21 (and not doubted on appeal: [2012] EWCA Civ 19; [2012] E.T.M.R. 14): the applicant knew of existing use of a similar mark by a competitor, but was bringing an action alleging that the competitor's use infringed a separate Community trade mark held by the claimant. The claimant's application was intended to strengthen its position in the forthcoming litigation. The judge held that the claimant's application was not in bad faith. The CJEU has ruled that applying for a mark with no intention of using it, but with the intention of using the mark as a basis for obtaining a top-level .eu domain name could amount to bad faith within the meaning of the relevant domain name regulation (Regulation 874/2004): *Internetportal und Marketing GmbH v Schlicht* (C-569/08) [2011] Bus. L.R. 726; [2010] E.T.M.R. 48 CJEU (Second chamber) June 3, 2010.

NOTE 360. Add at the end: It may be bad faith to apply for a mark over a much wider specification of goods or services than that for which the applicant intends to use the mark: *Laboratoire de la Mer trade marks* [2002] E.T.M.R. 34; [2002] F.S.R. 51.

(c) *Earlier rights*

Add at the end: National rights in "extended form" passing off were applicable in this context in *Tilda Riceland*, [2012] E.T.M.R. 15 General Court, concerning the term "basmati". See ch. 26 for further discussion of extended passing off. A rice-related trade mark was also invalid against earlier unregistered UK rights in *Tresplain Investments Ltd v OHIM* (C-76/11 P) [2012] E.T.M.R. 22.

NOTE 361. After initial reference insert: Note that the holder of the earlier mark may be required to prove genuine use—see para.**25–79** and Note 367.

Add at the end: The CJEU has given its views on the notion of "honest concurrent use" in *Budejovicky Budvar Narodni Podnik v Anheuser-Busch Inc* (C-482/09) [2012] E.T.M.R. 2 September 22, 2011. It ruled that the provisions of the Directive 2008/95/EC and Regulation (EC) 207/2009 do not allow a trade mark proprietor to prevent the use of an identical mark where there has been long concurrent use such that there is not likely to be any damage to the "essential function" of the earlier mark. Note that the case turned on its specific and rather unusual facts. The Court also ruled on the meaning of "acquiescence" as a concept of Community law. The Court of Appeal subsequently declined to remit the matter to the Trade Marks Registry: [2012] EWCA Civ 880; [2012] E.T.M.R. 48.

25–79   **Revocation for non-use, etc. and invalidity of registration.** NOTE 367. After initial reference add: See also the "use conditions" introduced into TMA 1994 ss.6A and 47 by the Trade Marks (Proof of Use) Regulations 2004/946.

Add at the end: Artice 15(1) of Regulation 207/2009 requires that the territorial borders of the Member States of the Community be disregarded for the purposes of assessing whether a trade mark has been put to genuine use—*Leno Merken BV v Hagelkruis Beheer BV* (C-149/11) [2013] E.T.M.R. 16 CJEU. Provisions of national law are irrelevant to the operation and scope of Regulation 207/2009 in relation to genuine use: *Rivella International AG v OHIM* (T-170/11) [2013] E.T.M.R. 4 General Court. Genuine use may be satisfied for a registered trade mark which has become distinctive as a result of use as part of a composite mark with other elements, even where it has only ever been used as part of that composite: *Colloseum Holding AG v Levi Strauss & Co* (C-12/12) [2013] E.T.M.R. 34. The use of FRUIT OF THE LOOM did not amount to genuine use of the mark FRUIT, since the additional words altered the distinctive character of the single word: *Fruit of the Loom Inc v OHIM* (T-514/10) [2012] E.T.M.R. 44 General Court.

For an example of an appeal against revocation for lack of genuine use, see *Galileo International Technology LLC v European Union (formerly European Community)* [2011] EWHC 35 (Ch); [2011] E.T.M.R. 22. The appeal was dismissed. Proof of use was in issue in *Environmental Manufacturing v OHIM & Société Elmar Wolf* (T-570/10) (OJ 2012 C200/14). For disputes about the evidence required to demonstrate use, see, e.g. *Centrotherm* (T-434/09) (OJ 2011 C311/43) General Court and *Völkl v OHIM* (T-504/09) (OJ 2012 C32/22) General Court. In *Redd Solicitors LLP v Red Legal Ltd* [2012] EWPCC 54; [2013] E.T.M.R. 13, the court held that even though the claimant used the mark primarily only in relation to intellectual property law, that did not mean that it would be fair to restrict the mark to that sphere of legal practice.

NOTE 369. Add at the end: Note the "use conditions" introduced by the Trade Marks (Proof of Use) Regulations 2004/946.

NOTE 370. Add at the end: The CJEU handed down a detailed decision on "use" on March 29, 2011: see *Anheuser-Busch Inc v Budejovicky Budvar Narodni Podnik* (C-96/09 P) [2011] E.T.M.R. 31.

NOTE 373. Second sentence. Delete and substitute: Application may be made to the UK Intellectual Property Office or to the High Court.

Last sentence. Delete the final reference and substitute: *Evans (t/a Firecraft) v Focal Point Fires Plc* [2009] EWHC 2784 (Ch); [2010] R.P.C. 15. This case is to be contrasted with the Court of Appeal decision in *Special Effects Ltd v L'Oréal SA* [2007] EWCA Civ 1; [2007] R.P.C. 15.

Licensing and assignment of registered trade marks. NOTE 377. Second **25–80** sentence. Add at the beginning of the sentence: Under s.25,
NOTE 379. Add at the end: For the contrast between this and the requirements of the Community Trade Mark Regulation (EC) 40/94 (codified in Regulation 207/2009), see *Jean Christian Perfumes Ltd v Thakrar (t/a Brand Distributor and/or Brand Distributors Ltd)* [2011] EWHC 1383 (Ch); [2011] F.S.R. 34: an oral licence was a sufficient basis for bringing an action.

(c) *Infringement of trade mark*

Infringement of registered trade mark. First sentence. Delete and substitute: **25–81** There are three ways in which a registered trade mark may be infringed, as well as ancillary torts relating to the affixation of trade marks in certain circumstances without consent.
Para. (c) Third sentence: Delete "repute or".
NOTE 385. After the sentence referring to *Rugby Football Union v Cotton Traders Ltd*, add: see *Unilever Plc v Griffin* [2010] EWHC 899 (Ch); [2010] F.S.R. 33, in which Arnold J. was sceptical about whether the inclusion of the trade mark MARMITE in a party political broadcast constituted use in the course of trade.
Insert before penultimate sentence: The CJEU has ruled that merely filling a package supplied by a customer does not amount to "use" of the marks borne on that package, but it does create the conditions for use to occur—see *Frisdranken Industrie Winters BV v Red Bull GmbH* (C-119/10) [2012] E.T.M.R. 16.
Final sentence. Delete and substitute: A large number of questions have been referred to the CJEU concerning trade mark use during searches on websites such as eBay and Google. The CJEU has given judgments in a number of cases, to which the reader should refer for full details. In the *Google France* cases (*Google France Sarl v Louis Vuitton Malletier SA* (C-236/08) [2010] E.T.M.R. 30 and two other joined cases: C-238/08 and C-237/08 [2010] E.T.M.R. 30), the CJEU ruled that Google itself did not infringe trade marks by allowing advertisers to purchase "keywords" that are also trade marks, but that advertisers who used such keywords *would* infringe if internet users could not readily ascertain the trade origin of the goods so advertised. See also *Portakabin Ltd v Primakabin BV* (C-558/08) [2010] E.T.M.R. 52; and *Die BergSpechte Outdoor Reisen und Alpinschule Edi Koblmuller GmbH v Guni* (C-278/08), [2010] E.T.M.R. 33. In *L'Oréal v eBay* (C-324/09 [2011] R.P.C 27, the court confirmed the approach of the *Google France* cases, and went into detail on the role of the online market-place in infringement. The court's decision in *Interflora Inc v Marks & Spencer Plc* (C-323/09), which concerned much the same set of issues, expanded on the ideas of infringement via damage to the advertising and investment functions of trade marks: see [2012] F.S.R. 3. These cases contain important developments in the concept of infringement which were usefully summarised by Arnold J.

when *Interflora* returned to the High Court (via two significant disputes about survey evidence which both went to the Court of Appeal)—see [2013] EWHC 1291 (Ch); [2013] E.T.M.R. 35. Arnold J. held that the use of "Interflora" as a keyword did infringe, since consumers were not able to tell, or could tell only with difficulty, that Marks & Spencer was not part of Interflora's network; however, the use of the mark did not take unfair advantage and was not without due cause.

NOTE 388. Add at the end: A thorough summary of the law was provided by Arnold J. in *Och-Ziff Management Europe Ltd v Och Capital LLP* [2010] EWHC 2599 (Ch); [2011] E.T.M.R. 1; [2011] F.S.R. 11 at [72] et seq. For recent discussions of issues surrounding infringement, see *32Red Plc v WHG (International) Ltd* [2011] EWHC 62 (Ch); [2011] E.T.M.R. 21; aff'd [2012] EWCA Civ 19; [2012] E.T.M.R. 14; and *Kingspan Group Plc v Rockwool Ltd* [2011] EWHC 250 (Ch). Note that evidence that the defendant has been "living dangerously" (trying to get as close to the claimant's mark as it believes it safely can) can make a finding of trademark infringement more likely: *Specsavers International Healthcare Ltd v Asda Stores Ltd* [2010] EWHC 2035 (Ch); [2011] F.S.R. 1. The Court of Appeal in *Specsavers* [2012] EWCA Civ 24; [2012] F.S.R. 19 allowed (in part) an appeal on certain issues of infringement, and referred a question to the CJEU about the scope of s.10(2) (i.e. art.9(1)(b) of Directive (EC) 207/2009) where a mark is registered without reference to colour but has in practice been used almost exclusively with a particular shade (in this case green for "Specsavers" word marks and overlapping ovals). For an illustration of the application of s.10(2) see *Samuel Smith Old Brewery (Tadcaster) v Lee (t/a Cropton Brewery)* [2011] EWHC 1879 (Ch); [2012] F.S.R. 7. For contrasting decisions about whether reusing a trade-marked product can give rise to infringement see *Schutz v Werit* [2011] EWHC 1712 (Ch) (in which infringement was found) and *Viking Gas A/S v Kosan Gas A/S*, Case C-46/10 [2011] E.T.M.R. 58 (no infringement, on the basis of exhaustion—see para.**25–82** below).

The Court of Appeal has given detailed guidance on the use of survey evidence in two decisions in *Interflora Inc v Marks &Spencer Plc* [2012] EWCA Civ 1501; [2013] F.S.R. 21; and [2013] EWCA Civ 319; [2013] F.S.R. 26. Survey evidence should not be admitted unless it is of real utility in the claim, and in such a way that justifies the cost of obtaining it. Lawyers preparing evidence should be careful not to mischaracterise the raw data—as to which see the judicial comment in *A&E Television Networks LLC v Discovery Communications Europe Ltd* [2013] EWHC 109 (Ch); [2013] E.T.M.R. 32.

NOTE 390. Add at the end: The nature of the *Intel* requirement for a change (or risk of change) in economic behaviour is perhaps not as strict as has been thought—see *Environmental Manufacturing LLP v OHIM, Société Elmar Wolf* (C-570/10) at [51] et seq. The Court of Justice in that case said that the economic effect is established if the proprietor of the earlier mark can show that the mark's ability to identify the goods or services for which it is registered as coming from that proprietor is weakened—essentially an aspect of dilution.

NOTE 391. Add at the end: See also the Court of Appeal's judgment following the CJEU verdict: [2010] EWCA Civ 535; [2010] E.T.M.R. 47. Unfair advantage was also considered in depth in the more recent *Red Bull GmbH v Sun Mark Ltd* [2012] EWHC 1929 (Ch), in which Arnold J. held that the strapline "NO BULL IN THIS CAN" infringed the claimant's RED BULL mark for energy drinks.

Limitations on the effect of a registered trade mark.   **25–82**

(a) *Reference to the proprietor's own goods—comparative advertising*

Last sentence of sub-para. (a): Reference to Directive 84/450 on comparative advertising should refer to the codified version of the Directive: 2006/114/EC.

NOTE 396: At the end of the sentence which reads "The provisions of s.10(6) are independent of the provisions of the Comparative Advertising Directive", insert: 2006/114/EC.

After the reference to *DSG Retail v Comet Group Plc*, insert: but contrast the decision in *Kingspan Group Plc v Rockwool Ltd* [2011] EWHC 250 (Ch), in which a claim for malicious falsehood failed, while the claim for infringement based on comparative advertising succeeded.

(b) *Descriptive use, use of own name, ancillary use, etc*

NOTE 401. Add at the end: In relation to Community trade marks (Regulation 207/2009), a company may rely on its trading name as well as its corporate name, depending on the circumstances: *Hotel Cipriani Srl v Cipriani (Grosvenor Street) Ltd* [2010] EWCA Civ 110; [2010] R.P.C. 16; it is submitted that the same would apply in relation to s.11(2). The High Court later held that the use of the statements "by G. Cipriani" and "Managed by Guiseppe Cipriani" breached injunctions preventing the use of the claimant's CIPRIANI Community trade mark, since in order to avoid infringement the defendant would need to establish that G. Cipriani was well known to the average consumer: *Hotel Cipriani Srl v Fred 250 Ltd (formerly Cipriani (Grosvenor Street) Ltd)* [2013] EWHC 70 (Ch); [2013] E.T.M.R. 18. For an example of a defendant choosing its company name with no good reason (and thereby having no defence to infringement) see *Smithkline Beecham Ltd v GSKline Ltd* [2011] EWHC 169 (Ch). The own-name defence was upheld in *Stichting BDO v BDO Unibank Inc* [2013] EWHC 418 (Ch); [2013] E.T.M.R. 31, and also in *A&E Television Networks LLC v Discovery Communications Europe Ltd* [2013] EWHC 109 (Ch); [2013] E.T.M.R. 32, in which DISCOVERY HISTORY did not infringe THE HISTORY CHANNEL.

NOTE 402. Add at the end: For use held not to be an honest indication of the kind of goods, see *Hasbro Inc v 123 Nahrmittel GmbH* [2011] EWHC 199 (Ch); [2011] E.T.M.R. 25 (product described as "play-dough"; claimant owned registered trade mark PLAY-DOH). The "indication of kind" defence was also rejected in *Bayerische Motoren Werke AG v Round & Metal Ltd* [2012] EWHC 2099; [2013] F.S.R. 18. Arnold J. held that the defendant could have described its replacement car wheels as "BMW style" rather than using the BMW mark, but in any event the court found that the use was not in accordance with honest practices in industrial or commercial matters.

(c) *Other exceptions to infringement*

NOTE 403. Delete and substitute: TMA 1994 s.11(3).

(d) *Exhaustion of rights*

NOTE 404. After the sentence beginning "The effect of the ECJ's judgment ..." insert: See the same reasoning in *Coty Prestige Lancaster Group GmbH v*

Simex Trading AG (C-127/09) [2010] E.T.M.R. 41, following *Makro Zelkbedeiningsgroothandel CV v Diesel SpA* (C-324/08) [2010] Bus. L.R. 608. In *Oracle America Inc v M-Tech Data Ltd* [2010] EWCA Civ 997; [2010] E.T.M.R. 64, the way in which the claimant marketed its goods was designed to make it difficult to tell if goods had first been marketed within the EEA; the Court of Appeal held that it was arguable that this was contrary to Community law on free movement of goods, but this has since been reversed following an appeal to the Supreme Court: [2012] UKSC 27; [2012] 1 W.L.R. 2026.

Add at the end: The CJEU held in *Viking Gas A/S v Kosan Gas A/S* (C-46/10) [2011] E.T.M.R. 58 that the proprietor of a shape mark for gas canisters had exhausted its rights in that mark by placing the product on the market in the EEA, and could not prevent customers exchanging empty canisters for ones refilled by a third party, absent any proper reason for objecting under art.7(2) of Directive (EC) 207/2009. The onus is on the defendant in an infringement action to put forward a defence of exhaustion: *Honda Motor Co Ltd v David Silver Spares Ltd* [2010] EWHC 1973 (Ch); [2010] F.S.R. 40.

(d) *Proceedings*

25–83   **Proceedings for trade mark infringement and remedies.** Add at the end: Trade mark infringement can be amenable to summary judgment: *British Sky Broadcasting Group Plc v Digital Satellite Warranty Cover Ltd (In Liquidation)* [2011] EWHC 2662 (Ch); [2012] F.S.R. 14. That case concerned s.10(1). Arnold J. also considered database right and passing off. For summary judgment on s.10(2) infringement see *Lewis v Client Connection Ltd* [2011] EWHC 1627; [2012] E.T.M.R. 6, and *United Airlines Inc v United Airways Ltd* [2011] EWHC 2411 (Ch).

NOTE 409. Add at the end: The fact that the mark alleged to infringe is itself registered is no bar to a finding of infringement, and the proprietor of the earlier mark need not first obtain a finding of invalidity against the later mark: *Fédération Cynologique Internationale v Federación Canina Internacional De Perros De Pura Raza* (C-561/11) [2013] E.T.M.R. 23 CJEU. This presents an apparent conflict with s.11(1) TMA 1994 which may have to be resolved in due course.

NOTE 410. After the reference to *Dormeuil v Ferraglow*, insert: In *National Guild of Removers and Storers Ltd v Jones (t/a ATR removals)* [2011] EWPCC 4 Patents County Court, damages for unlicensed use of the mark were awarded on the "user" principle of applying a royalty, the judge having noted that the relevant authorities did not forbid this approach (the case was reversed on appeal, but not affecting this point: [2012] EWCA Civ 216; [2012] 1 W.L.R. 2501). The user principle was considered and applied in *32Red Plc v WHG (International) Ltd* [2013] EWHC 815 (Ch). When conducting an account of profits, it is not appropriate simply to allocate a proportion of the infringer's general overheads to the infringing activity: the infringer must show what costs are properly attributable to the infringements—*Hollister Inc v Medik Ostomy Supplies Ltd* [2012] EWCA Civ 1419; [2013] F.S.R. 24.

NOTE 413. Add at the end: An injunction was refused in *Cowshed Products Ltd v Island Origins Ltd* [2010] EWHC 3357 (Ch); [2011] E.T.M.R. 42, after a detailed evaluation based on that same set of principles. Note that an injunction against infringement of a Community trade mark will, as a rule, extend to the entire European Union: *DHL Express France SAS v Chronopost SA* (C-235/09) [2011] E.T.M.R. 33. An injunction was also refused in *Protomed Ltd v Medication Systems Ltd* [2012] EWHC 3726 (Ch), where it was held that the claimant did not have a good arguable case on infringement.

Criminal offences and customs powers. NOTE 414. Add at the end: The   **25–84** court may make a confiscation order under the Proceeds of Crime Act 2002 in relation to trade mark offences—*R. v Kamran Hameed Ghori* [2012] EWCA Crim 1115. In a separate decision the Court of Appeal rejected arguments that such an order was oppressive: *R. v Beazley* [2013] EWCA Crim 567.

NOTE 417. Add at the end: As to the meaning of "counterfeit" in this context, Kitchin J. held in *Nokia Corp v Revenue and Customs Commissioners* [2009] EWHC 1903 (Ch); [2010] E.T.M.R. 59 that the goods in question had to infringe someone's trade marks in the relevant territory. The CJEU has ruled that goods brought into the EU customs area under a suspensive procedure (rather than being actually sold or advertised) cannot be classified as counterfeit or pirated goods: *Koninklijke Philips Electronics NV v Lucheng Meijing Industrial Co Ltd* (C-446/09), [2012] E.T.M.R. 13.

Action for groundless threats of trade mark infringement proceedings.   **25–86** NOTE 419. Add at the end: A Community-wide mark can found an action for threats of infringement proceedings under the 1994 Act, but only if the threat is in relation to proceedings within the United Kingdom: *Best Buy Co Inc v Worldwide Sales Corp España SL* [2011] EWCA Civ 618; [2011] F.S.R. 30.

9. PATENTS

(a) *Introduction*

Patents—scope of section. NOTE 421. Delete and substitute: See Miller,   **25–87** Burkhill, Birss & Campbell, *Terrell on the Law of Patents*, 17th edn (London: Sweet & Maxwell, 2010); *CIPA Guide to the Patents Acts*, 7th edn (London: Sweet & Maxwell, 2011); Clark, Jacob, Cornish, Hamer and Moody-Stuart, *Encyclopedia of United Kingdom and European Patent Law* (London: Sweet & Maxwell, looseleaf, last release March 2012). *Halsbury's Laws*, 4th edn, Vol. 11(1), (London: Lexis Nexis 2006 Reissue, "Copyright, Patents and Designs"). For procedure in infringement, etc. before the courts, including the Patent County Court, see Civil Procedure (Amendment 2) Rules (CPR) Pt.63, "Patents and Other Intellectual Property Claims", together with a supplementary Practice Directive, as amended in 2010. For procedure before the Intellectual Property Office (IPO (formerly the Patent Office)), see the Patents Rules 2007 and Patent (Fees) Rules 2007, as amended to October 1, 2011, and *The Manual of Patent Practice* (updated to October 1, 2011). All the above documents are available on the IPO's website: *http://www.ipo.gov.uk/tm/htm*.

25–88   **Introduction—the statutory framework.** Last sentence. Delete and substitute. Later laws, including the Copyright, Designs and Patents Act 1988, the Regulatory Reform (Patents Act) Order 2004, and the Patent Act 2004 have changed the 1977 Act.

Add: NOTE 421a. An unofficial consolidation of the Patents Act 1977 (as amended up to and including October 1, 2011) is available on the website of the Intellectual Property Office: *http://www.ipo.gov.uk/tm/htm*. See also the Patents (Convention Countries) Order 2007, SI 2007/276 (as amended by the Patents (Convention Countries) (Amendment) Order 2009 (SI 2009/2746) for the protection afforded to foreign nationals pursuant to the international obligations of the United Kingdom as a member of the EPC, PCT, Paris Convention for the Protection of Industrial Property and the World Trade Organisation (WTO).

25–90   **Application for a patent—priority date.** NOTE 424. Delete and substitute: See PA 1977 ss.14–24 for procedure.

NOTE 425. Add at beginning: EPC art.99.

NOTE 426. Delete and substitute: There is also the possibility of making an international application under the Patent Cooperation Treaty (PCT) 1970, which is administered by the World Intellectual Property Organization (WIPO) in Geneva. The PCT provides a unified procedure for obtaining patent protection in over 140 countries worldwide on the basis of a single application. Readers are referred to the above-mentioned specialist works for details.

25–91   **Term of Patent.** NOTE 429. Delete and substitute: See PA 1977 s.128B to which the EU Regulations 1768/92 (medicinal products) and 1610/96 (plant protection products) are scheduled. The law governing the grant of Supplementary Protection Certificates involves the overlap of the patent and regulatory regimes. It is a complex subject in its own right with extensive case law. The CJEU handed down three judgments on SPCs in 2011. Two established the principle that an application for an SPC must relate to a medicament (human or veterinary) "product" that: is protected by a patent; has been subject to an administrative authorisation procedure; and has not been placed on the market anywhere in the EEA as a medicinal product prior to being subject to safety and efficacy testing and a regulatory review (see *Generics (UK) Ltd v Synaptech Inc.* (C-427/09) [2012] 1 C.M.L.R. 4; [2012] R.P.C. 4 and *Synthon BV v Merz Pharma GmbH & Co. KGaA*, (C-195/09) [2012] R.P.C. 3). In the third case, the CJEU held that the competent industrial property office of a Member State is precluded from granting a supplementary protection certificate relating to active ingredients which are not specified in the wording of the claims of the basic patent relied on. A certificate may be granted, however, for a combination of two active ingredients where the medicinal product in question contains not only that combination but also other active ingredients (*Medeva BV v Comptroller General of Patents, Designs and Trade Marks* (C-322/10) [2012] R.P.C. 25). See also subsequent decision of the Court of Appeal [2012] EWCA Civ 523; [2012] 3 C.M.L.R. 9. The CJEU handed down a further judgment on July 19, 2012, in response to a request for a further preliminary ruling under art.267 TFEU in *Neurim Pharmaceuticals (1991) Ltd v Comptroller-General of Patents* (C-130/11) [2011] EWCA Civ 228; [2011] R.P.C. 19. The context of the case was a dispute between the parties as a result of the IPO refusing to grant a supplementary protection certificate for a second medical use protected by a European patent. Supplementary protection is only available when the marketing authorisation granted for the product is the first for that product. However, in its judgment dated July 19, 2012 ([2013] R.P.C. 23), the CJEU held that the mere existence of an earlier marketing authorisation obtained for a veterinary medicinal product does not preclude the grant of a supplementary protection certificate for a different application of the same product for human use for which a marketing authorisation has been granted. Thus, products relating to additional or second medical uses of an active ingredient are now eligible for supplementary protection.

Ownership, entitlement, licensing and employee inventions. NOTE 435. **25–92** Delete and substitute: There are provisions of EU competition law (especially art.101 of the Treaty on the Functioning of the European Union (TFEU) (ex art.81) and the Technology Transfer block exemption) which affect the terms that may be included in patent licences. The reader should consult specialist texts on EU competition law for details.

NOTE 438. Add at the end: In *Shanks v Unilever Plc* [2010] EWCA Civ 1283; [2011] R.P.C. 12, the Court of Appeal held that the term "That person" in PA 1977 s.41(2), referring to a person, connected to the employer of an inventor, to whom the rights in the invention had been assigned, meant the actual assignee with its actual attributes.

The specification—description and claims. First paragraph, fourth sentence. **25–93** Delete and substitute: An invention is taken to be that specified in the claims, as interpreted by the description and any drawings contained in the specification.

First paragraph, last sentence. Delete and substitute: This provides that: "Article 69 should not be interpreted as meaning that the extent of the protection conferred by a European patent is to be understood as that defined by the strict, literal meaning of the wording used in the claims, the description and drawings being employed only for the purpose of resolving an ambiguity found in the claims. Nor should it be taken to mean that the claims serve only as a guideline and that the actual protection conferred may extend to what, from a consideration of the description and drawings by a person skilled in the art, the patent proprietor has contemplated. On the contrary, it is to be interpreted as defining a position between these extremes which combines a fair protection for the patent proprietor with a reasonable degree of legal certainty for third parties."

Second paragraph, last sentence. Delete and substitute: In *Kirin-Amgen Inc v Hoechst Marion Roussel* Ltd,[442] the House of Lords revisited the *Catnic* principles stating that the principle of purposive construction established by *Catnic* was the bedrock of patent construction and was precisely in accordance with the Protocol on the Interpretation of art.69 of the European Patent Convention.

(b) *Validity*

Validity. **25–94**

(b) *Not obvious.*

The invention must involve an inventive step (i.e. it must not be obvious to a person skilled in the art).

(c) *Capable of industrial application*

NOTE 446. Second sentence, replace the brackets at the end: (PA 1977 s.4A). Add at end. See also the decision of the Supreme Court in *Human Genome Sciences Inc v Eli Lilly & Co* [2011] UKSC 51; [2012] 1 All E.R. 1154.

(d) *Not specifically excluded*

NOTE 447. Delete sub-para.(c) and substitute: "(c) a scheme, rule or method of performing a mental act, playing a game or doing business, or a programme for a computer. IPO practice on the patentability of mental acts is set out in a Practice Notice dated October 17, 2011. Its practice on patenting computer-implemented inventions (software patents) is based on *Aerotel Ltd v Telco Holdings and Macrossan's Application* [2006] EWCA Civ 1371; [2007] 1 All E.R. 225, and *Symbian Ltd's Application* [2008] EWCA Civ 1066; [2009] R.P.C. 1 (see Practice Notice of December 8, 2008, which should be read with Practice Notices dated November 2, 2006 and February 7, 2007 on patentable subject-matter. For EPO practice on this subject, see the EPO Enlarged Board of Appeal decision, G3/08 of May 12, 2010 (OJ EPO 1/2011, 10); or"

Second full paragraph. Delete the third sentence beginning: "The application of the exclusion . . ."

Add at the end: European Directive 98/44/EC on the patentability of biotechnological inventions has been implemented into UK law by amendment to the PA 1977 s.76A and Sch.A2. Section 3 of the Schedule provides that the following also are not patentable inventions: the human body, at the various stages of its formation and development, and the simple discovery of one of its elements, including the sequence or partial sequence of a gene; processes for cloning human beings; processes for modifying germ line genetic identity of human beings; uses of human embryos for industrial or commercial purposes and processes for modifying the genetic identity of animals which are likely to cause them suffering without any substantial medical benefit to man or animal, and animals resulting from such processes. In 2011 the CJEU delivered a judgment on the definition of the term "human embryo", *Oliver Brüstle v Greenpeace e.V.* (C-34/10), [2012] All E.R. (EC) 809; [2012] 1 C.M.L.R. 41, following which the IPO issued a Practice Notice "Inventions involving human embryonic stem cells" dated May 17, 2012. A new reference to the CJEU on the definition of human embryos and seeking clarification of the CJEU's decision in *Brüstle* was made by the Patent Court in *International Stem Cell Corp v Comptroller General of Patents* [2013] EWHC 807 (Ch).

25–96   **Revocation proceedings and other challenges to validity.** NOTE 461. Last sentence. Delete and substitute: If the opposition succeeds, the patent will be revoked (European Patent Convention art.101).

(c) *Infringement*

25–99   **Acts not constituting infringement.** NOTE 477. Add: and for use by a farmer of the product of his harvest for propagation or multiplication and of animal or animal reproductive material for an agricultural purpose where there has been a sale of plant propagating material or of breeding stock or other animal reproductive material by the proprietor of the patent or with his consent (PA 1977 s.60(5) (g) and (h)). An exception also applies to acts done in conducting a study, test or trial necessary for and conducted with a view to the application of certain provisions of EU Directives 2001/82/EC (as amended) and 2001/83/EC (as amended) concerning respectively veterinary medical products and medicinal products for human use (PA 1977 s.60(5)(i)).

Defences. Sub-paragraph (f), last sentence. Delete and substitute: In exceptional circumstances, the enforcement of a patent may constitute an abuse of a dominant position, contrary to art.102 of the Treaty on the Functioning of the European Union (TFEU) (ex art.82).   **25–102**

NOTE 489. Delete and substitute: This is a well-established principle of EU law: *Centrafarm v Sterling Drug* [1974] E.C.R. 1147. See for a comprehensive review of EU exhaustion principles: *Merck & Co Inc v Primecrown Ltd* (C-267/95 and C-268/95) [1997] F.S.R. 237 CJEU.

NOTE 494. Delete and substitute: PA 1977 s.44 (repealed).

Action for infringement, relief and remedies. NOTE 496. First sentence. Add: . . . (October 1, 2010).   **25–103**

Third and fourth sentences. Delete and substitute: If the defendant puts validity of the patent in issue, the statement of case must have a separate document attached to it headed "Grounds of Invalidity" (PD paras 4.1–4.6). There are provisions for case management, disclosure and inspection, experiments, use of models of apparatus, etc.

NOTE 497. First sentence. For PA 1977 s.61(1) substitute PA 1977 s.61(2).

Action to restrain unjustified threats of infringement proceedings. Fifth sentence. Delete and substitute: But merely providing factual information about the patent, or making enquiries about the patent for the sole purpose of discovering whether the patent has been infringed or making an assertion about the patent for the purpose of any such enquiry, is outside the section. Delete last sentence.   **25–107**

(d) *Special Regimes*

Compulsory licences, licences of right and Crown use. NOTE 522. First sentence. Delete and substitute: PA 1977 ss.48, 48A and 48B.   **25–108**

NOTE 523. First sentence. Delete and substitute: PA 1977 s.48A.

Plant Breeders' Rights. Second sentence. Delete and substitute: These rights are governed by the Plant Varieties Act 1997, which implements in the United Kingdom the 1991 International Convention for the Protection of New Varieties of Plants (UPOV). The 1997 Act also brings the UK law on this subject into line with EU Regulation 2100/94,[527] which established the European Union Plant Variety Right. The right granted primarily allows the holder to prevent others from producing, reproducing, using, conditioning or selling the protected variety.   **25–109**

The grant of EU rights gives protection throughout the European Union and it should be noted that EU rights and UK rights cannot operate simultaneously.[527a]

NOTE 527. [1995] O.J. L227/1.

Add. NOTE 527a. The UK and EU systems of plant breeders' rights are administered by the UK Plant Variety Office and the EU Plant Variety Office, respectively. For further information, see the UK Plant Variety Rights Office and Seeds Division of Defra: *http://www.fera.defra.gov.uk* [Accessed September 1, 2013].

CHAPTER 26

PASSING OFF

		PARA.
□	1. General principles	26–01
	2. Requirements	26–05
	■ (a) Goodwill	26–05
	■ (b) Misrepresentation	26–14
	■ (c) Damage	26–18
□	3. Remedies	26–19
	4. Defences	26–21
	5. Relationship to other rights	26–23

1. GENERAL PRINCIPLES

General principles. Add: *Yell Ltd v Giboin* [2011] EWPCC 009 H.H. Judge   **26–01**
Birss QC—the defendant was the owner and controller of a website outside
the United Kingdom but the services he advertised could be purchased in
the United Kingdom: the alleged passing off was within the jurisdiction of the
court.

Instruments of deception. In *SmithKline Beecham Ltd v GSKline Ltd* [2011]   **26–04**
EWHC 169 (Ch) at [23] Arnold J. applied *British Telecommunications Plc v One
in a Million* [1999] 1 W.L.R. 903.

NOTE 20. *L'Oreal SA v Bellure* was the subject of a further hearing by the
Court of Appeal ([2010] EWCA Civ 535; [2010] R.P.C. 23), but only with regard
to the registered trade mark claim.

2. REQUIREMENTS

(a) *Goodwill*

Goodwill. Add: In *Woolley v Ultimate Products Ltd* [2012] EWCA Civ 1038   **26–05**
the claimant sold watches under the name HENLEY; the defendants were a
wholesaler and retailer who used the name HENLEYS for their watches. Though
the defendant retailer had a reputation in the name HENLEYS for clothing it did
not have concurrent goodwill in the name HENLEYS on its own in the field of
watches.

In *Plentyoffish Media Inc v Plenty More LLP* [2011] EWHC 2568 (Ch); [2012]
R.P.C. 5 H.H. Judge Birss Q.C. (sitting as a judge of the High Court) the claimant
had a foreign-based dating website which had attracted visits or "hits" from UK
visitors, but there was no evidence any of them had become members. Held no

goodwill in the jurisdiction as the concept of customers required more than visiting a website. Also the claimant could not equate visitors with customers simply because the "hits" generated revenue from advertisers. Applied by Arnold J. in *Starbucks (HK) Ltd v British Sky Broadcasting Group Plc* [2012] EWHC 3074 (Ch); [2013] F.S.R. 29 Arnold J., especially at [125] and [130]. *W.S. Foster & Son Ltd v Brooks Brothers UK Ltd* [2013] EWPCC 18 Iain Purvis QC. Residual goodwill did not survive 40 years' non-use.

26–06 **Ownership of goodwill.** *Group Lotus Plc v 1 Malaysia Racing Team SDN BHD* [2011] EWHC 1366 (Ch); [2011] E.T.M.R. 62 at [153], Peter Smith J.: ownership where more than one company is involved in generating goodwill is a question of fact. *Fine & Country Ltd v Okotoks Ltd* [2013] EWCA Civ 672—a franchisor (providing a marketing umbrella for various independent estate agents) was capable of attracting goodwill, that goodwill being the ability to attract licence fees, at [56]–[58].

26–11 **Descriptive expressions.** In *Hasbro Inc v 123 Nahrmittel GmbH* [2011] EWHC 199; [2011] F.S.R. 21, the claimants had goodwill in the United Kingdom for their pre-mixed modelling compound, Play-Doh. The defendant had a similar product, Yummy Dough which they advertised as "the edible play dough". Floyd J. held this to be passing off. See also *Evegate Publishing Ltd v Newsquest Media (Southern) Ltd* [2013] EWHC 1975 (Ch) Asplin J. at [174]–[176]. On what does not constitute a descriptive phrase see *British Sky Broadcasting Group Plc v Microsoft Corp* [2013] EWHC 1826 (Ch), Asplin J. (especially at [247]).

26–12 **Get-up.** NOTE 75. Add: *Numatic International Ltd v Qualtex UK Ltd* [2010] EWHC 1237 (Ch); [2010] R.P.C. 25, Floyd J.—the shape of the claimant's vacuum cleaner (the "Henry") had acquired secondary meaning and the defendant's replica product constituted passing off.

(b) *Misrepresentation*

26–14 **Misrepresentation**
NOTE 95 Add: *Fine & Country Ltd v Okotoks Ltd* [2013] EWCA Civ 672 per Lewison L.J. (at [55]): ". . . the essence of the action is not confusion, but misrepresentation".

26–15 **Misrepresentations actionable as passing off.** Initial interest confusion (e.g. an advertisement not leading to a sale or customers not necessarily remaining confused at the time of any sale) is capable of constituting actionable passing off: see *Och–Ziff Management Europe Ltd v Och Capital LLP* [2010] EWHC 2599 (Ch); [2011] F.S.R. 11 Arnold J. at [155]–[157], citing (at [156]) para.7–39 of *Wadlow's Law of Passing Off: Unfair Competition by Misrepresentation*, 3rd edn (London: Sweet & Maxwell, 2003) where he notes: "the general principle is that if the defendant successfully induces the public to do business with him by making a misrepresentation then it ought not to matter that the falsity of the representation would become apparent at some stage." On initial interest confusion (or "switch selling") see also *Doosan Power Systems Ltd v Babcock International Group Plc* [2013] EWHC 1364 (Ch) Henderson J. The defendant argued that sophisticated clients (in the civil nuclear sector) were involved who would engage in extensive negotiations so that any alleged deception would be dispelled soon after contacting the defendant and prior to any contract. The judge found this to be an actionable misrepresentation, akin to the type of initial interest confusion discussed by Arnold J. in *Och-Ziff Management Europe Ltd v Och Capital LLP* [2010] EWHC 2599 (Ch); [2011] F.S.R. 11, so that "it matters not that the truth is subsequently discovered by the purchaser. From the point of view of the claimant, the damage has already been done and the distinctiveness of the goodwill has been eroded" (at [178]).

NOTE 98. On "connection" see Proudman J. in *Future Publishing Ltd v Edge Interactive Media Inc* [2011] EWHC 1489 (Ch); [2011] E.T.M.R. 50 at [71]: statements leading the public to believe the defendant's product "in some way approved or authorised" by the claimant. On an allegation that the defendant had decided to "live dangerously" see Mann J. in *Specsavers Int Healthcare Ltd v Asda Stores Ltd* [2010] EWHC 2035 (Ch); [2011] F.S.R. 1 at [193] (there was an appeal on the registered trade mark issues only: [2012] EWCA Civ 24; [2012] F.S.R. 19).

NOTE 106. Note in *Woolley v Ultimate Products Ltd* [2012] EWCA Civ 1038 Arden L.J. at [6] rejects "reverse passing off" in the sense of a misrepresentation that confuses the public into thinking that the goods of the claimant are the goods of the defendant. In *Doosan Power Systems Ltd v Babcock International Group Plc* [2013] EWHC 1364 (Ch) at [174] Henderson J. held there to be a "subtle" misrepresentation that the claimant's expertise was that of the defendant (rather than a source misrepresentation). The defendant group of companies had sold their civil nuclear business to the claimant, with an exclusive licence to use the name Babcock in relation to that business. Subsequently the defendant had made acquisitions in the civil nuclear sector and began to use the name Babcock in relation to this field. In its marketing and website material the defendant referred to Babcock's "50 years of experience" in the nuclear market.

"Extended passing off": product misdescription. *Diageo NA Inc v Intercontinental Brands (ICB) Ltd* [2010] EWCA Civ 920; [2011] 1 All E.R. 242: the extended form of passing off was not limited to products with "cachet". In *Fage UK Ltd v Chobani UK Ltd* [2013] EWHC 630 (Ch); [2013] E.T.M.R. 28 Briggs J. (there is an appeal to the Court of Appeal outstanding) the question was whether "Greek yoghurt" was a distinctive product for the purposes of extended passing off. The claimant contended that the term "Greek yoghurt", a thick and creamy yoghurt, could only be applied to strained yoghurt from Greece. Thick and creamy yoghurt could also be produced by the use of thickening agent, such yoghurt being sold as "Greek style yoghurt". The US defendant produced strained yoghurt but not from Greece and called it "Greek yoghurt". Held, Greek yoghurt was a distinctive product. To be a clearly defined class of goods, consumers did not have to know the manufacturing processes. As for geographical names, rather than any need to show strict regulations on the mode of manufacture of the product in question, "the fundamental question is whether the geographical trade name

26–16

has a pulling power that brings in customers . . ." (at [125]). With regard to a perception of distinctiveness, the test was whether a significant section of the public believed that the trading name denoted a sufficiently defined and distinctive class, with the requisite pulling power (*Chocosuisse Union des Fabricants Suisses de Chocolat v Cadbury Ltd* [1999] R.P.C. 826 applied). A substantial proportion of the yoghurt-eating population thought there was something special about Greek yoghurt (though this proportion of the relevant public was less than that found in cases concerning Champagne, Sherry and Swiss chocolate, [116]). Here, the market practice and labelling convention observed by the relevant market for over 25 years, the evidence of expert witnesses and the premium price commanded by a Greek yoghurt product were all relevant.

NOTE 109. Note the Court of Appeal decision now in *Diageo NA Inc v Intercontinental Brands (ICB) Ltd* [2010] EWCA Civ 920; [2011] 1 All E.R. 242.

26–17   **Proof of deception and confusion.** *Lumos Skincare Ltd v Sweet Squared Ltd* [2013] EWCA Civ 590—it was important in assessing who the claimant must show has been or would be misled by the defendant's representation to identify the market of each party and how the respective parties' products are used and sold.

NOTE 116. On the Whitford Guidelines in *Imperial Group v Philip Morris* [1984] R.P.C. 293, see also the guidance given by the Court of Appeal (Lewison L.J.) in *Marks and Spencer Plc v Interflora Inc* [2012] EWCA Civ 1501; [2013] F.S.R. 211 and *Interflora Inc v Marks and Spencer Plc* [2013] EWCA Civ 319; [2013] F.S.R. 26 (in the context of registered trade mark infringement). And see Lewison L.J. in *Fine & Country Ltd v Okotoks Ltd* [2013] EWCA Civ 672 at [72]. In *A&E Television Networks LLC v Discovery Communications Europe Ltd* [2013] EWHC 109 (Ch); E.T.M.R. 32; [2013] E.T.M.R. 32, at [129] Peter Smith J. adopted Lewison L.J.'s observations in *Marks and Spencer Plc v Interflora* in a passing off action. And see Hildyard J. in *Fage UK Ltd v Chobani UK Ltd* [2012] EWHC 3755 (Ch) and [2013] EWHC 298 (Ch) and Asplin J. in *Maier v ASOS Plc* [2012] EWHC 3456 (Ch).

(c) *Damage*

26–18   **Damage.** Add: In *British Sky Broadcasting Group Plc v Microsoft Corp* [2013] EWHC 1826 (Ch) at [250], Asplin J. noted "damage is inherently likely where frequently the customers of a business wrongly connect it to another". On dilution and loss of control see: *Redwood Tree Services Ltd v Apsay (t/a Redwood Tree Surgeons)* Unreported Patents CC Judge Birss QC; on dilution and substitution see: *Och–Ziff Management Europe Ltd v Och Capital LLP* [2010] EWHC 2599 (Ch); [2011] F.S.R. 11, Arnold J. at [158]–[160]. *Doosan Power Systems Ltd v Babcock International Group Plc* [2013] EWHC 1364 (Ch) Henderson J. at [180]: damage can include erosion of the goodwill attaching to a particular name (citing Laddie J. in *Irvine v Talksport Ltd* [2002] EWHC 367 (Ch); [2002] 1 W.L.R. 2355 at [38]). And in *Woolley v Ultimate Products Ltd* [2012] EWCA Civ 1038 at [7] Arden L.J. notes that the heads of damage for the tort include "an erosion or diminution in the value of goodwill".

3. Remedies

Injunctions. NOTE 132. In *Cowshed Products Ltd v Island Origins Ltd* [2010]   **26–20**
EWHC 3357 (Ch); [2011] E.T.M.R. 42 at [54] H.H. Judge Birss QC, the court
assessed the issue of unquantifiable harm and the balance of convenience.

CHAPTER 27

BREACH OF CONFIDENCE AND PRIVACY

		PARA.
■	1. General introduction	27–01
■	2. Action for breach of confidence (involving other than personal information)	27–05
■	(a) Information in respect of which an action for breach of confidence may arise	27–09
■	(b) Where an obligation of confidence arises	27–12
■	(c) Breach	27–19
	(d) Defences	27–25
	(i) Cessation of obligations	27–25
■	(ii) Public interest	27–26
■	(e) Remedies	27–32
■	3. The action for breach of personal confidence/privacy	27–36
■	(a) The reasonable expectation of privacy	27–39
■	(b) Competing interests	27–44
■	(c) Relevant statutory provisions	27–45
■	(d) Remedies	27–47

1. General Introduction

The traditional action for breach of confidence NOTE 1. Now see *Gurry* on   **27–01**
Breach of Confidence, 2nd edn (Oxford: Oxford University Press, 2012).

Juridical basis of the action. *Gray v News Group Newspapers Ltd* [2012]   **27–04**
UKSC 28; [2013] 1 A.C. 1: commercial (but not personal) confidential information obtained through phone hacking came within the definition of "commercial
information" and "intellectual property" for the purposes of s.72(5) of the Senior
Courts Act 1981 (so as to prevent the defendant from relying on the privilege
against self-incrimination: see the discussion by Lord Walker at [24]–[33]). In
Veolia ES Nottinghamshire Ltd v Notts CC [2010] EWCA Civ 1214; [2011] Env.
L.R. 12 (a case involving the interpretation of the public inspection provisions of
the Audit Commission Act 1988) Rix L.J. asserted (at [111]): ". . . confidential
information is a well recognised species of property, protected by the common
law . . ." and later (at [121]) noted he could see no reason why commercial confidential information should not be within the concept of "possessions" in art.1 of
the First Protocol to ECHR (which protects "peaceful enjoyment of possessions").
However, in *Force India Formula One Team Ltd v 1 Malaysia Racing Team Sdn
Bhd* [2012] EWHC 616 (Ch); [2012] R.P.C. 29 Arnold J. noted: "confidential
information is not property" (at [376], commenting on the view of Rix L.J., above,
at [417]). The Court of Appeal upheld the actual decision in this case, *Force
India Formula One Team Ltd v 1 Malaysia Racing Team Sdn Bhd* [2013]
EWCA Civ 780. It should be noted that Lewison L.J. commented (at [108]) that
he was "sceptical" about the assumption that the Enforcement Directive on the

enforcement of intellectual property rights (2004/48/EC) applied to the misuse of confidential information. In *Walsh v Shanahan* [2013] EWCA Civ 411 at [55] Rimer L.J. referred to "a case in tort arising out of their misuse of information belonging to [the claimant]".

Note that the decision of Arnold J. in *Vestergaard Frandsen A/S v BestNet Europe Ltd* (referred to in the Main Text) was in part reversed by the Court of Appeal ([2011] EWCA Civ 424); and now see *Vestergaard Frandsen A/S v Bestnet Europe Ltd* [2013] UKSC 31; [2013] 1 W.L.R. 1556, Lord Neuberger (discussed below, especially at para.**27–20**).

2. ACTION FOR BREACH OF CONFIDENCE
(INVOLVING OTHER THAN PERSONAL INFORMATION)

27–05   **Action for breach of confidence involving other than personal information.** *Vestergaard Frandsen A/S v Bestnet Europe Ltd* [2013] UKSC 31; [2013] 1 W.L.R. 1556, Lord Neuberger. Lord Neuberger: "an action in breach of confidence is based ultimately on conscience" (at [22]). The classic case of breach of confidence was that of recipient liability (at [23]) where the recipient of confidential information, who received it in circumstances where she had agreed, or ought to have appreciated, that it was confidential used it inconsistently with its confidential nature. But liability for breach of confidence could also arise where a defendant learns of a trade secret in circumstances where she reasonably does not appreciate that it is confidential, but subsequently appreciates that it is in fact confidential (at [25]). Lord Neuberger further noted "while a recipient of confidential information may be said to be primarily liable in a case of its misuse, a person who assists her in the misuse can be liable, in a secondary sense ... [though] she would normally have to know that the recipient was abusing confidential information" (at [26]). Knowledge in this context would include "blind-eye knowledge" (see Lord Nicholls in *Royal Brunei Airlines Sdn Bhd v Tan* [1995] 2 A.C. 378 PC, especially at 390F–391D). He also noted that even a person who did not know that the information which is being abused is confidential could nonetheless be liable if there were relevant additional facts, instancing vicarious liability.

Note *Ningbo Wentai Sports Equipment Co Ltd v Wang* [2012] EWPCC 51, Judge Birss QC. In proceedings to revoke the defendant's patent, the defendant counter-claimed for breach of confidence (in relation to prior disclosure) and breach of contract. When the patent was declared invalid, the issue was whether the PCC had jurisdiction to hear the counterclaim. Held, the PCC had jurisdiction to hear the claim for breach of confidence as it arose "out of the same subject-matter as a patent claim" (s.287 CDPA 1988 applied).

27–08   **Parties.** Add: *BSB Group Plc v Digital Satellite Warranty Cover Ltd* [2011] EWHC 2662 (Ch); [2012] F.S.R. 14 per Arnold J.: "... in principle a claimant could advance a case of joint liability for breach of an equitable obligation of confidence". And see Arnold J. in *Force India Formula One Team Ltd v 1 Malaysia Racing Team Sdn Bhd* [2012] EWHC 616 (Ch); [2012] R.P.C. 29 at [245] (the Court of Appeal upheld the actual decision in this case but did not comment on this point: [2013] EWCA Civ 780). In *Vestergaard Frandsen A/S v Bestnet Europe Ltd* [2013] UKSC 31; [2013] 1 W.L.R. 1556, Lord Neuberger (see para.**27–05**, above) the defendant was not liable under common design as for that she would have to share with the other party/parties each of the features of the design that made it wrongful (at [32]). Here she had neither received the trade secrets nor did she know they had been misused (*Unilever Plc v Gillette Ltd* [1989] R.P.C. 583, CA, a patent case, distinguished as not applying to confidential information, see [36]–[37]. cf. *Lancashire Fires Ltd v SA Lyons & Co* [1996] F.S.R. 629 where it had been conceded that the principle in *Unilever* applied to confidential information cases).

NOTE 38. And see *Abbey v Gilligan* [2012] EWHC 3217 (QB); [2013] E.M.L.R. 12 Tugendhat J. at [40]–[41].

(a) *Information (other than personal information) in respect of which an action for breach of confidence may arise*

The quality of confidence. In *BBC v HarperCollins Publishers Ltd* [2010]   **27–09**
EWHC 2424 (Ch); [2011] E.M.L.R. 6, the claimant sought to prevent the second defendant, the performer of the Stig character from the television programme Top Gear, from revealing his identity in an autobiography. The defendant had known that his identity was meant to be kept secret. Morgan J. refused an interim injunction, the defendant's identity having been extensively revealed in the press; *Schering Chemicals Ltd v Falkman Ltd* [1982] Q.B. 1 doubted (see Note 47).

Information protected by the action. NOTE 60. In *Bailey v Graham* [2011]   **27–10**
EWHC 3098 (Ch), Judge Pelling QC, questioned whether a recipe for sauce was sufficiently certain to have the necessary quality of confidence (at [104]), citing *De Maudsley v Palumbo* [1996] F.S.R. 447 that the material relied upon must be capable of being realised as an actuality (judgment upheld—on the issue of witness and parties' credibility—in [2012] EWCA Civ 1469).

(b) *Where an obligation of confidence arises*

Circumstances giving rise to an obligation of confidence. Add: In *Walsh v*   **27–12**
Shanahan [2013] EWCA Civ 411 (at [55]) Rimer L.J., citing Lord Nicholls in *Campbell v Mirror Group Newspapers* [2004] 2 A.C. 457, noted that the tort for which the claimant sued was one which had firmly shaken off the limiting constraint of the need for an initial confidential relationship and was "better encapsulated now as misuse of private information". In *Abbey v Gilligan* [2012] EWHC 3217 (QB); [2013] E.M.L.R. 12 at [63] Tugendhat J., with regard to the law of confidentiality and leaks to journalists, referred to his analysis in *Commissioner of Police of the Metropolis v Times Newspapers Ltd* [2011] EWHC 2705 (QB) (at [94]) and noted "a journalist considering whether or not to publish information must, in many cases, have an opportunity to read the information to make that decision. It cannot be right that the court should in such cases too readily find that the obtaining or reading of the information is a breach of confidence".

27–13 **Confidences arising from specific contractual provision or a relationship.** NOTE 89. With regard to legal professional privilege and "iniquity" see *BBGP Managing General Partner Ltd v Babcock & Brown Global Partners* [2010] EWHC 2176 (Ch); [2011] Ch. 296 Norris J.

NOTES 85 and 87. On the "Bolkiah" principle: an attempt to extend this principle to cover ordinary employees was rejected in *Caterpillar Logistics Services (UK) v Huesca de Crean* [2012] EWCA Civ 156; [2012] 3 All E.R. 129 ("confined to solicitors and the like . . ." per Stanley Burnton L.J. at [49]); whether the principle applied to a former in-house litigator as well as to independent litigators led to an obiter difference of views in the Court of Appeal in *Generics (UK) Ltd v Yeda Research & development Co Ltd* [2012] EWCA Civ 726; [2013] F.S.R. 13. Jacob L.J. believed it did; Etherton and Ward L.JJ. believed it did not (on the basis that the normal rule should apply to in-house litigators as applied to all ex-employees and that the existence of a fiduciary duty was central to the *Bolkiah* principle)

27–14 **Rights against employees.** Add: *Vestergaard Frandsen A/S v Bestnet Europe Ltd* [2013] UKSC 31; [2013] 1 W.L.R. 1556, Lord Neuberger. The defendant, a former employee of the claimant company, had established a competing company unaware that this new company's product had been developed using the claimant's confidential information. That confidential information had been in the form of a database created by the claimant for its consultant biologist who subsequently used it to develop products for the new company. Held that although she had been under a duty of confidence in her employment with the claimants, she was not liable under her contract duty either expressly or impliedly. The express terms of her contract did not cover the facts and it would be wrong in principle to imply an obligation that she would not assist another to misuse the claimant's trade secrets even though she did not know the trade secrets and was unaware that they were being misused (at [30]–[31]).

Saltri III Ltd v MD Mezzanine SA [2012] EWHC 1270 (Comm) Hamblen J.: where an employee was seconded to another employer, the documents produced during the secondment were prima facie confidential to the company to whom he had been seconded.

27–15 **Rights against ex-employees.** Add: *Vestergaard Frandsen A/S v Bestnet Europe Ltd* [2013] UKSC 31; [2013] 1 W.L.R. 1556, Lord Neuberger. Where an ex-employee set up a rival company using the former employer's consultant, the claimants sought to allege, inter alia what Lord Neuberger termed a "playing with fire allegation" [40]. But it was noted that merely taking a risk was insufficient for liability, though the fact that she took a risk might render it easier to hold that she was dishonest. The Supreme Court also underlined (at [44]–[45]) the need for the law to "maintain a realistic and fair balance" between protecting trade secrets and not inhibiting competition. So it should not "discourage former employees from benefiting society and advancing themselves by imposing unfair potential difficulties on their honest attempts to compete with their former employers".

With regard to restrictive covenants: Silber J. in *CEF Holdings Ltd v Munday* [2012] EWHC 1524 (QB); [2012] F.S.R. 35 discussed what is a protectable interest and why a restriction may be unreasonable. In *Force India Formula One Team Ltd v 1 Malaysia Racing Team Sdn Bhd* [2013] EWCA Civ 780 at [66]–[67]

Lewison L.J. discusses the approach to interpreting a covenant that deals with confidential information and the distinction between information and skill/ expertise.

Third party or confidential recipients of confidential information. See the discussion of *Vestergaard Frandsen A/S v Bestnet Europe Ltd* [2013] UKSC 31; [2013] 1 W.L.R. 1556, Lord Neuberger at para.**27–05**, above. With regard to bona fide purchasers without notice, note the views of Lord Neuberger M.R. in *Tchenguiz v Imerman* [2010] EWCA Civ 908; [2011] Fam. 116 at [74]. **27–16**

(c) *Breach*

Use and disclosure. Lord Neuberger M.R. in *Tchenguiz v Imerman* [2010] EWCA Civ 908; [2011] Fam. 116 at [69], said that it is a breach of confidence for a defendant without authority "to examine, or to make, retain or supply copies to a third party of a document, whose contents are, and were (or ought to have been) appreciated by the defendant to be, confidential to the claimant." **27–19**

Involuntary or accidental use. See *Vestergaard Frandsen A/S v Bestnet Europe Ltd* [2013] UKSC 31; [2013] 1 W.L.R. 1556, Lord Neuberger. *Seager v Copydex* [1967] 1 W.L.R. 923 (on which the judge at first instance had relied) was analysed and declared to be "an entirely orthodox application" of the approach set out by Lord Neuberger (see para.**27–05**, above). In *Seager*, "once it was found that they had received the information in confidence, their state of mind when using the information was irrelevant to the question of whether they had abused the confidence" (at [24]). **27–20**

(d) *Defences*

(ii) *Public interest*

Disclosure of matters of real public concern. Add: *Abbey v Gilligan* [2012] EWHC 3217 (QB); [2013] E.M.L.R. 12, Tugendhat J. If necessary, the court would have found that the public interest defence applied. The information published corrected a false image about a public figure and contributed to a public debate. **27–27**

Use and disclosure for other public purposes. Add: *Re General Dental Council's Application* [2011] EWHC 3011 (Admin); [2012] Med. L.R. 204 Sales J.: the GDC had a statutory authority (under s.27 of the Dentists Act 1984) to make use of a patient's dental records for the purpose of referring a complaint against a dentist to its investigating committee. This was a legitimate objective for the purposes of art.8. **27–29**

(e) *Remedies*

Injunction. In *BBC v HarperCollins Publishers Ltd* [2010] EWHC 2424 (Ch); [2011] E.M.L.R. 6, Morgan J. held that an injunction was not to be awarded **27–32**

to punish the defendant or deprive him of a benefit, as opposed to protecting the claimant against further harm, unlawfully caused. *Schering Chemicals Ltd v Falkman Ltd* [1982] Q.B. 1 was not to be relied upon as establishing that a court can award an injunction even after the material in question is no longer confidential (at [60]).

See also the Court of Appeal's decision in *Vestergaard Frandsen A/S v BestNet Europe Ltd* [2011] EWCA Civ 424 (in part reversing Arnold J.'s judgment, for which see Main Text) and now the Supreme Court judgment at [2013] UKSC 31; [2013] 1 W.L.R. 1556 Lord Neuberger.

27–33   **Damages or account of profits.** Add: In *Force India Formula One Team Ltd v 1 Malaysia Racing Team Sdn Bhd* [2013] EWCA Civ 780 the Court of Appeal held that the measure of damages was to be assessed to reflect the value of the unlawful use made of the confidential information. Here the cost of employing a consultant was the appropriate measure of compensation (see discussion at [103]). Lewison L.J. referred to the detailed discussion in the lower court ([2012] EWHC 616 (Ch); [2012] R.P.C. 29 at [374]–[424] Arnold J.) of the principles applicable to the assessment of damages or equitable compensation for breach of confidence but labelled this an unnecessary analysis (at [97]). In *Vestergaard Frandsen A/S v Bestnet Europe Ltd* [2013] UKSC 31; [2013] 1 W.L.R. 1556, Lord Neuberger noted that there was no entitlement to damages for losses suffered from misuse of trade secrets for the period when a particular defendant was honestly unaware of the fact that there was such misuse (see [39]).

Vestergaard Frandsen A/S v Bestnet Europe Ltd [2013] EWCA Civ 428: In a striking out application in a claim in an enquiry as to damages for breach of confidence, the court debated the correct approach to the assessment of damages where the misuse of the claimant's trade secrets resulted in the defendant's "derived product". (On the concept of a derived product see Laddie J. in *Ocular Sciences Ltd v Aspect Vision Care Ltd (No.2)* [1997] R.P.C. 289 at 396). The claimant had obtained an injunction to prevent the sale of the defendant's product that had been developed by misusing the claimant's confidential information. The defendant had subsequently developed two variants of this product, held to be sufficiently different from the claimant's product. The claimant sought lost profits damages for both the defendant's product that misused their confidential information and for the defendant's subsequent derived products. In relation to the derived products, the defendants contended that damages should be assessed only on a head start basis. Held, the decision in this case could only properly be made once the extent of the defendant's benefit had been established on the facts. However, the distinction the judge in the court below had drawn between the product and the derived products, granting an injunction only for the former, did not necessarily mean that only damages for a head start would be the method of assessment for the latter products. See also the discussion on the difference between lost profits/royalty/market value awards (at [21]–[22]) and the observation (at [119]–[120]) that on the measure of damages the underlying principles (as demonstrated in *Dowson & Mason v Potter* [1986] 1 W.L.R. 1419) were those expressed by Lord Wilberforce in *General Tire & Rubber Co v Firestone Tyre & Rubber Co* [1975] 1 W.L.R. 819 at 824 and Lord Shaw in *Watson, Laidlaw & Co Ltd v Potts, Cassels and Williamson* (1914) 31 R.P.C. 104 HL.

The "springboard doctrine". In *QBE Management Services (UK) Ltd v*   **27–34**
Dymoke [2012] EWHC 80 (QB); [2012] I.R.L.R. 458 Haddon-Cave J. provides a
summary of principles governing the grant of springboard relief. And see *Force
India Formula One Team Ltd v 1 Malaysia Racing Team Sdn Bhd* [2013] EWCA
Civ 780 at [72]–[76].

3. THE ACTION FOR BREACH OF PERSONAL CONFIDENCE/PRIVACY

The action for breach of personal confidence/privacy. Tugendhat J. in   **27–36**
Goodwin v News Group Newspapers Ltd [2011] EWHC 1437 (QB); [2011]
E.M.L.R. 27 at [85] analysed what the right to respect for private life involved.
Citing Warby, Moreham and Christie (eds), *Law of Privacy and the Media*, 2nd
edn (Oxford: Oxford University Press, 2011) he notes the two core components
are confidentiality and intrusion (at [85]). (He further noted, at [116], that the
protection against intrusion was also provided by the Protection from Harassment
Act 1997—see para.**27–46**, below, though accepting intrusion which the court
could protect against under HRA 1998 does not necessarily have to amount to
harassment as defined under the PHA 1997). The same judge in *Spelman v Express
Newspapers* [2012] EWHC 355 (QB) at [110]–[111], noted that though it was
often a strong argument that damages were not an adequate remedy where the
main interest was in keeping a secret, the position was less clear where the main
issue was intrusion. In *Goodwin v NGN Ltd* [2011] EWHC 1437 (QB); [2011]
E.M.L.R. 27 at [125] Tugendhat J. noted that there are different degrees of intrusion: "once a person's name appears in a newspaper or other media archive it may
well remain there indefinitely. Names mentioned on social networking sites are
less likely to be permanent".

The modern action for breach of personal confidence/privacy. *Ntuli v*   **27–37**
Donald [2010] EWCA Civ 1276; [2011] 1 W.L.R. 294 Maurice Kay L.J. at [10]:
"the basic principles of substantive law are now well settled"; and see also the
Court of Appeal in *ETK v News Group Newspapers Ltd* [2011] EWCA Civ 439;
[2011] 1 W.L.R. 1827 at [10]. Nicol J. in *Ferdinand v MGN Ltd* [2011] EWHC
2454 (QB) at [106], referred to the action for misuse of private information as "the
newer, human rights based, cause of action".
   NOTE 238. It was arguable that under art.8 the police had a duty to inform an
individual that they had been the victim of phone hacking: *R. (on the application
of Bryant) v Metropolitan Police Commissioner* [2011] EWHC 1314 (Admin);
[2011] H.R.L.R. 27, Foskett J.

European Court of Human Rights jurisprudence and the developing   **27–38**
action. In *Mosley v United Kingdom* (48009/08) [2011] ECHR 774; [2012]
E.M.L.R. 1 the ECtHR rejected the claim that the UK Government were obliged
to introduce a pre-notification duty in privacy cases involving intimate or sexual
details of private life. Note the discussion by the Grand Chamber of the ECtHR in
Von Hannover v Germany (No.2) [2012] E.M.L.R. 16 and *Axel Springer AG v
Germany* [2012] E.M.L.R. 15 about public figures and the contribution to a debate

of general interest. This court also reiterated the essential role the press played in a democratic society.

(a) *The reasonable expectation of privacy*

27–39   **The reasonable expectation of privacy.** In *Tchenguiz v Imerman* [2010] EWCA Civ 908; [2011] Fam. 116 at [66] Lord Neuberger M.R. noted that the "reasonable expectation of privacy" test in *Campbell v MGN Ltd* [2004] UKHL 22; [2004] 2 A.C. 457 "chimes well with the test suggested in classic commercial confidence cases, by Megarry J. in *Coco v AN Clark (Engineers) Ltd* [1969] R.P.C. 41 at 47, namely whether the information had the 'necessary quality of confidence' and had been 'imparted in circumstances importing an obligation of confidence.' " He also held that each spouse has a right of confidence against the other in regard to that part of their life which was separate and distinct from their shared married life. However, the fact that the parties live together, especially if married, civil partners or lovers, may affect the question of whether information is confidential as between them (at [84] and [87]). In the case itself, a wife in ancillary relief proceedings had to return confidential financial documents unlawfully extracted from her husband's computer: the so-called "Hildebrand" rules had no legal basis.

In *Hutcheson (formerly KGM) v News Group Newspapers Ltd* [2011] EWCA Civ 808; [2012] E.M.L.R. 2 the claimant had maintained that once art.8 was engaged (the information here relating to family life), there was automatically a reasonable expectation of privacy. However, it was held that such a reasonable expectation did not necessarily follow. Gross L.J. said, at [37], that: "there was an important distinction between not wanting publicity and having a reasonable expectation of privacy, such as to justify intervention on the part of the court". At [24] Gross L.J. noted the views of Laws L.J. in *R. (on the application of Wood) v CPM* [2009] EWCA Civ 414; [2010] 1 W.L.R. 123 at [22], that however "protean" art.8 may be it is important it should not be read so widely "that its claims become unreal and unreasonable". The views of Tugendhat J. in *LNS v Persons Unknown* [2010] EWHC 119 (QB); [2010] E.M.L.R. 16—emphasising the importance of public discussion and the freedom to criticise—were described as "powerful", at [29].

In *SKA v CRH* [2012] EWHC 766 (QB) Tugendhat J. held that the claimant was unlikely to succeed at trial in establishing they had a reasonable expectation of privacy in respect of the bare fact of the relationship at the heart of the allegation. This is in line with a series of cases where the court has distinguished between the reasonable expectation of keeping the *details* of a relationship private and the (less likely) reasonable expectation of keeping the *fact* of a realtionship private: see *Lord Browne of Madingley v Associated Newspapers Ltd* [2007] EWCA Civ 295; [2008] Q.B. 103; *Ntuli v Donald* [2010] EWCA Civ 1276; [2011] 1 W.L.R. 294; *Goodwin v News Group Newspapers Ltd* [2011] EWHC 1437 (QB); [2011] E.M.L.R. 27; *Trimingham v Associated Newspapers* [2012] EWHC 1296 (QB); [2012] 4 All E.R. 717 Tugendhat J.

With regard to reasonable expectation of privacy and photographs: see *Trimingham v Associated Newspapers Ltd* [2012] EWHC 1296 (QB); [2012] 4 All E.R. 717 Tugendhat J. at [316] and Nicol J., in *Ferdinand v MGN Ltd* [2011]

EWHC 2454 (QB) at [101]–[102], noting both the unacceptable intrusion into privacy that they may represent but also the need for an "intense focus" on the competing rights even if the photograph is of a private occasion (in *Ferdinand* the photograph was not covert and its publication would not have caused additional harm or embarrassment). In *AAA v Associated Newspapers* [2012] EWHC 2103 (QB); [2013] E.M.L.R. 2, Nicola Davies J., the publication of the child claimant's photograph was restrained, sufficient information on the allegations of the paternity of that child being included in the article itself. (The decision itself was affirmed by Court of Appeal: [2013] EWCA Civ 554). See also *Contostavlos v Mendahum* [2012] EWHC 850 (QB) Tugendhat J. concerning a "sex tape" involving the claimant.

In *ETK v News Group Newspapers Ltd* [2011] EWCA Civ 439; [2011] 1 W.L.R. 1827 the sexual relationship at the heart of the action was still essentially a private matter even though it had become known to work colleagues (dicta in *Browne v Associated Newspapers Ltd* [2007] EWCA Civ 295; [2008] Q.B. 103 at [61] cited). Ward L.J. stated (at [11]) that the claimant "was reasonably entitled to expect that his colleagues would treat as confidential the information they had acquired whether from their own observation ... or from tittle-tattle and gossip ... or from a confidential confession to a colleague. A reasonable person of ordinary sensibilities would certainly find the disclosure offensive." However, note *Goodwin v NGN Ltd* [2011] EWHC 1437 (QB); [2011] E.M.L.R. 27 Tugendhat J. where the name of the claimant's lover had already become known to some acquaintances so that the additional publication of her name that was likely to follow from the publication in the press of her role was "not likely to be so great a further intrusion into her private life as to make it necessary and proportionate to interfere with the art.10 rights of NGN" (at [122]). It should also be noted that in this case the claimant was a very senior executive and the lover was an executive of less senior rank. In *WXY v Gewanter* [2012] EWHC 1601 (QB) Slade J. commented that even where there has been publication in one forum, publication in another forum can be restrained, noting the difference in internet websites and the print media. She also noted (at [95]) that "There is utility in restraining the publishing of information which, even if once known is likely to have faded from memory because of the passage of time".

The court may have to consider the extent to which the relationship in question has been conducted in secrecy. In *Ntuli v Donald* [2010] EWCA Civ 1276; [2011] 1 W.L.R. 294 the claimant had been unable to demonstrate that the relationship had *not* been conducted openly. The issue is fact sensitive; as Eady J. noted in *KGM v News Group Newspapers Ltd* [2010] EWHC 3145 (QB) at [22]: "It certainly cannot be taken to mean that there is always a reasonable expectation of privacy in respect of any personal information merely because it has not been 'widely published in a newspaper'." In *Ferdinand v MGN Ltd* [2011] EWHC 2454 (QB) Nicol J. at [58] commented "it is not necessary to consider whether in an extreme case there would be some merit in the argument that widespread and extensive discussion by the person of similar aspects of their private life would disentitle them to a reasonable expectation of privacy". In the case itself the fact that articles about alleged affairs had previously been published about the claimant and he had not litigated such articles was not to be taken as tacit acceptance.

SKA v CRH [2012] EWHC 766 (QB) Tugendhat J.: the court must have regard to the art.8 rights of non-parties but he noted "such person should, if practicable, speak for themselves" (at [24]); and see *Hutcheson (formerly KGM) v News Group Newspapers Ltd* [2011] EWCA Civ 808; [2012] E.M.L.R. 2 at [26].

Abbey v Gilligan [2012] EWHC 3217; [2013] E.M.L.R. 12 (QB), Tugendhat J.—where the information concerned a company and was not personal to the claimant there was no reasonable expectation of privacy.

27–40 **Factors indicating a reasonable expectation of privacy.** NOTE 271. Add: But see *AAA v Associated Newspapers Ltd* [2013] EWCA Civ 554: in evaluating the strength of the child claimant's reasonable expectation of privacy the judge was entitled to take into account any relevant conduct of the parent(s).

27–41 **Public figures.** In *Goodwin v News Group Newspapers Ltd* [2011] EWHC 1437 (QB); [2011] E.M.L.R. 27 at [64] Tugendhat J. noted "in the law of privacy there has been some recognition in the authorities of the concept of a public figure, defined as those who exercise public or official functions". In the case itself, the chief executive of one of the largest publicly quoted companies was a public figure. At [103] Tugendhat J. noted sportsmen and celebrities do not come within that definition "but even in the case of sportsmen, there may be a public interest if the sexual relationship gives rise to conflicts with professional interests or duties, for example to his team". In *Ferdinand v MGN Ltd* [2011] EWHC 2454 (QB) Nicol J. noted that a factor in the defendant's article being in the public interest was that the claimant had voluntarily assumed the role of England captain, "a job that carried with it an expectation of high standards" (at [89]) and the issue was whether the article reasonably contributed to the debate as to his suitability for that role. Note also the ECtHR Grand Chamber decisions in *Von Hannover v Germany (No. 2)* [2012] E.M.L.R. 16 and *Axel Springer AG v Germany* [2012] E.M.L.R. 15 (above para.**27–38**). See *Abbey v Gilligan* [2012] EWHC 3217 (QB); [2013] E.M.L.R. 12, Tugendhat J. and reference there to *Porubova v Russia* (8237/03) [2009] ECHR 1477 at [45].

In *AAA v Associated Newspapers Ltd* [2013] EWCA Civ 554 the child claimant was associated with a public figure, being the result of that public figure's extra-marital affair. There was a public interest in the story as on the facts it raised issues concerning the fitness of that public figure for public office; and see *Trimingham v Associated Newspapers Ltd* [2012] EWHC 1296 (QB); [2012] 4 All E.R. 717 Tugendhat J.

(b) *Competing interests*

27–44 **Balancing art.8 and art.10.** In *Goodwin v NGN Ltd* [2011] EWHC 1437 (QB); [2011] E.M.L.R. 27 Tugendhat J. provides a useful summary of the approach on this balancing exercise at [62].

On the issue of the public interest in publication of private information note the following judgments: Ward L.J. in *ETK v News Group Newspapers Ltd* [2011] EWCA Civ 439; [2011] 1 W.L.R. 1827 at [21] ("Here there is no political edge to the publication. The organisation of the economic, social and political life of the country, so crucial to democracy, is not enhanced by publication. The intellectual, artistic or personal development of members of society is not stunted by ignorance of the sexual frolics of figures known to the public"); Eady J. in *CDE v MGN Ltd* [2010] EWHC 3308 (QB); [2011] 1 F.L.R. 1524 (who asked, at [73], whether the intrusive proposed revelations would be "likely" at trial to be held to be in the public interest "as contemplated, for example, in the Press Complaints Commission Code? Or would it contribute, in the words of the Court in Strasbourg, in *Von Hannover v Germany* (2005) 40 E.H.R.R. 1, to a 'debate of general interest to society'?"); Eady J. in *KGM v News Group Newspapers Ltd* [2010] EWHC 3145 (QB) at [39] ("There is . . . a potential public interest in the exposure of wrongdoing such as, for example, breach of fiduciary duty or the misappropriation of corporate funds, so as in certain circumstances to override an otherwise legitimate expectation of privacy: see e.g. *Lord Browne of Madingley v Associated Newspapers Ltd* . . . So too, there is a public interest in ensuring, so far as possible, that the public is not misled or given an unduly slanted picture through the public pronouncements of an individual who has become, for one reason or another, the focus of public attention: see *Campbell v MGN Ltd?*" (and on this "false image" point see *Ferdinand v MGN Ltd* [2011] EWHC 2454 (QB) Nicol J. at [65]).

However, in more recent cases there is an emphasis on the importance of public discussion. In *Ferdinand v MGN Ltd* [2011] EWHC 2454 (QB) at [64] Nicol J. noted that the court's assessment of whether there is a public interest in the publication "must acknowledge that in a plural society there will be a range of views as to what matters or is of significance"; and see similar sentiments on pluralism and freedom to criticise expressed by Tugendhat J. in *LNS v Persons Unknown* [2010] EWHC 119 (QB); [2010] E.M.L.R. 16, described as "powerful" by the Court of Appeal in *Hutcheson (formerly KGM) v NGN Ltd* [2011] EWCA Civ 808; [2012] E.M.L.R. 2 at [29]. In *Hutcheson* the Court of Appeal also stressed "the general public interest in having a thriving and vigorous newspaper industry, representing all legitimate opinions" (at [34]). Tugendhat J. in *Goodwin v NGN Ltd* [2011] EWHC 1437 (QB); [2011] E.M.L.R. 27 at [133] stated "the public interest cannot be confined to exposing matters which are improper only by existing standards and laws and not by standards as they ought to be, or which people can reasonably contend that they ought to be". On leaks to journalists see *Abbey v Gilligan* [2012] EWHC 3217 (QB); [2013] E.M.L.R. 12 Tugendhat J. at [49]–[50].

On the issue of children and the balance: see *K v News Group Newspapers Ltd* [2011] EWCA Civ 439; [2011] 1 W.L.R. 1827 at [19] per Ward L.J.: "the interests of children do not automatically take precedence over the Convention rights of others"; and *Spelman v Express Newspapers* [2012] EWHC 355 (QB) Tugendhat J.—injunction was refused where the child was 17 with a personality and public profile of his own.

See also the discussion of privacy injunctions, below.

NOTE 305. In *CDE v MGN Ltd* [2010] EWHC 3308 (QB); [2011] 1 F.L.R. 1524 the pressure placed on the second defendant by the first defendant newspaper was according to Eady J. a relevant consideration when making an assessment of proportionality.

NOTE 307. The fact that the proposed publication only concerns the "bare facts" of a relationship may sometimes involve a relatively low degree of intrusion (see *Ntuli v Donald* [2010] EWCA Civ 1276; [2011] 1 W.L.R. 294 and *KGM v News Group Newspapers Ltd* [2010] EWHC 3145 (QB) at [36]) and also feeds into what constitutes a reasonable expectation of privacy: see para.**27–39**, above.

NOTE 318. However, in *Ferdinand v MGN Ltd* [2011] EWHC 2454 (QB) at [84] Nicol J. stated that though the article was a "kiss and tell story" "stories may be in the public interest even if the reasons behind the informant providing the information are less than noble".

(c) *Relevant statutory provisions*

27–46   **Protection from Harassment Act 1997.** There have been a number of privacy cases where the application of this Act to intrusive behaviour by the defendant (involving publications in newspapers rather than "door-stepping") has been discussed: *AMP v Persons Unknown* [2011] EWHC 3454 (TCC) Ramsay J.; *AM v News Group Newspapers Ltd* [2012] EWHC 308 (QB) Tugendhat J.; *Trimingham v Associated Newspapers Ltd* [2012] EWHC 1296 (QB); [2012] 4 All E.R. 717, Tugendhat J. *APW v WPA* [2012] EWHC 3151 (QB) Tugendhat J. noted that sending distressing text messages was arguably a course of conduct amounting to harassment within the Protection from Harassment Act 1997 (at [43]). However, the context in which they were sent was significant. As the 1997 Act also created a criminal offence "the conduct in question must be serious enough to attract the sanction of the criminal law" (at [12]).

WXY v Gewanter [2012] EWHC 1601 (QB) Slade J., obiter, no defence under the Protection from Harassment Act 1997 to argue that the material is already in the public domain (at [100]); *WXY v Gewanter* [2013] EWHC 589 (QB) on assessment of damages, Tugendhat J.: it was appropriate to make a single award of damages for harassment and distress caused by misuse of confidential information, where the harassment consisted in that misuse of information. Tugendhat J. noted that the Court of Appeal gave guidance on damages for harassment in *Vento v CC of West Yorkshire Police* [2002] EWCA Civ 1871; [2003] I.C.R. 318. He awarded £24,950 damages (including £5,000 for aggravated damages) given that it was a serious case. The distress was not related to the number of persons who had read the offending website (see [54] for comparison with damages in a defamation case).

(d) *Remedies*

27–47   **Injunction.** Note the *Practice Guidance (HC Interim Non-Disclosure Orders)* [2012] 1 W.L.R. 1003 in relation to applications for interim non-disclosure orders in civil proceedings to restrain the publication of information (and note also the Committee on Super-Injunctions, headed by Lord Neuberger M.R., issued its report on May 20, 2011: *Super Injunctions, Anonymised Injunctions and Open Justice* (*http://www.judiciary.gov.uk/Resources/JCO/Documents/Reports/super-injunction-report-20052011.pdf* [Accessed September 1, 2013]). This states that open justice is a fundamental principle and derogations from this principle can only be justified in exceptional cases. Where justified they should be no more than strictly necessary to achieve their purpose. The parties must ensure that the interference with the art.10 rights of third parties is kept to as short a time as possible (and see *Giggs (formerly known as CTB) v News Group Newspapers Ltd* [2012] EWHC 431 (QB); [2013] E.M.L.R. 5 Tugendhat J. at [111]). This Practice

Guidance contains reference to leading case law and notes that such derogation from the principle of open justice is an obligation, if it is justified (see *AMM v HXW* [2010] EWHC 2457 (QB); (2010) 160 N.L.J. 1425 Tugendhat J. at [34]).

Case law had already established:

(i)   that the onus is on the applicant to show that derogation from the general principle of open justice is *strictly necessary*. See Sir Maurice Kay L.J. in *Ntuli v Donald* [2010] EWCA Civ 1276; [2011] 1 W.L.R. 294, [52]–[54]; (and see Tugendhat J. in *Gray v UVW* [2010] EWHC 2367 (QB) at [55]– [56], no more than is "necessary and proportionate");

(ii) that any application to derogate from the general principle must be the subject of "intense scrutiny" by the court. See *LNS v Persons Unknown* [2010] EWHC 119 (QB); [2010] E.M.L.R. 16, Tugendhat J. (in Main Text) at [108]; *JIH v News Group Newspapers Ltd* [2011] EWCA Civ 42; [2011] 1 W.L.R. 1645, Lord Neuberger M.R. at [21(4)];

(iii) that derogations must be kept to an absolute minimum. See *Ntuli v Donald* [2010] EWCA Civ 1276; [2011] 1 W.L.R. 294 at [54]. The court should ask whether a less drastic course of action could be adopted (*Ambrosiadou v Coward* [2011] EWCA Civ 409; [2011] E.M.L.R. 21 at [52]);

(iv) that the decision is case sensitive: *Ntuli v Donald* [2010] EWCA Civ 1276; [2011] 1 W.L.R. 294 at [54], Maurice Kay L.J. (and see the Court of Appeal in *Hutcheson (formerly KGM) v News Group Newspapers Ltd* [2011] EWCA Civ 808; [2012] E.M.L.R. 2 at [26]);

(v)   that the parties themselves could not agree to derogate: it was for the court to decide whether such a derogation from open justice is necessary. See *Goldsmith v BCD* [2011] EWHC 674 (QB), Tugendhat J. at [64]. The fact that there was a public interest in open justice and that the public had art.10 rights was noted by Lord Neuberger M.R. in *JIH v News Group Newspapers Ltd* [2011] EWCA Civ 42; [2011] 1 W.L.R. 1645 at [21(7)])—note the Practice Guidance refers to this case as providing the "proper approach" at para.14. (On the approach to be taken to post-settlement anonymity see *JIH v News Group Newspapers Ltd* [2012] EWHC 2179 (QB), Tugendhat J., based on the guidance of Lord Neuberger M.R. in *Hutcheson v Popdog Ltd* [2011] EWCA Civ 1580; [2012] 1 W.L.R. 782).

On the relationship of the action for misuse of private information and the action for defamation and the rule in *Bonnard v Perryman* (noted in the Main Text) see also *Spelman v Express Newspapers* [2012] EWHC 355 (QB) where, at [64], Tugendhat J. referred to the uncertain issue of principle raised by the defendant "whether, and if so when, a court should refuse an injunction on the basis of *Bonnard v Perryman* when it is sought by a claimant who advances his case only on the basis of privacy".

Since 2010 there have been a large number of cases concerning the award of injunctions in privacy disputes. In particular the courts have debated the award of anonymised injunctions and the award of super-injunctions.

Anonymity orders

It should be noted that the practice and procedure of anonymity orders were discussed by the Supreme Court in two cases in 2010 (neither involving the action for breach of confidence but both raising art.8 v art.10 issues): *Re Guardian News and Media* [2010] UKSC 1; [2010] 2 A.C. 697 [63]–[64], and *Seretary of State for Home Dept v AP (No.2)* [2010] UKSC 26; [2010] 1 W.L.R. 1652 (these cases have been cited in *Ntuli v Donald* [2010] EWCA Civ 1276; [2011] 1 W.L.R. 294; *DFT v TFD* [2010] EWHC 2335 (QB) Sharp J.; *JIH v News Group Newspapers Ltd* [2011] EWCA Civ 42; [2011] 1 W.L.R. 1645).

In *Goldsmith v BCD* [2011] EWHC 674 (QB) Tugendhat J., concern for the mental health of the defendant led to the anonymisation of that party. Concern over the impact on the parties' respective children may be significant (*Ntuli v Donald* [2010] EWCA Civ 1276; [2011] 1 W.L.R. 294 Maurice Kay L.J. at [24]; *ETK v News Group Newspapers* [2011] EWCA Civ 439; [2011] 1.W.L.R. 1827 Ward L.J. at [19]; cf. adult children: *KGM v News Group Newspapers Ltd* [2010] EWHC 3145 (QB) Eady J., at [28] and see para.**27–44** above). It is also the policy of the law to protect those alleging they are the victim of a blackmailer (e.g. *POI v Lina* [2011] EWHC 25 (QB) Tugendhat J. at [8]) but Tugendhat J. in *SKA v CRH* [2012] EWHC 766 (QB) did not accept that the alleged blackmailer forfeited his art.10 rights, it remaining necessary for the court "to consider the value of the speech that would be made if the defendants were permitted to make the disclosure they threaten to make" (at [74]). Anonymisation was ordered in *JIH v News Group Newspapers Ltd* [2011] EWCA Civ 42; [2011] 1 W.L.R. 1645 at [40] with a view to protecting the claimant's rights and to reduce the risk of jigsaw identification but in *Goodwin v New Group Newspapers Ltd* [2011] EWHC 1437 (QB); [2011] E.M.L.R. 27 Tugendhat J. held that though revealing the name of the colleague with whom the claimant had had a sexual relationship would be an intrusion on her art.8 rights, her job description could be revealed as an important feature of the defendant's article.

As for anonymity in the face of internet speculation or Parliamentary disclosure, see Eady J. in *CTB v News Group Newspapers Ltd* [2011] EWHC 1326 (QB) (refused to vary the order after widespread coverage of the claimant's name on the internet) and in *KGM v News Group Newspapers Ltd* [2010] EWHC 3145 (QB) at [30]. In *CTB v News Group Newspapers Ltd* [2011] EWHC 1334 (QB) Tugendhat J. refused to remove an anonymity order although the claimant's name had been revealed on the internet and by an MP in Parliament. He noted, at [3]: "in so far as its purpose is to prevent intrusion or harassment, it has not failed."

Super-injunctions

See Maurice Kay L.J. in *Ntuli v Donald* [2010] EWCA Civ 1276; [2011] 1 W.L.R. 294 for the general approach, especially [46]–[54]. Sometimes a super-injunction for a short period may be strictly necessary e.g. to prevent "tipping off". This is echoed in the Practice Guidance (see above).

Other issues

In *TUV v Person or Persons Unknown* [2010] EWHC 853 (QB); [2010] E.M.L.R. 19 at [26] Eady J., noted that it would not always be proportionate to require a claimant to give prior notice of the application for an injunction to all non-party media organisations. Rather "the law should only impose an obligation to notify those who are already believed to have shown some interest in publishing."

Sharp J. discussed factors relevant to the decision to make an order without notice to the respondent or media in *DFT v TFD* [2010] EWHC 2335 (QB), citing *ASG v GSA* [2009] EWCA Civ 1574.

Contra mundum injunctions

In *OPQ v BJM* [2011] EWHC 1059 (QB); [2011] E.M.L.R. 23 at [18], Eady J. held: ". . . the court's power to grant an injunction *contra mundum* is not confined to the wardship jurisdiction; nor to children; nor to 'individuals who cannot take care of themselves'. The remedy is available, wherever necessary and proportionate, for the protection of Convention rights whether of children or adults."

Damages. Add: *Mirror Group Newspapers Ltd v United Kingdom* (39401/04)   **27–48** (2011) 53 E.H.R.R. 5 substantial success fees were likely to violate art.10 freedom particularly in privacy and defamation cases.

In *Spelman v Express Newspapers* [2012] EWHC 355 (QB) at [114] Tugendhat J. discussing damages in relation to intrusion commented: "if a remedy in damages is to be an effective remedy, then the amount the court may award must not be subject to too severe a limitation" [noting the recent settlements in the phone hacking cases] . . . the sums awarded in the early cases such as *Campbell* were very low. But it can no longer be asumed that damages at these levels are the limit of the court's powers". In *Cooper v Turrell* [2011] EWHC 3269 (QB) Tugendhat J. held that the misuse of private medical information was of a high level of seriousness and there were aggravating circumstances: there had been an internet campaign against the claimant; the defendant knew the information was false and had targeted the release of the information to people whose good opinion was important to the claimant.

CHAPTER 28

DAMAGES

PARA.

■ 1. Introduction 28–01
   2. General principles 28–02
       (a) Form of damages... 28–02
       (b) General and special damages 28–05
       (c) General principle of compensation..................................... 28–07
       (d) Causation and remoteness... 28–08
   □ (e) Mitigation 28–09
   □ (f) Certainty 28–12
   3. Damages for personal injuries 28–20
       (a) Itemisation of awards 28–20
   □ (b) Medical and other expenses 28–23
       (c) Loss of earnings 28–28
               (i)   The "multiplier method" 28–29
               (ii) The "lost years" 28–31
           ■ (iii) The "discount" rate 28–32
               (iv) Loss of earning capacity 28–36
               (v)   Effect of taxation 28–37
               (vi) Receipt of social security benefits...................... 28–40
               (vii) Other collateral benefits.................................... 28–44
       (d) Non-pecuniary loss.. 28–54
               (i)   Pain and suffering 28–55
           ■ (ii) Loss of faculty and loss of amenity 28–56
   ■ (e) Damages for wrongful birth 28–59
       (f) Interest on damages... 28–66
       (g) Interim payments 28–70
       (h) Provisional damages 28–71
       (i) Structured settlements... 28–72
   □ (j) (Reviewable) periodical payments 28–75
   4. Death: survival of causes of action... 28–77
       (a) Law Reform (Miscellaneous Provisions) Act 1934 28–78
       (b) Assessing damages under the Law Reform Act 28–82
       (c) Instantaneous death... 28–84
   5. Death as a cause of action.. 28–85
       (a) Fatal Accidents Act 1976 28–86
   ■ (b) Dependants 28–87
       (c) Nature of Fatal Accidents Act claim................................. 28–88
   ■ (d) Damages for bereavement.. 28–92
       (e) Assessment of Fatal Accident Act damages 28–93
               (i)   Loss of pecuniary benefit.................................... 28–93
               (ii) Assessing dependants' prospects 28–96
               (iii) Assessing dependants' loss—the "multiplier method" 28–98
               (iv) Pecuniary gains 28–107
       (f) Settlement of Fatal Accident Act claims............................ 28–113
       (g) Special statutory provisions 28–114
       (h) Relationship between Law Reform Act and Fatal Accidents Act claims 28–119
   6. Destruction of or damage to goods.. 28–121
   □ (a) Destruction of goods... 28–121
   ■ (b) Damage to goods.. 28–124
       (c) Betterment... 28–129

7. Recovery of costs of action. 28–130
□ 8. Equitable damages 28–132
9. Exemplary damages 28–137
■ (a) Distinguished from aggravated damages 28–137
(b) Scope of exemplary damages 28–139
■ (i) Oppressive, arbitrary or unconstitutional action by the servants
of the government 28–141
□ (ii) Defendant's conduct has been calculated by him to make a
profit which may well exceed the compensation payable 28–143
□ (c) Rejection of the "cause of action test" 28–145
□ (d) Factors to be considered 28–148
□ 10. Restitutionary damages. 28–152
11. Appeals on quantum of damages 28–154

1. INTRODUCTION

28–01   **Scope of chapter.** NOTE 14. Add at the end: *Rabone v Pennine Care NHS Trust* [2012] UKSC 2; [2012] 2 W.L.R. 381; *R. (on the application of Faulkner) v Secretary of State for Justice* [2013] UKSC 23; [2013] 2 W.L.R. 1157. For criticism of the *Greenfield* case, see Burrows, "Damages and Rights" in Nolan and Robertson (eds), *Rights and Private Law* (Oxford: Mart Publishing, 2012), pp. 275, 290–303.

2. GENERAL PRINCIPLES

(e) *Mitigation*

28–09   NOTE 56. Add at the end: As emerges from *Sayce v TNT (UK) Ltd* [2011] EWCA Civ 1583; [2012] 1 W.L.R. 1261, some of the reasoning in *Copley v Lawn* [2009] EWCA Civ 580; [2009] P.I.Q.R. P21 is controversial.

28–10   NOTE 65. Insert after the first sentence: *Lagden v O'Connor* was applied in *W v Veolia Environment Services UK Plc* [2011] EWHC 2020 (QB); [2012] 1 All E.R. (Comm) 667 in holding that total hire fees of more than £138,000 to hire a replacement Bentley, while the claimant's Bentley was being repaired, were recoverable.

(f) *Certainty*

28–19   NOTE 100. Amend the reference as follows: *Sienkiewicz v Greif (UK) Ltd* [2011] UKSC 10; [2011] 2 A.C. 229. Add at the end: See further the detailed analysis of *Barker v Corus (UK) Plc* in *Durham v BAI (Run off) Ltd* [2012] UKSC 14; [2012] 1 W.L.R. 867 in the context of construing an employer's liability insurance policy.

3. Damages for Personal Injury

(b) *Medical and other expenses*

Claimant's needs supplied by a third party. The principle established in   **28–27**
Hunt v Severs [1994] 2 A.C. 350, that a claimant can recover damages for the loss
incurred by a third party in gratuitously caring for the claimant, was applied in
Drake v Foster Wheeler Ltd [2010] EWHC 2004 (QB); [2011] 1 All E.R. 63 so as
to allow the cost of care provided by a charitable hospice to be compensated. The
claimant was the estate of the deceased who had been cared for, prior to his death,
by the hospice. As the damages awarded for that care were subject to a trust in
favour of the hospice, it was ordered that the tortfeasor should pay the damages
direct to the hospice.

(c) *Loss of earnings*

(iii) *The "discount" rate*

It is significant that in *Simon v Helmot* [2012] UKPC 5; [2012] Med. L.R. 394,   **28–33**
on an appeal from Guernsey, where there is no legislation governing the discount
rate so that the courts must decide that rate, it was held that on the present
economic evidence a "negative discount rate" of minus 1.5 per cent should be
applied in assessing damages for loss of future earnings (i.e. in calculating the
multiplier, there should be an addition to, rather than a deduction from, the number
of years during which the loss would be suffered).

(d) *Non-pecuniary loss*

(ii) *Loss of faculty and loss of amenity*

The eleventh edition of the *Guidelines for the Assessment of General Damages*   **28–56**
in Personal Injury Cases was published in 2012. From April 1, 2013, when the
legislative changes to the costs regime recommended by Sir Rupert Jackson came
into force, damages for pain, suffering and loss of amenity (and indeed all awards
of damages for non-pecuniary loss) have been increased by 10 per cent (unless the
claimant falls within s.44(6) of the Legal Aid, Sentencing and Punishment of
Offenders Act 2012): *Simmons v Castle* [2012] EWCA 1039; [2012] EWCA Civ
1288; [2013] 1 W.L.R. 1239.

(e) *Damages for wrongful birth*

NOTE 314. See Scott, "Reconsidering 'Wrongful Life' in England after 30   **28–59**
Years" [2013] C.L.J. 115.

(j) *(Reviewable) periodical payments*

NOTE 378. Add at the end: Lewis, "The indexation of periodical payments of   **28–75**
damages in tort: the future assured?" (2010) 30 L.S. 391.

5. DEATH AS A CAUSE OF ACTION

(b) *Dependants*

28–87   NOTE 440. In *Swift v Secretary of State for Justice* [2013] EWCA Civ 193; [2013] P.I.Q.R. P14 the claimant's partner, with whom she had been living for about six months, was killed as a result of an admitted tort. While their son, who was born after that death, had a claim for pecuniary loss under the Fatal Accidents Act 1976, the claimant did not. This was because she had not been living with the deceased for two years prior to the death. She argued unsuccessfully that, in denying her a claim, the 1976 Act was incompatible with her right to family life under art. 8 of the ECHR as protected by the Human Rights Act 1998.

(d) *Damages for bereavement*

28–92   NOTE 468. The fixed sum for bereavement damages was raised to £12,980 for causes of action accruing on or after April 1, 2013 by the Damages for Bereavement (Variation of Sum) (England and Wales) Order 2013 (SI 2013/510).

6. DESTRUCTION OF OR DAMAGE TO GOODS

(a) *Destruction of goods*

28–121   NOTE 601. Add to the end of the first sentence: *Beechwood Birmingham Ltd v Hoyer Group UK Ltd* [2010] EWCA Civ 647; [2011] Q.B. 357, per Sir Mark Potter P. at [47].

(b) *Damage to goods*

28–124   In *Coles v Hetherton* [2012] EWHC 1599 (QB); [2013] 1 All E.R. (Comm) 453 it was held that a claimant is entitled to damages for the reasonable cost of repairing a car even though the actual cost of the repairs, whether incurred by the claimant or his insurer, are lower. Cooke J. was of the opinion that the reasoning of the Court of Appeal in *Darbishire v Warran* [1963] 1 W.L.R. 1067 could not stand in the light of later authorities. But, with respect, the reasonable cost of repairs is merely a starting point in measuring the claimant's loss and, where the claimant has carried out the repairs at a lower cost, the claimant has thereby mitigated some of his loss which should therefore be non-recoverable. Moreover, it is incorrect to assume, as Cooke J. appeared to do, that the diminution in value of a damaged car is always to be measured by the reasonable cost of repair as opposed to the car's diminished resale value (which may not be the same).

28–127   NOTE 630. Add to the end of the first sentence: *Beechwood Birmingham Ltd v Hoyer Group UK Ltd* [2010] EWCA Civ 647; [2011] Q.B. 357.

28–128   In *Beechwood Birmingham Ltd v Hoyer Group UK Ltd* [2010] EWCA Civ 647; [2011] Q.B. 357 it was held that the claimant company should have mitigated its loss by replacing the damaged car from its stock, rather than hiring in a replacement, during the period while the car was being repaired. But while the cost of hire could not therefore be recovered, damages for loss of use were awarded and these were to be measured by the interest on the capital value of a car of the type damaged, plus depreciation, over the repair period.

8. EQUITABLE DAMAGES

NOTE 673. Add: *Hkruk II (CHC) Ltd v Heaney* [2010] EWHC 2245 (Ch); **28–134** [2010] 3 E.G.L.R. 15.

Measure of damages. NOTE 687. Insert after the reference to the *Carr-Saunders* **28–136** case: *Jones v Ruth* [2011] EWCA Civ 804; [2012] 1 W.L.R. 1495, at [36]–[41].

9. EXEMPLARY DAMAGES

(a) *Distinguished from aggravated damages*

NOTE 690. Add Murphy, "The Nature and Domain of Aggravated Damages" **28–137** [2010] C.L.J. 353.

As aggravated damages are to compensate for injured feelings and mental **28–138** distress, they cannot be awarded in favour of a company: *Collins Stewart Ltd v The Financial Times Ltd* [2005] EWHC 262 (QB); [2006] E.M.L.R. 5; *Eaton Mansions (Westminster) Ltd v Stinger Compania de Inversion SA* [2012] EWHC 3354 (Ch).

(b) *Scope of exemplary damages*

(i) *Oppressive, arbitrary or unconstitutional actions by the servants of the government*

In *Lumba v Secretary of State for the Home Department* [2011] UKSC 12; **28–141** [2012] 1 A.C. 245 the claimants, who had been detained in breach of public law, were held entitled to damages for the tort of false imprisonment. But as they would have been detained in any event, had correct procedures been followed, the damages should be nominal only. There was no justification for exemplary damages even though the conduct of the Home Office officials had been deplorable. See further para.**15–135** of this Supplement.

Although in *Lumba v Secretary of State for the Home Department* [2011] **28–142** UKSC 12; [2012] 1 A.C. 245 three of the nine Supreme Court Justices (Lord Walker, Lord Hope and Baroness Hale) would have been willing to award "vindicatory damages" for the tort of false imprisonment, the majority did not think such damages were appropriate; and some of the judges, especially Lord Dyson giving the leading judgment, cast severe doubt on whether vindicatory damages are ever justified as a remedy in tort (as opposed to being given for the infringement of a constitutional right where there is a written constitution). See further para.**1–12** of this Supplement. See also Burrows, "Damages and Rights" in Nolan and Robertson (eds), *Rights and Private Law* (2012) pp. 275, 303–307.

(ii) *Defendant's conduct has been calculated by him to make a profit which may well exceed the compensation payable*

28–143   NOTE 729. Add at the end: *Ramzan v Brookwide Ltd* [2011] EWCA Civ 985; [2012] 1 All E.R. 903 where exemplary damages were awarded for the tort of trespass to land.

(c) *Rejection of the "cause of action test"*

28–146   Add: In New Zealand, it was previously decided in *A v Bottrill* [2002] UKPC 44; [2003] 1 A.C. 449 that, in the context of the tort of negligence, there could be outrageous conduct justifying exemplary damages, even without subjective reck-lessness. But that was departed from in *Couch v Attorney General* [2010] NZSC 27, so that subjective recklessness is a necessary minimum requirement for exemplary damages (albeit that the cause of action may be the tort of negligence).

(d) *Factors to be considered*

28–148   In *Ramzan v Brookwide Ltd* [2011] EWCA Civ 985; [2012] 1 All E.R. 903 the Court of Appeal, while upholding an award of exemplary damages for the tort of trespass to land as being justified to deter similar conduct, reduced the quantum of exemplary damages that had been awarded at first instance by two-thirds to £20,000. Rather confusingly, the Court of Appeal reasoned that one had to be careful to ensure that the award of exemplary damages did not infringe the principle, in relation to the concurrent claim for breach of trust, that the claimant must elect for either compensation or an account of profits.

28–151   **Several claimants.** In *Lumba v Secretary of State for the Home Department* [2011] UKSC 12; [2012] 1 A.C. 245 at [167] one of the reasons for not awarding exemplary damages was that there were others in the same position as the claimants who were not before the court.

10. RESTITUTIONARY DAMAGES

28–152   NOTE 764. Add at the end of the first sentence: *Stadium Capital Holdings (No.2) Ltd v St Marylebone Property Co Plc* [2010] EWCA Civ 952; *Ramzan v Brookwide Ltd* [2011] EWCA Civ 985; [2012] 1 All E.R. 903 (both of these cases concerned trespass to land). Add at the end: *Jones v Ruth* [2011] EWCA Civ 804; [2012] 1 W.L.R. 1495 at [36]–[41]. Amend the spelling of *Devenish*.

28–153   NOTE 767. Update reference to Burrows, *The Law of Restitution*, 3rd edn (Oxford: Oxford University Press, 2011), ch.24.
NOTE 768. Amend the spelling of *Devenish*.

CHAPTER 29

INJUNCTIONS

		PARA.
☐	1. Introduction	29–01
■	2. Prohibitory injunctions	29–05
	3. Mandatory injunctions	29–10
	4. Action quia timet.	29–14
	5. Interim injunctions	29–17
	(a) American Cyanamid	29–17
■	(b) Exceptional situations	29–19
	(c) Function of appellate court	29–27
■	(d) Undertaking as to damages	29–28
☐	(dd) Anonymised injunctions and super-injunctions	29–28A
	(e) Search orders.	29–29
	(i) Order for disclosure and interrogatories	29–33
	(ii) Full disclosure by claimant required	29–35
	(iii) Custody and non-use of items seized.	29–36
	(iv) Improperly obtained orders	29–37
	(v) Order after judgment	29–38
	(vi) Abuse of search orders.	29–39
	(f) Freezing injunctions	29–40
■	(i) A good arguable case	29–41
■	(ii) Real risk of defendant's assets being disposed of	29–42
	(iii) Undertaking in damages	29–43
☐	(iv) Defendant's business and living expenses or legal costs	29–44
	(v) Position of third parties	29–45
	(vi) Order for disclosure and interrogatories	29–46
	(vii) Order for delivery up of goods and entry to premises	29–47
	(viii) Full disclosure by claimant required.	29–48
	(ix) Duty to continue with claim.	29–49
☐	(x) Order after judgment	29–50
	(xi) Conclusion	29–51
	6. Injunctions and declarations against the Crown	29–52

1. Introduction

Torts of all kinds may be restrained by injunction where "just or conven-   **29–02**
ient". NOTE 4. Add at the end of the first sentence: (trespass to land); *Mayor of London v Hall* [2010] EWCA Civ 817; [2011] 1 W.L.R. 504 (trespass to land).

2. Prohibitory Injunctions

NOTE 21. Add: See similarly *HKRUK II (CHC) Ltd v Heaney* [2010] EWHC   **29–05**
2245 (Ch); [2010] 3 E.G.L.R. 15.

5. INTERIM INJUNCTIONS

(b) *Exceptional situations*

29–20   **Trial unlikely.** NOTE 95. Add at the end of the second sentence: *Serco Ltd v National Union of Rail, Maritime and Transport Workers* [2011] EWCA Civ 226; [2011] I.C.R. 848; [2011] 3 All E.R. 913 at [10]–[14].

29–22   **Freedom of speech** NOTE 105. Add at the end: Applications for interim injunctions by public figures, alleging breach of privacy in relation to newspaper articles, were refused in, e.g. *Ferdinand v MGN Ltd* [2011] EWHC 2454; *McClaren v News Group Newspapers Ltd* [2012] EWHC 2466; [2012] E.M.L.R. 33.

(d) *Undertaking as to damages*

29–28   In *Financial Services Authority v Sinaloa Gold Plc* [2013] UKSC 11; [2013] 2 W.L.R. 678 the Financial Services Authority (FSA), acting under its statutory powers under the Financial Services and Markets Act 2000, sought to continue a worldwide freezing injunction of a person's assets who was suspected of fraudulent share-dealing. The question was whether the FSA was required to give the usual cross-undertaking in damages for loss suffered by innocent third parties (e.g. banks) consequent on that freezing injunction. It was held that, applying *Hoffmann-La Roche & Co AG v Secretary for Trade and Industry* [1975] A.C. 295, no such cross-undertaking was required. The FSA was a public authority seeking to enforce the law in the interests of the public generally.

After para.**29–28** insert new para.**29–28A**:

(dd) *Anonymised injunctions and super-injunctions*

29–28A   A great deal of recent interest and controversy has been generated by the willingness of the courts to grant interim anonymised injunctions and, much more rarely, so-called "super-injunctions".[134a] Sought especially in relation to claims by public figures against the media for alleged breach of confidence or breach of privacy, the former type of interim injunction is one where, in granting the injunction, the court orders that the claimant or the defendant or both must not be named.[134b] The latter type of interim injunction is one where the court goes further and orders that the fact that the proceedings have taken place and that an injunction has been granted should not be publicised.[134c]

NOTE 134a. See generally *Report of the Committee on Super-Injunctions: Super-Injunctions, Anonymised Injunctions and Open Justice* (chaired by Lord Neuberger M.R., 2010). See further para.**27–47** of this Supplement.

NOTE 134b. See, e.g. *JIH v News Group Newspapers Ltd* [2011] EWCA Civ 42; [2011] 1 W.L.R. 1645; *ETK v News Group Newspapers Ltd* [2011] EWCA Civ 439; [2011] 1 W.L.R. 1827.

NOTE 134c. *Donald v Ntuli* [2010] EWCA Civ 1276; [2011] 1 W.L.R. 294 at [43]. It would appear that these are extremely rarely granted (the Neuberger

Report, see Note 134a above, was aware of only four having been granted) and thought that they were now generally only sought to stop a "tip-off".

(f) *Freezing injunctions*

(i) *A good arguable case*

NOTE 198. See also *Royal Bank of Scotland Plc v FAL Oil Co Ltd* [2012] **29–41** EWHC 3628 (Comm); [2013] 1 Lloyd's Rep. 327.

(ii) *Real risk of defendant's assets being disposed of*

NOTE 207. The defendant's rights under loan agreements were held not to be **29–42** "assets" within the meaning of the freezing injunction in *JSC BTA Bank v Ablyazov (No. 5)* [2012] EWHC 1819 (Comm); [2012] 2 All E.R. (Comm) 1243.

NOTE 209. While a maximum sum is usually inserted, in *JSC BTA Bank v Ablyazov (No.2)* [2009] EWHC 3267 (Comm); [2010] 1 All E.R. (Comm) 1040 the maximum sum (£175million) was limited to assets within England and Wales (i.e. the defendant was only free to deal with assets abroad if assets within the jurisdiction remained above the maximum sum).

NOTE 211. Add at the end: See also *Parbulk II AS v PT Humpuss Intermoda Transportasi TBK, The Mahakam* [2011] EWHC 3143 (Comm); [2012] 2 All E.R. (Comm) 513.

NOTE 212. Insert after the sentence dealing with *Federal Bank of the Middle East v Hadkinson* [2000] 1 W.L.R. 1695: But the standard terms have since been amended so that assets held by the defendant as a bare trustee are included as assets of the defendant: *JSC BTA Bank v Solodchenko* [2010] EWCA Civ 1436; [2011] 1 W.L.R. 888.

(iv) *Defendant's business and living expenses or legal costs*

NOTE 217. Add at the end: *Nomihold Securities Inc v Mobile Telesystems* **29–44** *Finance SA* [2011] EWCA Civ 1040; [2012] 1 All E.R. (Comm) 223.

(x) *Order after judgment*

NOTE 248. Add at the end: As regards a freezing injunction to aid enforcement **29–50** of an arbitration award, see *Nomihold Securities Inc v Mobile Telesystems Finance SA* [2011] EWCA Civ 1040; [2012] 1 All E.R. (Comm) 223.

CHAPTER 31

DISCHARGE OF TORTS

		PARA.
1.	Introduction..	31–01
2.	Waiver: election	31–02
3.	Accord and satisfaction...	31–07
4.	Release	31–13
5.	Judgment recovered	31–14
	□ (a) Damages for one cause of action must be recovered once and for all	31–15
	(b) Avoidance of the rule because different course of action	31–17
	(c) Solutions: other approaches to the problem	31–21
	(d) Satisfied judgments..	31–22
	□ (e) Judgment of foreign court.................................	31–23
6.	*Res judicata*..	*31–24*
	□ (a) Principle of *res judicata*	31–24
	(b) Contribution proceedings	31–29
	(c) Statutory defence to an action for assault......................	31–31
7.	Joint wrongdoers..	31–36
8.	Joint claimants	31–38

5. JUDGMENT RECOVERED

(a) *Damages for one cause of action must be recovered once and for all*

NOTE 68. Add at the end: *Noble v Owens* [2010] EWCA Civ 224; [2010] 1   **31–16**
W.L.R. 2491 (the question of whether the claimant had fraudulently misled the
trial judge as to his injuries could be referred back to the judge and, if proved, he
could reassess the damages).

(e) *Judgment of foreign court*

NOTE 104. Add at the end of the penultimate sentence: *Naraji v Shelbourne*   **31–23**
[2011] EWHC 3298 (QB).

6. RES JUDICATA

(a) *Principle of resjudicata*

NOTE 110. Add at the end of the penultimate sentence: *Naraji v Shelbourne*   **31–24**
[2011] EWHC 3298 (QB).
NOTE 111. Insert after the first sentence: The principle of res judicata also
extends to successive proceedings before non-statutory disciplinary or regulatory

tribunals: *R. (on the application of Coke-Wallis) v Institute of Chartered Accountants in England and Wales* [2011] UKSC 1; [2011] 2 A.C. 146.

Add at the end: For acceptance that a consent order can give rise to an estoppel by res judicata, see *Zurich Insurance Co Plc v Hayward* [2011] EWCA Civ 641; [2011] C.P. Rep. 39.

CHAPTER 32

LIMITATION

		PARA.
□	1. General	32–01
	(a) Limitation is a matter of practice and procedure	32–02
	(b) Burden of proof..	32–03
	(c) How time is computed	32–04
	(d) No suspension of limitation period once time has started to run	32–05
	(e) Starting the limitation period	32–06
	(i) Accrual of the cause of action..	32–07
■	(ii) The problem of latent damage	32–10
	(iii) Transfer of property which has sustained latent damage	32–16
	(iv) Concurrent liability in contract and tort................................	32–17
	(v) Parties in existence..	32–18
□	2. New claims in pending actions	32–19
□	3. Persons under a disability	32–21
■	4. Fraud, mistake and deliberate concealment..	32–23
	5. Extinction of title in conversion and detinue	32–30
	6. Limitation and dismissal for want of prosecution...................................	32–34
	7. Actions for personal injuries and death	32–37
	(a) General..	32–37
	(b) Claimant's knowledge..	32–41
	□ (i) Significant injury: s.14(1)(a)...	32–42
■	(ii) Injury attributable to the act or omission alleged to constitute negligence, nuisance or breach of duty: s.14(1)(b)...................	32–44
	(iii) Defendant's identity: s.14(1)(c)	32–48
	(iv) Vicarious liability etc: s.14(1)(d)	32–49
	(v) Ignorance of the law irrelevant	32–50
■	(vi) Distinguish "knowledge" and "belief"..................................	32–51
■	(vii) Constructive knowledge...	32–52
■	(c) The court's discretion..	32–55
	□ (i) The balance of prejudice...	32–57
■	(ii) The six listed factors	32–60
	(iii) Other factors..	32–67
	(iv) Role of the appellate courts..	32–68
	(d) Claims on behalf of the estate..	32–69
	(e) Fatal Accident Act claims	32–70
■	8. Negligence actions for latent damage (other than personal injury)	32–71
	9. Other special periods of limitation...	32–78
■	(a) Merchant Shipping Act 1995	32–78
	(b) Carriage by Air Act 1961	32–80
	(c) International Transport Conventions Act 1983	32–81
	(d) Defamation..	32–82
	(e) Consumer Protection Act 1987	32–83
	(f) Human Rights Act 1998..	32–84
	(g) Public authorities	32–85
	(h) Contribution between tortfeasors..	32–86
	(i) Other statutes	32–87

1. GENERAL

32–01   NOTE 1. Update the reference to McGee, *Limitation of Actions*, 6th edn (London: Sweet & Maxwell, 2010).

NOTE 8. Add at the end: See also *Page v Hewetts Solicitors* [2012] EWCA Civ 805.

(e) *Starting the limitation period*

(ii) *The problem of latent damage*

32–13   NOTE 59. Add: *Nouri v Marvi* [2010] EWCA Civ 1107; [2011] P.N.L.R. 7; *Green v Eadie* [2011] EWHC B24 (Ch); [2012] 2 W.L.R. 510; *Boycott v Perrins Guy Williams* [2011] EWHC 2969 (Ch); [2012] P.N.L.R. 25; *Lane v Cullens Solicitors* [2011] EWCA Civ 547; [2012] Q.B. 693 (in a claim by the administrator of an estate against his solicitor, for negligent failure to advise him not to distribute the estate, it was held that the claimant's loss was suffered when he distributed the estate).

2. NEW CLAIMS IN PENDING ACTIONS

32–20   NOTE 89. Add at the end: But in *Roberts v Gill* [2010] UKSC 22; [2011] 1 A.C. 240 the Supreme Court, in refusing the amendment sought, held that, although it was necessary to join the administrator for a representative action to carry on, the action that had been brought was in the claimant's personal capacity and there was no need to join the administrator for that action to carry on.

NOTE 90. Add at the end: See also *Lockheed Martin Corp v Willis Group Ltd* [2010] EWCA Civ 927; [2010] P.N.L.R. 34.

NOTE 93. Add at the end: See also *Berezovsky v Abramovich* [2011] EWCA Civ 153; [2011] 1 W.L.R. 2290.

3. PERSONS UNDER A DISABILITY

32–21   At the end of the first sentence, substitute the following for the words "of unsound mind": "lacks capacity (within the meaning of the Mental Capacity Act 2005) to conduct legal proceedings."

Insert before the penultimate sentence: It was also said in obiter dicta in *Toropdar v D* [2009] EWHC 567 (QB); [2010] Lloyd's Rep. I.R. 358 that a person could be granted a negative declaration that he was not liable to the injured party even though the limitation period had not, and would not, run out (because the injured party had suffered permanent brain damage). For criticism of this reasoning, see Patten, "When is a Limitation Period not a Limitation Period?" [2010] C.J.Q. 284.

NOTE 97. Delete the second sentence.

A person of unsound mind. This paragraph must now be read in the light of the   **32–22**
Mental Capacity Act 2005 and the consequent amendment made to the Limitation
Act 1980 s.38(2) and the repeal of s.38(3) and (4). The statute no longer refers to
"a person of unsound mind". Instead, by s.38(2) of the Limitation Act 1980, a
person is under a disability if under the age of 18 or if he "lacks capacity (within
the meaning of the Mental Capacity Act 2005) to conduct legal proceedings."

4. FRAUD, MISTAKE AND DELIBERATE CONCEALMENT

NOTE 115. Add at the end: In *The Test Claimants in the Franked Investment*   **32–23**
Group Litigation v Revenue and Customs Commissioners [2012] UKSC 19;
[2012] 2 W.L.R. 1149, it was authoritatively confirmed that s.32(1)(c) applies
only where mistake is an essential element of the cause of action (as, most obviously, where the claim is for restitution for unjust enrichment based on a mistake
of fact or law).

Deliberate concealment. NOTE 116. In *Williams v Lishman Sidwell Campbell*   **32–24**
& Price Ltd [2010] EWCA Civ 418; [2010] P.N.L.R. 25 it was suggested in obiter
dicta that, where there are subsequent causes of action for professional negligence, concealment of facts relevant to the first cause of action can carry on
through to constitute concealment of facts in relation to the second cause of action.

7. ACTIONS FOR PERSONAL INJURIES AND DEATH

(b) *Claimant's knowledge*

(i) *Significant injury: s.14(1)(a)*

NOTE 179. Delete the reference to: *AB v Ministry of Defence* [2009] EWHC   **32–42**
1225 (QB).

(ii) *Injury attributable to the act of omission alleged to constitue negigence, nuisance or breach of duty: s.14(1)(b)*

In *AB v Ministry of Defence* [2012] UKSC 9; [2013] 1 A.C. 78, at [68], Lord   **32–45**
Walker said that summaries, such as that by Brooke L.J. in *Spargo v North Essex*
District HA, "may be unhelpful if treated as if they were statutory texts."

(vi) *Distinguish "knowledge" and "belief"*

In *AB v Ministry of Defence* [2012] UKSC 9; [2013] 1 A.C. 78, the Supreme   **32–51**
Court (by a majority of four to three) held that claims for injury or death, allegedly
caused to ex-servicemen by radiation exposure during nuclear testing in the 1950s,
were time-barred. The majority held that a claimant must be treated as having the
requisite knowledge under s.14(1) once he issued proceedings. It could not be
correct that the weak case of the claimants should be regarded as not time-barred
because better evidence as to attributability might yet emerge. In the words of Lord

Wilson J.S.C., at [2], "it is a legal impossibility for a claimant to lack knowledge of attributability for the purpose of section 14(1) at a time after the date of the issue of his claim. By that date he must in law have had knowledge of it."

(vii) Constructive knowledge

32–53   NOTE 215. See also *Johnson v Ministry of Defence* [2012] EWCA Civ 1505; [2013] P.I.Q.R. P7.

(c) The court's discretion

32–55   NOTE 221. In holding that it was not equitable to allow the action for alleged hearing loss and tinnitus to proceed, the Court of Appeal in *Sayers v Hunters* [2012] EWCA Civ 1715; [2013] 1 W.L.R. 1695 clarified that it is incorrect to say that the burden on the claimant of displacing the limitation period is a heavy one. All that can be said is that the burden is on the claimant.

Amend the reference to *AB v Ministry of Defence* to: [2010] EWCA Civ 1317; (2011) 117 B.M.L.R. 101 at [96].

32–56   Applying *Horton v Sadler* [2006] UKHL 27; [2007] 1 A.C. 307, there is also no abuse of process, and the discretion in s.33 of the Limitation Act 1980 can be exercised, where a second claim form has been issued (outside the limitation period) and validly served, following the negligent failure to serve a first claim form in the time allowed for service: *Aktas v Adepta* [2010] EWCA Civ 1170; [2011] Q.B. 894.

In *Mutua v Foreign and Commonwealth Office* [2012] EWHC 2678 (QB) it was held that claims should be allowed to proceed under s.33 even though they were commenced 50 years after the expiry of the limitation period.

(i) The balance of prejudice

32–59   NOTE 237. Delete the reference to *AB v Ministry of Defence* [2009] EWHC 1225 (QB).

(ii) The six listed factors

32–61   **Length and reasons for the delay.** In *Cairns-Jones v Christie Tyler South West Wales Division Ltd* [2010] EWCA Civ 1642, it was confirmed that the delay, for the purposes of s.33(3)(a), means the delay after the expiry of the limitation period rather than delay since the claimant had actual or constructive knowledge.

8. NEGLIGENCE ACTIONS FOR LATENT DAMAGE (OTHER THAN PERSONAL INJURY)

32–75   **Claimant's knowledge.** NOTE 307. Add at the end: See, subsequent to *Haward v Fawcetts, Harris Springs Ltd v Howes* [2007] EWHC 3271 (TCC); [2008] B.L.R. 229; *Boycott v Perrins Guy Williams* [2011] EWHC 2969 (Ch); [2012] P.N.L.R. 25; *Integral Memory Plc v Haines Watt* [2012] EWHC 342 (Ch); [2012] S.T.I. 1385.

9. OTHER SPECIAL PERIODS OF LIMITATION

(a) *Merchant Shipping Act 1995*

NOTE 312. Add to the list of cases: *Gold Shipping Navigation Co SA v Lulu* **32–78**
Maritime Ltd [2009] EWHC 1365 (Admlty); [2010] 2 All E.R. (Comm) 64 (which
also clarified that the twoyear period extends to counterclaims.)

NOTE 316. Add: *Michael v Musgrove, The Sea Eagle* [2011] EWHC 1438 **32–79**
(Admlty); [2012] 2 Lloyd's Rep. 37.